KU-033-494

MiniAtlas
London

First published 2001 by

George Philip Ltd, a division of
Octopus Publishing Group Ltd
2–4 Heron Quays
London E14 4JP

First edition 2001
First impression 2001

ISBN 0 540 07813 1
© George Philip Ltd 2001

O|S Ordnance Survey

This product includes mapping data
licensed from Ordnance Survey®, with the
permission of the Controller of Her Majesty's
Stationery Office.© Crown copyright 2001.
All rights reserved.
Licence number 100011710

To the best of the Publishers' knowledge,
the information in this atlas was correct at
the time of going to press. No responsibility
can be accepted for any errors or their
consequences.

The representation in this atlas of a road,
track or path is no evidence of the existence
of a right of way.

Ordnance Survey and the OS symbol are
registered trademarks of Ordnance Survey,
the national mapping agency of Great Britain

This product contains driver restriction
information derived from Teleatlas
©TeleatlasDRI

Printed and bound in Spain
by Cayfosa-Quebecor.

Contents

II Key to map pages

IV Administrative and Postcode boundaries

VI Key to map symbols

1 Street maps

77 Keys to enlarged map pages and symbols

78 Enlarged street maps

174 Index

267 List of numbered locations

280 London Underground

282 Central London theatres and cinemas

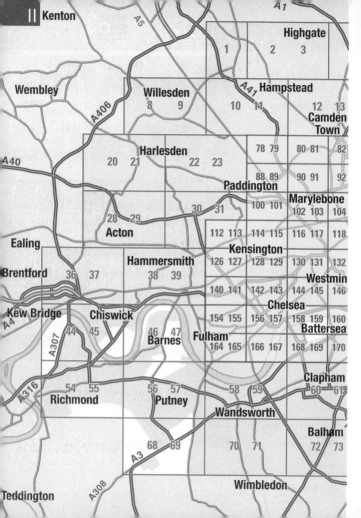

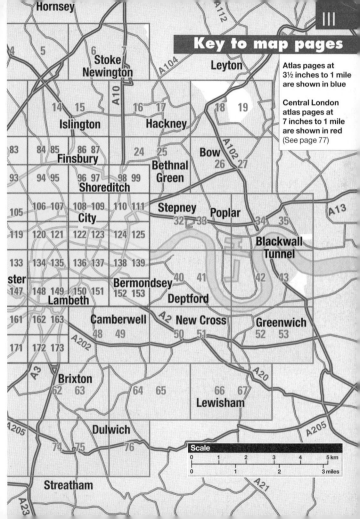

III

Key to map pages

Atlas pages at 3½ inches to 1 mile are shown in blue

Central London atlas pages at 7 inches to 1 mile are shown in red (See page 77)

Hornsey

A112

5

6 Stoke Newington 7

A104

Leyton

4

A10

14 15 16 17 18 19

Islington Hackney

83 84 85 86 87 24 25 Bow

Finsbury 26 27

A102

93 94 95 96 97 98 99

Shoreditch

Bethnal Green

105 106–107 108–109 110 111 Stepney Poplar A13

City 32 33 34 35

119 120 121 122 123 124 125

Blackwall Tunnel

133 134–135 136 137 138 139

40 41 42 43

ster 147 148 149 150 151 152 153 Bermondsey

Lambeth Deptford

161 162 163 Camberwell A2 New Cross Greenwich

48 49 50 51 52 53

171 172 173 A202

A20

64 65 66 67

Brixton Lewisham

A3 62 63

74 75 76

Dulwich A205

Streatham

A23 A21

Scale

0 1 2 3 4 5 km

0 1 2 3 miles

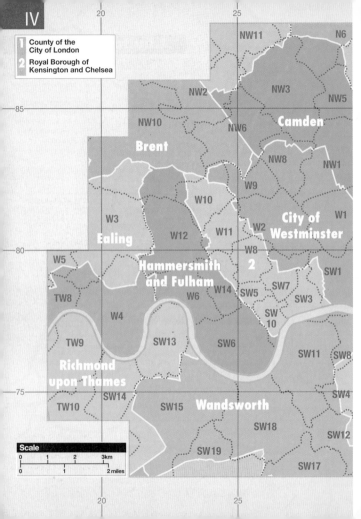

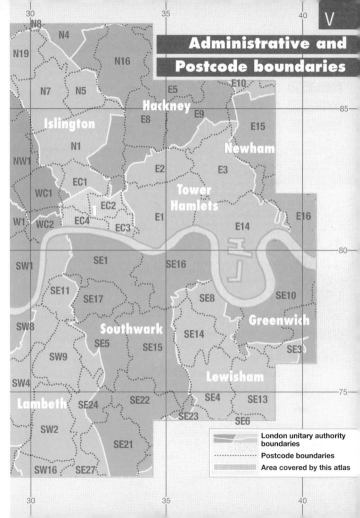

Administrative and Postcode boundaries

London unitary authority boundaries

Postcode boundaries

Area covered by this atlas

Key to map symbols

(22a)	Motorway with junction number
	Primary route – single, dual carriageway
	A road – single, dual carriageway
	B road – single, dual carriageway
	Through-route – single, dual carriageway
	Minor road – single, dual carriageway
	Road under construction
	Rural track, private road or narrow road in urban area
	Path, bridleway, byway open to all traffic, road used as public path
	Tunnel, covered road
	Gate or barrier, car pound
P P&R	Parking, park and ride
Three Legged Cross	Junction name
	Pedestrianised area
	Restricted access area
	Railway with station
	London Underground station
D	Docklands Light Railway station
	Bus or coach station

♦ ♦ ♦	Ambulance, police, fire station
H ✚	Hospital, accident and emergency entrance
⌂ 🗑	Market, public amenity site
i PO	Information centre, post office
VILLA House	Roman, non-Roman antiquity
100 ·304	House number, spot height – in metres
✝	Christian place of worship
☾ ✡	Mosque, synagogue
◘	Other place of worship
	Houses, important buildings
	Woods, parkland/common
65	Adjoining page number
NW6	Postcode boundaries
City of Westminster	Unitary authority boundaries
Barking Creek	Tidal water
	River or canal – major, minor
	Stream
	Water

Scale

3½ inches to 1 mile   1:18103

0	220yds	440yds	660yds	½ mile

0	250m	500m	750m	1km

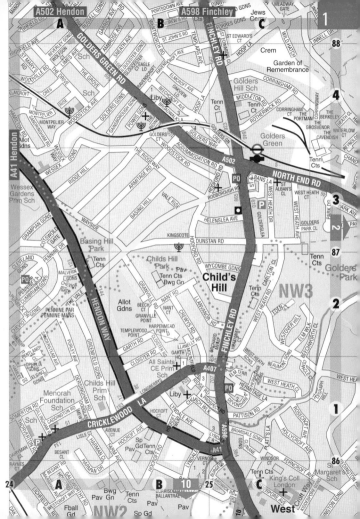

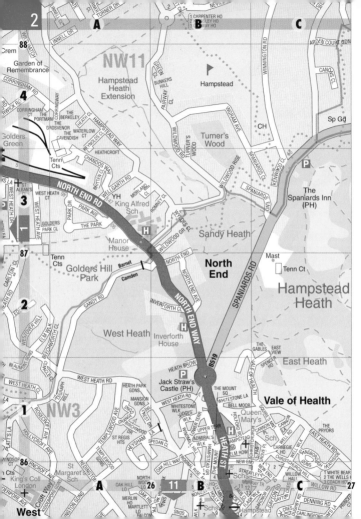

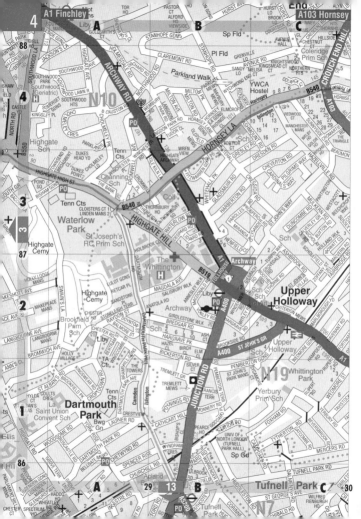

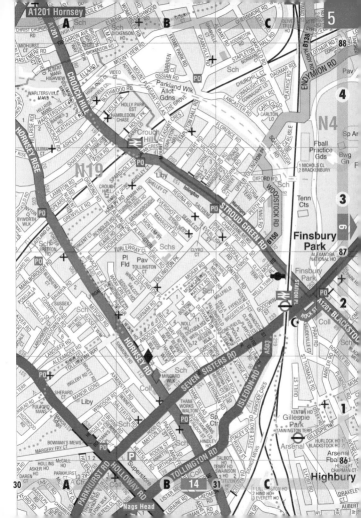

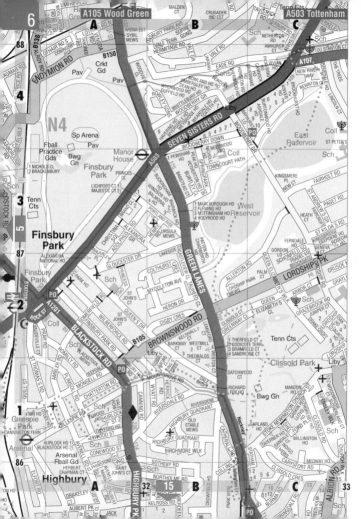

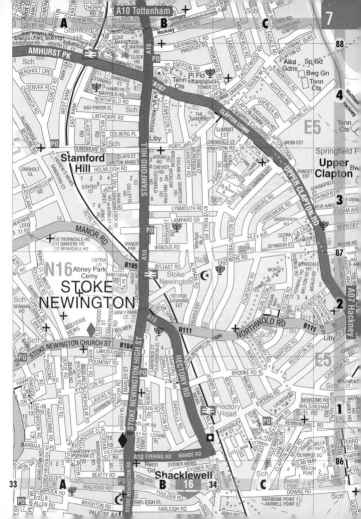

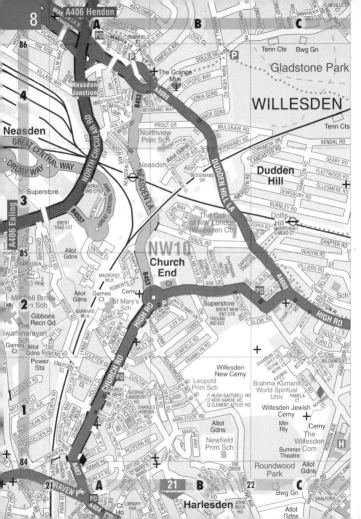

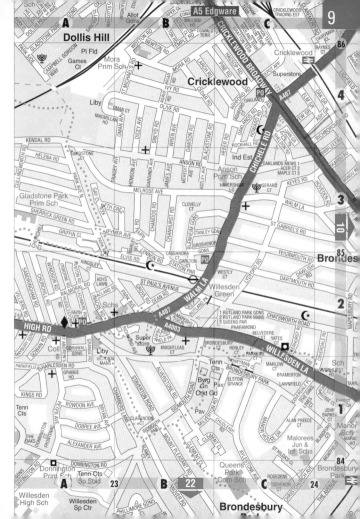

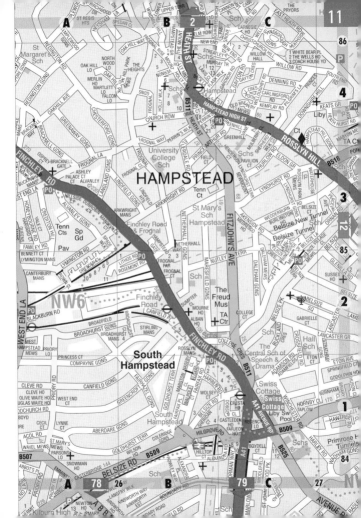

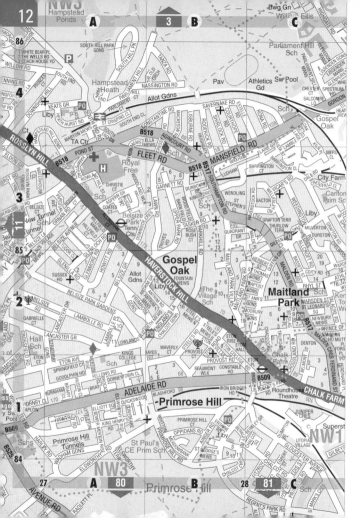

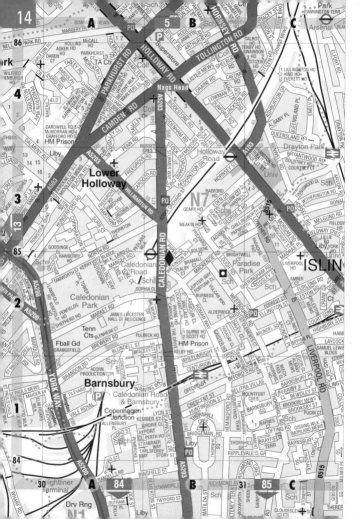

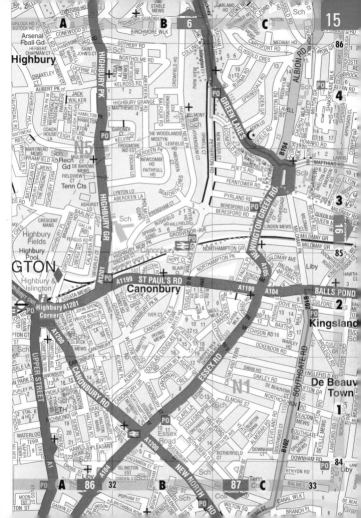

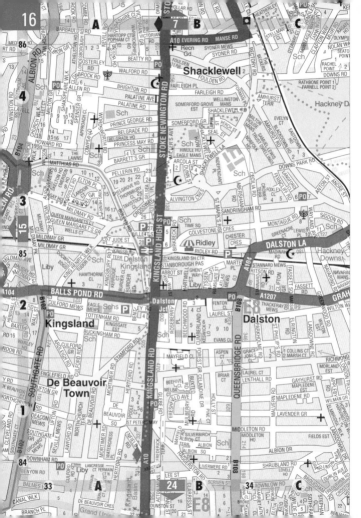

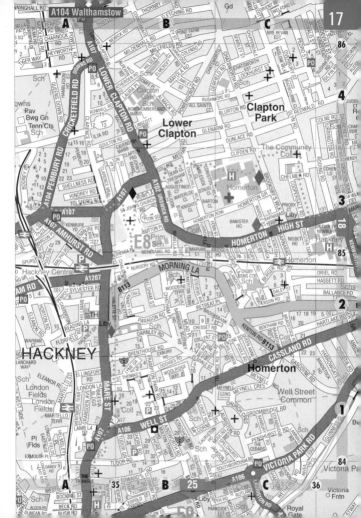

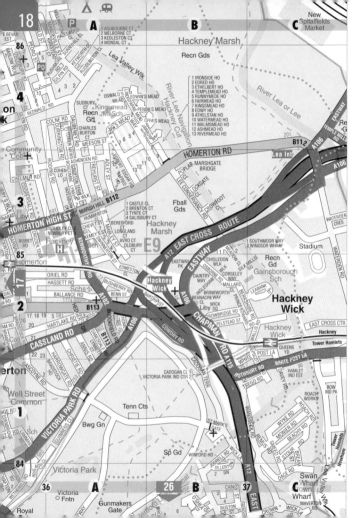

P A 1 ASHBOURNE CT B 2 MELBORNE CT C
2 MELBORNE CT
3 KEDLESTON CT
4 MONSAL CT

Hackney Marsh

Recn Gds

86

PO

4

on
k

Community
Col

CHELMER RD

3

85

17

2

84

36

26

37

SUDBURY
CT

Kingsmead
JMI Sch

Recn
Gd

Lea Valley Wlk

OSWALD'S
MEAD

EDWIN'S MEAD

PENDA'S MEAD

OFFA'S MEAD

CHARLES
BURTON
CT

MEESON ST

COLNE RD

River Lee Navigation Cut

River Lea or Lee

1 IRONSIDE HO
2 EDRED HO
3 ETHELBERT HO
4 TEMPLEMEAD HO
5 RUNNYMEDE HO
6 FAIRMEAD HO
7 KINGSMEAD HO
8 EDWY HO
9 ATHELSTAN HO
10 WATERMEAD HO
11 MALMSMEAD HO
12 ASHMEAD HO
13 RIVERMEAD HO

HOMERTON RD

B112

A106

Lea Int

201

EASTWAY

River Lea or Lee

TEMPLE MILL LA

Re

ASHENDEN RD

COHEN

CL

POPLAR
CL

MARSHGATE
BRIDGE

LEE CONSERVANCY RD

LEE CONSERVANCY RD

CROWFOOT
CL

Fball
Gds

MARSH HILL B112

HUMBERTON

1 CASTLE CL
2 BRENTON CT
3 TYNTE CT
4 SALISBURY CT

BERESFORD

LONGLAND
CT

AVRO CT

OLDBURY

Hackney
Marsh

E9

A12 EAST CROSS ROUTE

WATERDEN
CRES

WATERDEN RD

HOMERTON HIGH ST

Hackney

H

Homerton

CHEVET ST

EDMESTON
CL

ORIEL RD

HASSETT RD

Schs

A102

BALLANCE RD

B113

BUSHBERRY RD

BENN ST

NEWBURY CT

EASTWAY

EASTWAY

1 SOUTHMOOR WAY
2 WINDSOR WHARF

Recn
Gd

Gainsborough
Sch

Stadium

CHISLEDON
WLK

DAINTRY
WAY

OSBORNE RD

CORSELEY
WAY

SLIP
MILLS

SIDINGS

WAY

MALLARD

BRINKWORTH
WAY

BEANACRE WAY

Wick
Sq

Liby

Hackney
Wick

Hackney
Wick

LEABANK
CL

PERSHORE
RD

BRENTHOUSE
RD

BUNGALOW

RD

Hackney
Wick

Hackney

EAST CROSS CTR

2

ORIEL RD

HARTLAKE RD

17 18 19

20

BROOKENDALE RD

A102

B113

CASSLAND RD

SMARTHLOP ST

GOWBRIDGE RD

FELSTEAD ST

QUEENS
YD

WHITE POST LA

Tower Hamlets

CHAPMAN

RD A115

COWDRY RD

POST LA

HAMLET
IND EST

TREGO RD

White

Hackney
Wick

Tower
Hamlets

erton

21 22 23

THROWGATE RD

CHRISTIE RD

ANNIS RD

CADOGAN TER

CADOGAN CL 1
VICTORIA PARK IND CTR 2

VICTORIA PARK RD

GUINNESS CL

1

Well Street
Common

Sch

Tenn Cts

Bwg Gn

Sp Gd

WINFORD RD

WANSBECK RD

ROTHBURY RD

DAVEY ST

FOTHERGILL RD

A12

WYKE RD

MONIER RD

BEACHY RD

SHEEP

LANE

STOUR RD

DACE RD

ROACH

RD

ROACH
WORKS

WICK LA

BOW
IND PK

Tower
Hamlets

Newham

EAST

Victoria
Fntn

Gunmakers
Gate

Victoria Park

ST MARK'S
GATE

RUSTON

CROWN

OLLERTON

CAN21

MAVERTON RD

Swan
Wharf

Swan
Wharf

Royal

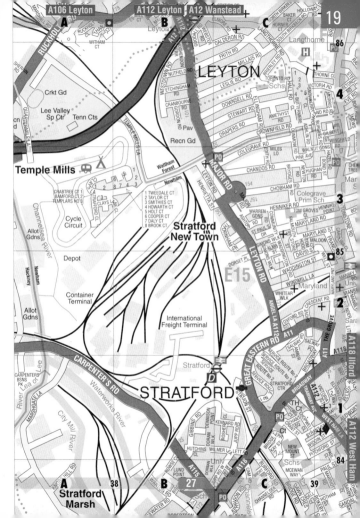

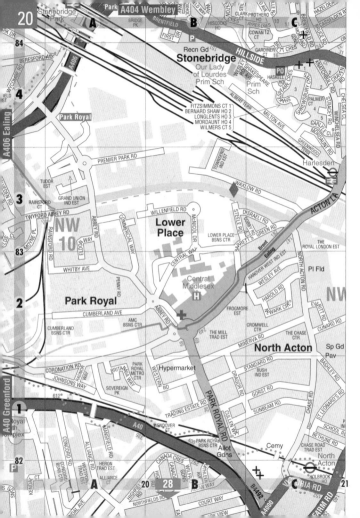

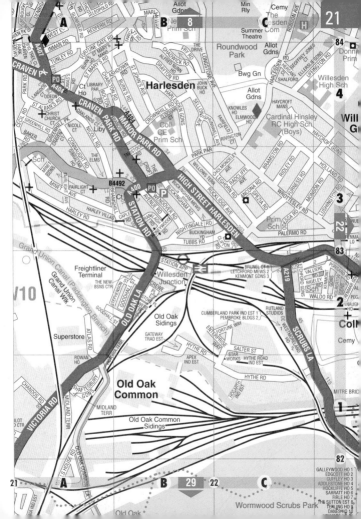

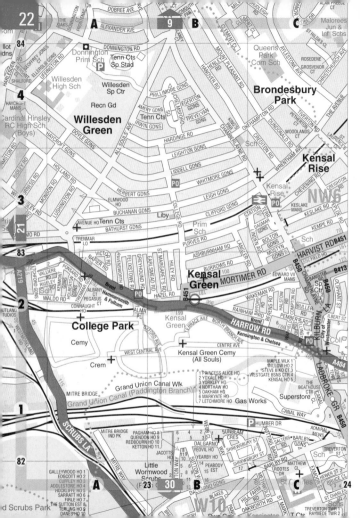

Malorees
Jun &
Inf Schs

DOBREE AVE

ALEXANDER AVE

9

The OAKS

GEOFFREY JONES CT

ELLERSLIE GDNS

HELMSDALE

DONNINGTON RD

Donnington
Prim Sch

Willesden
High Sch

Willesden
Sp Ctr

DONNINGTON RD

HANOVER RD

Queens
Park
Com Sch

ROSEDENE
CT

GROSVENOR
CT

CHRISTCHURCH AVE

84

lot
dns

HAYCROFT MANS

Cardinal Hinsley
RC High Sch
(Boys)

4

Willesden
Sp Ctr

Recn Gd

PHILLIMORE GDNS

AMERY GDNS

EGERTON
GDNS

Willesden
Green

Tenn Cts

CHELMSFORD GDNS

TREVELYAN
GDNS

OKEHAMPTON RD

CREDITON RD

PETHERTON RD

WOODLANDS CT

THE AVENUE

Brondesbury
Park

3

HAYCROFT GDNS

HOLLAND RD

RIDLEY RD

MONSON RD

LUSHINGTON RD

DOYLE GDNS

IRWIN GDNS

HARDINGE RD

LEIGHTON GDNS

LIDDELL GDNS

WHITMORE GDNS

HERBERT GDNS

ELMWOOD HO

BUCHANAN GDNS

COLLEGE RD

LEIGH GDNS

CLIFFORD GDNS

WRENTHAM AVE

Kensal
Rise

PO

Kensal
Rise

CHEVENING RD

CREIGHTON

NW6

KESLAKE MANS

KEMPE RD

KESLAKE RD

STATION

HARVIST RD

B451

21

83

MORA RD

Tenn Cts

Avenue Ho

Liby

BATHURST GDNS

Prim
Sch

DAGMAR

BOLTON

MOSTYN

GDNS

SHEFFIELD RD

B450

HARVIST RD

B413

TRENMAR
LO

VICTOR RD

NAPIER RD

PARKINSON CT

FELIXSTOWE RD

PURVES RD

ASHBURNHAM RD

BURROWS RD

ANGLER'S LA

EDWARD VII
MANS

BANBASTER

Sp Ctr

BULLER RD

KILBURN

A404

2

RUTLAND STUDIOS

A219

WESTBOURNE RD

VALLIERE

PANGBORNE

KEMMONT

POKESBOWN

TREHERNE

ALBANY

PEGASUS

CONNAUGHT

WALDO RD

GREYHOUND RD

St MARGARET'S RD

HILEY RD

HAZEL RD

Hammersmith
& Fulham

PO

Brent

ALMA
PL

Kensal
Green

B451

Kensal
Green

MORTIMER RD

GRACE AVE

NORTH BRANCH LA

RAINHAM RD

BAYFORD RD

WAKEMAN RD

BRENS RD

COMPTON RD

PEMBER RD

Brent

HARROW RD

Kensington & Chelsea

PO

Coll

of Westminster

LADBROKE GR

B450

College Park

Cemy

Crem

WEST CENTRAL AVE

CENTRE AVE

Kensal Green Cemy
(All Souls)

MAPLE WLK 1
WILLOW HO 2
STEVE BIKO CT 3
WESTGATE BSNS CTR 4
KENSAL HO 5

The BOATHOUSE
CT

Superstore

1

MITRE BRIDGE

Grand Union Canal Wlk

Grand Union Canal (Paddington Branch)

1 PRINCESS ALICE HO
2 YOXALL HO
3 YORKLEY HO
4 NORTHAM HO
5 OAKHAM HO
6 MARKYATE HO
7 LETCHMORE HO

Gas Works

CANAL WAY

ADMIRAL

82

SCRUBS LA

MITRE BRIDGE
IND PK

MITRE WAY

GALLEYWOOD HO 1
EDGCOTT HO 2
CUFFLEY HO 3
ADDLESTONE HO 4
HOCKLIFFE HO 5
SARRATT HO 6
FIRLE HO 7
THE SUTTON EST 8
TERLING HO 9
DANES HO 10

A

PAGHAM HO 8
QUENDON HO 9
REDBOURN HO 10
KETTON HO 11

JACOTTS

AYLTON

WEDB RD

SUNBEAM
CRES

DALGARNO

YEOVIL HO

YEARBY HO

15 EST

PEABODY
EST

WEBB RD

DALGARNO GDNS

SHREWSBURY RD

BARLBY

SALTERS RD

GDNS

MATTHEW

BOSWORTH RD

HILL FARM
LA

OAKWORTH RD

Sch

TREVERTON

HEWER ST

St CHARLES

BRUCE CL

TREVERTON TWR 1
RAYMEDE TWR 2

24

23

30

B

C

Little
Wormwood
Scrubs

d Scrubs Park

W10

BLAKES

Kensington

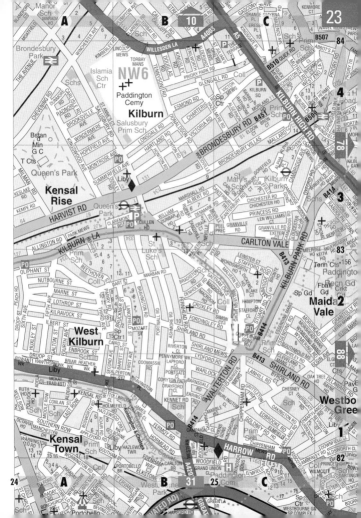

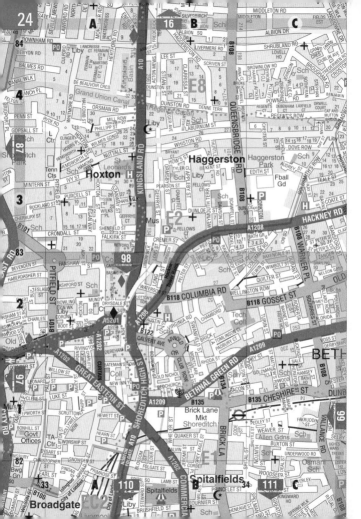

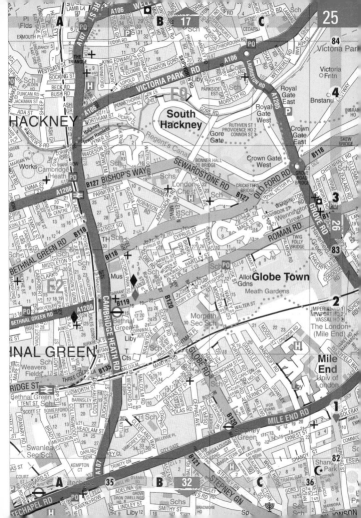

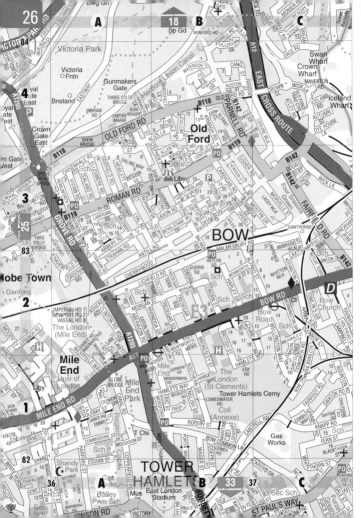

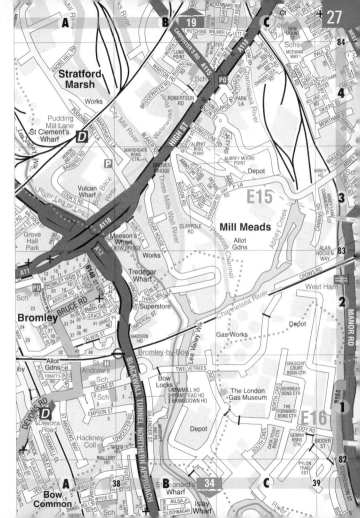

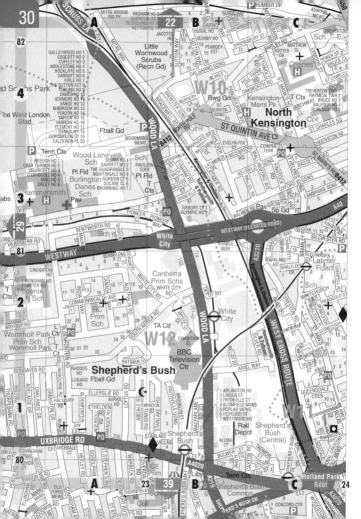

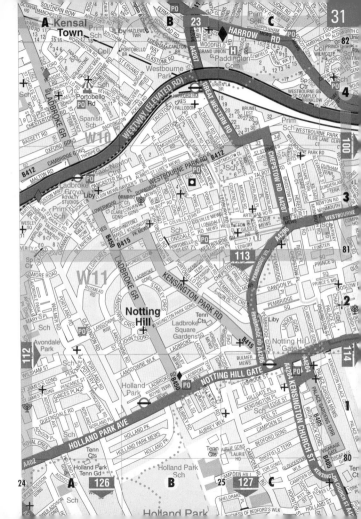

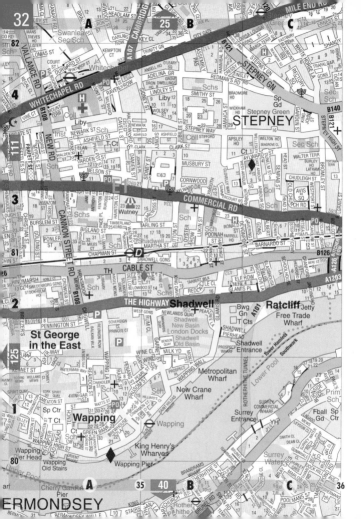

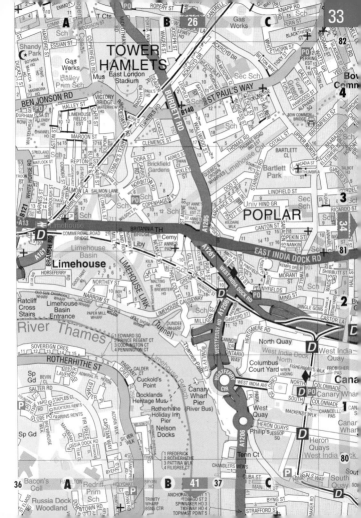

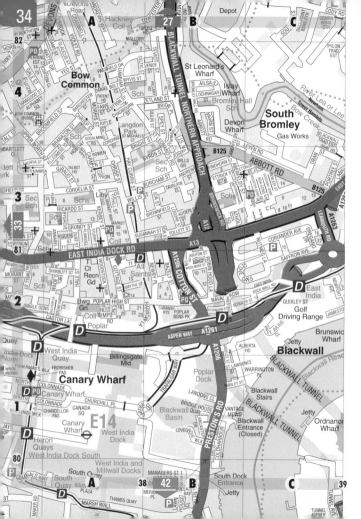

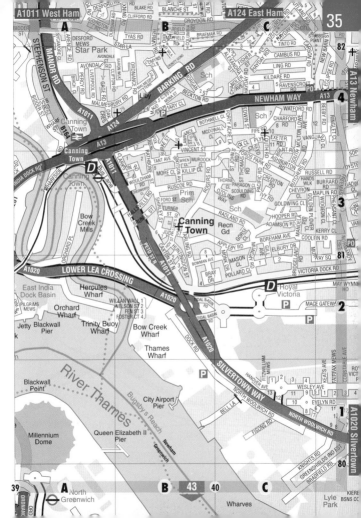

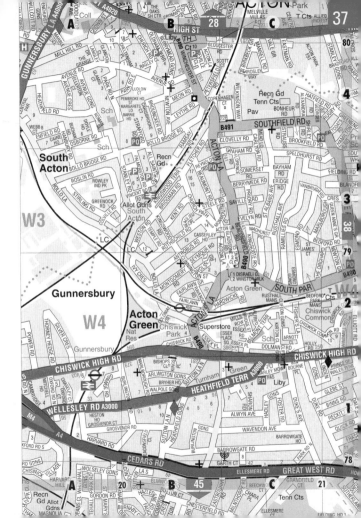

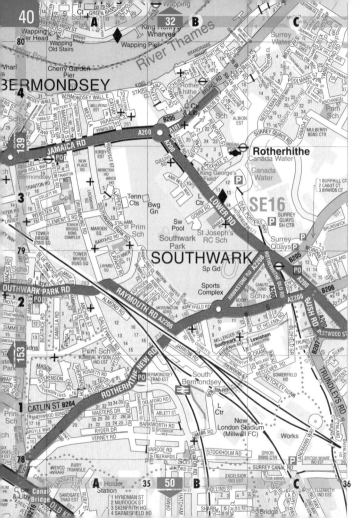

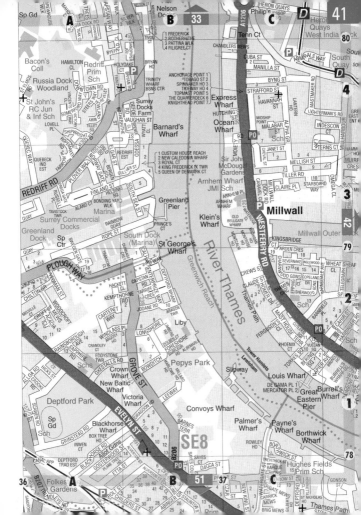

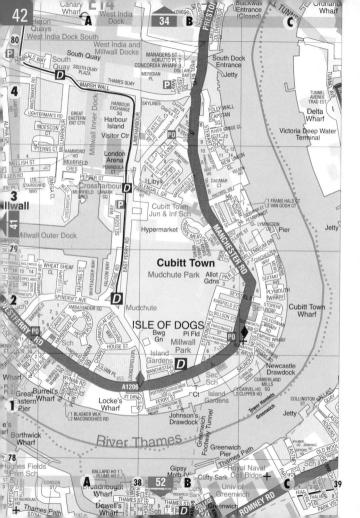

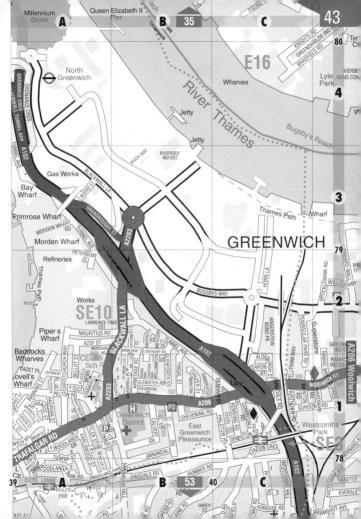

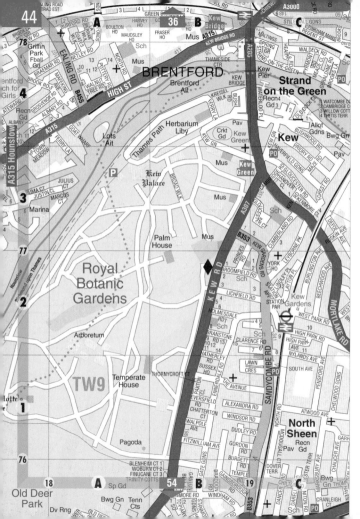

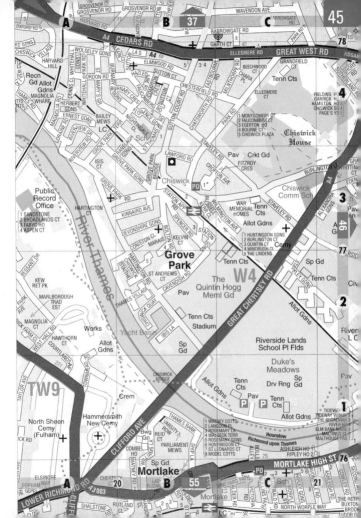

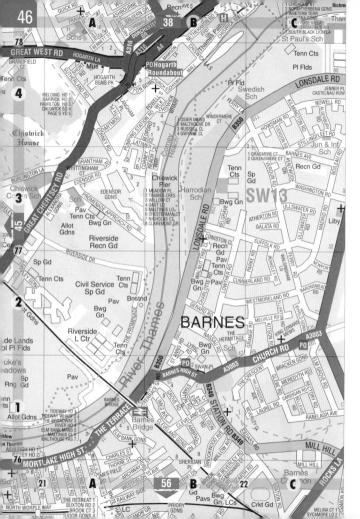

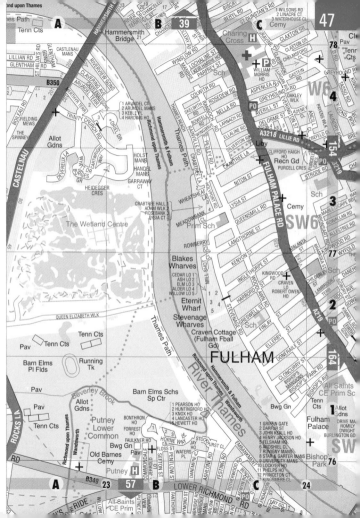

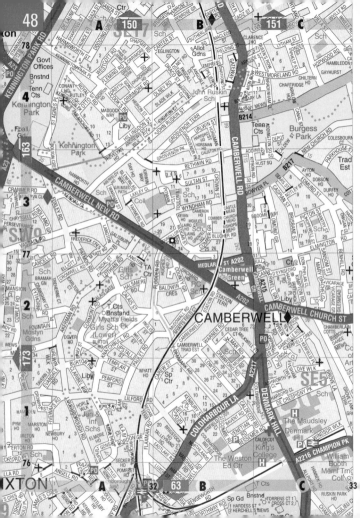

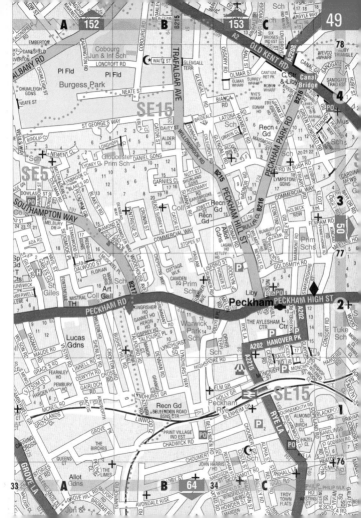

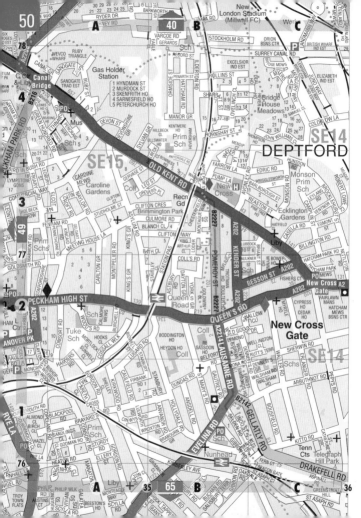

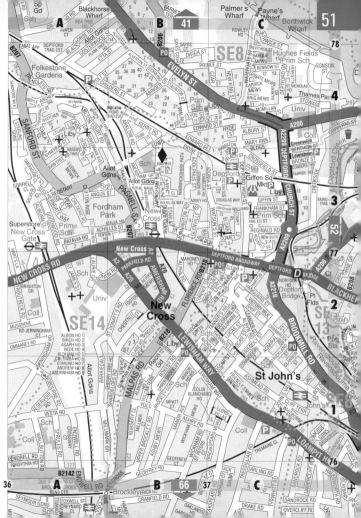

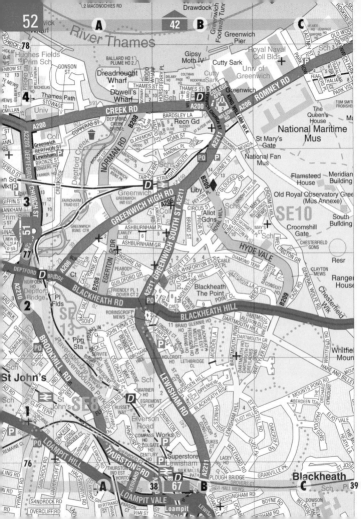

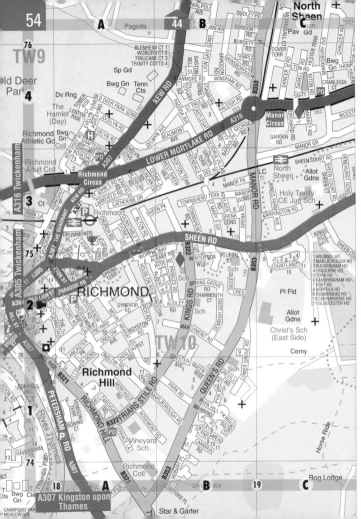

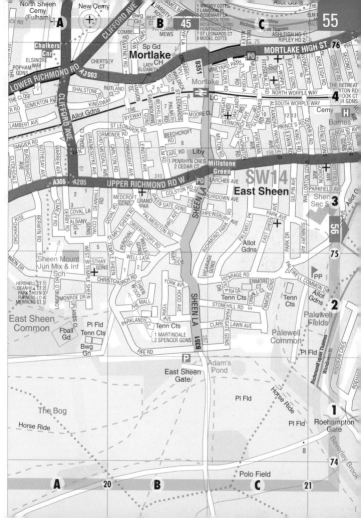

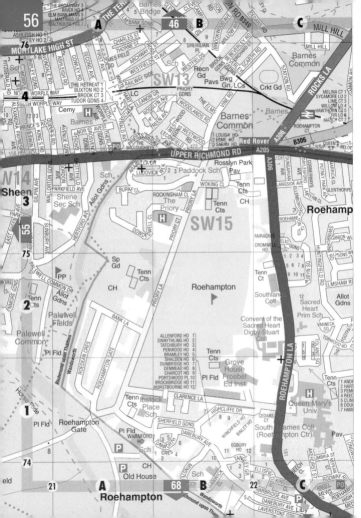

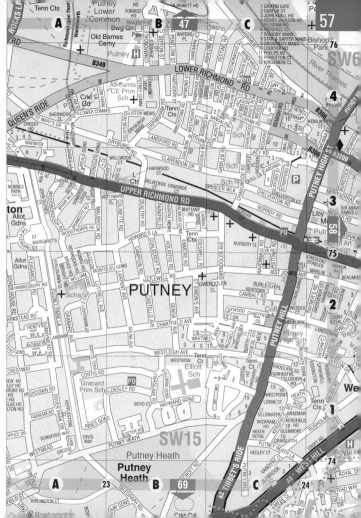

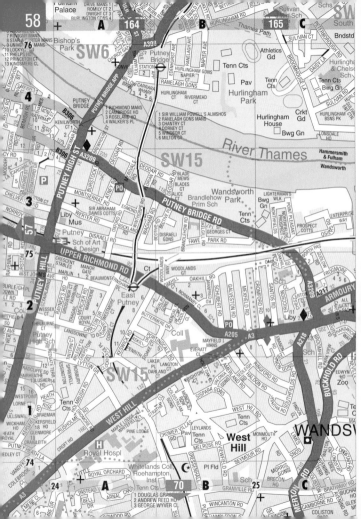

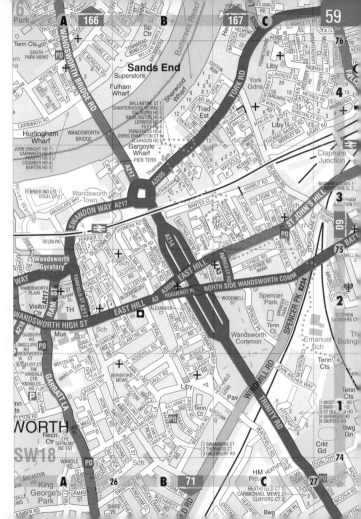

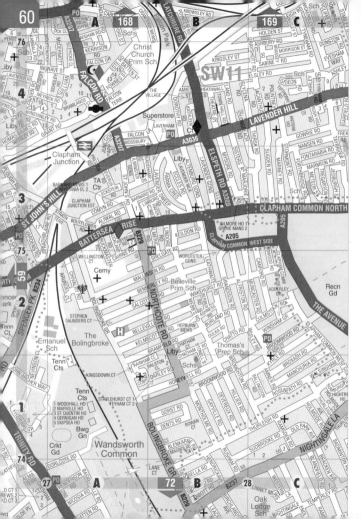

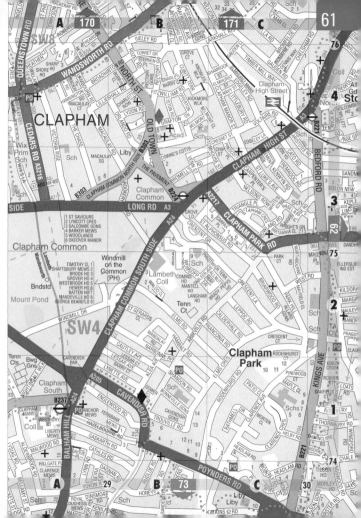

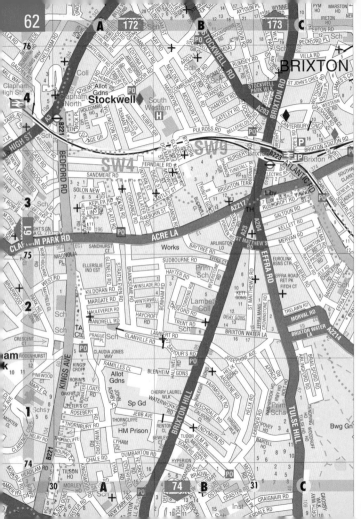

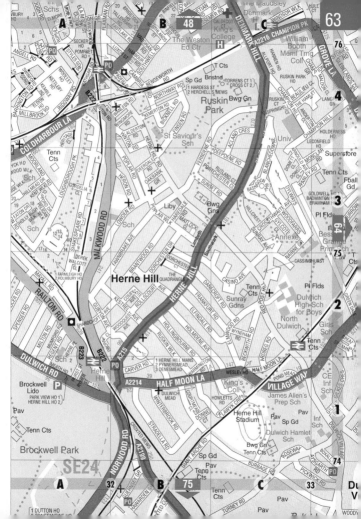

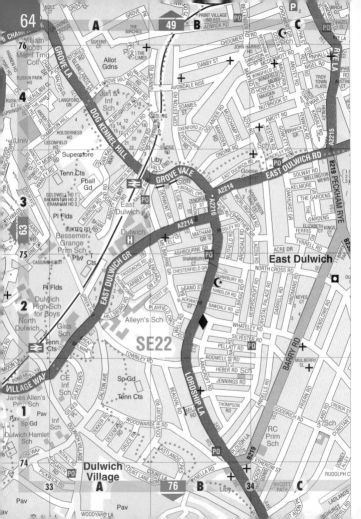

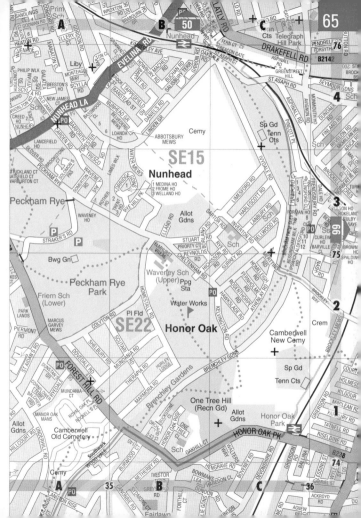

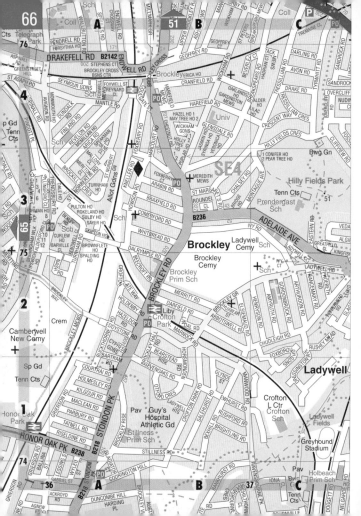

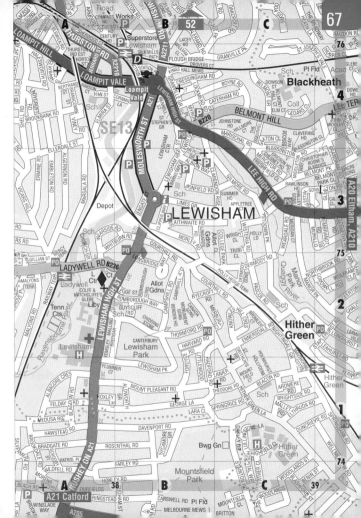

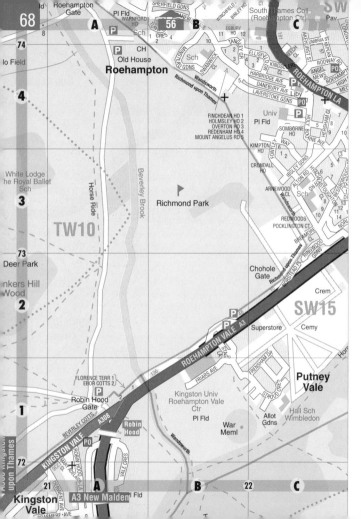

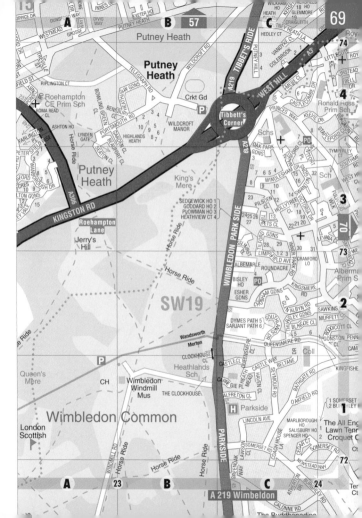

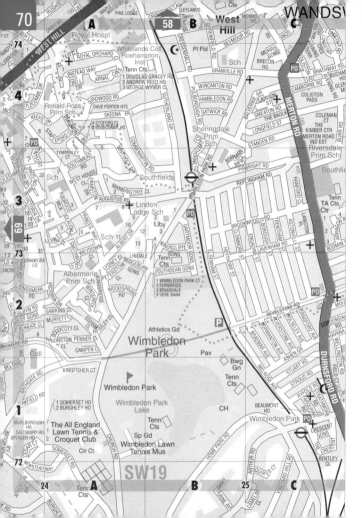

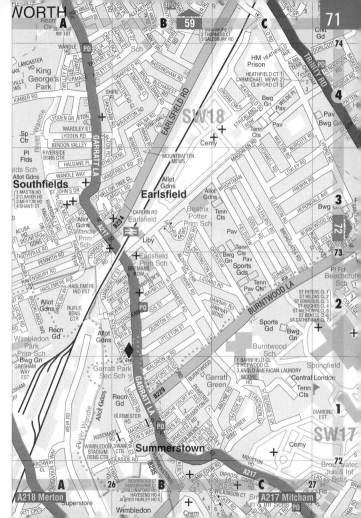

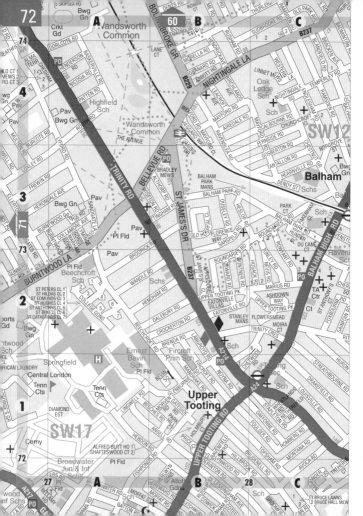

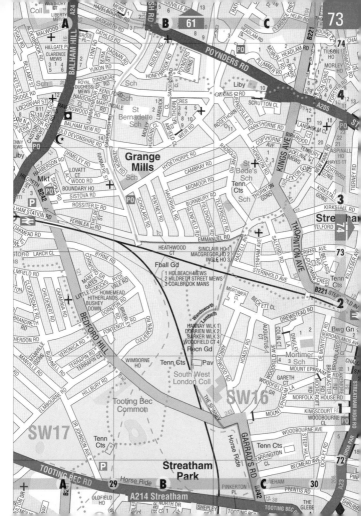

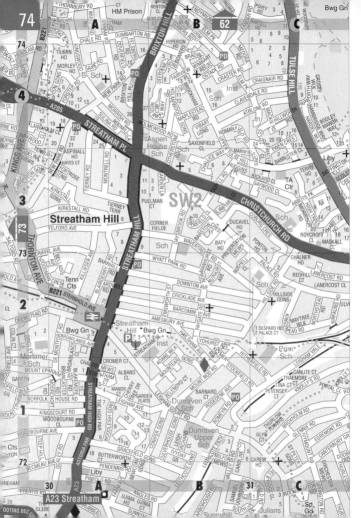

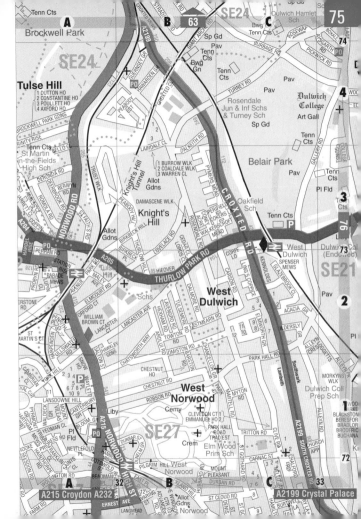

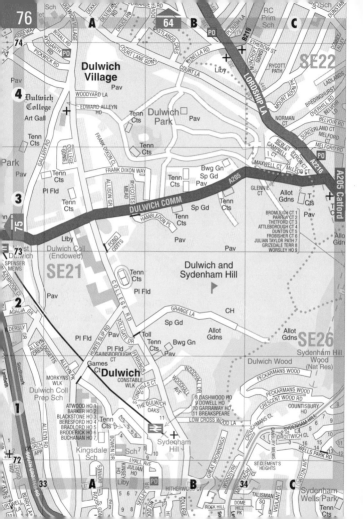

Key to enlarged map pages

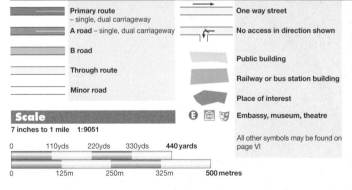

		Primrose Hill			Islington		
78 79	80–81	82 83	84 85	86 87			
Maida Vale			Finsbury	Shoreditch		Bethnal Green
88 89	90 91	92 93	94 95	96 97	98 99	
Paddington	Marylebone		Bloomsbury			
100 101	102 103	104 105	106–107 Holborn	108–109 City	110 111 Whitechapel
Notting Hill	Bayswater	Mayfair				
112 113	114 115	116 117	118 119	120 121	122 123	124 125
Kensington	Knightsbridge		Southwark			
126 127	128 129	130 131	132 133	134 135	136 137	138 139 Bermondsey
		Westminster		Lambeth		
140 141	142 143	144 145	146 147	148 149	150 151	152 153
Earl's Court	Chelsea	Belgravia				
154 155	156 157	158 159	160 161	162 163		
Fulham		Battersea	Nine Elms			
164 165	166 167	168 169	170 171	172 173 Stockwell		

Additional symbols on enlarged maps

Primary route – single, dual carriageway	One way street
A road – single, dual carriageway	No access in direction shown
B road	
	Public building
Through route	Railway or bus station building
Minor road	Place of interest
	E 🏛 🛡 Embassy, museum, theatre

Scale

7 inches to 1 mile 1:9051

0	110yds	220yds	330yds	**440 yards**

0	125m	250m	325m	**500 metres**

All other symbols may be found on page VI

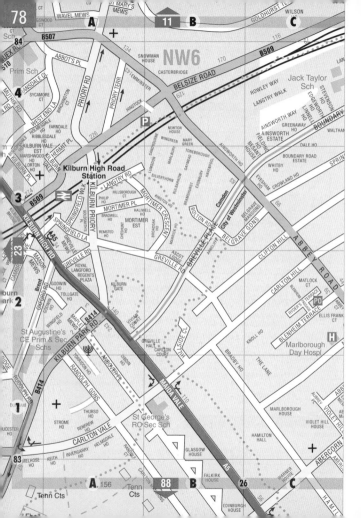

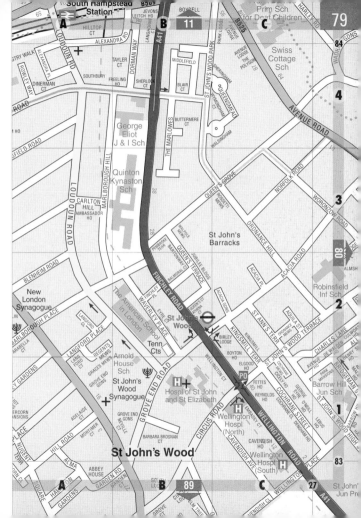

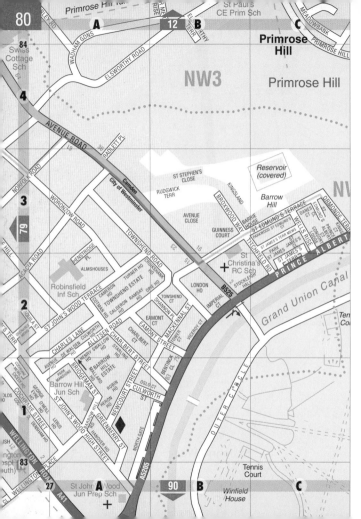

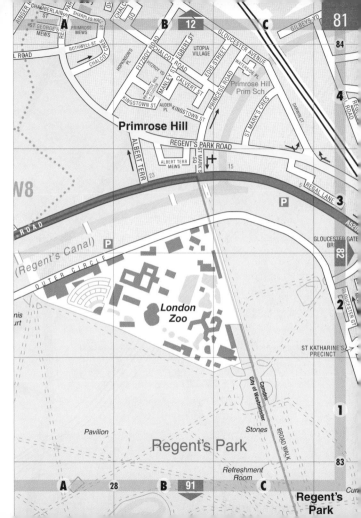

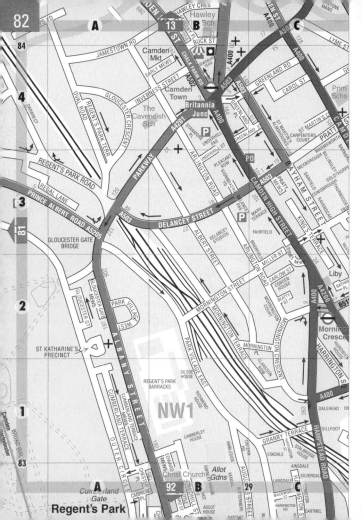

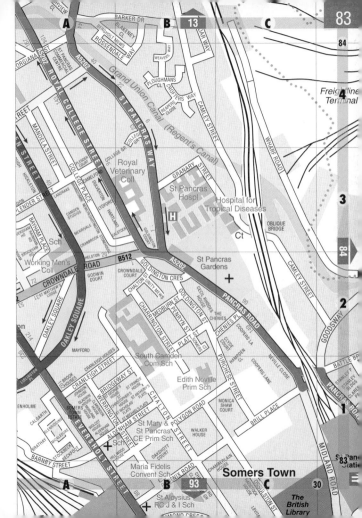

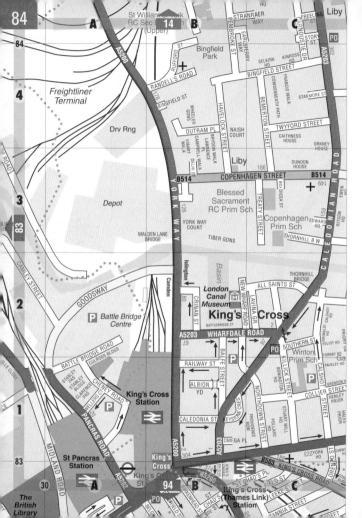

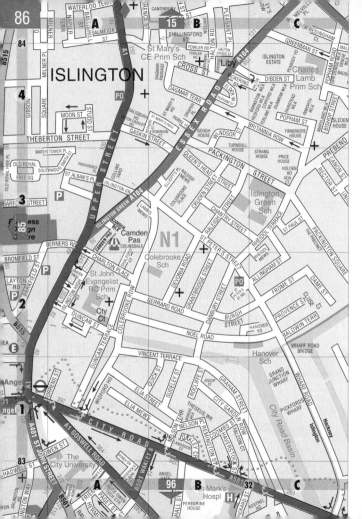

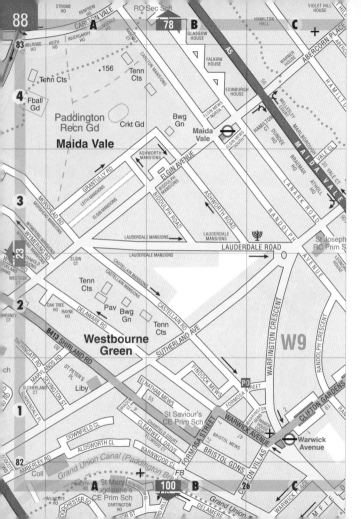

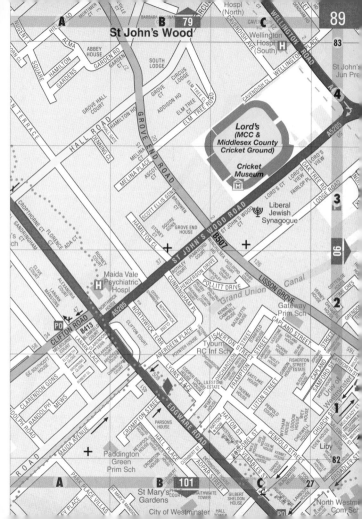

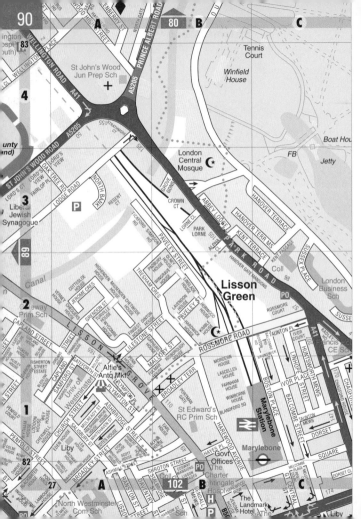

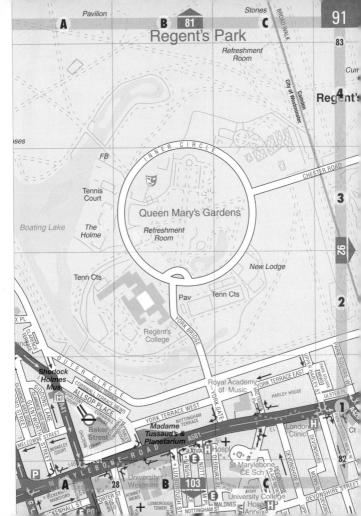

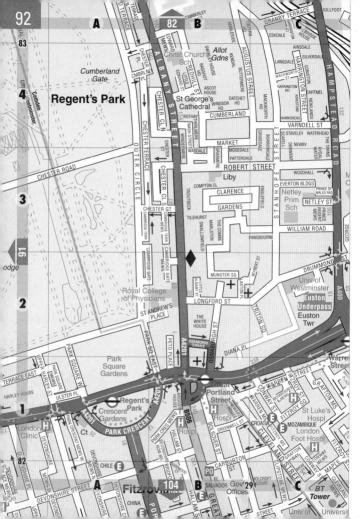

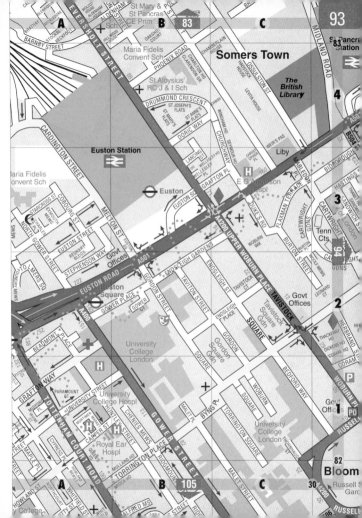

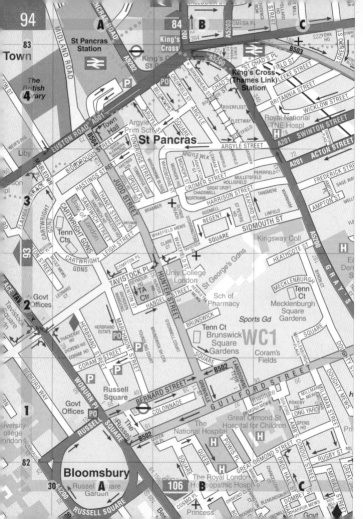

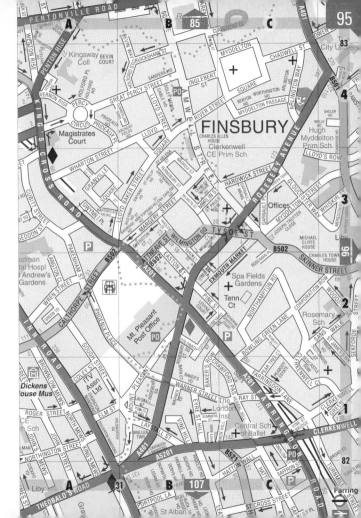

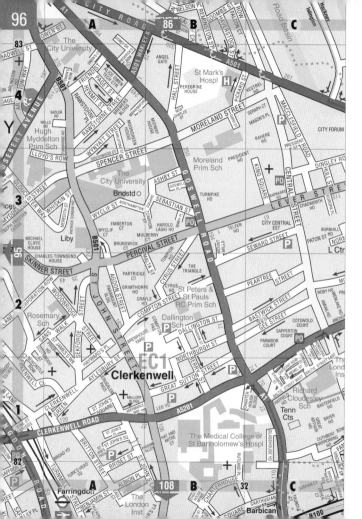

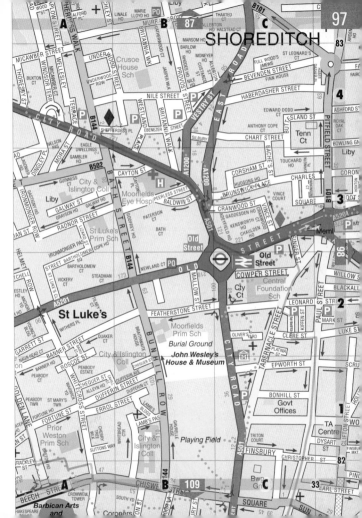

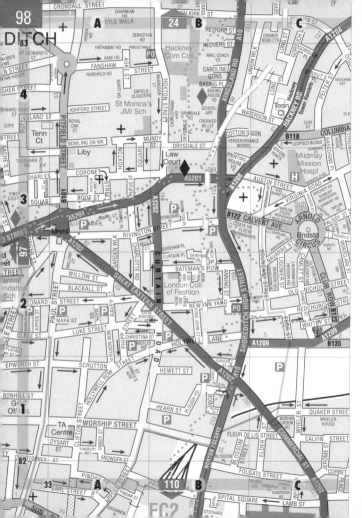

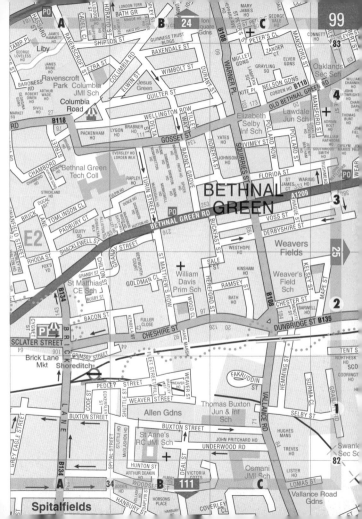

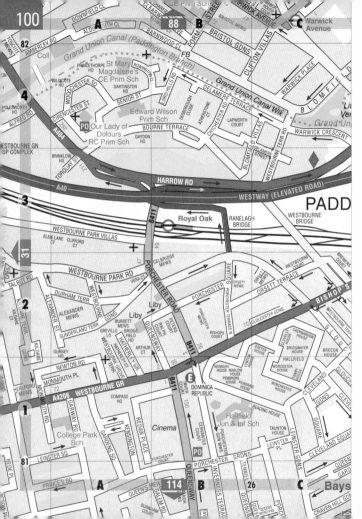

A MAIDA AVENUE
CROME
PARSONS HOUSE
B 89
WYTHAM HOUSE
COSWAY
C
PENFOLD STREET
82

PL PL ROAD

Paddington Green Prim Sch

HETHPOOL

HOMER ROW

CROMPTON HOUSE

CUTHBERT STREET

GILBERT STREET

DEVONSHIRE CLOSE

BOSCOBEL ST
VENABLES ST
WINDMILL DRIVE

BROAD

North Wes

PARK PLACE

HOWLEY PLACE

ST MARY'S MANSIONS

CROMPTON HOUSE

CUTHBERT COURT

ADPAR STREET

St Mary's Gardens

PHILIP COURT

BRAITHWAITE TOWER

GILBERT SHELDON HOUSE

POOL HOUSE

MILES PLACE

ST JAMES'S

4 m

Lis

City of Westminster Coll

HALL TOWER

PENFOLD PLACE

Edgware R

JOHN AIRD COURT

ST MARY'S SQ

PORTEUS RD

HOGAN MEWS

FLEMING COURT

ST MARY'S TER

PADDINGTON GREEN

A5

PO

MILES ST

Lis

HARROW RD
A404

Canal

ST MARY'S SQ

NEWCASTLE PL

Edgware R
(Bakerloo

HARROW ROAD
A404

HARROW ROAD (UNDER)

A40206

HARROW ROAD
A40

HARROW ROAD
A404

W2

INGTON
(Paddington)

HERMITAGE ST

DUDLEY ST

North Westminster Com Sch (Upper)

SIDDONS HOUSE

TARBET ROAD

A4206

Marylebone
Flyo

3

BISHOP'S ROAD BRIDGE

DUDLEY HOUSE

NORTH WHARF ROAD

Paddington Basin

102

Branch)

P

ST MICHA

BRIDGE ROAD
A4205

P

P

St Mary's Hosp

SOUTH WHARF ROAD

Medical Sch

H ✚

STAR STREET

2

WEST

TERRACE

EASTBOURNE TERRACE

Paddington Station 🚉

WINSLAND STREET

WINSLAND MEWS

PRAED STREET

PRAED MS

NORFOLK PLACE

BONVERIE PL

SOUTHWICK

RAMSBO

SOUTH

ELAND

CLEVELAND

EASTBOURNE MEWS

CHILWORTH MEWS

Paddington 🚉

A4205

LONDON MEWS

NORFOLK SQUARE

BOVMTON

RADNOR MEWS

ER MEWS TERRACE

GLOUCESTER MEWS

TERRACE

CHILWORTH MEWS

CONDUIT PL

TALBOT

SQUARE

SUSSEX GARDENS

RADNOR PLACE

SOMER

AND

DEVONSHIRE MEWS

GLOUCESTER ROAD

SMALLBROOK

CONDUIT MEWS

B410

SPRING ST

CONDUIT SQUARE

A4209

CLIFTON

SUSSEX MEWS

CHERWOOD

SUSSEX PLACE

GLOUCESTER

SQUARE

GLOUCESTER

ENS

CRAVEN HILL MS TERR

WESTBOURNE CRES

SUSSEX

BATHURST MEWS

CLIFTON PL

STRATHEA

ST

81

water

CRAVEN HILL

St James & ichael's CE Sch

A ✚

CRAVEN RD

CRAVEN CL

CRAVEN LODGE

BROOK MEWS NTH

B 115

SUSSEX

TERR

BOURN

SUSSEX SQUARE

STANHOPE TERRACE

HYDE PARK

C

SUSSEX

HYDE PARK, GARDENS

27

E SRI LAN

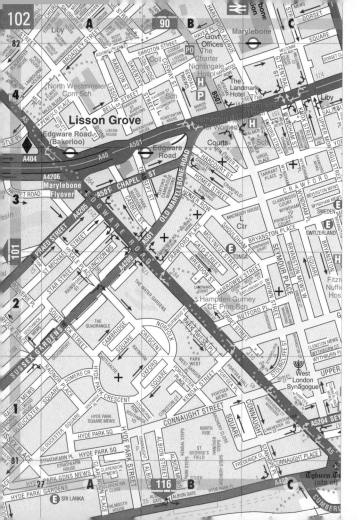

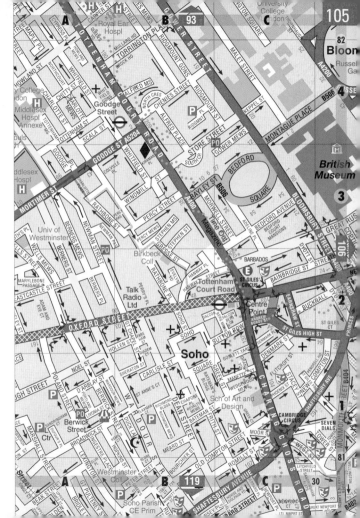

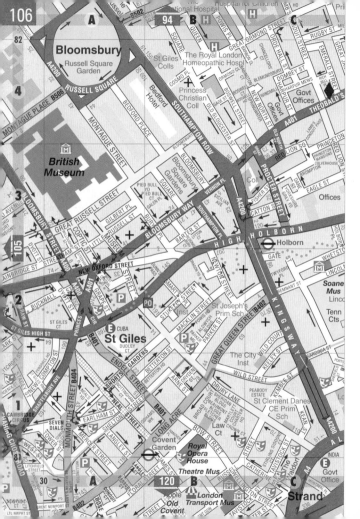

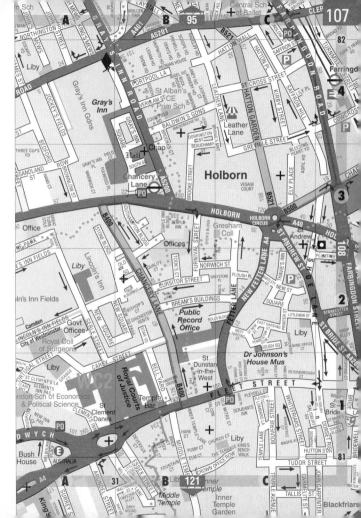

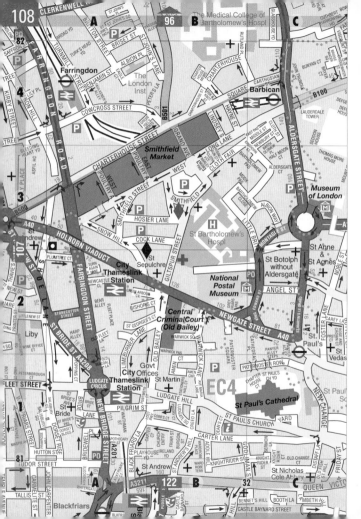

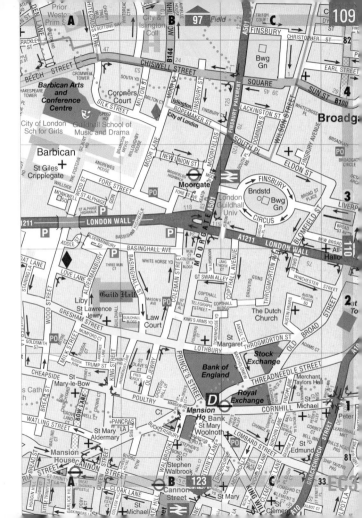

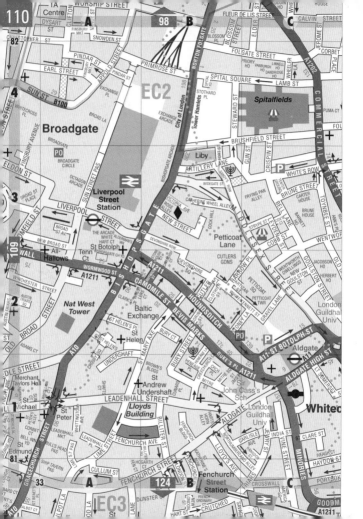

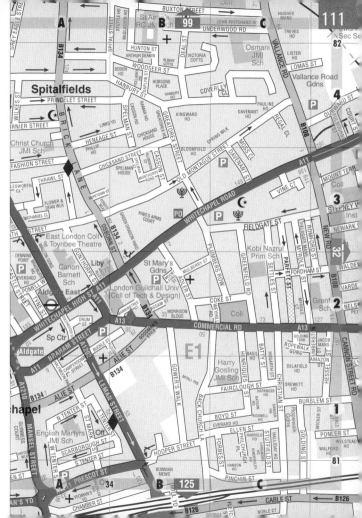

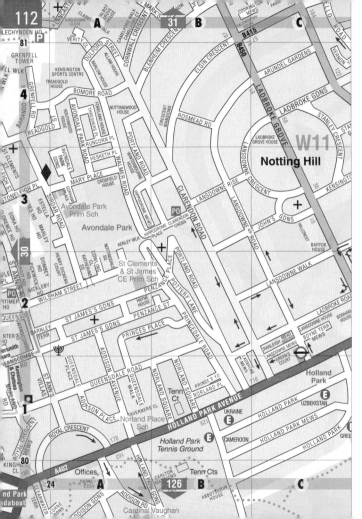

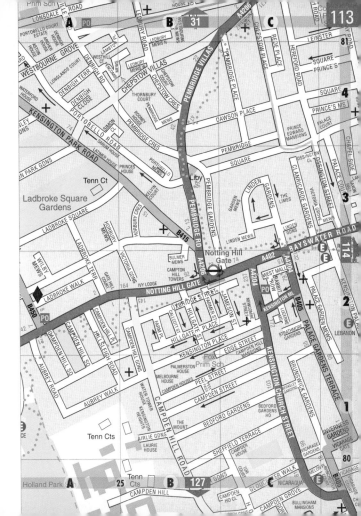

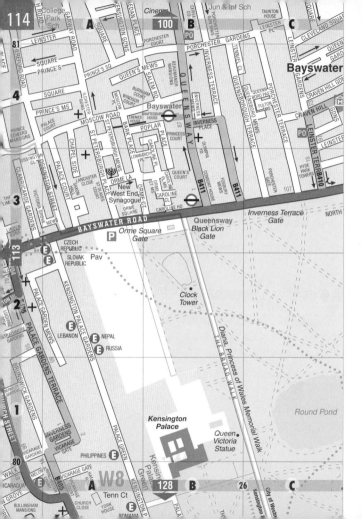

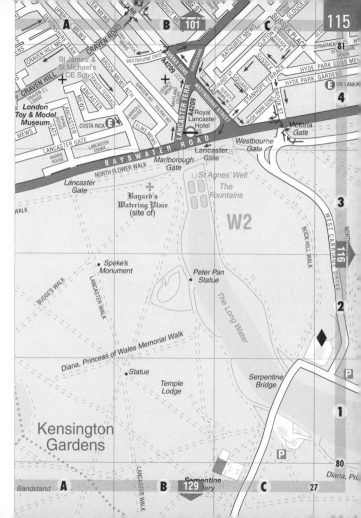

UPPER TER MS

DEVONSHIRE MEWS

CRAVEN HILL MS

CRAVEN ROAD

CONDUIT PAS

GLOUCE

SUSSEX PLACE

GLO

STRATHEARN PL

STRATHEARN

81

H

BATHURST MEWS

CLIFTON PL

SUSSEX SQ

SUSSEX MS E

Westbourne Cres

A4209

SUSSEX GDNS

SUSSEX LANE

BATHURST ST

SUSSEX SQUARE

4

St James' &
St Michael's
CE Scho

CRAVEN HILL

CRAVEN HILL MEWS

BROOK MEWS N

SMALLBROOK MS

BROADLEY

GARDEN MS

CRAVEN TERRACE

WESTBOURNE STREET

MAITLAND COURT

GILRAY RD

WESTBOURNE TERR

STANHOPE TERRACE

HYDE PARK GDNS ME

London
Toy & Model
Museum

CRAVEN CT

CRAVEN HILL GDNS

LANCASTER MEWS

LANCASTER GATE

BARRIE HOUSE

CARROLL HOUSE

ELMS MEWS

COSTA RICA **E**

HYDE PARK GARDENS

HYDE PARK CRESCENT

BROOK ST

HYDE PARK GDNS

E SRI LANKA

Royal
Lancaster
Hotel

LANCASTER COURT

⊖
Lancaster
Gate

B A Y S W A T E R   R O A D

Victoria
Gate

Westbourne
Gate

LANCASTER GATE

LANCASTER TERR

LANCASTER GATE

NORTH FLOWER WALK

Marlborough
Gate

Lancaster
Gate

Lancaster
Gate

St Agnes' Well

The
Fountains

W2

Bayard's
Watering Place
(site of)

3

WEST CARRIAGE DRIVE

BUCK HILL WALK

NORTH

116

WALK

BUDGE'S WALK

LANCASTER WALK

Speke's
Monument

Peter Pan
Statue

The Long Water

2

◆

Diana, Princess of Wales Memorial Walk

Statue

Temple
Lodge

Serpentine
Bridge

P

**Kensington
Gardens**

1

P

80

Diana, Pri

LANCASTER WALK

Serpentine
lery

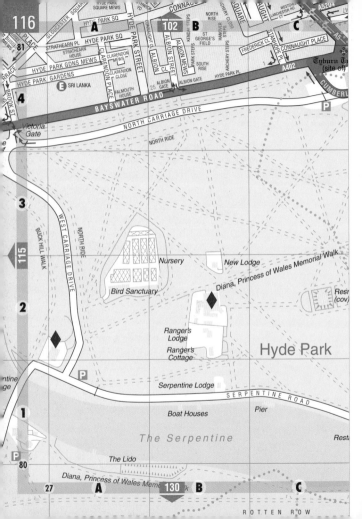

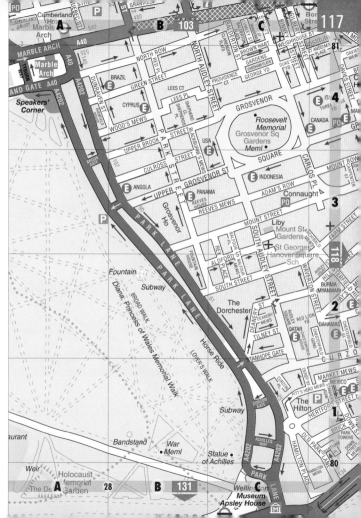

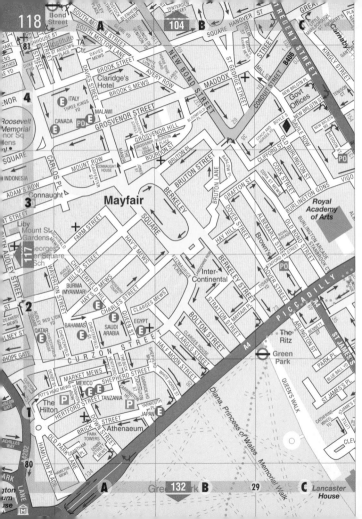

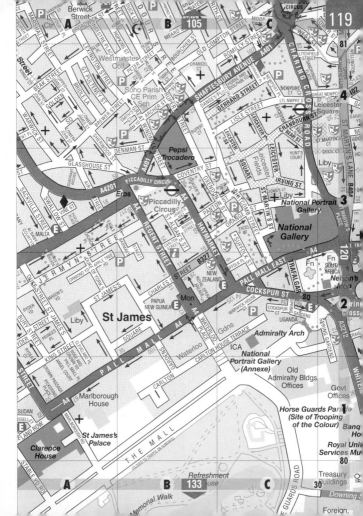

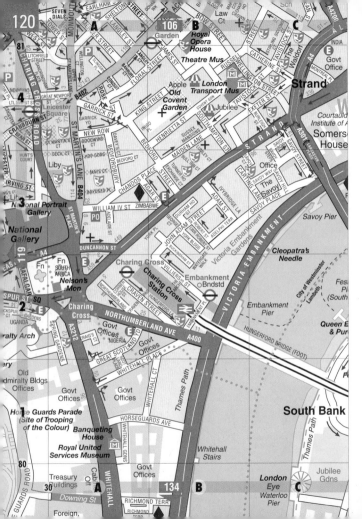

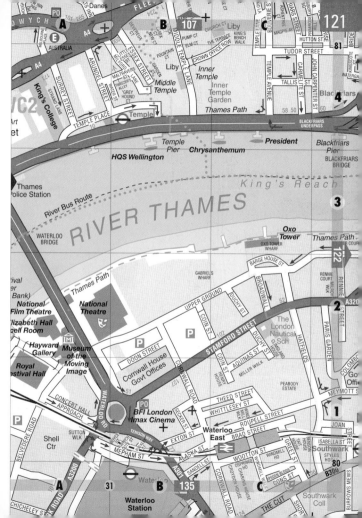

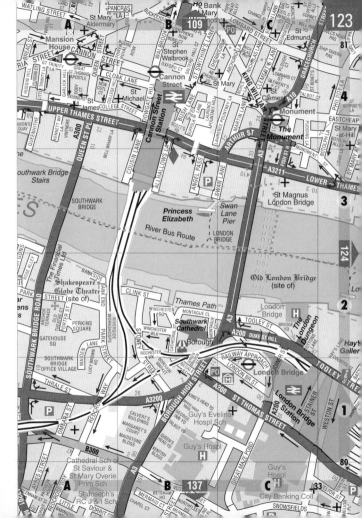

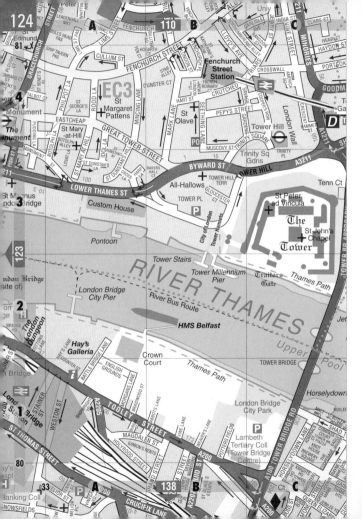

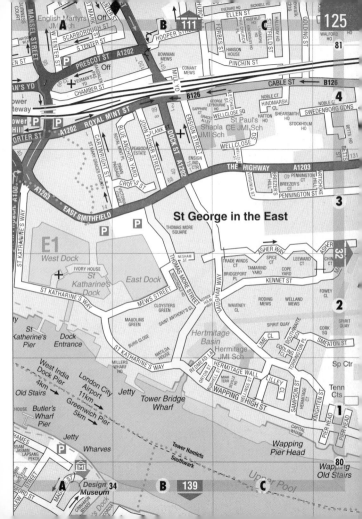

St George in the East

E1

West Dock

East Dock

St Katharine's Dock

IVORY HOUSE

THOMAS MORE SQUARE

THOMAS MORE STREET

St Katharine's Pier

Dock Entrance

West India Dock Pier 4km
Old Stairs

Butler's Wharf Pier

London City Airport 11km
Greenwich Pier 5km

Tower Bridge Wharf

Design Museum

Jetty

Jetty

Wharves

Tower Hamlets
Southwark

Upper Pool

Wapping Pier Head

Wapping Old Stairs

Hertmitage Basin

Hermitage JMI Sch

Hermitage Wall

WAPPING HIGH ST

ST KATHARINE'S WAY

MEWS STREET

CLOYSTERS GREEN

SAINT ANTHONY'S CL

MAUDLINS GREEN

BURR CLOSE

MATILDA HOUSE

MILLER'S WHARF HO

REDMEAD

OPTON SQ

BODMAN

MIAH TERR

LILLEY CL

VAUGHAN WAY

KENNET ST

TRADE WINDS PL

SPICE CT

LEEWARD CT

TAMARIND YARD

COPE YARD

BRIDGEPORT PL

WAVENEY CL

RODING MEWS

WELLAND MEWS

SPIRIT QUAY

LIME CL

SPIRIT QUAY

CORK SQ

SMEATON ST

COOLING CL

SOUTHWAITE

LODING TOW PL

FOWEY CL

CHIN CL

32

2

1

FISHER WAY

CAPITAL WHARF

PIER HEAD

PIER HEAD

Tenn Cts

Sp Ctr

80

English Martyrs
JMI

MANSEL STREET

SCARBOROUGH ST

S TENTER ST

W TENTER ST

PRESCOT ST

A1202

CHAMBER ST

Off

Off

BOWMAN MEWS

CONANT MEWS

MILL YD

CABLE ST ← B126

B126

ELLEN ST

EVERARD HO

BICKNELL HO

FORBES ST

HANSON HOUSE

PINCHIN ST

HOOPER STREET

SETFIELD ST

FIELD ST

HADFIELD HO

PHILCHURCH PL

HINMAN PL

SALBY

111

WALFORD HO

81

GOLDING ST

NOBLE CT

HINDMARSH CL

SHEARSMITH HO

HATTON HO

STOCKHOLM HO

SWEDENBORG GDNS

NOBLE CT

BETTS ST

131

4

3

ROYAL MINT ST

A1202

JOHN FISHER STREET

BLUE ANCHOR YARD

ENSIGN STREET

DOCK ST A1202

WELLCLOSE SQ

St Paul's
Shapla CE JMI Sch

WELLCLOSE SQ

Shapla JMI Sch

THE HIGHWAY A1203

VIRGINIA ST

PENNINGTON ST

Op PENNINGTON CT

BREEZER'S CT

PENNINGTON HILL

ARTICHOKE HILL

SWAN PASSAGE

GRACE ALLEY

SAPPHIRE CT

PEABODY ESTATE

ROYAL MINT PL

ENSIGN IND CTR

ENSIGN IND CTR

CROFTS

VICTORIA COURT

EAST SMITHFIELD

A1203

CARTWRIGHT ST

ST MARY GRACES COURT

TOWER GATEWAY

PORTER ST

GUINNESS TRUST

HAYDON ST

Tower Hill

ST KATHARINE'S WAY

A100

34

139

George Leybourne

CONANT MEWS

SAMPSON ST

HERMITAGE

KNIGHTEN ST

PELHAM ST

WAPPING

A

B

C

A

B

C

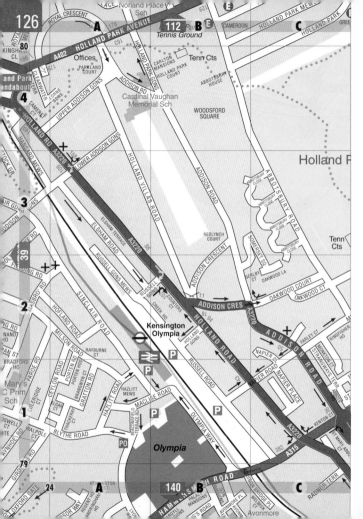

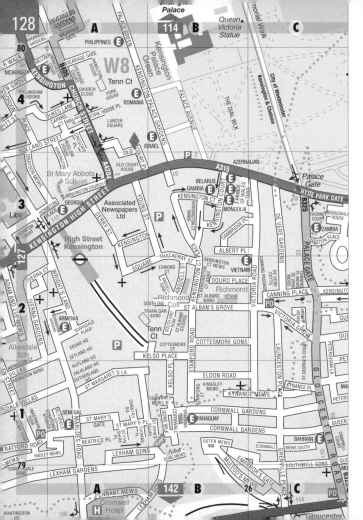

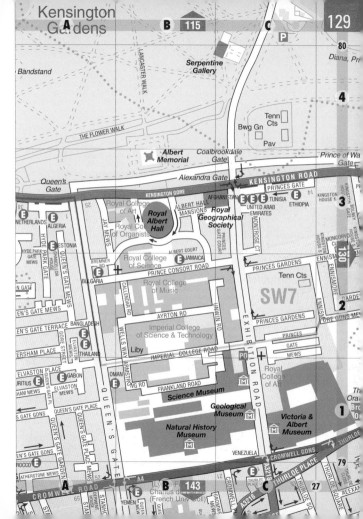

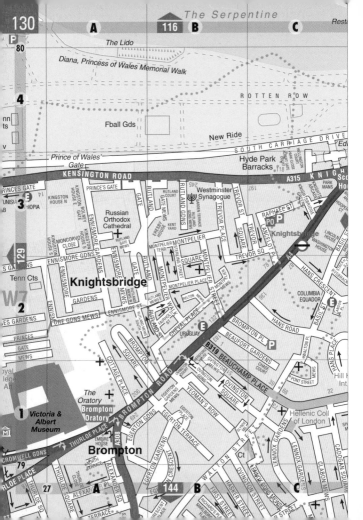

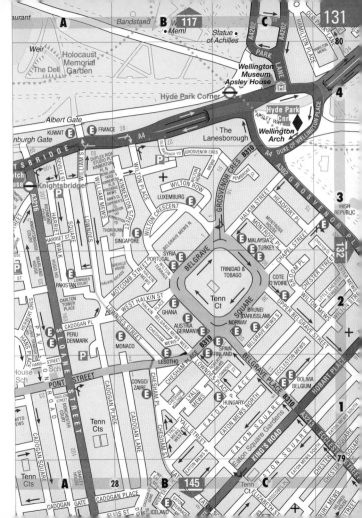

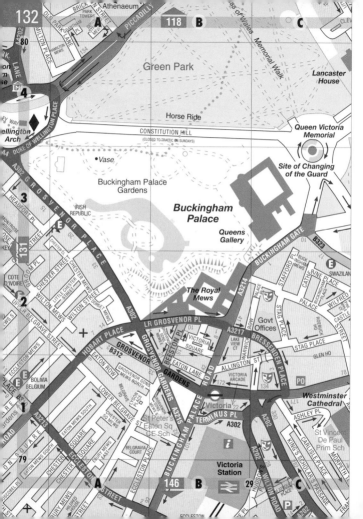

Atheneaum

BRICK ST
Park Terr
PARK TOWERS
OLD PARK LANE
CE METS
HAMILTON MEWS
MILTON PLACE
80

ss of Wales
Memorial Walk

CLEV

Green Park

Lancaster
House

EY WAY
4
Wellington
Arch

Horse Ride

DUKE OF WELLINGTON PLACE
A4

CONSTITUTION HILL
(CLOSED TO TRAFFIC ON SUNDAYS)

Queen Victoria
Memorial

A302 GROSVENOR PLACE

•Vase

Site of Changing
of the Guard

Buckingham Palace
Gardens

A44

HEADFORT PL
MONTROSE
HOUSE
KEY
131

3

IRISH
REPUBLIC

Buckingham
Palace

E
CHESTER ST
LITTLE CHESTER
CHESTER MEWS
DORSET MEWS

BUCKINGHAM GATE
B323

E
SWAZILAN

COTE
D'IVOIRE

GROOM PL

WILTON MEWS

WILTON STREET

Queens
Gallery

A3214
PALACE ST
STAFFORD PL
CATH
PINE PLACE
WILFRED
BUCK
INGHAM
PLACE

2

MEWS S

UPPER BELGRAVE STREET

The Royal
Mews

A3214
BOW
WARWICK
STAG
PLACE
ROEBUCK HO
CASTLE
STREET

LR GROSVENOR PL
A3217

Govt
Offices

STAG PLACE

GLEN HO

HOBART PLACE

BRESSENDEN PLACE

B312
EATON ROW
GROSVENOR GDNS
MEWS NORTH
BELGRAVE
LAKE
VIEW CT

VICTORIA
SQUARE

PO
78

E
BOLIVIA
BELGIUM

GROSVENOR GARDENS

BEESTON PL

VICTORIA
ARCADE

Westminster
Cathedral

1

LOWER BELGRAVE
CHESTER ROW
SQ SW1W8

EATON MEWS
ECCLESTON MEWS

BUCKINGHAM PALACE ROAD

EATON LANE

B216

ALLINGTON ST
VICTORIA
ST
172
134

ASHLEY PL

St Vincent
De Paul
Prim Sch

A3213 ROAD
79

CHESTER SQUARE
BELGRAVIA
COURT

ST EATON MEWS SOUTH
BURY MEWS EAST

St Peter's
ST Eaton Sq
CE Sch

TERMINUS PL

Victoria
A302

KING'S SCHOLARS PASSAGE
CARLISLE PLACE
MORPETH

CHESTER
BURY MEWS SOUTH
HILGROVE
STREET
ECCLESTON

Victoria
Station

i

P

A202 WILTON ROAD
HUDSON

A202
A202
S
ST Vincent
29

ECCLESTON

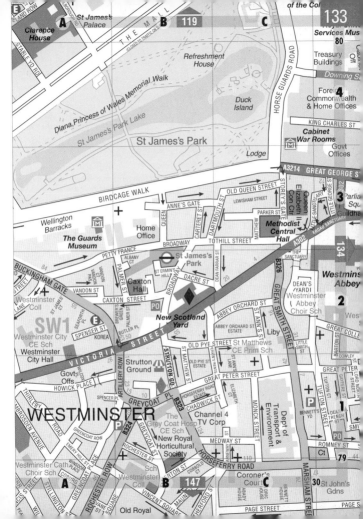

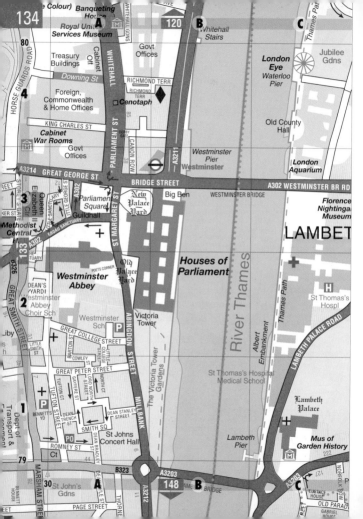

(e Colour)

Banqueting House

Royal United Services Museum

WHITEHALL GDNS

Whitehall Stairs

Thames Path

80

HORSE GUARDS ROAD

Cabinet Off

Treasury Buildings

WHITEHALL

Downing St

Govt Offices

RICHMOND TERR

RICHMOND TERR

■Cenotaph

London Eye

Waterloo Pier

Jubilee Gdns

4

Foreign, Commonwealth & Home Offices

PARLIAMENT ST

DERBY GATE

KING CHARLES ST

85

CANON ROW

Old County Hall

Cabinet War Rooms

Govt Offices

Queen Elizabeth

A3214 **GREAT GEORGE ST**

BRIDGE STREET

A3211

Westminster Pier

Westminster

London Aquarium

A302 WESTMINSTER BR RD

A302

STORY'S GATE

3

CAXTON STREET

LITTLE GEORGE ST

A302

A302

LITTLE SANCTUARY

Parliament Square

Guildhall

BROAD SANCTUARY

New Palace Yard

Big Ben

WESTMINSTER BRIDGE

WESTMINSTER BRIDGE

LAMBET

133

B326

GREAT SMITH STREET

Methodist Central

THE SANCTUARY

+

Houses of Parliament

River Thames

St Thomas's Hospl

H

2

POETS CORNER

Old Palace Yard

Westminster Abbey

DEAN'S YARD

Westminster Abbey Choir Sch

Westminster Sch

P

Thames Path

Albert Embankment

LAMBETH PALACE ROAD

LITTLE SMITH ST

COWLEY

GREAT COLLEGE STREET

COLLEGE MEWS

Victoria Tower

GREAT PETER STREET

NORTH CT

LORD NORTH ST

GAYFERE ST

ABINGDON STREET

The Victoria Tower Gardens

MILLBANK

St Thomas's Hospital Medical School

1

TUFTON STREET

P

BENNETTS YD

LITTLE SMITH ST

DEAN TRENCH ST

DEAN STANLEY STREET

SMITH SQ

Lambeth Palace

79

Dept of Transport & ~~company~~

MARSHAM STREET

PO

DEAN BRADLEY ST

ROMNEY ST

Ct

St Johns Concert Hall

Lambeth Pier

Mus of Garden History

■

30

St John's Gdns

DELL ST

BESSBOROUGH ST

THORNEY

B323

A3212

A3203

LAMBETH BRIDGE

A3203

NORFOLK ROW

EUSTACE HOUSE

OLD PARAD

GABRIEL HOUSE

PAGE STREET

BENNETT ST

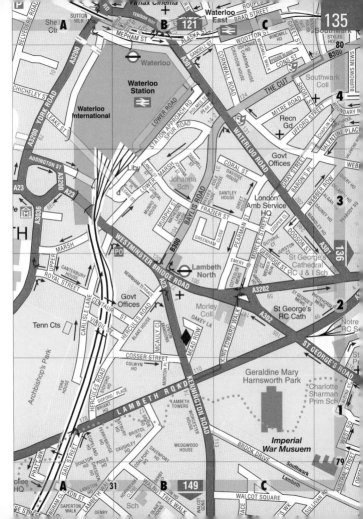

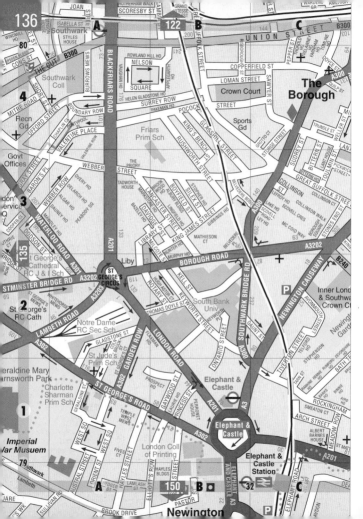

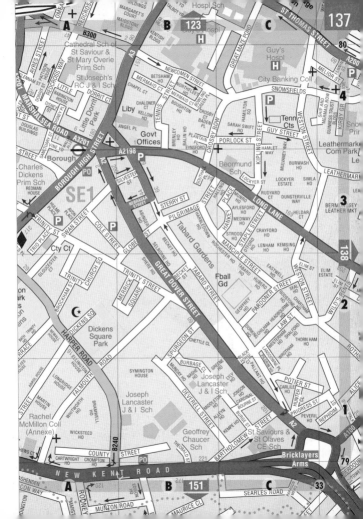

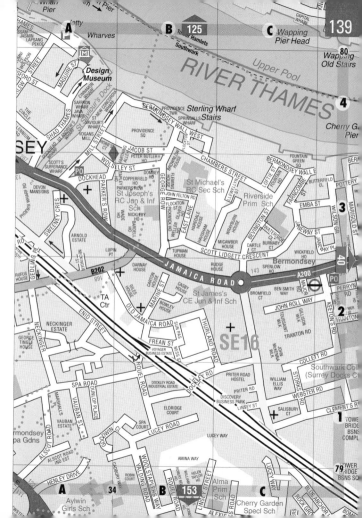

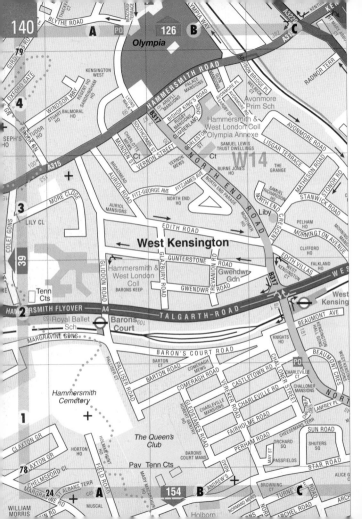

BLYTHE ROAD

79

KENSINGTON WEST

Olympia

OLYMPIA WAY

A3220

KENT

RADNOR TERR

OXFORD GATE

4

WINDSOR WAY

SANDRINGHAM HO

STUART BALMORAL HO

LYONS

CHARLOTTE Ct

HAMMERSMITH ROAD

B317

BISHOP KING'S ROAD

ARGYLL MANSIONS

VERNON STREET

VERNON MEWS

NORTH END ROAD

ADDISON BRIDGE PL

TALGAROM PL

PALACE MANSIONS

AVONMORE PL

AVONMORE

Avonmore Prim Sch

WEBBER HO

Hammersmith & West London Coll Olympia Annexe

SAMUEL LEWIS TRUST DWELLINGS

LISGAR TERRACE

AVONMORE ROAD

SEPH'S HO

A315

A315

TUDOR KENSINGTON

100

A315

CHARLOTTE Ct

SOUTHCOMBE ST

BROADMEAD

AURIOL ROAD

MUNDEN ST

FITZ-GEORGE AVE

GIRLSTONE Ct

CUMBERLAND Ct

BURNE JONES HO

SAMUEL RICHARDSON HO

THE GRANGE

W14

3

MORE CLOSE

LILY CL

AURIOL MANSIONS

FITZJAMES AVE

NORTH END PARADE

NORTH END

FITZJAMES AVE

NORTH END

MORTIMER

NORTH END Liby

NORTH END CRESCENT

STANWICK ROAD

PELHAM HO

MATHESON ROAD

STONOR RD

MORNINGTON MANS

COLET GDNS

39

EDITH ROAD

← **West Kensington**

GLIDDON ROAD

Hammersmith & West London Coll

BARONS KEEP

GUNTERSTONE

GLAZBURY ROAD

GWENDWR

TREVANION RD

ROAD

Gwendwr Gdn

GWENDWR

MORNINGTON AVENUE

CLIFFORD HO

EDITH VILLAS

FALKLAND HO

WEST KENSINGTON Ct

B317

WES

2

HAMMERSMITH FLYOVER A4

Royal Ballet Sch

163

Barons Court

TALGARTH ROAD

West Kensing

West Kensing

MARGRAVINE GDNS

Tenn Cts

BEAUMONT AVE

KNIGHTS HO

BEAUMONT CRES

KENSINGTON HALL GDNS

WEST KENSINGTON MANSIONS

NOR

PALLISER ROAD

BARON'S COURT ROAD

BARTON Ct

BARTON ROAD

COMERAGH MEWS

COMERAGH ROAD

CASTLETOWN ROAD

VEREKER ROAD

CHALLONER STREET

PO

CHARLEVILLE Ct

CHALLONER MANSIONS

LANFREY PL

1

Hammersmith Cemetery

GLIDDON ROBERTS RD GLAZBURY

CHARLEVILLE MANSIONS

CHARLEVILLE ROAD

FAIRHOLME ROAD

PERHAM ROAD

CHEESEMANS TERR

ORCHARD SQ

MAY ST

SUN ROAD

SHUTERS SQ

STAR ROAD

ALICE G

CLAXTON GR

78

HORTON HO

HOLMEAD HUNT

The Queen's Club

BARONS COURT MANS

Pav Tenn Cts

PASSFIELDS

CAXTON GR

CHELMSFORD CL

24 ST ALBANS TERR

COP

MARGRAVINE RD

MARY MACARTHUR

MUSCAL

BROWNING CT

TURNE

NORMAND MEWS

ARCHEL ROAD

ARCH

WILLIAM MORRIS

Holborn

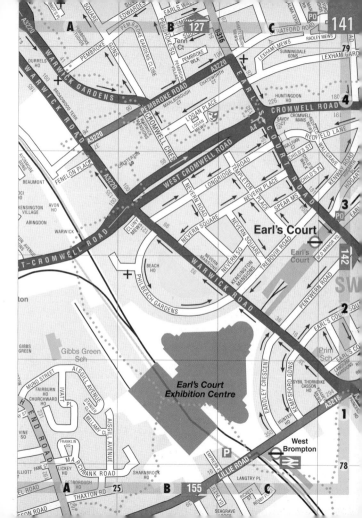

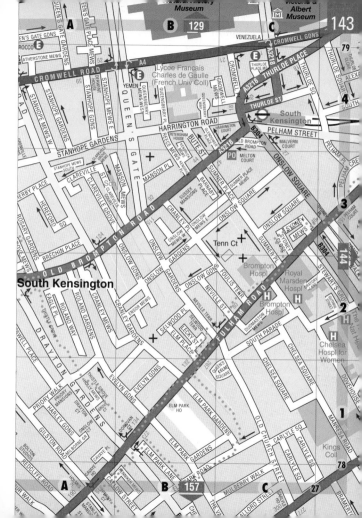

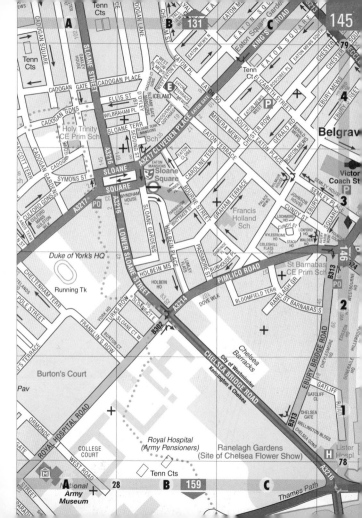

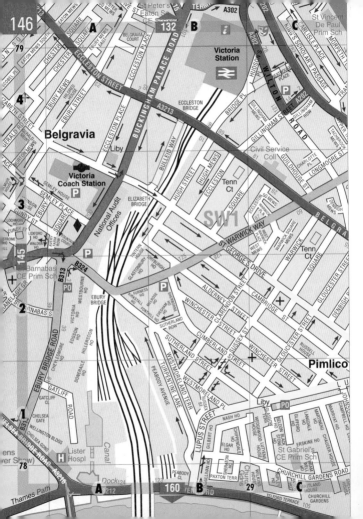

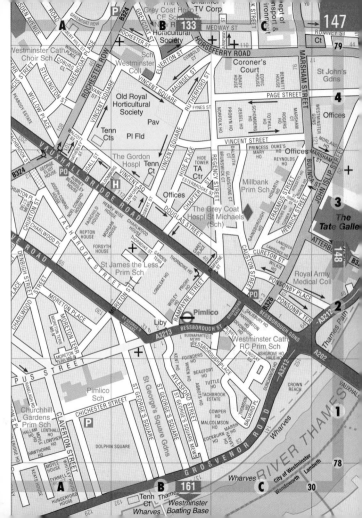

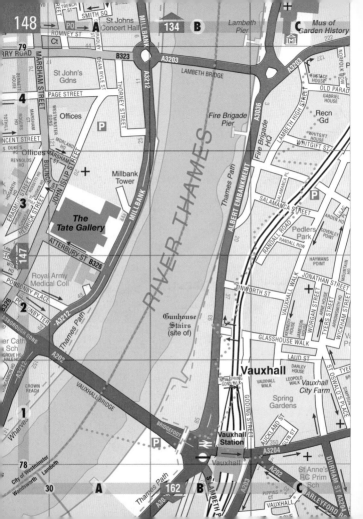

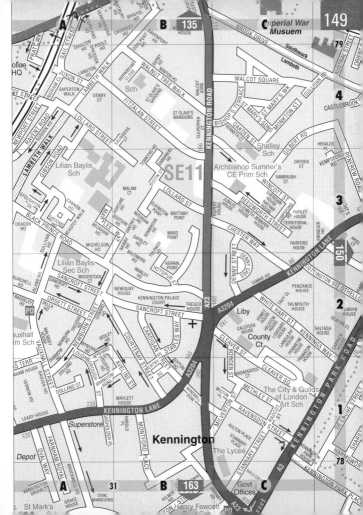

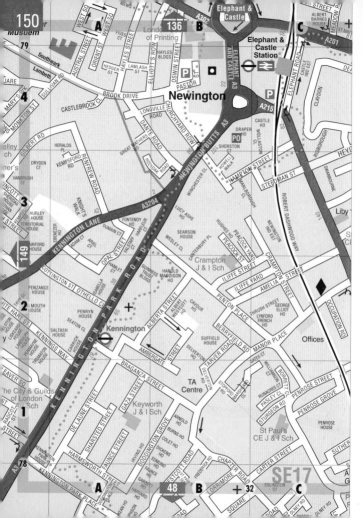

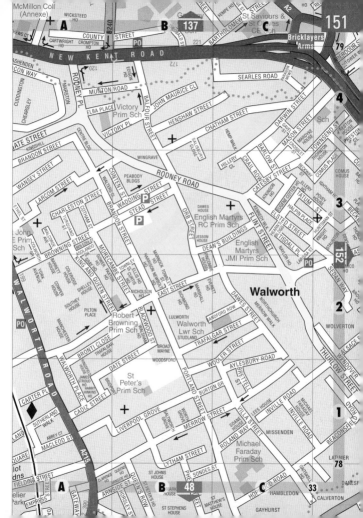

McMillon Coll
(Annexe)

WICKSTEED
HO

A COUNTY STREET **B** 137

CARTWRIGHT HO
CROMPTON HO
PO

St Saviours &
St f_____ es
Ch ___ ch

Bricklayers
Arms

79

NEW KENT ROAD

SEARLES ROAD

RODNEY PL
MUNTON ROAD

ELBA PLACE Victory
Prim Sch

VICTORY PL
JOHN MAURICE CL
HENSHAW STREET
CHATHAM STREET

DARWIN STREET
MASON STREET

4

Sch

WINGRAVE

HILLERY
CL

CRAIL ROW
CATESBY ST

CUDDINGTON
CHEARSLEY

DATE STREET
KINGSHILL
BRANDON STREET

WANSEY STREET
LARCOM STREET

St John
Prim
Sch

ETHEL ST

CHARLESTON STREET

BROWNING STREET

KING AND QUEEN STREET

COTHAM ST

WADDING STREET
STEAD STREET
BRANDON STREET

PEABODY
BLDGS

RODNEY ROAD

ORB STREET

DAWES
HOUSE

English Martyrs
RC Prim Sch

JESSON
HOUSE

DEAN'S BUILDINGS

English
Martyrs
JMI Prim Sch

FLINT STREET

HALF PIN PLACE
ELSTED STREET
TISDALL PL

PO

152

3

Walworth

MORECAMBE STREET
EAST STREET

Robert
Browning
Prim Sch

BRONTI CLOSE

DATE STREET

St Peter's
Prim Sch

CADIZ STREET

NICHOLSON ST

PILTON
PLACE

BLACKWOOD ST

BROAD
MAYNE

WOODSFORD

PORTLAND STREET

LULWORTH

Walworth
Lwr Sch
STUDLAND

TRAFALGAR STREET

WOOLER STREET

AYLESBURY ROAD

BURTON GR

DAWES STREET

MERROW WALK
NORTHCHURCH

WOLVERTON

THURLOW STREET
SEDAN WAY

2

CARTER PL

SUTHERLAND
WALK

ABBEY CT

MACLEOD ST

WALWORTH PLACE

LIVERPOOL GROVE

MERROW STREET

LYTHAM STREET

ROLAND WAY

Michael
Faraday
Prim Sch

INVILLE ROAD
MICHAEL
FARADAY ST

BEACONSFIELD

LATIMER
78

1

WALWORTH ROAD

A215

A ARNSIDE ST **B** 48

ST JOHNS
HOUSE
ST STEPHENS
HOUSE

QUEEN'S ROW

PHE ___ ROAD SONDES ST **C** 33

ST MATTHEW'S
HOUSE

HAMBLEDON

GAYHURST

CALVERTON

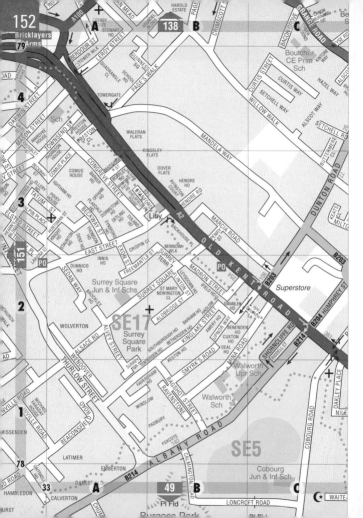

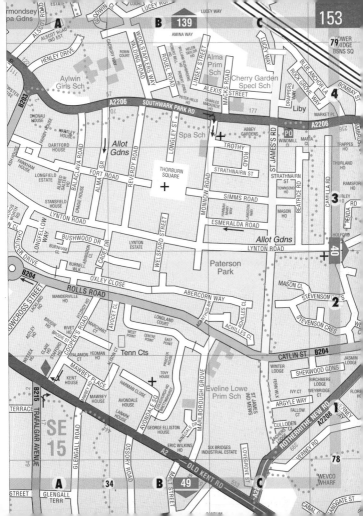

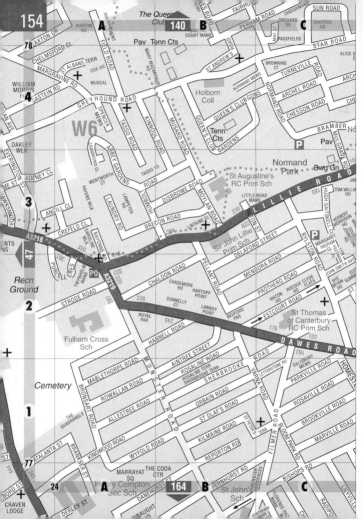

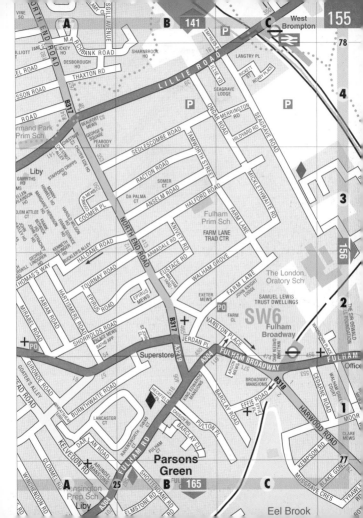

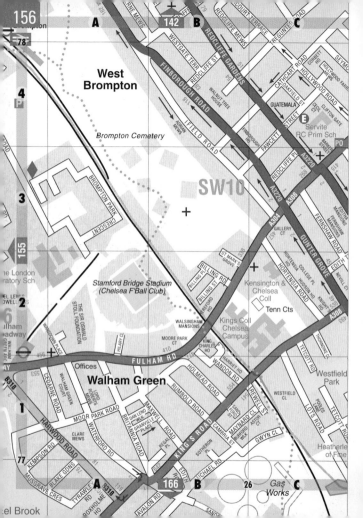

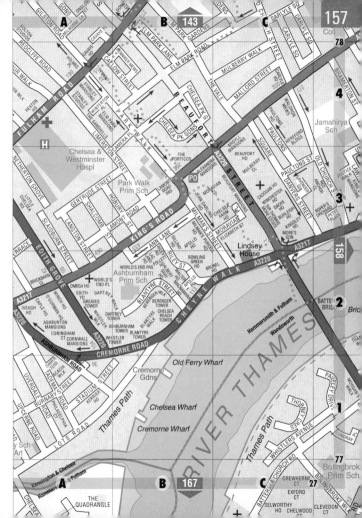

A
COLLEGE
COURT
WEST ROAD

Royal Hosp
(Army Pensioners)

Ranelagh Gardens
(Site of Chelsea Flower Show)

CHELSEA GDNS
A3216
ELLINGTON BL
Lister
Hosp

Tenn Cts

National
Army
Museum

Thames Path

4

EMBANKMENT GDNS

CHELSEA CT

DILKE ST

CHEL
BRIL

EMBANKMENT

Kensington & Chelsea

Wandsworth

HAMES
sea Reach

Thames Path

P
CARRIAGE DRIVE NORTH

3

QUEENS

160

The London Peace
Pagoda

THE PARADE

Tennis
Courts

Athletic
Ground

Pav

2

Tenn
Cts

Children's
Zoo

Tennis
Courts

Recn
Gd

War
Meml

CENTRAL AVENUE

CARRIAGE DRIVE EAST

Fountain
Lake

Recn
Gd

Pleasure
ens

CENTRAL AVENUE

Battersea Park

1

W11
Recn
Gd

Pav
Bwg
Gn

Boating Lake

P

77

A
28

B
169

C
CARRIAGE DR S

PRINCE OF WALES DR
PRINCE OF WALES MANS
ALBERT PALACE MANS

P

BATTERSEA

P

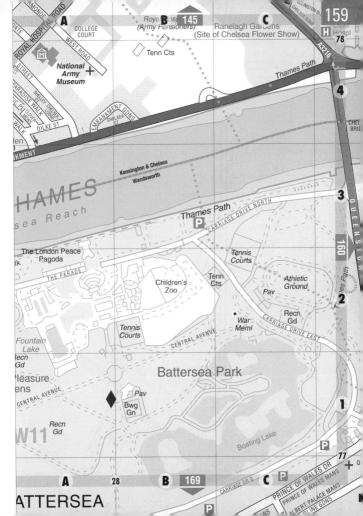

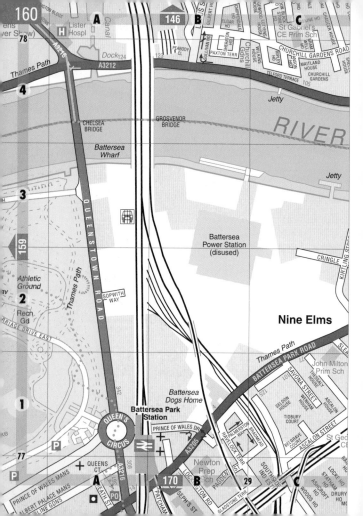

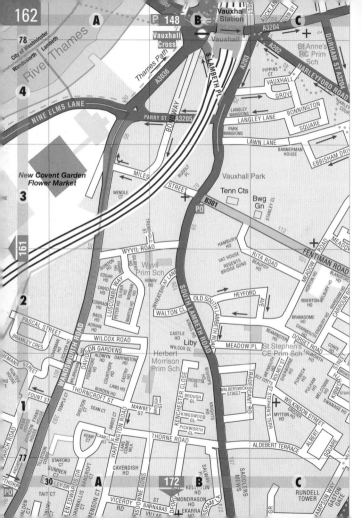

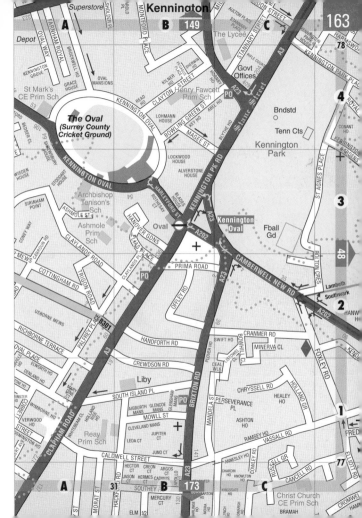

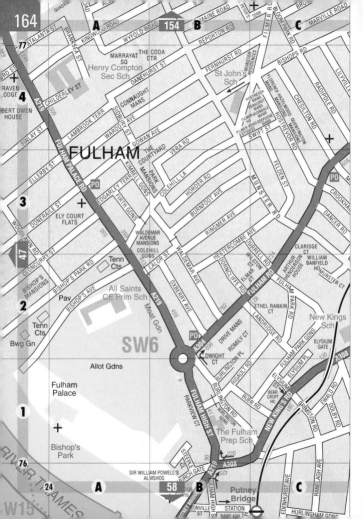

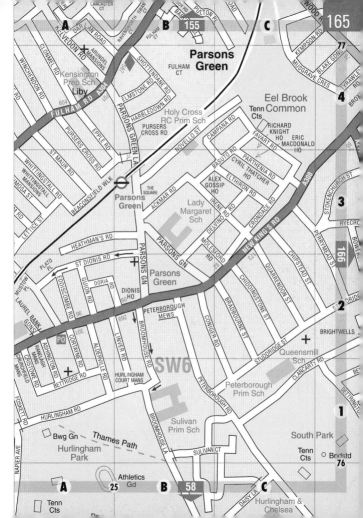

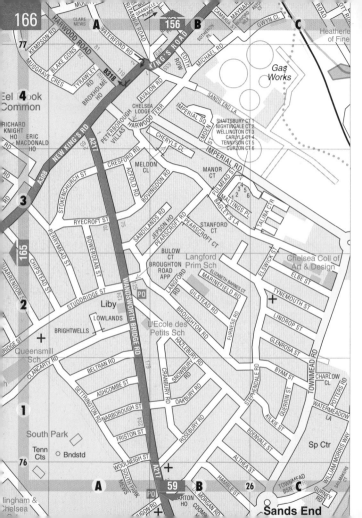

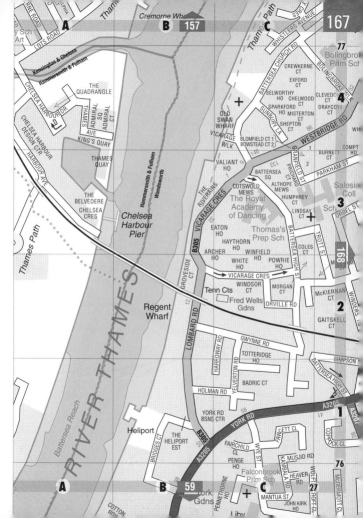

A · B · C

Cremorne Wh... · Thames Path · WHISTLERS AVENUE

77
Bolingbroh
Prim Sch

LOTS ROAD

Kensington & Chelsea
Hammersmith & Fulham

CHELSEA HARBOUR
CHELSEA HARBOUR DESIGN CTR

THE QUADRANGLE
ADMIRAL SQ · ADMIRAL CT
THAMES
AVE
KING'S QUAY
THAMES QUAY

THE BELVEDERE · CHELSEA CRES

Thames Path

Chelsea Harbour Pier

Hammersmith & Fulham
Wandsworth

CREWKERNE CT
EXFORD CT
SELWORTHY HO · CHELWOOD CT
SPARKFORD HO · MISTERTON CT
SHEPTON CT

BATTERSEA CHURCH RD

CLEVEDO CT · DRAYCOTT 4
COMPT BURNETT CT

WESTBRIDGE RD

OLD SWAN WHARF
VICARAGE WLK
BLOMFIELD CT 1 · BOWSTEAD CT 2
VALIANT HO
GRANFIELD · PRICHARD
PARKHAM ST

THE RIVERAINS
VICARAGE CRES
COTSWOLD MEWS
BATTERSEA SQ · ALTHOPE MEWS
HUMPHREY CT
LINDSAY CT

The Royal Academy of Dancing

Salesia Coll
Sch

ORBEL ST
TROTT ST

B305

EATON HO · HAYTHORN HO
ARCHER HO · WINFIELD HO
WHITE HO · POWRIE HO

Thomas's Prep Sch

BATTERSEA HIGH ST

COLES CT 168

GROVESIDE CT

VICARAGE CRES

WINDSOR CT
Tenn Cts
Fred Wells Gdns

MORGAN CT
ORVILLE RD

McKIERNAN CT
WINDERS 2
GAITSKELL CT

Regent Wharf

LOMBARD RD

GWYNNE RD
TOTTERIDGE HO

BATTERSEA HIGH ST
SIMPSON

HARROWAY RD · YELVERTON RD
BADRIC CT

HOLMAN RD

RIVER THAMES

Battersea Reach

YORK RD BSNS CTR
YORK RD
A3205

Heliport

BRIDGES CT
THE HELIPORT EST
B3205
A3205
WEST ST

FAIRCHILD CL
PENGE HO

FAWCETT CL

MUSJID RD
KAMBALA RD · HEAVER 27
WOLFT
COPCOCK CL

A321 1

76

Falconbrook Prim Sch
PENNETHORNE HO
MANTUA ST
JOHN KIRK
MCDERMOTT CL
WOLFT

A · B · 59 · ork Gdns · C

COTTON ROW
Libr

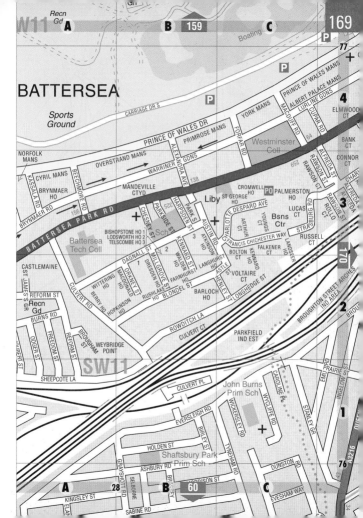

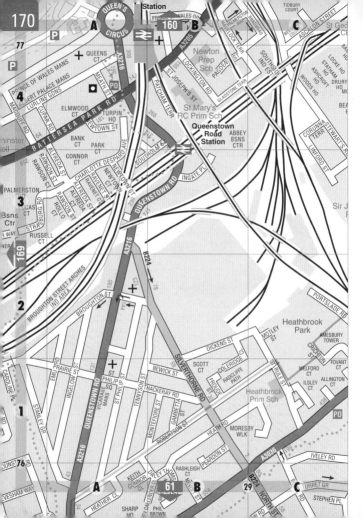

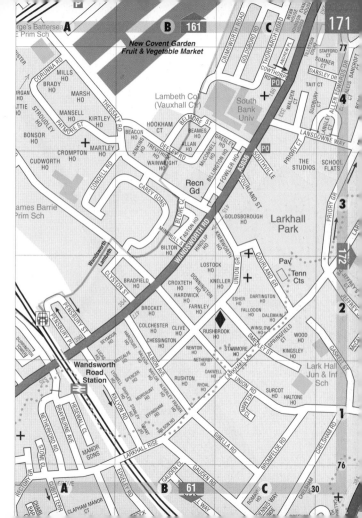

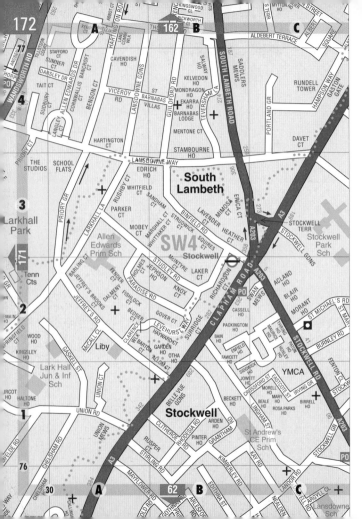

Index

Church Rd **6** Beckenham BR2..........**53** C6 **228** C6

Place name	Location number	Locality, town or village	Postcode district	Standard scale reference	Enlarged scale reference
May be abbreviated on the map	Present when a number indicates the place's position in a crowded area of mapping	Shown when more than one place (outside London postal districts) has the same name	District for the indexed place	Page number and grid reference for the standard mapping	Page number and grid reference for the central London enlarged mapping, underlined in red

Public and commercial buildings are highlighted in magenta
Places of interest are highlighted in blue with a star★

Index of localities, towns and villages

A
Acton 28 C1
Acton Green 37 B2

B
Balham 72 C3
Barbican 109 A3
Barnes 46 B2
Barnsbury 14 A1
Battersea 169 A4
Bayswater 114 C4
Bedford Park 38 A3
Belgravia 146 A4
Belsize Park 12 A3
Bermondsey 40 A4
Bethnal Green 25 A2
Blackheath
Vale 53 B1
Blackwall 34 C2
Bloomsbury 106 A4
Borough The 136 C4
Bow 26 B3
Bow Common 34 A4
Brixton 62 C4
Broadgate 110 A4
Brockley 66 B3
Bromley
(Tower Hamlets) . .27 A2
Brompton 130 A1
Brondesbury 10 A2
Brondesbury
Park 22 C4
Brook Green 39 C2

C
Camberwell 48 B2
Camden Town 13 A1
Canary Wharf 34 A1
Canning Town 35 B3
Canonbury 15 B2
Chelsea 144 B1
Child's Hill 1 C6
Chiswick 38 B1
Church End
(Brent) 8 B2
City of London 122 B4
Clapham 61 A4
Clapham
Common 61 A3
Clapham Junction . .60 A3
Clapham Park 61 C2
Clapton Park 17 C4
Clerkenwell 96 A1
College Park 22 A2
Covent Garden 120 B4
Cricklewood 9 B4
Cubitt Town 42 B2

D
Dalston 16 C2
Dartmouth Park 4 A1
De Beauvoir Town . .16 A1
Deptford 50 C3
Dollis Hill 9 A4
Dudden Hill 8 C3
Dulwich 76 A2
Dulwich Village 76 A4

E
Earl's Court 141 C2
Earlsfield 71 B3
East Acton 29 A1
East Dulwich 64 C2
East Sheen 55 C3
Euston 93 A3

F
Finsbury 95 C4
Finsbury Park 5 C3
Fitzrovia 104 A4
Fulham 47 C1

G
Globe Town 25 C2
Gospel Oak 12 B2
Greenwich 53 A4
Grove Park
(Hounslow) 45 B2
Gunnersbury 37 A2

H
Hackney 17 A2
Hackney Wick 18 C2
Haggerston 24 B3
Hammersmith 39 B2
Hampstead 11 B3
Harlesden 21 B4
Herne Hill 63 B2
Highbury 15 A4
Highgate 3 C4
Holborn 107 C3

H (cont.)
Homerton 17 C1
Honor Oak 65 B2
Hoxton 24 A3
Hyde Park 116 C2

I
Isle of Dogs 42 B2
Islington 14 C2

K
Kennington 149 B1
Kensal Green 22 B2
Kensal Rise 22 C3
Kensal Town 23 A1
Kensington 127 C3
Kentish Town 13 B2
Kew 44 C4
Kilburn 23 B4
King's Cross 84 C2
Kingsland 16 A2
Knightsbridge 130 A1

L
Ladywell 66 C1
Lambeth 134 C3
Lewisham 67 B3
Leyton 19 C4
Limehouse 33 A2
Lisson Green 90 B2
Lisson Grove 102 A4
Lower Clapton 17 B4
Lower Holloway 14 A3
Lower Place 20 B3

M
Maida Vale 88 A4
Maitland Park 12 C2
Marylebone 104 B2
Mayfair 118 A3
Mile End 26 A1
Mill Meads 27 C3
Millwall 41 C3
Mortlake 55 B4

N
New Cross 51 B2
New Cross Gate 50 C2
Newington 150 B4
Nine Elms 160 C2
North End 26 A1
North Kensington . .30 C4
North Sheen 44 C1
Notting Hill 112 C3
Nunhead 65 B3

O
Old Ford 26 B4
Old Oak Common . . .21 B1

P
Paddington 100 C3
Park Royal 20 A2
Parsons Green 165 B4
Peckham 49 A2
Pentonville 85 A1
Pimlico 146 C1

Poplar 33 C3	Shepherd's Bush ...30 A1	St James 119 B2	**T**	Wandsworth 58 C1
Primrose Hill 12 B1	Shoreditch 87 C1	St John's 51 C1	Temple Mills 19 A3	Wapping 32 A1
Putney 57 B2	Soho 105 B1	St John's Wood 79 B1	Tower Hamlets 33 B4	Waterloo 135 B4
Putney Heath 57 B1	Somers Town 93 C4	St Luke's 97 A2	Tufnell Park 13 C4	West Brompton ...156 A4
Putney Vale 68 C1	South Acton 37 A3	St Pancras 94 B4	Tulse Hill 75 A4	West Dulwich 75 A2
	South Bank 120 C1	Stamford Hill 7 A3		West Hampstead ...10 C4
R	South Bromley 34 C4	Stepney 32 C4	**U**	West Hill 58 B1
Ratcliff 32 C2	South Hackney 25 B4	Stockwell 62 A4	Upper Holloway 4 C2	West Kensington ..140 B3
Regent's Park 92 A4	South Hampstead ..11 B1	Stoke Newington ...7 A2	Upper Tooting 72 B1	West Kilburn 23 A2
Richmond 54 A2	South	Stonebridge 20 B4		West Norwood 75 B1
Richmond Hill 54 A1	Kensington 143 A3	Strand 120 C4	**V**	Westbourne Green ..88 A2
Roehampton 68 A4	South Lambeth 172 B3	Strand on	Vale of Health 2 C1	Westminster 133 A1
Rotherhithe 40 C3	Southfields 71 A3	the Green 44 C4	Vauxhall 148 B1	Whitechapel 110 C1
	Southwark 40 B2	Stratford 19 B1		Willesden 8 C4
S	Spitalfields 110 A4	Stratford Marsh ...27 A4	**W**	Willesden Green ...22 B4
Sands End 59 B4	St George in	Stratford New Town .19 B3	Walham Green 156 A1	Wimbledon Park ...70 B2
Shacklewell 16 B4	the East 32 A2	Streatham Hill 74 A3	Walworth 151 C2	
Shadwell 32 B2	St Giles 106 A2	Summerstown 71 B1		

Abbreviations used in the index

Acad	Academy	Ent Pk	Enterprise Park	Orch	Orchard
App	Approach	Est	Estate	Par	Parade
Arc	Arcade	Ex Ctr	Exhibition Centre	Pas	Passage
Art Gall	Art Gallery	Ex Hall	Exhibition Hall	Pav	Pavilion
Ave	Avenue	Fst	First	Pk	Park
Bglws	Bungalows	Gdn	Garden	Pl	Place
Bldgs	Buildings	Gdns	Gardens	Prec	Precinct
Bsns Ctr	Business Centre	Gn	Green	Prep	Preparatory
Bsns Pk	Business Park	Gr	Grove	Prim	Primary
Bvd	Boulevard	Gram	Grammar	Prom	Promenade
Cath	Cathedral, Catholic	Her Ctr	Heritage Centre	RC	Roman Catholic
CE	Church of England	Ho	House	Rd	Road
Cemy	Cemetery	Hospl	Hospital	Rdbt	Roundabout
Cir	Circus	Hts	Heights	Ret Pk	Retail Park
Circ	Circle	Ind Est	Industrial Estate	Sch	School
Cl	Close	Inf	Infant	Sec	Secondary
Cnr	Corner	Inst	Institute	Sh Ctr	Shopping Centre
Coll	College	Int	International	Sp	Sports
Com	Community	Intc	Interchange	Specl	Special
Comm	Common	Jun	Junior	Sports Ctr	Sports Centre
Comp	Comprehensive	Junc	Junction	Sq	Square
Con Ctr	Conference Centre	La	Lane	St	Street, Saint
Cotts	Cottages	L Ctr	Leisure Centre	Sta	Station
Cres	Crescent	Liby	Library	Stad	Stadium
Cswy	Causeway	Mans	Mansions	Tech	Technical/Technology
Ct	Court	Mdw/s	Meadow/s	Terr	Terrace
Ctr	Centre	Meml	Memorial	Trad Est	Trading Estate
Crkt	Cricket	Mid	Middle	Twr/s	Tower/s
Ctry Pk	Country Park	Mix	Mixed	Univ	University
Cty	County	Mkt	Market	Wlk	Walk
Ctyd	Courtyard	Mon	Monument	Yd	Yard
Dr	Drive	Mus	Museum		
Ent Ctr	Enterprise Centre	Obsy	Observatory		

A

Abady Ho SW1 ....147 C4
Abbess Cl SW2 .....75 A3
Abbeville Mews 3
SW4 ....61 C3
Abbeville Rd SW4 ...61 B2
Abbey Bsns Ctr
SW8 ....170 B4
Abbey Ct NW8 ......78 C2
SE17 ....151 A1
E6 12 ....32 B4
Abbey Gdns NW8 ....79 A1
SE16 ....153 C4
W6 ....154 A3
Abbey Ho NW8 ......89 A4
Abbey Lo NW8 ......90 B3
Abbey Orchard St
SW1 ....133 C2
Abbey Orchard Street
Est 133 C2
Abbey Rd NW8 ......78 C2
NW6 ....11 A1
NW10 ....20 A3
Abbey St SE1 ......138 C2
Abbeyfield Rd SE16 .40 B2
Abbot Ct SW8 .....162 A1
Abbot Ho E14 ......34 A2
Abbot St E8 ....16 B2
Abbot's Pl NW6 ....78 A4
Abbots Ho W14 ....126 C1
SW1 ....147 B1
Abbots La SE1 .....124 B1
Abbots Pk SW2 .....74 C3
Abbotsbury Cl
W14 ....126 C3
E15 ....27 B3
Abbotsbury Ho
W14 ....126 B4
Abbotsbury Mews
SE15 ....65 B4
Abbotsbury Rd
W14 ....126 C3
Abbotshade Rd 13
SE16 ....32 C1
Abbotstone Ho 4 5 7
SW15 ....57 B4
Abbotstone Rd
SW15 ....57 B4
Abbotswell Rd SE4 .66 B2
Abbotswood Rd
SE22 ....64 A3
SW16 ....73 C1
Abbott Ho SW12 ...72 B4
Abbott Rd E14 .....34 C3
Abbotts Cl N1 .....15 B2
Abchurch La EC2,
EC4 ....123 C4
Abchurch Yd EC4 ..123 B4
Abdale Rd W12 .....30 A1
Abel Ho SE11 .....163 B4
Aberavon Rd E3 ....26 A2
Abercorn Cl NW8 ..78 C1
Abercorn Mans
NW8 ....79 A1
Abercorn Pl NW8 ..78 C1
Abercorn Way SE1 .153 B2
Abercrombie Ho 11
W12 ....30 A2
Abercrombie St
SW11 ....168 B2

Aberdale Ct 22
SE26 ....40 C4
Aberdare Gdns
NW6 ....11 A1
Aberdeen Ct W2 ...89 B1
N5 ....15 B4
Aberdeen La N5 ....15 B3
Aberdeen Mans
WC1 ....94 A2
Aberdeen Pk N5 ....15 B3
Aberdeen Pl NW8 ..89 B2
Aberdeen Rd NW10 .8 B3
N5 ....15 B4
Aberdeen Terr SE3 .52 C1
Aberdour St SE1 ..152 A4
Aberfeldy Ho SE5 .48 A3
Aberfeldy St E14 ..34 B3
Abersham Rd E8 ....16 B3
Abingdon W14 ....141 A3
Abingdon Cl SE1 ..153 A2
NW1 ....13 C2
Abingdon Ct W8 ..127 C1
Abingdon Gdns
W8 ....127 C1
Abingdon Mans
W8 ....127 B2
Abingdon Rd W8 ..127 C1
N20 ....25 A3
Abingdon St SW1 .134 A2
Abingdon Villas
W8 ....127 C1
Abinger Gr SE8 ....51 B4
Abinger Ho SE1 ...137 B3
Abinger Mews W9 ..23 C1
Abinger Rd W4 .....38 A3
Ablett St SE16 ....40 B1
Abney Park Cemetery*
N16 ....7 A2
Abney Park Ct N16 .7 B2
Aboyne Rd SW17 ...71 C1
Abyssinia Cl SW11 .60 A3
Abyssinia Rd SW11 .60 A3
Acacia Cl SE8 .....41 A2
Acacia Gdns NW8 ..79 C2
Acacia Gr SE21 ....75 C2
Acacia Ho N16 .....6 C2
Acacia Pl NW8 ....79 C2
Acacia Rd NW8 ....79 C2
W3 ....28 B2
Acacia Wlk SW10 .157 A1
Academy Ct 18 E2 .25 B2
Academy The 2 E3 .26 B2
Acanthus Dr SE1 .153 B2
Acanthus Rd SW11 .60 C4
Accommodation Rd
NW11 ....1 B3
Acer Ct N1 ....15 B1
Acfold Rd SW6 ...166 A3
Achilles Cl SE1 ..153 C2
Achilles Ho 16 E2 .25 A3
Achilles Rd NW6 ..10 C3
Achilles St SE14 ..51 A3
Achilles Way W1 ..117 C1
Acklam Rd W10 ....31 B4
Ackmar Rd SW6 ..165 B3
Ackroyd Dr E3 .....33 C4
Acland Burghley Sch
NW5 ....13 A4
Acland Cres SE5 ...63 C4
Acland Ho SW9 ...172 C2
Acland Rd NW2 ....9 A2
Acol Ct 3 NW6 ....10 C1
Acol Rd NW6 ......11 A1
Acorn Gdns W3 ....28 C4
Acorn Par 7 SE15 .50 A3

Acorn Production Ctr
N7 ....14 A1
Acorn Wharf SE1 ..49 C4
Acorn Wlk SE16 ...33 A1
Acorns The 21
SW19 ....69 C3
Acre Dr SE22 ......64 C3
Acre La SW2 ....62 B3
Acris St SW18 .....59 B2
Acton Central Ind Est 9
...............28 A1
Acton Central Sta
W3 ....28 B1
Acton High Sch W3 .36 C4
Acton Hill Mews
W3 ....28 A1
Acton Ho E8 ......24 B4
5 W3 ....28 B3
Acton Hospl W3 ...36 C4
Acton La NW10 ....20 C3
W4 ....37 B2
W3 ....37 B3
Acton Main Line Sta
W3 ....28 B3
Acton Mews E8 ....24 B4
Acton Park Est W3 .37 C4
Acton St WC1 .....94 C3
Acton Town Sta W3 .36 C4
Acton Vale Ind Pk
W3 ....29 B1
Acuba Ho SW18 ...71 A3
Acuba Rd SW18 ...71 A2
Ada Ct N1 ....86 C3
W9 ....89 A3
Ada Gdns E14 .....34 C3
E15 ....27 A4
Ada Ho 28 E2 .....24 C4
Ada Kennedy Ct 6
SE10 ....52 B3
Ada Pl E2 ....24 C4
Ada Rd SE5 ....49 A3
Ada St E8 ....25 A4
Adair Ho SW3 ....158 B4
Adair Rd W10 .....23 A1
Adair Twr 7 W10 ..23 A1
Adam & Eve Ct
W1 ....105 A2
Adam & Eve Mews
W8 ....127 C2
Adam Ct SE11 ....150 A3
SW7 ....120 B3
Adam Wlk SW6 ....47 B3
Adam's Row W1 ..117 C3
Adamfields N11 ...11 C1
Adams Ct EC2 ....109 C2
Adams Gardens Est 3
SE16 ....40 B4
Adams Ho 3 E14 ..34 C3
Adams Pl N7 ......14 B3
Adamson Rd NW3 ..11 C1
E16 ....35 C3
Adare Wlk SW16,
SW2 ....74 B2
Adderley Gr SW11 .60 C2
Adderley St E14 ...34 B3
Addey & Stanhope Sch
SE14 ....51 C2
Addey Ho SE8 ....51 B3
Addington Ct 7
SW14 ....55 C4
Addington Ho 19
SW9 ....173 A1
Addington Rd E3 ..26 C2
Addington Sq SE5 .48 C3
Addington St SE1 .135 A3
Addison Ave
W11 ....31 A1 112 A1

Addison Bridge Pl
W14 ....140 C4
Addison Cres W14 .126 B2
Addison Gdns
W14 ....126 A3
W14 ....39 C3
Addison Gr W4 ....38 A3
Addison Ho 5 NW8 .89 B4
Addison Park Mans 12
W14 ....39 C4
Addison Pl
W11 ....31 A1 112 A1
Addison Prim Sch
W14 ....126 A2
Addison Rd W14 ..126 C2
Addle Hill EC4 ...108 B1
Addle St EC2 .....109 A3
Addlestone Ho W10 .30 B4
Addy Ho SE16 .....40 B2
Adela Ho 9 W6 ....39 B1
Adela St W10 .....23 A1
Adelaide Ave SE4 .66 C3
Adelaide Cl SW9 ..62 C3
Adelaide Ct NW8 ..79 A1
Adelaide Gr W12 ..29 C1
Adelaide Rd NW3 .12 A1
Richmond TW9 .....54 B3
2 SW18 ....58 C2
Adelaide St WC2 .120 A3
Adelaide Wlk SW9 .62 C3
Adelina Gr E1 ....32 B4
Adelina Mews
SW12 ....73 C3
Adeline Pl WC1 ..105 C3
Adelphi Ct SE16 ..40 C4
Adelphi Terr WC2 .120 B3
Aden Gr N16 ......6 C1
Aden Ho 12 E1 ....32 C4
Aden Lo N16 ......6 C1
Adeney Cl W6 .....47 C4
Adeyfield Ho EC1 .97 C3
Adie Rd W6 ....39 B2
Adisham Ho 4 E5 .17 A3
Adler St E1 ......111 B2
Adley St E5 ....18 A3
Admiral Ct SW10 .167 A4
SE16 ....40 A1
Admiral Hyson Ind Est
SE16 ....40 A1
Admiral Mews W10 .22 C1
Admiral Pl SE16 ..33 A1
Admiral Sq SW10 .167 A4
Admiral St SE8 ...51 C2
Admiral Wlk W9 ...23 C1
Admiral's Wlk NW3 .2 B1
Admirals Ct SE1 ..124 C1
52 SW19 ....69 C3
Admirals Way E14 .41 C4
Admiralty Arch*
SW1 ....119 C2
Admiralty Cl 1 SE8 .51 C2
Adolphus Rd N4 ...6 A2
Adolphus St SE8 ..51 B3
Adpar St W2 .....101 B4
Adrian Bolt Ho 2
E2 ....25 A2
Adrian Ho N1 .....85 A3
SW8 ....162 A2
Adrian Mews
SW10 ....156 B4
Adriatic Ho 18 E1 .25 C1
Adron Ho 6 SE16 .40 B2
Adstock Ho 5 N1 ..15 A1
ADT Coll SW15 ....58 B2
Adys Lawn NW2 ...9 A2
Adys Rd SE15 .....64 B4
Affleck St N1 .....85 A1

Afghan Rd SW11 ..168 A1
Agamemnon Rd
NW6 ....10 B2
Agar Gr NW1 ......13 C1
Agar Pl NW1 ......13 B1
Agar St WC2 .....120 B3
Agate Rd W6 ......39 B3
Agatha Cl E1 .....32 B1
Agave Rd NW2 ....9 B4
Agdon St EC1 .....96 A2
Agincourt Rd NW3 .12 B4
Agnes Ct 13 SW18 .59 C3
Agnes Ho 19 W11 .30 C2
Agnes Rd W3 ......38 B4
Agnes St E14 .....33 B3
Aigburth Mans
SW9 ....163 B1
Ailsa St E14 ......34 B4
Ainger Rd NW3 ....12 B1
Ainsdale NW1 .....92 C4
Ainsdale Dr SE1 ..153 A2
Ainsley St E2 .....25 A2
Ainsty St 14 SE16 .40 B4
Ainsworth Cl SE5 .49 A1
Ainsworth Est NW8 .78 C4
Ainsworth Ho NW8 .78 B3
Ainsworth Rd E9 ..17 B1
Ainsworth Way
NW8 ....78 C4
Aintree St SW6 ..154 B2
Air St W1 ....119 A3
Aird Ho SE11 .....136 C1
Airdrie Cl N1 .....14 B1
Airedale Ave W4 ..38 B1
Airedale Ave S W4 .38 B1
Airedale Rd SW12 .72 B4
Airlie Gdns
W8 ....31 C1 113 B1
Aisgill Ave SW5 ..141 A1
Aiten Pl W6 ......38 C2
Aithan Ho 9 E14 ..33 B3
Aitken Cl E8 ......24 C4
Ajax Ho 12 E2 ....25 A3
Ajax Rd NW6 .....10 C3
Akbar Ho 7 E14 ..42 A2
Akehurst St SW15 .68 C4
Akenside 3
NW3 ....11 C3
Akenside Rd NW3 .11 C3
Akerman Rd SW9 .48 A2
Akintaro Ho 7 SE8 .51 B4
Al Sadiq & Al Zahra
Schs NW6 ....23 A4
Alan Preece Ct NW6 .9 C1
Aland Ct SE16 ....41 A3
Alaska St SE1 ....121 B1
Alba Pl W11 ......31 B3
Albacore Cres SE13 .67 A1
Albans Cl SW16 ...74 A1
Albany W1 ....118 C3
Albany Cl SW14 ..55 A3
Albany Ct 12 NW10 .8 A4
NW8 ....22 A3
Albany Ctyd W1 ..119 A3
Albany Ho 3 TW8 .44 A4
Albany Mans SW11 158 B1
Albany Mews N1 ...14 C1
SE5 ....48 B4
Albany Par 4 TW8 .44 A4
Albany Pl N7 .....14 C4
Albany Rd SE5 ....49 A4
Richmond TW10 ....54 A2
Albany St NW1 ....92 B4
Albany Terr 6
TW10 ....54 B2

Albemarle SW19 ...69 C2
Albemarle Ho SE1 ...41 B2
Albemarle Mans
  NW3 ...11 A4
Albemarle St W1 ...118 C3
Albemarle Way EC1 ...96 A1
Albermarle Ho
  SW9 ...62 C4
Albermarle Prim Sch
  (Annexe) SW19 ...70 A2
Albermarle Prim Sch
  SW19 ...70 A2
Albert Ave SW8 ...162 C1
  SE1 ...136 C1
Albert Bigg Point
  E15 ...27 B4
Albert Bridge Rd
  SW11 ...158 C1
Albert Cl 1 E9 ...25 A4
Albert Cotts E1 ...111 B4
Albert Ct SW7 ...129 B3
  5 SW19 ...70 A3
Albert Dr SW19 ...70 A3
Albert Emb SE1 ...148 B3
Albert Gate Ct
  SW1 ...130 C3
Albert Gdns E1 ...32 C3
Albert Gray Ho
  SW10 ...157 B2
Albert Hall Mans
  SW7 ...129 B3
Albert Mans SW11 ...168 C4
  N8 ...5 A4
Albert Memorial*
  SW7 ...129 B3
Albert Mews W8 ...128 C2
Albert Palace Mans
  SW11 ...169 C4
Albert Pl W8 ...128 B3
Albert Rd N4 ...5 B4
  NW6 ...23 C2
  Richmond TW10 ...54 B2
Albert Sq SW8 ...162 C1
Albert St NW1 ...82 C3
Albert Starr Ho 7
  SE8 ...40 C2
Albert Studios
  SW11 ...168 C4
Albert Terr NW1 ...81 B3
  NW1 ...20 B4
Albert Terr Mews
  NW1 ...81 B3
Albert Westcott Ho
  SE17 ...150 B2
Alberta Ct 11 TW10 ...54 B2
Alberta Ho E14 ...34 B1
Alberta St SE17 ...150 B2
Albion Ave SW8 ...171 B1
Albion Cl W2 ...116 B4
Albion Ct 7 W6 ...39 A2
Albion Dr E8 ...16 C1
Albion Est SE16 ...40 B4
Albion Gate W2 ...116 B4
Albion Gr N16 ...16 A4
Albion Jun & Inf Sch
  SE16 ...40 B4
Albion Mews N1 ...85 B4
  W2 ...102 B1
Albion Pl EC1 ...108 A4
  EC2 ...109 C3
  W6 ...39 A2
Albion Rd N16 ...15 C4

Albion Sq E8 ...16 B1
Albion St W2 ...102 B1
  SE16 ...40 B4
Albion Terr E8 ...16 B1
Albion Way EC1 ...108 C3
  SE13 ...67 B3
Albion Wharf
  SW11 ...158 A2
Albion Yd N1 ...84 B1
Albon Ho SE14 ...51 B3
  SW18 ...59 A1
Albrighton Rd SE5,
  SE22 ...64 A4
Albury Bldgs SE1 ...136 B3
Albury Ct 7 SW2 ...74 B4
Albury St SE8 ...51 C4
Albyn Rd SE8 ...51 C2
Alconbury Rd E5 ...7 C2
Aldbourne Rd W12 ...29 C1
Aldbridge St SE17 ...152 B2
Aldburgh Mews
  W1 ...103 C2
Aldbury Ho SW3 ...144 A3
Aldebert Terr SW8 ...162 C1
Aldeburgh St SE18 ...43 C1
Alden Ho E8 ...25 A4
Aldenham Ho NW1 ...83 A1
Aldenham St NW1 ...83 B1
Aldensley Rd W6 ...39 A3
Alder Ho 1 NW3 ...12 B2
  SE15 ...49 B4
  SE4 ...66 C4
Alder Lo SW4 ...47 C2
Alder Mews 8 N19 ...4 B2
Alder Rd SW14 ...55 C4
Alderbrook Prim Sch
  SW12 ...73 A4
Alderbrook Rd
  SW12 ...61 A1
Alderbury Rd SW13 ...46 C4
Aldergrove Ho 3 E5 ...7 C2
Alderholt Way 9
  SE15 ...49 A3
Alderley Ho SW8 ...171 B1
Alderman's Wlk
  EC2 ...110 A3
Aldermanbury EC2 ...109 A2
Aldermanbury Sq
  EC2 ...109 A3
Aldermary Rd 10
  SE6 ...67 A4
Alderney Ho 21 N1 ...15 B2
Alderney Rd E1 ...25 C1
Alderney St SW1 ...146 B2
Aldersford Cl SE4 ...65 C3
Aldersgate St EC1 ...108 C3
Aldersgate St EC1 ...108 C2
Aldershot Rd NW6 ...23 B4
Alderson St W10 ...23 A1
Alderville Rd SW6 ...165 A2
Alderwick Ct N7 ...14 B2
Aldford St W1 ...117 C2
Aldgate EC3 ...110 B1
  EC3 ...111 A2
Aldgate East Sta
  ...111 A2
Aldgate High St
  EC3 ...110 C1
Aldgate Sta EC3 ...110 C1
Aldham Ho SE4 ...51 B2
Aldine Ct W12 ...30 B1
Aldine St W12 ...39 B4
Aldington Ct 8 E8 ...16 C1
Aldred Rd NW6 ...10 C3
Aldren Rd SW17 ...71 B1
Aldrich Terr SW18 ...71 B2

Aldrick Ho N1 ...85 A2
Aldridge Ct W11 ...31 B4
Aldridge Rd Villas
  W11 ...31 B4
Aldsworth Cl W9 ...88 A1
Aldworth Gr SE13 ...67 B1
Aldwych WC2 ...107 A1
Aldwych Bldgs
  WC2 ...106 B2
Aldwych Ho WC2 ...162 A1
Ale Gossip Ho
  SW6 ...165 B3
Alexander Ave NW10 ...9 A1
Alexander Ct SE3 ...53 C1
  SW18 ...59 B2
Alexander Ho 9
  E14 ...41 C3
Alexander Mews
  W2 ...100 A2
Alexander Pl SW7 ...144 A4
Alexander Rd N19 ...5 A1
Alexander Sq SW3 ...144 A4
Alexander St W2 ...31 C3
Alexander Mews
  SW1 ...169 B3
Alexandra Cotts
  SE14 ...51 B2
Alexandra Ct W9 ...89 A2
  W2 ...114 B4
  SW7 ...128 C2
Alexandra Gdns W4 ...46 A3
Alexandra Gr N4 ...6 A3
Alexandra Ho 15
  W6 ...39 B1
Alexandra Mans
  SW3 ...157 B3
  6 NW6 ...10 C3
Alexandra National Ho
  N4 ...6 A2
Alexandra Pl NW8 ...79 A4
Alexandra Rd NW8 ...11 C1
  W4 ...37 C4
  Richmond TW9 ...54 B4
  SW14 ...55 C4
Alexandra St E16 ...35 C4
  5 SE14 ...51 A3
Alexis St SE16 ...153 C4
Alfearn Rd E5 ...17 B4
Alford Ct N1 ...87 A1
Alford Pl N1 ...87 A1
Alfred Butt Ho
  SW17 ...72 B1
Alfred Cl W4 ...37 C2
Alfred Ho E9 ...18 A3
Alfred Mews W1,
  WC1 ...105 B4
Alfred Nunn Ho
  NW10 ...21 B4
Alfred Pl WC1 ...105 B4
Alfred Rd W3 ...28 B1
  W2 ...31 C4
Alfred Salter Ho
  SE1 ...153 A3
Alfred Salter Prim Sch
  SE16 ...40 C3
Alfred St E3 ...26 B2
Alfreda Ct SW11 ...170 A3
Alfreda St SW11 ...170 A3
Alfreton Cl SW19 ...69 C1
Alfriston Rd SW11 ...60 B2
Algar Ho SE1 ...136 A3
Algarve Rd SW18 ...71 A3
Algernon Rd NW6 ...23 C4
  SE13 ...67 A2
Algiers Rd SE13 ...66 C3
Alice Ct SW15 ...58 B3

Alice Gilliott Ct
  W14 ...155 A4
Alice La E3 ...26 B4
Alice Owen Tech Ctr
  EC1 ...96 A4
Alice Shepherd Ho 7
  E14 ...42 B4
Alice St SE1 ...138 A1
Alice Walker Cl 8
  SE24 ...63 A3
Alie St E1 ...111 A1
Alison Ct SE1 ...153 B1
Aliwal Rd SW11 ...60 A3
Alkerden Rd W4 ...38 A1
Alkham Rd N16 ...7 B2
All Saints CE Prim Sch
  SW6 ...164 A2
  SW15 ...57 B4
  W3 ...28 A1
  2 E14 ...34 A3
All Saints Ct E1 ...32 B2
All Saints Dr SE3 ...53 B1
All Saints Pas SW18 ...58 C2
All Saints Rd W11 ...31 B3
  W3 ...28 B3
All Saints St N1 ...84 C2
All Saints' CE Prim Sch
  NW2 ...1 B1
  SE3 ...53 A1
All Souls CE Prim Sch
  W1 ...104 C4
All Souls' Ave NW10 ...22 A4
All Souls Pl W1 ...104 B3
Allam Ho W11 ...112 A4
Allan Ho SW8 ...171 B4
Allan Way W3 ...28 B4
Allanbridge N16 ...7 A4
Allard Gdns SW4 ...61 C2
Allardyce St SW4,
  SW9 ...62 B3
Allbrook Ho 4
  SW15 ...68 C4
Allcroft Rd NW5 ...12 C3
Allen Edwards Dr
  SW8 ...172 A4
Allen Edwards Prim Sch
  SW4 ...172 A3
Allen Ho W8 ...127 C2
Allen Mans W8 ...127 C2
Allen Rd N16 ...16 A4
  E3 ...26 B3
Allen St W8 ...127 C1
Allendale Cl SE5 ...48 C1
Allendale Cl SW8 ...127 C2
Allenford Ho 1
  SW15 ...56 B1
Allensbury Pl
  NW1 ...13 C1
  NW1 ...14 A1
Allenswood 12
  SW19 ...70 A3
Allerdale Ho 7 N4 ...6 C4
Allerton Ho N1 ...87 C1
Allerton Rd N16 ...6 B2
Allerton St N1 ...97 C4
Allerton Wlk 11 N7 ...5 B2
Allestree Rd SW6 ...154 A1
Alleyn Cres SE21 ...75 C2
Alleyn Ho SE1 ...137 B2
  SE21 ...76 A1
Alleyn Park SE21 ...76 A1
Alleyn Rd SE21 ...76 A1
Alleyn's Sch SE22 ...64 A2

Allfarthing La SW18 ...59 B1
Allfarthing Prim Sch
  SW18 ...59 B1
Allgood St 10 E2 ...24 B3
Allhallows La EC4 ...123 B3
Alliance Ct W3 ...28 A4
Allied Ind Est W3 ...29 A1
Allied Way W3 ...29 A1
Allingham Ct NW3 ...12 A3
Allingham St N1 ...86 C2
Allington Ct SW8 ...170 C1
Allington Rd W10 ...23 A3
Allington St W1 ...132 B1
Allison Cl SE10 ...52 B2
Allison Gr SE21 ...76 A3
Allison Rd W3 ...28 B2
Allitsen Rd NW8 ...80 A2
Allnutt Way SW4 ...61 C2
Alloa Rd SE8 ...41 A1
Allom Ct SW4 ...172 B1
Allonby Ho E14 ...33 A4
Alloway Rd E3 ...26 A2
Allport Ho SE5 ...63 C4
Allsop Pl NW1 ...91 A1
Alma Birk Ho 1
  NW6 ...10 B1
Alma Gr SE1 ...153 A3
Alma Ho 7 TW8 ...44 A4
Alma Prim Sch
  SE16 ...153 C4
Alma Rd SW18 ...59 B2
Alma Sq NW8 ...89 A4
Alma Terr W8 ...127 C1
  E15 ...19 C2
Almack Rd E5 ...17 B4
Almeida St 10 N1 ...15 A1
Almeric Rd SW11 ...60 B3
Almington St N4 ...5 B3
Almond Ave W5 ...36 A3
Almond Cl SE15 ...49 C1
Almond Ho SE4 ...51 B1
Almond Rd SE16 ...40 A2
Almondsbury Ct 7
  SE15 ...50 B3
Almorah Rd N1 ...15 C1
Almshouses NW8 ...80 A2
Alperton St W10 ...23 B1
Alpha Cl NW1 ...90 B3
Alpha Ct 6 NW5 ...13 A2
Alpha Gr E14 ...41 C4
Alpha Ho NW6 ...23 C3
  NW6 ...90 B1
Alpha Pl SW3 ...158 B4
  NW6 ...23 C3
Alpha St SE15 ...49 C1
Alphabet Sq E3 ...33 C4
Alpine Rd SE16 ...40 C1
Alroy Rd N4 ...5 C4
Alsace Rd SE17 ...152 A2
Alscot Rd SE1 ...139 A1
Alscot Road Ind Est
  SE1 ...139 A1
Alscot Way SE1 ...152 C4
Altenburg Gdns
  SW11 ...60 B3
Althea St SW6 ...59 A4

Althorpe Mews
SW11 ....167 C3
Althorp Rd SW17 ....72 B3
Alton Ho 8 E3 ....28 A4
Alton Rd
Richmond TW10,TW9 ..54 A3
SW15 ....68 C3
Alton St E14 ....134 A4
Alumni C St E1 .....139 A4
Alvanley Ct NW3 .....11 A4
Alvanley Gdns NW6 ..11 A3
Alvanley Ho SW9 ...173 B4
Alverstone Ave
SW18,SW19 ....70 C2
Alverstone Ho
SE11 ....163 B3
Alverstone Rd NW2 ...9 B1
Alverton St SE8 .....51 B4
Alvey St SE17 .....152 A2
Alvington Cres E8 ..16 B3
Alwin Ave SW11 ......94 C3
Alwyn Gdns W3 ......28 A3
Alwyne La N1 ....15 A1
Alwyne Pl N1 ....15 B1
Alwyne Rd N1 ....15 B1
Alwyne Sq N1 ....15 B2
Alwyne Villas N1 ...15 A1
Alzette Ho 9 E2 ....25 C3
Amazon St E1 ....32 A3
Ambassador Ct 9
NW6 ....10 C3
Ambassador Ho
NW8 ....79 B4
Ambassador Sq E14 .42 A2
Amber Ct 7 N7 .....14 C2
Amber St E15 ....19 C2
Ambergate St
SE17 ....150 B2
Amberley Ct 2
SW9 ....63 A4
Amberley Rd W9 .....31 C4
Ambler JMI Sch N4 ..6 A2
Ambler Rd N4 ....6 A1
Ambleside NW1 .....82 B1
13 SW19 ....70 A3
Ambleside Cl E9 ....17 B3
Ambleside Point 1
SE15 ....50 B3
Ambleside Rd NW10 ..8 B1
Ambrosden Ave
SW1 ....133 A1
Ambrose Ho 4 E14 ..33 C4
Ambrose Mews
SW11 ....168 C2
Ambrose St SE16 ....40 A2
AMC Bsns Ctn NW10 20 A2
Amelia Ho 6 W6 ....39 B1
Amelia St
SE17 ....150 C2
Amen Cnr EC4 ......108 B1
Amen Ct EC4 ....108 B1
America Sq EC3 ....124 C4
America St SE1 ....122 C1
American Coll The
W1 ....103 C3
American Sch in London
The NW8 ....79 B2
Amerland Rd SW18 ..58 B1
Amersham Gr SE14 .51 B3
Amersham Rd SE14 .51 B2
Amersham Vale
SE14,SE8 ....51 B3
Amery Gdns NW10 ..22 A4

Amery Ho SE17 .....152 B2
Ames Cotts 14 E3 ...33 A4
Ames Ho 10 E2 .....25 C3
Amesbury Ave SW2 .74 B2
Amesbury Twr
SW8 ....170 C2
Amethyst Rd E15 ...19 C4
Amherst JMI Sch
E8 ....16 C3
Amherst Ho 4 ......16 C4
Amhurst Par N16 ....7 B4
Amhurst Pk N4,N16 ..7 A4
Amhurst Rd E8,N16 .16 C4
Amhurst Terr E8 ....16 C4
Amias Ho 7 EC1 ....96 C2
Amiel St 17 E1 .....25 B1
Amies St SW11 ......60 B4
Amigo Ho SE1 ......135 C2
Amina Way SE16 ...139 B1
Amner Rd SW11 .....60 C1
Amory Ho N1 ....85 A2
Amott Rd SE15 .....64 C4
Amoy Pl E14 ....33 C2
Ampton Pl WC1 .....94 C3
Ampton St WC1 .....94 C3
Amstel Ct 11 SE15 .49 B3
Amsterdam Rd E14 .42 B3
Amwell St EC1 ......95 B4
Amyruth Rd SE4 ....66 C2
Anatola Rd N19 .....4 B2
Anchor Ho EC1 .....96 C2
Anchor Mews SW12 .61 A1
Anchor St SE16 .....40 A2
Anchor Terr SE1 ...123 A2
Anchor Yd EC1 .....97 A2
Anchorage Point
E14 ....41 C4
Ancill Cl W6 ....154 A3
Ancona Rd NW10 ...21 C3
Andalus Rd SW9 ....62 A4
Andaman Ho 8 E1 ..33 A4
Anderson Cl W3 .....28 C3
Anderson Ho 10 E14 34 B2
Anderson Rd E9 ....17 C2
Anderson St SW3 ..144 C2
Anderston Cl SE5 ...63 C4
Andover Ho 6 N7 ...5 B2
Andover Pl NW6 ....78 A1
Andover Rd N7 ......5 B2
Andoversford Ct 7
SE15 ....49 A4
Andre St E8 ....16 C3
Andrew Borde St
WC2 ....105 C2
Andrew Ho SE4 .....11 B1
SW15 ....56 C2
N16 ....16 A4
Andrew Marvell Ho 9
N16 ....16 A4
Andrew Reed Ho
SW18 ....70 A4
Andrew St E14 ......34 B3
Andrew's Rd E8 ....25 A4
Andrewes Ho EC2 ..109 A3
Andrews Crosse
WC2 ....107 B1
Andrews Wlk SE17 ..48 A4
Anfield Cl SW12 ....73 B4
Angel N1 ....85 C1
Angel Alley E1 ....111 A2
Angel Ct EC2 ......109 C2
SW1 ....119 A1
Angel Gate EC1 .....96 B4
Angel Ho N1 ....85 C1
Angel La E15 ....19 C2

Angel Mews N1 .....85 C1
E1 ....32 A2
SW15 ....68 C4
Angel Pas EC4 ....123 B3
Angel Pl SE1 ......137 B4
Angel Prim Sch N1 .85 C2
Angel St EC1 ......108 C2
Angel Sta EC1 ......86 A1
Angel Wlk W6 ......39 B2
Angela Davis Ind Est 21
SW9 ....172 C2
Angelina Ho 2 ......49 C2
Angell Park Gdns 5
SW9 ....173 B2
Angell Rd SW9 ....173 A2
Angerstein Bsns Pk
SE10 ....43 C2
Angerstein La SE3 .53 B2
Anglebury 5 W2 ....31 C3
Anglers La NW5 ....13 A2
Anglesey Ho 9 E14 .33 C3
Anglia Ho 15 E14 ..33 A3
Anglo American Laundry
SW17 ....71 B1
Anglo Rd 24 E3 .....26 B3
Angrave Ct 8 E8 ...24 B4
Angrave Pas 5 E8 ..24 B4
Angus Ho 12 SW12 .73 C4
Angus St SE14 ......51 A3
Anhalt Rd SW11 ...158 B2
Anley Rd W14 ......39 C4
Ann La SW10 ......157 B3
Ann Moss Way SE16 40 B3
Ann's Cl SW1 ......131 B3
Ann's Pl E1 ....110 C3
Anna Cl E8 ....24 B4
Annabel Cl E14 .....34 A3
Annandale Prim Sch
SE10 ....43 B1
Annandale Rd W4 ..38 A1
SE10 ....43 B1
Anne Goodman Ho 3
E1 ....32 B3
Anne Kerr Ct 18
SW15 ....57 C1
Annesley Ho SW9 .163 C1
Annesley Wlk N19 ..4 B2
Annette Cres 9 N1 .15 B1
Annette Rd N7 ......5 B1
Annette Rd N7 ......14 B4
Annie Besant Cl E3 .26 B4
Anning St E2 ....98 B2
Annis Rd E9 ....18 A2
Ansdell Rd SE15 ....50 B1
Ansdell St W8 .....128 B2
Ansdell Terr W8 ...128 B2
Ansell Ho E1 ....32 B4
Ansell Rd SW17 ....72 B1
Anselm Rd SW6 ...155 B3
Ansleigh Pl W11 ...30 C2
Anslie Wlk 6 SW12 73 A4
Anson Ho SW1 ....160 C4
6 E1 ....26 A1
Anson Prim Sch NW2 9 C3
Anson Rd NW2 ......9 B3
N7 ....13 C4
Anstey Ct 6 W3 ....37 A4
Anstey Ho 8 E9 ....25 B4
Anstey Rd SE15 ....64 C4
Anstice Cl W4 ......46 A3
Antenor Ho 21 E2 ..25 A3
Anthony Cope Ct
N1 ....97 C4
Anthony Ho NW8 ....90 A1
Anthony St E1 ......32 A3

Antill Rd E3 ....26 A2
Antill Terr 8 E1 ....32 C3
Anton St E8 ....16 C3
Antony Ho 2 SE16 .40 B2
4 SE14 ....50 C3
Antrim Gr NW3 .....12 B2
Antrim Ho 8 E3 ....26 A3
SW11 ....60 C4
Antrim Mans NW3 ..12 B2
Antrim Rd NW3 ....12 B2
Antrobus Rd W4 ....37 B3
Apex Ind Est NW10 .21 B1
Aphrodite Ct E14 ..41 C2
Apollo Ct SW9 .....173 B4
Apollo Ho SW10 ...157 B3
N6 ....3 B4
31 E2 ....25 A3
Apollo Ind Bsns Ctr 20
SE8 ....50 C4
Apollo Pl SW10 ...157 B2
Apollo Studios 13
NW5 ....13 B3
Apothecary St EC4 108 A1
Appach Rd SW2 ....62 C1
Apple Mkt WC2 ....120 B4
Apple Tree Yd
SW1 ....119 A2
Appleby Rd E8 ......16 C1
E16 ....35 C3
Appleby St E2 ......24 B3
Appledore Cl SW12,
SW17 ....72 C2
Appleford 8 NW5 ..13 B3
Appleford Ho 6
W10 ....23 A1
Appleford Rd W10 ..23 A1
Applegarth Ho W14 136 B4
8 SE15 ....49 C3
Applegarth Rd W14 39 C3
Appleshaw Ho 4
SE5 ....64 A4
Appletree Ct SE13 ..67 C3
Appold St EC2 .....110 A4
Apprentice Way 6
E5 ....17 A4
Approach Cl N16 ...16 A4
Approach Rd E2 ....25 B3
Approach The 3 ....28 C3
April Ct 20 E2 ......24 C3
April St E8 ....16 B4
Apsley Ho E1 ......32 B4
Apsley Way W1 ....131 C4
Aquila St NW8 ......79 C2
Aquinas St SE1 ....121 C1
Arabella Ct NW8 ....79 A2
Arabella Dr SW15 ..56 A3
Arabian Ho 3 E1 ...26 A1
Arabin Rd SE4 ......66 B3
Aragon Twr SE8 ....41 B2
Arakan Ho 4 N16 ..15 C4
Aral Ho 4 E1 ....25 C1
Arapiles Ho 6 E14 .34 C3
Arbery Rd E3 ....26 A3
Arbon Ct N1 ....87 A3
Arbor Ct N16 ....6 C2
Arborfield Ho 6
E14 ....33 C2
Arbour Ho 3 E1 ....32 C3
Arbour Sq E1 ....32 C3
Arbourfield Cl SW2 .74 B3
Arbuthnot Rd SE14 .50 C1
Arbutus St E8 ......24 B4
Arcade The 22 ......109 C3
17 N7 ....14 A4
Arch St SE1 ....136 C1

Archangel St SE16 .40 C4
Archbishop Michael
Ramsey Tech Coll
SE5 ....48 A3
Archbishop Sumner's
CE Prim Sch
SE11 ....149 C3
Archbishop Tenison's
Sch SE11 ....163 A3
Archbishop's Pl 1
SW2 ....74 B4
Archdale Ct W12 ...30 A1
Archdale Ho SE1 ..138 A2
Archdale Rd SE22 ..64 B3
Archel Rd W14 ....154 C4
Archer Ho W11 ....113 A4
SW11 ....167 C3
25 N1 ....24 A4
Archer Sq SE14 ....51 A4
Archer St W1 ......119 B4
Archers Lo SE16 ...153 C1
Archery Cl W2 ....102 B1
Archery Fields Ho
WC1 ....95 B4
Archery Steps W2 ..116 B4
Arches The 20 ......120 B2
Archibald Mews
W1 ....118 A3
Archibald Rd N7 ...13 C4
Archibald St E13 ...26 C2
Archway N19 ......4 B2
Archway Cl W10 ....30 C4
N19 ....4 B2
Archway Hts 5 N19 .4 B3
Archway Rd N6 .....4 A4
Archway St SW13,
SW14 ....56 A4
Arcola St E8 ....16 B3
Arctic St NW5 ......13 A3
Ardbeg Rd SE24 ....63 C2
Arden 17 SW19 ....69 C3
Arden Cres E14 .....41 C2
Arden Ho SE11 ....148 C3
SW9 ....172 B1
21 N1 ....24 A3
Ardent Ho 28 E3 ...26 A3
Ardilaun Rd N5 .....15 B4
Ardleigh Rd N1 .....16 A2
Ardlui Rd SE27 .....75 B2
Ardmere Rd SE13 ..67 C1
Ardshiel Cl SW15 ..57 C4
Ardwell Rd SW2 ....74 A2
Ardwick Rd NW2 ...10 C4
Ares Ct 8 E14 ......41 C2
Arethusa Ho 8 E14 .42 A2
Argon Mews SW6 .155 C1
Argos Ct SW9 .....173 B4
Argos Ho 8 E2 .....25 A3
Argosy Ho W1 ......92 B1
SE8 ....41 A2
Argyle Ho E14 .....42 B3
Argyle Pl W6 ....39 A2
Argyle Prim Sch
WC1 ....94 A4
Argyle Rd E1 ....25 C1
Argyle Sq WC1 .....94 B4
Argyle St WC1 .....94 B4
Argyle Way SE16 ..153 C1
Argyle Wlk WC1 ....94 B3
Argyll Cl SW9 ......62 B4
Argyll Ct SW2 ......74 A4
Argyll Mans W14 ..140 B4
SW3 ....157 C4
Argyll Rd W8 ......127 C3

Argyll St W1 . . . .**104** C1
Arica Ho SE16 . . . . .40 A3
Arica Rd SE4 . . . . .66 A4
Ariel Ct SE11 . . . .**150** A3
  W12 . . . . .38 C3
Ariel Rd NW6 . . . . .10 C2
Ariel Way W12 . . . . .39 B4
Aristotle Rd SW4 . . . . . . .61 C4
Arkansas Ho **21** N19 . . . .4 C4
Arklow Ho SE17 . . . . .48 C4
Arklow Rd SE14 . . . . .51 B4
Arklow Road Trad Est
SE14 . . . . .51 B4
Arkwright Ho **28**
SW2 . . . . .74 A4
Arkwright Mans
NW3 . . . . .11 B3
Arkwright Rd NW3 . . . . .11 B3
Arlesey Cl SW15 . . . . .58 A2
Arlesford Rd SW9 . . . . . . .62 A4
Arlingford Rd SW2 . . . . . .62 C2
Arlington Ave N1 . . . . .87 A3
Arlington Gdns W4 . . . . . .37 B1
Arlington Ho EC1 . . . . .95 C4
  W12 . . . . .30 A1
 3 SE8 . . . . .51 B4
Arlington Lo SW2 . . . . . . .62 B3
Arlington Park Mans 1
W4 . . . . .37 B1
Arlington Pl 7
SE10 . . . . .52 B3
Arlington Rd NW1 . . . . . . .82 B3
Arlington Sq N1 . . . . .87 A3
Arlington St SW1 . . . . . .118 C2
Arlington Way EC1 . . . . . .95 C4
Armada Ct **11** SE8 . . . . .51 C4
Armada St **10** SE8 . . . . .51 C4
Armadale Rd SW6 . . . . . .155 B3
Armagh Rd E3 . . . . .26 B4
Arminger Rd W12 . . . . . . .30 A1
Armitage Rd NW11 . . . . . . .1 B3
  SE10 . . . . .43 B1
Armour Cl N7 . . . . .14 B2
Armoury Rd SE8 . . . . .52 A1
Armsby Ho **11** E1 . . . . . .32 B4
Armstrong Ho **8**
SW15 . . . . .57 C1
Armstrong Rd
SW7 . . . . .129 B1
  W3 . . . . .29 B1
Arnal Cres SW18 . . . . .70 A4
Arne Ho SE11 . . . . .149 A2
Arne St WC2 . . . . .106 B1
Arneway St SW1 . . . . .133 C1
Arnewood Cl SW15 . . . . . .68 C3
Arnhem Pl E14 . . . . .41 C3
Arnhem Way 3
SE22 . . . . .64 A2
Arnhem Wharf E14 . . . . . .41 C3
Arnhem Wharf JMI Sch
E14 . . . . .41 C3
Arnold Cir E2 . . . . .99 A3
Arnold Est SE1 . . . . . . .139 A3
Arnold Ho SE17 . . . . .150 B1
 7 N16 . . . . .6 C2
Arnold House Sch
NW8 . . . . .79 B1
Arnold Rd E3 . . . . .26 C2
Arnot Ho **27** SE5 . . . . . . .48 B3
Arnott Cl W4 . . . . .37 C2
Arnould Ave SE5 . . . . .63 C3
Arnside St SE17 . . . . .48 C4
Arnside St SE17 . . . . .48 C4
Arodene Rd SW2 . . . . .62 B1

Arragon Rd SW18 . . . . . . .70 C3
Arran Ho N16 . . . . .7 B3
Arran Wlk N1 . . . . .15 B1
Arrol Ho SE1 . . . . .137 A1
Arrow Ho **24** N1 . . . . . . .24 A4
Arrow Rd E3 . . . . .27 A2
Arrowe Ct **7** E5 . . . . .17 A4
Arrowsmith Ho
SE11 . . . . .148 C2
Arsenal Sta N5 . . . . .5 C1
Artemis Ct **8** E14 . . . . .41 C2
Artesian Rd W2 . . . . .31 C3
Arthur Ct W2 . . . . .100 A2
 10 W10 . . . . .30 C3
Arthur Deakin Ho
E1 . . . . .111 B4
Arthur Henderson Ho
SW6 . . . . .164 C2
 2 N19 . . . . .4 C4
Arthur Newton Ho **20**
SW11 . . . . .59 C4
Arthur Rd N7 . . . . .14 B4
Arthur St EC4 . . . . .123 C4
Arthur Wade Ho E2 . . . . .99 A4
Arthurdon Rd SE4 . . . . . . .66 C2
Artichoke Hill **8** E1 . . . .32 A2
Artichoke Mews 5
SE5 . . . . .48 C2
Artichoke Pl SE5 . . . . . . .48 C2
Artillery La E1 . . . . .110 B3
  W12 . . . . .29 C3
Artillery Row SW1 . . . .133 B1
Artizan St E1 . . . . .110 B2
Arton Wilson Ho **19**
SW15 . . . . .56 C2
Arts Educational Schs
The W4 . . . . .38 A2
Arundel Bldgs SE1 . . . . .138 B1
Arundel Cl SW11 . . . . .60 A2
Arundel Ct SW3 . . . . .144 B2
  SW13 . . . . .47 A4
  SW15 . . . . .57 C2
Arundel Gdns
W11 . . . .**31** B2 **112** C4
Arundel Gr N16 . . . . .16 A3
Arundel Ho N1 . . . . .86 B4
 3 W3 . . . . .37 A4
  Richmond TW10 . . . . . .54 C2
Arundel Mans
SW6 . . . . .165 A4
  SW13 . . . . .47 A4
Arundel Pl N1,N7 . . . . . . .14 C2
Arundel Sq N7 . . . . .14 C2
Arundel St WC2 . . . . .121 A4
Arundel Terr SW13 . . . . . .47 A4
Arvon Rd N5 . . . . .14 C3
Asaph Ho SE14 . . . . .51 B2
Ascalon Ct **16** SW2 . . . .74 B4
Ascalon Ho SE8 . . . . .160 A1
Ascalon St SW8 . . . . .160 A1
Ascot Ct NW8 . . . . .89 B3
 8 SW4 . . . . .62 A3
Ascot Ho NW1 . . . . .92 B4
 1 W9 . . . . .31 C4
Ascot Lo NW6 . . . . .78 B2
Ascot Par **9** SW4 . . . . . .62 A3
Ascott Ave W5 . . . . .36 A4
Asfil Ho EC1 . . . . .107 C3
Ash Ct W1 . . . . .102 C2
  N19 . . . . .4 B3
  SW11 . . . . .60 C2
Ash Gr NW2 . . . . .10 A4

Ash Gr continued
 8 E8 . . . . .25 A4
  W5 . . . . .36 A3
Ash Ho SE1 . . . . .153 A3
 3 E14 . . . . .42 B4
Ash Lo SW6 . . . . .47 C2
Ashbourne Ct E5 . . . . .18 A4
Ashbourne Gr W4 . . . . . . .38 A1
  SE22 . . . . .64 B3
Ashbridge St NW8 . . . . . . .90 A1
Ashbrook Rd N19 . . . . .4 C2
Ashburn Gdns
SW7 . . . . .142 C4
Ashburn Pl SW7 . . . . .142 C3
Ashburnham Gr
SE10 . . . . .52 A3
Ashburnham Pl
SE10 . . . . .52 A3
Ashburnham Prim Sch
SW10 . . . . .157 A1
Ashburnham Rd
SW10 . . . . .157 A1
Ashburnham Retreat **8**
SE10 . . . . .52 A3
Ashburnham Twr
SW10 . . . . .157 B2
Ashburton Gr N7 . . . . .14 C4
Ashburton Mans
SW10 . . . . .157 A2
Ashburton Rd E16 . . . . . . .35 C3
Ashby Ct NW8 . . . . .89 C2
Ashby Gr N1 . . . . .15 B1
Ashby Ho **2** SW9 . . . . . .48 A1
 3 SW9 . . . . .48 A1
Ashby Mews SE4 . . . . .51 B1
Ashby Rd SE4 . . . . .51 B1
Ashby St EC1 . . . . .96 B3
Ashchurch Ct W12 . . . . . .38 C3
Ashchurch Gr W12 . . . . . .38 C3
Ashchurch Park Villas
W12 . . . . .38 C3
Ashchurch Terr
W12 . . . . .38 C3
Ascombe Ct **4**
SW15 . . . . .58 B2
Ascombe Ho **32** E3 . . . .27 A2
Ascombe St SW6 . . . . . . .166 A1
Ashcroft Ho **5** SW8 . . .170 C4
Ashcroft Rd E3 . . . . .26 A2
Ashcroft Sq W6 . . . . .39 B2
Ashdale Ho N4 . . . . .6 C4
Ashdene **6** SE15 . . . . . . .50 A3
Ashdown Cres NW5 . . . . . .12 C3
Ashdown Ho **7** SW1 . . .147 B3
Ashdown Rd N10 . . . . .21 B4
Ashdown Way
SW17 . . . . .72 C2
Ashdown Wlk **15**
E14 . . . . .41 C2
Ashen Gr SW19 . . . . .70 C2
Ashenden SE17 . . . . .151 A4
Ashenden Rd E5 . . . . .18 A3
Ashentree Ct EC4 . . . . . .107 C1
Asher Way E1 . . . . .125 C3
Ashfield Ho **5** N5 . . . . . .15 B3
Ashfield Rd W3 . . . . .29 B1
Ashfield St E1 . . . . .32 A4
Ashford Ct NW2 . . . . .9 C4
Ashford Ho **11** SE8 . . . . .51 B4
 14 SW9 . . . . .63 A3
Ashford Rd NW2 . . . . .9 C4
Ashford St N1 . . . . .97 C4
Ashgrove Ct **2** W9 . . . . .31 C4
Ashgrove Ho SW1 . . . . . .147 C2

Ashington **1** NW5 . . . . . .13 A2
Ashington Ho **18** E1 . . . .25 A1
Ashington Rd SW6 . . . . . .165 B1
Ashland Pl W1 . . . . .103 B4
Ashleigh Ho SW14 . . . . . . .56 A4
Ashleigh Rd SW14 . . . . . . .56 A4
Ashley Cres SW11 . . . . . . .60 C4
Ashley Ct NW3 . . . . .11 A3
 13 N16 . . . . .16 A3
Ashley Pl SW1 . . . . .132 C1
Ashley Rd N19 . . . . .5 A4
  Richmond TW9 . . . . . . .54 A4
Ashlin Rd E15 . . . . .19 C4
Ashlone Rd SW15 . . . . . . .57 B4
Ashmead Bsns Ctr
E16 . . . . .27 C1
Ashmead Ho **9** E9 . . . . .18 A3
Ashmead Prim Sch
SE8 . . . . .51 C1
Ashmead Rd SE8 . . . . .51 C1
Ashmere Gr 11 SW2, ...
SW4 . . . . .62 A3
Ashmere Ho **10**
SW2 . . . . .62 A3
Ashmill St NW8 . . . . .102 A4
Ashmole Prim Sch
SW8 . . . . .163 A3
Ashmole St SW8 . . . . . . .163 A3
Ashmore NW1 . . . . .13 C1
Ashmore Ho **9** W14 . . . .126 B1
Ashmore Rd W9 . . . . .23 B2
Ashmount Prim Sch
N6 . . . . .4 B4
Ashmount Rd N19 . . . . .4 C4
Ashness Rd SW11 . . . . . . .60 B2
Ashpark Ho E14 . . . . .33 B3
Ashtead Ct **15** SW19 . . . .69 C3
Ashtead Rd E5 . . . . .7 C4
Ashton Ho SW9 . . . . .163 C1
  SW15 . . . . .69 B4
Ashton Rd E15 . . . . .19 C3
Ashton St E14 . . . . .34 B2
Ashurst Lo N5 . . . . .15 A3
Ashwin St E8 . . . . .16 B2
Ashworth Cl SE5 . . . . .48 C1
Ashworth Mans W9 . . . . . .88 B3
Ashworth Rd W9 . . . . .88 B3
Aske Ho N1 . . . . .98 A4
Aske St N1 . . . . .98 A4
Asker Ho N7 . . . . .14 A4
Askew Cres W12 . . . . .38 C4
  W12 . . . . .38 C4
Askew Rd W12 . . . . .38 C4
Aslett St SW18 . . . . .71 B4
Asmara Rd NW2 . . . . .10 A3
Asolando Dr SE17 . . . . . .151 A3
Aspen Ct **10** N19 . . . . . . .4 B2
  W5 . . . . .36 B2
Aspen Ct E8 . . . . .16 B3
  Richmond TW9 . . . . . . .44 C3
Aspen Gdns W6 . . . . .39 A2
Aspen Ho **4** SE15 . . . . . .50 B4
 8 SE15 . . . . .50 B4
Aspen House Sch
SW2 . . . . .74 B4
Aspen Way E14 . . . . .34 B2
Aspenlea Rd W6 . . . . .47 C4
Aspern Gr NW3 . . . . .12 A3
Aspinall Ho SW12 . . . . . . .74 A3
Aspinall Rd SE4 . . . . .65 C4
Aspinden Rd SE16 . . . . . . .40 A2
Aspley Rd SW18 . . . . .59 A2

Arg – Att 179

Assam SE1 . . . . .125 A1
Assam St E1 . . . . .111 B2
Assata Mews N1 . . . . .15 A2
Assembly Pas E1 . . . . .32 B4
Astbury Ho SE11 . . . . . . .135 B1
Astbury Rd SE15 . . . . .50 B2
Aste St E14 . . . . .42 B4
Astell St SW3 . . . . .144 B2
Astey's Row **3** N1 . . . . . .15 B1
Asthall Gdns IG6 . . . . .18 C4
Astle St SW11 . . . . .169 C2
Astley Ave NW2 . . . . .9 B3
Astley Ho SE1 . . . . .153 A2
Aston Ho W11 . . . . .113 A4
  SW8 . . . . .171 B3
Aston St E14 . . . . .33 A4
Astonville St SW18 . . . . . .70 C3
Astor Ct SW6 . . . . .156 C1
Astoria Mans **18**
SW16 . . . . .74 A1
Astoria Par SW16 . . . . . . .74 A1
Astoria Wlk SW9 . . . . .62 C4
Astra Ho N4 . . . . .5 B4
 4 E3 . . . . .26 B2
Astrop Mews W6 . . . . .39 B3
Astrop Terr W6 . . . . .39 B4
Astwood Mews
SW7 . . . . .142 C4
Asylum Rd SE15 . . . . .50 A3
Atalanta St SW6 . . . . . . .154 A1
Athelden Rd W18 . . . . .71 B3
Athelstan Gdns 6
NW6 . . . . .10 A1
Athelstan Ho N16 . . . . . . .16 A3
  E9 . . . . .18 A1
Athelstane Gr E3 . . . . .26 B3
Athelstane Mews N4 . . . . . .5 C3
Athena Ct NW8 . . . . .79 B2
Athenia Ho **7** E14 . . . . . .34 C3
Athenlay Rd SE15 . . . . . . .65 C2
Athenoeum Ct N5 . . . . . . .15 B4
Athens Gdns W9 . . . . .23 C1
Atherden Rd E5 . . . . .17 B4
Atherfield Ct SW18 . . . . . .59 A1
Atherfold Rd SW9 . . . . . . .62 A4
Atherstone Ct W2 . . . . . .100 B4
Atherstone Mews
SW7 . . . . .143 A4
Atherton Rd SW13 . . . . . .46 C3
Atherton St SW11 . . . . . .168 B2
Athlone Cl **22** E5 . . . . . . .17 A3
Athlone Ho **5** E1 . . . . . . .32 B3
 2 E1 . . . . .32 B3
Athlone House (The
Middlesex Hospl)
N6 . . . . .3 B3
Athlone Rd SW2 . . . . .74 C4
Athlone St NW5 . . . . .12 C2
Athol Sq E14 . . . . .34 B3
Atholl Ho W9 . . . . .88 C3
Atkins Rd SW4,SW12 . . . .73 C4
Atkinson Ho SE17 . . . . . .151 C3
 3 E2 . . . . .24 C3
 15 E2 . . . . .24 C3
Atlantic Ho **4** E1 . . . . . . .26 A1
 4 SW15 . . . . .58 B2
Atlantic Rd SW2,
SW9,SE24 . . . . .62 C3
Atlas Mews E8 . . . . .16 B2
Atlas Rd NW10 . . . . .21 A2
Atley Rd E3 . . . . .26 C4
Atney Rd SW15 . . . . .58 A3
Atterbury St SW1 . . . . . .148 A3
Attilburgh Ho SE1 . . . . . .138 C2

Attneave St WC1 ...95 B3
Atwater Cl SW2 ...74 C3
Atwell Rd 4 SE15 ...49 C1
Atwood Ave TW9 ...44 C1
Atwood Ho SE21 ...76 A1
Atwood Rd W6 ...39 A2
Aubert Ct N5 ...15 A4
Aubert Pk N5 ...15 A4
Aubert Rd N5 ...15 A4
Aubrey Beardsley Ho
SW1 ...147 A3
Aubrey Mans NW1 ...102 A4
Aubrey Moore Point
E15 ...27 B3
Aubrey Pl NW8 ...78 C1
Aubrey Rd
W14 ...31 B1 113 A1
Aubrey Wlk
W14 ...31 B1 113 A1
Auburn Cl SE14 ...51 A3
Aubyn Sq SW15 ...56 C2
Auckland Ho 11
W12 ...30 A2
Auckland Rd SW11 ...60 A3
Auckland St SE11 ...148 C1
Auden Pl NW1 ...81 B4
Audley Ct N1 ...118 A2
Audley Rd TW10 ...54 B2
Audley Sq W1 ...117 C2
Audrey St E2 ...24 C3
Augustus Cl W12 ...39 A3
Augustine Rd W14 ...39 C3
Augustines Ct 11 ...17 B3
Augustus Ct
8 SW19 ...70 A3
SW16 ...73 C2
Augustus Rd SW19 ...70 A3
Augustus St NW1 ...92 B4
Aulton Pl SE11 ...149 C1
Auriga Mews N1 ...15 C3
Auriol Mans W14 ...140 A3
Auriol Rd W14 ...140 A3
Austen Ho 2 NW6 ...23 C2
Austen Friars EC2 ...109 C2
Austin Friars Sq
EC2 ...109 C2
Austin Ho 11 SE14 ...51 B3
6 SW2 ...62 B2
Austin Rd SW11 ...169 B3
Austin St E2 ...98 C3
Austins Ct SE15 ...64 C4
Austral St SE11 ...150 A4
Australia Rd W12 ...30 A2
Autumn St E3 ...26 C4
Avalon Rd SW6 ...166 A4
Ave Maria La EC4 ...108 B1
Avebury Ct N1 ...87 B3
Avebury St N1 ...87 B3
Aveline St SE11 ...149 B1
Avenell Mans N5 ...15 A4
Avenell Rd N5 ...6 A1
Avening Rd SW18 ...70 C4
Avening Terr SW18 ...70 C4
Avenue Cl NW8 ...80 B3
Avenue Cres W3 ...37 A4
Avenue Gdns W3 ...37 A4
SW14 ...56 A4
NW2 ...1 A1
SW14 ...56 A4
N16 ...7 A4
NW10 ...22 A3

Avenue Lo NW8 ...79 C4
12 NW8 ...11 C1
Avenue Mans NW3 ...11 A3
Avenue Park Rd
SE21,SE22 ...75 A2
Avenue Rd NW8 ...80 A4
N6 ...4 C4
NW10 ...21 B3
W3 ...37 A4
Avenue The NW6 ...23 A4
W4 ...38 A3
Richmond TW9 ...44 B1
SW4 ...60 C2
SW18,SW12 ...72 A4
Averill St W6 ...47 C4
Avery Farm Row
SW1 ...145 C3
Avery Hill Coll (Mile End
Annexe) E3 ...26 C2
Avery Row W1 ...118 B4
Aviary Cl E16 ...35 B2
Avigdor (Jewish) JMI
Sch N16 ...6 C2
Avignon Rd SE4 ...65 C4
Avington Ct SE1 ...152 B3
Avis Sq E1 ...32 C3
Avoca Rd SW17 ...72 C1
Avocet Cl SE1 ...153 A2
Avon Ct 11 W3 ...28 B3
11 SW15 ...58 B2
Avon Ho W14 ...141 A3
14 N16 ...15 C4
Avon Pl SE1 ...137 A3
Avon Rd SE4 ...66 C4
Avondale Ct E16 ...35 A4
Avondale Ho SE1 ...153 B1
6 SW14 ...55 C4
Avondale Mans
SW6 ...164 C4
Avondale Park Gdns
W11 ...112 A3
Avondale Park Prim Sch
W11 ...31 A2 112 A4
Avondale Rd E16 ...35 A4
SW14 ...55 C4
Avondale Rise SE15 ...64 B4
Avonhurst Ho NW6 ...10 A1
Avonley Rd SE14 ...50 B3
Avonmore Gdns
W14 ...141 A3
Avonmore Pl W14 ...140 B4
Avonmore Prim Sch
W14 ...140 B4
Avonmore Rd W14 ...140 B4
Avonmouth St SE1 ...136 C2
Avriol Ho W12 ...30 A1
Avro Ct E9 ...18 A3
Axford Ho SW2 ...75 A3
Axminster Rd N7 ...5 B1
Aybrook St W1 ...103 B3
Aycliffe Rd W12 ...29 C1
Aylesbury Ho 16
SE15 ...49 C4
Aylesbury Rd SE17 ...151 C1
Aylesbury St EC1 ...96 A1
Aylesford St SW1 ...147 B1
Aylesham Centre The
SE15 ...49 C2
Aylestone Ave NW6 ...22 C4
Aylmer Ho SE10 ...42 C1
Aylmer Rd W12 ...38 B3
Aylton Est 22 SE16 ...40 B4

Aylward Ho 11 E14 ...33 A4
Aylward St E1 ...32 C3
Aylwin Est SE1 ...138 B2
Aylwin Girls Sch
SE11 ...153 A4
Aynhoe Mans W14 ...39 C3
Aynhoe Rd W14 ...39 C3
Ayres St SE1 ...137 A4
Ayrsome Rd N16 ...7 A1
Ayrton Gould Ho 9
E2 ...25 C2
Ayrton Rd SW7 ...129 B2
Aysgarth Rd SE21 ...76 A4
Ayston Ho 10 SE8 ...40 C2
Ayton Ho SE5 ...48 C3
Aytoun Ct SW9 ...173 A1
Aytoun Pl SW9 ...173 A1
Aytoun Rd SW9 ...173 A1
Azalea Ho SE14 ...51 B3
Azenby Rd SE15 ...49 B1
Azof St SE10 ...43 A2
Azov Ho 9 E1 ...26 A1

B

Baalbec Rd N5 ...15 A3
Babington Ho SE1 ...137 A4
Babmaes St SW1 ...119 A3
Bacchus Wlk 12 N1 ...24 A3
Bache's St N1 ...97 C3
Back Church La
E1 ...111 B1
Back Hill EC1 ...95 C1
Back La NW3 ...11 B4
Backhouse Pl SE1 ...152 B3
Bacon Gr SE1 ...138 C1
Bacon St E2 ...24 C1 99 B2
Bacon's Coll SE16 ...41 A4
Bacon's La N6 ...3 C3
Bacton NW5 ...12 C3
Bacton St E2 ...25 B2
Baddeley Ho SE11 ...149 A2
Baddow Wlk (off
Popham Rd) N1 ...86 C4
Baden Pl SE1 ...137 B4
Badminton Ct 9 N4 ...6 B4
Badminton Ho SE22 ...64 A3
Badminton Mews 10
E16 ...35 C1
Badminton Rd
SW12 ...60 C1
Badric Ct SW11 ...167 C1
Badsworth Rd 3
SE5 ...48 B2
Bagley's La SW6 ...166 B3
Bagshot Ho NW1 ...92 B4
Bagshot St SE17 ...152 A1
Baildon 28 E2 ...25 B3
Baildon St SE8 ...51 B3
Bailey Ct 9 W12 ...38 C4
Bailey Mews W4 ...45 A4
Bain Ho SW9 ...172 B2
Bainbridge St
WC1 ...105 C2
Baird Ho 20 W12 ...30 A2
Baird St EC1 ...97 A2
Baizdon Rd SE3 ...53 A1
Baker Ho 12 E3 ...27 A2
Baker Rd NW10 ...21 A4
Baker St W1 ...103 A4
Baker Street W1 ...91 A1
Baker's Mews W1 ...103 B2
Baker's Row EC1 ...95 B1

Baker's Yd EC1 ...95 B1
Bakers Field N7 ...14 A4
Bakers Hall Ct EC3 ...124 B3
Balaclava Rd SE1 ...153 A3
Balchier Rd SE22 ...65 A1
Balcombe Ho NW1 ...90 C1
11 SW2 ...74 B3
Balcombe St NW1 ...90 C1
Balcorne St E9 ...17 B1
Balderton Flats
W1 ...103 C1
Balderton St W1 ...103 C1
Baldock Ho 20 SE5 ...48 B1
Baldock St E3 ...27 A3
Baldrey Ho 11 SE10 ...43 B1
Baldwin Cres SE5 ...48 B2
Baldwin Ho 15 SW2 ...74 C3
Baldwin St EC1 ...97 B3
Baldwin Terr N1 ...86 C2
Baldwin's Gdns
EC1 ...107 B4
Baldwyn Gdns W3 ...28 C2
Bales Coll W10 ...22 C2
Balfe St N1 ...84 B1
Balfern Gr W4 ...38 A1
Balfern St SW11 ...168 B2
Balfour Ho W10 ...30 C4
Balfour Mews W1 ...117 C2
Balfour Pl W1 ...117 C3
SW15 ...57 A3
Balfour Rd N5 ...15 B4
W3 ...28 B4
Balfour St SE17 ...151 B4
Balfron Twr 2 E14 ...34 B3
Balham Gr SW12 ...72 C4
Balham High Rd
SW12,SW17 ...72 C3
Balham Hill SW12 ...61 A1
Balham New Rd
SW12 ...73 A4
Balham Park Mans
SW12 ...72 B3
Balham Park Rd
SW12,SW17 ...72 B3
Balham Sta SW12 ...73 A3
Balham Station Rd
SW12 ...73 A3
Balin Ho SE1 ...137 B4
Balkan Wlk 11 E1 ...32 A2
Ball Ct EC3 ...109 C1
Ball's Pond Pl 3
N1 ...16 A2
Ball's Pond Rd N1 ...16 A2
Ballance Rd E9 ...18 A2
Ballantine St SW18 ...59 B3
Ballantrae Ho NW2 ...10 B4
Ballard Ho SE10 ...52 A4
Ballast Quay SE10 ...42 C1
Ballater Rd SW2,
SW4 ...62 A3
Ballin Ct 9 E14 ...42 B4
Ballina St SE23 ...65 C1
Ballingdon Rd
SW11 ...60 C1
Ballinger Point 11
E3 ...27 A2
Balliol Ho 11 SW15 ...57 C1
Balliol Rd W10 ...30 C3
Ballogie Ave NW10 ...8 A4
Ballow Cl 22 SE5 ...49 A3
Balman Ho 3 SE16 ...40 C2
Balmer Rd E3 ...26 B3
Balmes Rd N1 ...87 C4
Balmoral Cl 1
SW15 ...57 C1
Balmoral Ct NW8 ...79 B2

Balmoral Ct continued
2 SE16 ...32 C1
Balmoral Gr N7 ...14 B2
Balmoral Ho 14
N4 ...6 B3
11
W12 ...38 B3
Balmoral Rd NW2 ...9 A2
Balmore St N19 ...4 A2
Balmuir Gdns SW15 ...57 B3
Balnacraig Ave
NW10 ...8 A4
Balniel Gate SW1 ...147 C2
Balsam Ho 8 E14 ...34 A2
Baltic Ho 7 SE5 ...48 B1
Baltic St E EC1 ...96 C1
Baltic St W EC1 ...96 C1
Baltimore Ho SE11 ...149 B2
Balvaird Pl SW1 ...147 C1
Balvernie Gr SW18 ...70 C4
Bamborough Gdns 15
W12 ...39 B4
Banbury Ct WC2 ...120 A4
Banbury Ho 8 E9 ...17 C1
Banbury Rd E9 ...17 C1
Banbury St SW11 ...168 B2
Bancroft Ct SW8 ...172 A4
Bancroft Ho 10 E1 ...25 B1
Bancroft Rd E1 ...25 C1
Banff Ho 11 NW3 ...12 A2
Bangabandhu JMI Sch
E2 ...25 B2
Bangalore St SW15 ...57 B4
Banim St W6 ...39 A2
Banister Ho SW8 ...171 A4
19 W10 ...23 A2
15 W10 ...23 A2
Bank Ct SW11 ...170 A4
Bank End SE1 ...123 A2
Bank La SW15 ...56 A2
Bank of England
EC2 ...109 B1
Bank Sta EC3 ...109 C1
Bank The N6 ...4 A3
Banks Ho SE1 ...136 C1
Bankside SE1 ...122 C3
SE1 ...123 A2
Bankside Pier SE1 ...122 C3
Bankton Rd SW2 ...62 C3
Banner Ho EC1 ...97 A1
Banner St EC1 ...97 A2
Bannerman Ho
SW8 ...162 C3
Banning Ho 4
SW19 ...69 C3
Banning St SE10 ...43 A1
Bannister Cl SW2 ...74 C3
Bannister Ho 88
SE14 ...51 A4
Banqueting House*
SW1 ...120 A1
Banstead Ct N4 ...65 B4
Banstead St SE15 ...65 B4
Bantock Ho 11 W10 ...23 A2
Bantry Ho 11 E1 ...25 C1
Bantry St SE5 ...48 C3
Banyan Ho 8 NW3 ...11 A2
Banyard Rd SE16 ...40 A3
Baptist Gdns NW5 ...12 C2
Barandon Wlk 6
W11 ...30 C2
Barb Mews W6 ...39 B3
Barbanel Ho 11 E1 ...25 B1

Barbara Brosnan Ct
NW8 . . . . .79 B1
Barbauld Rd N16 . . . . . . .7 A1
Barber Beaumont Ho 21
E1 . . . . .25 C2
Barbers Rd E15 . . . . . . .27 A3
Barbican ✻ EC2 . . . . . .109 A3
Barbican Arts & Con Ctr
EC2 . . . . .109 A4
Barbican Sta EC1 . . . . .106 C4
Barbon Cl WC1 . . . . . . .106 C4
Barbrook Ho E9 . . . . . . .17 B2
Barchard St SW18 . . . . .59 A2
Barchester St E14 . . . . .34 A4
Barclay Cl SW6 . . . . . . .155 B1
Barclay Ho 21 E9 . . . . . .17 B1
Barclay Rd SW6 . . . . . .155 C1
Barcombe Ave SW2 . . . .74 B2
Bard Rd W10 . . . . .30 C2
Bardell Ho 18 SE1 . . . .139 B3
Bardolph Rd N7 . . . . . . .14 A4
Richmond TW9 . . . . .54 B4
Bardsey Pl 63 E1 . . . . . .25 B1
Bardsey Wlk 6 N1 . . . .15 B2
Bardsley Ho 5
SE10 . . . . .52 B4
Bardsley La SE10 . . . . . .52 B4
Barents Ho 10 E1 . . . . . .25 C1
Barfett St W10 . . . . .23 B1
Barfleur Ho SE8 . . . . . . .41 B2
Barford Ho 19 E3 . . . . . .26 B3
Barford St N1 . . . . .85 C3
Barforth Rd SE15 . . . . . .65 A4
Barge House St
SE1 . . . . .121 C2
Barham Ho 9 SE17 . . .152 B2
Baring Ct N1 . . . . .87 B3
Baring Ho 11 E14 . . . . .33 C3
Baring St N1 . . . . .87 B3
Bark Pl W2 . . . . .114 A4
Barker Dr NW1 . . . . .13 C1
Barker Ho SE17 . . . . . .152 A3
SE21 . . . . .76 A1
Barker Mews SW4 . . . . .61 A3
Barker St SW10 . . . . . .156 C4
Barker Wlk SW16 . . . . . .73 C1
Barkston Gdns
SW5 . . . . .142 A3
Barkway Ct N4 . . . . .6 B2
Barkwith Ho 27
SE14 . . . . .50 C4
Barkworth Rd SE16 . . . .40 B1
Barlborough St
SE14 . . . . .50 C3
Barlby Gdns W10 . . . . . .22 C1
Barlby Prim Sch
W10 . . . . .22 C1
Barlby Rd W10 . . . . .30 C4
Barley Mow Pas
EC1 . . . . .108 B3
W4 . . . . .37 C1
Barleycorn Way E14 . . .33 B2
Barling 6 NW1 . . . . . . .13 A1
Barling Ct 5 SW4 . . . .172 A2
Barlings Ho 2 SE4 . . . .65 C3
Barloch Ho SW11 . . . . .169 B2
Barlow Ho N1 . . . . .97 B4
W11 . . . . .112 A4
14 SE16 . . . . .40 A2
Barlow Pl W1 . . . . .118 B3
Barlow Rd NW6 . . . . . . .10 B2
Barlow St SE17 . . . . . .151 C3
Barmouth Ho 6 N7 . . . .5 B2
Barmouth Rd SW18 . . . .59 B1
Barn Cl 13 NW5 . . . . . . .13 C3

Barn Field NW3 . . . . . . .12 B3
Barnabas Ho EC1 . . . . .96 C3
Barnabas Rd E9 . . . . . . .17 C3
Barnard Ho 12 E2 . . . . .25 A2
Barnard Lo 10 W9 . . . . .31 C4
Barnard Mews
SW11 . . . . .60 A3
Barnard Rd SW11 . . . . . .60 A3
Barnard's Inn
EC4 . . . . .107 C2
Barnardo Gdns 1
E1 . . . . .32 C2
Barnardo St E1 . . . . .32 C3
Barnbrough 4 NW1 . . . .82 C3
Barnby St NW1 . . . . . . .93 A4
Barnersbury Ho N7 . . . .14 A4
Barnes Ave SW13 . . . . . .46 C3
Barnes Bridge Sta
SW13 . . . . .46 A1
Barnes Common
SW13 . . . . .56 C4
Barnes Ct N1 . . . . .14 C1
Barnes High St
SW13 . . . . .46 B1
Barnes Ho N19 . . . . .4 C1
14 E2 . . . . .25 B3
28 SE14 . . . . .50 C4
Barnes Hospl SW14 . . . .56 A4
Barnes St E14 . . . . .33 A3
Barnes Terr SE8 . . . . . .41 B1
Barnet Gr E2 . . . .24 C2 99 B3
Barnet Ho 50 SE5 . . . . .48 B1
Barnett St 15 E1 . . . . . .32 A3
Barnett St 8 E1 . . . . . . .32 A3
Barnfield Cl N4 . . . . .5 A4
SW17 . . . . .71 B1
Barnfield Pl E14 . . . . . .41 C2
Barnham St SE1 . . . . . .138 B4
Barnsbury Gr N7 . . . . . .14 B1
Barnsbury Ho 16
SW4 . . . . .61 C1
Barnsbury Pk N1 . . . . . .14 C1
Barnsbury Rd N1 . . . . . .85 B3
Barnsbury Sq N1 . . . . . .14 C1
Barnsbury St N1 . . . . . .14 C1
Barnsbury Terr N1 . . . . .14 B1
Barnsdale Ave E14 . . . . .41 C2
Barnsdale Rd W9 . . . . . .23 B1
Barnsley St E1 . . . . .25 A1
Barnstaple La SE13 . . . .67 B3
Barnston Wlk N1 . . . . . .86 C4
Barnwell Ho 5 SE5 . . . .49 A2
Barnwell Rd SW2 . . . . . .62 C2
Barnwood Cl W9 . . . . . .88 B1
Baron Cl N1 . . . . .85 B2
Baron St N1 . . . . .85 B2
Baron Wlk E16 . . . . .35 B2
Baron's Court Rd
W14 . . . . .140 B2
Baron's Pl SE1 . . . . . . .135 C3
Baroness Rd E2 . . .99 A4 24 B3
Barons Court Mans
W14 . . . . .140 A1
Barons Court Sta
W14 . . . . .140 A1
Barons Gate 13 W4 . . . .37 B3
Barons Keep W14 . . . . .140 A2
Barons Lo 8 E14 . . . . . .42 B2
Baronsmead Rd
SW13 . . . . .46 C2
Baronsmere Rd N2 . . . . . . .36 B4

Barque Mews SE8 . . . . . .51 C4
Barratt Ho 15 N1 . . . . . .15 A1
Barratt Ind Pk E3 . . . . . .27 B1
Barret Ho NW6 . . . . . . .23 C4
2 SW9 . . . . .62 C4
Barrett Ho SE17 . . . . . .151 A2
Barrett St W1 . . . . .103 C1
Barrett's Gr N16 . . . . . . .16 A3
Barrett's Green Rd
NW10 . . . . .20 C3
Barrhill Rd SW2 . . . . . . .74 A2
Barridge Mews
NW6 . . . . .10 C3
Barrie Ho NW8 . . . . .80 A1
W2 . . . . .115 A3
8 N16 . . . . .7 A1
W3 . . . . .37 B4
Barriedale SE14 . . . . . . .51 A1
Barrington Cl NW5 . . . .12 C3
Barrington Ct NW5 . . . .12 C3
Barrington Rd SW9 . . . .63 A4
Barrow Hill Est
NW8 . . . . .80 A1
Barrow Hill Jun Sch
NW8 . . . . .80 A1
Barrow Hill Rd NW8 . . .80 A1
Barrowgate Ho W4 . . . .37 C1
Barrowgate Rd W4 . . . .37 C1
Barry Ct SW4 . . . . .61 B1
Barry Ho 4 SE16 . . . . . .40 A1
Barry Lo N4 . . . . .5 B4
Barry Par SE22 . . . . .64 C3
Barry Rd SE22 . . . . .64 C2
Barset Rd SE15 . . . . .65 B4
Barston Rd SE27 . . . . . .75 B1
Barstow Cres SW2 . . . . .74 B3
Bartell Ho SW2 . . . . . . .62 C1
Barter St WC1 . . . . . . .106 B3
Bartholomew Cl
EC1 . . . . .108 C3
SW18 . . . . .59 B3
Bartholomew Ct
EC1 . . . . .97 A2
Bartholomew Ho 20
SE5 . . . . .48 B1
Bartholomew La
EC2 . . . . .109 C1
Bartholomew Pas
EC1 . . . . .108 B3
Bartholomew Pl
EC1 . . . . .108 C3
Bartholomew Rd
NW5 . . . . .13 B2
Bartholomew Sq 18
E1 . . . . .25 A1
EC1 . . . . .97 A2
Bartholomew St
SE1 . . . . .137 C1
Bartholomew Villas
NW5 . . . . .13 B2
Bartle Rd W11 . . . . .31 A3
Bartlett Cl E14 . . . . .33 C3
Bartlett Ct EC4 . . . . . .107 C2
Bartok Ho W11 . . . . . . .112 C3
Bartolomew Sq EC1 . . .97 A2
Barton Cl E9 . . . . .17 B3
8 SE15 . . . . .65 A4
SW4 . . . . .172 A2
Barton Ho N1 . . . . .15 A1
8 E3 . . . . .27 A2
SW6 . . . . .59 A4
Barton Rd W14 . . . . . . .140 B1
Barton St SW1 . . . . . . .134 A2
Bartonway NW8 . . . . . . .79 B2
Bartram Rd SE4 . . . . . . .66 A1
Bartrip St E9 . . . . .18 B2

Barville Cl SE4 . . . . .66 A3
Barwell Ho E2 . . . . .99 B2
Barwick Ho 2 W3 . . . . . .37 B4
Barwick Rd E7 . . . . .37 B4
Bashley Rd NW10 . . . . . .20 C1
Basil Ho E1 . . . . .111 C2
SW8 . . . . .162 A2
Basil Mans SW1 . . . . . .130 C3
Basil St SW1,SW3 . . . . .130 C3
SW1 . . . . .130 C3
Basing Ct 12 SE15 . . . .49 B2
Basing Hill NW11 . . . . . . .1 B3
Basing House Yd
E2 . . . . .98 B4
Basing Pl E2 . . . . .98 B4
Basing St W11 . . . . .31 B3
Basingdon Way SE5 . . . .63 C3
Basinghall Ave
EC2 . . . . .109 B3
Basinghall St EC2 . . . .109 B2
Basire St N1 . . . . .87 A4
Baskerville Gdns
NW10 . . . . .8 A4
Baskerville Rd
SW18 . . . . .72 A4
Baslow Wlk E5 . . . . .17 C4
Basnett Rd 6 SW11 . . . .61 A3
Basque Ct 23 SE16 . . . .40 C4
Bassano St SE22 . . . . . .64 B2
Bassein Park Rd
W12 . . . . .38 B4
Bassett Rd W10 . . . . . . .30 C3
Bassett St NW5 . . . . . . .12 C2
Bassingbourn Ho 5
N1 . . . . .15 A1
Bassingham Rd
SW18 . . . . .71 B4
Bassishaw Highwalk
EC2 . . . . .109 B3
Basswood Cl SE15 . . . . .65 A4
Basterfield Ho EC1 . . . .96 C1
Bastwick St EC1 . . . . . .96 C2
Basuto Rd SW6 . . . . . .165 C3
Batavia Ho 1 SE14 . . . .51 A3
Batavia Mews 3
SE14 . . . . .51 A3
Batavia Rd SE14 . . . . . . .51 A3
Batchelor St N1 . . . . . . .85 C3
Bate St 10 E14 . . . . .33 B2
Bateman Ho 6
SE17 . . . . .48 A4
Bateman St W1 . . . . . .105 B1
Bateman's Bldgs
W1 . . . . .105 B1
Bateman's Row
EC2 . . . . .24 A1 98 B2
Bath Cl SE15 . . . . .50 A3
Bath Ct EC1 . . . . .95 B1
EC1 . . . . .97 B3
3 SE26 . . . . .76 C1
Bath Gr E2 . . . . .24 C3
Bath Ho E2 . . . . .24 C1 99 B2
Bath Pl EC2 . . . . .98 A3
8 W6 . . . . .39 B1
Bath Rd W4 . . . . .38 A2
Bath St EC1 . . . . .97 B3
Bath Terr SE1 . . . . .136 C2
Bathgate Ho 8
SW9 . . . . .48 A2
Bathgate Rd SW19 . . . . .69 C1
Baths App SW6 . . . . . . .155 A2
Bathurst Gdns
NW10 . . . . .22 A3
Bathurst Ho 12 W12 . . .30 A2
Bathurst Mews
W2 . . . . .101 C1

Bathurst Mews continued
W2 . . . . .115 C2
Batley Pl 3 N16 . . . . .7 B1
Batley Rd N16 . . . . .7 B1
Batman Cl W12 . . . . .30 A1
Batoum Gdns W6 . . . . . .39 B3
Batson Ho E1 . . . . .111 C1
Batson St W12 . . . . .38 C4
Batten Ho 12 W10 . . . . .23 A2
4 SW4 . . . . .61 B2
Batten St SW11 . . . . . . .60 A4
Battersea Bridge Rd
SW11 . . . . .158 A1
Battersea Church Rd
SW11 . . . . .167 C4
Battersea Dogs Home
SW8 . . . . .160 B1
Battersea High St
SW11 . . . . .167 C3
SW11 . . . . .167 A4
Battersea Park ✻
SW11 . . . . .159 B1
Battersea Park Rd
SW11,SW8 . . . . .169 A3
Battersea Park Sta
SW8 . . . . .160 A1
Battersea Power Station
(dis) SW8 . . . . .160 B3
Battersea Rise
SW11 . . . . .60 A3
Battersea Sq
SW11 . . . . .167 C3
Battersea Tech Coll
SW11 . . . . .169 A3
Battishill St 9 N1 . . . . .15 A1
Battle Bridge Ctr
NW1 . . . . .84 B2
Battle Bridge La
SE1 . . . . .124 A1
Battle Bridge Rd
NW1 . . . . .84 A2
Battle Ho 15 SE15 . . . . .49 C4
Battledean Rd N5 . . . . . .15 A3
Batty St E1 . . . . .111 C2
Baty Ho SW2 . . . . .74 B3
Baulk The SW18 . . . . . . .70 C4
Bavaria Rd N19 . . . . .5 A2
Bavent Rd SE5 . . . . .48 B1
Bawdale Rd SE22 . . . . . .64 B2
Bawtree Rd SE14 . . . . . .51 A3
Baxendale St
E2 . . . . .24 C2 99 B4
Baxter Ho 11 E3 . . . . . . .27 A2
Baxter Rd N1 . . . . .15 C2
Bay Ct 7 E1 . . . . .25 C1
W5 . . . . .36 A3
Baycliffe Ho 9 E9 . . . . .17 C2
Bayer Ho EC1 . . . . .96 C1
Bayes Ct NW3 . . . . .12 B1
Bayfield Ho 8 SE4 . . . .65 C3
Bayford Rd NW10 . . . . . .22 C2
Bayford St 2 E8 . . . . . .17 A1
Bayford St Ind Ctr 4 E8
. . . . .17 A1
Bayham Pl NW1 . . . . . . .83 A3
Bayham Rd W4 . . . . .37 C3
Bayham St NW1 . . . . . . .82 C3
Bayley St WC1 . . . . . . .105 B3
Baylis Rd SE1 . . . . .135 B3

Baynes Mews 2
NW3 ....11 C2
Baynes St NW1 ....13 B1
Bayon Ho 2 N19 ....4 C4
Bayonne Rd W6 ....154 A3
Bayston Rd N16 ....7 B1
Bayswater Rd W2 ....115 B3
Bayswater Sta W2 ...114 B4
Baythorne St 3 E3 ....33 B4
Bayton Ct 2 E8 ....16 C1
Baytree Rd SW2 ....62 B3
Bazalgette Ho NW8 ...89 C2
Bazeley Ho SE1 ....136 A3
Bazely St E14 ....34 B2

BBC Television Ctr
W12 ....30 B1
Beach Ho SW5 ....141 B2
Beachy Rd E3 ....18 C1
Beacon Gate SE14 .....65 C4
Beacon Hill N7 ....14 A3
Beacon Rd SE13 ......171 B4
Beaconsfield Terrace Rd
W14 ....126 A1
Beaconsfield Cl W4 ...37 B1
SE3 ....53 C4
Beaconsfield Rd
SE17 ....152 A1
NW10 ....8 B2
W4 ....37 C3
SE3 ....53 C3
Beaconsfield Wlk
SW6 ....165 A3
Beadon Rd W6 ....39 B2
Beak St W1 ....119 A4
Beale Ho SW9 ....172 C1
Beale Pl E3 ....26 B3
Beale Rd E3 ....26 B4
Beames Ho SW8 ......171 B4
Beaminster Ho
SW8 ....162 C2
Beamish Ho 6
SE16 ....40 B2
Beanacre Ct E9 ....18 B2
Bear Alley EC4 ....108 A2
Bear Croft Ho
SW6 ....164 C1
Bear Gardens Mus
SE1 ....122 C2
Bear Gdns SE1 ....122 C2
Bear St WC2 ....119 C4
Beardsley Way W3 ....37 C4
Bearstead Rise SE4 ..66 B2
Beatrice Ho 4 W6 .....39 B1
1 SW2 ....62 B2
Beatrice Pl W8 ....128 A1
Beatrice Rd SE1 ....153 C3
N4 ....5 C4
2 Richmond TW10 ....54 B2
Beatrice Tate Sch
E2 ....25 A2
Beatrice Webb Ho 3
E3 ....26 A3
Beatrix Ho SW5 ....142 B2
Beatrix Potter Prim Sch
SW18 ....71 B3
Beattie Ho SW8 ....171 A4
Beatty Rd N16 ....16 A4
Beatty St NW1 ....82 C2
Beauchamp Cl 8
W4 ....37 B3

Beauchamp Pl
SW3 ....130 B1
Beauchamp Rd
SW11 ....60 B3
Beauchamp St EC1 .107 B3
Beauclerc Ho W6 ......39 A3
Beauclerk Ho 10
W16 ....57 A4
Beaufort Ho SW1 ......74 B4
Beaufort Gdns
SW3 ....130 B2
Beaufort Ho SW1 ....147 B1
SW3 ....157 C3
SW11 ....168 A2
Beaufort Mans
SW6 ....155 A4
Beaufort St SW3 ......157 C3
Beaufoy Ho SW8 .....162 C2
2 SE27 ....75 A1
Beaufoy Wlk SE11 ...149 A3
Beaulieu Cl SE5 ....63 C4
Beaulieu Pl W4 ....37 B3
Beaumanor Mans
W2 ....114 B4
Beaumaris Twr 2
W3 ....37 A4
Beaumont W14 ....141 A3
SW15 ....58 A2
Beaumont Ave
W14 ....140 C2
Richmond TW9 ....54 B4
Beaumont Bldgs
WC2 ....106 B1
Beaumont Cres
W14 ....140 C1
Beaumont Ct 10 W4 .37 B1
Beaumont Gdns NW3 .1 C1
Beaumont Gr E1 ....25 C1
Beaumont Ho SW19 ..70 C1
2 SW2 ....74 A3
Beaumont Mews
W1 ....103 C4
Beaumont Pl NW1,
W1,W1 ....93 A2
Beaumont Rd W4 ....37 B3
SW15,SW19 ....70 A4
Beaumont Rise N19 ....4 C3
Beaumont Sq E1 ....32 C4
Beaumont St W1 ....103 C4
Beaumont Wlk NW3 .12 B1
Beauval Rd SE22 ....64 B1
Beauvale 6 NW1 ....12 C1
Beavis Ho N16 ....7 A1
Beavor La 4 W6 ....38 C1
Beccles St E14 ....33 B2
Beck Cl SE13 ....52 A2
Beck Ho N16 ....7 A1
Beckers The N16 ....16 C4
Becket Ho SE1 ....137 B3
Becket St SE1 ....137 B2
Beckett Cl NW10 ....8 A2
SW16 ....73 C2
Beckett Ho SW9 ......172 B1
2 E1 ....32 B4
Beckfoot NW1 ....83 A1
Beckford Ho 10 N16 .16 A3
Beckford Prim Sch
NW6 ....10 B3
Beckham Ho SE11 ...149 A3
Beckington 18 NW5 ..12 C2
Beckley Ho 5 E3 ....26 B1

Becklow Gdns W12 ...29 C1
1 W12 ....38 C4
Becklow Mews 7
W12 ....38 C4
Beckton Rd E16 ....35 B2
Beckway St SE17 .....152 A3
Beckwith Ho 22 E2 ...25 A3
Beckwith Rd SE24 .....63 C2
Bective Pl SW15 ....58 B3
Bective Rd SW15 ......58 B3
Bedale St SE1 ....123 B1
Bede Ho SE14 ....51 B2
5 SW15 ....57 C1
Bedefield WC1 ....94 B3
Bedford Ave WC1 ....105 C3
Bedford Cl W4 ....46 B4
Bedford Cnr 3 W4 .....38 A2
Bedford Court Mans
WC1 ....105 C3
Bedford Ct WC2 ....120 A3
6 Richmond TW9 ......54 B3
Bedford Gardens Ho
W8 ....113 C1
Bedford Gdns
W8 ....31 C1 113 C1
Bedford Hill SW12 ....73 A2
Bedford Ho 2 W4 ......38 A2
7 SW4 ....62 A3
Bedford Park Cnr 5
W4 ....38 A2
Bedford Park Mans
W4 ....38 A1
Bedford Pas SW6 ....154 B2
Bedford Rd W1 ....106 A4
Bedford Rd 4 W4 ......38 A3
SW2,SW4 ....62 A3
Bedford Row WC1 ...107 A3
Bedford Sq WC1 ......105 C3
Bedford St WC2 ....120 B3
Bedfordbury WC2 ....120 A3
Bedgebury Gdns
SW19 ....70 A2
Bedser Cl SE11 ....163 A4
Bedser Ct 4 SW4 .....172 B2
Bedwell Ho SW9 .....173 B1
Beech Ave W3 ....29 A1
Beech Cl SE8 ....51 B4
SW15 ....68 C4
Beech Croft Ct N5 .....15 A4
Beech Ct W1 ....102 C2
SE9 ....56 A4
6 NW2 ....9 B2
Beech Gdns W5 ....36 A3
Beech Ho N16 ....6 C2
8 NW3 ....11 C4
10 SE16 ....40 B4
Beech St EC2 ....109 A4
Beech Tree Cl N1 .....14 C1
Beechcroft Ave
NW11 ....1 B4
Beechcroft Cl 3
SW16 ....74 B1
Beechcroft Ct 3
NW11 ....1 B4
Beechcroft Rd
SW17 ....72 A2
Beechcroft Way N19 ..4 C3
Beechdale Rd SW2 ...62 B1
Beechdene 4 SE15 ...50 A2
Beeches Rd SW17 .....72 A1
Beeches The 1 N19 ...5 A3
Beechey Ho 30 E1 ....32 A1
Beechmore Rd
SW11 ....169 A3

Beechwood Ave
TW9 ....44 C2
Beechwood Ct N16 ....7 A4
W4 ....45 C4
Beechwood Gr W3 ....29 A2
Beechwood Ho 22
E2 ....24 C3
Beechwood Rd E8 ....16 B2
Beechworth Cl NW3 ...1 C2
Beecroft Rd SE4 ....66 A2
Beehive Cl E8 ....16 B1
Beehive Pl SW9 ....62 C4
Beeston Cl 5 E8 ....16 C3
Beeston Pl SW1 ....132 B2
Beeston's Ho SE15 ...65 A4
Beethoven St W10 ....23 A2
Begbie Ho SW9 ....173 A2
Begonia Wlk W12 .....29 B3
Beira St SW12 ....73 A4

Beis Rachel D'Satmar
Girls Sch N16 ....7 A3
Bekesbourne St 19
E14 ....33 A3
Beldanes Lo NW10 ....8 C1
Belenoyd Ct SW16 ...74 B1
Belfast Rd N16 ....7 B2
Belfont Wlk N7 ....14 A4
Belford Ho 7 E8 ....24 B4
Belfort Rd SE15 ....50 B1
Belfry Cl 33 SE16 ......40 A1
Belgrade Ho N16 ......16 A4
Belgrade Rd N16 ......16 A4
Belgrave Cl 1 W3 .....37 B4
Belgrave Ct 3 W4 .....45 B4
SW8 ....171 B4
Belgrave Gdns NW8 .78 C3
Belgrave Mans
NW8 ....78 C3
Belgrave Mews N
SW1 ....131 B3
Belgrave Mews S
SW1 ....131 C2
Belgrave Mews W
SW1 ....131 B2
Belgrave Pl SW1 ......131 C1
Belgrave Rd SW1 ....146 C3
SW13 ....46 B3
Belgrave Sq SW1 ....131 C2
Belgrave St E1 ....32 C3
Belgrave Yd SW1 ....132 A1
Belgravia Ct SW1 ....132 A1
Belgravia Ho 11
SW4 ....61 C1
Belgrove St WC1 ....94 B4
Belham Wlk 18 SE5 ..48 C2
Belinda Rd 8 SW9 ....63 A4
Belitha Villas N1 ....14 C1
Bell Dr SW18 ....70 A4
Bell Ho SE10 ....52 B4
19 SW2 ....74 C4
Bell Ind Est 2 W4 ......37 B2
Bell Inn Yd EC3 ....109 C1
Bell La E1 ....110 C3
E16 ....35 C1
Bell Moor NW3 ....2 B1
Bell St NW1 ....102 A4
Bell Wharf La EC4 ...123 A4
Bell Yd WC2 ....107 B2
Bellamy Cl SW5 ......141 A1
E14 ....41 C4
Bellamy Ho SW17 ....71 C1
Bellamy's Ct 18
SE16 ....32 C1
Bellasis Ave SW2 .....74 A2
Belle Vue Gdns
SW9 ....172 B1
Bellefields Rd SW9 ..62 B4

Bellenden Prim Sch
SE15 ....49 C1
Bellenden Rd SE15 ..49 B1
Bellenden Road Bsns
Ctr SE15 ....49 C2
Belleville Prim Sch
SW11 ....60 B2
Belleville Rd SW11 ...60 B2
Bellevue Pl E1 ....25 B1
Bellevue Rd SW13 ....46 C1
SW17 ....72 B3
Bellew St SW17 ....71 B1
Bellgate Mews NW5 ...4 A1
Bellina Mews NW5 .....4 A1
Bello Cl SE24,SW2 ...75 A3
Bellot Gdns 1 SE10 ..43 A1
Bellot St SE10 ....43 A1
Bellwood Rd SE15 ....65 C3
Belmont Cl SW4 ....61 B4
Belmont Ct 6 N16 ......7 A3
N5 ....15 B4
Belmont Gr SE13 ......67 C4
Belmont Hall Ct
SE13 ....67 C4
Belmont Jun & Inf Sch
W4 ....37 C2
Belmont Pk SE13 ......67 C3
Belmont Rd SW4 ......61 B4
Belmont St NW1 ....12 C1
Belmont Terr W4 ....37 C2
Belmore Ho N7 ....13 C3
Belmore St SW8 ......171 B4
Beloe Cl SW15 ....56 C3
Belsham St E9 ....17 B2
Belsize Ave NW3 ......11 C3

Belsize Court Garages
1 NW3 ....11 C3
Belsize Cres NW3 ....11 C3
Belsize Ct NW3 ....11 C3
Belsize Gr NW3 ....12 A2
Belsize La NW3 ....11 C3
Belsize Mews NW3 ...11 C3
Belsize Park Gdns
NW3 ....12 A2
Belsize Park Mews 1
NW3 ....11 C2
Belsize Park Sta
NW3 ....12 A3
Belsize Pk NW3 ....11 C3
Belsize Pk Mews
NW3 ....11 C3
Belsize Rd NW6 ....78 B4
Belsize Sq NW3 ....11 C2
Belsize Terr NW3 ......11 C2
Beltane Dr SW19 ......69 C1
Belthorn Cres SW12 .73 B4
Belton Rd NW2 ....9 A2
Belton Way E3 ....33 C4
Beltran Rd SW6 ....166 A1

Belvedere Bldgs
SE1 ....136 B3
Belvedere Ct 1 NW2 ...9 C2
5 SW15 ....57 B3
7 SW4 ....61 C1
Belvedere Mews
SE15 ....65 B4
Belvedere Pl SE1 .....136 B3
Belvedere Rd SE1 ...121 A1
Belvedere The
SW10 ....167 A3
Belvoir Lo SE22 ....76 C4
Belvoir Rd SE22 ....76 C4
Bembridge Cl NW6 ..10 A1
Bembridge Ho
8 SE8 ....41 B2
SW18 ....59 A1

Bemerton St N1 .... 84 C4
Bemish Rd SW15 .... 57 C4
Ben Ezra Ct SE17 ...... 151 A3
Ben Jonson Ct SE1 ....
N1 .... 24 A3
Ben Jonson JMI Sch
E1 .... 26 A1
Ben Jonson Rd E1 .... 32 C4
Ben Smith Way
SE16 .... 139 C2
Benabo Ct 8 E8 .... 16 C3
Benbow Ct 2 W6 .... 39 A3
Benbow Ho 12 SE8 .... 51 C4
Benbow Rd W6 .... 39 A3
Benbow St SE8 .... 51 C4
Bence Ho 3 SE8 .... 41 A2
Bendall Mews
NW1 .... 102 B4
Bendemeer Rd
SW15 .... 57 C4
Benden Ho SE13 .... 67 B2
Bendon Valley
SW18 .... 71 A4
Benedict Rd SW9 .... 62 B4
Benenden Ho SE17 ... 152 B2
Benfleet Ct 8 E8 .... 24 B4
Bengal Ct EC3 .... 109 C1
Bengal Ho E1 .... 32 C4
Bengeworth Rd SE5 .... 63 B4
Benham Cl 1 SW11 ..... 59 C3
Benham's Pl 6
NW3 .... 11 B4
Benhill Rd SE5 .... 48 C2
Benjamin Cl E8 .... 24 C4
Benjamin St EC1 ...... 108 A4
Benledi Ct E14 .... 34 C3
Benn Ho E2 .... 99 B3
Benn St E9 .... 18 A2
Bennelong Cl W12 ..... 30 A3
Bennerley Rd SW11 .... 60 B2
Bennet's Hill EC4 ..... 122 B4
Bennett Ct N7 .... 5 B1
NW6 .... 11 A2
7 W3 .... 37 A4
Bennett Gr SE13 .... 52 A2
Bennett St SW1 .... 118 C2
2 SW4 .... 73 C4
Bennett St SW1 .... 118 C2
W4 .... 38 A1
Bennett's Yd SW1 .... 133 C1
Bensbury CI SW15 ..... 69 B4
Benson Ct SW8 .... 172 A4
1 N19 .... 5 A2
Benson Ho E2 .... 98 C2
SE1 .... 121 C1
Benson Quay E1 .... 32 B2
Benthal Ct N16 .... 7 C1
Benthal JMI Schs
N16 .... 7 C1
Benthal Rd N16 .... 7 C1
Bentham Ct 10 N1 ..... 15 B1
Bentham Rd E9 .... 17 C2
Bentinck Cl NW8 ..... 80 B1
Bentinck Ho 4
W12 .... 30 A2
Bentinck Mans
W1 .... 103 C2
Bentinck Mews
W1 .... 103 C2
Bentinck St W1 .... 103 C2
Bentley Cl SW19 .... 70 C1
Bentley Ho 6 E3 ...... 26 C1
4 SE5 .... 49 A2
Bentley Rd N1 .... 16 A2
Bentworth Ct 2 E2 .... 99 B2

Bentworth Prim Sch
W12 .... 30 A3
Bentworth Rd W12 .... 30 A3
Benville Ho SW8 ...... 163 A1
Benwell Rd N7 .... 14 C3
Benwick Cl SE16 .... 40 A2
Benworth St E3 .... 26 B2
Benyon Ho EC1 .... 95 C4
Benyon Rd N1 .... 87 C4
Beormund Sch
SE1 .... 137 C3
Berber Rd SW11 .... 60 B2
Berberis Ho 8 E3 ...... 33 C4
Bere St 1 .... 32 C2
Berebinder Ho 7
E3 .... 26 B3
Berenger Twr
SW10 .... 157 B2
Berenger Wlk
SW10 .... 157 B2
Berens Rd NW10 ...... 22 C2
Beresford Ct E9 .... 18 A3
Beresford Ho SE21 .... 76 A1
Beresford Lo N4 .... 15 C2
Beresford Rd N5 ...... 15 C3
Beresford Terr 3
N5 .... 15 B3
Berestede Rd 4
W6 .... 38 B1
Bergen Ho 1 SE5 ...... 48 B1
Bergen Sq SE16 .... 41 A3
Berger JMI Sch E9 ... 17 C2
Berger Rd E9 .... 17 C2
Berghem Mews
W14 .... 39 C3
Bergholt Cres N16 ..... 7 A4
Bergholt Mews 4
NW1 .... 13 C1
Bering Sq E14 .... 41 C1
Berisford Mews
SW18 .... 59 B1
Berkeley Ct NW1 ...... 91 A1
1 NW11 .... 1 B4
18 SW2 .... 74 C3
Berkeley Gdns W8 ... 113 C1
Berkeley Ho 15 E3 .... 26 C2
8 SE8 .... 41 B1
Berkeley Mews
W1 .... 103 A1
Berkeley Rd SW13 .... 46 C2
Berkeley Sq W1 ...... 118 B3
Berkeley St W1 .... 118 B2
Berkeley The NW11 ... 2 A4
Berkeley Wlk 1 N7 ..... 5 B2
Berkeley Gr SW15 .... 57 C2
Berkley Gr NW1 .... 12 C1
Berkley Rd NW1 ...... 12 C1
Berkshire Ho E9 .... 18 B2
Berkeley Ct NW10 .... 8 B4
Bermans Way NW10 ... 8 B4
**Bermondsey Leather
Mkt** SE1 .... 138 A3
Bermondsey Mkt*
SE1 .... 138 B2
Bermondsey Sq
SE1 .... 138 B2
Bermondsey St
SE1 .... 138 B2
Bermondsey Trad Est
SE16 .... 40 B1
Bermondsey Wall E
SE16 .... 139 C3
SE16 .... 40 A4
Bermondsey Wall W
SE1,SE16 .... 139 B4

Bermondsey Sta
SE16 .... 139 C2
Bernard Angell Ho 4
SE10 .... 52 C4
Bernard Cassidy St 8
E16 .... 35 B2
Bernard Shaw Ct 3
N1 .... 13 B1
Bernard Shaw Ho 2
NW10 .... 20 C4
Bernard St WC1 .... 94 B1
Bernay's Gr SW9 ...... 62 B3
Berners Ho N1 .... 85 B2
Berners Mews W1 ... 105 A3
Berners Pl W1 .... 105 A2
Berners Rd N1 .... 86 A3
Berners St W1 .... 105 A2
Bernwood Ho 3
N4 .... 6 C4
Berridge Mews
NW6 .... 10 C3
Berriman Rd N7 .... 5 B1
Berry Cl NW10 .... 8 A1
Berry Ho SW11 ...... 169 A2
25 E1 .... 25 A1
Berry Pl EC1 .... 96 B3
Berry St EC1 .... 96 B1
Berry Way W5 .... 36 A3
Berryfield Rd SE17 . 150 B2
Berrymead Gdns
W3 .... 37 B4
Berrymede Inf Sch
W3 .... 37 A4
Berrymede Jun Sch
W3 .... 37 A4
Berrymede Rd W4 .... 37 C3
Bertha Neubergh Ho 1
SE5 .... 48 B2
Berthon St SE8 .... 51 C3
Bertie Rd NW10 .... 8 C2
Bertram House Sch
SW17 .... 72 C2
Bertram St N19 .... 4 A2
Bertrand Ho 11
SW16 .... 74 A1
Bertrand St SE13 ..... 67 A4
Berwick St W1 .... 105 A1
Berwyn Ho 3 N16 ..... 7 B3
Berwyn Rd
SW14,TW10 .... 55 A3
SE24 .... 75 A3
Beryl Rd W6 .... 39 C1
Besant Cl NW2 .... 1 A1
Besant Ct N1 .... 15 C3
Besant Ho NW8 .... 78 C3
Besant Rd NW2 .... 10 A4
Besant Wlk N7 .... 5 B2
Besford Ho 2 E2 ...... 24 C3
Bessant Dr TW9 ...... 45 A2
Bessborough Gdns
SW1 .... 147 C2
Bessborough Pl
SW1 .... 147 C2
Bessborough Rd
SW15 .... 68 C3
Bessborough St
SW1 .... 147 B2
Bessemer Ct 5
NW1 .... 13 B1
**Bessemer Grange Prim
Sch** SE5 .... 64 A3
Bessemer Park Ind Est
3 SE24 .... 63 A3
Bessemer Rd SE5 .... 48 B1
Bessingham Wlk
SE4 .... 65 C2
Besson St SE14 .... 50 C2
Bessy St E2 .... 25 B2
Bestwood Ho SE8 ..... 40 C2

Beswick Mews 1
NW6 .... 11 A2
Betchworth Ho
N7 .... 13 C3
Bethersden Ho
SE17 .... 152 B2
Bethlehem Ho 13
E14 .... 33 B2
**Bethnal Green Museum
of Childhood*** E2 . 25 B2
Bethnal Green Rd
E2 .... 24 B1 99 B3
Bethnal Green Sta
E1 .... 25 A1
E2 .... 99 A3
Bethune Rd N16 .... 7 A4
NW10 .... 20 C1
Bethwin Rd SE5 .... 48 B3
Betsham Ho SE1 .... 137 B4
Betterton Ho WC2 .. 106 B2
Betterton St WC2 ... 106 B1
Bettridge Rd SW6 .. 165 A1
Betts Ho E1 .... 32 A2
Betts St E1 .... 32 A2
Betty May Gray Ho 1
E14 .... 42 B2
Bev Callender Cl 3
SW8 .... 61 A4
Bevenden St N1 ...... 97 C4
Beveridge Rd 1
NW10 .... 8 A1
Beverley Cl SW13 .... 46 C1
6 SW11 .... 59 C3
Beverley Cotts
SW15 .... 68 A1
Beverley Ct N5 .... 15 A2
6 W4 .... 37 B1
12 SE4 .... 66 B4
Beverley Gdns NW11 .. 1 A4
SW13 .... 56 B4
Beverley Lo 6
TW10 .... 54 A2
Beverley Path 9
SW13 .... 46 B1
Beverley Rd SW4 .... 38 B1
SW13 .... 56 B4
Beversbrook Rd N19 .. 4 C1
Beverston Mews
NW1 .... 102 C3
Bevin Cl SE16 .... 33 A1
Bevin Ct WC1 .... 95 A4
Bevin Ho 6 E2 .... 25 B2
7 E3 .... 26 C2
Bevin Way WC1 .... 95 B4
Bevington Prim Sch
W10 .... 31 A4
Bevington Rd W10 .... 31 A4
Bevington St SE16 . 139 C3
Bevis Marks EC3 .... 110 B2
Bewdley Ho N4 .... 6 B4
Bewdley St N1 .... 14 C1
Bewick St SW8 ...... 170 B1
Bewley Ct SW2 .... 62 B1
Bewley Ho 7 E1 .... 32 A2
Bewley St E1 .... 32 A2
Bexhill Rd SW14 ...... 55 B4
SE4 .... 66 B1
Bexley Ho SE4 .... 66 A3

**BFI London Imax
Cinema** SE1 .... 121 B1
Bianca Rd SE1,SE15 .49 C4
Bicester Rd TW9 ..... 55 A4
Bickenhall Mans
W1 .... 103 A4
Bickenhall St W1 ... 103 A4
Bickerton Rd N19 .... 4 B2
Bicknell Ho E1 .... 111 C1
Bicknell Rd SE5 .... 63 B4
Bicknor Ho 2 E5 ...... 17 A3
Bidborough St N1,
WC1 .... 94 A3
Biddenham Ho 18
SE16 .... 40 C2
Bidder St E14 .... 35 A4
Biddesden Ho
SW3 .... 144 C3
Biddestone Rd N7 .... 14 B4
Biddulph Man W9 .... 88 B3
Biddulph Rd W9 ...... 88 B3
Bidwell St SE15 .... 50 A2
Big Ben* SW1 .... 134 B3
Bigg's Row SW15 .... 57 C4
Biggerstaff Rd E15 ... 27 B4
Biggerstaff St N4 ..... 5 C2
Bigland Green JMI Sch
E14 .... 32 A3
Bigland St E1 .... 32 A3
Bilberry Ho 3 E3 ...... 33 C4
Billing Ho 6 E1 .... 32 C3
Billing Pl SW10 ..... 156 B2
Billing Rd SW10 .... 156 B2
Billingford Cl SE4 .... 65 C3
Billingley NW1 .... 82 C3
Billington Ho SW8 .171 C3
Billington Rd SE14 .. 50 C3
Billiter Sq EC3 ...... 110 B1
Billiter St EC3 .... 110 B1
Billson St E14 .... 42 B2
Bilton Ho SW8 ...... 171 B3
Bilton Twrs W1 ...... 103 A1
Bina Gdns SW5 ..... 142 C3
Binbrook Ho W10 .... 30 B4
Binden Rd W12 .... 38 B3
Binfield Ct SE5 .... 48 B1
Binfield Rd SW4 .... 172 B3
Bingfield St N1 .... 84 C4
Bingham Pl W1 ...... 103 B4
Bingham St N1 .... 15 C2
Binley Ho SW15 ...... 56 B1
Binney St W1 .... 103 C1
Binnie Ho SE1 .... 136 C1
Binns Rd W4 .... 38 A1
Binns Terr 3 W4 ...... 38 A1
Binstead Ho SW18 ... 59 A1
Binyon Ho 5 N16 .... 16 A4
Birch Cl N19 .... 4 B2
E16 .... 35 A4
Birch Ho SE14 .... 51 B2
8 SW2 .... 62 C1
Birch Vale Ct NW8 .. 89 C2
Bircham Path SE4 ... 65 C3
Birchdown Ho 32
E3 .... 27 A2
Birches The SE5 ...... 49 A1
Birchfield Ho 2
E14 .... 33 C2
Birchfield St E14 ..... 33 C2

Birchin La EC3 .....109 C1
Birchington Ct NW6 .78 A4
Birchington Ho 8
  E5 .....17 A3
Birchington Rd
  NW6 .....23 C4
Birchlands Ave
  SW12 .....72 B4
Birchmere Lo 18
  SE16 .....40 A1
Birchmere Row SE3 .53 B1
Birchmore Wlk N5 ...6 B1
Birchwood Dr NW3 .2 A1
Bird in Bush Rd
  SE15 .....49 C3
Bird in Hand Yd 11
  NW3 .....11 B4
Bird St W1 .....103 C1
Birdcage Wlk SW1 .133 B3
Birdhurst Rd SW18 .59 B2
Birdlip Cl SE15 .....49 A4
Birdsall Ho 5 SE5 ..64 A4
Birdsfield La E3 ....26 B4
Birkbeck Ave 3 .....28 B2
Birkbeck Coll W1 ..105 B2
Birkbeck Ct 3 .....28 C1
Birkbeck Gr W3 .....37 C4
Birkbeck Hill SE21 .75 A3
Birkbeck Mews 5
  E8 .....16 B3
Birkbeck Pl SE21 ...75 B2
Birkbeck Rd E8 .....16 B3
  W3 .....28 C1
Birkbeck St 2 .....25 A2
Birkdale Cl 50 SE16 .40 A1
Birkenhead Ho 11
  N7 .....14 C3
Birkenhead St WC1 .94 B4
Birkwood Cl SW12 ..73 C4
Birley Lo NW8 .....79 C2
Birley St SW11 ....169 B1
Birnam Rd N4 .....5 B2
Birrell Ho SW9 ....172 C1
Birse Cres NW10 ....8 A4
Birtwhistle Ho 5
  E3 .....26 B4
Biscay Ho 11 E1 ....25 C1
Biscay Rd W6 .....39 C1
Biscoe Way SE13 ...67 C4
Biscott Ho 3 E3 ...27 A1
Bisham Gdns N6 ....3 C3
Bishop Challoner Sec
  Sch E1 .....32 B3
Bishop Duppa's
  Almshouses 7
  TW10 .....54 A2
Bishop King's Rd
  W14 .....140 B4
Bishop St N1 .....86 C4
Bishop Way NW10 ..8 A1
Bishop Wilfred Wood Cl
  SE15 .....49 C1
Bishop's Ave SW6 .164 A2
Bishop's Bridge Rd
  W2 .....100 C2
Bishop's Cl N19 ....4 B1
Bishop's Ct WC2 ...107 B2
  EC4 .....108 A2
Bishop's Mans SW6 .47 C1
Bishop's Park Rd
  SW6 .....47 C1
Bishop's Park Rd
  SW6 .....164 A2

Bishop's Terr
  SE11 .....149 C4
Bishop's Way E2 ....25 B3
Bishopsgate 22 N1 ..24 A1
Bishops Ct W4 .....37 B1
Bishops Ho SW8 ...162 B1
Bishops Mead SE5 ..48 B3
Bishops Rd SW6 ...164 C4
Bishopsdale Ho 8
  NW6 .....23 C4
Bishopsgate Arc
  EC2 .....110 B3
Bishopsgate Church Yd
  EC2 .....110 A2
Bishopstone Ho
  SW11 .....169 B2
Bishopswood Rd N6 .3 B4
Bisley Ho SW19 .....69 C2
Bisson Rd E15 .....27 B3
Bittern Ct 8 SE8 ...51 C4
Bittern St SE1 ....136 C3
Black Friars La
  EC4 .....108 A1
Black Horse Ct
  SE1 .....137 C2
Black Lion La W6 ...38 C2
Black Lion Mews 4
  W6 .....38 C2
Black Prince Rd
  SE1,SE11 .....149 A3
Black Roof Ho 9
  SE5 .....48 A2
Black Swan Yd
  SE1 .....138 A4
Black's Rd W6 .....39 B2
Blackall St EC2 .....98 A2
Blackburne's Mews
  W1 .....117 B3
Blackdown Ho E8 ...16 C4
Blackett St SW15 ...57 C4
Blackfriars Bridge
  EC4 .....122 A3
  SE1 .....122 A3
Blackfriars Pas
  EC4 .....122 A4
Blackfriars Pier
  EC4 .....122 A3
Blackfriars Rd SE1 .122 A2
Blackfriars Sta
  EC4 .....122 A4
Blackheath SE3 .....53 A1
Blackheath Bsns Est
  SE10 .....52 B2
Blackheath Gr SE3 .53 B1
Blackheath High Sch
  SE3 .....53 B1
Blackheath High Sch
  (Girls) SE3 .....53 B1
Blackheath High School
  GPDST (Jun Dept)
Blackheath Hill
  SE10 .....52 B2
Blackheath Pk SE3 .53 C1
Blackheath Rd SE10 .52 A2
Blackheath Rise
  SE13 .....52 B1

Blackheath Vale
  SE3 .....53 A1
Blackheath Village
  SE3 .....53 B1
Blackhorse Rd SE8 .51 A4
Blacklands Terr
  SW3 .....145 A3
Blackmore Ho N1 ...85 A3
  2 SW18 .....59 A2
Blackmore Twr 3
  W3 .....37 B3
Blackpool Rd SE15 .50 A1
Blackstock Ho N5 ...6 A1
Blackstock Mews N4 .6 A1
Blackstock Rd N4,N5 .6 A2
Blackstone Ho
  SW1 .....146 C1
  SE21 .....76 A1
Blackthorn Ct
  2 E15 .....19 C3
  10 SE15 .....49 B3
Blackthorn St E3 ...26 C1
Blacktree Mews 12
  SW9 .....62 C4
Blackwall La SE10 ..43 B2
Blackwall Sta E14 ..34 B2
Blackwall Trad Est
  E14 .....34 C4
Blackwall Tunnel
  E14,SE10 .....34 C1
Blackwall Tunnel App
  SE10 .....43 A4
Blackwall Tunnel
  Northern Approach
  E14,E3 .....27 B1
Blackwall Way E14 .34 B2
Blackwater Ho
  NW8 .....101 C4
Blackwater St SE22 .64 B2
Blackwell Cl 10 E5 .17 C4
Blackwell Ho 4
  SW4 .....61 C1
Blackwood Ho 11
  E1 .....25 A1
Blackwood St
  SE17 .....151 B2
Blade Mews SW15 ..58 B3
Bladen Ho 4 E1 ....32 C3
Blades Ct SW15 ....58 B3
Blades Ho SE11 ....163 B3
Blagdon Rd SE13 ...67 A1
Blagrove Rd 1 W10 .31 A4
Blair Cl N1 .....15 B2
Blair Ct NW8 .....79 B4
Blair St E14 .....34 C3
Blairderry Rd SW2 .74 A2
Blake Ct NW6 .....23 C2
  8 SE16 .....40 A1
Blake Gdns SW6 ...166 A4
Blake Ho
  1 .....135 B2
  11 N19 .....4 C1
  14 N16 .....16 A4
  2 SE8 .....51 C4
Blake's Rd SE15 ....49 A3
Blakemore Rd
  SW16 .....74 A1
Blakeney Cl 5 NW1 .13 C1
  4 E8 .....16 C3
Blakenham Ct W12 .29 C1
Blaker Rd E15 .....27 B4
Blakes Cl W10 .....30 B4
Blanca Ho 16 N1 ...24 A3
Blanch Cl SE15 .....50 B3
Blanchard Way E8 ..16 C2

Blanche Ho NW8 ....90 A1
Blanchedowne SE5 .63 C3
Bland Ho SE11 ....149 A2
Blandfield Rd SW12 .72 C4
Blandford Ct NW6 ..10 A1
  6 N1 .....16 A1
Blandford Ho SW8 .162 C2
Blandford Rd W4 ...38 A3
Blandford Sq NW1 ..90 B1
Blandford St W1 ...103 B3
Blaney Pl 1 N7 ....14 C2
Blantyre St SW10 ..157 B2
Blantyre Twr
  SW10 .....157 B2
Blantyre Wlk
  SW10 .....157 B2
Blashford NW3 .....12 B1
Blasker Wlk E14 ...42 A1
Blaxland Ho 12 W12 .30 A2
Blechynden Ho 17
  W10 .....30 C3
Blechynden St W10 .30 C2
Bledlow Ho NW8 ...101 C4
Bleeding Heart Yd
  EC1 .....107 C3
Blemundsbury
  WC1 .....106 C4
Blendworth Point 4
  SW15 .....69 A3
Blendworth Way
  SE15 .....49 A3
Blenheim 26 SW19 .69 C3
Blenheim Cres
  W11 .....31 A3 112 B4
Blenheim Ct N19 ...5 A2
  N7 .....14 A2
  17 SE16 .....32 C1
  Richmond TW9 .....54 B4
Blenheim Gdns NW2 .9 B3
  SW2 .....74 B4
Blenheim Gr SE15 ..49 C1
Blenheim Pas NW8 .78 C2
Blenheim Rd NW8 ..79 A2
  W4 .....38 A3
Blenheim St W1 ...104 A1
Blenheim Terr NW8 .78 C2
Blenkarne Rd SW11 .60 B1
Blessed John Roche RC
  Sec Sch E14 .....33 C3
Blessed Sacrament RC
  Prim Sch N1 .....84 C3
Blessington Cl SE13 .67 C4
Blessington Rd
  SE13 .....67 C3
Bletchley Ct N1 ....87 B1
Bletchley St N1 ....87 A1
Bletsoe Wlk N1 ....87 A2
Blick Ho 11 SE16 ..40 B3
Blincoe Cl SW19 ...69 C2
Blissett St SE10 ....52 B2
Blisworth Ho 12 E2 .24 C4
Blithfield St W8 ...128 A1
Bloemfontein Ave
  W12 .....30 A1
Bloemfontein Rd
  W12 .....30 A2
Blomfield Mans
  W12 .....30 B1
Blomfield Rd W9 ...100 C4
Blomfield St EC2 ...109 C3
Blomfield Villas
  W9 .....100 C4
Blondel St SW11 ...169 B2
Blondin St E3 .....26 C3

Bloom Gr SE27 .....75 A1
Bloom Park Rd
  SW6 .....154 C1
Bloomburg St
  SW1 .....147 A3
Bloomfield Ho 11
  E1 .....111 B3
Bloomfield Pl W1 ..118 B4
Bloomfield Terr
  SW1 .....145 C2
Bloomsbury Ct
  WC1 .....106 B3
Bloomsbury Ho 10
  SW4 .....61 C1
Bloomsbury Pl
  WC1 .....106 B3
  SW18 .....59 B2
Bloomsbury Sq
  WC1 .....106 B3
Bloomsbury St
  WC1 .....105 C3
Bloomsbury Way
  WC1 .....106 B3
Blore Cl SW8 .....171 B3
Blore Ct W1 .....119 B4
Blossom Cl W5 .....36 A4
Blossom St 1 E1 ...98 B1
Blossom St
  E1 .....24 A1 98 B1
Blount Ho 18 E14 ..33 A4
Blount St E14 .....33 A3
Blucher Rd SE5 ....48 B3
Blue Anchor Alley 4
  TW9 .....54 A3
Blue Anchor La
  SE16 .....40 A2
Blue Anchor Yd E1 .125 B4
Blue Ball Yd SW1 ..118 C1
Blue Gate Field JMI
  Schs E1 .....32 B2
Blundell St N7 .....14 A2
Blurton Rd E5 .....17 C4
Blyth Cl 4 E14 ....42 C2
Blyth's Wharf E14 ..33 A2
Blythe Ho SE11 ....163 C4
Blythe Mews 2
  W14 .....39 C3
Blythe Rd W14 ....126 A1
Blythe St E2 .....25 A2
Blythendale Ho 31
  E2 .....24 C3
Blythwood Rd N4 ...5 A4
Boadicea St N1 ....84 C3
Boardley St SE17 ..152 A3
Boat Lifter Way 13
  SE16 .....41 A2
Boathouse Ctr The
  W10 .....22 C1
Bob Marley Way 11
  SE24 .....62 C3
Bobbin Cl SW4 .....61 B4
Bobington Cl WC1 .106 B4
Bocking St E8 .....25 A4
Boddicott Cl SW19 .70 A2
Boddington Ho
  SE14 .....50 B2
Boden Ho 11 E1 ...111 B4
Bodeney Ho 10 SE5 .49 A2
Bodington Ct 2
  W12 .....39 C4
Bodley Manor Way
  SE24 .....74 C4
Bodmin St SW18 ...70 C3
Bodney Mans 21 E8 .17 A3
Bodney Rd E5,E8 ...17 A3
Bohemia Pl 1 E8 ...17 A2

Boileau Rd SW13 ...47 A4
Boilerhouse SE1 ...124 C1
Boisseau Ho 27 E1 ...32 B4
Bolden St SE8 ...52 A1
Bolden Pl NW8 ...90 A1
Boleyn Rd N16 ...16 A3
Bolina Rd SE16 ...40 B1
Bolingbroke Gr
  SW11 ...60 B1
Bolingbroke Hospl The
  SW11 ...60 A2
Bolingbroke Prim Sch
  SW11 ...168 A4
Bolingbroke Rd
  W14 ...39 C3
Bolingbroke Wlk
  SW11 ...168 A4
Bollo Bridge Rd W3 ...37 B4
Bollo Ct 2 W3 ...37 B3
Bollo La 1 W3 ...37 A3
Bolney Gate SW7 ...130 A3
Bolney St SW8 ...162 C1
Bolsover St W1 ...92 B1
Bolt Ct EC4 ...107 C1
Bolton Cres SE5 ...48 A3
Bolton Ct SE15 ...50 B3
Bolton Gdns SW5 ...142 C2
  NW10 ...22 C3
Bolton Gdns Mews
  SW10 ...142 C2
Bolton Ho 4 SE10 ...43 A1
Bolton Rd NW8 ...78 B3
  NW10 ...21 A4
  W4 ...45 B3
Bolton St W1 ...118 B2
Bolton Studios
  SW10 ...143 A1
Bolton Wlk N7 ...5 B2
Boltons Ct SW5 ...142 C2
Boltons The SW10 ...142 C2
Bombay St SE16 ...40 A2
Bomore Rd
  W11 ...31 A2 112 A4
Bonar Rd SE15 ...49 C3
Bonchurch Rd W10 ...31 A4
Bond Ct EC4 ...109 B1
Bond Street Sta
  W1 ...103 C1
Bonding Yard Wlk
  SE16 ...41 A3
Bondway SW8 ...162 B4
Bonfield Rd SE13 ...67 B3
Bonham Ho W11 ...112 C3
Bonham Rd SW2 ...62 B2
Bonheur Rd W4 ...37 C4
Bonhill St EC2 ...97 C1
Bonington Ho N1 ...84 C1
Bonner Ho 3 SW15 ...56 C2
Bonner Rd E2 ...25 B3
Bonner St E2 ...25 B3
Bonneville Gdns
  SW4 ...61 B1
Bonneville Prim Sch
  SW4 ...61 B2
Bonnington Sq
  SW8 ...162 C4
Bonny St NW1 ...13 B1
Bonsor Ho SW8 ...171 A4
Bonsor St SE5 ...49 A3
Bonthron Ho SW15 ...47 B1
Booker Cl 15 E3 ...33 B4
Boot St N1 ...98 A3
Booth Cl 16 E9 ...25 A4

Booth Ho 2 SW2 ...74 C4
Booth La EC4 ...122 C4
Booth's Pl W1 ...105 A3
Boothby Rd N19 ...4 C2
Bordon Wlk 8
  SW15 ...68 C4
Boreas Wlk N1 ...86 B1
Boreham Ave E16 ...35 C3
Boreman Ho 10
  SE10 ...52 B4
Borland Rd SE15 ...65 B3
Borneo St SW15 ...57 B4
Borough High St
  SE1 ...123 B1
Borough Mkt*
  SE1 ...123 B1
Borough Rd SE1 ...136 B2
Borough Sq SE1 ...136 C3
Borough Sta SE1 ...137 A3
Borrett Cl SE17 ...150 C1
Borrodaile Rd SW18 ...59 A1
Borrowdale NW1 ...92 C3
Borthwick St SE8 ...41 C1
Boscastle Rd NW5 ...4 A1
Boscobel Ho 8 E8 ...17 A2
Boscobel Pl SW1 ...145 C4
Boscobel St NW8 ...89 C1
Boscombe Cl E5 ...18 A3
Boscombe Rd W12 ...38 C4
Boss Ho SE1 ...138 C4
Boss St SE1 ...138 C4
Boston Gdns W4 ...46 A4
Boston Ho N1 ...90 C2
  SW5 ...142 B3
  22 SE5 ...48 B1
Boston Pl NW1 ...90 C1
Bosun Cl 22 E14 ...41 C4
Boswell Ct
  WC1 ...106 B4
  14 W14 ...39 C3
Boswell Ho WC1 ...106 B4
Boswell St WC1 ...106 B4
Bosworth Ho 4
  W10 ...23 A1
Bosworth Rd W10 ...23 A1
Bothnia Ho E1 ...33 A4
Bothwell Cl E16 ...35 B2
Bothwell St 4 W6 ...47 C4
Botolph Alley EC3 ...124 A4
Botolph La EC3 ...124 A4
Bott's Mews W2 ...31 C3
Boughton Ho SE1 ...137 B4
Boulcott St E1 ...32 C3
Boulevard The 4
  SW17 ...72 A2
Boulogne Ho SE1 ...138 C2
Boulter Ho SE14 ...50 B2
Boundaries Mans 8
  SW12 ...72 C3
Boundaries Rd
  SW12 ...72 C3
Boundary Ho
  13 SE5 ...48 B3
Boundary La SE17 ...48 B4
Boundary Pas E2 ...98 C2
Boundary Rd NW8 ...79 A4
Boundary Rd Est
  NW8 ...78 C3
Boundary Row
  SE1 ...136 A4
Boundary St
  E2 ...24 B1 98 C2
Bourchier St W1 ...119 B4
Bourdon Pl W1 ...118 B4
Bourdon St W1 ...118 B3

Bourke Cl NW10 ...8 A1
  SW4 ...62 A1
Bourlet Cl W1 ...104 C3
Bourne Ct W4 ...45 B4
Bourne Mews W1 ...103 C1
Bourne Pl W4 ...37 C1
Bourne St SW1 ...145 B3
Bourne Terr W2 ...100 B4
Bournemouth Cl
  SE15 ...49 C1
Bournemouth Rd
  SE15 ...49 C1
Bousfield Prim Sch
  SW10 ...142 C2
Bousfield Rd SE14 ...50 C1
Boutcher CE Prim Sch
  SE1 ...152 C4
Boutflower Rd
  SW11 ...60 A3
Bouverie Mews N16 ...7 A2
Bouverie Pl W2 ...101 C2
Bouverie Rd N16 ...7 A2
Bouverie St EC4 ...107 C1
Boveney Rd SE23 ...65 C1
Bovingdon Cl 3 N19 ...4 B2
Bovingdon Rd
  SW6 ...166 B3
Bow Boys Sec Sch
  E3 ...26 C2
Bow Brook The 20
  E2 ...25 C3
Bow Church Sta E3 ...26 C2
Bow Churchyard
  EC2,EC4 ...109 A1
Bow Common La
  E3 ...26 B1
Bow La EC2,EC4 ...109 A1
Bow Rd E3 ...26 C2
Bow Road Sta E3 ...26 C2
Bow St WC2 ...106 B1
Bow Triangle Bsns Ctr
  E3 ...26 C2
Bowater Cl SW2 ...62 A1
Bowater Ho EC1 ...97 A1
Bowden St SE11 ...149 C1
Bowditch SE8 ...41 B1
Bowen Ct 2 N5 ...15 A4
Bowen Dr SE21 ...76 A1
Bowen St E14 ...34 A3
Bowen Ave SE3 ...53 A3
Bower Ho SE14 ...50 C2
Bower Ave SE3 ...32 C3
Bowerdean St
  SW6 ...166 A3
Bowerman Ave
  SE14 ...51 A4
Bowerman Ct 11 N19 ...4 C2
Bowes Rd W3 ...29 A2
Bowfell Rd W6 ...47 B4
Bowhill Cl SW9 ...163 C2
Bowie Cl SW4 ...73 C4
Bowl Ct EC2 ...98 B1
Bowland Ho N4 ...6 B4
Bowland Rd SW4 ...61 C3
Bowland Yd SW1 ...131 A3
Bowles Rd 1 SE1 ...49 C4
Bowley Ho SE16 ...139 B2
Bowley St E14 ...33 B2
Bowling Green Cl
  SW19 ...69 A4
Bowling Green Ho
  SW10 ...157 B2

Bowling Green La
  EC1 ...95 C2
Bowling Green Pl
  SE1 ...137 B4
Bowling Green St
  SE11 ...163 B4
Bowling Green Wlk
  N1 ...98 A4
Bowman Ave E16 ...35 B2
Bowman Mews E1 ...125 B4
  SW18 ...70 B3
Bowman's Mews N7 ...5 A1
Bowman's Pl N7 ...5 A1
Bowmore Wlk NW1 ...13 C1
Bowness Cl 5 E8 ...16 B2
Bowness Ho SE15 ...50 B3
Bowood Rd SW11 ...60 C2
Bowry Ho 14 E14 ...33 B4
Bowsprit Point 5
  E14 ...41 C3
Bowstead Ct SW11 ...167 C3
Bowyer Ho 20 N1 ...24 A4
  SW18 ...59 A1
Bowyer Pl SE5 ...48 B3
Bowyer St 15 SE5 ...48 B3
Box Tree Ho SE8 ...41 A1
Boxall Rd SE21 ...64 A1
Boxley Ho 5 E5 ...17 A3
Boxmoor Ho 16 E2 ...24 C4
  W11 ...30 C1
Boxworth Gr N1 ...85 A4
Boyce Ho 7 W10 ...23 B2
Boyce St E1 ...121 B1
Boyd St E1 ...111 C1
Boydell Ct NW8 ...11 C1
Boyfield St SE1 ...136 B3
Boyle St W1 ...118 C4
Boyne Ct NW10 ...8 C1
Boyne Rd SE13 ...67 C4
Boyne Terr Mews
  W11 ...31 B1 112 C2
Boyson Rd 10 SE17 ...48 C4
Boyton Cl E1 ...25 C1
Boyton Ho NW8 ...79 C2
  SE11 ...149 B1
Brabazon St E14 ...34 A4
Brabner Ho 2 E2 ...99 B4
Brabourn Gr SE15 ...50 B1
Bracer Ho 1 N1 ...24 A3
Bracewell Rd W10 ...30 B4
Bracey St N4 ...5 A2
Bracken Ave SW12 ...72 C4
Bracken Gdns SW13 ...46 C1
Bracken Ho 15 E3 ...33 C4
Brackenbury N4 ...5 B3
Brackenbury Gdns
  W6 ...39 A3
Brackenbury Prim Sch
  W6 ...39 A2
Brackenbury Rd
  W6 ...39 A3
Brackley Ct NW8 ...89 C2
Brackley Rd W4 ...38 A1
Brackley St EC1 ...109 A4
Brackley Terr 6
  W4 ...38 A1
Bracklyn Ct N1 ...87 B2
Bracklyn St N1 ...87 B2
Bracknell Gate
  NW3 ...11 A3
Bracknell Gdns
  NW3 ...11 A4
Bracknell Way
  NW3 ...11 A4
Brad St SE1 ...121 C1
Bradbeer Ho 24 E2 ...25 B2

Bradbourne St
  SW6 ...165 C2
Bradbury Ct 2 SE3 ...53 C3
Bradbury Ho E1 ...111 A2
Bradbury St 8 N16 ...16 A3
Braddon Rd TW9 ...54 B4
Braddyll St SE10 ...43 A1
Braden St W9 ...88 A1
Bradenham 11 SE17 ...48 C4
Bradenham Cl SE17 ...48 C4
Bradfield Ct 14
  NW1 ...13 A1
Bradfield Ho 5
  SW8 ...171 B2
Bradfield Rd E16 ...35 C1
Bradford Ho 6
  W14 ...39 C3
Bradford Rd W3 ...38 A4
Bradgate Rd SE6 ...67 A1
Brading Rd SW2 ...74 B4
Brading Terr W12 ...38 C3
Bradiston Rd W9 ...23 B2
Bradley Cl N7 ...14 B2
Bradley Ho 6 E3 ...27 A2
  SE16 ...40 A2
Bradley Mews SW12 ...72 B3
Bradley's Cl N1 ...85 C2
Bradmead SW8 ...160 C1
Bradmore Ho 6 E1 ...32 B4
Bradmore Park Rd
  W6 ...39 A2
Bradshaw Cl SW19 ...70 C2
Bradstock Ho E9 ...18 A1
Bradstock Rd E9 ...17 C2
Bradwell Ho 6 NW6 ...78 A3
Brady Ho SW8 ...171 A4
  SW4 ...61 C2
Brady St E1 ...25 A1
Braefoot Ct SW15 ...57 C2
Braemar SW15 ...57 C1
Braemar Ave SW19 ...70 C2
Braemar Ho W9 ...88 C3
Braemar Mans W8 ...128 B1
Braemore Ho 20
  SE15 ...49 C3
Braes St N1 ...15 A1
Braganza St SE17 ...150 A1
Braham Ho SE11 ...149 A1
Braham St E1 ...111 A1
Brahma Kumaris World
  Spiritual Univ NW10 ...8 C1
Braid Ave W3 ...29 A3
Braid Ho SE10 ...52 B2
Braidwood St SE1 ...124 A1
Brailsford Rd SW2 ...62 C1
Braintree Ho 5 E1 ...25 B1
Braintree St E2 ...25 B2
  14 E14 ...34 C3
Braithwaite Ho EC1 ...97 B2
Braithwaite Twr
  W2 ...101 B4
Bramah Gn SW9 ...173 C4
Bramall Ct N7 ...14 B2
Bramber WC1 ...94 A3
Bramber Ct TW8 ...36 A2
Bramber Rd W14 ...154 C4
Bramble Gdns W12 ...29 B2
Bramble Ho 12 E3 ...33 C4
Brambledown N4 ...5 A4
Brambling Ct 25
  SE8 ...51 B4

Bramcote Gr SE16 . .40 B1
Bramcote Rd SW15 . .57 A3
Bramerton NW6 . . . . . .9 C1
Bramerton St SW3 158 B4
Bramfield Ct N4 . . . . . .6 B2
Bramfield Rd SW11 .60 B2
Bramford Rd SW18 .59 B3
Bramham Gdns
SW5 . . . . .142 B2
Bramham Ho SE22 .64 A3
Bramlands Cl SW11 .60 A4
Bramley Cres SW8 .161 C2
Bramley Ho W10 . . .30 C3
5 SW15 . . . . .56 B1
Bramley Rd W10 . . .30 C3
Bramshaw Rd E9 . . .17 C2
Bramshill Gdns NW5 . .4 A1
Bramshill Rd NW10 .21 C3
Bramshot Ave SE3 . .53 C4
Bramshurst NW8 . . .78 B3
Bramston Rd NW10 .21 C3
SW17 . . . . .71 B1
Bramwell Ho SE1 . .137 A1
SW1 . . . . .160 C4
Bramwell Mews N1 .85 A4
Brancaster Ho N5 . . .15 A3
22 E1 . . . . .25 C2
Brancaster Rd
SW16 . . . . .74 A1
Branch Pl N1 . . . . . .87 C4
Branch Rd E14 . . . . .33 A2
Branch St SE15 . . . .49 A3
Brand Cl N4 . . . . .6 A3
Brand St SE10 . . . . .52 B3
Brandlehow Prim Sch
SW15 . . . . .58 B3
Brandlehow Rd
SW15 . . . . .58 B3
Brandon Mews
EC2 . . . . .109 B4
Brandon Rd N7 . . . . .14 A1
Brandon St SE17 . .151 A3
Brandrams Wharf
SE16 . . . . .40 B4
Brandreth Rd SW17 .73 A2
Brangton Rd SE11 .149 A1
Brangwyn Ct W14 126 A1
Branksea St SW6 . .154 A1
Branksome Ho
SW8 . . . . .162 C2
Branksome Rd SW2 .62 A2
Bransby Ct 4 N16 . .16 A4
Branscombe NW1 . . .83 A3
Branscombe St
SE13 . . . . .67 A4
Bransdale Cl NW6 . .23 C4
Branston Ho N7 . . . .14 C3
Branstone St 8
TW9 . . . . .44 B2
Branston Ho TW9 . .44 B2
Brantwood Ho 9
SE5 . . . . .48 B3
Brantwood Rd SE24 .63 B2
Brass Talley Alley 11
SE16 . . . . .40 C4
Brassey Ho 1 E14 . .42 A2
Brassey Rd NW6 . . .10 B2
Brassey Sq SW11 . . .60 C4
Brassie Ave W3 . . . .29 A3
Brathay NW1 . . . . . .83 A1
Brathway Rd SW18 .70 C4
Bratley St E1 . . . . . .99 B1
Bravington Pl W9 . . .23 B1

Bravington Rd W9 . .23 B2
Brawne Ho 12 SE17 .48 A4
Braxfield Rd SE4 . . .66 B3
Bray NW3 . . . . .12 A1
Bray Cres SE16 . . . .40 C4
Bray Dr E16 . . . . . . .35 B2
Bray St SW1 . . . . . .144 C3
Brayard's Rd SE15 . .50 A1
Braybrook St W12 . .29 B3
Brayburne Ave
SW4 . . . . .171 A1
Braydon Rd N16 . . . . .7 C3
Brayfield Terr N1 . . .14 C1
Brayford Sq 1 E1 . .32 B3
Bread St EC2,EC4 . .109 A1
Breakspeare SE21 . .76 B1
Breakspears
Mews 1 SE4 . . . . . .51 C1
Breakspears Rd SE4 66 C4
Breakwell Ct 18
W10 . . . . .23 A1
Bream St E3 . . . . . . .18 C1
Bream's Bldgs
EC4 . . . . .107 B2
Breamore Cl SW15 . .68 C3
Breamore Ho 22
SE15 . . . . .49 C3
Breasley Cl SW15 . . .57 A3
Brecknell Ho E9 . . . .17 C2
Brecknock Prim Sch
NW1 . . . . .13 C2
Brecknock Rd N19 . .13 C3
Brecon Ho W2 . . . .100 C2
N16 . . . . .7 B3
SW18 . . . . .70 C4
Brecon Rd W6 . . . .154 B3
Bredel Ho 1 E14 . . .33 C4
Bredgar SE13 . . . . . .67 A2
Bredgar Rd N19 . . . . .4 B2
Bredinghurst SE22 . .76 C4
Bredinghurst Sch
SE15 . . . . .65 C3
Breer St SW6 . . . . . .59 A4
Breezer's Ct 1 E1 . .125 C3
Breezer's Hill E1 . . .125 C3
Bremans Row SW18 .71 B2
Bremner Rd SW7 . .129 A2
Brenchley Gdns
SE15,SE22,SE23 . . . .65 C1
Brenda Rd SW17 . . . .72 B2
Brendon Ave NW10 . . .8 A4
Brendon Ho N1 . . . .103 B4
Brendon St W1 . . . .102 B2
Brenley Ho SE1 . . . .137 B4
Brent Ct 5 W12 . . . .38 A3
Brent Ho 19 E9 . . . . .17 B2
Brent New Ent Ctr
NW10 . . . . .8 B2
Brent Rd E16 . . . . . .35 C4
Brent Trad Est NW10 .8 A3
Brentford Fountain
Leisure Centre W4 .36 C1
Brenthouse Rd E9 . .17 B2
Brenthurst Rd NW10 . .8 B2
Brenton Ct E9 . . . . . .18 A3
Brenton St E14 . . . . .33 A3
Brentwick Gdns
TW8 . . . . .36 A2
Brereton Ho 4
SW2 . . . . .74 C4
Bressenden Pl
SW1 . . . . .132 C2
Breton Ho EC2 . . . . .97 A1
SE1 . . . . .138 C2
Brett Cl N16 . . . . .7 A2
Brett Cres NW10 . . .20 C4
Brett Ho 1 SW15 . . .69 C4

Brett House Cl 2
SW15 . . . . .69 C4
Brett Manor E8 . . . .17 A3
Brett Pas 28 E8 . . . .17 A3
Brett Rd E8 . . . . .17 A3
Brettell St SE17 . . .151 C1
Brettinghurst SE1 . .153 B1
Bretton Ho N19 . . . . .5 A3
Brewer St W1 . . . . .119 A4
Brewer's Gn SW1 . .133 B2
Brewer Sq 2 . . . . . .100 C2
Brewery Rd N7 . . . . .14 A2
Brewery Sq SE1 . . .124 C1
Brewhouse La E1 . . .32 A1
Brewhouse St SW15 58 A4
Brewhouse Wlk
SE16 . . . . .33 A1
Brewhouse Yd EC1 . .96 A2
Brewster Gdns W10 .30 B4
Brewster Ho SE1 . .153 A4
E14 . . . . .33 B2
Briant Ho SE1 . . . . .135 A1
Briant St SE14 . . . . .50 C3
Briar Ct E8 . . . . .16 B1
Briar Rd NW2 . . . . . . .9 B4
Briar Wlk W10 . . . . .23 A1
SW15 . . . . .57 A3
Briardale SW19 . . . .70 B3
Briardale Gdns NW3 . .1 C1
Briardale Ho N16 . . . .7 A3
Briarwood Rd SW4 .61 C2
Briary Cl NW3 . . . . . .12 A1
Brick Ct EC4 . . . . . .107 B1
Brick Farm Cl TW9 . .45 A2
Brick La E1 . . . . .99 A2
E2 . . . . .24 B2 99 A3
Brick St W1 . . . . . . .118 A1
Brickbarn Cl SW10 157 A2
Bricklayers Arms
SE1 . . . . .137 C1
Brickworth Ho 1
SW9 . . . . .173 C4
Bride Ct EC4 . . . . . .108 A1
Bride La EC4 . . . . . .108 A1
Bride St N7 . . . . .14 B2
Brideale Cl SE15 . . . .49 B4
Bridewain St SE1 . .138 C2
Bridewell Pl EC4 . . .108 A1
20 E1 . . . . .32 A1
Bridford Mews W1 .104 B4
Bridge App NW3 . . . .11 C1
Bridge Ave W6 . . . . .39 B1
Bridge Avenue Mans 3
W6 . . . . .39 B1
Bridge Ct 7 E14 . . . .33 A2
Bridge Field Ho
W2 . . . . .100 A2
Bridge Ho 1 NW1 . . .12 C1
5 SE4 . . . . .51 B1
Bridge House Quay
E14 . . . . .34 B1
Bridge La SW11 . . . .168 B3
Bridge Meadows
SE14 . . . . .50 C4
Bridge Pk 7 SW18 . .58 C2
Bridge Pl SW1 . . . .146 B4
Bridge Rd NW10 . . . . .8 A2
E15 . . . . .27 C4
Bridge St SW1 . . . . .134 B3
W4 . . . . .37 C2
Bridge Terr E15 . . . .19 C1
Bridge Wharf 10 E2 .25 C3
Bridge Yd SE1 . . . . .123 C2
Bridgefoot SE1 . . . .148 B1

Bridgeland Rd E16 . .35 C2
Bridgeman Ho 19
E9 . . . . .17 B1
Bridgeman Rd N1 . . .14 B1
Bridgeman St NW8 . .80 A1
Bridge Pk 3 E14 . . . . .41 C2
Bridgen Ho 1 E1 . . .32 A3
Bridgend Rd SW18 . .59 B3
Bridgeport Pl E1 . . .125 C2
Bridges Ct 1 . . . . . .167 B1
Bridges Ho 15 SE5 . .48 C3
Bridgeview 6 . . . . . . .39 B1
Bridgewater Rd E15 .27 C4
Bridgewater Sq
EC2 . . . . .108 C4
Bridgewater St
EC2 . . . . .108 C4
Bridgeway St NW1 . .83 A1
Bridgford St SW17, . .
SW18 . . . . .71 B1
Bridgman Rd W4 . . .37 B3
Bridgnorth Ho 10
SE15 . . . . .49 C4
Bridgwater Ho W2 .100 C2
Bridle La W1 . . . . . .119 A4
Bridlington Ho
SW18 . . . . .59 B3
Bridport SE17 . . . . .151 A1
Bridport Ho N1 . . . . .87 C3
Bridport Pl N1 . . . . . .87 C3
Bridstow Pl W2 . . . .31 C3
Brief St SE5 . . . . . . .48 A2
Brierfield NW1 . . . . . .82 C3
Brierley Rd E11 . . . .19 C4
SW12 . . . . .73 B2
Brierly Gdns E2 . . . .25 B3
Brig Mews SE8 . . . . .51 C4
Brigade St SE3 . . . . .53 B1
Briggeford Cl 5 E5 . . .7 C2
Briggs Ho 2 . . . . .99 A4
Bright St E14 . . . . . .34 A4
Brightling Rd SE4 . . .66 B1
Brightlingsea Pl 8 . . .
E14 . . . . .33 B2
Brightman Rd SW18 .71 C3
Brighton Bldgs
SE1 . . . . .138 A1
Brighton Gr SE14 . . .51 A2
Brighton Ho 52 SE5 .48 C2
Brighton Rd N16 . . . .16 A4
Brighton Terr SW9 . .62 B3
Brightside Rd SE13 .67 C1
Brightwell Ct N7 . . .14 B3
Brightwells SW6 . . .166 A2
Brigstock Ho SE5 . . .48 B1
Brill Pl NW1 . . . . . . .83 C1
Brimsdown Ho E3 . . .27 B1
Brindley Ho 22 . . . . .
SW12 . . . . .74 A4
Brine Ho 10 E3 . . . . .26 A3
Brinklow Ho W2 . . .100 A3
Brinkworth Way E9 .18 B2
Brinsley Ho 17 E1 . . .32 B3
Brinsley St 29 E1 . . . .32 A3
Brinton Wlk SE1 . . .122 A1
Brion Pl E14 . . . . . . .34 B4
Brisbane Ho 8 . . . . . .
W12 . . . . .30 A2
Brisbane St SE5 . . . .48 C3
Briset St EC1 . . . . . .96 A1
Briset Way N7 . . . . . .5 B2
Bristol Gdns W9 . . . .88 B1
Bristol Ho SE11 . . . .135 B1
Bristol Mews W9 . . .88 B1
Britannia Cl SW4 . . .61 C3

Britannia Gate 12
E16 . . . . .35 C1
Britannia Junc NW1 .82 B4
Britannia Rd 6
E14 . . . . .41 C2
Britannia Row N1 . . .86 C4
Britannia St WC1 . . .94 C4
Britannia Way
NW10 . . . . .20 A1
Britannia Wlk N1 . . .97 B4
British Gr W4 . . . . . .38 B1
British Grove Pas 2 . . .
W4 . . . . .38 B1
British Library The 4
NW1 . . . . .93 C4
British Mus* WC1 . .106 A3
British St E3 . . . . . . .26 B2
British Wharf Ind Est
SE14 . . . . .50 C4
Britley Ho 10 E14 . . .33 B3
Brittany Ho SW15 . . . .
Brittany Point
SE11 . . . . .149 B3
Britten Cl NW11 . . . . .2 A3
Britten House
SW3 . . . . .144 B2
Britten St SW3 . . . .144 A2
Britton St EC1 . . . . . .96 A1
Brixton Day Coll
SW9 . . . . .62 A4
Brixton Hill SW2 . . .62 B1
Brixton Hill Ct 5 . . . . .
SW2 . . . . .62 B2
Brixton Hill Pl SW2 .74 A4
Brixton Mkt SW9 . . .62 C3
Brixton Oval 3 . . . . . .
SW2 . . . . .62 C3
Brixton Rd SW9 . . . .173 B2
Brixton Sta SW9 . . . .62 C3
Brixton Station Rd
SW9 . . . . .62 C3
Brixton Water La
SW2 . . . . .62 B2
Broad Bridge Cl
SE3 . . . . .53 C3
Broad Common Est
N16 . . . . .7 C3
Broad Ct WC2 . . . . .106 B1
Broad La EC2 . . . . . .110 A4
Broad Sanctuary
SW1 . . . . .134 A3
Broad St Ave EC2 . .110 A3
Broad St Pl EC2 . . .109 C3
Broad Wlk NW1 . . . .81 C1
W1 . . . . .117 B2
Brindley Ho 22 . . . . . .
SW12 . . . . .74 A4
Broadbent Cl N6 . . . . .4 A3
Broadbent St W1 . . .118 A4
Broadfield NW6 . . . .11 A2
Broadfield La NW1 . .14 A1
Broadfields Way
NW10 . . . . .8 B3
Broadford Ho 11 E1 . .26 A1
Broadgate EC2 . . . .110 A4
Broadgate Circ
EC2 . . . . .110 A3
Broadgates Ct
SE11 . . . . .149 C1
Broadgates Rd
SW18 . . . . .71 C3
Broadhinton Rd
SW4 . . . . .61 B4

Broadhurst Cl NW6 ...11 B2
  9 Richmond TW10 ...54 B2
Broadhurst Gdns
  NW6 ....11 A2
Broadhurst Mans
  NW6 ....11 A2
Broadlands N6 ....3 C4
Broadlands Ave
  SW16 ....74 A2
Broadlands Cl N6 ....3 C4
  SW16 ....74 A2
Broadlands Ct NW9 ..44 C3
Broadlands Lo N6 ....3 B4
Broadlands Mans 2
  SW16 ....74 A2
Broadlands Rd N6 ....3 B4
Broadley St NW8 ...102 A4
Broadley Terr NW1 ..90 B1
Broadmayne SE17 ...151 B2
Broadmead W14 .....140 A3
Broadoak Ho 5
  SW9 ....62 C4
Broadoak Ho NW6 ...78 B3
Broadstone Ho
  SW8 ....162 C1
Broadstone Pl W1 ...103 B3
Broadwalk Ho
  SW7 ....128 C3
Broadwall La NW11 ..1 B4
Broadwall SW1 .....133 B2
  E15 ....19 C1
Broadway Arc 3
  W6 ....39 A2
Broadway Ho 2 E8 ..25 A4
Broadway Mans
  SW6 ....155 C1
Broadway Market
  E8 ....25 A4
Broadway Market Mews
  18 E8 ....25 A4
Broadway Mews E5 ..7 B4
Broadway Mo W3 ...36 C4
  SW13 ....46 A1
Broadwick St W1 ...105 A1
Broadwood Terr
  W14 ....141 A4
Brocas Cl NW3 ....12 A1
Brock Ho WC1 ......105 B4
Brock Pl E3 ....27 A1
Brock St SE5 ....49 A1
Brockbridge Ho 6
  SW15 ....56 B1
Brocket Ho 8 SW8 ..171 B2
Brockham Dr SW2 ...74 B4
Brockham Ho NW1 ..83 A3
  11 SW2 ....74 B4
Brockham St SE1 ...137 A2
Brockhurst Ho N4 ...6 C4
Brockill Cres SE4 ....66 A3
Brocklebank Rd
  SW18 ....71 B4
Brocklehurst St
  SE14 ....50 C3
Brockley Cross SE4 ..66 B4
Brockley Cross Bsns Ctr
  SE4 ....66 B4
Brockley Gdns SE4 ..51 B1
Brockley Gr SE4 .....66 C2
Brockley Hall Rd
  SE4 ....66 A2
Brockley Ho SE17 ...152 A2
Brockley Mews SE4 ..66 A2
Brockley Prim Sch
  SE4 ....66 B3
Brockley Rd SE4 .....66 B2

Brockley Sta SE4 ....66 A4
Brockley Way SE4 ...66 A2
Brockmer Ho 5 E1 ..32 A2
Brockweir 20 E2 .....25 B3
Brockwell Ct 2
  SW2 ....62 C2
Brockwell Ho
  SE11 ....163 A4
Brockwell Park
Brockwell Park Gdns
  SE24 ....63 B2
Brockwell Prim Schs
  SW2 ....62 C2
Broderick Ho SE21 ..76 A1
Brodia Rd N16 ....7 A1
Brodick Ho 11 E3 ....26 B3
Brodlove La E1 ......32 C2
Brodie Ho SE1 ......153 A2
Brodie St SE1 ....153 A2
Broke Wlk E8 ....24 B4
  11 E8 ....24 B4
Broken Wharf EC4 ..122 C4
Brokesley St E3 ......26 B2
Bromar Rd SE5 ......64 A4
Bromehead St 8
  E1 ....32 B3
Bromell's Rd SW4 ...61 B3
Bromfelde Rd
  SW4 ....171 C1
Bromfield Ct SE16 ..139 C2
Bromfield St N1 .....85 C2
Bromleigh Ho SE1 ..138 C2
Bromley Ct SE13 ....67 C2
Bromley Hall Rd
  E14 ....34 B4
Bromley Hall Sch
  E14 ....34 B4
Bromley High St E3 ..27 A2
Bromley Lo 2 W3 ...28 B3
Bromley PI W1 .....104 C4
Bromley St E1 ....32 C4
Bromley-by-Bow Sta
  E3 ....27 A2
Brompton WC1 .....106 C3
Brompton Arc
  SW1 ....131 A3
Brompton Hospl
  SW3 ....143 C2
Brompton Oratory
  SW3 ....130 A1
Brompton Park Cres
  SW6 ....156 A3
Brompton PI SW3 ...130 B1
Brompton Rd SW3 ..130 A1
Brompton Sq SW3 ...130 A2
Bromstone Ho
  SW9 ....173 B3
Bromwich Ave N6 ....3 C2
Bromwich Ho 3
  TW10 ....54 A1
Bromyard Ave W3 ...29 A2
Bromyard Ho 3
  SE15 ....50 A3
Bron Ct NW6 ....23 C4
Brondesbury Ct NW2 ..9 C2
Brondesbury Mews 11
  NW6 ....10 B1
Brondesbury Park Sta
  NW6 ....23 A4
Brondesbury Pk NW2 ..9 C2
Brondesbury Rd
  NW6 ....23 B3
Brondesbury Sta
  NW6 ....10 B1

Brondesbury Villas
  NW6 ....23 C3
Bronsart Rd SW6 ...154 A1
Bronte Ct 8 W14 ....39 C3
Bronte Ho 6 N16 ...16 A3
  NW6 ....23 C2
Bronti Cl SE17 ......151 A2
Bronwen Ct NW8 ....89 B3
Bronze St SE8 ....51 C3
Brook Ct SW14 ......56 A4
Brook Dr SE11 ......150 A4
Brook Gate W1 .....117 A3
Brook Gdns SW13 ...56 B4
Brook Gn W6 ....39 C2
Brook Green Flats 11
  W14 ....39 C3
Brook Ho W3 ....36 C4
  4 W6 ....39 B3
  5 SW4 ....61 B2
Brook Hos NW1 .....83 A1
Brook Mews N W2 ..115 A4
Brook St W2 ....115 C4
  W1 ....118 A3
Brook's Mews
  W1 ....118 A4
Brookbank Rd SE13 ..66 C4
Brookdale Rd SE6 ...67 A1
Brooke Rd E5,N16 ...7 C1
Brooke St EC1 ......107 B3
Brooke's Mkt EC1 ...107 C4
Brookes Ct EC1 .....107 B4
Brookfield
  11 N4 ....5 C2
  W5 ....36 A3
Brookfield Ho 5 E2 ..24 C3
Brookfield Pk NW5 ...4 A1
Brookfield Prim Sch
  N19 ....4 A2
Brookfield Rd E9 ....18 A2
  W4 ....37 C4
Brookgate Ho
  SW18 ....71 A2
Brooklands Ave
  SW18 ....71 A2
Brooklands Court
  Apartments 3
  NW6 ....10 B1
Brooklands Ct 2
  NW6 ....10 B1
Brooklyn Ct W12 ....30 B1
Brookmarsh Ind Est
  SE10 ....52 A3
Brookmill Rd SE8 ...51 C2
Brooks Ct 5
  SW4 ....172 A2
Brooks Ho 6 SW2 ..74 C3
Brooks La W4 ....44 C4
Brooks Rd W4 ....36 C1
Brooksbank Ho 7
  E9 ....17 B2
Brooksbank St 9
  E9 ....17 B2
Brooksby Mews N1 ..14 C1
Brooksby St N1 ......14 C1
Brooksby's Wlk E9 ...17 C3
Brookside Rd N19 ....4 B2
Brookstone Ct SE15 ..65 A3
Brooksville Ave
  NW6 ....23 A4
Brookville Rd SW6 ..154 C1
Brookwood Ave
  SW13 ....46 B1
Brookwood Ho
  SE1 ....136 B3
Brookwood Rd
  SW18 ....70 C3
Broome Ct 3 TW9 ...44 C2
Broome 7 E5 ....17 A3

Broome Way SE5 ....48 C3
Broomfield 7 NW1 ..12 C1
Broomfield
  SE17 ....152 A3
Broomfield House Sch
  TW9 ....44 B2
Broomfield Rd TW9 ..44 B2
Broomfield St E14 ...34 A4
Broomgrove Rd
  SW9 ....173 A1
Broomhill Rd SW18 ..58 C2
Broomhouse La
  SW6 ....58 C4
Broomhouse Rd
  SW6 ....165 B1
Broomsleigh St
  NW6 ....10 B3
Broomwood Rd
  SW11 ....60 C2
Brough Cl SW8 .....162 B1
Brough St SW8 .....162 B1
Brougham Rd E8 ....24 C4
  W3 ....28 B3
Brougham St
  SW11 ....169 A2
Broughton Dr 20
  SW9 ....63 A3
Broughton Rd
  SW6 ....166 B2
Broughton Road App
  SW6 ....166 A2
Broughton St SW8 ..170 A2
Broughton Street
  Arches Ind Area
  SW8 ....170 A2
Brouncker Rd W3 ...37 B4
Brown Hart Gdns
  W1 ....103 C1
  W1 ....117 C4
Brown St W1 ....102 C2
Brown's Bldgs
  EC3 ....110 B1
Browne Ho 13 SE8 ..51 C3
Brownfield St E14 ...34 B3
Brownflete Ho SE4 ..66 A3
Browning Cl W9 .....89 A1
Browning Ct W14 ...154 C4
Browning Ho
  W1 ....103 C3
  6 SE14 ....51 B2
  3 N16 ....16 A4
  W12 ....30 B3
Browning Mews
  W1 ....103 C3
Brownlow Ho 16 SE16 ..139 B3
Brownlow Mews
  WC1 ....95 A1
Brownlow Rd NW10 ..107 A3
  E8 ....24 C4
Brownswood Rd N4 ..6 B2
Broxash Rd SW11 ...60 C1
Broxbourne Ho 3
  E3 ....27 A1
Broxholm Rd SE27,
  SW16 ....74 C1
Broxholme Ho
  SW6 ....166 A4
Broxwood Way
  NW8 ....80 B3
Bruce Cl W10 ....30 C4
Bruce Glasier Ho 13
  N19 ....5 A3
Bruce Ho W10 ......30 C4
  4 SW4 ....61 C1
Bruce Rd E3 ....27 A2

Bruckner St W10 ....23 B2
Brudenell Rd SW17 ..72 C1
Bruges PI 13 NW1 ...13 B1
Brune Ho E1 ....110 C3
Brune St E1 ....110 C3
  8 NW6 ....46 B1
Brunel Ct 3
  SW13 ....46 B1
Brunel Est W2 ....31 C4
Brunel Ho SW10 ...157 C2
  4 NW5 ....13 A4
  E14 ....42 A1
  25 SW2 ....74 A4
Brunel Rd W3 ....29 A4
  SE16 ....32 B1
Brunel St E16 ....35 B1
Brunlees Ho SE1 ...137 A1
Brunswick Ct EC1 ..96 A3
  SE1 ....138 B4
  3 SW1 ....147 C3
Brunswick Gdns
  W8 ....31 C1 113 C4
Brunswick Ho 12 W9 ..90 C2
  4 E2 ....24 B3
Brunswick Mews
  W8 ....103 A2
Brunswick Park Prim
  Sch SE5 ....48 C3
Brunswick Pk SE5 ..49 A2
Brunswick PI N1 .....97 C3
Brunswick Quay
  SE16 ....40 C3
Brunswick Rd E14 ...34 B3
Brunswick Sh Ctr
  WC1 ....94 B2
Brunswick St E17 ...38 A3
Brunswick Villas 2
  SE5 ....49 A2
Brunton PI E14 ......33 A3
Brushfield St E1 ....110 C4
Brushwood Ho 4
  E14 ....34 A4
Brussels Rd SW11 ...59 C3
Bruton La W1 ....118 B3
Bruton PI W1 ....118 B3
Bruton St W1 ....118 B3
Bryan Ave NW10 .....9 A1
Bryan Ct W1 ....102 C2
Bryan Ho SE16 ......41 B4
Bryan Rd SE16 ......41 B4
Bryanston Ct W1 ...102 C2
Bryanston Ho 11
  SE15 ....49 B2
Bryanston Mans
  W1 ....102 C4
Bryanston Mews E
  W1 ....102 C3
Bryanston Mews W
  W1 ....102 C3
Bryanston PI W1 ...102 C3
Bryanston Sq W1 ...102 C2
Bryanston St W1 ...103 A1
Bryant Ct E2 ....24 B3
  W3 ....28 B1
Bryantwood Rd N5,
  N7 ....14 C3
Bryce Ho 23 SE14 ..50 C4
Brydale Ho 20 SE16 ..40 C2
Brydges PI WC2 ....120 A3
Brydges Rd E15 .....19 C3
Brydon Wlk N1 ......84 B4
Bryer Ct EC2 ....108 C4
Bryett Rd N7 ....5 A1
Bryher Ho W4 ....37 B1
Brymay Cl E3 ....26 C3

Brymon Ct W1 .... **103** B3
Brynmaer Ho SW11 .... **169** A3
Brynmaer Rd SW11 .... **169** A3
Bryony Rd W12 .... 29 C2
BT Tower* W1 .... **104** C4
Buccleuch Ho E5 .... 7 C4
Buchan Ho W3 .... 37 A4
Buchan Rd SE15 .... 65 B4
Buchanan Ct **16** SE16 .... 40 C2
Buchanan Gdns NW10 .... 22 A3
Buchan Ho SW18 .... 70 C4
SE21 .... 76 B1
Bucharest Rd SW18 .... 71 A4
Buck Hill Wlk W2 .... **115** C3
Buck St NW1 .... 13 A1
Buckfast St E2 .... 24 C2 **99** C3
Buckhold Rd SW18 .... 58 C1
Buckhurst Ho **15** N7 .... 13 C3
Buckhurst St E1 .... 25 A1
Buckingham Gate SW1 .... **133** A2
Buckingham Ho **4** 6 B3
Richmond TW10 .... 54 C2
Buckingham Mans NW6 .... 11 A3
Buckingham Mews SW1 .... **132** C2
NW10 .... 21 B3
Buckingham Palace* SW1 .... **132** C3
Buckingham Palace Rd SW1 .... **146** B3
Buckingham Pl SW1 .... **132** C2
Buckingham Rd N1 .... 16 A2
NW10 .... 21 B3
Buckingham St WC2 .... **120** B3
Buckingham Yd SW1 .... 21 B3
Buckland Cres SW3 .... 11 C2
Buckland Ct **6** N1 .... 24 A3
Buckland St N1 .... **87** C1
Buckland Wlk **2** W3 .... 28 A1
Buckle St E1 .... **111** A2
Buckler's Alley SW6 .... **155** A2
Bucklersbury EC2, EC4 .... **109** B1
Buckley Ct **5** NW6 .... 10 B1
Buckley Rd NW6 .... 10 B1
Buckley St SE1 .... **121** B1
Buckmaster Ho **1** N7 .... 14 B4
1 SW9 .... 62 C4
Buckmaster Rd SW11 .... 60 A3
Bucknall St WC1 .... **106** A2
Bucknell Cl SW2 .... 62 B3
Buckner Rd SW2 .... 62 B3
Buckridge Ho EC1 .... **107** B4
Buckshead Ho **19** W2 .... 31 C4
Buckstone Cl SE23 .... 65 B1
Buckters Rents SE16 .... 33 A1
Buckthorne Rd SE4 .... 66 A1

Budge Row EC4 .... **109** B1
Budge's Wlk W2 .... **115** A2
Budleigh Ho **19** SE15 .... 49 C3
Buer Rd SW6 .... **164** C1
Bugsbys Way SE10 .... 43 B2
Buick Ho **4** E3 .... 26 C1
Bulinca St SW1 .... **147** C3
Bull Inn Ct WC2 .... **120** B3
Bull Yd SE15 .... 49 C2
Bull's Gdns SW3 .... **144** B4
Bullace Row SE5 .... 48 C2
Bullards Pl **15** E2 .... 25 C2
Bulleid Way SW1 .... **146** B3
Bullen Ho **15** E1 .... 25 A1
Bullen St SW11 .... **168** B2
Buller Cl SE15 .... 49 C4
Buller Rd NW10 .... 22 C2
Bullfinch Ct **3** SE21 75 C2
Bullingham Mans W8 .... **127** C4
Bullivant St **4** E14 .... 34 B2
Bulls Alley SW14 .... 45 C1
Bulls Head Pas EC3 .... **110** A1
Bulmer Mews W11 .... 31 C1 **113** B2
Bulstrode Pl W1 .... **103** C3
Bulstrode St W1 .... **103** C2
Bulwer St W12 .... 30 B1
Bunbury Ho SE15 .... 49 C3
Bunhill Row EC1 .... **97** B1
Bunhouse Pl SW1 .... **145** C2
Bunkers Hill NW11 .... 2 B4
Bunning Ho N7 .... 14 A4
Bunning Way N7 .... 14 A4
Bunsen Ho **1** E3 .... 26 A3
Bunsen St **2** E3 .... 26 A3
Bunyan Ct EC2 .... **108** C4
Buonaparte Mews SW1 .... **147** B2
Burbage Cl SE1 .... **137** B1
Burbage Ho N1 .... **87** C3
16 SE14 .... 50 C3
Burbage Jun & Inf Sch N1 .... 24 A3
Burbage Rd SE21, SE24 .... 75 C4
Burcham St E14 .... 34 B3
Burchell Ho **10** SE11 **149** A2
Burchell Rd SE15 .... 50 A2
Burcote Rd SW18 .... 71 C4
Burden Ho **5** SW8 **162** A1
Burdenshott Ave TW10 .... 55 A3
Burder Cl N1 .... 16 A2
Burder Rd N1 .... 16 A2
Burdett Coutts CE Prim Sch SW1 .... **147** B4
Burdett Mews **4** W2 **100** A2
Burdett Rd E3 .... 33 B4
Richmond TW9 .... 44 B3
1 Brentford TW8 36 A1
Burford Ho **6** TW8 36 A1
Burford Rd E15 .... 27 C4
Burford Wlk SW6 .... **156** B1
Burgate Ct **10** SW9 62 C4
Burge St SE1 .... **137** C1
Burges Gr SW13 .... 47 A3
Burgess Ho **5** SE5 .... 48 B3
Burgess Park Mans NW6 .... 10 C4
Burgess St E14 .... 33 C4
Burgh St N1 .... **86** B2

Burghley Ho SW19 .... 70 A1
Burghley Rd NW5 .... 13 A4
Burghley Twr W3 .... 29 B1
Burgon St EC4 .... **108** B1
Burgos Gr SE10 .... 52 A2
Burgoyne Rd SW9 .... 62 B4
Burhan Uddin Ho E1 .... **98** C1
Buriton Ho **9** SW15 69 A3
Burke Cl SW15 .... 56 A3
Burke St E16 .... 35 B2
Burland Rd SW11 .... 60 B2
Burleigh Ho SW3 .... **157** C3
W10 .... 30 C4
Burleigh Pl SW15 .... 57 C2
Burleigh St WC2 .... **120** C4
Burley Ho E1 .... 32 C3
Burlington Arc W1 .... **118** C3
Burlington Ave TW9 44 C2
Burlington Cl W9 .... 23 B1
Burlington Ct W4 .... 45 B3
Burlington Danes Sch W12 .... 30 A3
Burlington Gdns W1 .... **118** C3
SW6 .... **164** B1
W3 .... 28 B1
W4 .... 37 B1
Burlington Ho NW3 11 C3
Burlington La W4 .... 45 C3
Burlington Mews SW15 .... 58 B2
1 W3 .... 28 B1
Burlington Pl SW6 **164** B1
Burlington Rd W4 .... **164** B1
Burma Rd N16 .... 15 C4
Burmarsh **8** NW5 .... 12 C2
Burmester Ho SW17 71 B1
Burmester Rd SW17 71 B1
Burn's Ho NW10 .... 21 A4
Burn's Rd NW10 .... 21 B4
Burnaby Cres W4 .... 45 B4
Burnaby Ct SE16 .... **139** C3
Burnaby Gdns W4 .... 45 A4
Burnand Ho **3** W14 39 C3
Burnaston Ho **5** E5 .. 7 C1
Burnbury Rd SW12 73 B3
Burne Jones Ho W14 .... **140** B3
Burne St NW1 .... **102** A4
Burnell Ho **10** SW2 .... 74 C3
Burnell Wlk SE1 .... **152** C4
Burness Cl N7 .... 14 B2
Burnett Cl E9 .... 17 B3
Burnett Ho **6** SE13 .. 52 B1
Burney St SE10 .... 52 B3
Burnfoot Ave SW6 .. **164** B3
Burnham NW3 .... 12 A1
Burnham Cl SE1 .... **153** A3
Burnham Ct W2 .... **114** B4
Burnham Est **8** E2 .. 25 B2
Burnham St E2 .... 25 B2
Burnhill Ho EC1 .... **96** C3
Burnley Rd SW9 .... **172** C2
NW10 .... 8 C3
Burns Ho **10** E2 .... 25 B2
16 N16 .... 16 A4
18 SE17 .... 48 A4
Burns Rd SW11 .... **168** C2
Burnsall St SW3 .... **144** B2

Burnside Cl SE16 .... 32 C1
Burnthwaite Rd SW6 .... **155** A1
Burntwood Cl SW18 72 A3
Burntwood Ct SW17 71 B1
Burntwood Grange Rd SW18 .... 72 A3
Burntwood La SW17 .... 71 C2
Buross St E1 .... 32 A3
Burr Cl E1 .... **125** B2
Burr Rd SW18 .... 70 C4
Burrage Ct **17** SE16 .. 40 C2
Burrard Ho **8** E2 .... 25 B3
Burrard Rd NW6 .... 10 C4
Burrell St SE1 .... **122** A2
Burrell's Wharf Sq E14 .... 42 A1
Burrhill Ct SE16 .... 40 C3
Burrow Ho SW9 .... **173** A1
Burrow Rd SE22 .... 64 A3
Burrow Wlk SE21 .... 75 B4
Burrows Mews SE1 .... **136** A4
Burrows Rd NW10 .. 22 B2
Bursar St SE1 .... **124** A1
Burstock Rd SW15 .. 58 A3
Burston Rd SW15 .. 57 C2
Burtley Ct N4 .... 6 B3
Burton Bank N1 .... 15 C1
Burton Ct SW3 .... **145** A2
Burton Gr SE17 .... **151** B1
Burton Ho **6** SE16 .. 40 A4
Burton La SW9 .... **173** C2
Burton Lo **5** SW15 .. 58 B2
Burton Mews SW1 .. **145** C3
Burton Pl WC1 .... **93** C3
Burton Rd SW9 .... **173** B2
NW6 .... 10 B1
Burton Road SW9 .. 48 A1
Burton St WC1 .... **93** C2
Burtons Ct E15 .... 19 C1
Burtonwood Ho N4 .. 6 C4
Burtt Ho N1 .... **98** A4
Burwash Ho SE1 .... **137** C3
Burwell Cl **25** E1 .... 32 A3
Burwell Wlk **3** E3 .. 26 C1
Burwood Ct SE22 .. 65 B1
Burwood Ho **3** SW9 .... 63 A3
Burwood Pl W2 .... **102** B2
Bury Cl SE16 .... 32 C1
Bury Ct EC3 .... **110** B2
Bury Pl WC1 .... **106** B3
Bury St EC3 .... **110** B2
SW1 .... **119** A2
Bury Wlk SW3 .... **144** A2
Busbridge Ho **6** E14 .... 33 C4
Busby Pl NW5 .... 13 C2
Busby St E2 .... **99** A2
Bush Cotts **12** SW18 58 C2
Bush Ct **7** W12 .... 39 C4
Bush La EC4 .... **123** B4
Bush Rd E8 .... 25 A4
SE8 .... 40 C2
Richmond TW9 .... 44 B4
Bushbaby Cl SE1 .... **138** A1
Bushberry Rd E9 .... 18 A2
Bushell Cl SW2 .... 74 B2
Bushell St E1 .... **125** C1
Bushey Down SW12 73 A2
Bushey Hall SE5 .... 48 B2

Bushey Hill Rd SE5 .. 49 B2
Bushfield Ho N5 .... 15 B3
Bushnell Rd SW17 .. 73 A1
Bushwood Dr SE1 .. **153** A3
Bushwood Rd TW9 .. 44 C3
Business Design Ctr* N1 .... **85** C3
Buspace Studios **2** W10 .... 23 A1
Butcher Row E1 .... 32 C3
Butchers Rd E16 .... 35 C3
Bute Gdns W6 .... 39 C2
Bute House Prep Sch W6 .... 39 C2
Bute St SW7 .... **143** B4
Butfield Ho **6** E9 .... 17 B2
Butler Ho **32** E2 .... 25 B2
15 E14 .... 33 B3
8 SW9 .... 48 A2
Butler Pl SW1 .... **133** B2
Butler Rd NW10 .... 8 B1
Butler St **33** E2 .... 25 B2
Butler's Wharf W SE1 .... **124** C1
Butley Ct **23** E3 .... 26 A3
Butterfield Cl **3** SE16 .... 40 A4
Butterfly Wlk **2** SE5 .... 48 C2
Buttermere NW1 .... **92** B4
Buttermere Cl SE1 .. **152** C3
E11 .... 19 C4
Buttermere Ct NW8 **79** B4
Buttermere Dr SW15 .... 58 A2
Buttermere Ho **11** E3 .... 26 B2
Buttermere Wlk **8** E8 .... 16 B2
Butterwick W6 .... 39 B2
Butterworth Ct SW16 .... 74 A1
Buttesland St N1 .... **97** C4
Buxhall Cres E9 .... 18 B2
Buxted Rd E8 .... 16 B1
SE22 .... 64 A3
Buxton Ct N1 .... **97** A4
Buxton Gdns W3 .... 28 A2
Buxton Ho **3** SW11 59 C3
Buxton Rd N19 .... 4 C3
NW2 .... 9 A2
SW14 .... 56 A4
Buxton St E1 .... 24 C1 **99** B1
Byam Shaw Sch of Art N19 .... 4 C2
Byam St SW6 .... **166** C1
Byards Ct SE16 .... 40 C3
Byas Ho **6** E3 .... 26 B2
Bye The W3 .... 29 A3
Byefield Cl SE16 .... 41 A4
Byelands Cl **1** SE16 32 C1
Byeway The SW14 .. 55 B4
Byfeld Gdns SW13 .. 47 A2
Bygrove Prim Sch E14 .... 34 A3
Bygrove St E14 .... 34 A3
Byng Pl WC1 .... **93** B1
Byng St E14 .... 41 C4
Byrne Ho **11** SW2 .. 62 B2
Byrne Rd SW12 .... 73 A2
Byron Cl E8 .... 24 C4
Byron Ct WC1 .... **94** C2
SW3 .... **144** B3
NW6 .... 11 B1
W9 .... 23 C1
SE21 .... 76 C3
Byron Mews NW3 .. 12 A4

Byron St E14 ....34 B3
Bythorn St SW9 ....62 B3
Byward St EC3 ....124 B3
Bywater Pl SE16 ....33 A1
Bywater St SW3 ....144 C2
Bywell Pl W1 ....104 C3
Byworth Wlk N19 ....5 A3

C

Cabbell St NW1 ....102 A3
Cabinet Office
  SW1 ....134 A4
Cabinet War Rooms ★
  SW1 ....133 C3
Cable Ho WC1 ....95 B4
Cable Pl SE10 ....52 B2
Cable St E1 ....111 C1
Cabot Ct SE16 ....40 C3
Cabot Sq E14 ....33 C1
Cabul Rd SW11 ....168 B1
Cactus Cl SE5 ....49 B1
Cadbury Way SE16 ......153 B4
Caddington Rd NW2 ......1 A1
Cade Rd SE10 ....52 C2
Cade Tyler Ho ⓒ
  SE10 ....52 B2
Cadell Cl E2 ....24 B3
Cadell Ho E2 ....24 B3
Cader Rd SW18 ....59 B1
Cadet Dr SE1 ....153 A2
Cadet Pl SE10 ....43 A1
Cadiz St SE17 ....151 A1
Cadmore Ho ⓸ N1 ......15 A1
Cadmus Cl SW4 ....173 B4
Cadnam Point ⓲
  SW15 ....69 A3
Cadogan Ct ⓴ SE16 ....40 B4
Cadogan Ct SW3 ....144 C3
Cadogan Ct Gdns
  SW1 ....145 B4
Cadogan Gate
  SW1 ....145 B4
Cadogan Gdns
  SW3 ....145 A3
Cadogan Ho SW3 ....157 C3
Cadogan La SW1 ....131 B1
Cadogan Pl SW1 ....131 A1
Cadogan Sq SW1 ....144 C3
Cadogan Terr E9 ....18 B1
Caedmon Rd N7 ....14 B4
Caernarvon Ho
  W2 ....100 C2
Cahill St EC1 ....97 A1
Cahir St E14 ....42 A2
Caine Ho ⓷ 14 B1
Caird St W9 ....23 B2
Cairns Ho ⓵ N7 ....14 B4
Cairns Rd SW11 ....60 A2
Caister Ho N7 ....14 B2
  ⓸ SW12 ....73 A4
Caister Mews SW12 .....73 A4
Caistor Ho SW12 ....73 A4
Caithness Ho N1 ....84 C4
Caithness Rd W14 ......39 C3
Calabria Rd N5 ....15 A3
Calais Gate SE5 ....48 A2
Calais St SE5 ....48 A2
Calbourne Rd SW12 .....72 C4
Calcraft Ho ⓶ E2 ....25 B3
Caldecot Ct SE5 ....48 B1
Caldecot Rd SE5 ....48 B1
Calderon Ho NW8 ......80 A2
Calderon Pl W10 ....30 B4
Caldervale Rd SW4 .....61 C2
Caldew St SE5 ....48 C3
Caldwell St SW9 ....163 B1
Caldy Wlk ⓲ N1 ....15 B2
Cale St SW3 ....144 A2
Caleb St SE1 ....137 A4
Caledonia Ho ⓲
  E14 ....33 A3
Caledonia St N1 ....84 B1
Caledonian Market
  SE1 ....138 B2
Caledonian Rd N1 ....84 C3
  N7 ....14 B2
Caledonian Road &
  Barnsbury Sta N7 ...14 B1
Caledonian Road Sta
  N7 ....14 B2
Caledonian Wharf Rd
  E14 ....42 C2
Caletock Way SE10 ....43 B1
Calgarth NW1 ....83 A1
Calgary Ct ⓴ SE16 .....40 B4
Caliban Twr ⓳ N1 ......24 A3
Calico Ho ⓸ SW11 ......59 B4
Calico Row ⓹ SW11 ....59 B4
Calidore Cl SW2 ....62 B1
Callaby Terr ⓯ N1 .....15 C2
Callahan Cotts ⓼
  E1 ....32 B4
Callcott Ct NW6 ....10 B1
Callcott Rd NW6 ....10 B1
Callcott St W8 ....113 B2
Callendar Rd SW7 .....129 B2
Callingham Cl ⓲
  E14 ....33 B4
Callingham Ho ⓲
  SW4 ....172 A2
Callow St SW3 ....157 B3
Calmington Rd
  SE5 ....152 B1
Calshot Ho N1 ....84 C2
Calshot St N1 ....84 C1
Calstock Ho ⓸
  SW11 ....149 C2
Calthorpe St WC1 ......95 A2
Calver ⓲ NW5 ....13 A4
Calverley Gr N19 ....4 C3
Calvert Ct ⓲ N19 ......4 C3
  ⓹ Richmond TW9 .....54 B3
Calvert Ho ⓴ W12 ......30 A2
Calvert Rd SE10 ....43 B1
Calvert St NW1 ....81 B4
Calvert's Bldgs
  SE1 ....123 B1
Calverton SE5 ....49 A4
Calvin St E1 ....24 B1 98 C1
Calypso Way SE16 ......41 B2
Cam Ct ⓶ SE15 ....49 B4
Cam Rd E15 ....27 C4
Cambalt Ho ⓷
  SW15 ....57 C2
Cambalt Rd SW15 ......57 C2
Cambay Ho ⓸ E1 ....26 A1
Camber Ho ⓸ SE15 ....50 B4
Camberley Ho
  NW1 ....82 B1
Camberwell Church St
  SE5 ....48 C2
Camberwell Coll of Arts
  SE5 ....49 A2
  SE5 ....49 B3
Camberwell Glebe
  SE5 ....49 A2
Camberwell Gn SE5 ....48 C2
Camberwell Gr SE5 ....49 A1
Camberwell Green
  SE5 ....48 B2
Camberwell New Rd
  SE5 ....163 C2
Camberwell Rd SE5 ....48 B3
Camberwell Station Rd
  SE5 ....48 C2
Camberwell Trad Est
  SE5 ....48 B2
Camborne Rd SW18 ....70 C4
Cambourne Mews ⓺
  W11 ....31 A3
Cambria Ho ⓸ E14 ....33 A3
Cambria Rd SE5 ....63 B4
Cambria St SW6 ....156 B1
Cambrian Cl SE27 ......75 A1
Cambrian Rd TW10 .....54 B1
Cambridge Ave
  NW6 ....23 C3
Cambridge Cir
  WC2 ....105 C1
Cambridge Cotts
  TW9 ....44 C4
Cambridge Cres ⓳
  E2 ....25 A3
Cambridge Ct N16 .....7 A4
  ⓶ E2 ....25 A3
  ⓳ W2 ....102 A2
Cambridge Gardens
  NW6 ....23 C3
Cambridge Gate
  NW1 ....92 A2
Cambridge Gate Mews
  NW1 ....92 B2
Cambridge Gdns
  NW6 ....23 C3
  ⓹ W10 ....31 A4
Cambridge Gr W6 ......39 A2
Cambridge Heath Rd
  E1,E2 ....25 A3
Cambridge Heath Sta
  E2 ....25 A3
Cambridge Ho SW6 ....58 A4
Cambridge Mans
  SW11 ....168 C3
Cambridge Pas ⓽
  E9 ....17 B1
Cambridge Pl W8 .....128 B3
Cambridge Rd
  SW11 ....168 C3
  NW6 ....23 C2
  NW6 ....23 C3
  Richmond TW9 ....44 C3
  SW13 ....46 B1
Cambridge Rd N
  W4 ....37 A1
Cambridge Rd S ⓶
  W4 ....37 A1
Cambridge Sch W2 ....102 A2
Cambridge St SW1 ....146 C2
Cambridge Terr
  NW1 ....92 A3
Cambridge Terr Mews
  NW1 ....92 B3
Cambus Rd E16 ....35 C4
Camden Gdns NW1 ....13 A1
Camden High St
  NW1 ....82 C3
Camden Ho ⓳ SE8 ....41 B1
Camden Lock Pl
  NW1 ....13 A1
Camberwell Church St
Camden Mews NW1 ....13 C2
Camden Mkt ★ NW1 ....82 B4
Camden Park Rd
  NW1 ....13 C2
Camden Pas N1 ....86 A3
Camden Rd NW1 ....82 C4
Camden Road Sta
  NW1 ....13 B1
Camden Row SE3 ......53 A1
Camden Sq NW1 ....13 C2
Camden St NW1 ....83 A4
Camden Studios
  NW1 ....83 A3
Camden Town Sta
  NW1 ....82 C3
Camdenhurst St
  E14 ....33 A3
Camelford Ct ⓴
  SW12 ....74 A4
Camelford NW1 ....83 A3
Camelford Wlk ⓼
  W11 ....31 A3
Camellia Ho SE8 ....51 B3
Camellia St SW8 ......162 A1
Camelot Ho ⓶ N1 .....13 C2
Camelot Prim Sch
  SE15 ....50 A4
Camera Pl SW10 ......157 B4
Cameret Ct ⓺ W11 ....39 C4
Cameron Ct ⓹
  SW19 ....70 A3
Cameron Ho ⓼ SE5 ...48 B3
Cameron Ho ⓲ NW8 ...80 A2
Cameron Cl ⓸ E16 ....16 A2
Camilla Rd SE16 ......40 A2
Camlet St E2 ....98 C2
Camley St NW1 ....83 B4
Camomile St EC3 .....110 B2
Campaign Ct W9 ....23 B1
Campana Rd SW6 .....165 C4
Campbell Ct SW7 .....128 C1
  SE21 ....76 C3
Camperdown St
  E1 ....111 A1
Campion Ho ⓲ N16 ...16 A3
Campion Rd SW15 .....57 B2
Camplin St SE14 ......50 C3
Campshill Pl SE13 .....67 B2
Campshill Rd SE13 ....67 B2
Campton Hill Towers
  W8 ....113 B2
Camsey Ho ⓸ SW2 ....62 B2
Canada Cres W3 ....20 B1
Canada Gdns SE13 ....67 B2
Canada Rd W3 ....28 B4
Canada Sq E14 ....34 A1
Canada St SE16 ....40 C4
Canada Way W12 ......30 A2
Canal App SE8 ....51 A4
Canal Bridge SE15 ....49 C4
Canal Cl W10 ....22 C1
  E1 ....26 A1
Canal Gr SE15 ....50 A4
Canal Path ⓶ E2 ......24 B4
Canal Rd E1 ....26 A1
Canal Side Wlk
  W9 ....90 A2
Canal St SE5 ....48 C4
Canal Way W10 ....22 C1
Canal Wlk N1 ....87 C4
Canalside Studios ⓷
  N1 ....24 A4
Canary Wharf ★ E14 ...34 A1
Canary Wharf Pier
  (River Bus) E14 .....33 B1
Canary Wharf Sta
  E14 ....34 A1
Canberra Prim Schs
  W12 ....30 A2
Canbury Mews
  SE26 ....76 C1
Cancell Rd SW9 ......173 C4
Candahar Rd
  SW11 ....168 B1
Candida Ct ⓲ NW1 ....13 A1
Candishe Ho SE1 .....138 C4
Candover St W1 ......104 C3
Candy St E3 ....26 B4
Canfield Gdns NW6 ....11 A1
Canfield Pl NW6 ....11 B2
Canford Rd SW11 .....60 C2
Canham Rd W3 ....38 A4
Canning Cross SE5 ....49 A1
Canning Ho ⓲ W12 ....30 A2
Canning Pas W8 ......128 C2
Canning Pl W8 ....128 C2
Canning Pl Mews
  W8 ....128 C2
Canning Rd N5 ....6 A1
Canning Town E16 .....35 A4
Canning Town Sta
  E16 ....35 A4
Cannington ⓮ NW5 ....12 C2
Cannock Ho N4 ....6 C4
Cannon Dr ⓲ E14 .....33 C2
Cannon Hill NW6 ......10 C3
Cannon Ho SE11 .....149 A3
Cannon La NW3 ....2 C1
Cannon Pl NW3 ....2 C1
Cannon St EC4 ....123 A4
Cannon Street Rd
  E1 ....32 A3

Cannon Street Sta
EC4 .... **123** B4
Cannon Wharf Bsns Ctr
🖹 SE8 .... 41 A2
Canon Barnett CE Prim
Sch E1 .... **111** A2
Canon Beck Rd
🖹 40 B4
Canon Murnane Rd
SE1 .... **138** C1
Canon Row SW1 ...... 134 A4
Canon St N1 .... **86** C3
Canonbury Cres N1 .. 15 B1
Canonbury Ct 🔟 N1 .. 15 B1
Canonbury La N1 .... 15 B1
Canonbury Pk N N1 .. 15 B2
Canonbury Pk S N1 .. 15 B2
Canonbury Pl N1 .... 15 A2
Canonbury Prim Sch
N1 ....
Canonbury Rd N1 .... 15 A1
Canonbury Sq N1 .... 15 A1
Canonbury St N1 .... 15 B1
Canonbury Sta N1,
N5 .... 15 B3
Canonbury Villas
N1 .... 15 A1
Canons Cl N2 ....
Canrobert St E2 .... 25 A2
Cantelowes Rd
NW1 .... 13 C2
Canterbury SE13 .... 67 B2
Canterbury Cl 🔟
SE5 .... 48 B1
Canterbury Cres
SW9 .... 62 C4
Canterbury Ct NW6 .. 23 C3
Canterbury Gr SE27,
SW16 .... 74 C1
Canterbury Ho
SE1 .... 135 A2
🖻 E3 .... 27 A2
Canterbury Ind Pk 🖻
SE15 .... 50 B4
Canterbury Mans
NW6 .... 11 A2
Canterbury Pl
SE17 .... 150 B3
Canterbury Rd NW6 .. 23 C3
Canterbury Terr
NW6 .... 23 C3
Cantium Ret Pk SE1 49 C4
Canton St E14 ...... 33 C3
Cantrell Rd E3 ...... 26 C1
Canute Ct SW16 .... 74 C1
Canute Gdns SE16 .. 40 C2
Canvey St SE1 ...... 122 C2
Capel Ho 🖻 E9 ...... 17 B1
Capel Lo
🖻 Richmond TW9 .... 44 B2
🔟 SW2 .... 74 B4
Capener's Cl SW1 .. 131 B3
Capern Rd SW18 .... 71 B3
Capital Interchange Way
TW8 ....
Capital Wharf E1 ...125 C1
Capland Ho 🖻 NW8 89 C2
Capland St NW8 .... 89 C2
Caple Ho SW10 .... 157 A2
Caple Rd NW10 .... 21 B3
Capper St WC1 ...... 93 A1
Capstan Ho 🖻 E14 .. 42 B2

Capstan Rd SE8 .... 41 B2
Capstan Sq E14 .... 42 B4
Capstan Way SE16 .. 33 A1
Capulet Mews 🖻
E16 .... 35 C1
Caradoc Cl W2 ...... 31 C3
Caradoc St SE10 .... 43 A1
Caravel Cl E14 ...... 41 C3
Caravel Mews 🔟
SE8 .... 41 B2
Caraway Hts E14 .... 34 B2
Carbery Ave W3 .... 36 B4
Carbis Rd E14 ...... 33 B3
Carbroke Ho 🔟 E9 .. 25 B4
Carburton St W1 .... 92 B1
Cardale St 🔳 E14 .. 42 B3
Cardiff Ho 🔳 SE15 .. 49 C4
Cardigan Rd E3 .... 26 B3
Cardigan Rd
 Richmond TW10 .... 54 A1
Cardigan St SE11 .. 149 B2
Cardigan Wlk 🔟 N1 15 B1
Cardinal Bourne St
 SE1 .... 137 C1
Cardinal Cap Alley
 SE1 .... 122 C2
Cardinal Hinsley RC
 High Sch (Boys)
 NW10 .... 21 C4
Cardinal Pl SW15 .. 57 C3
Cardinal Pole Sch
 (Lower) E9 .... 17 C1
Cardinal Pole Sch
 (Upper) E9 .... 18 A3
Cardinal Vaughan
 Memorial Sch
 W14 .... 126 A4
Cardinals Way N19 .. 4 C3
Cardine Mews SE15 50 A3
Cardington St NW1 .. 93 A3
Cardozo Rd N7 ...... 14 A3
Cardross St 🔳 W6 .. 39 A3
Cardwell Rd 🔳 N7 .. 14 A4
Career Ct 🔟 SE16 .. 40 C4
Carew Cl N7 .... 5 B2
Carew Ct 🔳 SE14 .. 50 C4
Carew Ho NW16 .... 74 C1
Carew St SE5 .... 48 B1
Carey Ct 🔳 SE5 .... 48 B3
Carey Gdns SW8 .. 171 B3
Carey La EC2 ...... 108 C2
Carey Pl SW1 ...... 147 B3
Carey St WC2 ...... 107 A1
Carfax Pl SW4 ...... 61 C3
Carfree Cl 🔳 N1 .. 14 C1
Cargill Rd SW18 .... 71 B3
Carinbrook St
 Carisbrook Ct 🔳
 .... 74 B1
Carisbrook Rd SW16
🖻 SW3 .... 37 B4
Carisbrooke Gdns
 SE15 .... 49 B3
Carisbrooke Ho
 TW10 .... 54 C2
Carleton Gdns N19 13 B3
Carleton Rd N7 .... 13 C3
Carlile Cl E3 .... 26 B3
Carlile Ho SE1 .... 137 C1
Carlingford Rd
 .... 74 B1
Carlisle Ave EC3 .. 110 C1
Carlisle La SE1 .... 135 A2
Carlisle Pl SW1 .... 132 C1
Carlisle Rd N4 ...... 5 C4
NW6 .... 23 A4

Carlisle St W1 ...... 105 B1
Carlisle Wlk 🔳 E8 .. 16 B2
Carlos Pl W1 ...... 118 A3
Carlow St NW1 ...... 82 C4
Carlton Cl NW6 .... 78 B2
NW2 ....
Carlton Ct SW9 .... 48 A2
Carlton Dr SW15 .. 58 A2
Carlton Gdns SW1 119 B1
Carlton Gr SE15 .. 50 A2
🔳 SE15 .... 50 B2
Carlton Hill NW8 .. 78 C2
Carlton Ho 🔳
NW6 .... 23 B3
Carlton Ho 🔳
 Richmond TW9 .... 44 C2
Carlton House Terr
 SW1 .... 119 C1
Carlton Lo 🔟 5 C4
Carlton Mans W9 .. 88 B4
W14 .... 126 B4
N16 .... 7 B4
🔳 SW2 .... 62 C1
Carlton Prim Sch
 NW5 .... 12 C3
Carlton Rd N4 ...... 5 C4
 🔳 W4 .... 37 C4
SW14 .... 55 B3
Carlton Sq E1 ...... 25 C1
Carlton St SW1 .... 119 B3
Carlton Tower Pl
 SW1 .... 131 A2
Carlton Vale NW6 .. 23 C2
Carlton Vale Inf Sch
 .... 23 B2
Carltons The 🔳
SW15 .... 57 C1
Carlyle Cl N2 ...... 20 C4
Carlyle Ct SW6 .... 166 B3
Carlyle Ho 🔳 SW3 157 C4
🔳 N16 .... 7 A3
🖻 SE5 .... 48 B3
Carlyle Mans SW3 158 A3
Carlyle Pl SW15 .... 57 C3
Carlyle Rd 🔳 E12 .. 35 B4
Carlyle's Ho 🔳 SW3 158 A3
Carmalt Gdns SW15 57 B3
Carmarthen Ho 🔳
 SW15 .... 69 B4
Carmarthen Pl
 SE1 .... 138 A4
Carmel Ct W8 ...... 128 A4
Carmelite St EC4 .. 121 C4
Carmen St E14 .... 34 A3
Carmichael Cl 🖻
SW11 .... 59 C4
Carmichael Ct 🔳
SW13 .... 46 B1
Carmichael Ho 🔳
E14 .... 34 B2
Carmichael Mews
 SW18 .... 71 C4
Carminia Rd SW17 73 A2
Carnaby St* W1 .. 104 C1
Carnac St SE21,SE27 75 C1
Carnegie Ho NW3 .. 2 C1
Carnegie Pl SW19 .. 69 C1
Carnegie St N1 .... 85 A3
Carnicot Ho 🔳
 SE15 .... 50 A2
Carnoustie Dr N1 .. 84 C4

Carol St NW1 ...... 82 C4
Caroline Cl W2 .... 114 B3
SW16 .... 74 B1
Caroline Gdns E2 .. 98 B4
Caroline Ho W2 .... 114 B3
🔳 W6 .... 39 B1
Caroline Martyn Ho 🖻
N19 .... 4 C4
Caroline Pl W2 .... 114 B3
SW11 .... 169 C1
Caroline Pl Mews
 W2 .... 114 B3
Caroline St E1 ...... 32 C3
Caroline Terr SW1 145 B3
Caroline Wlk W6 .. 154 A3
Carpenter Ho
 🔳 E14 .... 33 C4
 🔟 NW11 .... 1 C3
Carpenter St W1 .. 118 A3
Carpenter's Pl SW4 61 C3
Carpenter's Rd E15 19 A1
Carpenters Bsns Pk
 E15 .... 19 A1
Carpenters Prim Sch
 E15 .... 19 C1
Carr St 🔳 E14 ...... 33 A3
Carrara Wharf SW6 58 A4
Carrara Wlk 🔟 SW9 63 A3
Carriage Dr E
 SW11 .... 159 C2
Carriage Dr N
 SW11 .... 158 C2
SW8 .... 159 C3
Carriage Dr S
 SW11 .... 169 B4
Carriage Dr W
 SW11 .... 158 C1
Carrick Ho N7 .... 14 B2
🔳 SE11 .... 150 A2
Carrick Mews SE8 51 C4
Carrington Ho W1 .. 118 A1
Carrington Lo 🔳
 TW10 .... 54 A2
Carrington Rd
 TW10 .... 54 C3
Carrol Cl NW5 ...... 13 A4
Carroll Ho W2 .... 115 B4
Carron Cl E14 ...... 34 A3
Carroun Rd SW8 .. 162 C2
Carslake Rd SW15 57 B1
Carson Rd E16 .... 35 C4
 SE21 .... 75 C2
Carter Ct 🔳 EC4 .. 108 B1
Carter Ho 🔳 110 C3
Carter La EC4 ...... 108 B1
Carter Pl SE17 .... 151 A1
Carter St SE17 .... 150 C1
Carter's Yd SW18 38 C2
Carteret Ho 🔳 W12 30 A2
Carteret St SW1 .. 133 B3
Carteret Way SE8 .. 41 A2
Carthew Rd W6 .... 39 A3
Carthew Villas W6 39 A3
Carthusian St EC1 108 C4
Cartier Circ E14 .. 34 B1
Carting La WC2 .. 120 B3
Cartmel NW1 ...... 92 C4
Carton Ho SE16 .. 139 B2
🔳 W11 .... 30 C2
Cartwright Gdns
 WC1 .... 94 A3
Cartwright Ho SE1 137 A1

Cartwright St E1 .. 125 B3
Cartwright Way
 SW13 .... 47 A3
Carvel Ho E14 ...... 42 B1
Carver Rd SE24 .... 63 B1
Carville Cres TW8 .. 36 A2
Caryl Ho 🖻 SW19 .. 70 A3
Carysfort Rd N16 .. 15 C4
Casby Ho SE16 .. 139 B2
Casella Rd SE14 .. 50 C3
Casino Ave SE24 .. 63 C2
Caspian Ho 🔟 E1 .. 32 C4
Caspian St SE5 .... 48 C3
Cass Ho 🞬 E9 ...... 17 C2
Cassandra Ct W12 .. 30 B3
Casselden Rd NW10 8 A1
Cassell Ho 🔳 SW9 172 B2
Casserley Ho W4 .. 37 C3
Cassidy Rd SW6 .. 155 B1
Cassinghurst SE24 63 C2
Cassland Rd E9 .... 17 C2
Casson Ho 🔳 111 A4
Casson St E1 ...... 111 B3
Castalia Sq 🔳 E14 42 B4
Castell Ho 🔳 SE8 .. 51 C3
Castellain Mans W9 88 A2
Castellain Rd W9 .. 88 B2
Castellan Ave 🔳 .. 88 C1
Castello Ave SW15 57 B2
Castelnau SW13 .. 47 A3
Casterbridge Ho 🖻
 🔳 W11 .... 31 C3
Casterton St 🔳 E8 17 A2
Castle Baynard St
 EC4 .... 122 C4
Castle Cl E9 .... 18 A3
SW19 .... 69 C1
Castle Ho EC3 .... 109 C1
Castle Ho SE1 .... 150 C4
SW8 .... 162 B2
Castle Ind Est
 SE17 .... 150 C4
Castle La SW1 .... 132 C2
Castle Mead SE5 .. 48 B3
Castle Mews NW1 .. 13 A2
Castle Pl 🔳 W4 .... 38 A2
Castle Rd NW1 ...... 13 A2
 N6 .... 3 C4
Castle Way SW19 .. 69 C1
Castle Yd SE1 .... 122 B2
🔳 N6 .... 3 C4
Castlebrook 🔳
SE11 .... 150 A4
Castlecombe Dr
 SW19 .... 69 C4
Castleden Ho NW6 11 C1
Castleford Ct NW8 .. 89 C2
Castlefrank Ho 🔳 98 B4
Castlegate TW9 .... 54 B4
Castlehaven Rd
 NW1 .... 13 A1
Castlemaine SW11 169 A2
Castlemain Gdns
 SW13 .... 47 A4
Castlereagh St W1 102 C2
Castleton Ho 🔳 E14 42 B2
Castletown Rd
 W14 .... 140 B1
Castleview Cl N4 .. 6 B2
Castor La E14 ...... 34 A2
Caterham Rd SE13 67 C4
Catesby Ho 🔳 E9 .. 17 B1
Catesby St SE17 .. 151 C3

Cathay Ho SE16 ....40 A4
Cathay St 9 SE16 ......40 A4
Cathcart Hill N19 ......4 B1
Cathcart Rd SW10 .156 C4
Cathcart St 4 NW5 ...13 A2
Cathedral Pl EC4 ....108 C2
Cathedral Sch of St
  Saviour & St Mary
  Overie Prim Sch
SE1 ....137 A4
Cathedral St SE1 .123 B2
Catherall Rd N5,N16 ..6 B1
Catherine Baird Ct 12
SW12 ....73 A4
Catherine Dr TW9 ...54 A3
Catherine Gr SE10 ...52 A2
Catherine Griffiths Ct
EC1 ....95 C2
Catherine Ho 16 N1 ..24 A4
Catherine Pl SW1 ..132 C2
Catherine St WC2 ...120 C4
Catherine Wheel Alley
E1 ....110 B3
Catherine Wheel Yd
SW1 ....118 C4
Catherwood Ct N1 ...87 B1
Cathles Rd SW12 ......61 A1
Cathnor Rd W12 ......39 A4
Catinthia Ct 5 SE8 ..41 A2
Catlin St SE16 ....40 A1
Cato Rd SW4 ....61 C3
Cato St W1 ....102 B2
Cator St SE15 ....49 B4
                          .49 B3
Catton St WC1 ....106 C3
Caughley Ho SE11 ..135 B1
Caulfield Ct 12 NW1 ..13 B1
Caulfield Rd SE15 ....50 A1
Causeway The
SW18 ....59 A2
Causton Cotts 3
E14 ....33 A3
Causton Ho SE5 ......48 B3
Causton Rd N6 ....4 A4
Causton St SW1 .....147 C2
Cautley Ave SW4 ......61 B2
Cavalry Gdns SW15 ..58 B2
Cavan Ho 2 E2 ....24 B4
Cavaye Ho SW10 ...157 A4
Cavaye Pl SW10 .....143 A1
Cavell Ho 6 N1 ....24 A4
Cavell St E1 ....32 A4
Cavendish Ave NW8 .79 C1
Cavendish Cl NW6 ....10 B2
                          .10 B2
Cavendish Ct EC2 ...110 B2
Cavendish Gdns
SW4 ....61 B1
Cavendish Ho NW8 ...79 C1
SW8 ....172 A4
Cavendish Jun & Inf Sch
W4 ....46 A3
Cavendish Mans
EC1 ....95 B1
8 NW6 ....10 C3
5 ....17 B3
Cavendish Mews N
W1 ....104 B4
Cavendish Mews S
W1 ....104 B3
Cavendish Par
SW12 ....61 A1
Cavendish Pl W1 ....104 B2

Cavendish Rd NW6 ...10 B1
W4 ....45 B2
SW12 ....61 B1
Cavendish Sch The
NW1 ....82 B4
Cavendish Sq W1 ...104 B2
Cavendish St N1 ....87 B1
Cavendish Terr 10
E3 ....26 B2
Cavendish The NW11 ..2 A4
Caversham Ho 7
SE15 ....49 C4
Caversham Rd NW5 ..13 B2
Caversham St
SW3 ....158 C4
Caverswall St W12 ...30 B3
Cavour Ho SE17 .....150 B2
Caxton Gr E3 ....26 C2
Caxton Hall SW1 ....133 B2
Caxton Rd W12 ....39 C4
SW19 ....70 C1
Caxton St SW1 ......133 B2
Caxton St N E8 ....16 C1
Cayford Ho 5 NW5 ...13 B3
Cayley Sch E14 ....33 A3
Cayton Pl EC1 ....97 B3
Cayton St EC1 ....97 B3
Cazenove Mans 4
N16 ....7 C2
Cecil Ct WC2 ....120 A3
SW10 ....156 C4
N8 ....5 A4
W3 ....28 B4
Cecil Mans 2 SW17 ..72 C2
Cecil Rd NW10 ....21 A4
W3 ....28 B4
Cecil Rhodes Ho
NW1 ....83 A2
Cecilia Rd E8 ....16 C3
Cedar Cl SE21 ....75 B2
Cedar Ct 1 N1 ....15 B1
E3 ....26 B2
SW19 ....70 A3
SE13 ....67 C4
W4 ....45 B4
Cedar Gr W5 ....36 A3
Cedar Ho W8 ....128 A2
18 SE16 ....40 C4
2 E14 ....42 B4
SE14 ....50 C2
Cedar Hts NW2 ....10 B2
Cedar Lo NW6 ....9 C1
Cedar Rd NW2 ....9 B4
Cedar Terr TW9 ....54 A3
Cedar Tree Ct SE5 ...48 B2
Cedar Way NW1 ....83 B4
Cedarne Rd SW6 ....156 A1
Cedars Cl SE13 ....67 C4
Cedars Ct SW15 ....56 C1
Cedars Mews SW4 ...61 A3
Cedars Rd W4 ....45 B4
SW13 ....46 C1
Cedars The E9 ....17 C1
Cedra Ct N16 ....7 C3
Cedric Chambers
NW8 ....89 B2
Celandine Cl E3,E14 ..33 C4
Celandine Dr E8 ....16 B1
Celbridge Mews
W2 ....100 B2
Celestial Gdns SE13 .67 C3
Celia Ct 7 TW9 ....44 B2
Celia Ho 10 N1 ....24 A3
Celia Rd N19 ....13 B4
Celtic St E14 ....34 A4
Cenacle Cl NW3 ....1 C1
Cenotaph* SW1 .....134 A4

Centaur Ct 3 TW8 ...36 A1
Centaur St SE1 .....135 A2
Central Ave SW11 ...159 A1
Central Bsns Ctr
NW10 ....20 B1
Central Criminal Court
  (Old Bailey)*
EC4 ....108 B2
Central Foundation
  Lower Sch E3 ....26 A2
Central Foundation Sch
EC2 ....97 C2
Central Foundation
  Upper Sch E3 ....26 B2
Central Middlesex Hospl
NW10 ....20 B2
Central Par W3 ....28 C1
Central Sch of Ballet
EC1 ....95 C1
Central Sch of Speech &
  Drama The NW3 .....11 C1
Central St EC1 ....96 C3
Central St Martin's Sch
  of Art & Design
W1 ....105 C1
Central St Martins Coll
  of Art & Design (The
  London Institute)
WC1 ....106 C3
Central Way NW10 ...20 B2
Centre Ave NW10 ....22 B2
W3 ....28 B1
Centre Bldg SE17 ...151 A4
Centre Hts 5 NW3 ...11 C1
Centre Point SE1 ....153 B2
Centre St E2 ....25 A3
Centurion Cl N7 ......14 B1
Centurion La E3 ......26 B3
Century Ho SE13 .....52 A1
Cephas Ave E1 ....25 B1
Cephas Ho 8 E1 ......25 B1
Cephas St E1 ....25 B1
Cerise Rd SE15 ....49 C2
Cerney Mews W2 ...115 B4
Cervantes Ct W2 ...100 B1
Ceylon Rd W14 ......126 A1
                          .39 C3
Chadbourn St E14 ...34 A4
Chaddacre Ho 10
SW9 ....63 A3
Chadston Ho 17 N1 ..15 B2
Chadswell Heights
WC1 ....94 B3
Chadwell St EC1 ......95 C4
Chadwick Rd NW10 ..21 B4
SE15 ....49 B1
Chadwick St SW1 ..133 B1
Chagford Ho NW1 ....90 C1
8 E3 ....27 A2
Chagford St NW1 ....91 A1
Chalbury Ho 3
SW9 ....62 B3
Chalbury Wlk N1 ......85 B2
Chalcot Cres NW1 ...81 A4
Chalcot Gdns NW3 ...12 B2
Chalcot Mews
SW16 ....74 A1
Chalcot Rd NW1 ......81 B4
Chalcot Sch NW1 .....13 A1
Chalcot Sq NW1 ......81 B4
Chale Rd SW2 ....62 A1
Chalfont Ct NW1 ......91 A1

Chalfont Ho 2
SE16 ....40 A3
Chalford Ct 15
SW15 ....57 C1
Chalford Rd SE21 .....75 C1
Chalgrove Rd E9,E17 ..17 B2
Chalk Farm Rd NW1 ..12 C1
Chalk Farm Sta
NW3 ....12 C1
Chalk Hill Rd W6 .....39 C2
Chalkers Cnr TW9 ...55 A4
Chalkwell Ho 9 E1 ...32 C3
Challenger Ho 7
E14 ....33 A2
Challice Way SW2 ...74 B3
Challoner Cres
W14 ....140 C1
Challoner Mans
W14 ....140 C1
Challoner St W14 ...140 C1
Chalmer's Wlk 14
SE17 ....48 A4
Chalmers Ho 13
SW11 ....59 B4
Chalner Ho SW2 ......74 C3
Chalton St NW1 ....83 B1
Chamber St E1 ......125 A4
Chamberlain Cotts
SE5 ....48 C2
Chamberlain Ho
1 E1 ....32 B2
Chamberlain St 7
NW1 ....12 C1
Chamberlayne Mans 5
NW10 ....22 C2
Chamberlayne Rd
NW10 ....22 B4
Chambers La NW10 ..9 B1
Chambers Rd N7 .....14 A4
Chambers St SE16 ..139 C3
Chambon Pl 6 W6 ...38 C2
Chambord Ho 2 E2 ..99 A3
Chambord St E2 ......99 A3
Champion Gr SE5 ....63 C4
Champion Hill SE5 ...63 C4
Champion Pk SE5 ....48 C1
Champlain Ho 28
W12 ....30 A2
Chance St E2 ....98 C2
Chancel Ct 1 W1 ....119 B4
Chancel St SE1 ......122 A1
Chancellor Gr SE21 .75 B1
Chancellor Ho
SW7 ....129 A2
1 E1 ....32 A1
Chancellor Pas E14 .33 C1
Chancellor's Rd W6 .39 B1
Chancellors St W6 ...39 B1
Chancellors Wharf 3
W6 ....39 B1
Chancellors' Ct
WC1 ....106 C4
Chancery Bldgs 13
E1 ....32 B2
Chancery La EC4 ...107 B2
Chancery Lane Sta
WC1 ....107 B3
Chandler Ave E14 ...33 C4
Chandler St E1 ....32 A1
Chandler Way SE15 .49 B3
Chandlers Mews
E14 ....41 C4

Chandlers Way 11
SE24 ....74 C4
Chandos Pl WC2 ....120 A3
Chandos Rd E15 ......19 C3
E15 ....27 C3
NW10 ....21 A1
NW2 ....9 B3
Chandos St W1 ......104 B3
Chandos Way NW11 ..2 A3
Change Alley EC3 ...109 C1
Channel Ho E14 ......33 A4
Channelsea Rd E15 ..27 C4
Channing Sch N6 ......4 A3
Chant Sq E15 ....19 C1
Chant St E15 ....19 C1
Chantrey Rd SW9 ....62 B4
Chantry Cl W9 ....23 B1
Chantry St N1 ....86 B3
Chantry Sq W8 ......128 A1
Chantry St N1 ....86 B3
Chapel Ct EC2 ....98 A3
SE1 ....137 B4
Chapel House St
E14 ....42 A2
Chapel Market 1 N1 .85 B2
Chapel Pl N1 ....85 C2
EC2 ....98 A3
W1 ....104 A1
Chapel Side W2 .....114 A3
Chapel St NW1 ......102 A3
SW1 ....131 C3
Chapleton Ho SW2 ..62 C2
Chaplin Cl SE1 ....136 A4
Chaplin Ho 6 SW9 ...62 C3
Chaplin Rd NW2 ......8 C2
Chapman Ho 21
2 E2 ....25 A2
Chapman Rd E9 ......18 B2
Chapman St E1 ....32 A2
Chapmans Park Ind Est
NW10 ....8 B2
Chapone Pl W1 ......105 B1
Chapter Cl 13 W4 ....37 B3
Chapter House Ct
EC4 ....108 C1
Chapter Rd SE17 ...150 B1
NW2 ....9 A3
SE17 ....150 B1
Chapter St SW1 .....147 B3
Chara Pl W4 ....45 C4
Charcot Ho 9
SW15 ....56 B1
Charcroft Ct 11
W14 ....39 C4
Chard Ho 7 N7 ....5 B2
Chardin Rd 1 W4 .....38 A2
Chardmore Rd N16 ...7 C3
Charecroft Way
W12 ....39 C4
Charfield Ct W9 ....88 B1
Charford Rd E16 .....35 C4
Chargrove Cl 24
SE16 ....40 C4
Charing Cross
SW1 ....120 A2
Charing Cross Hospl
W6 ....39 C1
Charing Cross Rd
WC2 ....105 C1
Charing Cross Sta
WC2 ....120 B2
Charing Ho SE1 .....135 C4
Charlbert Ct NW8 ....80 A2

Charlbert St NW8 ....**80** A2
Charles Allen Ho
EC1 ....**95** B4
Charles Auffray Ho 8
E1 ....**32** B4
Charles Barry Cl
SW4 ....**61** B4
Charles Burton Ct
E5 ....**18** A4
Charles Coveney Way 4
SE15 ....**49** B2
Charles Darwin Ho 8
E2 ....**25** A2
Charles Dickens Ho
E2 ....**99** C4
1 E2 ....**25** A2
Charles Dickens Prim
Sch SE1 ....**136** C3
Charles Edward Brooke
Girls Sch (Lower)
SE5 ....**48** A2
Charles Edward Brooke
Girls Sch (Upper)
SW9 ....**48** A1
Charles Flemmell Mews
3 E16 ....**35** C1
Charles Hobson Ho
NW10 ....**21** A3
Charles Hocking Ho 4
W3 ....**37** B4
Charles II Pl SW3 ..**144** C1
Charles II St SW1 ..**119** B2
Charles La NW8 .....**80** A2
Charles Lamb Prim Sch
N1 ....**86** C4
Charles Mackenzie Ho
SE16 ....**153** C4
Charles Pl NW1 ......**93** A3
Charles Rowan Ho
WC1 ....**95** B3
Charles Sq N1 ....**97** C3
Charles St W1 ....**118** A2
SW13 ....**46** A1
Charles Townsend Ho
EC1 ....**96** A2
Charleston St
SE17 ....**151** A3
Charlesworth Ho 2
E14 ....**33** C3
Charleville Ct SW5 **140** C1
Charleville Mans
W14 ....**140** B1
Charleville Rd
W14 ....**140** B1
Charlotte Despard Ave
SW11 ....**169** C3
SW11 ....**170** A3
Charlotte Ho Ho 6 W6 ..**39** B1
Charlotte Mews
W1 ....**105** A4
W14 ....**140** A4
W10 ....**30** C4
Charlotte Pl W1 ....**105** A3
SW1 ....**146** C3
Charlotte Rd
EC2 ......**24** A1 **98** A2
SW13 ....**46** B2
Charlotte Row SW4 ..**61** B4
Charlotte Sharman Prim
Sch SE11 ....**136** A1
Charlotte Sq 5
TW10 ....**54** B1
Charlotte St W1 ...**105** A4

Charlotte Terr N1 ...**85** A3
Charlow Cl SW6 ....**166** C1
Charlton Ct 17 N7 ..**13** C3
25 E2 ....**24** B4
Charlton Ho NW1 ....**93** B4
1 Brentford TW8 ...**44** A4
Charlton King's Rd
NW5 ....**13** C3
Charlton Pl N1 ....**86** A2
Charlton Rd NW10 ..**21** A4
SE3 ....**53** C3
Charlton Way SE10,
SE3 ....**53** A2
Charlwood Ho
SW1 ....**147** B3
1 SW2 ....**74** B3
Charlwood Pl SW1 .**147** A3
Charlwood Rd
SW15 ....**57** C3
Charlwood Terr 5
SW15 ....**57** C3
Charman Ho 10 SW8 **162** A2
Charmian Ho 10 N1 ..**24** A3
Charmouth Ct TW10 ..**54** B2
Charmouth Ho
SW8 ....**162** C2
Charnock Ho 22
W12 ....**30** A2
Charnwood Gdns
E14 ....**41** C2
Charrington Ho NW1 ..**83** B2
Chart Pl N1 ....**97** C4
Chart St N1 ....**97** C4
Charter Ct W1 ......**102** B2
Charter Ho WC2 ....**106** B1
Charter Nightingale
Hospl The NW1 ....**102** B4
Charterhouse Bldgs
EC1 ....**96** C1
Charterhouse Mews
EC1 ....**108** A4
Charterhouse Sq
EC1 ....**108** A4
Charterhouse St
EC1 ....**108** A4
Charteris Rd N4 ......**5** C3
NW6 ....**23** B4
Chartes Ho SE1 .....**138** B2
Chartfield Ave
SW15 ....**57** B2
Chartfield Sch
SW15 ....**57** A2
Chartfield Sq SW15 ..**57** C2
Chartham Ct 13
SW9 ....**62** C4
Chartham Gr SE27 ..**75** A1
Chartham Ho SE1 ...**137** C2
Cartridge SE17 .....**48** C4
Chase Ct SW3 ....**130** C1
Chase Ctr The
NW10 ....**20** C2
Chase Rd NW10 .....**20** C1
Chase Road Trad Est
NW10 ....**20** C1
Chase The SW4 ......**61** A4
Chaseley Ct W4 .....**37** A1
Chaseley St E14 ....**33** A3
Chasemore Ho
SW6 ....**154** B2
Chater Ho 6 E2 .....**25** C2
Chatfield Rd SW11 ..**59** B4
Chatham Ct SW11 ..**60** B2
Chatham Ho 7 SE5 ..**49** A1
Chatham Pl E9 ......**17** B2

Chatham Rd SW11 ...**60** B2
Chatham St SE17 ...**151** C4
Chatsworth Ct W8 ..**141** B4
E5 ....**17** C4
Chatsworth Est E5 ..**17** C4
Chatsworth Gdns
W3 ....**28** A1
Chatsworth Ho
1 W4 ....**37** C1
Chatsworth Rd NW2 ..**9** C2
E5 ....**17** B4
Chatsworth Way
SE27 ....**75** B1
Chattenden Ho 8
N4 ....**6** C4
Chatterton Ct TW9 ..**44** B1
Chatterton Rd N4 ....**6** A1
Chatto Rd SW11 .....**60** B2
Chaucer Ave TW9 ...**44** C1
Chaucer Ct N16 .....**16** A4
Chaucer Dr SE1 ....**153** A3
Chaucer Ho SW1 ...**146** C1
Chaucer Rd W3 ......**28** B1
SE24 ....**63** A2
Chauldon Ho EC1 ...**97** C3
Cheadle Ct NW8 .....**89** C2
Cheadle Ho 11 E14 ..**33** B3
Cheam St 4 SE15 ....**65** A4
Cheapside EC2 .....**109** A1
Chearsley SE17 ....**151** A4
Cheddington Ho 9
E2 ....**24** C4
Chedworth Cl E16 ...**35** B1
Chedworth Ho 6
E5 ....**17** A3
N7 ....**14** B4
Cheesemans Terr
W14 ....**140** C1
Chelmer Rd E9 ......**17** C3
Chelmsford Cl W6 ..**47** C4
Chelmsford Ho 5
N7 ....**14** B4
Chelmsford Sq
NW10 ....**22** B4
Chelsea & Westminster
Hospl SW10 ....**157** A3
Chelsea Barracks
SW1 ....**145** C1
Chelsea Bridge
SW1 ....**160** A4
Chelsea Bridge Rd
SW1 ....**145** C1
Chelsea Cl NW10 ....**20** C4
Chelsea Cloisters
SW3 ....**144** B3
Chelsea Coll of Art &
Design
SW3 ....**144** A1
SW6 ....**59** A4
Chelsea Cres
SW10 ....**167** A3
Chelsea Ct SW3 ....**159** B4
Chelsea Emb SW3 ..**158** C3
Chelsea Est SW3 ...**158** A3
Chelsea Farm Ho
SW10 ....**157** C3
Chelsea Gate SW1 .**145** C1
Chelsea Gdns SW1 .**145** C1
Chelsea Harbour Design
Ctr SW10 ....**167** A4
Chelsea Harbour Dr
SW10 ....**167** A4
Chelsea Harbour Pier
SW10 ....**167** B3

Chelsea Hospl for
Women SW3 ....**144** A2
Chelsea Lo SW3 ....**159** A4
SW6 ....**166** A4
Chelsea Manor Ct
SW3 ....**158** B4
Chelsea Manor Gdns
SW3 ....**144** B1
Chelsea Manor St
SW3 ....**144** B1
Chelsea Manor Studios
SW3 ....**144** B1
Chelsea Park Gdns
SW3 ....**157** B4
Chelsea Physic Gdn★
SW3 ....**158** C4
Chelsea Reach Twr
SW10 ....**157** B2
Chelsea Sq SW3 ....**143** C1
Chelsea Twrs SW3 .**158** B4
Chelsfield Ho
SE17 ....**152** A3
Chelsfield Point 3
SW17 ....**17** C2
Chelsham Ho 1
SW4 ....**61** C4
Cheltenham Pl 1
W3 ....**37** A4
Cheltenham Rd
SE15 ....**65** B2
Cheltenham Terr
SW3 ....**145** A2
Chelverton Ct SW15 **57** C3
Chelverton Rd
SW15 ....**57** C3
Chelwood NW5 ......**12** C3
Chelwood Ct
SW11 ....**167** C4
Chelwood Gdns
TW9 ....**44** C1
Chelwood Ho 2
W2 ....**101** C1
Cheney Ho NW1 .....**84** A1
Chenies Ho 2 W4 ..**114** A4
Chenies Mews WC1 ..**93** B1
Chenies Pl NW1 .....**83** C2
Chenies St WC1 ....**105** B4
Chenies The NW1 ...**83** C2
Cheniston Gdns
W8 ....**128** A2
Chepstow Cl SW15 ..**58** A2
Chepstow Cres
W11 ....**31** C2 **113** B4
Chepstow Ct W11 ..**113** B4
Chepstow Pl
W2 ....**31** C2 **113** C4
Chepstow Rd W2 ....**31** C3
Chepstow Villas
W11 .....**31** C2 **113** B4
Chepstow Way SE15 **49** B2
Chequer St EC1 .....**97** A1
Chequers Ho NW8 ..**90** A2
Cherbury Ct N1 .....**87** C1
Cherbury St N1 .....**87** C1
Cheriton Ho 8 E5 ...**17** A3
Cherry Cl 12 SW2 ..**74** C4
Cherry Ct W3 ....**29** A1
Cherry Garden Ho
SE16 ....**40** A4
Cherry Garden Specl
Sch SE16 ....**153** C4
Cherry Garden St
SE16 ....**40** A4
Cherry Laurel Wlk
SW2 ....**62** B1

Cherry Tree Dr
SW16 ....**74** A1
Cherry Tree Ho
SE14 ....**51** B1
Cherry Tree Terr
SE1 ....**138** B4
Cherry Tree Wlk
EC1 ....**97** A1
Cherrytree Ho 8
W10 ....**22** C2
Cherrywood Cl E3 ...**26** A2
Cherrywood Dr
SW15 ....**57** C2
Chertsey Ct SW14 ..**55** A4
Chertsey Ho 2 E2 ...**98** C3
Cherwell Ho NW8 ...**89** C1
Cheryls Cl SW6 ....**166** B4
Chesham Cl SW1 ...**131** B1
Chesham Ct SW18 ..**71** C4
Chesham Flats W1 **117** C4
Chesham Mews
SW1 ....**131** B2
Chesham Pl SW1 ...**131** B1
Chesham St SW1 ...**131** B1
Cheshire St
E2 ....**24** C1 **99** B2
Chesholm Rd N16 ....**7** A1
Cheshunt Ho NW6 ..**78** A3
Chesil Ct SW3 ......**158** B4
18 E2 ....**25** B3
Chesilton Rd SW6 ..**164** C4
Chesney Ct W9 .....**23** C1
Chesney St SW11 ..**169** B3
Chessington Ho
SW8 ....**171** B2
Chester Ave TW10 ..**54** B1
Chester Ct NW1 ....**92** B4
5 SE5 ....**48** C3
Chester Gate NW1 ..**92** B3
Chester Ho N19 .....**4** A2
1 SE8 ....**51** B4
Chester Mews
SW1 ....**132** A2
Chester Pl NW1 .....**92** A4
Chester Rd NW1 ....**91** C4
N19 ....**4** A2
Chester Row SW1 ..**145** C4
Chester Sq SW1 ...**146** A4
Chester Sq Mews
SW1 ....**132** A1
Chester St E2 **24** C1 **99** C2
SW1 ....**131** C2
E2 ....**24** C4
Chester Terr NW1 ...**92** A4
Chester Way SE11 .**149** C3
Chesterfield Gdns
W1 ....**118** A2
SE10 ....**52** C3
Chesterfield Gr
SE22 ....**64** B2
Chesterfield Hill
W1 ....**118** A2
Chesterfield Ho
W1 ....**117** C2

Chesterfield Rd W4 .45 B4
Chesterfield St
W1 ....118 A2
Chesterfield Way
SE15 ....50 B3
Chesterford Gdns
NW3 ....11 A4
Chesterman St E4 .54 B2
Chesterton CI SW18 58 C2
Chesterton Ho
3 W10 ....31 A4
5 W11 ....31 C4
Chesterton Prim Sch
SW11 ....169 B3
Chesterton Rd W10 31 A4
Chesterton Sq W8 .141 B3
Chestnut Alley
SW6 ....155 A3
Chestnut Ave **11**
SW14 ....55 C4
Chestnut CI **1** N16 .6 C2
SE14 ....51 A2
Chestnut Gr SW6 .155 A4
Chestnut Gr SW12 .72 C3
Chestnut Grove Sch
SW12 ....72 C3
Chestnut Ho
7 NW3 ....12 B2
3 W4 ....38 A2
SE4 ....66 B4
SE27 ....75 B1
Chestnut Rd SE21,
SE27 ....75 B1
Chestnuts The **1**
N5 ....15 A4
Chettle CI SE1 .....137 B2
Chetwode Ho NW8 .90 A2
Chetwode Rd SW17 72 B1
Chetwynd Rd NW5 ..4 A1
Cheval Ct SW15 .....57 A3
Cheval Pl SW7 ....130 B2
Cheval St E14 ....41 C3
Chevening Rd NW6 .23 A4
NW10 ....22 B2
SE10 ....43 B1
Cheverell Ho **8** E2 .24 C3
Cheverton Rd N19 ...4 C3
Chevet St E9 ....18 A3
Chevington NW2 ...10 B2
Cheviot Ct **16** SE14 .50 B3
Cheviot Gate NW2 ...1 A2
Cheviot Gdns NW2 ...1 A2
Cheviot Ho N16 ......7 B3
Chevron CI E16 .....35 C3
Cheylesmore Ho
SW1 ....146 A2
Cheyne Gdns SW3 .158 C4
Cheyne Gdns SW3 .158 B3
Cheyne Mews SW3 .158 C4
Cheyne Row SW3 ..158 A3
Cheyne Wlk SW10 .157 B2
Cheyney Ho **2** E9 .17 C2
Chichele Rd NW2 ....9 C3
Chicheley St SE1 ..135 A4
Chichester Ho NW6 .23 C3
Chichester Rd W2 ..100 B4
NW6 ....23 C3
Chichester Rents
WC2 ....107 A2
Chichester St SW1 .147 A1
Chichester Way E14 42 C2
Chicksand St E1 ...111 B3
Chicksand St E1 ...111 B3
Chiddingstone
SE13 ....67 B2
Chiddingstone St
SW6 ....165 C2
Chigwell Hill E1 ....32 A2

Chilam Ho **5** SE15 .50 B4
Chilcombe Ho **6**
SW15 ....68 C4
Chilcot CI **11** E14 ..34 A3
Child's Pl SW5 .....141 C3
Child's St SW5 .....141 C3
Childs Wlk SW5 ....141 C3
Childeric Prim Sch
SE14 ....51 A3
Childeric Rd SE14 ..51 A3
Childerley St SW6 .164 A4
Childers St SE8 .....51 A4
Childs Hill Prim Sch
NW2 ....1 A1
Chilham Ct **14** SW9 .62 C4
Chilham Ho **1** 137 C2
Chillingworth Rd
N7 ....14 C3
Chiltern Ct NW1 ....91 A1
15 SE14 ....50 B3
Chiltern Ho **5** N16 .7 B3
4 W10 ....31 A4
SE17 ....48 C4
Chiltern Rd E3 ....26 C1
Chiltern St W1 .....103 B4
Chilton Gr SE8 ......41 A2
Chilton Rd TW9 .....54 C4
Chilton St E2 .24 B1 99 A2
Chilver St SE10 ......43 B1
Chilworth Ct **8**
SW19 ....69 C3
Chilworth Mews
W2 ....101 B1
Chilworth St W2 ...101 A1
Chimney Ct **2** E1 .32 A1
China Ct **1** E1 ......32 A1
Chindit Ho **1** N16 .15 C4
Chinnocks Wharf
E14 ....33 A2
Chip St SW4 ....61 C3
Chipka St E14 ....42 B4
Chipley St SE14 .....51 A4
Chippendale Ho
SW1 ....146 B1
Chippenham Gdns
NW6 ....23 C2
Chippenham Mews
W9 ....23 C1
Chippenham Rd W9 23 C1
Chipstead Ho **4**
SW2 ....74 B3
Chipstead St SW6 .165 C2
Chisenhale JMI Sch
E3 ....26 A3
Chisenhale Rd E3 ..26 A3
Chisholm Ct **16**
W4 ....38 C1
Chisholm Rd **13**
TW10 ....54 B1
Chislehurst Rd
TW10 ....54 A2
Chislet **5** NW5 ...12 C2
Chiswell St EC1 ....109 B4
Chiswick Comm Sch
W4 ....37 C1
Chiswick Common Rd
W4 ....38 A2
Chiswick High Rd
W4 ....36 C1
Chiswick High Road
(North Circular Rd)
W4 ....36 C1
Chiswick House★
W4 ....45 C4
Chiswick La W4 .....38 A1

Chiswick La S W4 ...46 B4
Chiswick Mall W4 ...38 B1
Chiswick Maternity
Hospl W4 ....38 B1
Chiswick Park Sta
W4 ....37 B2
Chiswick Pier W4 ...46 B3
Chiswick Plaza W4 .45 B4
Chiswick Quay W4 ..45 B2
Chiswick Rd W4 ....37 B2
Chiswick Rdbt W4 ..36 C1
Chiswick Sta W4 ....45 B3
Chiswick Sta W4 ....45 B3
Chiswick Staithe
W4 ....45 B2
Chiswick Terr **6**
W4 ....37 B2
Chiswick Village
W4 ....37 A1
Chiswick Wharf W4 .46 B4
Chitty St W1 ....105 A4
Chivalry Rd SW11 ..60 A2
Chivelston **20** SW19 69 C3
Chobham Gdns
SW19 ....69 C2
Chobham Rd E15 ...19 C3
Cholmeley Cres N6 ..4 A4
Cholmeley Lo N6 ....4 A3
Cholmeley Pk N6 ....4 A3
Cholmley Gdns
NW6 ....10 C3
Cholmondeley Ave
NW10 ....21 C3
Chopin's Ct **1** E1 .32 A1
Chopwell CI E15 ....19 C1
Choumert Gr SE15 ..49 C1
Choumert Mews
SE15 ....49 C1
Choumert Rd SE15 .49 B1
Choumert Sq **2**
SE15 ....49 C1
Chow Sq **3** E8 .....16 B3
Chrisp Ho SE10 .....53 A4
Chrisp St E14 ....34 A3
Christ Church Bentinck
CE Prim Sch NW1 102 B4
Christ Church CE JMI
Sch SE10 ....42 C1
Christ Church CE Prim
Sch
NW1 ....92 B4
SW9 ....173 C4
NW3 ....2 C1
SW3 ....158 D4
SE23 ....65 C1
Christ Church Ct
NW6 ....10 A1
NW10 ....21 A4
Christ Church JMI Sch
E1 ....111 A3
Christ Church Prim Sch
SW11 ....60 A4
Christ Church Sq **4**
E9 ....25 B4
Christ the King Coll
SE13 ....67 C4
Christ the King RC Prim
Sch N4 ....5 B3
Christ's Coll SE3 ....53 C2
Christ's Sch (East Side)
SW14 ....56 A4
Christ's Sch (West Side)
TW10 ....54 B2
Christchurch Ave
NW6 ....10 A1
Christchurch Hill
NW3 ....2 C1
Christchurch Ho **2**
SW2 ....74 B3

Christchurch Pas
NW3 ....2 B1
Christchurch Prim Sch
SW3 ....158 C4
Christchurch Rd
SW14 ....55 B2
SE27 ....74 C1
Christchurch St
SW3 ....158 C4
Christchurch Terr
SW3 ....158 C4
Christchurch Way
SE10 ....43 A1
Christian Ct SE16 ..33 B1
Christian St E1 .....111 C1
Christie **1 11** N19 ...5 A2
NW3 ....2 A2
Christie Ho **2** SE10 43 B1
Christie Rd E9 ....18 A2
Christina Sq N4 .....6 A3
Christina St EC2 ....98 A2
Christopher Boone's
Almshouses 67 C3
Christopher CI SE16 40 C4
Christopher Le N4 ...6 C4
Christopher PI NW1 .93 C3
Christopher St EC2 .97 C1
Chryssell Rd SW9 .163 C1
Chubworth St
SE14 ....51 A4
Chudleigh Rd NW6 ..9 C1
NW6 ....10 A1
SE4 ....66 C2
Chudleigh St E1 .....32 C3
Chumleigh Gdns
SE5 ....49 A4
Chumleigh St SE5 ..49 A4
Church Almshouses **8**
TW9 ....54 B3
Church App SE21 ...75 C1
Church Ave NW1 ...13 A2
SW14 ....55 C4
Church CI W8 ......128 A3
Church Cres E9 .....17 C1
Church Ct EC4 .....107 C1
Church Entry EC4 ..108 B1
Church Garth **9** N19 4 C2
Church Gate SW6 .164 B1
Church Gn SW9 ....173 C2
Church Gr SE13 ....67 A2
Church Green **1**
W4 ....38 A2
Church Mead SE5 ..48 B3
Church Path NW4 ...37 B3
Church PI SW1 .....119 A3
Church Rd NW10 ...8 A2
N1 ....15 B2
SW13 ....46 C2
SW19 ....70 A1
W4 ....37 B3
Church Row NW3 ...11 B4
Church St NW8 ......90 A1
W4 ....46 B4
Church Wlk NW2 ....1 B1
N16 ....16 A4
Churchcroft CI
SW12 ....72 C4
Churchdale Ct **1**
W4 ....37 A1
Churchfield Ho W2 .89 B1
Churchfield Mans
SW6 ....165 A1
Churchfield Rd W3 .28 B1
Churchfields SE10 ..52 B4
Churchill Ct N4 .....5 C4

Churchill Gardens Prim
Sch SW1 ....147 A1
Churchill Gdns
SW1 ....160 C4
Churchill Gdns Rd
SW1 ....160 C4
Churchill Pl E14 ....34 A1
Churchill Rd NW2 ...9 A2
NW5 ....13 A4
Churchill Wlk E9 ...17 B3
Churchmead Rd
NW10 ....8 C2
Churchward Ho
SW5 ....141 A1
SE17 ....48 A4
Churchway NW1 ....93 C4
Churchyard Row
SE11 ....150 B4
Churnfield **2** N4 ...5 C2
Churston CI **17** SW2 74 C3
Churston Mans
WC1 ....95 A1
Churton PI SW1 ...147 A3
Churton St SW1 ...147 A3
Chute Ho **10** SW9 .173 B1
Chuter Ede Ho
SW6 ....155 A3
Cicada Rd SW18 ....59 B2
Cicely Ho NW8 ......79 C1
Cicely Rd SE15 .....49 C2
Cinnamon Row **3**
SW11 ....59 B4
Cinnamon St E1 ....32 A1
Cinnamon Wharf
SE1 ....139 A4
Circle Ho **15** E14 ..34 C3
Circle The SE1 ....139 A4
Circus Lodge NW8 .89 B4
Circus Mews **1**
W1 ....102 C4
Circus PI EC2 ......109 C3
Circus St SE10 ......52 B3
Cirencester St W2 .100 A4
Cissbury Ho **6**
SE26 ....76 C1
Citizen Ho **1** N7 ..14 C4
Citizen Rd N7 ....14 C4
Citron Terr **3** SE15 65 A4
Citrus Ho **14** SE8 ...41 B1
City & Guilds of London
Art Sch The SE11 149 C1
City & Islington Coll
N4 ....5 B1
N1 ....87 B3
EC1 ....97 A3
N7 ....14 C3
N1 ....6 A2
N4 ....6 A3
City Airport Pier
E16 ....35 C2
City Banking Coll
SE1 ....138 A4
City Bsns Ctr **20**
SE16 ....40 B4
City Central Est EC1 96 C3
City Forum EC1 .....96 C4
City Garden Row
N1 ....86 B1
City Gate E1 ....25 B1
City Institute The
WC2 ....106 C2
City Literature Inst The
WC2 ....106 B2

City of London Sch
EC4 ....**122** C4
City of London Sch for
Girls EC2 ....**109** A4
City of Westminster
Coll W10 ....**23** A2
City of Westminster
Coll
W2 ....**101** B4
NW1 ....**102** B4
W9 ....**23** C2
City Rd EC1 ....**97** A4
City Thameslink Sta
EC4 ....**108** A1
City Univ The EC1 ....**96** A3
City Univerity The
EC1 ....**96** A4
Civil Service Coll
SW1 ....**119** B3
Clabon Mews SW1 ...**144** C4
Clack St SE16 ....**40** B4
Claire Ct NW2 ....**10** A2
Clairre Pl E14 ....**41** C3
Clancarty Rd SW6 ...**165** C1
Clandon Cl W3 ....**37** A4
Clandon St SE8 ....**51** C1
Clanfield Ho **12**
SW15 ....**69** A3
Clanfield Way **12**
SE15 ....**49** A3
Clanricarde Gdns
W2 ....**31** C2 **113** C3
Clapham Common*
SW4 ....**61** B4
Clapham Common North
Side SW4 ....**60** C3
Clapham Common
South Side SW4 .....**61** B2
Clapham Common Sta
SW4 ....**61** B3
Clapham Common West
Side
SW4,SW11 ....**60** C2
SW11 ....**60** C2
Clapham Court Terr **2**
SW4 ....**62** A2
Clapham Cres SW4 ..**61** C3
Clapham Ct **3** SW4 .**62** A2
Clapham High St
SW4 ....**61** C4
Clapham High Street Sta
SW4 ....**61** C4
Clapham Junction Est
SW11 ....**60** A3
Clapham Junction Sta
SW11 ....**60** A3
Clapham Manor Ct **4**
SW4 ....**61** B4
Clapham Manor Prim
Sch SW4 ....**61** B4
Clapham Manor St
SW4 ....**61** C4
Clapham Mans SW4 .**61** A1
Clapham North Sta
SW4 ....**62** A4
Clapham Park Rd
SW4 ....**61** C3
Clapham Park Sch
SW4 ....**62** A2
Clapham Park Terr **4**
SW2 ....**62** A2
Clapham Rd SW9 ...**173** A4
Clapham South Sta
SW4 ....**61** A1

Clapton Comm E5 .....**7** C4
Clapton Girls Sch
E5 ....**17** B4
Clapton Pas E5 ......**17** B3
Clapton Sq E5 ....**17** B3
Clapton Terr E5 ....**7** C1
Clapton Way E5 ....**7** C1
Clara Grant JMI Sch
E14 ....**26** C1
Clare Cl WC1 ....**94** B3
Clare Gdns **11** E5 .....**31** A3
Clare Grant Ho **8**
E14 ....**41** C4
Clare Ho SE1 ....**153** A2
Clare La N1 ....**15** B1
Clare Lawn Ave
SW14 ....**55** C2
Clare Mews SW6 ....**156** A1
Clare Mkt WC2 ....**107** A1
SE14 ....**51** B2
Clare Rd NW10 ....**8** C1
Clare St E2 ....**25** A3
Claredale Ho **3** E2 ...**25** A3
Claredale St E2 ....**24** C3
Claremont CI N1 ....**85** C1
E4 ....**9** C4
SW2 ....**74** B3
Claremont Ct **1** NW2 .**9** A2
Claremont Gr W4 .....**46** A3
Claremont Rd N6 .....**4** A4
W13 ....**21** A1
Claremont Sq N1 .....**85** B1
Claremont St SE10 ..**52** A4
Claremont Ave **1**
SW4 ....**61** C1
Clarence Gate Gdns
NW1 ....**91** A1
Clarence Gdns
NW1 ....**92** B3
Clarence Ho*
SW1 ....**119** A1
SE17 ....**48** B4
Clarence Mews **1**
1 SE16 ....**32** C1
SW12 ....**73** A4
Clarence Pas NW1 ..**84** A1
Clarence Pl **2** E5 ....**17** A3
Clarence Rd NW6 ....**10** B1
E5 ....**17** A4
W4 ....**36** C1
Richmond TW9 ....**44** C2
Clarence St **1** TW9 ..**54** A3
Clarence Terr NW1 ..**91** A2
Clarence Way NW1 ..**13** A1
Clarence Wlk SW4 ..**172** A2
Clarendon Cl W2 ...**116** A4
Clarendon Cross
W11 ....**112** B3
Clarendon Ct **1** **89** A2
NW2 ....**9** B1
1 Richmond TW9 ...**44** C2
Clarendon Dr SW15 .**57** B3
Clarendon Flats
W1 ....**103** C1
Clarendon Gdns
W9 ....**89** A1
Clarendon Gr NW1 ...**93** A4
Clarendon Ho **1**
NW1 ....**83** A1
Clarendon Mews
W2 ....**116** A4
Clarendon Pl **3** W2 .**116** A4
Clarendon Rd
W11 ....**31** A1 **112** B3
Clarendon Rise
SE13 ....**67** B3

Clarendon St SW1 ..**146** B2
Clarendon Terr W9 ..**89** A2
Clarendon Wlk **10**
W11 ....**31** A3
Clareville Ct **1** SW7 .**143** A3
Clareville Gr SW7 ..**143** A3
Clareville Grove Mews
SW7 ....**143** A3
Clareville St SW7 ..**143** A3
Clarewood Ct W1 ...**102** C3
Clarewood Wlk
SW9 ....**62** C3
Clarges Ho W1 ......**118** B2
Clarges Mews W1 ..**118** A2
Clarges St W1 ....**118** B2
Claribel Rd SW9 .....**48** A1
Claridge Ct SW6 ....**164** C3
Clarissa Ho **7** E14 ..**34** A3
Clarissa St E8 ....**24** B4
Clark Lawrence Ct **11**
SW11 ....**59** C4
Clark St E1 ....**32** B4
Clark's Pl EC2 ....**110** A2
Clarke Ho **3** SW4 ...**61** C3
Clarke Path N16 ......**7** C3
Clarkes Mews W1 ..**103** C4
Clarkson Ho SW11 ..**59** C3
Clarkson Rd E16 .....**35** B1
Clarkson Row NW1 ..**82** C1
Clarkson St E2 ....**25** A2
Classic Mans **33** E9 .**17** B1
Classinghall Ho **14**
SW15 ....**57** C1
Claude Rd SE15 ......**50** A1
Claude St E14 ....**41** C2
Claudia Jones Way
SW2 ....**62** A1
Claudia Pl SW19 .....**70** A3
Clave St E1 ....**32** B1
Clavell St **7** SE10 ...**52** B4
Claverdale Rd SW2 .**74** C4
Clavering Ave SW13 .**47** A4
Clavering Ho SE13 ..**67** C3
Claverton St SW1 ..**147** A1
Claxton Gr W6 ......**140** A2
Clay St W1 ....**103** A3
Claybank Gr SE13 ..**67** A4
Claybrook Rd W6 ...**47** C4
Claydon SE17 ....**150** C4
Clayhall Ct **16** E3 ....**26** B3
Claylands Pl SW8 ..**163** B2
Claylands Rd SW8 .**163** A3
Claypole Rd E15 .....**27** B3
Clayp003 Ave TW8 .**36** A2
Clayp003 Hospl & Day
Treatment Ctr
TW8 ....**36** A1
Clayp003 La TW8 ....**36** A1
Clays Ct N16 ....**7** B3
Clays La E15 ....**19** A3
Clays Lane Cl E15 ...**19** A3
Clayton Ct N16 ....**7** C4
Clayton Ho **2** E9 ....**17** B1
Clayton Mews SE10 .**52** C2
Clayton Rd SE15 ....**49** C2
Clayton St SE11 ....**163** B4
Clearbrook Way **3**
E1 ....**32** B3
Clearwater Ho **6**
TW10 ....**54** A2
Clearwater Terr **4**
W11 ....**39** C4
Clearwell Dr W9 .....**88** B1
Cleaver Ho **6** NW3 ..**12** B1
Cleaver Sq SE11 ...**149** C1
Cleaver St SE11 ....**149** C2

Cleeve Ho **2** **98** B3
Cleeve Workshops
E2 ....**98** B3
Clegg St **18** E1 ......**32** A1
Cleland Ho **10** E2 ...**25** B3
Clem Attlee Ct
SW6 ....**155** A3
Clematis St W12 .....**29** C2
Clemence St E14 .....**33** B4
Clement Attlee Ho
NW10 ....**8** B1
Clement Ave SW4 ...**61** C3
Clement Cl NW6 .....**9** C1
W4 ....**37** C2
Clement Ho W10 .....**30** B4
14 SE8 ....**41** A2
Clement's La EC2,
EC4 ....**123** C4
Clement's St E16 ....**40** A3
Clements Ave **1**
E16 ....**35** C2
Clements Inn WC2 .**107** A1
Clements Inn Pas
WC2 ....**107** A1
Clemson Ho **8** E8 ..**24** B4
Clenham St SE1 ...**137** A4
Clenston Mews
W1 ....**102** C2
Clent Ho **4** N16 ....**7** B3
Cleopatra's Needle*
WC2 ....**120** C3
Clephane Rd **8** N1 ..**15** B2
Clephane Rd N N1 ...**15** B2
Clephane Rd S N1 ...**15** C2
Clere Pl EC2 ....**97** C2
Clere St EC2 ....**97** C2
Clerkenwell Cl EC1 ..**95** C1
Clerkenwell Gn EC1 .**96** A1
Clerkenwell Parochial
CE Prim Sch EC1 ....**95** B4
Clerkenwell Rd EC1 .**96** A1
Clermont Rd E9 ....**25** B4
Cleve Ho NW6 ....**11** A1
Cleve Rd NW6 ....**11** A1
Clevedon Cl SW11 .**168** A4
Clevedon Ct SW11 ..**75** C1
SW11 ....**75** C1
Clevedon Mans
NW5 ....**12** C4
Cleveland Ave **4** .**38** B2
Cleveland Gdns
W2 ....**100** C1
SW13 ....**46** B1
Cleveland Gr **53** E1 .**25** B1
Cleveland Mans
SW9 ....**163** B1
5 ....**10** B1
Cleveland Mews
W1 ....**104** C4
Cleveland Pl SW1 ..**119** A2
Cleveland Rd N1 ....**15** C1
14 W4 ....**37** B3
SW13 ....**46** B1
Cleveland Row
SW1 ....**119** A1
Cleveland Sq W2 ..**100** C1
Cleveland St W1 ....**92** C1
Cleveland Terr W2 .**101** A2
Cleveland Way E1 ...**25** B1
Clevedon Cl N16 .....**7** B1
Cleverly Cotts W12 .**29** B1
Cleverly Est W12 ....**29** C2
Cley Ho SE4 ....**65** C3
Clichy Ho **2** E1 ......**32** B4
Clifden Rd E5 ....**17** C3
Cliff Ct **5** NW1 ......**13** C2

Cliff Rd NW1 ....**13** C2
Cliff Terr SE8 ....**51** C1
Cliff Villas NW1 ......**13** C2
Cliff Wlk E16 ....**35** B2
Cliffe Ho **4** SE10 ...**43** B1
Clifford Ct SW14,
TW10,TW9 ....**45** B1
Clifford Ct W2 ....**100** A3
NW10 ....**8** A4
SW18 ....**71** C4
Clifford Dr SW9 ......**63** A3
Clifford Gdns NW10 .**22** B3
Clifford Haigh Ho
SW6 ....**47** C3
Clifford Ho W14 ....**140** C3
Clifford St W1 ......**118** C3
Clifford Way NW10 ...**8** B4
Clifford's Inn Pas
EC4 ....**107** B1
Cliffsend Ho SW9 ..**173** C3
Cliffview Rd SE13 ....**66** C4
Clifton Ave W12 .....**29** B1
Clifton Cres SE15 ...**50** A3
Clifton Ct NW8 ....**89** B2
SE15 ....**50** A3
SW15 ....**57** C2
Clifton Gate SW10 **156** C4
Clifton Gdns **11** N15 .**88** C3
W4 ....**37** C2
Clifton Gr E8 ....**16** C2
Clifton Hill NW8 ......**78** C3
Clifton Ho **2** E2 ....**98** C2
Clifton Mans **4**
SW9 ....**62** C3
Clifton Pl W2 ....**101** C1
SE16 ....**40** B4
Clifton Rd W9 ....**89** A2
NW10 ....**21** C3
E16 ....**35** A4
Clifton Rise SE14 ....**51** A3
Clifton St EC2 ...**24** A1 **98** A1
Clifton Terr N4 ....**5** C2
Clifton Villas W9 ...**100** C4
Clifton Way SE15 ....**50** B3
Clinstand Ho SE1 ..**121** C2
Clinch Ct **11** E16 ....**35** C4
Cline Ho SW15 ....**56** C2
Clinger Ct N1 ....**24** A4
Clink St SE1 ....**123** B2
Clinton Rd E3 ....**26** A2
Clipper Cl **3** SE16 ..**40** C4
Clipper Ho SE14 .....**42** B1
Clipper Way SE13 ...**67** B3
Clipstone Ho **10**
SW15 ....**68** A3
Clipstone Mews
W1 ....**104** C4
Clipstone St W1 ....**104** C4
Clissold Cres N16 ..**15** C4
Clissold Ct N4 ....**6** B2
Clissold Ho **4** N16 ..**6** C2
Clissold Rd N16 ......**6** C1
Clitheroe Rd SW9 ..**172** B1
Clive Ho **2** **43** C2
Clive Ct W9 ....**89** A2
SE10 ....**52** B4
Clive Rd SE21,SE27 .**75** C1
Cliveden Pl SW1 ...**145** B4
Cloak La EC4 ....**123** A4
Clochar Ct NW10 ....**21** B4
Clock Ho N16 ....**7** C4
Clock Tower Mews
N1 ....**87** A3
Clock Tower Pl N7 ...**14** A2

Clockhouse Cl SW19 ....69 B2
Clockhouse Pl SW15 ....58 A1
Clockhouse The SW19 ....69 B1
Cloister Rd NW2 ....1 B2
W3 ....28 B4
Cloisters Ct N6 .....4 A4
Cloisters The SW9 ..173 C3
Clonbrock Rd N16 ..16 A4
Cloncurry St SW6 ...47 C1
Clone Ct W12 ....38 A3
Clonmel Rd SW6 ...165 A4
Clonmore St SW18 ..70 B3
Clorane Gdns NW3 ...1 C1
Close The TW9 ......55 A4
Cloth Ct EC1 ....108 B3
Cloth Fair EC1 .....108 B3
Cloth St EC1 ....108 C4
Clothier St EC3 ....110 B2
Cloudesdale Rd SW17 ....73 A2
Cloudesley Mans N1 ....85 C3
Cloudesley Pl N1 ...85 C3
Cloudesley Rd N1 ...85 C3
Cloudesley Sq N1 ...85 C3
Cloudesley St N1 ...85 C3
Clove Cres E14 .....34 C2
Clovelly Ct NW2 ....9 B3
Clovelly Ho W2 ....100 C2
Clovelly Way E1 ....32 B3
Clover Mews SW3 ..159 A4
Clowes Ho 3 SW4 ..62 A3
Cloysters Gn E1 ...125 B2
Club Row 2 E2 ....24 B1 98 C2
Clunbury St N1 .....87 C1
Clunie Ho SW1 ....131 A2
Cluny Mews SW5 ...141 B3
Cluny Pl SE1 ......138 A2
Cluse Ct N1 ....86 C2
Clutton St E14 .....34 A4
Clyde Ct NW1 ......83 C2
Clyde Flats SW6 ..154 C2
Clyde St SE8 ....51 B4
Clydesdale Gdns TW10 ....55 A3
Clydesdale Ho 3 W11 ....31 B3
Clydesdale Rd W11 .31 B3
Clynes Ho 3 E2 ...25 C2
N1 ....15 B1
Clyston St SW8 ....171 A2
Coach & Horses Yd W1 ....118 C4
Coach House La N5 ..15 A4
SW19 ....69 C1
Coach House Yd NW3 ....11 C4
Coal Wharf Rd W12 .30 C1
Coalbrook Mans 3 SW12 ....73 A4
Coaldale Wlk SE21 .75 B4
Coalecroft Rd SW15 57 B2
Coalport Ho SE11 ..149 B4
Coate St E2 ....24 C3
Coates Ct NW3 .....12 A3
Coates Wlk TW8 ...36 A1
Cobb's Ct EC4 .....108 B1
Cobb's Hall 1 SW6 .47 C4
Cobbett St SW8 ....163 A1
Cobble Mews N4,N5 .6 B1

Cobbold Ct SW1 ...147 B4
Cobbold Mews W12 .38 B4
Cobbold Rd NW10 ...8 B2
W12 ....38 B4
Cobden Bldgs WC1 ..94 C4
Cobden Ho 5 NW1 ..82 C2
E2 ....99 C4
Cobham Cl SW11 ...60 A1
Cobham Mews 3 NW1 ....13 C1
Coborn Rd E3 ......26 B2
Coborn St E3 ......26 B2
Cobourg Jun & Inf Sch SE5 ....49 B4
Cobourg Rd SE5 ....49 B4
Cobourg St NW1 ....93 A3
Coburg Cl SW1 ....147 A4
Coburg Cres SW2 ..74 C3
Coburg Dwellings 10 E1 ....32 B2
Coburn Mews 6 E1 .25 A1
Cochrane Cl NW8 ...79 C1
Cochrane Mews NW8 ....79 C1
Coci Ho W14 ......141 A3
Cock Hill E1 ......110 B3
Cock La EC1 ....108 B3
Cockburn Ho SW1 .147 C1
Cockpit Yd WC1 ...107 A4
Cockspur Ct SW1 ..119 C2
Cockspur St SW1 ..119 C2
Coda Ctr The SW6 .164 B4
Code St E1 ....24 B1 99 A1
Codicote Ho 5 SE8 .40 C2
Codicote Terr N4 ...6 B2
Codling Cl E1 .....125 C2
Codrington Ct SE16 .33 A1
Codrington Ho 7 E1 ....25 A1
Codrington Mews W11 ....31 A3
Cody Rd E16 ....27 C1
Cohen Lo E15 ......19 C4
Coity Rd NW5 .....12 C2
Coke St E1 ....111 C2
Cokers La SE21 ....75 C3
Colas Mews 7 NW6 23 C4
Colbeck Mews SW5 ....142 B3
Colbeck Rd W14 ...140 A4
Colberg Pl N16 .....7 B4
Colborne Ho 8 E14 .33 C2
Colchester Ho 3 SW8 ....171 B2
Colchester St E1 ...111 A2
Coldbath Sq EC1 ...95 B3
Coldbath St SE13 ...52 A1
Coldblow La SE14 ..50 C4
Coldharbour E14 ...34 B1
Coldharbour Ind Est SE5 ....48 B1
Coldharbour La SW9 ....63 A4
Coldharbour Pl SE5 48 C1
Coldstream Gdns SW18 ....58 B1
Cole Ho SE1 ......135 C3
Cole St SE1 ....137 A3
Colebert Ave E1 ....25 B1
Colebert Ho 9 E1 ..25 B1
Colebrook Cl SW19 .70 C4
Colebrook Ct SW3 .144 B3

Colebrook Ho 1 E14 ....34 A3
Colebrooke Pl N1 ...86 B3
Colebrooke Rd NW10 .8 B2
W12 ....38 B4
Colebrooke Row N1 ....86 B3
Colebrooke Sch N1 ..86 B2
Coleby Path 21 SE5 .48 C3
Colechurch Ho 4 SE1 ....153 B1
Coleford Rd SW18 ..59 B2
Colegrave Prim Sch E15 ....19 C3
Colegrave Rd E15 ..19 C3
Colegrove Rd SE15 .49 B4
Coleherne Ct SW5 ....142 B2
Coleherne Mans SW5 ....142 B3
Coleherne Mews SW10 ....142 A2
Coleherne Rd SW10 ....142 A1
Colehill Gdns SW6 .164 A3
Colehill La SW6 ...164 B4
Coleman Ct SW18 ..70 C4
Coleman Fields N1 ..87 A4
Coleman Mans N19 ..5 A4
Coleman Rd SE5 ....49 A3
Coleman St EC2 ...109 B2
Coleman St Bldgs EC2 ....109 B2
Colenso Rd E5 .....17 B4
Coleraine Rd SE3 ..53 B4
Coleridge Cl SW8 .170 B1
Coleridge Ct W14 ..39 C3
Coleridge Gdns NW6 ....11 B1
Coleridge Ho SW1 .147 A1
SE17 ....151 A2
Coleridge Prim Sch N8 ....4 C4
Coleridge Rd N4,N7 .5 C2
Coles Ct SW11 ....167 C3
Colestone Ct SE15 ..49 C2
Coleshill Flats SW1 ....145 C3
Colestown St SW11 ....168 B2
Colet Gdns W14 ....39 C2
Colet Ho SE17 .....150 B1
Colette Ct 8 SE16 .40 C4
Coley St WC1 ......95 A1
Colfe & Hatchcliffe's Glebe Sch 2 SE13 ....67 A2
Colfe Rd SE23 .....66 A1
Colin Blanchard Ho SE4 ....51 C1
Colin Ct SW16 .....73 C2
Colin Rd NW10 .....9 A2
Colin Winter Ho 17 E1 ....25 B1
Colinette Rd SW15 ..57 B3
Colinsdale N1 ......86 A3
Coliston Pass SW18 .70 C4
Coliston Rd SW18 ..70 C4
Coll of NW London (Willesden Centre) The NW10 ....22 B4
Coll Sharp Ct 20 E2 .98 C3
Collamore Ave SW18 ....72 A3
Collard Pl NW1 .....13 A1
College App SE10 ..52 B4
College Cl E5 ......17 B3
College Cres NW3 ..11 C2

College Cross N1 ...14 C1
College Ct SW3 ....145 A1
NW3 ....11 C2
6 W6 ....39 B1
College Gdns SW17 .72 A3
SE21 ....76 A3
College Gr 1 NW1 ..83 B4
College Hill EC4 ...123 A4
College La NW5 ....13 A4
College Park Cl SE13 ....67 C3
College Park Sch W2 ....100 A1
College Pl NW1 ....83 A3
SW10 ....156 C2
College Rd NW10 ..22 B2
SE19,SE21 .....76 A2
College St EC4 ....123 A4
College Terr E3 ....26 B2
Collent Ho 10 E9 ...17 B2
Collent St E9 ......17 B2
Colley Ho 12 N7 ...13 C3
Collier St N1 ....84 C1
Collingbourne Rd W12 ....30 A1
Collingham Gdns SW5 ....142 B3
Collingham Pl SW5 ....142 B3
Collingham Rd SW5 ....142 B4
Collington Ho 27 E1 ....25 A1
Collingwood Ho 24 E1 ....25 A1
Collins Ct E8 ......16 C2
Collins Ho 4 E14 ..34 B2
5 SE10 ....43 B1
Collins Rd N5,N16 ..15 B4
Collins Sq SE3 .....53 B1
Collins St SE3 .....53 A1
Collins Yd N1 ......86 A3
Collinson Ct SE1 ..136 C3
Collinson Ho 13 SE15 ....49 C3
Collinson St SE1 ..136 C3
Collinson Wlk SE1 .136 C3
Collyer Pl SE15 ....49 C2
Colman Wharf 5 E14 ....34 A4
Colmar Ct 5 E2 ...25 C1
Colnbrook St SE1 ..136 A2
Colne Ho NW8 .....89 C1
Colne Rd E5 ....18 A4
Cologne Rd SW11 ..59 C3
Colomb St SE10 ....43 A1
Colombo St SE1 ...122 A1
Colonades The 2 SE5 ....48 C2
Colonial Dr W4 ....37 B2
Colonnade WC1 ....94 B1
Colonnades The 2 E8 ....17 A2
Colonnade The W9 ....88 C3
Colroy Ct 3 NW6 ..10 A1
Colston Rd SW14 ..55 B3
Colthurst Cres N4 ...6 B2
Coltman Ho 1 E14 .33 A3
SE10 ....52 B4
Columba Ho SE14 ..51 B2
Columbia Ho 3 E3 .26 C2
Columbia JMI Sch

Columbia Point 7 SE16 ....40 B3
Columbia Rd E2 ....98 C4
E2 ....24 B2 99 A4
Colverson Ho 10 E1 .32 B4
Colvestone Cres E8 .16 B3
Colville Ho 2 E2 ...25 B1
W11 ....31 B3
Colville Mews W11 .31 B3
Colville Pl W1 ....105 A3
Colville Prim Sch W11 ....31 B3
Colville Rd W11 ...31 B3
W3 ....37 A3
Colville Sq W11 ...31 B3
Colville Terr W11 ..31 B3
Colwall Ho SW9 ...173 A1
Colwell Rd SE22 ...64 B2
Colwick Cl N6 .....4 C4
Colwith Rd W6 ....47 B4
Colworth Gr SE17 .151 A3
Colwyn Ho SE1 ...135 B1
Colyton Rd SE22 ..65 A2
Com Coll Sixth Form Ctr The E9 ....17 C2
Combe Ave SE3 ....53 B3
Combe Ho 22 W2 ..31 C4
SW14 ....45 B1
Combe Mews 4 SE3 ....53 B3
Combe The NW1 ...92 B3
Combedale Rd SE10 43 C1
Combemartin Rd SW18 ....70 A3
Comber Gr 2 SE5 ..48 B3
Comber Grove Jun & Inf Sch SE5 ....48 B3
Comber Ho SE5 ....48 B3
Combermere Rd SW9 ....62 B4
Comeragh Mews W14 ....140 B1
Comeragh Rd W14 140 B1
Comerford Rd SE4 .66 B3
Comet Pl SE8 ......51 C3
Comet St SE8 ......51 C3
Comins Ho SW4 ....61 B2
Commercial Rd E1 .111 C2
E1 ....32 B3
Commercial St E1 ..110 C4
Commercial Way NW10 ....20 A3
SE15 ....49 C3
Commerell Pl SE10 .43 B1
Commerell St SE10 .43 A1
Commodore Ct SE8 .51 C2
Commodore Ho 7 E14 ....34 B2
Commodore St E1 ..26 A1
Common Rd SW13 ..56 C4
Common View SW15 ....57 B4
Commondale SW15 .57 B4
Commonwealth Ave 21 W12 ....30 A2
Community Coll The E9 ....17 C2
E9 ....25 C3

Community Rd E15 ...19 C3
Compania Bldg
E1 ....32 C2
Compass Ct SE1 ...124 C1
Compass Ho ...100 A1
SE8 ....52 A1
Compass Point
E14 ....33 C2
Compayne Gdns
NW6 ....11 A1
Compton Ave N6 ...3 A4
N1 ....15 A2
Compton Cl NW1 ...92 B3
Compton Cres W4 ...45 B4
Compton Ho SW11 168 A4
Compton Pas EC1 ...96 B2
Compton Pl WC1 ...94 A2
Compton Rd N1 ...15 A2
NW10 ....22 C2
Compton St EC1 ...96 B2
Compton Terr N1 ...15 A2
Comus Ho SE17 ...152 A3
Comus Pl SE17 ...152 A3
Comyn Rd SW11 ...60 A3
Comyns Cl E16 ...35 B2
Conant Ho SE11 ...148 A4
Conant Mews E1 ...125 B4
Concanon Rd SW2,
SW4 ....62 B3
Concert Hall App
SE1 ....121 A1
Concord Bsns Ctr
W3 ....28 A4
Concord Ctr W12 ...39 C4
Concord Rd W3 ...20 A1
Concordia Wharf
E14 ....34 B1
Condell Rd SW8 ...171 A4
Conder St E14 ...33 A3
Condray Pl SW11 ...158 A1
Conduit Ct WC2 ...120 A4
Conduit Ho SE10 ...52 C2
Conduit Mews W2 ...101 B1
Conduit Pas W2 ...101 B1
Conduit Pl W2 ...101 B1
Conduit St W1 ...118 C4
Conewood St N5 ...6 A1
Coney Acre SE21 ...75 B3
Coney Way SW8 ...163 A3
Congers Ho SE8 ...51 C3
Congreve Ho
N16 ....16 A3
Congreve St SE17 ...152 A3
Conifer Ct SW19 ...69 C3
Conifer Gdns SW16 ...74 B1
Conifer Ho SE4 ...66 B3
Coniger Rd SW6 ...165 B2
Coningham Ct
SW10 ....157 A2
Coningham Mews
W12 ....29 C1
Coningham Rd W12 ...39 A4
Coningsby Rd N4 ...6 A4
Conington Rd SE13 ...52 B1
Conisbrough NW1 ...82 C3
Coniston NW1 ...92 C4
Coniston Cl W4 ...45 B3
SW13 ....46 B3
Coniston Ct W2 ...102 B1
SE16 ....40 C4
Coniston Ho E3 ...26 B2
SE5 ....48 B3
Coniston Wlk E9 ...17 B3

Conistone Way N7 ...14 A1
Conlan St W10 ...23 A1
Conley Rd NW10 ...8 A2
Conley St SE10 ...43 A1
Connaught Ave
SW14 ....55 B3
Connaught Cl W2 ...102 A1
Connaught Ho W1 ...118 A3
NW10 ....22 A2
Richmond TW10 ...54 A2
Connaught Lo N4 ...5 C4
Connaught Mans
SW6 ....164 B3
SW11 ....168 B3
N16 ....15 C4
SW9 ....62 C3
Connaught Pl W2 ...102 C1
Connaught Rd N4 ...5 C4
NW10 ....21 A3
Richmond TW10 ...54 B2
Connaught Sq W2 ...102 C1
Connaught St W2 ...102 B1
Connell Ct SE14 ...50 C4
Connett Ho E2 ...25 A3
Connor Ct SW11 ...170 A3
Connor St E9 ...25 C4
Conrad Ho SW8 ...162 A2
N16 ....16 A3
SE16 ....33 A2
Cons St SE1 ...135 C4
Consort Ho W2 ...114 B3
Consort Lo NW8 ...80 C3
Consort Rd SE15 ...50 A1
Constable Ct
SE16 ....40 A1
Constable Ho NW3 ...12 B1
Constable Wlk SE21 ...76 A1
Constant Ho E14 ...34 A2
Constantine Ho
SW2 ....75 A3
Constantine Rd
NW3 ....12 A4
Constitution Hill
SW1,W1 ....132 B4
Consul Ho E3 ...26 C1
Content St SE17 ...151 B3
Convent Gdns W11 ...31 B3
Convent of Jesus &
Mary CE Inf Sch
NW2 ....9 B2
Convent of Jesus &
Mary Language Coll for
Girls The NW10 ...21 B4
Convent of the Sacred
Heart Digby-Stuart
Coll SW15 ....56 B2
Conway Gr W3 ...28 C4
Conway Ho SW3 ...144 C2
SW2 ....74 A4
Conway Mews W1 ...92 C1
Conway St W1 ...92 C1
Conybeare NW3 ...12 A1
Conyer St E3 ...26 A3
Cook's Rd E15 ...27 A3
Cookham Cres SE16 ...40 C4
Cookham Ho E2 ...98 C2
Coomassie Rd W9 ...23 B1
Coombe Ho N7 ...13 C3
Coomber Ho SW6 ...59 A4
Coombs St N1 ...86 B1
Coomer Mews
SW6 ....155 A3
Coomer Pl SW6 ...155 A3
Cooper Cl SE1 ...135 C3
Cooper Ct E15 ...76 B3
Cooper Ho NW8 ...89 B1

Cooper Rd NW10 ...8 C3
Cooper St E16 ...35 B2
Cooper's Ct SE1 ...153 A2
Cooper's Row
EC3 ....124 C4
Cooperage The
SE1 ....124 C1
Coopers Cl E1 ...25 B1
Coopers La NW1 ...83 C2
Coopersale Rd E9 ...17 C3
Cope Ho EC1 ...97 A3
Cope Pl W8 ...127 B1
Cope St SE16 ...40 C2
Cope Yd E1 ...125 C2
Copeland Dr E14 ...41 C2
Copeland Ho SE11 ...135 A1
Copeland Rd SE15 ...50 A1
Copenhagen Ho N1 ...85 B3
Copenhagen Pl E14 ...33 B3
Copenhagen Prim Sch
N1 ....84 C3
Copenhagen St N1 ...84 C3
Copford Wlk N1 ...86 C4
Copleston Rd SE15 ...64 B4
Copley Cl SE17 ...48 A4
Copley St E1 ...32 C4
Copnor Way
SE15 ....49 A3
Coppedhall SE21 ...75 C2
Copper Beech N6 ...3 C4
Copperas St SE8 ...52 A4
Copperfield Ho
SE1 ....139 B3
Copperfield St
SE1 ....136 A4
Copperfields Ct W3 ...36 C4
Coppice Dr SW15 ...57 A1
Coppin Ho SW2 ...75 A3
Coppock Cl SW11 ...168 A1
Copse Ct SW15 ...58 A2
Copthall Ave EC2 ...109 C2
Copthall Bldgs
EC2 ....109 C2
Copthall Cl EC2 ...109 B2
Copthorne Ave
SW12 ....73 C3
Coptic St WC1 ...106 A3
Copton Cl E3 ...33 C4
Coral Ho E1 ...26 A1
Coral St SE1 ...135 C3
Coram Ho WC1 ...94 A2
W4 ....38 A1
Coram St WC1 ...94 A1
Corbden Cl SE15 ...49 B2
Corbet Ct EC3 ...109 C1
Corbet Ho N1 ...85 B3
Corbet Pl E1 ...110 C4
Corbett Ho SW10 ...156 C2
Corbett's La SE16 ...40 B2
Corbiere Ho N1 ...24 A4
Corbin Ho E3 ...27 A2
Corbridge Cres E2 ...25 A3
Corby Ho NW10 ...20 C3
Corby Way E3 ...26 C1
Corbyn St N4,N19 ...5 A3
Cord Way E14 ...41 C3
Cordelia Cl SE24 ...63 A3
Cordelia Ho N1 ...24 A3
Cordelia St E14 ...34 A3
Cording St E14 ...34 A4
Cordova Rd E3 ...26 A2
Cordwainers Coll
E8 ....17 A1
Cordwainers Ct
Corfe Ho SW8 ...162 C2

Corfe Lo SE21 ...75 C2
Corfe Twr W3 ...37 B4
Corfield St E2 ...25 A2
Coriander Ave E14 ...34 C3
Corinne Rd N19 ...13 B4
Cork Sq E1 ...32 A1
Cork St W1 ...118 C3
Cork St Mews W1 ...118 C3
Corlett St NW1 ...102 A4
Cormont Rd SE5 ...48 A2
Cormorant Ct
SE8 ....51 B4
SE21 ....75 C2
Cornbury Ho SE8 ...51 B4
Cornelia St N7 ...14 B2
Corner Gn SE3 ...53 C1
Corner House St
WC2 ....120 A2
Cornerways SW6 ...154 A4
Corney Rd W4 ...46 A4
Corney Reach Way
W4 ....46 A3
Cornflower Terr
SE22 ....65 A1
Cornford Gr SW12 ...73 A2
Cornhill EC3 ...109 C1
Cornick Ho SE16 ...40 A3
Cornish Ho
Brentford TW8 ...36 B1
SE17 ....48 A4
Cornmill La SE13 ...67 B4
Cornmow Dr NW10 ...8 C3
Cornwall Ave E2 ...25 B2
Cornwall Cres
W11 ....112 A4
W11 ....31 A3
Cornwall Gdns
SW7 ....128 B1
NW10 ....9 A2
Cornwall Gdns Wlk
SW7 ....128 B1
Cornwall Gr W4 ...38 A1
Cornwall Ho NW1 ...91 A1
SW15 ....69 B4
Cornwall Mans
NW1 ....91 A1
SW10 ....157 A2
Cornwall Mews S
SW7 ....128 C1
Cornwall Mews W
SW7 ....128 B1
Cornwall Rd SE1 ...135 C4
N4 ....5 C4
N15,N4 ....? A2
Cornwall Sq SE11 ...150 A2
Cornwall St E1 ...32 A2
Cornwall Terr NW1 ...91 A1
Cornwall Terr Mews
NW1 ....91 A1
Cornwallis Ct SW8 ...172 A4
Cornwallis Ho
W12 ....30 A2
Cornwallis Rd N19 ...5 A2
Cornwallis Sq N19 ...5 A2
Cornwood Dr E1 ...32 B3
Coronation Ave
N16 ....16 B4
Coronation Ct W10 ...30 B4
Coronet St N1 ...98 A3
Corporation Row
EC1 ....95 C2
Corporation St N7 ...14 A3
Corpus Christi RC Prim
Sch SW2 ....62 B2
Corrance Rd SW2,
SW4 ....62 A3
Corringham Ct NW11 ...1 C4

Corringham Ho
E1 ....32 C3
Corringham Rd
NW11 ....1 C4
Corringway NW11 ...2 A4
Corry Ho E14 ...34 A2
Corseley Way E9 ...18 B2
Corsham St N1 ...97 C3
Corsica St N5 ...15 A2
Cortis Rd SW15 ...57 A1
Cortis Terr SW15 ...57 A1
Corunna Rd SW8 ...171 A4
Corunna Terr SW8 ...170 C4
Corvette Sq SE10 ...52 C4
Coryton Path W9 ...23 B1
Cosbycote Ave SE24 ...63 B2
Cosgrove Ho E2 ...24 C4
Cosmo Pl WC1 ...106 B4
Cosmur Cl W12 ...38 B3
Cossall Wlk SE15 ...50 A2
Cosser St SE1 ...135 B2
Costa St SE15 ...49 C1
Coston Wlk SE4 ...65 C3
Cosway Mans NW1 ...102 B4
Cosway St NW1 ...102 B4
Cotall St E14 ...33 C3
Cotes Ho NW8 ...90 A1
Cotham St SE17 ...151 A3
Cotherstone Rd
SW2 ....74 B3
Cotleigh Rd NW6 ...10 C1
Cotman Cl SW15 ...57 C2
Cotman Ho NW8 ...80 A2
Cotswold Ct EC1 ...96 C2
Cotswold Gate NW2 ...1 A3
Cotswold Ho N16 ...7 B3
Cotswold Mews
SW11 ....167 C3
Cottage Gn SE5 ...48 C3
Cottage Gr SW9 ...62 A4
Cottage Pl SW3 ...130 A1
Cottage St E14 ...34 A2
Cottage Wlk N16 ...7 B1
SE15 ....49 B2
Cottenham Ho
N19 ....5 A2
Cottesbrook St
SE14 ....51 A3
Cottesloe Ho NW8 ...90 A2
Cottesloe Mews
SE1 ....135 C2
Cottesmore Ct
W8 ....128 B2
Cottesmore Gdns
W8 ....128 B2
Cottingham Rd
SW8 ....163 A2
Cottington St SE11 ...150 A2
Cotton Ave W3 ...28 C3
Cotton Ho W12 ...38 B4
SW2 ....74 A4
Cotton Row SW11 ...59 C4
Cotton St E14 ...34 B2
Cotton's Gdn E2 ...98 B4
Cottons La SE1 ...123 C2
Couchman Ho
SW4 ....61 B1
Coulgate St SE4 ...66 A4
Coulson St SW3 ...144 C2
Coulter Rd W6 ...39 A3
Coults Cres NW5 ...3 C1
Councillor St SE5 ...48 B3
Counter Ct SE1 ...123 B2
Counter St SE1 ...124 A1
Counters Ct W14 ...126 B2
Countess Rd NW5 ...13 B3

Countisbury Ho
  SE26 ....76 C1
County Gr SE5 ....48 B2
County Pk SW9 ....173 B4
County St SE1 ....137 A1
Courier Ho 17 SW2 ....74 C4
Courland Gr SW8 ......171 C3
Courland St SW8 ......171 C3
Court Gdns N7 ....14 C2
Court La SE21 ....76 A4
Court Lane Gdns
  SE21 ....76 A4
Court Mans ⑥ W6 ......38 C2
Court Royal SW15 ......58 A2
Court St E1 ....96 A2
Court Way W3 ....28 C4
Courtauld Ho 11 E2 ..24 C3
Courtauld Inst of Art★
  W1 ....103 A2
  WC2 ....120 C4
Courtauld Rd N19 ......5 A3
Courtenay Ave N6 ......3 A4
Courtenay Sq 14 SE11 149 B1
Courtenay St SE11 ..149 B2
Courtfield Gdns
  SW5 ....142 B3
Courtfield Ho 1 EC1 ..107 B4
Courtfield Mews
  SW7 ....142 B3
Courtfield Rd SW7 ..142 C3
Courthill Rd SE13 ......67 B3
Courthope Ho
  SW8 ....162 A1
  16 SE16 ....40 B3
Courthope Rd SW3 ..12 B4
Courtlands SW10 ......54 C2
Courtlands Ave
  TW9 ....45 A1
Courtmead Cl SE24 ....63 B1
Courtnell St W2 ....31 C3
Courtney Ct N7 ....14 C3
Courtney Ho N14 ....4 C3
Courtrai Rd SE23 ......66 A1
Courtville Ho 9
  W10 ....23 A2
Courtyard The
  SW6 ....164 A3
  N1 ....14 B1
  18 SW18 ....59 C3
Cousin La EC4 ....123 B3
Couzens Ho 3 E3 ......33 B4
Coval Gdns SW14 ......55 A3
Coval La SW14 ....55 A3
Coval Rd SW14 ....55 A3
Covent Garden Sta
  WC2 ....106 B1
Coventry Cl NW6 ......23 C4
Coventry Rd E1 ....25 A1
Coventry St W1 ....119 B3
Coverdale Rd NW6 ......9 C1
Coverdale Rd NW2 ....10 A2
  W12 ....39 A4
Coverham Ho 5
  SE4 ....65 C3
Coverley Cl E1 ....111 C4
Coverley Point
  SE11 ....148 C3
Cowcross St EC1 ......108 A4
Cowdenbeath Path
  N1 ....84 C4
Cowdry Hall Coll of
  Nursing W1 ....104 A2
Cowdray Ho 23
  SE22 ....64 A4
Cowdry Rd E9 ....18 B2

Cowley Rd SW9 ....173 C4
  W3 ....29 B1
Cowley St SW1 ....134 A1
Cowling Cl W11 ....112 A2
Cowper Ho SW1 ......147 C1
  SE17 ....151 A2
Cowper Rd N16 ....16 A4
  W3 ....28 C1
Cowper St EC1,EC2 ..97 C2
Cowper Terr W10 ......30 C4
Cowper's Ct EC3 ......109 C1
Coxhoe Rd 5
  SW8 ....171 C4
Cox Ho W6 ....154 A4
Cox's Ct E1 ....110 C3
Coxson Way SE1 ......138 C3
Coysh Ct 5 SW15 ......58 A2
Crabtree Ct E15 ....18 C4
Crabtree Ct E15 ....19 C3
Crabtree Hall SW6 ....47 B3
Crabtree La SW6 ......47 C3
Craddock St NW5 ....12 C2
Craig's Ct SW1 ....120 A2
Craigie Ho EC1 ....43 C3
Craigleith SW15 ....57 C1
Craignair Rd SW2 ....74 C4
Craik Ct NW6 ....23 B3
Crail Row SE17 ....151 C3
Cramer St W1 ....103 C3
Crammond Cl W6 ......154 A3
Crampton Jun & Inf Sch
  SE17 ....150 B2
Crampton St SE17 ..150 C2
Cranbourn Alley
  WC2 ....119 C4
Cranbourn Ho 4
  SE16 ....40 A4
Cranbourn St SE16 ..119 C4
Cranbourne Ct
  SW11 ....158 B2
Cranbourne Rd E15 ..76 B4
Cranbrook Ho 11
  E5 ....17 A3
  8 W6 ....39 B1
Cranbrook Rd W4 ....38 A1
  SE8 ....51 C2
Cranbrook St E2 ....25 C3
Cranbury Rd SW6 ....166 B1
Crandale Ho 8 E5 ....17 A3
Crandley Ct SE8 ....41 A2
Crane Ave W3 ....28 B2
Crane Ct EC4 ....107 C1
  7 W12 ....38 A4
Crane Gr N7 ....14 C2
Crane Ho 22 E3 ....26 B3
  9 SE15 ....49 B2
Crane Mead SE16 ....40 C2
Crane St SE15 ....49 B2
Cranfield Ct NW1 ....102 B3
Cranfield Rd SE4 ......66 B4
Cranfield Cotts 8
  E1 ....32 C2
Cranford Lo SW19 ....69 C2
Cranford St E1 ....32 C2
Cranhurst Rd NW2 ....9 B3
Cranleigh W11 ....31 B2
Cranleigh Ct 4 N16 ..7 A3
  Richmond TW9 ......54 C4
Cranleigh Hos NW1 ..83 A1
Cranleigh Mews
  SW11 ....168 B1
Cranleigh St NW1 ....83 A1
Cranley Gdns SW7 ..143 B2
Cranley Mews
  SW7 ....143 A2

Cranley Pl SW7 ....143 B3
Cranmer Ct SW3 ......144 B3
Cranmer Ho SW11 ..168 A4
Cranmer Rd SW9 ......163 C2
Cranswick Rd SE16 ..40 A1
Cranwell Cl E3 ....27 A1
Cranwich Rd N16 ......7 A4
Cranwood Ct EC1 ....97 C3
Cranwood St EC1 ....97 C3
Cranworth Gdns
  SW9 ....173 B4
Cranworth Ho 6
  N7 ....14 B4
Craster Rd SW2 ....74 C4
Craston Ho 2 SE5 ....49 A1
Craven Cl N16 ....7 C4
Craven Cottage (Fulham
  FC) SW6 ....47 C2
Craven Ct NW10 ......21 A4
Craven Hill W2 ....115 A4
Craven Hill Gdns
  W2 ....114 C4
Craven Hill Mews
  W2 ....115 A4
Craven Ho 2 SW14 ..55 C4
Craven Lo 2 W2 ......115 A4
  SW6 ....47 C2
Craven Mews 6
  SW11 ....60 C4
Craven Park Mews
  NW10 ....21 A4
Craven Park Rd
  NW10 ....21 A4
Craven Pas WC2 ......120 A2
Craven Pk NW10 ......21 A4
Craven Rd W2 ....101 A1
  NW10 ....20 C4
Craven St W2 ....120 A2
Craven Terr W2 ....115 A4
Craven Wlk E5,N16 ....7 C4
Crawford Bldgs
  NW1 ....102 B3
Crawford Jun & Inf Sch
  SE5 ....48 B2
Crawford Mews
  W1 ....102 C3
Crawford Pas EC1 ....95 C1
Crawford Pl W1 ......102 B3
Crawford Place
  Dwellings NW1 ....102 B3
Crawford Point 4
  E16 ....35 B1
Crawford Rd SE5 ....48 B1
Crawford St W1 ......102 C3
Crawshay Ct SW9 ..173 C4
Crawshay Ho 2
  N16 ....15 C4
Crawthew Gr SE22 ..64 B3
Crayford Ho SE1 ......137 C3
  N7 ....14 A4
Crayford Rd N7 ....14 A4
Crayle Ho EC1 ....96 B2
Crealock St SW18 ....59 A1
Creasy Est SE1 ....138 A1
Crebor St SE22 ....64 C1
Credenhill Ho 2
  SE15 ....50 A3
Crediton Hill NW6 ....11 A3
Crediton Rd NW10 ..22 B4
  E16 ....35 C3
Credon Rd SE16 ....40 A1
Creechurch La
  EC3 ....110 B1
Creechurch Pl EC3 ..110 B1
Creed Ho SE15 ....65 A4
Creed La EC4 ....108 B1

Creek Ho W14 ....126 B2
Creek Rd SE10,SE8 ..52 A4
Creekside SE8 ....52 A3
Crefeld Cl W6 ....154 A3
Creighton Rd NW10 ..22 B3
Creighton Rd NW6 ..22 C3
Cremer Bsns Ctr 8
  E2 ....24 B3
Cremer Ho 9 SE8 ....51 C3
Cremer St E2 ....24 B3
Cremorne Rd
  SW10 ....157 B2
Creon Ct SW9 ....173 B4
Crescent EC3 ....124 C4
Crescent Ct SW4 ....61 C2
Crescent Gdns
  SW19 ....70 C1
Crescent Gr SW4 ....61 B3
Crescent Ho SE13 ..52 A1
Crescent La SW4 ......61 C2
Crescent Mans
  W11 ....112 B4
  N5 ....15 A3
Crescent Pl SW3 ....144 B4
Crescent Row EC1 ..96 C1
Crescent St N1 ....14 B1
Crescent Stables
  SW15 ....58 A2
Crescent The W3 ......29 A3
Crescent The SW13 ..46 C1
  SW19 ....70 C1
Crescent Way SE4 ..66 C4
Crescent Wood Rd
  SE21,SE26 ....76 C1
Cresford Rd SW6 ....166 A3
Cressage Ho 9
  TW8 ....44 A4
Cressall Ho 8 E14 ....41 C3
Cresset Ho 8 E9 ......17 B2
Cresset Rd E9 ....17 B2
Cresset St SW4 ....61 C4
Cressfield Cl NW5 ....12 C3
Cressida Rd N19 ......4 C3
Cressingham Rd
  SE13 ....67 B4
Cressington Cl 4
  N16 ....16 A3
Cresswell Gdns
  SW5 ....142 C2
Cresswell Pl SW10 ..143 A2
Cressy Ct E1 ....32 B4
  W6 ....39 A3
Cressy Hos 2 E1 ......32 B4
Cressy Pl E1 ....32 B4
Cressy Rd NW3 ....12 B4
Cresta Ho NW6 ....11 C1
  7 E3 ....26 C1
Crestfield St N1,
  WC1 ....94 B4
Crestview NW5 ....4 A1
Creswick Ct W3 ....28 A2
Creswick Rd W3 ......28 A2
Creswick Wlk 6 E3 ..26 C2
Crewdson Rd SW9 ..163 B1
Crewe Pl NW10 ....21 B2
Crewkerne Ct
  SW11 ....167 C4
Crews St E14 ....41 C2
Crewys Rd NW2 ......1 B2
  SE15 ....50 A1
Crichton St SW8 ......170 C2

Cricketers Mews 4
  SW18 ....59 A2
Cricketfield Rd E5 ....17 A4
Cricklade Ave SW2 ..74 B2
Cricklewood Broadway
  NW2 ....9 C4
Cricklewood La NW2 ..1 B1
Cricklewood
  Sta 9 C4
Crieff Rd SW18 ....59 B1
Criffel Ave SW2 ......73 C3
Crimscott St SE1 ....138 B1
Crimsworth Rd
  SW8 ....161 C1
Crinan St N1 ....84 B2
Cringle St SW8 ....160 C2
Cripplegate
  EC1 ....109 A4
Crispe Ho N1 ....85 A2
Crispe Ho N1 ....85 A3
Crispian Cl NW10 ....8 A4
Crispin Ct SE17 ......152 A3
Crispin St E1 ....110 C3
Cristowe Rd SW6 ..165 A1
Criterion Mews N19 ..4 C2
Crockerton Rd
  SW17 ....72 B2
Croft Ho 12 W10 ......23 A2
  SW15 ....58 A1
Croft St SE8 ....41 A2
Croft The NW10 ......21 B3
Croftdown Rd NW5 ..4 A1
Crofters Ct 9 SE8 ....41 A2
Crofters Way NW1 ..83 B4
Crofton Ave W4 ......45 C3
Crofton Gate Way
  SE4 ....66 A2
Crofton L Ctr SE4 ....66 C1
Crofton Park Rd
  SE4 ....66 B1
Crofton Park Sta
  SE4 ....66 B1
Crofton Rd SE5 ....49 A1
Crofton Sch SE4 ......66 B1
Crofton Terr E5 ....18 A3
  Richmond TW9 ......54 B3
Crofts Ho 13 E2 ......24 C3
Crofts St E1 ....125 B3
Crogsland Rd NW1 ..12 C1
Cromartie Rd N19 ....4 C4
Cromarty Ho 8 E1 ....33 A4
Crombie Mews
  SW11 ....168 B2
Cromdale Ct N16 ......7 C4
Cromer Ct SW18 ......58 B1
  SW16 ....74 A1
Cromer St WC1 ....94 B3
Cromer Terr E8 ....16 C3
Cromer Villas Rd
  SW18 ....58 B1
Cromford Path 11
  E5 ....17 C4
Cromford Rd SW18 ..58 C2
Crompton Ct SW3 ..144 A4
Crompton Ho N1 ......89 B1
  SE1 ....137 A1
  SW8 ....171 A3
Crompton St W2 ......89 B1
Cromwell Ave N6 ......4 A3
  W6 ....39 A2
Cromwell Cl W3 ......28 B1
  2 W4 ....37 C1

Cromwell Cres
SW5 .... 141 B4
Cromwell Ct NW10 .20 C2
Cromwell Gdns
SW7 .... 129 C1
Cromwell Gr W6 ....39 B3
Cromwell Ho
SW11 .... 169 C3
SW15 ....56 C3
Cromwell Lo 🔲 E1 .25 B1
Cromwell Mans
SW5 .... 141 C4
Cromwell Mews
SW7 .... 143 C4
Cromwell Pl SW7 .143 C4
N6 ....4 B4
🔲 W3 ....28 B1
SW14 ....55 B4
Cromwell Rd
SW5,SW7 .... 142 B4
SW9 .... 173 A4
Cromwell Twr EC2 109 A4
Crondace Rd SW6 165 C3
Crondall Ct 🔟 N1 ...24 A3
Crondall Ho SW15 ..68 C3
Crondall Pl 🔟 N1 ...24 A3
Crondall St N1 ......87 C1
............................24 A3
Crone Ct 🔟 NW6 ....23 B3
Cronin St SE15 ......49 B3
Crooke Rd SE8 ......41 A1
Crooked Billet Yd
E2 ....98 B4
Crookham Rd SW6 164 C3
Croom's Hill SE10 ..52 C3
Croom's Hill Gr
SE10 ....52 B3
Cropley Ct N1 ....87 B2
Cropley St N1 ....87 B2
Cropthorne Ct W9 ..89 A3
Crosby Ct SE1 ...... 137 B4
Crosby Row SE1 ... 137 B4
Crosby Sq EC3 ......110 A2
Crosby Wlk 🔟 E8 ...16 B2
............................74 C4
Crosfield Ct 🔟 W10 .30 C3
Crosfield Ho W11 .. 112 A3
Crosland Pl 🔟
SW11 ....60 C4
Cross Cl SE15 ....50 A1
Cross Ct SE5 ....63 C4
Cross Keys Cl W1 . 103 C3
Cross La EC3 .... 124 A3
Cross Rd SE5 ....49 A1
Cross St N1 ....86 B4
SW13 ....56 A4
Crossbow Ho 🔟 N1 .24 A4
Crossfield Rd NW3 .11 C2
Crossfield St SE8 ...51 C3
Crossford St SW9 . 172 C1
Crossharbour & London
Arena Sta 🔟 E14 ...42 A3
Crossleigh Ct 🔟
SE14 ....51 B3
Crosslet St SE17 .. 151 C4
Crosslet Vale SE10 .52 A2
Crossley St N7 ....14 C2
Crossman Hos 🔟
SW12 ....74 A4
Crossmount Ho 🔟
SE5 ....48 B3

Crossthwaite Ave
SE5,SE24 ....63 C3
Crosswall EC3 ...... 124 C4
Crossway E8,N16 ...16 A3
Crossway Ct SE4 ....51 A1
Croston St E8 ....24 C4
Crouch End Hill N8 ..4 C4
Crouch Hall Ct N19 ..5 B3
Crouch Hall Rd
N19 ....5 A3
Crouchmans Cl
SE21,SE26 ....76 C1
Crowder St E1 ....32 A2
Crowfield Ho N5 .....15 B4
Crowfoot Cl E9 ....18 B3
Crowhurst Cl SW9 173 C2
Crowhurst Ho 🔟
SW9 .... 173 A1
Crowland Ho NW8 ..78 C3
Crowland Terr N1 ...15 C1
Crowline Wlk 🔟 N1 .15 B2
Crown Cl NW6 ....11 A2
E3 ....26 C4
Crown Close Bsns
Ctr E3 ....26 C4
Crown Ct WC2 ..... 106 B1
EC4 .... 109 A1
🔟 SW15 ....57 C3
Crown Lo SW3 ..... 144 B3
Crown Office Row
EC4 .... 121 B4
Crown Pas SW1 ... 119 A1
Crown Pl NW5 ....13 A2
Crown Reach SW1 147 C1
Crown St W3 ....28 A1
SE5 ....48 B3
Crown Terr NW1 ....54 B3
Crowndale Ct NW1 .83 A2
Crowndale Rd NW1 .83 A2
Crownfield Rd E15 ..19 C4
Crownhill Rd NW10 21 B4
Crownleigh Ct SW2 62 C2
Crownstone Ct 🔟
SW2 ....62 C2
Crownstone Rd
SW2 ....62 C2
Crows Rd E15 ....27 C2
Crowther Ave 🔟 TW8 .36 A2
Crowthorne Cl
SW18 ....70 B3
Crowthorne Rd
W10 ....30 C3
Croxley Rd W9 ....23 B2
Croxted Cl SE21 .....75 B4
Croxted Mews SE24 .63 B1
Croxted Rd SE21,
SE24 ....
Croxteth Ho 🔟 SW8 171 B2
Croydon Ho 🔟 SE1 135 C4
Crozier Ho SW8 ... 162 C1
Crozier Terr E9 ......17 C3
Crucifix La SE1 .... 138 A4
Cruden Ho 🔟 E2 ....26 B3
🔟 SE17 ....48 A4
Cruden St N1 ....86 B3
Cruickshank St
WC1 ....95 A4
Cruikshank Ho NW8 80 B2
Crusoe House Sch
N1 ....97 A4
Crusoe Mews N16 ...6 C2
Crutched Friars
EC3 .... 124 B4
Crystal Palace Rd
SE22 ....64 C2
Cuba St E14 ....41 C4
Cubitt Ho 🔟 SW4 ...61 B1

Cubitt St WC1 ....95 A3
Cubitt Terr SW4 .....61 B4
Cubitt Town Jun & Inf
Sch E14 ....42 B3
Cuddington SE17 .. 151 A4
Cudworth Ho 🔟 SW8 171 A3
Cudworth St E1 ......25 A1
Cuff Pt E2 ....98 C4
Cuffley Ho 🔟 W10 ..30 B4
Culand Ho SE17 ... 152 A3
Culford Gdns SW3 145 A3
Culford Gr N1 ....16 A2
Culford Mans SW3 145 A3
Culford Mews N1 ...16 A2
Culford Rd N1 ....16 A1
N1 ....16 A2
Culham Ho E2 ....98 C3
🔟 W2 ....31 C4
Cullen Ho W9 ....31 C4
Cullen Way NW10 ..20 B1
Culling Rd SE16 .....40 B3
Cullingworth Rd
NW10 ....9 A3
Culloden Cl 🔟 SE16 153 C1
Culloden JMI Sch
E14 ....34 B3
Cullum St EC3 ..... 124 A4
Culmore Rd SE15 ...50 B3
Culmstock Rd SW11 60 C2
Culpeper Ct SE11 . 149 B4
Culpeper Ho 🔟
E14 ....33 A3
Culpin Ho E2 ....26 C2
Culross Bldgs NW1 84 A2
Culross St W1 ...... 117 B3
Culver Ct SW18 .....59 A1
Culverden Rd SW12 73 B2
Culverhouse WC1 . 106 C3
Culverhouse Gdns
SW16 ....74 B1
Culvert Ct SW11 .. 169 B2
Culvert Pl SW11 ... 169 B2
Culvert Rd SW11 .. 169 A2
Culworth Ho NW8 ..80 A2
Culworth St NW8 ...80 A1
Cumber Ho SW18 ..70 C3
Cumberland Ave
NW10 ....20 A2
Cumberland Bsns Ctr
Cumberland Cl 🔟 E8 .16 B2
Cumberland Comp Sch
E16 ....35 A4
Cumberland Cres
W14 .... 140 B4
Cumberland Ct
W1 .... 103 A1
Cumberland Gate
W1 .... 117 A4
Cumberland Gdns
WC1 ....95 A4
Cumberland Ho 🔟
SW15 ....69 B4
Cumberland Mans
W1 .... 102 C2
🔟 NW6 ....10 C3
Cumberland Market
NW1 ....92 B4
Cumberland Mills Sq
E14 ....42 C1
Cumberland Park Ind
Est NW10 ....21 C2
Cumberland Pk W3 28 B2
Cumberland Pl
NW1 ....92 A4
Cumberland Rd W3 28 B2

Cumberland Rd continued
Richmond TW9 ......44 C3
SW13 ....46 C2
Cumberland Sch
E16 ....35 B2
Cumberland St
SW1 .... 146 B2
Cumberland Terr
NW1 ....82 A1
Cumberland Terrace
Mews NW1 ....82 A1
Cumberland Villas
W3 ....28 B2
Cumbria Ho 🔟
SW15 ....58 B2
Cumbrian Gdns NW2 1 A2
Cumming St N1 ......85 A1
Cumnor Cl SW9 ... 173 A2
Cunard Pl EC3 ..... 110 B1
Cunard Rd NW10 ...20 C2
Cunard Wlk 🔟 SE16 41 A2
Cundy St SW1 ..... 145 C3
Cunningham Ct W2 89 B1
Cunningham Ho 🔟
SE5 ....48 C3
Cunningham Pl
NW8 ....89 B2
Cunnington St W4 ..37 B2
Cupar Rd SW11 ... 169 C4
Cureton St SW1 ... 147 C3
Curlew Ho 🔟 SE15 . 49 B2
SE4 ....66 A3
Curlew St SE1 ..... 139 A4
Curness St SW13 . 144 A3
Curnick's La 🔟 SE27 75 B1
Curran Ho SW3 ... 144 A3
Curricle St W3 ....29 A1
Currie Ho 🔟 SW12 .73 C4
Cursitor St EC4 .... 107 B2
Curtain Pl EC2 ....98 B2
Curtain Rd
EC2 ....24 A1 98 B2
Curtis Dr W3 ....28 C3
Curtis Ho SE17 .... 151 B2
Curtis St SE1 .... 152 C4
Curtis Way SE1 .... 152 C4
Curve The W12 ....30 A2
Curwen Rd W12 .....38 C4
Curzon Cres NW10 ..8 A1
Curzon Gate W1 .. 117 C1
Curzon St W1 ...... 118 A2
Custance Ho N1 .....87 B1
Custance St N1 ......97 B4
Custom House
............................124 A3
Custom House Reach
SE16 ....41 B3
Cut The SE1 .... 135 C4
Cutbush Ho N7 .....13 C3
Cutcombe Mans 🔲
SE5 ....48 B1
Cutcombe Rd SE5 ..48 B1
Cuthbert Harrowing Ho
EC1 ....96 C1
Cuthbert Ho 🔟 W2 101 B4
Cuthbert St W2 ......89 C1
Cuthill Wlk 🔟 SE5 ..48 C2
Cutler St EC2 .... 110 B2
Cutlers Gdns EC2 . 110 B2
Cutlers Sq E14 ......41 C2
Cutty Sark★ SE10 ..52 B4
Cutty Sark Sta SE10 52 B4
Cuxton Ho SE17 ... 152 B2
Cyclops Mews 🔟
E14 ....41 C2
Cygnet St E1 ....99 A2

Cygnus Bsns Ctr
NW10 ....8 B2
Cynthia St N1 ....85 A1
Cypress Ct 🔟 E11 ..19 C4
Cypress Gdns SE4 ..66 A2
Cypress Ho SE14 ...50 C2
Cypress Pl W1 ....93 A1
Cypress Pl 🔟 E2 .....25 B3
Cyprus Pl 🔟 E2 .....25 B3
Cyprus St E2 ....25 B3
Cyrena Rd SE22 .....64 B2
Cyril Jackson JMI Sch
E14 ....33 B2
Cyril Jackson Sch
E14 ....33 B2
Cyril Mans SW11 . 169 A3
Cyril Thatcher Ho
SW6 .... 165 C3
Cyrus Ho EC1 ....96 B2
Cyrus St EC1 ....96 B2
Czar St SE8 ....51 C4

D

D'arblay St W1 ..... 105 A1
D'eynsford Rd SE5 ..48 C2
D'Oyley St SW1 ... 145 B4
Da Palma Ct SW6 . 155 B3
Da Vinci Ct 🔟 SE16 40 A1
Dabb's La EC1 ....95 C1
Dabin Cres SE10 ...52 B2
Dacca St SE8 ....51 B4
Dace Rd E3 ....26 C4
Dacre Ho SW3 ..... 157 C3
Dacre St SW1 ...... 133 B2
Daffodil St W12 .....29 B2
Daffome Rd SW17 ..72 C1
Dagmar Ct E14 .....42 B3
Dagmar Gdns NW10 22 C3
Dagmar Pas N1 .....86 B3
Dagmar Rd N4 ....5 C4
............................49 A2
Dagmar Terr N1 .....86 B3
Dagnall St SW11 .. 169 B3
Dagnan Rd SW12 ..73 B4
Dagobert Ho 🔟 E1 .32 B4
Daimler Ho 🔟 E3 ...26 C1
Dainton Ho 🔟 W2 ..31 C4
Daintry Way E9 .....18 B2
Dairyman Cl NW2 ...1 A1
Daisy Dormer Ct 🔟
SW9 ....62 B3
Daisy La SW6 ....58 C4
Dalberg Rd SW2 ...62 C2
Dalbury Ho 🔟 SW9 .62 B3
Dalby Rd SW18 .....59 B3
Dalby St NW5 ....13 A2
Dale Croft N4 ....6 B1
Dale Ho NW8 ....78 C4
SE4 ....66 A3
Dale Lo NW5 ....47 A4
SE17 ....48 A4
Dale Row W11 ....31 A3
Dale St W4 ....38 A1
Dalebury Rd SW17 .72 B2
Dalehead NW1 ......82 C1
Daleham Gdns NW3 11 C2
Daleham Mews
NW3 ....11 C2
Dalemain Ho 🔟 SW8 171 C2
Dalemain Mews 🔟
E16 ....35 C1
Daley Ho W12 ....30 A3
Daley St E9 ....17 C2
Daley Thompson Way 🔟
SW8 ....61 A4
Dalgarno Gdns W10 30 B4

Dalgarno Way W10 .22 B1
Daling Way E3 .26 A3
Dalkeith Ct SW1 .147 C3
Dalkeith Ho [5] SW9 .48 A2
Dalkeith Rd SE21 .75 B4
Dalling Rd W6 .39 A2
Dallington Sch EC1 .96 B2
Dallington St EC1 .96 B2
Dalmeny Ave N7 .13 C4
Dalmeny Ct SW4 .172 A2
Dalmeny Rd N7 .13 C4
Dalmore Rd SE21 .75 B2
Dalrymple Rd SE4 .66 A3
Dalston Jct E8 .16 B2
Dalston Kingsland Sta
E8 .16 B3
Dalston La E8 .16 C3
Dalton Ho E3 .26 A3
[19] E14 .50 C4
[5] SW12 .73 A4
Dalton St SE27 .75 A1
Dalwood St SE5 .49 A2
Daly Ct E15 .76 A3
Dalyell Rd SW9 .62 B4
Damascene Wlk
SE21 .75 B3
Dame St N1 .86 C2
Damer Ho [9] TW10 .54 B1
Damer Terr SW10 .157 A1
Damien Ct E1 .32 A3
Damien St E1 .32 A3
Damory Ho [3] SE16 .40 B2
Dan Bryant Ho [6]
SW4 .156 A1
Dan Leno Wlk
SW6 .156 A1
Danbury St N1 .86 B2
Danby Ho [22] E9 .17 B1
[3] W10 .23 A1
Danby St SE15 .64 B4
Dancer Rd SW6 .164 C3
Mortlake TW9 .54 C4
Dandridge Cl SE10 .43 B1
Dandridge Ho E1 .110 C4
Dane Ho [13] SE5 .48 B1
Dane Pl E3 .26 B3
Dane St WC1 .106 C3
Danebury W10 .30 A4
Danebury Ave SW15 .56 B1
Danebury Prim Sch
SW15 .68 B4
Danecroft Rd SE24 .63 C2
Danehurst St SW6 .164 A4
Danemere St SW15 .57 B4
Danes Ct NW8 .80 C3
Danes Ho W10 .30 B4
Danesdale Rd E9 .18 A2
Danesfield SE5 .49 A4
Daneville Rd SE5 .48 C2
Daniel Bolt Cl E14 .34 A4
Daniel Ct W3 .29 A2
Daniel Gdns SE15 .49 B3
Daniel's Rd SE15 .65 B4
Daniell Ho N1 .87 C2
Dansey Pl W1 .119 B4
Dante Rd SE11 .150 A4
Danube Ct [15] SE15 .49 B3
Danube St SW3 .144 B3
Danvers Ho [4] E1 .111 C1
Danvers St SW3 .157 C3
Daphne St SW18 .59 B1
Daplyn St E1 .111 B4
Darcy Ho E8 .25 A4
Darell Prim Sch
TW9 .54 C4

Darell Rd TW9 .54 C4
Daren Ct N7 .14 A4
Darent Ho NW8 .101 C4
Darenth Rd N16 .7 B3
Darfield NW1 .82 C3
Darfield Rd SE4 .66 B2
Darfield Way W10 .30 C3
Darfur St [5] SW15 .57 C4
Darien Ho [8] E1 .32 C4
[17] SW11 .59 C4
Darien Rd SW11 .59 C4
Daring Ho [21] E3 .26 A3
Darlan Rd SW6 .155 A1
Darland Ct SW15 .58 B1
Darley Ho SE11 .148 C1
Darley Rd SW11 .60 B1
Darling Rd SE4 .66 C4
Darling Row E1 .25 A1
Darlington Ho
SW8 .161 C1
Darnay Ho SE16 .139 B2
Darnell Ho [4] SE10 .52 B3
[9] SE10 .52 B3
Darnley Ho [8] E14 .33 A3
Darnley Rd E9 .17 B2
Darnley Terr [12]
W11 .30 C1
Darrell Rd SE22 .64 C2
Darren Cl N4 .5 A4
Darsley Dr SW8 .172 A4
Dart St W10 .23 B2
Dartford Ho SE1 .153 A4
Dartford St SE17 .48 B4
Dartington NW1 .83 A3
Dartington Ho W2 .100 A4
Dartle Ct [2] SE16 .139 C3
Dartmoor Wlk [17]
E14 .41 C2
Dartmouth Cl W11 .31 C3
Dartmouth Ct SE10 .52 B2
Dartmouth Gr SE10 .52 B2
Dartmouth Hill
SE10 .52 B2
Dartmouth Ho N19 .4 A2
Dartmouth Park Ave
NW5 .4 A1
Dartmouth Park Hill
N19 .4 A2
Dartmouth Park Rd
NW5 .4 A1
Dartmouth Pl W4 .46 A4
Dartmouth Rd NW2 .9 C2
Dartmouth Row
SE10 .52 B2
Dartmouth St SW1 .133 C3
Dartmouth Terr
SE10 .52 C2
Darton St W3 .28 B3
Dartrey Twr SW10 .157 B2
Dartrey Wlk SW10 .157 A2
Darul Ammah Private
Sch E1 .32 A3
Darville Rd N16 .7 B1
Darwen Pl E2 .25 A4
Darwin Ct NW1 .81 C4
Darwin St SE17 .151 C4
Daryngton Ho
SW8 .162 A1
Dashwood Ho SE21 .76 B1
Data Point Bsns Ctr
E16 .27 C1
Datchelor Pl [14] SE5 .48 C2
Datchet Ho [11] NW1 .92 B4
Datchett Ho [2] E2 .98 C3
Datchwood Ct N4 .6 B1

Datchworth Ho [8]
N1 .15 B1
Date St SE17 .151 B1
Daubeney JMI Sch
E5 .18 A4
Daubeney Rd E5 .18 A4
Daubeney Twr [2]
SE8 .41 B1
Dault Rd SW18 .59 B1
Dauney Ho SE1 .136 A3
Dave Adams Ho [7]
E3 .26 B3
Dave Porter Hts
SW19 .70 A4
Davenant Ho E1 .111 C4
Davenant Rd N19 .4 C2
Davenant St E1 .111 C3
Davenport Ho
SE11 .135 B1
Davenport Rd SE6 .67 B1
Daventry St NW1 .102 A4
Daver Ct SW3 .144 B1
Davern Cl SE10 .43 B2
Davet Ct SW4 .172 C4
Davey Cl N7 .14 B2
Davey Rd E9 .18 C1
Davey St SE15 .49 B4
Davey's Ct WC2 .120 A4
David Devine Ho [6]
E8 .16 C3
David Ho SW8 .162 A2
[3] SW15 .56 C2
David Mews W1 .103 A4
David St E15 .19 C3
Davidge Ho SE1 .135 C3
Davidge St SE1 .136 B3
Davidson Gdns
SW8 .162 A2
Davidson Ho [7] N19 .13 B4
Davies Mews W1 .118 A4
Davies St W1 .118 A4
W1 .118 A4
Davis Ho W12 .30 A2
Davis Rd W3 .38 B4
Davisville Rd W12 .38 C4
Dawes Ho SE17 .151 B3
Dawes Rd SW6 .154 C2
Dawes St SE17 .151 C2
Dawlish Ave SW18 .71 A2
Dawlish Rd NW2 .9 C2
Dawn Cres E15 .27 C4
Dawnay Gdns SW18 .71 C2
Dawnay Rd [13] SW18,
SW19 .71 C2
Daws Ho [8] W12 .30 A2
Dawson Ho [22] E2 .25 B2
[3] SE5 .49 A2
Dawson Pl
W2 .31 C2 113 C4
Dawson Rd NW2 .9 B4
Dawson St E2 .24 B3
Day Ho [5] SE5 .48 B3
Daylesford Ave
SW15 .56 C3
Daynor Ho [4] NW6 .23 C4
Daysbrook Rd SW2 .74 B3
Dayton Gr SE15 .50 B2
De Barowe Mews
N5 .15 A3
De Beauvoir Cres
N1 .24 A4
De Beauvoir Ct N1 .15 C1

De Beauvoir JMI Sch
N1 .16 A2
De Beauvoir Pl [5]
N1 .16 A2
De Beauvoir Prim Sch
N1 .16 A1
De Beauvoir Rd N1 .16 A1
De Beauvoir Sq N1 .16 A1
De Crespigny Pk
SE5 .48 C1
De Gama Pl E14 .41 C1
De Laune St SE17 .150 A1
De Montfort Par [1]
SW16 .74 A1
De Montfort Rd
SW16 .74 A2
De Morgan Rd SW6 .59 A4
De Quincey Mews [3]
E16 .35 C1
De Vere Cotts W8 .128 C2
De Vere Gdns W8 .128 C3
De Vere Mews W8 .128 C2
De Walden Ho NW8 .80 A2
De Walden St W1 .103 C3
Deacon Ho SE11 .149 A3
Deacon Mews N1 .15 C1
Deacon Rd NW2 .8 C2
Deacon Way SE17 .151 A4
Deal Ho SE17 .152 B2
SE15 .50 C4
Deal Porters Way
SE16 .40 C3
Deal St E1 .111 B4
Deal Wlk SW9 .163 C1
Dealtry Rd SW15 .57 B3
Dean Bradley St
SW1 .134 A1
Dean Cl E9 .17 B3
[9] SE16 .32 C1
Dean Ct SW8 .162 A1
Dean Farrar St
SW1 .133 C2
Dean Ho N4 .6 B4
[18] E1 .32 B3
Dean Rd NW2 .9 B2
Dean Ryle St SW1 .148 A4
Dean St W1 .105 B1
Dean Stanley St
SW1 .134 A1
Dean Trench St
SW1 .134 A1
Dean's Bldgs
SE17 .151 C3
Dean's Ct EC4 .108 B1
Dean's Mews W1 .104 B2
Deancross St E1 .32 B3
Deanery Mews W1 .117 C2
Deanery St W1 .117 C2
Deanhill Ct [2]
SW14 .55 A3
Deanhill Rd SW14 .55 A3
Deans Cl W4 .45 A4
Deanshanger Ho [21]
SE8 .41 B1
Dearmer Ho [6]
SW2 .74 C4
Deason St E15 .27 B4
Deauville Ct
[4] SE16 .40 C4
[14] SW4 .61 B1
Deauville Mans [13]
SW4 .61 B1
Debdale Ho [20] E2 .24 C4
Debenham Ct E8 .24 C4
Debnams Rd SE16 .40 B2
Decima St SE1 .138 A2

Deck Cl SE16 .32 C1
Dee Rd TW9 .54 B3
Dee St E14 .34 B3
Deeley Rd SW8 .171 B4
Deepdale N4 .6 A1
Deepdene Gdns
SW2 .74 B4
Deepdene Ho N16 .6 C3
Deepdene Lo [5]
SW2 .74 B4
Deepdene Mans
SW6 .164 C4
Deepdene Rd SE5,
SE24 .63 C3
Deer Lo SW6 .58 A4
Deerbrook Rd SE24,
SW2 .75 B3
Deerdale Rd SE24 .63 B3
Deerhurst Ho [6]
SE5 .49 C4
Deerhurst Rd NW2 .9 C2
Deeside Rd SW17 .71 C1
Defoe Ave TW9 .44 C3
Defoe Ho EC2 .108 C4
[2] N16 .6 C2
Defoe Pl EC2 .108 C4
Defoe Rd N16 .7 A1
[5] SE16 .41 B4
Dekker Ho [19] SE5 .48 C3
Dekker Rd SE21 .64 A1
Delafield Ho E1 .111 C1
Delaford Rd SE16 .40 A1
Delaford St SW6 .154 B3
Delamere Ho [4] N4 .6 C4
Delamere Rd W5 .36 A4
Delamere St W2 .100 C3
Delamere Terr W2 .100 B4
Delancey Pas [9]
NW1 .82 B3
Delancey St NW1 .82 B3
Delancey Studios
NW1 .82 B3
Delany Ho SE10 .52 B4
Delarch Ho SE1 .136 A3
Delaware Rd W9 .88 A2
Delawyk Cres SE24 .63 C1
Delft Way [2] SE22 .64 A2
Delhi St N1 .84 B3
Delia St SW18 .71 A4
Delius Gr E15 .27 C4
Dell Cl E15 .27 C4
Dell's Mews SW1 .147 A3
Dellafield N4 .5 C2
Dellow Ho [6] E1 .32 A2
Dellow St E1 .32 A2
Delmaine Ho [4] E14 .33 A3
Deloraine Ho SE8 .51 C2
Deloraine St SE8 .51 C2
Delorme St W6 .47 C4
Delta Bldg [4] E14 .34 B3
Delta Pk SW18 .59 A3
Delta St E2 .99 B4
Delverton Ho SE17 .150 B2
Delverton Rd SE17 .150 B1
Delvino Rd SW6 .165 C3
Dempster Rd SW18 .59 B2
Denbigh Cl
W11 .31 B2 113 A4
NW10 .8 A1
Denbigh Gdns TW10 .54 B2
Denbigh Ho W11 .113 A4
SW1 .131 A2
[7] W11 .31 B3

Denbigh Mews SW1 ....146 C3
Denbigh Pl SW1 ....146 C2
Denbigh Rd
W11 ....31 B2 113 A4
Denbigh St SW1 ....147 A2
Denbigh Terr
W11 ....31 B2 113 A4
Denbury Ho 48 E3 ....27 A2
Denby Ct SE11 ....149 A4
Dence Ho E2 ....99 B3
Denchworth Ho
SW9 ....173 B1
Dendy St SW12 ....72 C3
Dene Cl SE4 ....66 A3
Dene Mans 1 NW6 ....10 C2
Denehurst Gdns
W3 ....28 A1
Mortlake TW10 ....54 C3
Denesmead SE24 ....63 B2
Denewood Ho N6 ....3 B4
Dengie Wlk (off Maldon
Cl) N1 ....86 C4
Denham Ho 82 W12 ....30 A2
Denham St SE10 ....43 C1
Denholme Rd W9 ....23 B2
Denland Ho SW8 ....163 A1
Denman Ho N16 ....7 A2
Denman Rd SE15 ....49 B1
Denman St W1 ....119 B3
Denmark Gr N1 ....85 C2
Denmark Hill SE5 ....48 C1
Denmark Hill Sta
SE5 ....48 B1
Denmark Mans 1
SE5 ....48 B1
Denmark Pl WC2 ....105 C2
Denmark Rd NW6 ....23 B3
SE5 ....48 B1
Denmark St WC2 ....105 C2
Denmead Ho 8
SW15 ....56 B1
Denmead Way SE15 ....49 B3
Denne Terr E8 ....24 B4
Dennett's Gr SE14 ....50 C1
Dennett's Rd SE14 ....50 B2
Denning Cl NW8 ....89 A3
Denning Point E1 ....111 A2
Denning Rd NW3 ....11 C4
Dennington Park Rd
NW6 ....10 C2
Dennis Ho 4 E3 ....26 B3
Dennis Way SW4 ....61 C4
Dennison Point E15 ....19 B1
Denny Cres SE11 ....149 C2
Denny St SE11 ....149 C2
Densham Ho NW8 ....79 C1
Denstone Ho 5
SE15 ....49 C4
Dent Ho SE17 ....152 A3
Denton NW1 ....12 C2
Denton Ho N1 ....15 A1
Denton St SW18 ....59 A1
Dents Rd SW11 ....60 B1
Denver Rd N16 ....7 A4
Denyer Ho 1 NW5 ....13 A4
Denyer St SW3 ....144 B4
Denys Ho EC1 ....107 B4
Denzil Rd NW10 ....8 B3
Deodar Rd SW15 ....58 A3
Depot App NW2 ....9 C4
Depot Rd W12 ....30 B2

Depot St SE5 ....48 C4
Dept of Transport &
Environment
SW1 ....133 C1
Deptford Bridge
SE8 ....51 C2
Deptford Bridge Sta
SE8 ....51 C2
Deptford Broadway
SE8,SE14 ....51 C2
Deptford Church St
SE8 ....51 C3
Deptford Ferry Rd 14
E14 ....41 C2
Deptford Gn SE8 ....51 C4
Deptford Green Sch
SE14 ....51 B3
Deptford Green Sch
(Annexe) SE14 ....51 A3
Deptford High St
SE8 ....51 C3
Deptford Park Prim
Schs SE8 ....41 A1
Deptford Trad Est SE8 ....51 A4
Deptford Trad Est
SE14 ....51 A4
Deptford Wharf SE8 ....41 B2
Derby Ct 5 E5 ....17 C4
Derby Gate SW1 ....134 A4
Derby Ho SE11 ....149 B4
Derby Rd E9 ....25 C4
SW14 ....55 A3
Derby St W1 ....117 C1
Derbyshire
E2 ....24 C2 99 C3
Dereham Ho 7 SE4 ....65 C3
Dereham Pl E2 ....98 B2
EC2 ....98 B3
Derek Walcott Cl
SE24 ....63 A2
Dericote St E8 ....25 A4
Dering St W1 ....104 B1
Dermody Gdns
SE13 ....67 C2
Dermody Rd SE13 ....67 C2
Deronda Rd SE24, ...
Derrick Ho 13 SW2 ....74 C3
Derry St W8 ....128 A3
Derrycombe Ho
W11 ....31 B4
18 W2 ....31 C4
Dersingham Rd NW2 ....1 A1
Derwent NW1 ....92 C3
Derwent Ct 3 W6 ....38 C2
8 SE16 ....40 C4
Derwent Gr SE22 ....64 B3
Derwent Ho SW7 ....143 A4
E3 ....26 B1
Derwent St SE10 ....43 A1
Derwentwater Mans 2
W3 ....28 B1
Derwentwater Prim Sch
W3 ....28 B1
Derwentwater Rd
W3 ....28 B1
Desborough Cl
W2 ....100 B4
Desborough Ho
W14 ....155 A4
Desenfans Rd SE21 ....64 A1
Design Museum*
SE1 ....139 A4

Dethick Ct E3 ....26 A4
Detling Ho SE17 ....152 A3
Devas St E3 ....27 A1
Deventer Cres 8
SE22 ....64 A2
Deverell St SE1 ....137 B1
Devereux Ct WC2 ....107 B1
Devereux Ho 7
SW15 ....56 C2
Devereux La SW13 ....47 A3
Devereux Rd SW11 ....60 B1
Devitt Ho 4 E14 ....34 A2
Devizes St N1 ....87 C3
Devon Mans SE1 ....138 B4
Devon St SE15 ....50 A4
Devonhurst Pl 4
W4 ....37 C1
Devonia Rd N1 ....86 B2
Devonport W2 ....102 A2
Devonport Ho
W2 ....31 C4
Devonport Rd W12 ....39 A4
Devonport St E1 ....32 C3
Devons Rd E3 ....27 A1
Devons Road Sta
E3 ....27 A1
Devonshire Cl W1 ....104 A4
Devonshire Ct 6
TW9 ....44 C2
Devonshire Dr SE10 ....52 A2
Devonshire Gdns
W4 ....45 B3
Devonshire Gr SE15 ....50 A4
Devonshire Hall 14
E9 ....17 B2
Devonshire Ho
SE1 ....101 C4
SW1 ....136 C2
SW1 ....147 C2
2 SW15 ....69 B4
14 SW12 ....73 A4
Devonshire Hospl
W1 ....103 C4
Devonshire Mews 5
W4 ....38 A1
Devonshire Mews N
W1 ....104 A4
Devonshire Mews S
W1 ....104 A4
Devonshire Mews W
NW1 ....104 A4
W1 ....128 A1
Devonshire Place Mews
W1 ....103 C4
Devonshire Rd W4 ....38 A1
SE23 ....65 C1
Devonshire Row
EC2 ....110 B3
Devonshire Row Mews
W1 ....92 B1
Devonshire Sq
EC2 ....110 B2
Devonshire St W1 ....104 A4
W4 ....38 A1
Devonshire Terr
W2 ....101 A1
Dewar St SE15 ....64 C4
Dewberry St E14 ....34 B4
Dewey Rd N1 ....85 B2
Dewhurst Rd W14 ....39 C3
Dewsbury Ct 5 W4 ....37 B2

Dewsbury Rd NW10 ....8 C3
Dewsbury Terr NW1 ....82 B4
Dhonau Ho SE16 ....153 A4
Diadem Ct W1 ....105 B2
Dial Wlk The W8 ....128 B4
Diamond Ho 20 E3 ....26 A3
Diamond St SE17 ....152 A3
Diamond St SE15 ....49 A3
Diamond Terr SE10 ....52 B2
Diana Ho 6 SW13 ....46 B2
Diana Pl NW1 ....92 B2
Diana, Princess of
Wales Memorial Walk
W2 ....114 C1
Dibden Ho 6 SE5 ....49 A3
Dibden St N1 ....86 C4
Dibdin Ho W9 ....78 A1
Dicey Ave NW2 ....9 B4
Dick Sheppard Sch
SE24 ....63 A2
Dickens Ho NW8 ....89 C2
WC1 ....94 A2
SE17 ....150 B1
NW6 ....23 C2
WC1 ....95 A1
Dickens Mus* The
WC1 ....95 A1
Dickens Sq SE1 ....137 A2
Dickens St SW8 ....170 B2
Dickenson Rd N8 ....5 A4
Dickinson Ho 2
E2 ....99 B3
Dicksee Ho NW8 ....89 B1
Dickson 15 E1 ....32 A3
Didbin Ho N7 ....5 B2
Digby Bsns Ctr 19 ....17 C2
Digby Cres N4 ....6 B2
Digby Mans W6 ....39 B1
Digby Rd E9 ....17 C2
Digby St E2 ....25 B2
Diggon St 16 E1 ....32 C4
Dighton Ct SE17 ....48 B4
Dighton Rd SW18 ....59 B3
Dignum St N1 ....85 B2
Digswell St N7 ....14 C2
Dilke St SW3 ....159 A4
Dilston Gr SE16 ....40 B2
Dilton Gdns SW15 ....69 A3
Dimes Pl 1 W6 ....39 A2
Dimson Cres E3 ....26 C2
Dinerman St NW8 ....79 A4
Dingle Gdns E14 ....33 C2
Dingley La SW16 ....73 C2
Dingley Pl EC1 ....97 A3
Dingley Rd EC1 ....96 C3
Dingwall Rd SW18 ....71 B4
Dinmont Ho 23 E2 ....24 C3
Dinmont St 1 E2 ....25 A3
Dinmore Ho 8 E9 ....25 B4
Dinnington Ho 17
E1 ....25 A1
Dinsdale Rd SE3 ....53 B4
Dinsmore Rd SW12 ....73 A4
Dinton Ho NW8 ....90 A2
Dinwiddy Ho N1 ....84 C1
Dionis Ho SW6 ....166 B2
Disbrowe Rd W6 ....154 B3
Discovery Bsns Pk
SE16 ....139 C1
Discovery Ho 1
E14 ....34 B2
Disney Pl SE1 ....137 A4
Disney St SE1 ....137 A4
Disraeli Cl 1 W4 ....37 C2
Disraeli Gdns SW15 ....58 B3
Disraeli Rd NW10 ....20 C3
SW15 ....58 A3
Diss St E2 ....98 C4

Distaff La EC4 ....122 C4
Distillery La W6 ....39 B1
Distillery Rd W6 ....39 B1
Distillery Wlk 14
TW8 ....44 A4
Distin St SE11 ....149 B3
Ditchburn St E14 ....34 B2
Ditton Ho 10 E5 ....17 A3
Divis Way SW15 ....57 A1
Dixon Clark Ct N1 ....15 A2
Dixon Rd SE14 ....51 A2
Dobree Ave NW10 ....9 A1
Dobson Cl NW6 ....11 C1
Dobson Ho SE5 ....48 C3
18 SE16 ....40 C4
Doby Ct EC4 ....123 A4
Dock Hill Ave SE16 ....40 C4
Dock Offices 12
SE16 ....40 B3
Dock Rd E16 ....35 B2
Dock St E1 ....125 B4
Dockers Tanner Rd 10
E14 ....41 C2
Dockhead SE1 ....139 A3
Dockhead Wharf
SE1 ....139 A4
Docklands Heritage Mus*
SE16 ....33 B1
Dockley Rd SE16 ....139 B1
Dockley Road Ind Est
SE16 ....139 B1
Doctor Spurstowe
Almshos 9 E8 ....17 A2
Docura Ho N7 ....5 B2
Docwra's Bldgs N1 ....16 A2
Dod St E14 ....33 C3
Dodbrooke Rd SE27 ....75 A1
Dodd Ho 18 SE16 ....40 A2
Doddington Gr
SE17 ....150 B1
Doddington Pl 4
SE17 ....48 A4
Dodson St SE1 ....135 C3
Dog Kennel Hill
SE22 ....64 A4
Dog Kennel Hill Jun &
Inf Sch SE22 ....64 A4
Dog La NW10 ....8 A4
Doggett Rd SE4 ....66 C3
Dolben Ct SE8 ....41 B2
Dolben St SE1 ....122 B1
Dolby Rd SW6 ....164 C1
Dolland Ho SE11 ....149 A1
Dolland St SE11 ....149 A1
Dollar Bay E14 ....42 B4
Dollis Hill Sta NW2 ....8 C3
Dolman Rd W4 ....37 C2
Dolman St SW4 ....62 B3
Dolphin Cl 2 SE16 ....40 C4
Dolphin Ct N7 ....13 C4
Dolphin La E14 ....34 A2
Dolphin Sq SW1 ....147 A1
Dolphin Twr 21 SE8 ....51 B4
Dombey Ho SE1 ....139 B3
4 W11 ....30 C1
Dombey St WC1 ....106 C4
Dome Hill Pk SE26 ....76 C1
Domelton Ho SW18 ....59 A1
Domett Cl SE5 ....63 C3
Domfe Pl E5 ....17 B4
Domingo St EC1 ....96 C1
Dominion St EC2 ....109 C4
Don Phelan Cl SE5 ....48 C2
Donaghue Cotts 13
E14 ....33 A4
Donaldson Rd NW6 ....23 B4
Donegal Ho 2 E1 ....25 B1

Donegal St N1 .....85 A1
Doneraile Ho SW1 .146 A1
Doneraile St SW6 .164 A3
SW6 .....47 C2
Donkey Alley SE22 .64 C1
Donkin Ho 15 SE16 .40 A2
Donne Ct SE24 .63 B1
Donne Ho 18 N16 .15 C4
7 E14 .....33 C3
14 SE14 .....50 C4
Donne Pl SW3 .144 B4
Donnelly Ct SW6 .154 B2
Donnington Ct NW10 .9 A1
1 NW1 .....13 A1
Donnington Ho
SW8 .....171 B2
Donnington Prim Sch
NW10 .....22 A4
Donnington Rd
NW10 .....22 A4
Donovan Ct SW7 .143 B1
Donovan Ho 3 E1 .32 B2
Doon St SE1 .121 B2
Dora Ho 9 W11 .30 C2
1 E14 .....33 B3
Dora St E14 .33 B3
Doradus Ct 20
SW19 .....69 C3
Doran Wlk E15 .76 B1
Dorando Cl W12 .30 A2
Dorcas Ct 9 SW18 .59 C3
Dorchester Ct
SW1 .....131 A1
SE24 .....16 A1
N1 .....64 B3
6 SW16 .74 A2
Dorchester Dr SE24 .63 B2
Dorchester Gr W4 .38 B1
Dordrecht Rd W3 .29 A1
Doria Rd SW6 .165 A2
Doric Ho 7 E2 .25 C3
Doric Way NW1 .93 B4
Doris Emmerton Ct
SW18 .....59 B3
Dorking Cl SE8 .51 B4
Dorking Ho SE1 .137 C2
Dorlcote Rd SW18 .72 A4
Dorleston Ct N1 .87 C4
Dorman Way NW8 .79 B4
Dormay St SW18 .59 A2
Dormstone Ho
SE17 .....152 A3
Dornan Wlk E15 .27 B4
Dornberg Cl SE3 .53 C3
Dorncliffe Rd SW6 .164 B2
Dorney NW3 .12 A1
Dorney Ct SW6 .58 A4
Dornfell St NW6 .10 B3
Dornoch Ho 3 E3 .26 B3
Dornton Rd SW12,
SW17 .....73 B2
Dorothy Charrington Ho
1 SE22 .64 C2
Dorothy Rd SW11 .60 B4
Dorrien Wlk SW16 .73 C2
Dorrington Point 20
E3 .....27 A2
Dorrington St EC1 .107 B4
Dorrit Ho 2 W11 .30 C1
Dorrit St SE1 .137 A4
Dorset Bldgs EC4 .108 A1
Dorset Cl NW1 .102 C4
Dorset Ct 3 N1 .16 A1
Dorset Mans W6 .47 C4
Dorset Mews SW1 .132 A2
Dorset Pl E15 .19 C2

Dorset Rd SW8 .162 C2
Dorset Rise EC4 .108 A1
Dorset Sq NW1 .90 C1
Dorset St W1 .103 A3
Dorville Cres W6 .39 A3
Doughty Ct 11 E1 .32 A1
Doughty Mews WC1 .94 C1
Doughty St WC1 .94 C1
Douglas Bldgs SE1 .137 A4
Douglas Ct 5 NW6 .10 C1
Douglas Gracey Ho
SW18 .....70 A4
Douglas Ho SW15 .56 C1
Douglas Johnstone Ho
SW6 .....154 C3
Douglas Mews NW2 .1 A1
Douglas Rd N1 .15 B1
5 E16 .....35 C4
Douglas Rd S N1 .15 B2
Douglas St SW1 .147 B3
Douglas Waite Ho
NW6 .....11 A1
Douglas Way SE8 .51 B3
Doulton Ho SE11 .149 A4
Doulton Mews 4
NW6 .....11 A2
Dounesforth Gdns
SW18 .....71 A3
Douro Pl W8 .128 B2
Douro St E3 .26 C3
Douthwaite Sq 1 E1 .125 C2
Dove Mews SW7 .143 A2
Dove Rd N1 .15 C2
Dove Row E2 .24 C4
Dove Wlk SW1 .145 B2
Dovecote Gdns 3
SW14 .....55 C4
Dovedale Cotts
SW11 .....168 C2
Dovedale Ho N16 .6 C4
Dovedale Rd SE22 .65 A1
Dovehouse St
SW3 .....144 A1
Dover Ct SE10 .52 A2
Dover Flats SE1 .152 B3
Dover Ho SE5 .48 A2
SE15 .....50 B4
Dover House Rd
SW15 .....57 A2
Dover Park Dr
SW15 .....57 A1
Dover St W1 .118 C2
Dover Terr TW9 .44 C1
Dover Yd W1 .118 C2
Dovercourt Rd SE22 .64 B1
Doverfield Rd SW2 .74 A4
Doveton Ho 6 E1 .25 B1
Doveton St 5 E1 .25 B1
Dowdeswell Cl
SW15 .....56 A3
Dowding Ho N6 .3 C4
Dowell Ho SE21 .76 B1
Dowes Ho 15 SW16 .74 A1
Dowgate Hill EC4 .123 B4
Dowlas St SE5 .49 A3
Down Pl W6 .39 A1
Down St Mews
W1 .....118 A1
Downbarton Ho
SW9 .....173 B4

Downbury Mews 18
SW18 .....58 C2
Downend Ct 8
SE15 .....49 A4
Downer's Cotts SW4 .61 B3
Downey Ho 6 E1 .25 C1
Downfield Cl W9 .88 A1
Downham Ct 1 N1 .15 C1
Downham Rd N1 .15 C1
Downing Ho
2 W10 .30 C2
4 SW15 .56 C2
Downing St* SW1 .134 A4
Downs Ct 18 E8 .17 A3
Downs La 4 E5 .17 A4
Downs Park Rd E5,
.....16 C3
Downs Rd E5,N16 .16 C4
Downs Side JMI Sch
E5 .....16 C3
Downsell Jun & Inf Schs
E15 .....19 C4
Downsell Rd E15 .19 C4
Downshire Hill
NW3 .....11 C4
Downside 2 SW15 .58 A2
Downside Cres
NW3 .....12 A3
Downsview Sch 5 E5 .17 A4
Downton Ave SW2 .74 B2
Downtown Rd SE16 .41 A4
Dowrey St N1 .85 B4
Dowson Cl SE5 .63 C3
Dowson Ct SE13 .67 C4
Dowson Ho 5 E1 .32 C3
Doyce St SE1 .136 C4
Doyle Gdns NW10 .22 A4
Doyle Ho W3 .37 A4
Doynton St N19 .4 A2
Dr Johnson Ave
SW17 .....73 A1
Dr Johnson's Ho*
EC4 .....107 C1
Draco St SE17 .48 B4
Dragon Yd WC1 .106 B2
Dragoon Rd SE8 .41 B1
Dragor Rd NW10 .20 B1
Drake Croft N16 .6 C2
Drake Ct 5 E12 .39 A4
Drake Ho 17 E1 .32 B4
2 E14 .....33 A2
Drake Rd SE4 .66 C4
Drake St WC1 .106 C3
Drakefell Rd SE4,
SE14 .....66 B2
Drakefield Rd SW17 .72 C1
Drakeley Ct N5 .15 A4
Drakes Ctyd NW6 .10 B1
Draldo Ho 5 SW15 .58 A2
Draper Ho SE1 .150 B4
Draper Pl N1 .86 B4
Drapers Almshouses 5
E3 .....27 A2
Drapers Gdns EC2 .109 C2
Drapers Rd E15 .19 C4
Drappers Way
SE16 .....153 C4
Dray Gdns SW2 .62 B2
Draycott Ave SW3 .144 B3
Draycott Cl SW11 .144 B4
Draycott Ho SW3 .144 C3
Draycott Pl SW3 .144 C3
Draycott Terr SW3 .145 A3
Drayford Cl W9 .23 B1
Drayson Mews W8 .127 C3
Drayton Ct SW10 .143 A1

Drayton Gdns
SW10 .....143 A1
Drayton Ho 11 SE5 .48 C3
Drayton Park Prim Sch
N5 .....14 C3
Drayton Park Sta
N5 .....14 C3
Drayton Pk N5,N7 .14 C4
Drayton Rd NW10 .21 B4
Dreadnought St
SE10 .....43 A3
Dresden Cl NW6 .11 A2
Dresden Ho SE11 .149 A4
SW11 .....169 B2
Dresden Rd N19 .4 C3
Dressington Ave
SE4 .....66 C1
Drew Ho 9 SW16 .74 A1
Drewett Ho E1 .111 C1
Drewstead Rd
SW16 .....73 C2
Driffield Rd E3 .26 A3
Driftway Ho 21 E3 .26 B3
Drinkwater Ho 11
SE5 .....48 C3
Drive Mans SW6 .164 B2
Drive The NW11 .1 A4
N7 .....14 B2
W3 .....28 B3
Droitwich Cl SE26 .76 C1
Dromore Rd SW15 .58 A1
Dron Ho E1 .32 B4
Droop St W10 .23 A1
Drovers Ct SE13 .67 B4
Drovers Pl SE15 .50 A3
Druce Rd SE21 .64 A1
Druid St SE1 .138 C3
Drum St E1 .111 A2
Drummer Lo N7 .5 B1
Drummond Cres
NW1 .....93 B4
Drummond Gate
SW1 .....147 C2
Drummond Ho 12
E2 .....24 C3
Drummond Rd SE16 .40 A3
Drummonds Pl TW9 .54 A3
Drury Ho SW8 .170 C4
Drury La WC2 .106 B1
Dryad St SW15 .57 C4
Dryburgh Ho SW1 .146 B2
Dryburgh Mans
SW15 .....57 B4
Dryburgh Rd SW15 .57 B4
Dryden Ct SE11 .149 C3
Dryden Ho 18 N16 .16 A4
6 SE5 .....49 A2
Dryden St WC2 .106 B1
Dryer's Bldgs EC1 .107 B3
Dryfield Wlk 8 SE8 .51 C4
Drysdale Flats 3
E8 .....16 B3
Drysdale Ho 1 E2 .24 B3
Drysdale Pl N1 .24 A3
Drysdale St N1 .24 A3
Du Cane Ct SW12 .72 C3
Du Cane Rd W12 .29 C3
Du Cros Rd W3 .29 A1
Du Maurier Ho 2
NW3 .....12 B3
Dublin Ave E8 .24 C4
Ducal St E2 .99 A3
Ducane Cl W12 .30 B3
Ducavel Ho SW2 .74 B3

Duchess Mews W1 .104 B3
Duchess of Bedford Ho
W8 .....127 B3
Duchess of Bedford's
Wlk W8 .....127 B3
Duchess St W1 .104 B3
Duchy St SE1 .121 C2
Ducie Ho 7 SW15 .57 B2
Ducie St SW4 .62 B3
Duck La W1 .105 B1
Duckett St E1 .33 A4
Dudden Hill La NW10 .8 B3
Dudley Ct W1 .102 C1
WC2 .....106 A2
Dudley Ho W2 .101 B3
SW9 .....173 B2
Dudley Rd NW6 .23 B3
Richmond TW9 .44 B1
Dudley St W2 .101 B3
Dudmaston Mews
SW3 .....143 C2
Duff St E14 .34 A3
Duffell Ho SE11 .149 A1
Dufferin Ave EC1 .97 B1
Dufferin St EC1 .97 A1
Duffield Ho N4 .6 B4
Dufour's Pl W1 .105 A1
Dugdale Ho 10 N7 .13 C3
Duke Humphrey Rd
SE3 .....53 A1
Duke of Wellington Pl
SW1,W1 .....131 C4
Duke of York St
SW1 .....119 A2
Duke St W1 .103 C1
Duke St Hill SE1 .123 C2
Duke St Mans W1 .103 C1
Duke St St James's
SW1 .....119 A2
Duke's Ave W4 .37 C1
Duke's Head Yd N6 .4 A3
Duke's Mews W1 .103 C2
Duke's Pl EC3 .110 B1
Duke's Rd WC1 .93 C3
Duke's Yd W1 .117 C4
Dukes Ct SE13 .52 B1
SE22 .....65 A2
Dukes Gate 4 W4 .37 B2
Dukes Head Yd N6 .4 A3
Dukes La W8 .128 A4
Dukes Point N6 .4 A3
Dulas St N4 .5 B3
Dulford St W11 .31 A2 112 A4
Dulka Rd SW11 .60 B2
Dulverton NW1 .83 A3
Dulverton Mans
WC1 .....95 A1
Dulwich Coll (Endowed)
SE21 .....76 A3
Dulwich Coll Picture
Gall SE21 .....76 A3
Dulwich Coll Prep Sch
SE21 .....76 A1
Dulwich Comm
SE21 .....76 A3
Dulwich Hamlet Jun &
Inf Sch SE21 .....63 C1

Dulwich High Sch for
Boys SE21 . . . . 63 C2
Dulwich Hospl SE22 64 A3
Dulwich Mead SE24 63 B1
Dulwich Mews 1
SE22 . . . . 64 B3
Dulwich Oaks The
SE21 . . . . 76 B1
Dulwich Rd SE24 . . . 63 A1
Dulwich Village
SE21 . . . . 64 A3
Dulwich Village CE Inf
Sch SE21 . . . . 64 A3
Dumain Ct SE11 . . . 150 A3
Dumbarton Ct
SW2 . . . . 74 A4
Dumbarton Rd SW2 62 A1
Dumont Rd N16 . . . . .7 A1
Dumphreys Ho 5
SW4 . . . . 73 C4
Dumpton Pl NW1 . . .12 C1
Dunbar St SE27 . . . . .75 B1
Dunboyne Rd NW3 . .12 B3
Dunbridge Ho 7
SW15 . . . . 56 B1
Dunbridge St E2 . . . .25 A1
E2 . . . . 99 B2
Duncan Gr 3 W3 . . . 29 A3
Duncan Ho 4 SW1 . .12 B1
Duncan Rd E8 . . . . . . .25 A4
Richmond TW9 . . . . . .54 A3
Duncan St N1 . . . . . . .86 A2
Duncan Terr N1 . . . . .86 A2
Duncannon Ho
SW1 . . . . 147 C1
Duncannon St
WC2 . . . . 120 A3
Dunch St 55 E1 . . . . .32 A3
Duncombe Ho 2
SW19 . . . . .69 C3
Duncombe Prim Sch
N19 . . . . .4 C3
Duncombe Rd N19 . . .4 C3
Duncrievie Rd SE13 .67 C1
Dundalk Ho 2 E1 . . .32 B3
Dundalk Rd SE4 . . . . 66 A4
Dundas Ho 12 E2 . . . 25 B3
Dundas Rd SE15 . . . .50 B1
Dundee Ct 28 E1 . . . .32 A1
Dundee Ho W9 . . . . . 88 C4
Dundee St E1 . . . . . . .32 A1
Dundee Wharf E14 . .33 B2
Dundonald Rd
NW10 . . . . .22 C4
Dundry Ho 5 SE26 . .76 C1
Dunelm Gr SE27 . . . .75 B1
Dunelm St E1 . . . . . . .32 C3
Dunford Rd N7 . . . . . 14 B4
Dungarvan Ave
SW15 . . . . .56 C3
Dungeness Ho
SW18 . . . . .59 B3
Dunhill Point 2
SW15 . . . . .69 A3
Dunkeld Ho 12 E14 . .34 C3
Dunlace Rd E5 . . . . . .17 C4
Dunlin Ct 11 SE21 . 175 C2
Dunlin Ho 6 SE16 . . .40 C2
Dunloe Ct 7 E2 . . . . .24 B3
Dunlop Pl SE16 . . . . 139 A1
Dunmore Pt E2 . . . . . 98 C4
Dunmore Rd NW6 . . .23 A4

Dunmow Ho SE11 . . 149 A2
Dunmow Rd E15 . . . .19 C4
Dunmow Wlk N1 . . . .86 C4
Dun St SE18 . . . . .16 B3
Dunn's Pas WC1 . . . 106 B2
Dunnage Cres SE16 . 41 A2
Dunnet Ho 20 E3 . . . .26 B3
Dunnico Ho SE17 . . 152 A2
Dunnock Ct 15 SE21 75 C2
Dunollie Pl NW5 . . . .13 B3
Dunollie Rd NW5 . . .13 B3
Dunoon Ho N1 . . . . . .84 C3
Dunraven Ho 1
TW9 . . . . 44 B2
Dunraven Lower Sch
SW16 . . . . .74 A1
Dunraven Rd W12 . .29 C1
Dunraven St W1 . . . 117 A4
Dunraven Upper Sch
SW16 . . . . .74 A1
Dunrobin Ct NW3 . . .11 A3
Dunsany Rd W14 . . . 39 C3
Dunsfold Ho 4
SW2 . . . . 74 B3
Dunsford Way
SW15 . . . . .57 A1
Dunsmure Rd N16 . . .7 A3
Dunstable Ct 3
SE3 . . . . 53 C3
Dunstable Mews
W1 . . . . 103 C4
Dunstable Rd TW10,
Richmond TW9 . . . . . .54 A3
Dunstall Ho 9 SE15 .49 C2
Dunstan Ho 6 E1 . . .32 B4
Dunstan Hos 5 E1 . . 32 B4
Dunstan Rd NW11 . . .1 C3
Dunstan's Gr SE22 . .65 A1
Dunstan's Rd SE22 . 64 C1
Dunster Ct 3 E14 . . 34 A2
Dunster Gdns NW6 . .10 B1
Dunsterville Way
SE1 . . . . 137 C3
Dunston Rd SW11 . . 169 C1
E8 . . . . 24 B4
Dunston St E8 . . . . . .24 B4
Dunton Ho 16 SW4 . .73 C4
Dunton Rd SE1 . . . . 152 C3
Dunthill Rd 6 E16 . . 35 A4
Dunworth Mews 6
W11 . . . . 31 B3
Duplex Ride SW1 . . 131 A3
Dupont St 13 E14 . . .33 A3
Durand Gdns SW9 . 173 A3
Durand Prim Sch
SW9 . . . . 173 B4
Durant St E2 . . . . 24 C2
Durban Ho 20 W12 . .30 A2
Durdans Ho 5 NW1 .13 B1
Durfey Ho SE5 . . . . . 48 C3
Durford Cres SW15 . 69 A3
Durham Ct 3 NW6 . .23 C3
Durham House St
WC2 . . . . 120 B3
Durham Pl SW3 . . . 144 C1
Durham Rd N4,N7 . . .5 B2
Durham Row E1 . . . . 33 A4
Durham St SE11 . . . 162 C4
Durham Terr W2 . . . 100 A2
Durley Rd N16 . . . . . . .7 A4
Durlock Ho NW9 . . . 173 B4
Durlston Rd E5 . . . . . . .7 C2
Durnford St 3 SE10 52 B4
Durnsford Ave
SW18,SW19 . . . . .70 C2

Durnsford Rd SW18,
SW19 . . . . .70 C1
Durrell Rd SW6 . . . . 164 C3
Durrels Ho W14 . . . . 141 A4
Durrington Rd E5 . . .18 A4
Durrington Twr
SW8 . . . . 171 A2
Durrisdeer Ho NW2 . 10 B4
Dursley Cl SE3 . . . . .53 C1
Dursley Ct 2 SE15 . .49 A3
Durston NW5 . . . . . . .12 C3
Durward St E1 . . . . . .32 A4
Durweston Mews
W1 . . . . 103 A4
Durweston St W1 . . 103 A4
Dutch Yd SW18 . . . . .58 C2
Dutton Ho SW2 . . . . .75 A3
Dutton St SE10 . . . . .52 B2
Dwight Ct SW6 . . . . 164 B2
Dycer Ho 4 E9 . . . . . 17 B1
Dye House La E3 . . . 26 C4
Dyer's La SW15 . . . . .57 A3
Dykes Ct 1 SW2 . . . .74 B3
Dylan Rd 3 SE24 . . . 63 A3
Dylways SE5 . . . . .63 C3
Dymchurch Ho 12
E5 . . . . 17 A3
Dymes Path SW19 . .69 C2
Dymock St SE15 . . . 115 B3
Dymock St SW6 . . . . 59 A4
Dyne Rd NW6 . . . . . . .10 B1
Dynevor Rd N16 . . . . .7 B1
Richmond TW10 . . . .54 A2
Dynham Rd NW6 . . . . 10 C1
Dyott St WC1,
WC1,WC2 . . . . 106 A2
Dysart St EC2 . 24 A1 98 A1
Dyson Ho 3 SE10 . . . 43 B1

E

Eade Rd N4 . . . . .6 B4
Eagle Cl SE16 . . . . . . 40 B1
Eagle Ct EC1 . . . . . . 108 A4
E3 . . . . 97 A4
Eagle Ho 22 E1 . . . . .25 A1
Eagle Hts 10 SW11 . .60 A4
Eagle Lo NW11 . . . . . .1 B4
Eagle Mans N16 . . . .16 B3
Eagle Mews N1 . . . . .16 A2
Eagle Pl SW1 . . . . . . 119 A3
SW7 . . . . 143 A2
Eagle St WC1 . . . . . . 106 C3
Eagle Wharf Rd N1 . 87 A2
Eagle Works E1 . . . . .99 A3
Ealing Tertiary Coll
W3 . . . . 28 A1
Eamann Casey Ho
SW9 . . . . 173 C3
Eamont Ct NW8 . . . . .80 B2
Eamont St NW8 . . . . .80 B2
Eardley Cres SW5 . . 141 C1
Earl Ho NW1 . . . . .90 B1
Earl Rd SW14 . . . . . . .55 B3
Earl St EC2 . . . . 110 A4
Earl's Court Ctr ★
SW5 . . . . 141 B1
Earl's Court Gdns
SW5 . . . . 142 A3
Earl's Court Rd
SW5,W8 . . . . 141 C4
Earl's Court Sq
SW5 . . . . 142 A2
Earl's Court Sta
SW5 . . . . 141 C3

Earldom Rd SW15 . . 57 B3
Earlham St WC2 . . . 106 A1
Earlom Ho WC1 . . . . 95 B3
Earlom Rd SW1 . . . . 127 A1
Earls Terr W8 . . . . . . 127 A4
Earls Wlk W8 . . . . . . 127 B1
Earlsferry Way N1 . . 14 A1
Earlsfield Prim Sch
SW18 . . . . 71 B2
Earlsfield Rd SW18 . 71 B4
Earlsfield Sta SW18 71 B3
Earlsmead Rd NW10 22 B2
Earlsthorpe Mews 3
SW12 . . . . 60 C1
Earlstoke St EC1 . . . 96 A4
Earlston Gr E9 . . . . . . 25 A4
Earlswood Cl 10
SE10 . . . . 43 A1
Earlswood Ho 2
SW2 . . . . 74 B3
Earlswood St SE10 . . 43 A1
Early Mews NW1 . . . 82 B4
Earnshaw St WC2,
WC2 . . . . 105 C2
Earsby St W14 . . . . . 140 B4
Eashing Point 5
SW15 . . . . 69 A3
Easleys Mews W1 . . 103 C2
East Acton Arc W3 . . 29 B3
East Acton Ct 5 W3 . 29 A2
East Acton La W3 . . . 29 A1
East Acton Prim Sch
W3 . . . . 29 A2
East Acton Sta W3 . . 29 B3
East Arbour St E1 . . . 32 C3
East Bank N16 . . . . . . .7 A4
East Block 5 SE1 . . . 121 C3
East Churchfield Rd
W3 . . . . 28 C1
East Cross Ctr E15 . . 18 C2
East Cross Route
E9 . . . . 18 B3
E3 . . . . 18 B1
East Dulwich Gr
SE22 . . . . 64 A2
East Dulwich Rd
SE15,SE22 . . . . 64 C3
East Dulwich Sta
SE22 . . . . 64 A3
East Ferry Rd E14 . . . 42 A2
East Harding St
EC4 . . . . 107 C2
East Heath Rd NW3 . .2 C1
East Hill SW18 . . . . . 59 B2
East India Bldgs 8
E14 . . . . 33 C2
East India Dock Basin
★ E14 . . . . 35 A1
East India Dock Rd
E14 . . . . 34 A2
East India Dock Road
Tunnel 17 E14 . . . . . . 35 A2
East India Dock Wall Rd
E14 . . . . 34 C2
East India Sta E14 . . 34 C2
East La 20 SE16 . . . 139 B3
East London Coll for
Toynbee Theatre
E1 . . . . 111 A3
East London Stadium
E3 . . . . 33 B4
East Mount St E1 . . . 32 A4
East Pas EC1 . . . . . . 108 C4
East Point SE1 . . . . . 153 B2
East Poultry Ave
EC1 . . . . 108 A3

East Putney Sta
SW15 . . . . 58 B2
East Rd N1 . . . . 97 C4
East Row W10 . . . . . . 23 A1
East Sheen Ave
SW14 . . . . 55 C3
East Sheen Prim Sch
SW14 . . . . 56 A3
East Smithfield E1 . 125 A3
East St SE17 . . . . . . 151 B2
East Surrey Gr SE15 49 B3
East Tenter St 1 . . . 111 A1
East View NW5 . . . . . .2 C2
Eastbourne Ave W3 . 29 A3
Eastbourne Gdns
SW14 . . . . 55 B4
Eastbourne Mews
W2 . . . . 101 A2
Eastbourne Rd W4 . . 45 B4
Eastbourne Terr
W2 . . . . 101 A2
Eastbury Gr W4 . . . . 38 A1
Eastbury Terr E1 . . . . 25 C1
Eastcastle St W1 . . . 105 A2
Eastcheap EC3 . . . . 124 A4
Eastcote St SW9 . . . 172 C1
Eastdown Ho E8 . . . . 16 C4
Eastdown Pk SE13 . . 67 C3
Eastern Rd SE4 . . . . . 66 C3
Eastfields Rd W3 . . . 28 B4
Eastlake Ho NW8 . . . 89 C1
Eastlake Rd SE5 . . . . 48 B1
Eastlands Cres SE21 64 B1
Eastleigh Wlk 9
SW15 . . . . 68 C4
Eastman Dental Hospl
WC1 . . . . 94 C2
Eastman Ho 7 SW4 . 61 B1
Eastmearn Rd SE21,
SE21 . . . . 75 B2
Eastney St SE10 . . . . 42 C1
Easton Ho 4 SE27 . . 75 A1
Easton St WC1 . . . . . 95 B3
Eastry Ho SW8 . . . . 162 A2
Eastvale W3 . . . . 29 B1
Eastway E9,E10 . . . . .18 C4
Eastway Pk E9 . . . . . .18 B2
Eastwell Ho SE1 . . . 137 C2
Eastwick Ct 2
SW19 . . . . 69 C3
Eaton Cl SW1 . . . . . 145 B3
Eaton Dr SW9 . . . . . . 63 A3
Eaton Gate SW1 . . . 145 B4
Eaton House The Manor
Sch SW4 . . . . 61 A3
Eaton La SW1 . . . . . 132 B1
Eaton Mans SW1 . . 145 B3
Eaton Mews N
SW1 . . . . 131 C1
Eaton Mews S
SW1 . . . . 132 A1
Eaton Mews W
SW1 . . . . 145 C4
Eaton Pl SW1 . . . . . 131 C1
Eaton Row SW1 . . . 132 A1
Eaton Sq SW1 . . . . . 131 C1
Eaton Terr SW1 . . . . 145 C4
Eaton Terr Mews
SW1 . . . . 145 B4
Eatonville Rd SW17 . 72 B2
Eatonville Villas
SW17 . . . . 72 B2

Ebbisham Dr SW8 .....162 C3
Ebbsfleet Rd NW2 ......10 A4
Ebenezer Ho SE11 ....150 A3
Ebenezer Mussel Ho **5**
E2 ....25 B3
Ebenezer St N1 ....97 B4
Ebley Cl SE15 ....49 B4
Ebner St SW18 ....59 A2
Ebony Ho **10** NW3 ....11 A2
Ebor Cotts SW15 ....68 A1
Ebor St E1,E2 ....98 C2
Eburne Rd N7 ....5 A1
Ebury Bridge Rd
SW1 ....146 B1
Ebury Mews SW1 ......146 A4
Ebury Mews E
SW1 ....132 A1
Ebury Sq SW1 ....146 A2
Ebury St SW1 ....146 A4
Eccles Rd SW11 ....60 B3
Ecclesbourne Prim Sch
N1 ....15 C1
Ecclesbourne Rd
N1 ....15 C1
Eccleston Ho **1**
SW2 ....62 C1
Eccleston Mews
SW1 ....131 C1
Eccleston Pl SW1 .....146 A4
Eccleston Sq SW1 ....146 B3
Eccleston Sq Mews
SW1 ....146 C3
Eccleston St SW1 .....146 A4
Eckersley St E1 ....99 A1
Eckford St N1 ....85 B2
Eckstein Rd SW11 .....60 A3
Edans Ct W12 ....38 B4
Edbrooke Rd W9 ....23 C1
Eddisbury Ho **7**
SE26 ....76 C1
Eddiscombe Rd
SW6 ....165 A2
Eddystone Rd SE4 .....66 A2
Eddystone Twr SE8 ....41 A1
Eden Cl W8 ....127 C2
NW3 ....2 B2
Eden Gr N7 ....14 B3
Eden Ho NW8 ....90 A1
15 SW11 ....60 A4
Eden Mews SW17 ......71 B1
Edenbridge Cl **8**
SE16 ....40 A1
Edenbridge Rd E9 ....17 C1
Edendale W3 ....28 A2
Edenham Way WU10 ..31 B4
Edenhurst Ave SW6 ...58 B4
Edensmuir Ct SE3 ......53 C3
Edensor Gdns W4 ......46 A3
Edensor Rd W4 ....46 A3
Edenvale St SW6 ......166 B2
Edgar Ho SW8 ....162 A2
E9 ....18 A3
Edgar Kail Way
SE22 ....64 A3
Edgar Rd E3 ....27 A2
Edgarley Terr SW6 ...164 A3
Edgcott Ho W10 ....30 B4
Edge St W8 ..31 C1 113 C2
Edgecombe Ho
4 SE5 ....49 A1
SW19 ....70 A3
Edgecote Cl **7** W3 ..28 B1
Edgehill Ho **7** SW9 ..48 A1
Edgel St SW18 ....59 A3
Edgeley La SW4 ....61 C4
Edgeley Rd SW4 ....61 C4

Edgeworth Ho NW8 ....78 C4
Edgson Ho **1** SW1 ..146 A2
Edgware Rd W1,
W2,NW1,NW8 ....102 A3
Edgware Road Sta
(Bakerloo) NW1 ....102 A3
Edgware Road Sta
(Ham,Distr,Circle)
NW1 ....102 B3
Edinburgh Cl **7** E2 ..25 B3
Edinburgh Ct **10**
SE16 ....32 C1
Edinburgh Ho W9 ......88 B4
11 W3 ....28 C3
Edington **20** NW5 ....12 C2
Edis St NW1 ....81 C4
Edison Ho SE1 ....151 B4
Edith Gr SW10 ....157 A2
Edith Ho **6** W6 ....39 B1
Edith Neville Prim Sch
NW1 ....83 B1
Edith Ramsay Ho
E1 ....33 A4
Edith Rd W14 ....140 B3
E15 ....19 C3
Edith Row SW6 ....166 B4
Edith St E2 ....24 C3
Edith Summerskill Ho
SW6 ....154 C2
Edith Terr SW10 ......156 C2
Edith Villas W14 ......140 C2
Edith Yd SW10 ....157 A2
Editha Mans SW10 ..156 C3
Edmeston Cl E9 ....18 A2
Edmond Ct SE14 ....50 B2
Edmond Ho **5**
SE16 ....40 C3
Edmonton Ct **5**
SE16 ....40 B3
Edmund Ho SE17 .....150 B1
SE14 ....50 B3
Edmund St SE5 ....48 C3
Edmund Waller Jun &
Inf Schs SE14 ....50 C1
Edna St SW11 ....168 A3
Ednam Ho SE15 ....49 C4
Edred Ho E9 ....18 A4
Edric Ho SW1 ....147 C4
Edric Rd SE14 ....50 C3
Edrich Ho SW4 ....172 A3
Edridge Ho **9** SE27 ..75 A1
Edward Alleyn Ho
SE21 ....76 A4
Edward Dodd Ct N1 ..97 C4
Edward Edward's Ho
SE1 ....122 A1
Edward Friend Ho **4**
N16 ....7 A1
Edward Ho **2**
SW1 ....89 B1
Edward Kennedy Ho **18**
W10 ....23 A1
Edward Mann Cl **12**
E1 ....32 C3
Edward Mews NW1 ....82 B1
Edward Pl SE8 ....51 B4
Edward Robinson Ho **5**
SE14 ....50 C3
Edward Sq N1 ....84 C3
SE16 ....33 A1
Edward St SE14 ....51 B3
Edward VII Mans
NW10 ....22 C2
Edward Wilson Prim Sch
W2 ....100 A4

Edward's Cotts **11**
N1 ....15 A1
Edward's La N16 ....7 A2
Edwardes Sq W8 .....127 A1
Edwards Mews
N1 ....103 B1
W1 ....103 C1
Edwin Ho SE15 ....49 C3
Edwin St E1 ....25 B1
E16 ....35 C4
Edwin's Mead E9 ......18 A4
Edwyn Ho SW18 ....59 A1
Effie Pl SW6 ....155 C1
Effie Rd SW6 ....155 C1
Effingham Ho SW8 ...171 B1
Effra Cft SW2 ....62 C2
Effra Mans SW2 ....62 C2
Effra Par SW2 ....62 C2
Effra Rd SW2 ....62 C2
Effra Road Ret Pk
SW2 ....62 C2
Egbert Ho E9 ....18 A3
Egbert St NW1 ....81 B4
Egbury Ho SW15 ......56 B1
Egerton Cres SW3 ...144 B4
Egerton Ct **5** W10 ..54 A2
Egerton Dr SE10 ....52 A2
Egerton Gdns SW3 ..130 A1
NW10 ....22 B4
Egerton Gdns Mews
SW3 ....130 B1
Egerton Ho **3** W4 ..45 B4
Egerton Pl SW3 ....130 B1
Egerton Rd N16 ....7 B4
Egerton Terr SW3 ....130 B1
Egham Cl SW19 ....70 A2
Eglantine Rd SW18 ..59 B2
Eglington Ct SE17 ....48 B4
Egliston Mews
SW15 ....57 B4
Egliston Rd SW15 ......57 B4
Egmont St SE14 ....50 C3
Egremont Ho SE13 ....52 A1
Egremont Rd SE27 ....74 C1
Egret Ho **11** SE16 ...40 C2
Ekarra Ho SW8 ....172 B4
Elaine Ct **13** NW3 ...12 B2
Elaine Gr NW5 ....12 C3
Elaine Ho N4 ....5 A3
Elam Cl SE5 ....48 A1
Elam St SE5 ....48 A1
Elan Ct E1 ....32 A4
Eland Rd SW11 ....60 B4
Elba Pl SE17 ....151 A4
Elbe St SW6 ....166 C2
Elborough St SW18 ..70 C3
Elbury Dr E16 ....35 C3
Elcho St SW11 ....158 B1
Elcot Ave SE15 ....50 A3
Elder Ct **32** SE8 ......51 B4
Elder St E1 ....24 B1 98 C1
Elder Wlk N1 ....86 B4
Elderberry Rd W5 .....36 A4
Elderfield Ho **3**
E14 ....33 C2
Elderfield Rd E5 ....17 B4
Eldon Ct NW6 ....23 C4
Eldon Gr NW3 ....11 C3
Eldon Ho SW9 ....63 A4
Eldon Rd W8 ....128 B1
Eldon St EC2 ....109 C3
Eldridge Ct SE16 .....139 B1
Eleanor Cl SE16 ....40 C4
Eleanor Ct **13** E2 ....24 C4

Eleanor Gr SW13 ......56 A4
Eleanor Ho **1** NW5 ..13 B3
18 W6 ....39 B1
Eleanor Palmer Prim
Sch NW5 ....13 B4
Eleanor Rathbone Ho **1**
N6 ....4 C4
Eleanor Rd E8 ....17 A1
E8 ....17 A2
Eleanor St E3 ....26 C2
Electric Ave SW9 ......62 C3
Electric Ho **13** E3 ....26 C2
Electric La **2** SW9 ..62 C3
Electric Mans **1**
SW9 ....62 C3
Elephant & Castle
SE1 ....136 B1
SE1 ....136 B3
Elephant & Castle Sta
SE1 ....136 B1
SE17 ....150 C4
Elephant La SE16 ......40 B4
Elephant Rd SE17 ....150 C4
Elf Row E1 ....32 B2
Elfindale Rd SE24 .....63 B2
Elfort Rd N5 ....14 C4
Elgar Ave W5 ....36 A4
Elgar Cl SE8 ....51 C3
Elgar Ct W14 ....126 A1
Elgar Ho SW1 ....146 B1
NW6 ....11 B1
Elgar St SE16 ....41 A3
Elgin Ave W9 ....88 B4
W12 ....39 A3
Elgin Cres
W11 ....31 A2 112 B4
Elgin Ct W9 ....88 A2
Elgin Ho **8** E14 ....34 A3
Elgin Mans W9 ....88 A3
Elgin Mews W11 ....31 A3
Elgin Mews N W9 .....88 B4
Elgin Mews S W9 ......88 B4
Elgood Ho NW8 ....79 C1
Elham Ho **15** E5 ....17 A3
Elia Mews N1 ....86 A1
Elia St N1 ....86 A1
Elias Pl SW8 ....163 B3
Elim Est SE1 ....138 A2
Elim St SE1 ....138 A2
Eliot Ct SW18 ....59 A1
Eliot Gdns SW15 ....56 C3
Eliot Hill SE13 ....52 B1
Eliot Ho **10** TW10 ....54 A1
Eliot Mews NW8 ....78 C2
Eliot Pk SE13 ....52 B1
Eliot Pl SE3 ....53 A1
Eliot Vale SE3 ....52 C1
Elizabeth Ave N1 ......87 A4
Elizabeth Barnes Ct
SW6 ....166 B2
Elizabeth Cl **5**
W9 ....89 A1
12 E14 ....34 A3
Elizabeth Cotts **5**
TW9 ....44 C2
Elizabeth Ct SW1 .....133 C1
SW10 ....157 C3
SE22 ....64 C3
Elizabeth Finn Ho
W12 ....38 C3
Elizabeth Garrett
Anderson Hospl
NW1 ....93 C3
Elizabeth Garrett
Anderson Sch N1 .....85 C2
Elizabeth Gdns W3 ...29 B1
Elizabeth Ho SW1 ...149 C3

Elizabeth Ho continued
46 E3 ....27 A2
19 W6 ....39 B1
Elizabeth Ind Est
SE14 ....50 C4
Elizabeth Kenny Ho
N1 ....15 B2
Elizabeth Mews
NW3 ....12 B2
Elizabeth Selby Inf Sch
E2 ....24 C2 99 C4
Elizabeth Sq **3**
SE16 ....33 A2
Elizabeth St SW1 ....145 C4
Elkington Point
SE11 ....149 B3
Elkstone Ct **1** SE15 ..49 A4
Elkstone Rd W10 ......31 B4
Ella Rd N4,N8 ....5 C4
Ellacombe Ho **1**
SW2 ....74 C4
Ellaline Rd W6 ....47 C4
Elland Ho **15** E14 ....33 B3
Elland Rd SE15 ....65 B3
Ellen St **1** 111 C1
Ellen Wilkinson Ho
SW6 ....155 A3
2 E2 ....25 C2
Ellenborough Pl
SW15 ....56 C3
Ellerby St SW6 ....164 A3
Ellerdale Rd NW3 .....11 B3
Ellerdale St SE13 .....54 A1
Ellerker Gdns TW10 ..54 A1
Ellerslie Gdns
NW10 ....21 C4
Ellerslie Ind Est
SW2 ....62 A2
Ellerslie Rd W12 ....30 A1
Ellerton Ct W3 ....37 A4
Ellerton Rd SW13 ......46 C2
SW17,SW18 ....71 C3
Ellery Ho SE17 ....151 C3
Ellery St SE15 ....50 A1
Ellesmere Ct W4 ......45 C4
Ellesmere Rd NW10 ..8 C3
E3 ....26 A3
Ellesmere Rd (Great
West Rd) W4 ....45 C4
Ellesmere St E14 ......34 A3
Ellingfort Rd E8 ....17 A1
Ellingham Rd E15 .....19 C4
W12 ....38 C4
Ellington Ho SE1 .....137 A1
Ellington St N7 ....14 C2
Elliot Rd SW9 ....48 A3
Elliott Sch SW15 ......57 B1
Elliott Sq NW3 ....12 A1
Elliott's Pl N1 ....86 B3
Elliott's Row SE11 ...150 B4
Ellis Franklin Ct
NW8 ....78 C2
Ellis Ho SE17 ....151 B2
Ellis St SW1 ....145 B4
Ellisfield Dr SW15 ....68 C4
Ellison Ho **1** SE13 ...52 B1
Ellison Rd SW13 ....46 B1

Ellsworth St E2 ...25 A2
Ellwood Ct W9 ...88 B1
Elm Bank Gdns
  SW13 ...46 A1
Elm Bank Mans
  SW13 ...46 A1
Elm Cl N19 ...4 B2
Elm Court Sch SE27 ...75 B2
Elm Cres W5 ...36 A4
Elm Ct EC4 ...121 B4
  SW9 ...173 B4
  SE13 ...67 C4
Elm Friars Wlk
  NW1 ...13 C1
Elm Gn W3 ...29 A3
Elm Gr NW2 ...9 C4
  SE15 ...49 C1
Elm Grove Rd W5 ...36 A4
  SW13 ...46 C1
Elm Ho E14 ...42 B4
Lo SW6 ...47 C2
Elm Park Gdns
  SW10 ...143 B1
Elm Park Ho SW10 ...143 B1
Elm Park La SW3 ...143 B1
Elm Park Mans
  SW10 ...157 A4
Elm Park Rd SW3 ...157 B4
Elm Pk SW7 ...74 B4
Elm Pl SW7 ...143 B2
Elm Quay SW8 ...161 B3
Elm Rd SW14 ...55 B3
Elm Row NW3 ...2 B1
Elm St WC1 ...95 A1
Elm Terr NW2 ...1 C1
Elm Tree Cl NW8 ...89 B4
Elm Tree Ct NW8 ...89 B4
  5 SE5 ...48 B2
Elm Tree Rd NW8 ...89 B4
Elm Way NW10 ...1 A2
Elm Wlk NW3 ...1 C2
Elm Wood Prim Sch
  SE27 ...75 A2
Elmar Ct W6 ...164 B2
Elmbourne Rd
  SW17 ...73 A1
Elmbridge Wlk E8 ...16 C1
Elmcourt Rd SE21,
  SE27 ...75 A2
Elmcroft N6 ...4 B4
Elmcroft Ave NW11 ...1 B4
Elmcroft Cres NW11 ...1 A4
Elmcroft St E5 ...17 B4
Elmer Ho NW1 ...102 A4
Elmfield Ho N6 ...15 B3
  W9 ...23 C1
Elmfield Mans 5
  SW17 ...72 C2
Elmfield Rd SW17 ...73 A2
Elmfield Way W9 ...31 C4
Elmhurst Mans
  SW4 ...61 C4
Elmhurst St SW4 ...61 C4
Elmhurst Villas
  SE15 ...65 B3
Elmington Rd SE5 ...48 C3
Elmira St SE13 ...67 A4
Elmore Ho SW9 ...48 A1
Elmore St N1 ...15 C1
Elms Cres SW4 ...61 C1
Elms Mews W2 ...115 B4
Elms Rd SW4 ...61 B2
Elms The NW11 ...21 A3

Elms The continued
  SW13 ...56 B4
Elmshaw Rd SW15 ...56 C2
Elmslie Point 2 E3 ...33 B4
Elmstone Rd SW6 ...165 B4
Elmton Ct NW8 ...89 B2
Elmton Way E5 ...7 C1
Elmwood Ct 1 SW11 ...170 A4
Elmwood Ho NW10 ...21 C4
  NW10 ...22 A3
Elmwood Rd W4 ...45 B4
  SE24 ...63 C2
Elmworth Gr SE21 ...75 C2
Elnathan Mews W9 ...88 B1
Elphinstone St N5 ...15 A4
Elrington Rd E8 ...16 C2
Elsa St E1 ...33 A4
Elsdale St E9 ...17 B2
Elsden Mews 6 E2 ...25 B3
Elsenham St SW18,
  SW19 ...70 B2
Elsfield NW5 ...13 A3
Elsham Rd W14 ...126 A2
Elsham Terr W14 ...126 A2
Elsie Lane Ct W2 ...100 A3
Elsie Rd SE22 ...64 B3
Elsiemaud Rd SE4 ...66 B2
Elsinore Gdns NW2 ...1 A1
Elsinore Ho N1 ...85 B3
  12 SE5 ...48 B1
Elsinore Way TW9 ...55 A4
Elsley Rd SW11 ...60 C4
Elspeth Rd SW11 ...60 B3
Elstead Ho 9 SW2 ...74 B4
Elsted St SE17 ...151 C3
Elstow Grange NW6 ...9 C1
Elswick Rd SE13 ...52 A1
Elswick St SW6 ...166 C2
  SW6 ...166 C2
Elsworthy Rd NW3 ...80 A4
Elsworthy Rise NW3 ...12 A1
Elsworthy Terr NW3 ...12 A1
Elsynge Road Mans
  SW18 ...59 C2
Elthiron Rd SW6 ...165 C3
Elthorne Rd N19 ...4 C2
Elthruda Rd SE13 ...67 C1
Elton Ho 3 E3 ...26 B4
Elton Pl N16 ...16 A3
Elton St 11 N16 ...16 A3
Eltringham St SW18 ...59 B3
Elvaston Mews
  SW7 ...129 A2
Elvaston Pl SW7 ...129 A1
Elveden Ho 17 SW9 ...63 A3
Elver Gdns 2 E2 ...24 C2
Elverson Rd SE8 ...52 A1
Elverson Rd Sta
  SE8 ...52 A1
Elverton St SW1 ...147 B4
Elvin Ho 2 E9 ...17 B2
Elvis Rd NW2 ...9 B2
Elwin St E2 ...24 C2 99 B4
Elwood St N4,N5 ...6 A1
Elworth Ho SW8 ...163 A1
Ely Cottages SW8 ...162 C1
Ely Court Flats
  SW6 ...164 C3
Ely Ho 22 SE15 ...49 C3
Ely Pl EC1 ...107 C3
Elysium Gate SW6 ...164 C2
Elysium Pl SW6 ...164 C1
Elysium St 6 SW6 ...164 C1

Elystan Pl SW3 ...144 C2
Elystan St SW3 ...144 B3
Elystan Wlk N1 ...85 B3
Elyston Ct SW15 ...57 A2
Emanuel Ave W3 ...28 B3
Emanuel Ct W3 ...28 C3
Emanuel Sch SW11 ...60 A2
Emba St SE16 ...139 C3
Embankment SW15 ...47 C1
Embankment Gdns
  SW3 ...159 A4
Embankment Pier
  WC2 ...120 B2
Embankment Pl
  WC2 ...120 B2
Embankment Sta
  WC2 ...120 B2
Embassy Ct NW8 ...79 C1
Embassy Ho 4 NW6 ...10 C1
Ember Ct 2 W12 ...38 A3
Emberton SE5 ...49 A4
Emberton Ct EC1 ...96 A3
Embleton Rd SE13 ...67 A3
Embley Point 3 E5 ...17 A4
Emden St SW6 ...166 B4
Emerald St WC1 ...106 C4
Emerson Ho N16 ...16 A3
Emerson St SE1 ...122 C2
Emery Hill St SW1 ...133 A1
Emery St SE1 ...135 C2
Emily Pl N7 ...14 C4
Emily St 2 E16 ...35 B1
Emlyn Gdns 3 W12 ...38 A3
Emlyn Rd W12 ...38 B3
Emmanuel CE Prim Sch
  NW6 ...10 C3
Emmanuel Ho
  SE11 ...149 B3
  SE21 ...75 C1
Emmanuel Rd SW12 ...73 C3
Emminster NW6 ...78 A4
Emmott Cl E1 ...26 A1
Emperor's Gate
  SW7 ...142 C4
Empingham 20
  SE8 ...40 C2
Empire Ho SW3 ...130 A1
Empire Wharf E3 ...26 A4
Empire Wharf Rd
  E14 ...42 C2
Empress Pl SW5 ...141 B1
Empress St SE17 ...48 B4
Empson St 3 E3 ...27 A1
Emsworth St 2 SW2 ...74 B2
Emu Rd SW8 ...170 A1
Enard Ho 27 E3 ...26 B3
Enbrook St W10 ...23 A2
Endeavour Way
  SW18 ...71 A1
Endell St WC2 ...106 A1
Enderby St SE10 ...43 A1
Endlesham Ct 2
  SW12 ...72 C4
Endlesham Rd
  SW12 ...72 C4
Endsleigh Gdns
  WC1 ...93 B2
Endsleigh Mans 4
  SW16 ...74 A1
Endsleigh Pl WC1 ...93 C2
Endsleigh St WC1 ...93 C2
Endwell Rd SE4 ...51 A1
Endymion Rd N4 ...6 A4
  SW2 ...62 B1

Energen Cl NW10 ...8 A1
Enfield Cloisters
  N1 ...98 A4
Enfield Ho SW9 ...172 B2
Enfield Rd E8,N1 ...16 A1
  W3 ...37 A4
Enford St W1 ...102 C4
Engadine St SW18 ...70 C3
Engate St SE13 ...67 B3
England's La NW3 ...12 B2
Englefield NW1 ...92 C3
Englefield Rd N1 ...16 A1
Englewood Rd
  SW12 ...61 B1
English Grounds
  SE1 ...124 A1
English Martyrs JMI
  Prim Sch SE17 ...151 C3
English Martyrs JMI Sch
  E1 ...111 A1
English Martyrs RC Sec
  Sch SE17 ...151 C3
Enid St SE16 ...138 C2
Enid Staff Ho 11
  N19 ...4 C4
Enmore Ct SW14 ...55 C2
Enmore Gdns SW14 ...55 C2
Enmore Rd SW15 ...57 B2
Ennerdale Ho 3 N4 ...6 C4
Ennerdale Rd TW9 ...44 C1
Ennersdale Prim Sch
  SE13 ...67 C2
Ennersdale Rd SE13 ...67 C2
Ennis Ho 18 E14 ...34 A3
Ennis Rd N4 ...5 C3
  SW7 ...130 A3
Ennismore Ave W4 ...38 B2
Ennismore Gdns
  SW7 ...130 A3
Ennismore Gdns Mews
  SW7 ...130 A2
Ennismore Mews
  SW7 ...130 A2
Ennismore St
  SW7 ...130 A2
Ensbury Ho SW8 ...162 C2
Ensign Ind Ctr 1 ...125 B3
Ensign St E1 ...125 B4
Ensor Mews SW7 ...143 B2
Enterprise Way
  NW10 ...21 C2
  SW18 ...58 C3
Enterprise Way SE8 ...41 B2
Epirus Mews SW6 ...155 A2
Epirus Rd SW6 ...155 A2
Epping Cl E14 ...41 C2
Epping Ho 5 E5 ...7 C2
Epping Pl N1 ...14 C2
Epple Rd SW6 ...165 A4
Epworth St EC2 ...97 C1
Equity Sq E2 ...99 A3
Erasmus St SW1 ...147 C3
Erconwald St W12 ...29 B3
Eresby Ho SW7 ...130 B3
Eresby Pl NW6 ...10 C1
Eric Fletcher Ct 7
  N1 ...15 B1
Eric Macdonald Ho
  SW6 ...165 C3
Eric Rd NW10 ...8 B2
Eric St E3 ...26 B1
Eric Wilkins Ho
  SE1 ...153 B1
Erica Ct SW4 ...172 B3
Erica Ho SE4 ...66 B4
Erica St W12 ...29 C2
Ericcson Cl SW18 ...58 C2

Ericson Ho N16 ...7 B3
  SE13 ...67 C3
Eridge Ho SE22 ...64 B4
Eridge Rd W4 ...37 C3
Erlanger Rd SE14 ...50 C1
Ermine Rd SE13 ...67 A3
  N15 ...
Ernest Bevin Sch
  SW17 ...72 A1
Ernest Gdns W4 ...45 A4
Ernest Simmonds Ho
  SE14 ...50 B1
Ernest St E1 ...25 C1
Ernshaw Pl SW15 ...58 A2
Eros (Shaftesbury
  Meml)* W1 ...119 B3
Erpingham Rd
  SW15 ...57 B4
Errington Rd W9 ...23 B1
Errol St EC1 ...97 A1
Erskine Ho SW1 ...146 C1
Erskine Rd NW3 ...12 B1
Escuan Lo N5 ...15 B3
Esker Gdns SW19 ...69 C2
Esher Ho SW8 ...171 C2
Esk Ho E3 ...26 B1
Eskdale NW1 ...82 C1
Esme Ho SW15 ...56 B3
Esmeralda Rd SE1 ...153 C3
Esmond Ct W8 ...128 B2
Esmond Gdns W4 ...37 C2
Esmond Rd NW6 ...23 B4
  W4 ...37 C2
Esmond St SW15 ...58 A3
Esparto St SW18 ...71 A4
Essendine Mans
  W9 ...23 C2
Essendine Prim Sch
  W9 ...23 C2
Essendine Rd W9 ...23 C2
Essex Ct EC4 ...107 B1
  W6 ...39 B3
  SW13 ...46 B3
Essex Ho 2 E14 ...34 A3
Essex Park Mews
  W3 ...29 A1
Essex Pl W4 ...37 B2
Essex Place Sq 4 W4 ...37 C2
Essex Rd N1 ...86 B4
  NW10 ...8 A1
  W3 ...28 B2
  W4 ...37 C2
Essex Road Sta N1 ...15 B1
Essex St WC2 ...121 B4
Essex Villas W8 ...127 B3
Essian St E1 ...33 A4
Essington SW15 ...58 A1
Estcourt Rd SW6 ...154 C2
Este Rd SW11 ...60 A4
Estella Ho W11 ...30 C2
Estelle Rd NW3 ...12 B4
Esterbrooke St
  SW1 ...147 B3
Estoria Cl 22 SW2 ...74 C4
Etal Ho N1 ...15 A1
Etchingham Rd E15 ...76 B4
Ethel Rankin Ct
  SW6 ...164 C2
Ethel St SE17 ...151 A3
Ethelbert Ho E9 ...18 A4
Ethelbert St SW12 ...73 A3
Ethelburga Prim Sch
  SW11 ...168 B4
Ethelburga St
  SW11 ...168 B4
Ethelburga Tower
  SW11 ...168 B4

Ethelbank Rd W12	.30	A1
Ethelworth Ct **4**		
SW2	.74	C3
Etherow St SE22	.76	C4
Ethnard Rd SE15	.50	A4
Eton Ave NW3	.12	A1
Eton Cl SW18	.71	A4
Eton College Rd		
NW3	.12	B2
Eton Ct NW3	.11	C1
Eton Garages **11**		
	.12	A2
Eton Hall NW3	.12	B2
Eton Ho N5	.15	A4
Eton Pl NW1	.12	C1
Eton Rd NW3	.12	B2
Eton Rise NW3	.12	B2
Eton St TW10	.54	A2
Eton Villas NW3	.12	B2
Etta St SE8	.51	A4
Ettrick St E14	.34	B3
Eugene Cotter Ho		
SE17	**.151**	C3
Eugenia Rd SE16	.40	B2
Euro Cl NW10	.8	C2
EuroInk Bsns Ctr		
SW2	.62	C2
Europa Pl EC1	**.96**	C3
Eustace Ho SE11	**.148**	C4
Eustace Rd SW6	**.155**	B2
Euston Rd NW1	.93	A2
Euston Sq NW1	.93	B3
Euston Square Sta		
WC1	**.93**	A2
Euston Sta NW1	**.93**	B3
Euston Sta NW1	**.93**	B3
Euston Underpass		
NW1	**.92**	C2
Evandale Rd SW9	**.173**	C2
Evangelist Rd NW5	.13	A4
Evans Cl E8	.16	B2
Evans Ho SW8	**.161**	C1
34 W12	.30	A2
Evelina Mans **5**		
SE5	.48	C3
Evelina Rd SE15	.50	B1
Evelyn Lowe Prim Sch		
SE1	**.153**	C1
Evelyn Ct N1	**.87**	B1
W1	**.102**	C1
E8	.16	C4
Evelyn Denington Ct **2**		
N1	.15	A1
Evelyn Fox Ct W10	.30	B4
Evelyn Gdns SW7	**.143**	B1
Richmond TW9	.54	A2
Evelyn Ho W12	.38	B4
3 SW2	.62	B2
Evelyn Rd W4	.37	C3
Richmond TW9	.54	A4
Evelyn Terr TW9	.54	A4
Evelyn Wlk N1	**.87**	B1
Evelyn Yd W1	**.105**	B2
Evenwood Cl SW15	.58	A2
Everard Ho **1** EC1	**.111**	C1
Everatt Cl SW18	.58	B2
Everdon Rd SW13	.46	C4
Everest Pl E14	.34	B4
Everett Ho SE17	**.151**	B2
N7	.14	C4
Everilda St N1	**.85**	A3
Everington Rd N10	.20	C2
Everington St W6	.47	C4
Everitt Rd NW10	.20	C2
Everleigh St N4	.5	B3

Eversfield Rd TW9	.44	B1
Evershed Ho E1	**.111**	A2
Eversholt St NW1	**.83**	A1
Evershot Rd N4	.5	B3
Eversleigh Rd		
SW11	**.169**	B1
Everthorpe Rd SE15	.64	B4
Everton Bldgs NW1	**.92**	C3
Evesham Ho NW8	**.78**	C3
1 SE15	.49	C4
3 E2	.25	B3
Evesham St W11	.30	C2
Evesham Way SW11	.60	C4
Evesham Wlk SW9	**.173**	B2
SE5	.48	C1
Ewald Rd SW6	**.164**	C1
Ewart Pl **10** E3	.26	B3
Ewe Cl N7	.14	A2
Ewen Cres SW2	.74	C4
Ewen Ho N1	**.84**	C3
Ewer St SE1	**.122**	C1
Ewhurst **10** SW15	.57	C1
Ewhurst Cl E1	.32	B4
Ewhurst Rd SE4	.66	B1
Exbury Ho **9**	.17	B2
SW9		
Excel Ct WC2	**.119**	C3
Excelsior Gdns SE13	.52	B1
Excelsior Ind Est		
SE16	.40	C1
Exchange Arc EC2	**.110**	B4
Exchange Ct WC2	**.120**	B3
Exchange Mans **2**		
NW11	.1	B4
Exchange Pl EC2	**.110**	A4
Exeter Ct NW6	.23	C3
Exeter Ho **2** SE15	.49	C4
11 SE15	.49	C4
SW15	.57	B1
Exeter Mans NW2	.10	A2
Exeter Mews SW6	**.155**	B2
E16	.35	C4
Exeter Rd NW2	.10	A3
E16	.35	C4
Exeter St WC2	**.120**	C4
Exeter Way SE14	.51	B3
Exford Ct SW11	**.167**	C4
Exhibition Cl W12	.30	B2
Exhibition Rd SW7	**.129**	C3
Exmoor Ho **23** E3	.26	A3
Exmoor St W10	.30	C4
Exmouth Ho **6** E14	.42	A2
Exmouth Market		
EC1	**.95**	C2
Exmouth Mews		
NW1	**.93**	A3
Exmouth Pl E8	.17	A1
Exmouth St E1	.32	B3
Exon St SE17	**.152**	A3
Exonbury NW8	**.78**	B3
Exton St SE1	**.121**	B1
Eynella Rd SE21	.76	B4
Eynham Rd W12	.30	B3
Eynsford Ho SE1	**.137**	B4
SE17	**.152**	A3
12 SE15	.50	B4
Eyot Gdns W6	.38	B1
Eyot Gn W4	.38	B1
Eyre Ct NW8	**.79**	B2
Eyre St Hill EC1	**.95**	B1
Eythorne Rd SW9	**.173**	C3
Ezra St E2	**.99**	A3

Fabyc Ho TW9	.44	C3
Fair St SE1	**.138**	C4
Fairacres SW15	.56	C3
Fairbairn Gn **1**		
SW9	.48	A2
Fairbridge Rd N19	.4	C2
Fairburn Ct SW15	.58	A2
Fairburn Ho SW5	**.141**	A1
7 N16	.7	A3
Fairby Ho SE1	**.153**	A4
Faircharm Trad Est		
SE8	.52	A4
Fairchild Cl SW11	**.167**	C3
Fairchild Ho N1	.98	A4
SW1	**.147**	A3
13 E9	.17	B1
Fairchild Pl EC2	.98	B1
Fairchild St EC2	.98	B1
Fairclough St E1	**.111**	C1
Faircourt NW3	.12	B2
Faircroft N16	.6	C3
Fairdale Gdns SW15	.57	A3
Fairdene Ct N7	.14	A3
Fairfax Ho SW9	**.173**	C1
Fairfax Mews SW15	.57	A3
Fairfax Pl NW6	.11	B1
W14	.38	A3
Fairfax Rd NW6	.11	B1
W4	.38	A3
Fairfield **4**	**.82**	C4
4 E1	.32	B4
Fairfield Ct NW10	.21	C4
1 SW18	.59	A2
Fairfield Dr SW18	.59	A2
Fairfield Rd E3	.26	C3
Fairfield St SW18	.59	A2
Fairfoot Rd E3	.26	C1
Fairford Ho SE11	**.149**	C3
Fairhall Ct SW6		
Fairhazel Gdns		
NW6	.11	B1
Fairheathe SW15	.57	C1
Fairholme Rd W14	**.140**	B1
Fairholt Cl N16	.7	A3
Fairholt Rd N16	.6	C3
Fairholt St SW7	**.130**	B2
Fairhurst **13** NW6	.10	C3
Fairlawn Ave W4	.37	B2
Fairlawn Ct **3** W4	.37	B2
Fairlawn Gr W4	.37	B2
Fairlawn Mans SE14	.50	C2
Fairlawns SW15	.57	C2
Fairlie Ct **1** N7	.13	C4
22 E3	.27	A2
Fairlight Ave NW10	.21	A3
Fairlight Ct NW10	.21	A3
Fairlop Pl NW8	**.89**	C3
Fairmead Ho E9	.18	A4
Fairmead Rd N7,N19	.5	A1
Fairmont Ho **3** E3	.26	C1
Fairmount Rd SW2	.62	B1
Fairstead Wlk N1	**.86**	C4
Fairthorn Rd SE7,		
SE10	.43	C1
Fairview Ho **14** SW2	.74	B3
Fairview Pl SW2	.74	B4
Fairwall Ho **5** SE5	.49	A2
Fairway Cl NW11	.2	B4
Fairway Ct **15** SE16	.40	C4
Fairway The W3	.29	A3
Fairweather Ho N7	.14	A4
Faith Ct NW2	.9	A2
Faithfull Ho N5	.15	B3
Fakruddin St		
E1	.24	C1 **99** C1
Falcon Cl SW14	.45	B1
W4	.45	B4

Falcon Ct N1	**.86**	B1
EC4	**.107**	B1
8 SE21	.75	C2
Falcon Gr SW11	.60	A4
Falcon Ho **10** SE15	.49	B2
Falcon La SW11	.60	A4
Falcon Lo N1	.11	A4
11 W9	.31	C4
Falcon Point SE1	**.122**	B3
Falcon Rd SW11	.60	A4
Falcon Terr SW11	.60	A4
Falcon Way E14	.42	A2
Falconberg Ct W1	**.105**	C2
Falconberg Mews		
W1	**.105**	C2
Falconbrook Prim Sch		
SW11	.59	C4
Falconer Wlk **12** N7	.5	B2
Falconwood Ct SE3	.53	B1
Falkener Ct SW11	**.170**	A3
Falkirk Ct **11** SE16	.32	C1
Falkirk Ho W9	**.88**	B4
Falkirk St N1	.24	A3
Falkland Ho W8	**.128**	A1
W14	**.140**	C2
Falkland Pl **2** NW5	.13	B3
Falkland Rd NW5	.13	B3
Falladon Ho **3** W11	.31	B4
Fallodon Ho SW11	**.171**	C2
Fallow Ct SE16	**.153**	C1
Fallowfield N4	.5	B2
Falmouth Ho **2** W2	**.116**	A4
SE11	**.149**	C2
Falmouth Rd SE1	**.137**	A1
Falmouth St E15	.19	C3
Falstaff Ct SE11	**.150**	A3
Falstaff Ho **1** N1	.24	A3
Fane Ho **23** E2	.25	B4
Fane St W14	**.155**	A4
Fann St EC1	**.97**	A1
Fanshaw St N1	**.98**	A4
Fanthorpe St SW15	.57	B4
Faraday Cl N7	.14	B2
Faraday Ho **6** NW5	.13	A4
W10	.31	A4
14 E14	.33	B2
11 SW12	.73	A4
Faraday Rd W10	.31	A4
W3	.28	B2
Fareham Ho **15**		
SW15	.68	C3
Fareham St W1	**.105**	B2
Farjeon Ho NW6	.11	C1
Farleigh Pl N16	.7	B1
Farleigh Rd N16	.7	B1
Farley Ct NW1	**.91**	B1
W14	**.126**	C2
Farley Ho SE26	.76	C1
Farley Rd SE6	.67	B1
Farlington Pl SW15	.69	A4
Farlow Rd SW15	.57	C4
Farlton Rd SW18	.71	A4
Farm Ave NW2	.1	B1
Farm Cl SW6	**.155**	C2
Farm La SW6	**.155**	C2
Farm Lane Trad Ctr		
SW6	**.155**	C3
Farm Pl W8	**.113**	B2
Farm St W1	**.118**	A3
Farmdale Rd SE10	.43	C1
Farmer Ho **4** SE16	.40	A3
Farmer St W8	**.113**	B2
Farmleigh Ho SW9	.63	A2
Farnaby Ho **2** W10	.23	B2
Farnborough Ho **1**		
SW15	.68	C3

Farnborough Way **10**		
SE15	.49	A3
Farncombe St		
SE16	**.139**	C3
Farndale Ho **6**	**.78**	A4
Farnell Mews SW5	**.142**	A2
Farnell Point E5	.16	C4
Farnfield Ho **12**		
SW2	.62	B2
Farnham Ct **2** N16	.7	A3
Farnham Ho NW1	.90	B1
SE1	**.122**	C1
Farnham Pl SE1	**.122**	B1
Farnham Royal		
SE11	**.149**	A1
Farnhurst Ho		
SW11	**.169**	B2
Farningham Ho **9**		
N4	.6	C4
Farnley Ho SW8	**.171**	B2
Farnworth Ho **5**		
E14	.42	C2
Faroe Rd W14	.39	C3
Farquhar Rd SW19	.70	C1
Farrance St E14	.33	C3
Farrant Ho **15** SW11	.59	C4
Farrell Ho E1	.32	B3
Farrer Ho SE8	.51	C3
Farrier St NW1	.13	B1
Farrier Wlk SW10	**.156**	C4
Farringdon La EC1	**.95**	C1
Farringdon Rd EC1	**.95**	C1
Farringdon St EC4	**.108**	A2
Farringdon Sta		
EC1	**.108**	A4
Farrins Rents SE16	.33	A1
Farrow La SE14	.50	B3
Farrow Pl SE16	.41	A3
Farthing Alley SE1	**.139**	B3
Farthing Fields **8**		
E1	.32	A1
Fashion St E1	**.111**	A3
Fassett Rd E8	.16	C2
Fassett Sq E8	.16	C2
Fauconberg Ct W4	.45	B4
Fauconberg Rd W4	.45	B4
Faulkner Ho SW15	.47	B1
Faulkner St SE14	.50	B2
Faulkner's Alley		
EC1	**.108**	A4
Faunce Ho **1** SE17	.48	A4
Faunce St SE17	**.150**	A1
Favart Rd SW6	**.165**	C4
Fawcett Cl SW11	**.167**	C1
Fawcett Est E5	.7	C3
Fawcett Ho **9** SW9	**.172**	B2
Fawcett Rd NW10	.8	B1
Fawcett St SW10	**.156**	C4
Fawe Park Rd SW15	**.58**	B3
Fawe St E14	.34	A4
Fawkham Ho SE1	**.153**	A3
Fawley Ct **1** SE14	.42	C2
Fawley Rd NW6	.11	A3
Fawnbrake Ave		
SE24	.63	B2
Fayetville Ho **20** N19	.4	C4
Faygate Rd SW2	.74	B2
Fearnley Ho SE5	.49	A1
Fearon St SE10	.43	C1
Feathers Pl SE10	.52	C4

Featherstone St
EC1 .....**97** B2
Featley Rd SW9 .....63 A4
Felbridge Ho **22**
SE22 .....64 A4
Felday Rd SE13 .....67 B2
Felden St SW6 .....**164** C3
Feldman Cl N16 .....7 C3
Felgate Mews **4**
W6 .....39 A2
Felix St **11** E2 .....25 A3
Felixstowe Rd
NW10 .....22 A2
Fellbrigg Rd SE22 .....64 B2
Fellbrigg St **21** E1 .....25 A1
Fellows Ct E2 .....24 A3
Fellows Rd NW3 .....12 A1
Fells Haugh **6** W3 .....28 B3
Felltram Way SE7 .....43 C1
Felmersham Cl **2**
SW4 .....61 C3
Felsberg Rd SW2 .....74 A4
Felsham Ho SW15 .....57 C4
Felsham Rd SW15 .....57 C4
Felstead St E9 .....18 B2
Felstead Wharf E14 .....42 B1
Felton Ho N1 .....**87** C3
Felton St N1 .....**87** C3
Fen Ct EC3 .....**124** A4
Fen St E16 .....35 A2
Fenchurch Ave
EC3 .....**110** A1
Fenchurch Bldgs
EC3 .....**110** B1
Fenchurch PI EC3 .....**124** B4
Fenchurch St EC3 .....**124** A4
Fenchurch Street Sta
EC3 .....**124** A4
Fendall St SE1 .....**138** B1
Fender Ct SW4 .....**172** A2
Fendt Cl **8** E16 .....35 B3
Fenelon PI W14 .....**141** A3
Fenham Rd SE15 .....50 A3
Fenn St E9 .....17 B3
Fenner Cl SE16 .....40 A2
Fenner Ho **23** E1 .....32 A1
Fenner Sq **10** SW11 .....59 C4
Fenning St SE1 .....**138** A4
Fenstanton Prim Sch
SW2 .....74 C3
Fentiman Rd SW8 .....**162** C2
Fenton Cl SW9 .....**172** C1
E8 .....16 B2
Fenton Ho SE14 .....51 A3
Fenton St E1 .....32 A3
Fentons SE3 .....53 B3
Fenwick Gr SE15 .....64 C4
Fenwick PI SW9 .....62 A4
Fenwick Rd SE15 .....64 C4
Ferdinand Ho **1**
NW1 .....13 A1
Ferdinand PI NW1 .....12 C1
Ferdinand St NW1 .....12 C1
Ferguson Dr W3 .....28 C3
Ferguson Ho SE10 .....52 B2
Ferguson's Cl E14 .....41 C2
Fermain Ct E N1 .....24 A4
Fermain Ct N N1 .....24 A4
Fermain Ct W N1 .....24 A4
Fermoy Rd W9 .....23 B1
Fern Cl **3** N1 .....24 A3

Fern Ct SE14 .....50 C1
Fern St E3 .....26 C1
Fern Wlk SE16 .....**153** C1
Fernbank Mews
SW12 .....61 B1
Ferncliff Rd E8 .....16 C3
Ferncroft Ave NW3 .....10 C4
Ferndale Ct **3** SE3 .....53 B3
Ferndale Ho N16 .....6 C3
Ferndale Rd SW4,
SW9 .....62 B3
Ferndene Rd SE24 .....63 B3
Fernhead Rd W9 .....23 B2
Fernhill Ho E5 .....7 C2
Fernholme Rd SE15 .....65 C2
Fernhurst Rd SW6 .....**164** B4
Fernie Ho SE22 .....64 B4
Fernlea Rd SW12 .....73 A3
Fernsbury St WC1 .....**95** B3
Fernshaw Mans
SW10 .....**156** C3
Fernshaw Rd
SW10 .....**156** C3
Fernside Rd SW12 .....72 C4
Ferntower Rd N5 .....15 C3
Fernwood SW19 .....70 B3
Ferny Rd N1 .....14 C1
Ferrier Ind Est
?? 59 A3
Ferrier Point **6**
E16 .....35 C4
Ferrier St SW18 .....59 A3
Ferrings SE21 .....76 A1
Ferris Rd SE22 .....64 C3
Ferry La
Brentford TW8 .....44 A4
Richmond TW9 .....44 C3
Ferry Rd SW13 .....46 C2
Ferry Sq **1** TW8 .....44 A4
Ferry St E14 .....42 B1
Ferrybridge Ho
SE11 .....**135** A1
Festing Rd SW15 .....57 C4
Festival Pier SE1 .....**120** C2
Festival Pleasure Gdns
SW11 .....**158** C2
Fetter La EC4 .....**107** C2
Fettes Ho NW8 .....**79** C1
Ffinch St SE8 .....51 C3
Field Ct WC1 .....**107** A3
NW3 .....11 B3
N7 .....14 A3
SW19 .....70 C1
Field Rd W6 .....**154** A4
Field St WC1 .....**94** C4
Fieldgate Mans E1 .....**111** C3
Fieldgate St E1 .....**111** C3
Fieldhouse Rd
SW12 .....73 B3
Fielding Ho NW8 .....**78** C4
3 NW6 .....23 C2
W4 .....46 A4
Fielding Mews
SW13 .....47 A4
Fielding Rd W4 .....38 A3
W14 .....39 C3
Fielding St SE17 .....48 B4
Fields Est E8 .....16 C1
Fieldsway Ho N5 .....14 C3
Fieldview SW17,
SW18 .....71 C3
Fieldview Ct N5 .....15 A3
Fieldway Cres N5,
?? .....
Fieldwick Ho **14** E9 .....17 C2

Fife Rd E16 .....35 C4
SW14 .....55 B2
Fife Terr N1 .....**85** A2
Fig Tree Cl NW10 .....21 A4
Filey Ave N16 .....7 C3
Filey Ho SW18 .....59 B3
Filigree Ct SE16 .....33 B1
Filmer Ho SW6 .....**164** B4
Filmer Mews SW6 .....**164** C4
Filmer Rd SW6 .....**154** C1
Filmer Road Studios
SW6 .....**164** B4
Filton Ct **14** SE14 .....50 B3
Finborough Ho
SW10 .....**156** C4
Finborough Rd
SW10 .....**156** B4
Finch Ho **1** SE8 .....52 A3
Finch La EC2,EC3 .....**109** C1
Finch Lo **19** W9 .....31 C4
Finch Mews **3** SE15 .....49 B2
Finch's Ct **9** E14 .....34 A2
Finchdean Ho SW15 .....68 B4
Finchley Pl NW8 .....**79** B2
Finchley Rd NW8 .....**79** B2
Finchley Road & Frognal
Sta NW3 .....11 B3
Finchley Road Sta
NW3 .....11 B2
Findhorn St E14 .....34 B3
Findon Cl SW18 .....58 C1
Findon Rd W12 .....38 C4
Fineran Ct **16** SW11 .....59 C3
Fingal St SE10 .....43 B1
Fingest Ho NW8 .....**90** A2
Finland Rd SE4 .....66 A4
Finland St SE16 .....41 A3
Finlay St SW6 .....47 C2
Finley Ct **21** SE5 .....48 B3
Finmere Ho **4** N4 .....6 B4
Finn Ho N1 .....**97** C4
Finnemore Ho N1 .....**86** C4
Finnis St E2 .....25 A1
Finsbury Ave EC2 .....**109** C3
Finsbury Cir EC2 .....**109** C3
Finsbury Ct EC2 .....**109** B4
Finsbury Market
EC2 .....**110** A4
Finsbury Mkt EC2 .....**98** A1
Finsbury Park Rd N4,
N5 .....6 A2
Finsbury Park Sta
N4 .....5 C2
Finsbury Pavement
EC2 .....**109** C4
Finsbury Sq EC2 .....**109** C4
Finsbury St EC2 .....**109** B4
Finsen Rd SE5 .....63 B4
Finstock Rd W10 .....30 C3
Finton House Sch
SW17 .....72 B2
Finucane Ct TW9 .....54 B4
Finwhale Ho E14 .....42 A3
Fiona Ct **9** NW6 .....23 C3
Fir Lo SW15 .....57 A3
Fir Tree Ho **11** SE14 .....50 B3
Fir Trees Cl SE16 .....33 A1
Firbank Rd SE15 .....50 A1
Fircroft N1 .....**86** B4
Fircroft Prim Sch
SW17 .....72 B1
Fircroft Rd SW17 .....72 B1
Fire Brigade Pier
SE1 .....**148** A4
Firecrest Dr NW3 .....2 A1

Firle Ho W10 .....30 B4
Firmston Ho **9**
SW14 .....55 C4
Firs Ave SW14 .....55 B3
Firsby Rd N16 .....7 C3
First Ave W10 .....23 B1
W3 .....29 B1
SW14 .....56 A4
First St SW3 .....**144** B4
Firth Gdns SW6 .....**164** A3
Fish St Hill EC3 .....**123** C3
Fisher Ho N1 .....**85** B3
2 N19 .....4 B1
8 E1 .....32 B2
Fisher's La W4 .....37 C2
Fisherman's Wlk
E14 .....33 C1
Fishermans Dr SE16 .....40 C4
Fishers Ct SE14 .....50 C2
Fisherton St NW8 .....**89** C2
Fisherton Street Est
NW8 .....**89** C1
Fishlock Ct SW4 .....**172** A2
Fishponds Rd SW17 .....72 A1
Fisons Rd E16 .....35 C1
Fitch Ct SW2 .....62 C2
Fitz-George Ave
W14 .....**140** A3
Fitzalan St SE11 .....**149** B4
Fitzgerald Ave
SW14 .....56 A4
Fitzgerald Ho SW9 .....**173** B1
14 E14 .....34 A3
Fitzgerald Rd SW14 .....55 C4
Fitzhardinge Ho
W1 .....**103** B2
Fitzhardinge St
W1 .....**103** B2
Fitzherbert Ho **11**
TW10 .....54 B1
Fitzhugh Gr SW18 .....59 C1
Fitzjames Ave
W14 .....**140** B3
Fitzjohn's Ave NW3 .....11 C3
Fitzjohns Prim Sch
NW3 .....11 C3
Fitzmaurice Ho **7**
SE16 .....40 A2
Fitzmaurice PI W1 .....**118** B2
Fitzneal St W12 .....29 B3
Fitzroy Cl N6 .....3 B3
Fitzroy Cres W4 .....45 C3
Fitzroy Ct W1 .....**93** A1
Fitzroy Ho SE1 .....**153** A2
14 E14 .....33 B3
Fitzroy Mews W1 .....**92** C1
Fitzroy Nuffield Hosp
W1 .....**102** C2
Fitzroy Pk N6 .....3 B3
Fitzroy Rd NW1 .....**81** B4
Fitzroy Sq W1 .....**92** C1
Fitzroy St W1 .....**92** C1
Fitzroy Yd NW1 .....**81** B4
Fitzsimmons Ct **1**
NW10 .....20 C4
Fitzwarren Gdns N19 .....4 B3
Fitzwilliam Ave
TW9 .....44 B1
Fitzwilliam Mews
E16 .....35 C1
Fitzwilliam Rd SW4 .....61 B4
Fives Ct SE11 .....**136** A1
Fiveways Rd SW9 .....**173** C1

Flamborough Ho **11**
SE15 .....49 C2
Flamborough St
E14 .....33 A3
Flamingo Ct **2** SE8 .....51 C3
Flamsted House
SE10 .....52 C3
Flanchford Rd W12 .....38 B3
Flanders Mans **1**
W4 .....38 B2
Flanders Rd W4 .....38 A2
Flanders Way E9 .....17 C2
Flank St E1 .....**125** B4
Flansham Ho **2**
E14 .....33 B3
Flask Wlk NW3 .....11 C4
Flavell Mews SE10 .....43 A1
Flaxman Ct W1 .....**105** B1
Flaxman Ho **1** **136** B2
10 W4 .....38 A1
Flaxman Rd SE5 .....48 A1
Flaxman Terr WC1 .....**93** C3
Flecker Ho **8** SE5 .....48 C3
Fleece Wlk N7 .....14 A2
Fleet Ct **1** W12 .....38 A3
Fleet Ho **4** E14 .....33 A2
6 SW2 .....62 C2
Fleet PI EC4 .....**108** A2
Fleet Prim Sch NW3 .....12 B3
Fleet Rd NW3 .....12 B3
Fleet Sq WC1 .....**95** A3
Fleet St EC4 .....**107** C1
Fleet Street Hill E1 .....**99** B1
Fleetfield WC1 .....**94** B4
Fleetway WC1 .....**94** B4
Fleetwood Rd NW10 .....8 C3
Fleetwood St N16 .....7 A2
Fleming Ct W2 .....**101** B4
Fleming Ho SE16 .....**139** B3
N4 .....6 C4
Fleming Rd SE17 .....48 A4
Fletcher Bldgs
WC2 .....**106** B1
Fletcher Ct **9** NW5 .....13 A4
Fletcher Ho **16** N16 .....16 A4
Fletcher Path **7**
SE8 .....51 C3
Fletcher Rd W4 .....37 B3
Fletcher St E1 .....**125** C4
Fleur Gates **7**
SW19 .....69 C4
Flinders Ho **28** E1 .....32 A1
Flint St SE17 .....**151** C3
Flinton St SE17 .....**152** B2
Flitcroft St WC2 .....**105** C1
Flitton Ho **7** N1 .....15 A1
Flock Mill PI SW18 .....71 A3
Flockton St SE16 .....**139** B3
Flodden Rd SE5 .....48 B2
Flood St SW3 .....**158** A4
Flood Wlk SW3 .....**158** A4
Flora Cl E14 .....34 A3
Flora Gardens Prim Sch
W6 .....39 A2
Flora Gdns **2** W6 .....39 A2
Floral St WC2 .....**120** A4
Florence Ct W9 .....**89** A3
Florence Gdns W4 .....45 B4
Florence Ho
10 W11 .....30 C2
20 SE16 .....40 A1
7 SW2 .....74 B3
2 SW2 .....62 B2

Florence Mans
SW6 ....164 C4
Florence Nightingale Ho
SW8 ....162 C2
Florence Nightingale
Mus SE1 ....135 A3
Florence Rd N4 ....5 C4
W4 ....37 C3
SE14 ....51 B2
Florence St N1 ....15 A1
Florence Terr SE14 ..51 B2
SW15 ....68 A1
Florence Way SW12 ..72 B3
Flores Ho E1 ....32 C4
Florfield Rd E8 ......17 A2
Florian SE5 ....49 A2
Florian Rd SW15 .....58 A3
Florida St E2 .....24 C2 99 C3
Florys Ct SW19 ......70 A3
Floss St SW15 ....57 B4
Flower & Dean Wlk
E1 ....111 A3
Flower Wlk The
SW7 ....129 A4
Flowers Mews [1]
N19 ....4 B2
Flowersmead SW17 ...72 C2
Fluer De Lis St E1 ....98 C1
Flynn Ct [8] E14 .....33 C2
Foley Ho [6] E1 ....32 B3
Foley St W1 ....104 C3
Folgate St E1 ....110 C4
Foliot Ho N1 ....84 C2
Foliot St W12 ....29 B3
Folland SW9 [10] 163 C1
Follett St E14 ....34 B3
Folly Wall E14 ......42 B4
Fontarabia Rd
SW11 ....60 C3
Fontenelle SE5 ....49 A2
Fontenoy Ho SE11 ...150 A3
Fontenoy Rd SW12,
SW17 ....73 B2
Fonthill Ho SW1 ....146 B2
Fonthill Mews N4 .....5 B2
Fonthill Rd N4 ....5 C2
Fontley Way SW15 ...68 C4
Footpath The SW15 ..56 C2
Forber Ho [5] E2 .....25 B2
Forbes Ho [2] W4 ....36 C1
Forbes St E1 ....111 C1
Forburg Rd N16 ....7 C3
Ford Cl [11] E3 ....26 A3
Ford Rd E3 ....26 A3
Ford Sq E1 ....32 A4
E16 ....35 B1
Fordcombe [13] NW5 .12 C2
Fordham St E1 ....111 C2
Fordingley Rd W9 ....23 B2
Fords Park Rd E16 ....35 C3
Fordwych Ct NW2 ....10 A2
Fordwych Rd NW2 ....10 A3
Fordyce Rd SE13 ......67 B2
Fore St EC2 ....109 A3
Fore St Ave EC2 .....109 B3
Foreign, Commonwealth
& Home Offices
SW1 ....134 A4
Foreland Ho W11 ....112 A4
Foreshore SE8 ....41 B2
Forest Gr E8 ....16 B1
Forest Hill Rd SE22 ..65 A1
Forest Rd E8 ....16 B2
Forest TW9 ....44 C3
Forest Way [1] N19 ..4 B2

Forester Rd SE15 .....65 A4
Forfar Rd SW11 .....169 C4
Forge Pl NW1 ....12 C2
Forman Ho SE4 ....65 C3
Forman Pl [2] N16 ....16 B4
Formby Ct [2] N7 .....14 B3
Formosa Ho [1] E1 ....26 A1
Formosa St W9 ....88 B1
Formunt Cl E16 ....35 B2
Forres Gdns SE17 ....48 A4
Forset Ho SW15 ....47 B1
Forset Ct W1 ....102 B2
Forset St W1 ....102 B2
Forster Rd SW2 ....74 A4
Forston St N1 ....87 A2
Forsyth Gdns SE17 ...48 A4
Forsyth Ho SW1 .....147 A3
E9 ....17 B1
Forsythia Ho SE4 .....66 A4
Fort Rd SE1 ....153 A3
Fort St E1 ....110 B3
E16 ....35 C1
Fortescue Ave [1]
E8 ....17 A1
Fortess Gr NW5 ....13 B3
Fortess Rd NW5 ....13 B4
Fortess Wlk NW5 .....13 A3
Forth Ho [5] E3 ....26 B2
Forthbridge Rd
SW11 ....60 C3
Forties The NW5 .....13 B3
Fortior Ct N6 ....4 B4
Fortnam Rd N19 ....4 C2
Fortrose Gdns
SW12,SW2 ....74 A3
Fortuna Cl N7 ....14 B2
Fortune Gate Rd
NW10 ....21 A4
Fortune Green Rd
NW6 ....10 C4
Fortune Ho EC1 ....97 A1
SE11 ....149 B3
Fortune St EC1 ....97 A1
Fortune Way NW10 ...21 C2
Forty Acre La E16 ....35 C4
Forward Bsns Ctr The
E16 ....27 C1
Fosbrook Ho SE8 .....162 A1
Fosbury Ho [7] SW9 ..62 B3
Fosbury Mews W2 ...114 B3
Foscote Mews W9 ....31 C4
Foskett Rd SW6 ......165 A1
Fossil Rd SE13 ....66 C4
Foster Ct [4] NW1 ....13 B1
E16 ....35 B2
Foster Ho SE14 ......108 C4
Foster La EC2 ....108 C2
Foster Rd W3 ....29 A2
W4 ....37 C1
Foubert's Pl W1 .....104 C1
Foulden Rd N16 ....16 B4
Foulden Terr N16 .....16 B4
Foulis Terr SW7 .....143 C2
Foulser Rd SW17 .....72 C1
Foundary Ho [7] E14 .34 A4
Founders Ct EC2 .....109 B2
Founders Ho SW1 ...147 B2
Foundling Ct WC1 ......94 A2
Foundry Cl SE16 ....33 A1
Foundry Mews NW1 ..93 A2
Fount St SW8 ....161 C2
Fountain Ct EC4 .....121 B4
SW1 ....146 A3
Fountain Green Sq
SE16 ....139 C3
Fountain Ho [1] W1 ..117 B2

Fountain Ho *continued*
SE16 ....139 C3
SW6 ....164 B3
[1] NW6 ....10 A1
Fountain Mews
N5 ....15 B4
NW3 ....12 B2
Fountayne Rd N16 .....7 C2
Fournier St E1 ....111 A4
Fourth Ave W10 ......23 A2
Fovant Ct SW8 ......170 C1
Fowey Cl E1 ....32 A1
Fowey Ho SE11 ......149 C2
Fowler Cl SW11 ....59 C4
Fowler Ho N1 ....86 B4
SE5 ....49 A1
SW8 ....171 C3
Fowler Rd N1 ....86 B4
Fownes St SW18 ......59 A1
Fox & Knot St EC1 ...108 B4
Fox Cl E1 ....25 B1
E16 ....35 C4
Fox Ho SW11 ....59 C3
Fox Prim Sch
W8 ....31 C1 113 B3
Fox Rd E16 ....35 B2
Fox's Yd E2 ....99 A2
Foxberry Ct SE4 ....66 B3
Foxberry Rd SE4 ......66 A4
Foxborough Gdns
SE4 ....66 C2
Foxbourne Rd
SW17 ....72 C2
Foxcombe Rd [6]
SW15 ....68 C3
Foxcote SE5 ....152 B3
Foxcroft N1 ....85 A1
Foxglove St W12 .....29 B2
Foxham Rd N19 ....4 C1
Foxley Cl E8 ....16 C3
Foxley Ho [4] E3 ......27 A2
Foxley Rd SW9 ....48 A3
Foxley Sq [3] SW9 ...48 A2
Foxmore St SW11 ...168 C3
Foxwell Mews SE4 ....66 A4
Foxwell St SE4 ....66 A4
Foyle Rd SE3 ....53 B4
Fradel La N16 ....6 C3
Framfield Rd N5 ....15 A3
Frampton NW1 ....13 C1
Frampton Ct [3] W3 ..37 B4
Frampton Ho NW8 ....89 C1
Frampton Park Rd
E9 ....17 B1
Frampton St NW8 .....89 C1
Francemary Rd SE4 ...66 C2
Franche Court Rd
SW17 ....71 B1
Francis Chichester Way
SW11 ....169 C3
Francis Cl [6] E14 ....42 C2
Francis Ct [12] SE14 ..50 C4
Francis Ho NW10 ......21 B4
[1] N1 ....24 A4
Francis Holland CE Sch
for Girls NW1 ....90 C2
Francis Holland Sch
SW1 ....145 C3
Francis Snary Lo [1]
SW18 ....58 C2
Francis St SW1 ....147 A4
E15 ....19 C3
Francis Terr N19 ....4 B1
Francis Wlk N1 ....84 C4
Franconia Rd SW4 ....61 C2

Frank Barnes Prim Sch
for Deaf Children
NW3 ....11 C1
Frank Beswick Ho
SW6 ....155 A3
Frank Dixon Cl
SE21 ....76 A3
Frank Dixon Way
SE21 ....76 A3
Frank Douglas Ct
W6 ....162 A2
Frank Ho SW8 ....162 A2
Frank Soskice Ho
SW6 ....155 A3
Frank Whymark Ho [4]
SE16 ....40 B4
Frankfurt Rd SE24 ....63 B2
Frankham Ho [3]
SE8 ....51 C3
Frankham St SE8 ......51 C3
Frankland Cl SE16 ....40 A2
Frankland Ho [4]
SW12 ....73 A4
Frankland Rd SW7 ...129 B1
Franklin Cl SE13 ......52 A2
SE27 ....75 A1
Franklin Ho [3] E1 ...125 C2
Franklin Sq SW5 ......141 A1
Franklin St [3] E3 ....27 A2
Franklin's Row
SW3 ....145 A2
Franklyn Rd NW10 ...8 B2
Frans Hals Ct E14 ....42 C3
Fraser Ct SW11 ......168 A4
Fraser Ho SW8 ....171 B1
Brentford TW8 ....36 B1
Fraser Regnart Ct [8]
NW5 ....12 B3
Fraser St W4 ....38 A1
E3 ....26 A3
Frazier St SE1 ....135 B3
Frean St SE16 ....139 B2
Frearson Ho WC1 ......95 A4
Freda Corbett Cl [9]
SE15 ....49 C3
Frederic Mews
SW1 ....131 B3
Frederica St N7 ....14 B1
Frederick Cl W2 ......116 C4
Frederick Charrington
Ho [3] E1 ....25 B1
Frederick Cl W2 .....102 C1
W2 ....116 C4
Frederick Cres SW9 ..48 A3
Frederick Rd SE17 ..150 B1
Frederick Sq [11]
SE16 ....33 A2
Frederick St WC1 .....94 C3
Frederick Terr E8 .....16 B1
Frederick's Pl
EC2 ....109 B1
Frederick's Row
EC1 ....96 A4
Freedom St SW11 ...169 A2
Freegrove Rd N7 .....14 A3
Freeling Ho NW8 ......79 B4
Freeling St [1] N1 ....14 B1
Freeman Ho [7]
SW2 ....74 A4
Freemantle St
SE17 ....152 A2
Freemens Hos [3]
SW9 ....62 B3
Freke Rd SW11 ....60 C4
Fremantle Ho [14] E1 ..25 A1

Fremont St E9 ....25 B4
French Ordinary Ct
EC3 ....124 B4
French Pl E1 ....98 B2
Frendsbury Rd SE4 ...66 A3
Frensham Ct N5 ....15 B3
Frensham Dr SW15 ...68 C2
Frensham St SE15 ....49 C4
Frere St SW11 ....168 B2
Freshfield Ave E8 .....16 B1
Freshfield Cl SE13 ....67 C3
Freshford St SW17,
SW18 ....71 B1
Freston Rd W10,
W11 ....30 C2
Freswick Ho [6] SE8 ..41 A2
Freud Mus The
NW3 ....11 B2
Frewell Ho EC1 ....107 B4
Frewin Rd SW18 ....71 C3
Friar Mews SE27 .....75 A1
Friar St EC4 ....108 B1
Friars Ave SW15 .....58 B1
Friars Cl SE1 ....122 B1
Friars Gdns W3 ....28 C3
Friars Mead E14 ......42 B3
Friars Place La W3 ....28 C2
Friars Prim Sch
SE1 ....136 B3
Friars Stile Pl [9]
TW10 ....54 A1
Friars Stile Rd
TW10 ....54 A1
Friars Way W3 ....28 C3
Friary Park Ct W3 .....28 B3
Friary Rd W3 ....28 C3
SE15 ....49 C3
Friday St EC4 ....122 C4
Frideswide Pl NW5 ...13 B3
Friend St EC1 ....96 A4
Friendly Pl SE13 ......52 A2
Friendly St SE8 ....51 C2
Friendly Street Mews
SE8 ....51 C1
Friern Rd SE22 ....64 C1
Friern Sch (Lower)
SE22 ....65 A2
Frigate Ho [8] E14 ...42 B2
Frigate Mews SE8 .....51 C4
Frimley Cl SW19 ......70 A2
Frimley Way E1 ....25 C1
Frinstead Ho
W10 ....30 C2
Friston St SW6 ....166 A1
Frith Ho NW8 ....89 C1
E2 ....24 C2 99 B3
Frith Rd E11 ....19 C4
Frith St W1 ....105 B1
Frithville Ct W12 ......30 B1
Frithville Gdns W12 ..30 B1
Frobisher Ct [3]
W12 ....39 B4
Frobisher Ho [27] E1 ..32 A1
Frobisher Pas E14 ....33 C1
Frobisher Sq [1]
SE10 ....43 B3
Frobisher St SE10 ....53 C4
Frogley Rd SE22 ....64 B3
Frogmore SW18 ....58 C2
Frogmore Est
NW10 ....20 B2
Frogmore Ind Est
N5 ....15 B4
Frognal NW3 ....11 B3

Frognal Cl NW3 ....11 B3
Frognal Ct NW3 ....11 B2
Frognal Gdns NW3 ..11 B4
Frognal La NW3 .....11 A3
Frognal Par NW3 ....11 B3
Frognal Rise NW3 ...11 B4
Frognal Way NW3 ...11 B4
Frome Ho SE15 ....65 B3
Frome St N1 ....86 C2
Frontenac NW10 ....
Froude St SW8 .....170 B1
Fry Rd NW10 ....21 B4
Frye Ct E3 ....
Frying Pan Alley
  E1 ....110 C3
Fulbeck Ho N7 ....
Fulbourne St E1 ....32 A4
Fulbrook Rd N19 ...13 B4
Fulcher Ho 10 N1 ..24 A4
  13 SE8 ....41 B1
Fulford Mans N19 ...5 A4
Fulford St SE16 .....40 A4

Fulham Broadway
  SW6 ....155 C1
Fulham Broadway Sta
  SW6 ....155 C2
Fulham Cross Sch
  SW6 ....154 A2
Fulham Ct SW6 ....165 B4
Fulham High St
  SW6 ....164 B1
Fulham Palace ★ ..164 A1
Fulham Palace Rd
  SW6 ....164 A3
Fulham Park Gdns
  SW6 ....164 C2
Fulham Park Rd
  SW6 ....164 C2
Fulham Prep Sch The
  SW6 ....155 B3
Fulham Prim Sch
  SW6 ....155 B3
Fulham Rd SW10 ..157 A4
  SW6 ....165 A4
Fuller Cl E2 ....99 B2
Fullers Ho 6 SW18 .58 C2
Fullerton Rd SW18 .59 B2
Fullwood's Mews
  N1 ....97 C4
Fulmar Ct 5 SE21 ..75 C2
Fulmar Ho NW8 ....90 B1
  12 SE16 ....40 C2
Fulmead St SW6 ...166 B3
Fulneck 6 E1 ......32 B4
Fulthorp Rd SE3 ....53 C1
Fulton Mews W2 ...114 C4
Fulwood Pl WC1 ...107 A3
Fulwood Wlk SW19 .70 A3
Furber St W6 ......39 A3
Furley Ho 7 SE15 ..49 C3
Furley Rd SE15 ....49 C3
Furlong Rd N7 .....14 C2
Furmage St SW18 ..71 A4
Furness Ho SW1 ...146 A2
Furness La 4 SW14 .56 A3
Furness Rd NW10 .21 C3
  NW10 ....22 A2
Furnival St EC4 ...107 B2
Furrow La E9 ......17 B3
Fursecroft W1 .....102 C2
Furze St E3 ....33 C4
Fyfield N4 ....5 C2
Fyfield Rd 5 SW9 ..62 C4
Fynes St SW1 .....147 B4

G

Gable Ho 15 W4 ...38 A2
Gables Cl SE5 .....49 A2
Gables The NW3 ....
  3 W4 ....38 A2
Gabriel Ho SE11 ..148 C4
Gabriel's Wharf
  SE1 ....121 B2
Gabrielle Ct NW3 ..11 C2
Gaddesden Ho EC1 .97 C3
Gadsden Ho 10 E9 ..17 C2
  8 W10 ....23 A1
Gagarin Ho SW11 ..59 C4
Gage Rd E16 ....35 A4
Gainford Ho 18 E2 .25 A2
Gainford St N1 .....85 B4
Gainsborough Ct
  W12 ....39 B4
  15 SE16 ....40 A1
  SE21 ....76 A2
Gainsborough Gdns
  NW11 ....1 B4
  NW3 ....2 C1
Gainsborough Ho
  SW1 ....147 C3
  N4 ....5 B3
  3 NW3 ....11 B4
  14 E14 ....42 B4
Gainsborough Prim Sch
  E9 ....18 C2
Gainsborough Rd
  W4 ....38 B2
  Richmond TW9 ....54 B4
Gainsford St SE1 ..139 A4
Gairloch Ho 2 ....
  NW1 ....13 C1
Gairloch Rd SE5 ...49 A1
Gaisford St NW5 ...13 B2
Gaitskell Ct SW11 .168 A2
Gaitskell Ho SE17 ..48 C4
Galata Rd SW13 ...46 C3
Galatea Sq SE15 ...65 B4
Galbraith St E14 ...42 B3
Gale Ho 10 SW2 ...62 B2
Gale St E3 ....34 A4
Galen Pl WC1 .....106 B3
Galena Ho 6 W6 ...39 A2
Gales Gdns E2 .....25 A2
Galesbury Rd SW18 71 B4
Galgate Cl 4 SW19 .70 A3
Galleon Cl 16 SE16 .40 C4
Galleon Ho 7 E14 .42 B2
Gallery Ct SW10 ..156 C3
Gallery Rd SE21 ...75 C3
Galleywall Prim Sch
  SE16 ....40 A2
Galleywall Rd SE16 40 A2
Galleywall Road Trad
  Est 12 SE16 ....40 A2
Galleywood Ho W10 30 B4
Gallia Rd N5 ....15 A3
Galleon Cl SE16 ...40 C4
Galloway Rd W12 ..29 C1
Galsworthy Ho 2 ....
  W11 ....31 A3
Galsworthy Rd NW2 10 A4
Galton St W10 .....23 A2
Galveston Ho 2 E1 .26 A1
Galveston Rd SW15 58 B2
Galway Cl 29 SE16 .40 A1

Galway Ho EC1 ....97 A3
  4 E1 ....32 C4
Galway St EC1 ....97 A3
Gambetta St SW8 .170 B1
Gambia St SE1 ....122 B1
Gambier Ho EC1 ...97 A3
Gamlen Rd SW15 ..57 C3
Ganley Ct 13 SW11 .59 C4
Gannet Ct 4 SE21 ..75 C2
Gannet Ho SE15 ...49 B2
Ganton St W1 .....105 A1
Garbett Ho 2 SE17 .48 A4
Garbutt Pl W1 ....103 C3
Gard St EC1 ....96 B4
Garden Cl SW15 ...69 A4
Garden Ct NW8 ...89 B4
  EC4 ....121 B4
  12 W4 ....44 B2
  3 Richmond TW9 ..44 B2
Garden Flats SW16 .74 A1
Garden Ho 6 SW9 .172 B2
Garden La SW2 ....74 B3
Garden Mews W2 ..113 C3
Garden Rd NW8 ...89 A4
  Mortlake TW9 .....54 C4
Garden Royal 18 ....
  SW15 ....57 C1
Garden St E1 ......32 C4
Garden Terr SW1 ..130 B3
  SW1 ....147 B2
Garden Wlk
  EC2 ......24 A2 98 A2
Gardens The N16 ....7 B4
  SE22 ....64 C3
Gardiner Ave NW2 ..9 B3
Gardiner Ct NW10 .20 C4
Gardiner Ho SW11 168 A4
Gardner Ct N5 .....15 B4
Gardners La 4 EC4 122 C4
Gardnor Mans 10 ....
  NW3 ....11 B4
Gardnor Rd NW3 ...11 C4
Gareth Ct SW16 ...73 C2
Garfield Rd SW11 ..60 C4
Garford St E14 ....33 C2
Garland Ho N16 .....6 C1
Garlick Hill EC4 ...123 A4
Garlinge Ho SW9 ..173 B4
Garlinge Rd NW2 ..10 B2
Garnault Mews EC1 .95 C3
Garnault Pl EC1 ...95 C3
Garner St E2 ......24 C3
Garnet Rd NW10 ..8 A2
Garnet St E1 ......32 B2
Garnett Ho 5 NW3 .12 B3
Garnett Rd NW3 ...12 B3
Garnham St N16 ....7 B2
Garnham St 6 N16 ..7 B2
Garnies Cl SE15 ...49 B3
Garrad's Rd SW16 .73 C1
Garrard Wlk NW10 ..8 A2
Garratt Ho 8 N16 ...7 A3
Garratt La SW18 ...71 A3
Garratt Park Sec Sch
  SW18 ....71 A2
Garraway Ct SW13 .47 B3
Garraway Ho SE21 .76 A1
Garrett Cl W3 .....28 C4
Garrett Ho W12 ...30 A3
Garrett St EC1 .....97 A2
Garrick Cl SW18 ...59 B3
Garrick Ho W1 ....118 A1
  W4 ....46 A4
Garrick Rd TW9 ...44 C1
Garrick St WC2 ...120 A4

Garrick Yd WC2 ...120 A4
Garsington Mews
  SE4 ....66 B4
Garson Ho W2 ....115 B4
Garston Ho 6 N1 ..15 A1
Garter Way SE16 ..40 C4
Garth Ct W4 ....45 B4
Garth Ho NW2 ......1 B2
Garth Rd NW2 ......1 B2
  8 W4 ....37 C1
Gartmoor Gdns
  SW19 ....70 B3
Garton Ho 6 N6 .....4 C4
Garton Pl SW18 ...59 B1
Gartons Way SW11 .59 B4
Garway Rd W2 ....100 A1
  W2 ....114 A4
Gascoigne Pl 12 ...98 C3
Gascony Ave NW6 .10 C1
Gascoyne Ho 2 E9 .17 C1
Gascoyne Rd E9 ...17 C1
Gaselee St E14 ....34 B2
Gasholder Pl SE11 149 A1
Gaskarth Rd SW12 .61 A1
Gaskell St SW4 ...172 A2
Gaskin Ho N16 .....6 C1
Gaskin St N1 ......86 B4
Gaspar Cl SW7 ....142 B4
Gaspar Mews SW5 142 B4
Gasson Ho 24 SE14 .50 C4
Gastein Rd W6 ...154 A4
  W6 ....47 C4
Gastigny Ho EC1 ..97 A3
Gaston Bell Cl TW9 .54 B4
Gaston Gate West 12 .72 C4
Gataker Ho 8 SE16 .40 A3
Gataker St 9 SE16 .40 A3
Gatcliff Cl SW1 ...145 C1
Gatcombe Ho 20 ....
  SE22 ....64 A4
  9 N19 ....13 B4
Gate Hill Ct W11 ..113 A2
Gate Mews SW7 ..130 B3
Gate St WC2 ......106 C2
Gatebeck Ho 21 ....
  SE22 ....64 A4
Gatefield Ct SE15 ..64 C4
Gateforth St NW8 .90 A1
Gatehouse Sch E2 .25 C3
Gatehouse Sq SE1 123 A2
Gateley Ho 6 SE4 .65 C3
Gateley Rd SW9 ...62 B4
Gates SE17 ....150 C2
Gatesborough St
  EC2 ....98 A2
Gatesden WC1 ....94 B3
Gateside Rd SW17 .72 B1
Gateway SE17 .....48 B4
Gateway Mews 4 ....
  E8 ....16 B3
Gateway Prim Sch
  NW8 ....89 C2
Gateway Trad Est
  NW10 ....21 B2
Gateways The
  SW3 ....144 B3
Gathorne St 2 E2 ..25 C3
Gatliff Rd SW1 ....146 A1
Gatonside Ho W12 .30 A2
Gatwick Ho 9 E14 .33 B3
Gatwick Rd SW18 .70 B4
Gauden Cl SW4 ...61 C4
Gauden Rd SW4 ...61 C4
Gaugin 13 SE16 ...40 A1
Gaunt St SE1 .....136 C2
Gautrey Rd SE15 ..50 B1

Gavel St SE17 ....151 C4
Gaviller Pl 8 E5 ...17 A4
Gavrelle Ho EC1 ...97 B3
Gawber St E2 .....25 B2
Gawthorne Ct E3 ..26 C3
Gay Cl NW2 ....9 A3
Gay Ho N16 ....16 A3
Gay Rd E15 ....27 C3
Gay St SW15 ......57 C4
Gaydon Ho W2 ...100 A4
Gayfere St SW1 ...134 A1
Gayford Rd W12 ...38 B4
Gayhurst SE17 ....48 C4
Gayhurst Ho NW8 .90 B2
Gayhurst Prim Sch
  E8 ....16 C1
Gayhurst Rd E8 ...16 C1
Gaymead NW8 ....78 B3
Gaysley Ho SE11 .149 B3
Gayton Cres NW3 .11 C4
Gayton Ho 3 ....11 C4
Gayton Rd NW3 ...11 C4
Gayville Rd SW11 .60 B1
Gaywood Cl SW2 ..74 C3
Gaywood St SE1 ..136 B1
Gaza St SE17 .....150 A1
Gaze Ho 10 E14 ...34 C3
Gean Ct 2 E11 ....19 C4
Geary Ho N7 ....14 B3
Geary Rd NW10 ....8 C3
Geary St N7 ....14 B3
Gedling Ho SE22 ..64 B4
Gedling Pl SE1 ...139 A2
Gee St EC1 ....96 C2
Gees Ct W1 ....103 C1
Geffrye Ct N1 .....24 A3
Geffrye Mus ★ E2 .24 B3
Geffrye St E2 .....24 B3
Geldart Rd SE15 ...50 A3
Geldeston Rd E5 ...7 C2
Gellatly Rd SE14 ..50 C1
Gemini Bsns Ctr
  E16 ....27 C1
Gemini Ho 10 E1 ..26 A1
General Hospl NW1 82 B4
General Wolfe Rd
  SE10 ....52 C2
Geneva Ct N16 ....6 C3
  8 SW15 ....57 C2
Geneva Dr SW9 ...62 C3
Genoa Ave SW15 ..57 B2
Genoa Ho 10 E1 ...25 C1
Geoffrey Chaucer Sch
  SE1 ....137 B1
Geoffrey Cl SE5 ...48 B1
Geoffrey Ct SE4 ...66 B4
Geoffrey Ho SE1 ..137 C2
Geoffrey Jones Ct
  NW10 ....21 C4
Geoffrey Rd SE4 ..66 B4
Geological Mus
  SW7 ....129 C3
George Beard Rd 10 ....
  SE8 ....41 B2
George Beare Lo 9 ....
  SW4 ....61 B2
George Belt Ho 15 ....
  E2 ....25 C2
George Ct WC2 ...120 B3
George Downing Est
  N16 ....7 B2
George Eliot Ho
  SW1 ....147 A3
George Eliot Jun & Inf
  Sch NW8 ....79 B4

George Elliot Ho
SE17 .... **150** C2
George Elliston Ho
SE1 .... **153** B1
George Eyre Ho
NW8 .... **79** C1
George Green's Sec Sch
E14 .... 42 B1
George Inn Yd SE1 **123** B1
George La SE13 .... 67 B1
George Lansbury Ho
NW10 .... 8 A1
☐ E3 .... **26** B2
George Lashwood Ct ☐ ☐
SW9 .... 62 B3
George Leybourne Ho
E1 .... **125** C4
George Lindgren Ho
SW6 .... **155** A2
George Loveless Ho
E2 .... 99 A4
George Mews W1 **92** C3/4
George Orwell Sch
N6 .... 5 B3
George Row SE16 **139** B3
George Sq ☐ SW1 **103** A2
☐ E16 .... 35 C1
George Tingle Ho
SE1 .... **139** B3
George Vale Ho ☐
E2 .... 24 C3
George Walter Ho ☐
SE16 .... 40 B2
George Wyver Cl
SW18 .... 59 A3
George Yd EC3 .. **109** C1
W1 .... **117** C4
George's Rd N7 ...... 14 B3
George's Sq SW6 **155** A4
Georgette Pl SE10 .... 52 B3
Georgiana St NW1 .... 83 A4
Georgina Gdns ☐ ☐
E2 .... 99 A4
Gerald Mews SW1 **145** C4
Gerald Rd SW1 .... **145** C4
Geraldine Rd W4 ...... 44 C4
SW18 .... 59 B2
Geraldine St SE11 **136** A1
Gerard Ct NW2 .... 9 C3
Gerard Rd SW13 ...... 46 B2
Gerards Cl SE16 ...... 40 C4
Gernigan Ho SW18 .... 59 C1
Gernon Rd E3 .... 26 A3
Gerrard Ho ☐ SE14 .. 50 C3
Gerrard Pl W1 ...... **119** C4
Gerrard Rd N1 .... 86 B2
Gerrard St W1 ...... **119** C4
Gerridge Ct SE1 .... **135** C2
Gerridge St SE1 .... **135** C2
Gertrude St SW10 **157** A3
Gervase St SE15 ...... 50 A3
Ghent Way E8 .... 16 B2
Giant Arches Rd
SE24 .... 63 B1
Gibbings Ho SE1 **136** A3
Gibbins Rd E15 ...... 76 B1
Gibbon Ho NW6 ...... 89 C1
Gibbon Rd W3 .... 29 A2
SE15 .... 50 B1
Gibbon Wlk SW15 .. 56 C3
Gibbon's Rents
SE1 .... **124** A1
Gibbons Rd NW10 .... 8 A2
Gibbs Gn W14 ...... **141** A2
Gibbs Green Sch
W14 .... **141** A2

Gibbs Ho ☐ SW12 .. 73 A4
Gibraltar Ho N1 .... **21** A3
Gibraltar Wlk E2 .... 99 A3
Gibson Cl E1 .... 25 B1
Gibson Gdns N16 .... 7 B2
Gibson Sq N1 .... **85** C4
Gibson St SE10 ...... 43 A1
Gideon Rd SW11 .... 60 C4
Giesbach Rd N19 .... 4 C2
Giffen Square Mkt
SE8 .... 51 C3
Giffin St SE8 .... 51 C3
Gifford Ho SE10 .... 42 C1
☐ SW4 .... 61 C3
Gifford St N1 .... 14 A1
Gilbert Ho EC2 .... **109** A3
SW1 .... **146** B1
SW8 .... **162** A2
☐ E2 .... 25 C2
SE8 .... 51 C4
Gilbert Pl WC1 .... **106** A3
Gilbert Rd SE11 .. **149** C4
Gilbert Sheldon Ho
W2 .... **101** C4
Gilbert St W1 ...... **103** C1
Gilbertson Ho ☐
E14 .... 41 C3
Gilbys Yd NW1 ...... 12 C1
Gilbey Ho ☐ E9 ...... 17 C2
Gilda Cres N16 ...... 7 C3
Gildea St W1 .... **104** B3
Gilden Cres NW5 .... 12 C3
Giles Ho SE16 .... **139** B2
W11 .... 31 C2/3
Gilesmead SE5 ...... 48 C2
Gilkes Cres SE21 .... 64 A1
Gilkes Pl SE21 ...... 64 A1
Gill Ave E16 .... 35 C3
Gill St E14 .... 33 B2
Gillam Ho ☐ SE16 .. 40 B2
Gillender St ☐ E3 .. 27 C1
Gillespie Prim Sch
N5 .... 6 A1
Gillespie Rd N4,N5 .. 6 A1
Gillet Pl ☐ E2 .... 99 B3
Gillett Pl ☐ E8 ...... **16** A3
Gillett St E8,N16 .... 16 A3
Gillfoot NW1 .... **82** C1
Gillian St SE13 ...... 67 A2
Gillies Ho NW6 ...... 11 C1
Gilling Ct ☐ NW3 .. 12 A2
Gillingham Mews
SW1 .... **146** C4
Gillingham Rd NW2 .. 1 A1
Gillingham Row
SW1 .... **146** C4
Gillingham St
SW1 .... **146** C4
Gillison Wlk SE16 **139** C2
Gillman Ho ☐ E2 .. 24 C3
Gillray Ho SW10 .. **157** B3
Gilmore Ho SW4 .... 60 B3
Gilmore Rd SE13 .... 67 C3
Gilpin Ave SW14 .... 55 C3
Gilpin Cl W2 .... **101** A4
Gilray Ho W2 ...... **115** B4
Gilstead Rd SW6 .. **166** B2
Gilston Rd SW10 .. **143** A1
Giltspur St EC1 .... **108** B2
Gilwell Cl ☐ E4 ...... 17 A4
Gipsy Corner W3 .... 28 C4
Gipsy La SW15 ...... 57 A4
Gipsy Moth IV SE10 52 B4
Giraud St E14 .... 34 A3
Girdlers Rd W14 .... 39 C2
Girdlestone Wlk N19 .4 B2

Girdwood Rd SW18,
SW19 .... 70 A4
Girling Ho ☐ N1 .... 24 A4
Girnock Av SE6 .... **155** A1
Girton Ho SW15 .... 57 C1
Girton Villas ☐
W10 .... 30 C3
Gissing Wlk N1 ...... 14 C1
Gladiator St SE23 .. 66 A1
Glading Terr N16 .... 7 B1
Gladsmuir Rd N19 .... 4 B3
Gladstone Ct
SW1 .... **147** C3
NW2 .... 9 A3
Gladstone Ho ☐
E14 .... 33 C3
Gladstone Park Prim
Sch NW10 .... 9 A4
Gladstone St SE1 .. **136** A2
Gladstone Terr
SW8 .... **170** B4
Gladwin Ho NW1 .... **83** A1
Gladwyn Rd SW15 .. 57 C4
Gladys Rd NW6 .... 10 C1
Glaisher St SE10 .... 52 B3
Glamis Ct W3 .... 37 A4
Glamis Est ☐ E1 .... 32 C2
Glamis Pl E1 .... 32 B2
Glamis Rd E1 .... 32 B2
Glanville Ho ☐
SW12 .... 73 B4
Glanville Rd SW2 .... 62 A2
Glasbury Ho ☐ SW9 62 B3
Glaserton Rd N16 .... 7 A4
Glasgow Ho W9 ...... **78** B1
Glasgow Terr SW1 **146** C1
Glass St ☐ E2 .... 25 A1
Glasshill St SE1 .... **136** B4
Glasshouse Fields
E1 .... 32 C2
Glasshouse St ☐
W1 .... **119** A3
Glasshouse Wlk
SE11 .... **148** C2
Glasshouse Yd
EC1 .... **96** C1
Glastonbury Ct ☐
SE14 .... 50 B3
Glastonbury Ho
SW1 .... **146** A2
Glastonbury St NW6 10 B3
Glaucus St E3 .... 34 A4
Glazbury Rd W14 .... 140 B2
Glazebrook Cl SE21 75 C2
Glebe Cl ☐ W4 ...... 38 A1
Glebe Ho ☐ SE16 .. 40 A3
Glebe Pl SW3 ...... **158** A4
Glebe Rd NW10 ...... 8 C2
E8 .... 16 B1
SW13 .... 47 A1
Glebe St W4 .... 38 A1
Glebelands Cl SE5 .. 64 A4
Gledhow Gdns
SW5 .... **142** C3
Gledstanes Rd
W14 .... **140** B1
Glen Albyn Rd
SW19 .... 69 C2
Glen Ho ☐ SW1 .... **132** C4
Glen Terr E14 .... 42 B4
Glenaffric Ave E14 .. 42 C2
Glenalmond Ho ☐
SW15 .... 56 C2
Glenarm Rd E5 ...... 17 C4
Glenbrook Rd NW6 .. 10 C3

Glenburnie Rd
SW17 .... 72 B1
Glencoe Mans
SW9 .... **163** B1
Glendall St SW9 .... 62 B3
Glendarvon
SW15 .... 57 C4
Glendower Gdns ☐☐
SW14 .... 55 C4
Glendower Pl SW7 **143** B4
Glendower Rd
SW14 .... 55 C4
Glendown Ho ☐ E8 16 C3
Glendun Ct W3 ...... 29 A2
Glendun Rd W3 ...... 29 A2
Gleneagles Cl ☐
SE16 .... 40 A1
Glenelg Rd SW2 .... 62 A2
Glenfield Rd SW12 .. 73 B3
Glenfinlas Way SE5 .. 48 A3
Glenforth St SE10 .. 43 B1
Glengall Gr E14 ...... 42 B3
Glengall Pass ☐
NW6 .... 23 C4
Glengall Rd SE15 .... 49 B4
SE15 .... 49 B4
Glengall Terr SE15 .. 49 B4
Glengarnock Ave
E14 .... 42 B2
Glengarry Rd SE22 .. 64 B2
Glenhurst Ave NW5 .. 12 C4
Glenilla Rd NW3 .... 12 A2
Glenloch Rd NW3 .. 12 A2
Glenlock Rd NW3 .. 12 A2
Glenluce SE13 ...... 52 C1
Glenmore SW15 .... 57 C1
Glenmore Ho ☐
TW10 .... 54 A1
Glenmore Rd NW3 .. 12 A2
Glennie Ct SE21 .... 76 C3
Glennie Ho SE10 .... 52 B2
Glenridding NW1 .... **82** C1
Glenrosa St SW6 .. **166** C2
Glenroy St W12 ...... 30 B3
Glensdale Rd SE4 .. 66 B4
Glenshaw Mans
SW9 .... **163** B1
Glentanner Way
SW17 .... 71 C1
Glentham Gdns
SW13 .... 47 A4
Glentham Rd SW13 47 A4
Glenthorne Mews
W6 .... 39 A2
Glenthorne Rd W6 .. 39 A2
Glenthorpe SW15 .. 56 C3
Glentworth St NW1 **91** A1
Glenville Gr SE8 .... 51 B3
Glenville Mews
SW18 .... 70 C4
Glenworth Ave E14 .. 42 C2
Gliddon Rd W14 .. **140** A3
Glifford Rd SW11 .. **146** C1
Globe JMI Sch E2 .. 25 B2
Globe Pond Rd
SE16 .... 33 A1
Globe St SE1 ...... **137** B3
Globe Terr ☐ E2 .... 25 B2
Globe Theatre The*
SE1 .... **122** C3
Globe Yd W1 ...... **104** A1

Geo – God   209

Gloucester Ave
NW1 .... **81** C4
Gloucester Cir SE10 52 B3
Gloucester Cres
NW1 .... **82** A4
Gloucester Ct SE1 **124** B3
SE1 .... **137** C2
NW11 .... 1 B4
Richmond TW9 ...... 44 C3
Gloucester Dr N4 .... 6 A2
Gloucester Gate
NW1 .... **82** A2
Gloucester Gate Mews
NW1 .... **82** A2
Gloucester Gdns
W2 .... **100** C2
NW11 .... 1 B4
Gloucester Ho NW6 .. 23 C3
Richmond TW10 .... 54 C2
Gloucester Mews
W2 .... **101** A1
Gloucester Mews W
W2 .... **101** A1
Gloucester Pk
SW7 .... **142** C4
Gloucester Pl W1 **103** A4
Gloucester Pl Mews
W1 .... **103** A3
Gloucester Prim Sch
SE15 .... 49 A3
Gloucester Rd
SW7 .... **142** C4
W3 .... 37 B3
Richmond TW9 ...... 44 C3
Gloucester Road Sta
SW7 .... **142** C4
Gloucester Sq W2 **101** C1
☐ E2 .... 24 C4
Gloucester St SW1 **146** C1
Gloucester Terr
W2 .... **101** A1
Gloucester Way
EC1 .... **95** C3
Gloucester Wlk
W8 .... **127** C4
Glover Ho ☐ NW6 .. 11 B1
SE15 .... 65 A3
Glycena Rd SW11 .. 60 B4
Glyn Ct SE27 .... 74 C1
Glyn Mans W14 .... **140** B4
Glyn Rd E5 .... 17 C4
Glynde Mews SW3 **130** B1
Glynde Reach WC1 **94** B3
Glynde St SE4 ...... 66 B1
Glynfield Rd NW10 .. 8 A1
Goat Wharf TW8 .... 44 A4
Goater's Alley
SW6 .... **155** A1
Godalming Rd E14 .. 34 A4
Godbold Rd SW19 .. 69 C2
Goddard Pl N19 ...... 4 B1
Godfrey Ho EC1 .... **97** B3
Godfrey St SW3 .. **144** B2
E15 .... 27 B3
Goding St SE11 .... **148** B1
Godley Rd SW18 .. **71** C3
Godliman St EC4 .. **122** C4
Godman Rd SE15 .. 50 A1
Godolphin & Latymer
Sch W6 .... 39 A2
Godolphin Ho NW3 12 A1
☐ SW2 .... 74 C3

Godolphin Pl W3 . . . .28 C2
Godolphin Rd W12 . . . .39 A4
Godson St N1 . . . . .85 B2
Godstone Ct **1** N16 . . . .7 A3
Godstone Ho **1** SE1 . . .137 C2
Godwin Cl N1 . . . . .87 A2
Godwin Ho NW6 . . . . . .78 B3
2 E2 . . . . .24 B3
Goffers Ho SE3 . . . . . . .53 A1
Goffers Rd SE3,SE13 . . .53 A1
Goffton Ho SW9 . . . . .173 A1
Golborne Gdns
8 W10 . . . . .23 A1
W10 . . . . .23 A1
Golborne Mews **9**
W10 . . . . .31 A4
Golborne Rd W10 . . . .31 A4
Golden Hind Pl **4**
SE8 . . . . .41 B2
Golden La EC1 . . . . . . .97 A1
Golden Plover Cl
E16 . . . . .35 C3
Golden Sq W1 . . . . . .119 A4
Golders Ct NW11 . . . . . .1 B4
Golders Gdns NW11 . . .1 B4
Golders Green Cres
NW11 . . . . .1 C4
Golders Green Rd
NW11 . . . . .1 A4
Golders Green Sta
NW11 . . . . .1 C3
Golders Hill Sch
NW11 . . . . .1 C4
Golders Park Cl
NW11 . . . . .1 C3
Golders Way NW11 . . . .1 B4
Goldhawk Ind Est The
W6 . . . . .39 A3
Goldhawk Mews **7**
W12 . . . . .39 A4
Goldhawk Rd W12 . . . .38 C3
Goldhawk Road Sta
W12 . . . . .39 B4
Goldhurst Terr NW6 . . .11 B1
Goldie Ho N19 . . . . .4 C4
Golding St E1 . . . . . . .111 C1
Golding Terr E1 . . . . . .111 C1
Goldington Cres
NW1 . . . . .83 B2
Goldington Ct NW1 . . .83 B3
Goldington St NW1 . . .83 B3
Goldman Cl
E2 . . . . .24 C1 99 B2
Goldney Rd W9 . . . . . . .23 C1
Goldsboro Rd SW8 . . .161 C1
Goldsborough Ho
SW8 . . . . .171 C3
Goldsmith Ave W3 . . .28 C2
Goldsmith Ct WC1 . . .106 B2
Goldsmith Rd W3 . . . . .28 C2
SE15 . . . . .49 C2
Goldsmith St EC2 . . . .109 A2
Goldsmith's Pl
NW6 . . . . .78 A3
Goldsmith's Row E2 . . .24 C3
Goldsmith's Sq **1**
E2 . . . . .24 C3
Goldsmiths Bldgs
3 W3 . . . . .28 C1
Goldsmiths Cl W3 . . . .28 C1
Goldsworthy Gdns
SE16 . . . . .40 B1

Goldthorpe NW1 . . . . .82 C3
Goldwell Ho SE22 . . . . .64 A4
Goldwin Cl SE14 . . . . . .50 B2
Goldwing Cl **10** E16 . . .35 C3
Gomm Rd SE16 . . . . . . .40 B3
Gondar Gdns NW6 . . . .10 B3
Gondar Mans NW6 . . . .10 B3
Gonson St SE8 . . . . . . .52 A4
Gonston Cl SW19 . . . . .70 A2
Gonville Ho **6**
SW15 . . . . .56 C2
Gonville St SW6 . . . . . .58 A4
Gooch Ho EC1 . . . . . .107 B4
Good Hart Pl E14 . . . . .33 A2
Goodall Ho **10** SE4 . . . .65 C3
Goodfaith Ho **9**
E14 . . . . .34 A2
Goodge Pl W1 . . . . . . .105 A3
Goodge St W1 . . . . . . .105 A3
Goodge Street Sta
W1 . . . . .105 A3
Goodhall St NW10 . . . .21 B2
Goodhope Ho **18**
E14 . . . . .34 A2
Gooding Cl N7 . . . . . . .14 A2
Goodinge Cl N7 . . . . . .14 A2
Goodman Cres SW2 . . .73 C2
Goodman's Stile
E1 . . . . .111 B2
Goodman's Yd E1, . . .124 C4
Goodrich Ct **9** W10 . . .30 C3
Goodrich Ho N16 . . . . . .7 A4
21 E2 . . . . .25 B3
Goodrich Prim Sch
SE22 . . . . .64 C1
Goodrich Rd SE22 . . . . .64 C1
Goodson Rd NW10 . . . . .8 A1
Goodsway NW1 . . . . . . .84 A2
Goodway Gdns E14 . . . .34 C3
Goodwill Ho **19** E14 . . .34 A2
Goodwin Cl SE16 . . . .139 A1
Goodwin Ho **2**
SE15 . . . . .65 A4
Goodwin Rd W12 . . . . .38 C4
Goodwins Ct WC2 . . . .120 A4
Goodwood Ct **1** W1 . .104 B4
Goodwood Ho **3**
W4 . . . . .37 B1
Goodwood Mans **4**
SW9 . . . . .62 C4
Goodwood Rd SE14 . . .51 A3
Goosander Ct **13**
E3 . . . . .26 C3
Goose Green Trad Est
SE22 . . . . .64 C3
Gophir La EC4 . . . . . . .123 B4
Gopsall St N1 . . . . .87 C3
Gordon Ave SW14 . . . .56 A3
Gordon Ct **10** W12 . . . .30 B3
Gordon Gr SE5 . . . . . . .48 A1
Gordon Ho **16** E1 . . . . .32 B2
3 SE10 . . . . .52 C3
Gordon Hospl The
SW1 . . . . .147 B3
Gordon House Rd
NW5 . . . . .12 C4
Gordon Lo N16 . . . . .6 C4
Gordon Pl W8 . . . . . . .127 C4
Gordon Rd
Richmond TW9 . . . . . .44 B1
W4 . . . . .45 A4
SE15 . . . . .50 A1
E15 . . . . .76 B4
Gordon Sq WC1 . . . . . .93 C2

Gordon St WC1 . . . . . . .93 B2
Gordonbrock Jun & Inf
Sch SE4 . . . . .66 C2
Gordonbrock Rd
SE4 . . . . .66 C2
Gordondale Rd
SW18,SW19 . . . . .70 C2
Gore Rd E9 . . . . .25 B4
Gore St SW7 . . . . .129 A2
Gorefield Ho NW6 . . . . .23 C3
Gorefield Pl NW6 . . . . .23 C3
Gorham Ho **12** SW4 . . .61 B1
Gorham Pl W11 . . . . . .112 A4
Goring St EC3 . . . . . . .110 B2
Gorleston St W14 . . . .140 B4
Gorse Cl E16 . . . . .35 C3
Gorsefield Ho **5**
E14 . . . . .33 C2
Gorst Rd NW10 . . . . . . .20 C1
SW11 . . . . .60 B1
Gorsuch Pl E2 . . . . .98 C4
Gorsuch St E2 . . . . .98 C4
Gosberton Rd SW12 . . .72 C3
Gosfield St W1 . . . . . .104 C3
Gosford Ho **3** E3 . . . . .26 B3
Gosling Ho **2** E1 . . . . .32 B2
Gosling Way SW9 . . . .173 B4
Gospel Oak Prim Sch
NW5 . . . . .12 C4
Gospel Oak Sta
NW5 . . . . .12 C4
Gosport Ho **3**
SW15 . . . . .68 C3
Gosport Way **5**
SE15 . . . . .49 B3
Gosset St E2 . . . .24 C2 99 B4
Gosterwood St SE8 . . . .51 A4
Goswell Pl EC1 . . . . . . .96 B3
Goswell Rd EC1 . . . . . . .96 B3
Gothic Ct **17** SE5 . . . . .48 B3
Gottfried Mews
NW5 . . . . .13 B4
Gough Ho N1 . . . . .86 B4
Gough Sq EC4 . . . . . . .107 C2
Gough St WC1 . . . . .95 A1
Gough Wlk **11** E14 . . . .33 C3
Gould Terr **22** E8 . . . . .17 A3
Goulden Ho SW11 . . . .168 A2
Gouldman Ho **33** E1 . . .25 B1
Goulston St E1 . . . . . . .110 C2
Goulton Rd E5 . . . . .17 A4
Govan St E2 . . . . .24 C4
Gover Ct SW4 . . . . . . .172 B2
Gowan Ave SW6 . . . . .164 A4
Gowan Rd NW10 . . . . . . .9 A2
Gower Ct WC1 . . . . .93 B3
Gower Ho SE17 . . . . . .151 A2
Gower Mews WC1 . . . .105 C4
Gower Pl NW1,WC1 . . .93 B3
Gower St WC1 . . . . .93 B2
Gower's Wlk E1 . . . . . .111 B1
Gowlett Rd SE15 . . . . . .64 C4
Gowrie Rd SW11 . . . . . .60 C4
Grace Ho SE11 . . . . . .163 A4
Grace Jones Cl E8 . . . .16 C2
Grace Pl E3 . . . . .27 A2
Grace St E3 . . . . .27 A2
Grace's Mews SE5 . . . . .49 A1
Grace's Rd SE5 . . . . . . .49 A1
Gracechurch St
EC3 . . . . .109 C1
Gracefield Gdns
SW16 . . . . .74 A1

Gracehill **2** E1 . . . . . . .32 B4
Graces Alley E1 . . . . . .125 B4
Graces Mews NW8 . . . .79 A1
SE5 . . . . .49 A1
Graemesdyke Ave
SW14 . . . . .55 A3
Grafton Cres NW1 . . . . .13 A2
Grafton Ct **10** E8 . . . . .16 C3
Grafton Ho **3** E3 . . . . .26 C2
12 SE8 . . . . .41 B1
Grafton Mews W1 . . . . .92 C1
Grafton Pl NW1 . . . . . . .93 C3
Grafton Prim Sch N7 . . .5 A1
Grafton Rd NW5 . . . . . .12 C3
W3 . . . . .28 B2
Grafton Sq SW4 . . . . . .61 B4
Grafton St W1 . . . . . . .118 B3
Grafton Terr NW5 . . . . .12 C3
Grafton Way W1 . . . . . .93 A1
Grafton Yd NW5 . . . . . .13 A2
Graham Ct **5** SE14 . . . .50 C4
Graham Ho **2** N19 . . . .13 C4
5 SW12 . . . . .73 A4
Graham Mans **2** E8 . . .17 A2
Graham Rd E8 . . . . .16 C2
Graham St N1 . . . . .86 B1
Graham Terr SW1 . . . . .145 C3
Grainger Ct **22** SE5 . . .48 B3
Grampian Gdns NW2 . . .1 A3
Grampians The **10**
W14 . . . . .39 C4
Granard Ave SW15 . . . .57 A2
Granard Ho **20** E9 . . . . .17 C2
Granard Prim Sch
SW15 . . . . .57 A1
Granard Rd SW11,
SW12 . . . . .72 B4
Granary Rd E1 . . . . .25 A1
Granary St NW1 . . . . . .83 B3
Granby Pl SE1 . . . . . . .135 B3
Granby St E2 . . . . .99 A2
E2 . . . . .24 A1 99 B3
Granby Terr NW1 . . . . . .82 C1
Grand Ave EC1 . . . . . . .108 B4
Grand Junction Wharf
N1 . . . . .86 C1
Grand Par SW14 . . . . . .55 B3
Grand Union Cl W9 . . . .31 B4
Grand Union Cres
E8 . . . . .24 C4
Grand Union Ind Est
NW10 . . . . .20 A3
Grand Vitesse Ind Est
SE1 . . . . .122 B1
Grandfield Ct W4 . . . . . .45 C4
Grandison Rd SW11 . . .60 B2
Granfield St SW11 . . . .167 C3
Grange Ct WC2 . . . . . .107 A1
SE15 . . . . .49 B1
Grange Gr N1 . . . . .15 B2
Grange Ho NW10 . . . . . .9 A1
SW13 . . . . .47 A3
Grange La SE21 . . . . . . .76 B2
Grange Mills SW12 . . . .73 B3
Grange Mus of
Community History The
NW10 . . . . .9 A3
Grange Pl NW6 . . . . . . .10 C1
Grange Prim Sch
SE1 . . . . .138 A1
Grange Rd SE1 . . . . . . .138 C1
NW10 . . . . .9 A1
W4 . . . . .37 A1
SW13 . . . . .46 C2
Grange St N1 . . . . .87 C3

Grange The SE1 . . . . . .138 C2
W14 . . . . .140 C3
19 NW3 . . . . .12 B2
7 W4 . . . . .37 A1
W3 . . . . .39 A3
Grange Wlk SE1 . . . . . .138 C1
Grange Yd SE1 . . . . . . .138 C1
Grangecourt Rd N16 . . .7 A3
Grangefield NW1 . . . . . .14 A1
Grangemill **11** NW5 . . .13 A4
Grangeway NW6 . . . . . .10 C1
Gransden Ave E8 . . . . . .17 A1
Gransden Ho **8** SE8 . . .41 B1
Grant Ho SW8 . . . . . . .171 B1
Grant St SW11 . . . . .60 A4
N1 . . . . .85 B2
Grantbridge St N1 . . . . .86 B2
Grantham Ct **5**
SE16 . . . . .40 C4
Grantham Ho **12**
SE15 . . . . .49 C4
Grantham Pl W1 . . . . . .118 A1
Grantham Rd SW9 . . . .172 B1
W4 . . . . .46 A3
Grantley Ho
2 SE14 . . . . .50 C4
5 SW19 . . . . .69 C3
Grantley St E1 . . . . .25 C1
Grantully Rd W9 . . . . . .88 A3
Granville Ct N1 . . . . . . .87 C4
8 SE14 . . . . .51 B3
Granville Gr SE13 . . . . .67 B4
Granville Ho **18** E14 . . .33 C3
Granville Mans **8**
W12 . . . . .39 B4
Granville Pk SE13 . . . . .67 C4
Granville Pl W1 . . . . . .103 B1
SW6 . . . . .156 A1
Granville Point NW2 . . .1 B2
Granville Rd NW2 . . . . . .1 B2
NW6 . . . . .23 C3
SW18 . . . . .70 B4
Granville Sq WC1 . . . . .95 A3
SE15 . . . . .49 A3
Granville St WC1 . . . . . .95 A3
Grape St WC2 . . . . . . .106 A2
Grasmere NW1 . . . . . . .92 B3
Grasmere Ave W3 . . . . .28 C2
Grasmere Ct SW13 . . . .46 C4
Grasmere Ho **18**
N16 . . . . .15 C4
Grasmere JMI Sch
SE15 . . . . .50 B3
Grasmere Point **2**
SE15 . . . . .50 B3
Grately Ho **10** SW15 . . .68 C3
Gratton Rd W14 . . . . . .126 A1
Gravel La E1 . . . . .110 C2
Graveley Ho **7** SE8 . . . .41 B2
Gravesend Rd W12 . . . .29 C2
Gray Ho SE17 . . . . . . .151 A2
Gray St SE1 . . . . .135 C3
Gray's Inn* WC1 . . . . .107 A4
Gray's Inn Pl WC1 . . . .107 A3
Gray's Inn Rd WC1 . . . .95 A2
Gray's Yd W1 . . . . .103 C2
Grayfriars Pas EC1 . . . .108 B2
Grayling Ho N16 . . . . . . .6 C2
Grayling Sq
E2 . . . . .24 C2 99 C4
Grayshott Rd SW11 . . . .60 C4
Grayson Ho EC1 . . . . . . .97 A3

Grayswood Point 14
SW15 .... 68 C3
Grazebrook JMI Sch
N16 .... 7 A2
Grazebrook Rd N16 ..... 7 A2
Great Arthur Ho
EC1 .... 96 C1
Great Bell Alley
EC2 .... 109 B2
Great Brownings
E15 .... 76 B1
Great Castle St
W1 .... 104 C2
Great Central St
NW1 .... 102 C4
Great Chapel St
W1 .... 105 B2
Great Chertsey Rd
SW14,W4 .... 45 C2
Great Church La
W6 .... 39 C1
Great College St
SW1 .... 134 A2
Great Croft WC1 ..... 94 B3
Great Cumberland Mews
W1 .... 102 C2
Great Cumberland Pl
W1 .... 103 A1
Great Dover St
SE1 .... 137 B2
Great Eastern Bldgs 10
E8 .... 17 A2
Great Eastern Ent Ctr
E14 .... 42 A4
Great Eastern Pier
E14 .... 41 C1
Great Eastern Rd
E15 .... 19 C2
Great Eastern St
EC2 .... 24 A1 98 A2
Great Eastern Wharf
SW11 .... 158 B1
Great Field 7 NW5 ... 13 B3
Great George St
SW1 .... 134 A3
Great Guildford Bsns Sq
SE1 .... 122 C1
Great Guildford St
SE1 .... 122 C1
Great James St
WC1 .... 106 C4
Great Marlborough St
W1 .... 104 C1
Great Mathers Rd
SE11 .... 150 A4
Great Maze Pond
SE1 .... 137 C4
Great New St EC4 .. 107 C2
Great Newport St
WC2 .... 120 A4
Great Ormond St
WC1 .... 94 C1
Great Ormond St Hospl
for Children WC1 .. 94 C1
Great Percy St WC1 . 95 B4
Great Peter St
SW1 .... 133 C1
Great Portland St
W1 .... 104 B4
Great Portland Street
Sta W1 .... 92 B1
Great Pulteney St
W1 .... 119 A4
Great Queen St
WC2 .... 106 B2

Great Russell St
WC1 .... 106 A3
Great Scotland Yd
SW1,WC2 .... 120 A2
Great Smith St
SW1 .... 133 C2
Great Spilmans
SE22 .... 64 A2
Great St Helen's
EC3 .... 110 A2
Great St Thomas
Apostle EC4 .... 123 A4
Great Suffolk St
SE1 .... 122 B1
Great Sutton St EC1 . 96 B1
Great Swan Alley
EC2 .... 109 B2
Great Titchfield St
W1 .... 104 C3
Great Tower St
EC3 .... 124 A4
Great Trinity La
EC4 .... 123 A4
Great Turnstile
WC2 .... 107 A3
Great West Rd W4,
W6 .... 45 C4
Great West Road Cedars
Rd W4 .... 45 C4
Great West Road
Hogarth La W4 ..... 46 A4
Great Western Rd
W2,W9 .... 31 B4
Great Winchester St
EC2 .... 109 C2
Great Windmill St
W1 .... 119 B4
Great Yd SE1 .... 138 B4
Greatfield Cl 4 N19 . 13 B4
SE4 .... 66 C3
Greatham Wlk 8
SW15 .... 68 C3
Greatorex Ho 9
E1 .... 111 B3
Greatorex St 2
E1 .... 111 B3
Greaves Cotts 12
E14 .... 33 A3
Greaves Twr SW10 . 157 A2
Grebe Ct 1 E14 ... 42 B4
28 SE8 .... 51 B4
Greek Ct W1 .... 105 C1
Greek St W1 .... 105 C1
Green Arbour Ct
EC1 .... 108 A2
Green Bank E1 ...... 32 A1
Green Cl NW11 .... 2 B4
Green Dale SE22 ... 64 A2
Green Dragon Ct
SE1 .... 123 B1
Green Dragon Jun & Inf
Sch TW8 .... 44 A4
Green Dragon La
TW8 .... 36 B1
Green Dragon Yd
E1 .... 111 B3
Green Ho The 5
SW19 .... 70 A3
Green Hundred Rd
SE15 .... 49 C4
Green Lanes N4,N8,
N15 .... 6 A4
Green Park SW1,
W1 .... 118 C2
Green Park Sta
W1 .... 118 C2
Green St W1 .... 117 B4
Green Terr EC1 ...... 95 C3

Green The W3 .... 29 A3
Green Wlk SE1 ...... 138 A1
Green Wood NW5 .. 13 B3
Green Yd WC1 .... 95 A2
Green's Ct W1 ...... 112 C1
Greenacre Ct E3 ... 26 B3
Greenacre Sq 16
SE16 .... 40 C4
Greenaway Gdns
NW3 .... 11 A4
Greenaway Ho NW8 70 C3
WC1 .... 95 B3
Greenberry St NW8 . 80 A1
Greencoat Pl SW1 . 147 A4
Greencoat Row
SW1 .... 133 A1
Greencroft Gdns
NW6 .... 11 A1
Greene Ct 20 SE14 150 C4
Greene Ho SE1 ..... 137 B1
Greenend Rd W4 ... 38 A4
Greener Ho 8 SW4 . 61 C4
Greenfell Mans
SE8 .... 52 A4
Greenfield Ho 28
SW19 .... 69 C3
Greenfield Rd E1 .. 111 C2
Greenham Cl SE1 . 135 B3
Greenham Ho 6 E9 25 B4
Greenheath Bsns Ctr 2
E2 .... 25 A1
Greenhill NW3 ...... 11 C4
Greenhill Pk NW10 . 21 A4
Greenhill Rd NW10 . 21 A4
Greenhill's Rents
EC1 .... 108 A4
Greenhills Terr 16
N1 .... 15 C2
Greenland Ho 4 E1 . 26 C2
4 E8 .... 24 B4
Greenland Mews
SE8 .... 40 C1
Greenland Pl NW1 . 82 B4
Greenland Quay
SE16 .... 40 C2
Greenland Rd NW1 . 82 B4
Greenleaf Cl 8
SW2 .... 74 C4
Greenman St N1 .... 86 C4
Greenock Rd 11 W3 37 B3
Greens Ct W1 ...... 119 B4
Greenside Prim Sch
W12 .... 29 C4
Greenside Rd W12 . 38 C4
Greenstead Gdns
SW15 .... 57 A2
Greenstreet Hill
SE4 .... 65 C4
Greenway Cl N4 .... 6 B2
Greenwell St W1 ... 92 B1
Greenwich Bsns Ctr
SE10 .... 52 A3
Greenwich Bsns Pk
SE10 .... 52 A3
Greenwich Church St
SE10 .... 52 B4
Greenwich Ct 13 E1 . 32 A3
Greenwich District
Hospl SE10 .... 43 B1
Greenwich High Rd
SE10 .... 52 A3
Greenwich Ind Est
SE10 .... 52 A3

Greenwich Mkt 1
SE10 .... 52 B4
Greenwich Park
SE10 .... 53 A3
Greenwich Park Sch
SE10 .... 53 A3
Greenwich Park St
SE10 .... 52 C4
Greenwich South St
SE10 .... 52 B2
Greenwich Sta SE10 52 A3
Greenwich View
E14 .... 42 A3
Greenwood 6
SW19 .... 69 C4
Greenwood Ho 4
8 SE4 .... 65 C3
Greenwood Pl NW5 . 13 A3
Greenwood Rd E8 .. 16 C2
Greenwood Terr
NW10 .... 20 C3
Greet Ho SE1 .... 135 C3
Greet St SE1 .... 121 C1
Gregor Mews SE3 . 53 C3
Gregory Pl W8 ...... 128 A4
Greig Terr SE17 ... 48 A4
Grena Gdns TW9 ... 54 B3
Grena Rd TW10,TW9 54 B3
Grenada Ho 19 E14 33 B2
Grenade St E14 .... 33 B2
Grendon Ho N1 .... 84 C1
7 E9 .... 25 B4
Grendon St NW8 .. 90 A2
Grenfell Ho SE5 .... 48 B3
Grenfell Rd W11 .... 30 C2
Grenfell Sch Ed 32 A3
Grenfell Twr 5
W11 .... 30 C2
Grenfell Wlk 4
W11 .... 30 C2
Grenville Ho 20 E3 . 26 A3
8 SE8 .... 51 C4
Grenville Ho N6 .... 4 A4
Grenville Mews
SW7 .... 143 A3
Grenville Pl SW7 . 142 C4
Grenville Rd N19 .. 5 A3
Grenville St WC1 .. 94 B1
Gresham Almshouses 3
SW9 .... 62 B3
Gresham Coll EC1 . 107 C3
Gresham Rd SW9 . 62 C4
Gresham St EC2 .. 109 A2
Gresham Way SW19 70 C1
Gresham Way Est
SW19 .... 71 A1
Gresley Ho SW8 ... 171 C4
Gresley Rd N19 .... 4 B4
Gresse St W1 .... 105 B2
Gressenhall Rd
SW18 .... 70 B4
Greswell St SW6 .. 47 C2
Gretton Ho 2 E2 ... 25 B2
Greville Hall NW6 .. 78 B2
Greville Ho SW1 .. 131 B2
SW15 .... 57 C4
Greville Lo 2 W2 . 100 A2
Greville Mews 4
NW6 .... 78 A3
Greville Pl NW6,
NW8 .... 78 A2
Greville Rd NW6 ... 78 A2
NW6 .... 78 A3
Richmond TW10 .... 54 B1
Greville St EC1 ..... 107 C4
Grey Coat Hospital CE
Sch The SW1 .... 133 B1

Grey Coat Hospital St
Michaels The
SW1 .... 147 B3
Grey Eagle St
E1 .... 24 B1 99 A1
Grey Ho 22 W12 .... 30 A2
Grey Turner Ho
W12 .... 29 C3
Greycoat Pl SW1 . 133 B1
Greycoat St SW1 . 133 B1
Greyfriars 18 SE26 76 C1
Greyfriars Ho SE3 . 53 B4
Greyhound Ct WC2 121 B4
Greyhound Rd W6 154 A4
NW10 .... 22 A2
Greyladies Gdns
SE10 .... 52 B2
Greystoke Ho SE15 49 C4
Greystoke Pl EC4 . 107 C2
Grice Ct N1 .... 15 B2
Grierson Rd SE23 . 65 C1
Griffin Cl NW10 ..... 9 A3
Griffin Ct W12 .... 30 A1
W4 .... 38 B1
13 Brentford TW8 .. 44 A4
Griffin Gate SW15 . 57 C4
Grifton Ho 3 SW11 . 60 A4
Grigg's Pl SE1 ..... 138 B1
Grimaldi Ho N1 .... 84 C2
Grimsby St E2 ...... 99 A2
Grimsel Path SE5 . 48 A3
Grimshaw Cl N6 .... 3 C4
Grimston Rd SW6 . 164 C1
Grimthorpe Ho EC1 96 A2
Grimwade Cl SE15 . 65 B4
Grindal St SE1 ..... 135 B3
Grindall Ho 28 E1 . 25 A1
Grindley Ho 8 E3 . 33 B4
Grinling Gibbons Prim
Sch SE8 .... 51 B4
Grinling Pl SE8 ..... 51 C4
Grinstead Rd SE8 . 41 A1
Grisedale NW1 ...... 92 C4
Grittleton Rd W9 .. 23 C1
Grocers' Hall Ct
EC2 .... 109 B1
Groom Cres SW18 . 71 C4
Groom Pl SW1 ..... 131 C2
Groombridge Rd E9 17 C1
Groome Ho SE11 . 149 A3
Grosse Way SW15 . 57 A1
Grosvenor Av N5 .. 15 B3
Richmond TW10 .... 54 A2
SW14 .... 56 A4
Grosvenor Bridge
SW1 .... 160 B4
Grosvenor Cotts
SW1 .... 145 B4
Grosvenor Cres
SW1 .... 131 C3
Grosvenor Cres Mews
SW1 .... 131 B3
Grosvenor Ct NW6 22 C4
W4 .... 37 A1
2 Richmond TW10 . 54 B1
SW15 .... 58 A2
Grosvenor Ct Mans
W2 .... 102 C1
Grosvenor Gdns
SW1 .... 132 B1
9 B3
NW2 .... 9 B2
SW14 .... 56 A4

Grosvenor Gdns Mews E
SW1 .... 132 B2
Grosvenor Gdns Mews N
SW1 .... 132 B2
Grosvenor Gdns Mews S
SW1 .... 132 B2
Grosvenor Hill W1 ....118 A4
Grosvenor Hill Ct
W1 .... 118 A4
Grosvenor Ho E5 ....7 C3
Grosvenor Park SE5 48 B3
Grosvenor Pier
SW1 .... 161 B4
Grosvenor Pk SE5 ....132 A3
Grosvenor Pl SW1 ....132 A3
Grosvenor Rd SW1 161 A4
W4 ....37 B1
Richmond TW10 ....54 A3
Grosvenor Residences
E14 ....42 C2
Grote's Bldgs SE3 ......53 A1
Grote's Pl SE3 ....53 A1
Groton Rd SW18 ....71 A2
Grotto Ct SE1 ....136 C4
Grotto Pas W1 ....103 C4
W1 ....103 C4
Grove Crescent Rd
E15 ....19 C2
Grove Ct NW8 ....89 B4
SW10 ....143 A1
SW4 ....61 A4
SW4 ....61 B4
Grove Dwellings E1 ..32 B4
Grove End NW5 ....13 A4
Grove End Gdns
NW8 ....79 A1
Grove End Ho NW8 ....89 B3
Grove End Rd NW8 ....89 B3
Grove Gdns NW8 ....90 B3
Grove Hall Ct NW8 ....89 A4
Grove Hill Rd SE5 ......64 A4
Grove Ho SW3 ....158 B4
SE3 ....53 B1
Grove House Froebel Ed
Inst SW15 ....56 B1
Grove House Prim Sch
SE22 ....75 A2
Grove Jun & Inf Sch
W11 ....45 A4
Grove La SE5 ....64 A4
Grove Lane Terr
SE5 ....48 C1
Grove Lo SW4 ....61 B3
Grove Mans E8 ....16 B3
N16 ....7 A4
2 W6 ....39 B4
....60 B3
Grove Mews W6 ....39 B3
Grove Park Bridge
W4 ....45 B3
Grove Park Gdns
W4 ....45 A3
Grove Park Mews
W4 ....45 B3
Grove Park Rd W4 ....45 A3
Grove Park Terr
W4 ....45 A4
Grove Pk SE5 ....49 A1
Grove Pl NW3 ....2 C1
W3 ....28 B1
SW12 ....61 A1

Grove Rd NW2 ....9 B2
E3 ....26 A3
W3 ....28 B1
SW13 ....46 B1
Richmond TW10 ....54 B1
Grove St SE8 ....41 B1
Grove The NW11 ....1 A4
N6 ....3 C3
5 B4
SE21 ....76 C3
Grove Vale SE22 ....64 B3
Grove Vale Prim Sch
SE22 ....64 B3
Grovedale Rd N19 ......4 C2
Groveland Ct EC4 ....109 A1
Grovelands Cl SE5 ......49 A1
Groveley Ho 7 N4 ....6 B4
Grover Ho SE11 ....149 A1
SW4 ....61 B2
Groveside Ct
SW11 ....167 B2
Groveway SW9 ....173 A3
Grovewood 9 TW9 ......44 C2
Grummant Rd SE15 ..49 B2
Grundy St E14 ....34 A3
Guardian Angels RC JMI
Sch E3 ....26 A2
Guards Mus The
SW1 ....133 A3
Gubyon Ave SE24 ......63 A2
Guerin Sq E3 ....26 B2
Guernsey Gr SE24 ......75 B4
Guernsey Ho 1 N1 ....15 B2
Guernsey Rd 2 N1 ....15 B2
Guy Hall* EC2 ....109 A2
Guildford Gr SE10 ......52 A2
Guildford Ho 24 SE5 48 B1
Guildford Rd SW8 ...172 B4
Guildford St WC1 ......94 B1
Guildhall Bldgs
EC2 ....109 B2
Guildhall Sch Music &
Drama EC2 ....109 A3
Guildhall Yd EC2 ......109 A2
Guildhouse St
SW1 ....146 C3
Guinness Cl E9 ....18 A1
Guinness Ct NW8 ......80 A2
EC1 ....97 A3
E1 ....111 A1
SW3 ....144 C3
Guinness Sq SE1 .....152 A4
Guinness Trust Bldgs
SE1 ....138 A4
SE1 ....138 A4
SE11 ....150 A2
W6 ....39 B1
W6 ....39 B1
Guion Rd SW6 ....165 A2
Gujarat Ho 1 N16 ....7 A1
Gulland Wlk 20 N1 ....15 B2
Gullane Ho 22 E3 ....26 B3
Gulliver St SE16 ....41 B3
Gulston Wlk SW3 ....145 A3
Gun St E1 ....110 C3
Gun Wharf E1 ....32 B1
E3 ....33 B4
Gunmakers La E3 ......26 A4
Gunners Rd SW18 ......71 C2

Gunnersbury Avenue
(North Circular Rd)
W3 ....36 C3
Gunnersbury Cl 8
W4 ....37 A1
Gunnersbury Cres
W3 ....36 C4
Gunnersbury Ct 8
W3 ....37 A4
Gunnersbury Dr W5 36 B4
Gunnersbury Gdns
W3 ....36 C4
Gunnersbury La W3 36 C3
Gunnersbury Mews 6
W4 ....37 A1
Gunnersbury Park
W3 ....36 C3
Gunnersbury Park Mus
W3 ....36 C3
Gunnersbury Sta
W4 ....37 A1
Gunpowder Sq
EC4 ....107 C2
Gunstor Rd N16 ....16 A4
Gunter Gr SW6 ....156 C2
Gunterstone Rd
W14 ....140 B2
Gunthorpe St E1 ....111 A2
Gunwhale Cl SE16 ....32 C1
Gurdon Ho 8 E14 ......33 C3
Gurdon Rd SE7 ....43 C1
Gurney Ho 2 E2 ....24 C3
4 W2 ....100 A2
Guthrie Ct SE1 ....135 C3
Guthrie St SW3 ....144 A2
Gutter La EC2 ....108 C2
Guy St SE1 ....137 C4
Guy's Evelina Hospl
Sch SE1 ....123 C1
Guy's Hospl SE1 ......123 C2
Guyscliff Rd SE13 ......67 B2
Gwalior Rd SW15 ....57 C4
Gwendolen Ave
SW15 ....57 C2
Gwendolen Cl SW15 57 C2
Gwendwr Rd W14 ....140 B2
Gwent Ct 18 SE16 ......32 C1
Gwilym Maries Ho 5
E2 ....25 A2
Gwyn Cl SW6 ....156 C1
Gwynne Cl W4 ....46 B3
Gwynne Ho WC1 ....95 B3
6 SW2 ....74 B4
Gwynne Pl WC1 ....95 A3
Gwynne Rd SW11 ....167 C2
Gye Ho 2 SW4 ....62 A3
Gylcote Cl SE5 ....63 C3

H

Haarlem Rd 12 W14 39 C3
Haber Dasher Pl N1 ..98 A4
Haberdasher St N1 ....97 C4
Haberdashers' Aske's
Hatcham Coll SE4 51 A2
Haberdashers' Aske's
Hatcham Coll (Boys)
E8 ....51 A2
Habington Ho 9
SE5 ....48 C3
Hackett Cl SE8 ....41 B2
Hackford Rd SW9 ....173 B4
Hackford Wlk SW9 ..173 B3
Hackney Central Sta
E8 ....17 A2

Hackney Coll (Poplar
Centre) E3 ....27 A1
Hackney Com Coll
N1 ....98 B4
Hackney Downs Sch
E5,E8 ....16 C3
Hackney Downs Sta
E8 ....17 A3
Hackney Free &
Parochial CE Sch
(Secondary) E9 .....17 B2
Hackney Gr E8 ....17 A2
Hackney Hospl E9 ....18 A3
Hackney Rd E2 ....24 C3
Hackney Wick E9 ......18 B2
Hackney Wick Sta
E9 ....18 C2
Hackworth Point 24
E3 ....27 A2
Haddington Ct 4
SE10 ....52 A3
Haddo Ho NW5 ....13 A4
SE10 ....52 A4
Haddo St SE10 ....52 B4
Haddon Ct W3 ....29 B2
Haden Ct N4 ....5 C2
Hadfield Ho 6 E1 .....111 C1
Hadleigh Cl 16 E1 ....25 B1
Hadleigh Ho 15 E1 ....25 B1
Hadleigh St E2 ....25 B2
Hadley Ct N16 ....7 C3
Hadley Gdns W4 ....37 C1
Hadlow Ho SE17 .....152 B2
Hadrian Cl 8 E3 ....26 C4
Hadrian Est 20 E2 ....24 C3
Hadrian St SE10 ....43 A1
Hadstock Ho N1 ....93 C4
Hadyn Park Ct 13
W12 ....38 C4
Hadyn Park Rd W12 38 C4
Hafer Rd SW11 ....60 B3
Haggerston Rd E8 ......24 B4
Haggerston Sch E2 ..24 B3
Hague JMI Sch E3 ......26 B1
Hague St 2 E2 ....99 C3
Haig Ho 2 E2 ....24 C3
Hailsham Ave SW2 ..74 B2
Hailsham Ho NW8 ......90 A1
Hainford Cl SE4 ....65 C3
Haining Cl 3 W4 ....36 C1
Hainthorpe Rd SE27 75 A1
Hainton Cl E1 ....32 A3
Halcomb St N1 ....24 A4
Halcrow St E1 ....32 A4
Haldane Pl SW18 ......71 A3
Haldane Rd SW6 ......155 A3
Haldon Rd SW18 ......58 B1
Hale Ho SW1 ....147 C2
Hale St E14 ....34 A2
Hales Ho 8 SW12 ......73 A4
Hales Prior N1 ....84 C1
Hales St SE8 ....51 C3
Halesworth Rd
SE13 ....67 A4
Half Moon Cr N1 ....85 A4
Half Moon Ct EC1 ....108 C3
Half Moon La SE24 ..63 B1
Half Moon St W1 .....118 B1
Halfmoon Pas E1 .....111 A1
Halford Ho 6 SW15 ..57 C2
Halford Rd SW6 ....155 B3
Richmond TW10 ....54 A2
Haliday Ho N1 ....15 C2
Haliday Wlk 4 N1 ......15 C2
Halidon Cl E9 ....17 B3

Haliwell Ho NW6 ......78 A3
Halkett Ho 11 E2 ......25 B4
Halkin Arc SW1 ....131 A2
Halkin Mews SW1 ...131 B2
Halkin Pl SW1 ....131 B2
Halkin St SW1 ....131 C3
Hall Gate NW8 ....89 A4
Hall Jun Sch The
NW3 ....11 C2
Hall Oak Wlk NW6 ...10 B2
Hall Pl W2 ....89 B1
Hall Rd NW8 ....89 A4
E15 ....19 C4
Hall Sch Wimbledon
SW15 ....68 C1
Hall St EC1 ....96 B4
Hall Twr W2 ....101 C4
Hallam Ct W1 ....104 B4
Hallam Ho SW1 ....147 A1
SW9 ....173 B4
Hallam Mews W1 ....104 B4
Hallam Rd SW13 ....57 A4
Hallam St W1 ....92 B1
Halley Ho 15 E2 ....24 C3
8 SE10 ....43 B1
Halley Prim Sch
E14 ....33 A4
Halley St E14 ....33 A4
Hallfield W2 ....100 C1
Hallfield Jun & Inf Sch
W2 ....100 C1
Halliday Ho E1 ....111 C1
Hallifield St N1 ....15 C1
Halling Ho SE1 ....137 C3
Halliwell Ct 8 SE22 64 C2
Halliwell Rd SW2 ......62 B1
Hallsville Prim Sch
E16 ....35 C3
Hallsville Rd E16 ....35 B3
Halpin Pl SE17 ....151 C3
Halsbury Ho 4 N7 .....14 B4
Halsbury Rd W12 ......30 A1
Halsey St SW3 ....144 C4
Halsmere Rd SE5 ......48 A2
Halstead Ct N1 ....87 C1
Halston Cl SW11 ....60 B1
Halstow 12 NW5 ....12 C2
Halstow Prim Sch
SE10 ....43 C1
Halstow Rd NW10 ....22 C2
SE3,SE10 ....43 C1
Halton Cross St N1 ..86 B4
Halton Ho 22 N1 ....15 A1
Halton Mans N1 ....15 A1
Halton Pl N1 ....86 B4
Halton Rd N1 ....86 B4
Haltone Ho SW4 ....171 C1
Halyard Ho E14 ....42 B3
Ham Yd W1 ....119 B4
Hambalt Rd SW4 ......61 B2
Hamble St SW6 ....59 A4
Hambledon SE17 ......48 C4
Hambledon Chase
N4 ....5 A4
Hambledon Ho E5 ......17 A4
Hambledon Pl SE21 76 B3
Hambledon Rd
SW18 ....70 B4
Hambley Ho 5
SE16 ....40 A2
Hamblyn Ct N16 ....7 B4
Hambridge Way
SW2 ....74 C4

Hambrook Ct 12
NW5 ....13 A4
Hambury Ho SW8 .162 B3
Hamers Ho 18 SW2 .74 B3
Hamilton Ct NW8 ...89 B3
SE16 ....41 A4
Hamilton Ct W9 ...88 B4
Hamilton Gdns
NW8 ....89 A4
Hamilton Hall NW8 .78 C3
Hamilton Ho NW8 ..89 B4
W8 ....128 A4
19 E3 ....26 B2
11 E14 ....27 B2
10 Richmond TW9 .54 A4
W4 ....46 A4
SW15 ....56 C2
Hamilton La N5 ....15 A4
Hamilton Lo 32 E1 ..25 B1
Hamilton Mews
W1 ....132 A4
Hamilton Pk N5 ....15 A4
Hamilton Pk W N5 .15 A4
Hamilton Pl W1 ...117 C1
Hamilton Rd NW11 .1 A4
W4 ....38 A4
Hamilton Sq SE1 ..137 C4
Hamilton St SE8 ...51 C4
Hamilton Terr NW8 .89 A4
Hamlet (Day) Hospl The
TW9 ....44 C1
Hamlet Ct SE11 ...150 A2
10 W6 ....38 C2
Hamlet Gdns W6 ...38 C2
Hamlet Ind Est E9 .18 C1
Hamlet Sq NW2 ....1 A1
Hamlet The SE5 ....63 C4
Hamlet Way SE1 ..137 C4
Hamlets Way E3 ...26 B1
Hammelton Gn 2
SW9 ....48 A2
Hammersley Ho 8
SE14 ....50 B3
Hammersmith & West
London Coll
W14 ....140 A2
W12 ....39 A4
Hammersmith & West
London Coll Olympia
Annexe W14 ....140 B4
Hammersmith Bridge Rd
W6,SW13 ....39 B1
Hammersmith Broadway
5 W6 ....39 B2
Hammersmith Flyover
W14 ....140 A2
10 W6 ....39 B1
Hammersmith Gr
W6 ....39 B3
Hammersmith Hospl
W12 ....30 A3
Hammersmith Rd
W14 ....140 B4
10 W6 ....39 C2
Hammersmith Sta
W6 ....39 C2
Hammersmith Terr
W6 ....38 C1
Hammett St EC3 ..124 C4
Hammond Ho E14 ..42 A3
10 SE14 ....50 B3
Hammond Lo 6
W9 ....31 C4
Hammond St NW5 .13 B2
Hamond Sq N1 .....24 A3

Hampden Cl NW1 ...83 C2
Hampden Gurney CE
Prim Sch W1 ......102 B2
Hampden Gurney St
W1 ....102 C1
Hampden Ho SW9 .173 C1
Hampden Rd N19 ...4 C2
Hampshire Ct 6
SW13 ....46 B1
Hampshire Hog La 11
W6 ....39 A2
Hampshire St 7
NW5 ....13 C2
Hampson Way
SW8 ....172 C4
Hampstead Gate
NW3 ....11 B3
Hampstead Gn NW3 .12 A3
Hampstead Gr NW3 ..2 C1
Hampstead Heath *
NW3 ....2 C2
Hampstead Heath Sta
NW3 ....12 B4
Hampstead High St
NW3 ....11 C4
Hampstead Hill Gdns
NW3 ....12 A4
Hampstead Hill Sch
NW3 ....12 A3
Hampstead La N6 ...3 A4
Hampstead Parochial CE
Sch NW3 ....11 B4
Hampstead Rd NW1 .92 C4
Hampstead Sch
NW2 ....10 B4
Hampstead Sq NW3 .2 B1
Hampstead Sta
NW3 ....11 C4
Hampstead West 4
E3 ....26 B4
Hampton Cl NW6 ..23 C2
Hampton Ct N1 ....15 A2
10 SE16 ....32 C1
Hampton St SE1 ...150 B3
Hananel St 6 E16 ..35 B3
Hanbury Ho 5 E1 ..111 B4
Hanbury Rd W3 ....37 A4
Hanbury St E1 .....111 A4
Hancock Nunn Ho 1
NW3 ....12 B1
Hancock Rd E3 ....27 B2
Hand Ct WC1 ......107 A3
Handa Wlk 3 N1 ...15 B2
Handel Mans SW13 .47 B3
Handel St WC1 .....94 B2
Handforth Rd SW9 .163 B2
Handley Rd E9 .....25 B4
Hands Wlk E16 .....35 C3
Hanford Cl SW18 ..70 C3
Hankey Pl SE1 ....137 C3
Hanley Gdns N4 ....5 B3
Hanley Rd N4,N19 ..5 A3
Hanmer Wlk N7 .....5 B2
Hannah Mary Way 5
SE1 ....153 C3
Hannay La N8 ....4 C4
Hannay Wlk N16 ...73 C2
Hannell Rd SW6 ..154 B2
Hannen Ho SE5 ....49 A1
Hannen Rd SE27 ...75 A1
Hannibal Rd E1 .....32 B4
Hannington Rd
SW4 ....61 A4
Hanover Ave E16 ..35 C1
Hanover Cl TW9 ...44 C3

Hanover Ct N16 .....7 B4
11 W12 ....29 C1
Hanover Gate Mans
NW1 ....90 B2
Hanover Gdns
SE11 ....163 B3
Hanover Ho NW8 ...80 A1
Hanover Mans 5
SW2 ....62 C2
Hanover Pk SE15 ..49 C2
Hanover Pl 2 WC2 .106 B1
Hanover Rd NW10 .22 B4
Hanover Sch N1 ...86 C2
Hanover St W1 .....104 B1
Hanover St 11 W6 ..39 A1
Hanover Steps 3 W2 .102 B1
Hanover Terr NW1 ..90 C3
Hanover Terr Mews
NW1 ....90 B3
Hanover West Ind Est
NW10 ....20 C2
Hanover Yd N1 .....86 C2
Hans Cres SW1 ...130 C2
Hans Pl SW1 ....130 C2
Hans Rd SW3 ......130 C2
Hans St SW1 ....131 A1
Hansard Mews W14 .39 C4
Hansler Rd SE22 ...64 B2
Hanson Cl SW14 ...55 B4
SW12 ....73 A4
Hanson Ho 1 E1 ...125 C4
Hanson St W1 .....104 C4
Hanway Ho 11 SW9 .173 C4
Hanway Pl W1 .....105 B2
Hanway St W1 .....105 B2
Hanworth Ho 20 SE5 .48 A3
Harben Rd NW6 ....11 B1
Harberson Rd SW12 .73 A3
Harberton Rd N19 ..4 B3
Harbet Rd W2 .....101 C3
Harbin Ho 3 SW2 ..74 C3
Harbinger JMI Sch
E14 ....42 A2
Harbinger Rd E14 ..42 A2
Harbledown Ho
SE1 ....137 B3
Harbledown Rd
SW6 ....165 B4
Harbord Cl SE5 .....48 C1
Harbord Ho 6 SE16 .40 C2
Harbord St SW6 ...47 C2
Harborough Sch N19 .4 C2
Harbour Ave SW10 .167 A3
Harbour Exchange Sq
E14 ....42 A4
Harbour Rd SE5 ...63 B4
Harbridge Ave
SW15 ....68 C4
Harbut Rd SW11 ..59 C3
Harcombe Rd N16 ..7 A1
Harcourt Ho 1 W1 .104 A2
SW8 ....171 B2
Harcourt Rd SE4 ...66 A3
Harcourt St W1 ...102 B3
Harcourt Terr
SW10 ....142 B1
Hardcastle Ho 8
SE15 ....49 C2
Hardel Rise SW2 ...75 A3
Hardel Wlk SE24,
SW2 ....74 C4
Harden Ho SE5 ....49 A1
Harders Rd SE15 ..50 A1
Hardess St SE24 ...63 B4

Hardham Ho 5
SW2 ....62 C1
Harding Cl SE17 ...48 B4
Harding Ho SW13 ..47 A4
Hardinge Rd NW10 .22 B4
Hardinge St E1 .....32 B3
Hardington 2 NW1 .12 C1
Hardwick Ho NW8 ..90 B2
SW8 ....171 B2
Hardwick St EC1 ...95 C3
Hardwick's Way
SW18 ....58 C2
Hardwicke Ho 14
E3 ....27 A2
Hardwicke Mews
WC1 ....95 A3
Hardwicke Rd W4 ..37 C2
Hardwidge St SE1 .138 A4
Hardy Ave 16 E16 ..35 C1
Hardy Cl SE16 .....40 C4
Hardy Cotts 2 SE10 .52 C4
Hardy Rd SE3 ......53 B4
Hare & Billet Rd
SE3 ....52 C1
Hare Ct EC4 ....107 B1
Hare Marsh
E2 ....24 C1 99 B2
Hare Pl EC4 ....107 C1
Hare Row E2 ....25 A3
Hare Wlk N1 ....24 A3
Harecourt Rd N1 ...15 B2
Haredale Ho 16
SE16 ....139 B3
Haredale Rd SE24 ..63 B3
Harefield Mews SE4 .66 B4
Harefield Rd SE4 ..66 B4
Harewood Ave NW1 .90 B1
Harewood Pl W1 ..104 B1
Harewood Row
NW1 ....102 B3
Harfield Gdns 1
SE5 ....64 A4
Harfleur Ct SE11 ..150 A3
Harford Ho W11 ....31 B4
SE5 ....48 B4
Harford St E1 ......26 A1
Hargrave Mans 2
N19 ....4 C2
Hargrave Park Prim Sch
N19 ....4 B2
Hargrave Pk N19 ...4 B2
Hargrave Pl N7 ....13 C3
Hargrave Rd N19 ...4 B2
Hargraves Ho 3
W12 ....30 A2
Hargwyne St SW9 .62 B4
Harkness Ho 1 E1 .111 C1
Harlech Twr 3 W3 .37 B4
Harlescott Rd SE15 .65 C3
Harlesden Gdns
NW10 ....21 B4
Harlesden Prim Sch
NW10 ....21 A3
Harlesden Rd NW10 .21 C4
Harlesden Sta
NW10 ....20 C3
Harley Gdns SW10 .143 A1
Harley Gr E3 ....26 B2
Harley Ho NW1 ....91 C1
Harley Pl W1 ......104 A3
Harley St NW1 ....104 A3
Harley Villas NW10 .21 A3
Harleyford Rd SW8 .162 C4

Harleyford Manor 6
W3 ....28 B1
Harleyford Rd
SE11 ....162 C4
Harleyford St SE11 .163 B3
Harling Ct 5 SW11 .168 C2
Harling Rd E16 .....35 C1
Harling St SW11 ...168 C2
Harlowe Ho 19 SE5 .24 B4
Harlynwood 19 SE5 .48 B3
Harman Cl E1 ......153 B1
NW2 ....1 A1
Harman Dr NW2 ...10 A4
Harman Ho 6 SE8 .41 B2
Harmood Gr NW1 ..13 A1
Harmood Ho 2
NW1 ....13 A1
Harmood St NW1 ..13 A1
Harmsworth St
SE17 ....150 A1
Harold Ct 14 SE16 .40 C4
Harold Est SE1 ...138 B1
Harold Ho 10 E2 ...25 C3
Harold Laski Ho
EC1 ....96 B3
Harold Maddison Ho
SE17 ....150 B2
Harold Pl SE11 ....149 B1
Harold Rd NW10 ...20 C2
Harold Wilson Ho
SW6 ....155 A3
Harp Alley EC4 ...108 A2
Harp La EC3 ......124 A3
Harpenden Rd SE27,
.......................75 A2
Harpenmead Point
NW2 ....1 B2
Harper Ho 3 SW9 .63 A4
Harper Mews SW17 .71 B1
Harper Rd SE1 ...137 A2
Harpley Sch E1 ....25 C1
Harpley Sq E1 .....25 C1
Harpsden St SW11 .169 B3
Harpur Mews WC1 .106 C4
Harpur St WC1 ....106 C4
Harrier Ho 9 SW11 .60 A4
Harriet Cl E8 ......24 C4
Harriet Ho SW6 ...156 B1
Harriet St SW1 ....131 A3
Harriet Tubman Cl 21
SW2 ....74 C4
Harriet Wlk SW1 ..131 A3
Harrington Ct
SW7 ....143 C4
9 W9 ....23 B2
Harrington Gdns
SW7 ....142 C3
Harrington Ho NW1 .92 C4
SW1 ....147 C2
Harrington Rd
SW7 ....143 B4
Harrington Sq NW1 .82 C1
Harrington St NW1 .92 C4
Harriott Cl SE10 ...43 B2
Harriott Ho 11 E1 ..32 B3
Harris Ho 10 E3 ....26 C2
SW9 ....62 C4
Harris St SE5 ......48 C3
Harrison Ho SE17 .151 B2
Harrison St WC1 ...94 B3
Harrisons Ct 1
SE14 ....50 C4
Harrodian Sch
SW13 ....46 B3
Harrogate Ct 2
SE26 ....76 C1

Harrold Ho **1** NW3 ...11 B1
Harrow La E14 ...34 B2
Harrow Pl E1 ...110 B2
Harrow Rd W2 ...101 B3
W2,W9 ...23 C1
Harrow St NW1 ...102 A4
Harroway Rd
SW11 ...167 C2
Harrowby St W1 ...102 B2
Harrowgate Ho **2**
E9 ...17 C2
Harrowgate Rd E9 ...18 A1
Harry Gosling JMI Sch
E1 ...111 C1
Harry Hinkins Ho
SE17 ...151 A1
Harry Lambourn Ho **10**
SE15 ...50 A3
Hart Ho SW2 ...74 C3
Hart St EC3 ...124 B4
Hart's La SE14 ...51 A2
Hartfield Terr E2 ...25 C3
Hartham Cl N7 ...14 A3
Hartham Rd N7 ...14 A3
W4 ...45 A3
Hartington Rd
SW8 ...162 A1
W4 ...45 B2
Hartismere Rd
SW6 ...155 A2
Hartlake Rd E9 ...18 A2
Hartland NW1 ...83 A3
Hartland Rd NW1 ...13 A1
NW6 ...23 B4
Hartley Ho SE1 ...153 A4
SW15 ...56 C2
Hartley St E2 ...25 B2
Hartnoll Ho **4** N7 ...14 C3
Hartnoll St N7 ...14 C3
Harton Lo **2** SE8 ...51 C2
Harton St SE8 ...51 C2
Hartop Ct N16 ...7 A1
Hartop Point
SW6 ...154 B2
Hartshorn Alley
EC3 ...110 B1
Hartswood Ho **10**
SW2 ...74 A3
Hartswood Rd W12 ...38 B3
Hartwell St E8 ...16 B2
Harvard Ct NW6 ...11 A3
Harvard Hill W4 ...45 A4
Harvard Ho **5** SE17 ...48 A4
SW15 ...57 C1
Harvard Mans **8**
SW11 ...59 C3
Harvard Rd W4 ...37 A1
11 W4 ...37 B1
SE13 ...67 B2
Harvey Ct SW11 ...168 B4
Harvey Ho N1 ...87 C3
1 E1 ...25 A1
SW1 ...147 C1
3 E14 ...33 C3
Brentford TW8 ...36 A1
Harvey Lo **8** W9 ...31 C4
Harvey Point **6** E16 ...35 C4
Harvey Rd **15** SE5 ...48 C2
Harvington Wlk E8 ...16 C1
Harvist Rd NW6 ...23 A3
Harwood Ct N1 ...87 C3
SW15 ...57 B3

Harwood Rd SW6 ...156 A1
Harwood Terr
SW6 ...166 A4
Hascombe Ho **11**
SW15 ...69 A3
Hascombe Terr **2**
SE5 ...48 C1
Haselrigge Prim Sch
SW4 ...61 C3
Haselrigge Rd SW4 ...61 C3
Haskell Ho NW10 ...20 C4
Hasker St SW3 ...144 B4
Haslam Cl N1 ...14 C1
Haslam Ho **1** N1 ...15 B1
Haslam St SE15 ...49 B2
Haslemere Ave
SW18 ...71 A2
Haslemere Ind Est
SW18 ...71 A2
Haslemere Rd N8 ...5 A4
Hassard St E2 ...24 B3
Hassett Rd E9 ...18 A2
Hassop Rd NW2 ...9 C4
Hastings Cl **16** SE15 ...49 C3
Hastings Ho **5** W12 ...30 A2
Hastings Hos WC1 ...94 A3
Hastings St WC1 ...94 A3
Hat & Mitre Ct EC1 ...96 B1
Hatcham Mews Bsns Ctr
SE14 ...50 C2
Hatcham Park Mews
SE14 ...50 C2
Hatcham Park Rd
SE14 ...50 C2
Hatcham Rd SE15 ...50 B4
Hatcham Wood Sch
SE14 ...51 A1
Hatchard Rd N19 ...5 A2
Hatcliffe Almshouses
SE10 ...43 A1
Hatcliffe St SE10 ...43 B1
Hatfield Cl SE14 ...50 C3
Hatfield Ct SE3 ...53 C3
Hatfield Ho EC1 ...96 C1
Hatfield Rd W4 ...37 C4
Hatfields SE1 ...121 C2
Hathaway Ho N1 ...98 A4
Hatherley Ct W2 ...100 A2
Hatherley Gr W2 ...100 A2
Hatherley Rd TW9 ...44 B2
Hatherley St SW1 ...147 A3
Hathersage Rd N1 ...15 C3
Hathersley Ho **3**
SW2 ...74 C4
Hathersley Ho **3**
SE5 ...50 A1
Hatherton Cl **3**
SE5 ...50 A1
Hathway St **4** SE15 ...50 B1
Hathway Ho **3**
SE15 ...50 B1
Hatteraick St **6**
SE16 ...40 B4
Hatton Gdn EC1 ...107 C4
Hatton Ho **1** E1 ...125 C4
Hatton Pl EC1 ...107 C4
Hatton Row NW8 ...89 C1
Hatton St NW8 ...89 C1
Hatton Wall EC1 ...107 C4
Haunch of Venison Yd
W1 ...104 A1
Hauteville Court Gdns **1**
W6 ...38 B3
Havana St E14 ...41 C4

Havant Way **8** SE15 ...49 B3
Havelock Cl **13** W12 ...30 A2
Havelock St N1 ...84 B4
Havelock Terr
SW8 ...160 B1
Haven Cl SW19 ...69 C1
Haven St **17** NW1 ...13 A1
Haven The TW9 ...54 C4
Havenpool NW8 ...78 B3
Havercourt **3** NW3 ...12 A2
Haverfield Gdns
TW9 ...44 C3
Haverfield Rd E3 ...26 A2
Haverhill Rd SW12 ...73 B3
Havering **2** NW1 ...13 A1
Havering Ho N4 ...6 B4
Havering St E1 ...32 C3
Haversham Lo NW2 ...9 C2
Haversham Pl N6 ...3 B2
Haverstock Hill
NW3 ...12 B2
Haverstock Rd NW5 ...12 C3
Haverstock Sch
NW1 ...12 C2
Havil St SE5 ...49 A2
Havisham Ho **16** SE16 ...139 B3
Hawarden Gr SE24 ...75 B4
Hawberry Ho N7 ...14 A2
Hawes St N1 ...15 A1
Hawgood St E3 ...33 C4
Hawk Ho **7** SW11 ...60 A4
Hawke Ho **20** E1 ...25 C1
Hawke Pl **22** SE16 ...40 C4
Hawke Twr **4** SE14 ...51 A4
Hawkesbury
Rd SW15 ...57 A2
Hawkesworth Ho **5**
SW4 ...61 B1
Hawkins Ho **3** SE8 ...51 C4
Hawkley Gdns SE27 ...75 A2
Hawkridge **19** NW5 ...12 C2
Hawks Mews **10**
SE10 ...52 B3
Hawkshaw Cl **23**
SW2 ...74 A4
Hawkshead NW1 ...92 C4
Hawkshead Rd NW10 ...8 B1
Hawksley Rd N16 ...7 A1
Hawksmoor Ho **8**
E14 ...33 A4
Hawksmoor Mews
E1 ...32 A2
Hawksmoor St **5**
W6 ...47 C4
Hawkstone Rd SE16 ...40 B2
Hawkwell Wlk (off
Maldon Cl) N1 ...87 A4
Hawley Cres NW1 ...13 A1
Hawley Inf Sch
NW1 ...13 A1
Hawley Mews **4**
NW1 ...13 A1
Hawley Rd **3** NW1 ...13 A1
Hawley St NW1 ...13 A1
Haworth Ct E15 ...76 B3
Haworth Ho **7** SW2 ...62 C1
Hawstead Rd SE6 ...67 A1
Hawthorn Ct
Richmond TW9 ...45 A2
SW15 ...57 A4
Hawthorn Rd NW10 ...8 C1
Hawthorn Wlk W10 ...23 A1
Hawthorne Cl N1 ...16 A2
Hawthorne Ho
SW1 ...147 A1

Hawtrey Rd NW3 ...12 A1
Hay Currie St E14 ...34 A3
Hay Hill W1 ...118 B3
Hay St E2 ...24 C4
Hay's Galleria*
SE1 ...124 A2
Hay's La SE1 ...124 A2
Hay's Mews W1 ...118 A2
Haycroft Gdns
NW10 ...22 A4
Haycroft Mans
NW10 ...21 C4
Haycroft Rd SW2 ...62 A2
Hayday Rd E16 ...35 C4
Hayden's Pl W11 ...31 B3
Haydon St E1,EC3 ...124 C4
Haydon Way SW11 ...59 C3
Haydon Wlk E1 ...111 A1
Hayes Ct **23** SE5 ...48 B3
SW12 ...74 A3
Hayes Pl NW1 ...90 B1
Hayfield Ho **38** E1 ...25 B1
Hayfield Pas E1 ...25 B1
Hayles Bldgs SE11 ...150 B4
Hayles St SE11 ...150 A4
Hayling Cl **28** N16 ...16 A3
Haymans Point
SE11 ...148 C2
Haymarket SW1 ...119 B3
Haymerle Ho **6**
SE15 ...49 C3
Haymerle Rd SE15 ...49 C4
Haymerle Sch SE15 ...49 C4
Hayne Ho W11 ...112 A2
Hayne St EC1 ...108 B4
Haynes Ho **8** E9 ...17 C2
Hayter Ho W12 ...29 C2
Hayter Rd SW2 ...62 B2
Haythorn Ho NW11 ...1 A1
Hayward Ct SW4 ...172 B2
Hayward Gallery*
SE1 ...121 A2
Hayward Gdns
SW15 ...57 B1
Hayward Ho N1 ...85 B2
Hayward's Pl EC1 ...96 A2
Haywood Lo **23** N7 ...13 C3
Hazel Cl N19 ...4 B2
SE15 ...49 C1
Hazel Ho **12** NW3 ...12 B2
SE4 ...66 B4
Hazel Rd NW10 ...22 B2
Hazel Way SE1 ...152 C4
Hazelbourne Rd
SW12 ...61 A1
Hazeldon Rd SE4 ...66 A2
Hazellville Rd N19 ...4 C3
Hazelmere Ct **10**
SW2 ...74 B3
Hazelmere Rd NW6 ...23 B4
Hazelwood Cl W5 ...36 A4
Hazelwood Ho **11**
SE8 ...41 A2
Hazelwood Mans
SW6 ...164 C4
Hazlebury Rd SW6 ...166 B2
Hazledene Rd W4 ...45 B4
Hazlewell Rd SW15 ...57 B2
Hazlewood Cres
W10 ...23 A1
Hazlewood Twr
W10 ...23 A1
Hazlitt Mews W14 ...126 A1
Hazlitt Rd W14 ...126 A1
Head St E1 ...32 C3

Headbourne Ho
SE1 ...137 C2
Headcorn **16** NW5 ...12 C2
Headfort Pl SW1 ...131 C3
Headington Rd
SW18 ...71 B2
Headlam Rd SW4 ...73 C4
Headlam St E1 ...25 A1
Heads Mews W11 ...31 C3
Heald St SE8,SE14 ...51 C2
Healey Ho SW9 ...163 C1
2 E3 ...26 C1
Healey St NW1 ...13 A2
Heanor Ct E5 ...17 C4
Hearn St EC2 ...24 A1 98 B1
Hearn's Bldgs
SE17 ...151 C3
Hearne Rd W4 ...44 C4
Hearnshaw Ho **8**
E14 ...33 A4
Hearnville Prim Sch
SW12 ...72 C3
Hearnville Rd SW12 ...72 C3
Heath Brow NW3 ...2 B1
Heath Cl NW11 ...2 A4
Heath Ct NW11 ...1 C4
6 SE15 ...6 C3
8 NW3 ...11 B2
Heath Hurst Rd
NW3 ...12 A4
Heath La SE3 ...52 C1
Heath Mans **4** NW3 ...11 B4
SW15 ...57 C4
Heath Mead SW19 ...69 C1
Heath Park Gdns
NW3 ...2 A1
Heath Rd SW8 ...170 B1
Heath Rise SW15 ...57 C1
Heath Royal SW15 ...57 C1
Heath St NW3 ...2 B1
Heath View NW5 ...12 C4
Heathbrook Prim Sch
SW4 ...170 C1
Heathcote St WC1 ...94 C3
Heathcroft NW11 ...2 A3
Heather Cl SW8 ...61 A4
SE13 ...67 C1
Heather Ct SW8 ...61 A4
Heather Ho **6** E14 ...34 B3
Heather Lo N16 ...7 A3
Heather Wlk W10 ...23 A1
Heatherley Ct N16 ...7 C1
Heatherley Sch of Fine
Art SW10 ...157 A1
Heathfield Ave
SW18 ...71 C4
Heathfield Ct
6 W4 ...37 C1
SE14 ...50 C3
Heathfield Gdns
NW11 ...1 A4
W4 ...37 B1
Heathfield Ho SE3 ...53 A1
Heathfield Pk NW2 ...9 B2
Heathfield Rd W3 ...37 A4
SW18 ...59 C1
Heathfield Sq SW18 ...71 C4
Heathfield Terr W4 ...37 C1
Heathland Rd N16 ...7 A3
Heathman's Rd
SW6 ...165 A3
Heathmere Prim Sch
SW15 ...68 C3
Heathpool Ct **6** E1 ...25 A1
Heathshot **8** TW10 ...54 A1

Heathside NW3 ....11 C4
Heathside Prep Sch
NW3 ....11 C4
Heathstan Rd W12 ....29 C3
Heathview St SW19 ..69 C2
Heathview Gdns
SW15 ....69 B4
Heathville Rd N4,N19 .5 A4
Heathwall St SW11 ...60 B4
Heathway 6 SE3 ......53 B3
SE3 ....53 C3
Heathway St SW4 ....157 A4
Heathwood Ct
SW12 ....73 B3
Heaton Ho SW10 ....157 A4
6 SE15 ....50 A1
Heaton Rd SE15 ....50 A1
Heaver Rd 2 SW11 ..59 C4
Hebden Ct 2 E2 ....24 B4
Hebdon Rd SW17 .....72 A1
Heber Prim Sch
SE22 ....64 B1
Heber Rd NW2 ....9 C4
SE22 ....64 B1
Hebron Rd W6 ....39 A3
Heckfield Pl SW6 ....155 B1
Heckford St E1 ....32 C2
Hector Ct SW9 ....173 B4
SW15 ....57 C2
Hector Ho 12 E2 ....25 A3
Heddington Gr N7 ....14 B3
Heddon St W1 ....118 C4
Hedger St SE11 ......150 A4
Hedger's Gr E9 ....18 A2
Hedingham Cl 6
N1 ....15 B1
Hedley Ct SW15 .....57 C1
Hedley Ho E14 ....42 B3
Hedley Row N5,N16 .15 C3
Hedsor Ho E2 ....98 C2
Heidegger Cres
SW13 ....47 A3
Heighate Pl NW3 .....12 B4
Heights The NW3 .....11 B4
Heiron St SE17 ....48 A4
Helby Rd SW4 ....61 C1
Heldar Ct SE1 ....137 C3
Helen Gladstone Ho
SE1 ....136 A4
Helen Ho 6 E2 ....25 A3
Helen Mackay Ho
E14 ....34 C3
Helen Peele Cotts 2
SE16 ....40 B3
Helen Taylor Ho
SE16 ....153 B4
Helen's Pl E2 ....25 B2
Helena Rd NW10 ....9 A3
Helena Sq 15 SE16 ..33 A2
Helenslea Ave NW11 .1 C3
Heliport Est The
SW11 ....167 B1
Helix Gdns SW2 ....62 B1
Helix Rd SW2 ....62 B1
Hellenic Coll of London
SW1 ....130 C1
Hellings St E1 ....125 C1
Helmet Row EC1 ......97 A2
Helmsdale Ho NW6 ..78 A1
Helmsley Pl E8 ....17 A1
Helmsley St 7 E8 ....17 A1
Helsby Ct NW8 ....89 B2
Helsinki Sq SE16 .....41 A3
Helston NW1 ....83 A2
Helston Ho SE11 ....149 C2
Hemans Est SW8 ....161 C1

Hemans St SW8 .....161 C1
Hemberton Rd SW9 .62 A4
Hemingford Rd N1 ..85 A4
Hemlington Ho 11
E14 ....33 A4
Hemlock Rd W12 ....29 B2
Hemming St
E1 ....24 C1 99 C1
Hemp Wlk SE17 ....151 C4
Hemstal Rd NW6 .....10 C1
Hemsworth Ct N1 ...24 A3
Hemsworth St N1 ...24 A3
Hemus Pl SW3 ....144 B1
Henchman St W12 ..29 B3
Henderson Ct NW3 ..11 C3
1 SE14 ....50 C4
Henderson Dr NW8 ..89 B2
Henderson Rd
SW18 ....72 A4
Hendre Ho SE1 ......152 B3
Hendre Rd SE1 ......152 B3
Hendrick Ave SW12 .72 B4
Heneage La EC3 ...110 B1
Heneage Pl EC3 ....110 B1
Heneage St E1 ....111 A4
Henfield Cl N19 ....4 C3
Hengrave Rd SE23 ..65 C1
Henley Cl SE16 ....40 B4
Henley Ct NW2 ....9 C2
SE15 ....64 C4
Henley Dr SE1 ......153 A4
Henley Ho E2 ....99 A2
Henley Prior N1 ....84 C1
Henley Rd NW10 ......22 B4
Henley St SW11 ....169 C2
Henniker Mews
SW3 ....157 B4
Henniker Rd E15 ....19 C3
Henning St SW11 ...168 A3
Henrietta Ho 11 W6 .39 B1
Henrietta Mews
WC1 ....94 B2
Henrietta Pl W1 ....104 A2
Henrietta St E15 .....19 B3
WC2 ....120 B4
Henriques St E1 .....111 C1
Henry Cavendish Prim
Sch SW12 ....73 B3
Henry Compton Sec Sch
SW6 ....164 A4
Henry Dickens Ct
W11 ....112 A4
Henry Fawcett Prim Sch
SE11 ....163 B4
Henry Ho NW8 ....90 A1
SE1 ....121 C1
SW8 ....162 A2
Henry Jackson Ho
SW15 ....57 C4
Henry Jackson Rd
SW15 ....57 C4
Henry Rd N4 ....6 B3
Henry Wise Ho
SW1 ....147 A3
Henryson Rd SE4 ....66 C2
Henshall Point 10
E3 ....27 A2
Henshall St N1 ....15 C2
Henshaw St SE17 ..151 B4
Henslow Ho 11
SE15 ....49 C3
Henslowe Rd SE22 ..64 C2
Henson Ave NW2 ......9 B3
Henson Ct 3 N5 ....15 B4

Henstridge Pl NW8 ..80 A2
Henty Cl SW11 ......168 B4
Henty Wlk SW15 .....57 A2
Hepburn Mews
SW11 ....60 B2
Hepplestone Cl
SW15 ....57 A1
Hepscott Rd E9 ....18 C1
Hera Ct 7 E14 ....41 C2
Herald St 5 E2 ....25 A1
Heralds Pl SE11 ....150 A4
Herbal Hill EC1 ....95 C1
Herbert Chapman Ct
N5 ....15 A4
Herbert Cres SW1 ..131 A2
Herbert Gdns NW10 .22 A3
1 W4 ....45 A4
Herbert Ho E1 ....110 C2
Herbert Morrison Ho
SW6 ....154 C3
Herbert Morrison Prim
Sch SW8 ....162 B1
Herbert St NW5 ....12 C2
Herbrand Est WC1 ..94 A2
Herbrand St WC1 ....94 A2
Hercules Pl N7 ....5 A1
Hercules Rd SE1 ...135 A1
Hercules St N7 ....5 A1
Hercules Twr SE14 ..51 A4
Hereford Bldgs
SW3 ....157 C4
Hereford Ho 5 NW6 .130 B2
SW3 ....156 B2
28 SE5 ....48 B1
1 SW2 ....62 C3
Hereford Mans 11
W2 ....31 C3
Hereford Mews 11
W2 ....31 C3
Hereford Pl SE14 ....51 B3
Hereford Rd
W2 ....31 C3 113 C4
2 W3 ....28 B2
Hereford Retreat 5
SE15 ....49 C3
Hereford Sq SW7 ..143 A3
Hereford St
E2 ....24 C1 99 B2
Heritage Cl SW9 .....63 A4
Heritage Ct SE8 ......40 C1
Heritage Ho 22
SW19 ....70 A3
Herm Ho 10 N1 ....15 B2
Hermes Cl 3 W9 .....23 C1
Hermes Ct SW9 .....173 B4
Hermes St N1 ....85 B1
Hermit Pl NW6 ....78 A3
Hermit St EC1 ....96 A4
Hermitage Ct 2
E1 ....125 C1
2 NW2 ....1 C1
Hermitage Gdns
NW2 ....1 C1
Hermitage La NW2 ...1 C1
Hermitage Row 9
E8 ....16 C3
Hermitage St W2 ....101 B3
Hermitage The
SW13 ....46 B2
Richmond TW10 ....54 A2
Hermitage Wall
E1 ....125 C1
Herndon Rd SW18 ..59 B2
Herne Hill SE24 ....63 B2
Herne Hill Ho SE24 ..63 A1

Herne Hill Mans
SE24 ....63 B1
Herne Hill Rd SE24 ..63 B2
Herne Hill Sta SE24 .63 A1
Herne Hill Stadium
SE24 ....63 C1
Herne Pl SE24 ....63 A2
Heron Cl NW10 ....8 A2
Heron Ct 14 E14 .....42 B3
6 E5 ....17 A3
5 SE21 ....75 C2
Heron Dr N4 ....6 B2
Heron Ho NW8 ....80 A1
11 SW11 ....168 B4
SE15 ....49 C4
Heron Ind Est E15 ..27 A3
Heron Pl W1 ....103 C2
SE16 ....33 A1
Heron Quays E14 ...33 C1
Heron Quays Sta
E14 ....33 C1
Heron Rd SE24 ....63 B3
Heron Trad Est 3
NW10 ....20 A4
Herondale Ave
SW18 ....72 A3
Herongate N1 ....87 A4
Herrick Ho 11 N16 ..16 A3
5 SE5 ....48 C3
Herrick Rd N5 ....6 B1
Herrick St SW1 ......147 C3
Herries St W10 ....23 A3
Hersant Cl NW10 ....21 C4
Herschell Mews 2
SE5 ....63 B4
Hersham Cl SW15 ..68 C4
Hershell Ct 1
SW14 ....55 A3
Hertford Ave SW14 .56 A3
Hertford Ct 16
SW11 ....60 A4
Hertford Lo 10
SW19 ....70 A3
Hertford Pl W1 ....93 A1
Hertford Rd N1 ....24 A4
Hertford St W1 ......118 A1
Hertmitage The 4
SE13 ....52 B1
Hertslet Rd N7 ....5 B1
Hertsmere Rd E14 ..33 C2
Hesewall Cl SW4 ..171 A1
Hesketh Pl W11 ....112 A3
Heslop Ct 1 SW12 ..72 C3
Heslop Rd SW12 ....72 B3
Hesper Mews SW5 .142 A3
Hesperus Cres E14 .42 A2
Hessel St 4 E1 ....32 A3
Hester Rd SW11 ....158 A1
Hester Terr 1 TW9 ..54 C4
Hestercombe Ave
SW6 ....164 B3
Heston Ho W4 ....37 A1
6 SE8 ....51 C2
Heston St SE14 ....51 C2
Hetherington Rd
SW2,SW4 ....62 A3
Hethpool Ho 2
W2 ....89 B1
Hetley Rd W12 ....39 A4
Hevelius Cl SE10 ....43 B1
Hever Ho SE15 ....50 C4
Heversham Ho SE15 .50 B4
Hewer Ho 6 SW4 ....61 B2
Hewer St W10 ....30 C4
Hewett St
EC2 ....24 A1 98 B1
Hewison St 3 E3 .....26 B3
Hewlett Rd E3 ....26 A3
Hewling Ho 8 N16 ..16 A3

Hewett Ho SW15 .....47 B1
Hexagon The N6 ....3 B3
Hexham Rd SE27 ....75 B2
Hey Bridge 9 NW1 ..13 A2
Heydon Ho SE14 .....50 B2
Heyford Ave 5 SW8 162 B2
Heygate St SE17 ...151 A4
Heylyn Sq E3 ....26 B2
Heysham La NW3 .....2 A1
Heythorp St SW18 ..70 B2
Heywood Ho
8 SE14 ....50 C4
6 SW2 ....62 C1
Heyworth Rd E5 ......17 A4
Hibbert St SW11 .....59 C4
Hichisson Rd SE15 ..65 B2
Hickes Ho 6 NW6 ...11 C1
Hickey's Almshouses 7
TW9 ....54 B3
Hickin Cl SE7 ....43 B3
Hickleton NW1 ....83 A3
Hickling Ho 11 SE16 .40 A3
Hicks Cl SW11 ....60 A4
Hicks St SE8 ....41 A1
Hide Pl SW1 ....147 B3
Hide Twr SW1 ....147 B3
Hieover SE21 ....75 B2
Higgins Ho 7 N1 .....24 A4
Higginson Ho 2
NW3 ....12 B1
High Bridge 43 A4
High Holborn WC1 ..106 C3
High London N6 ....4 C4
High Par The TW9 ...44 C2
High Park Ave TW9 .44 C2
High Park Rd TW9 ...44 C2
High Point N6 ....3 C4
High Rd NW10 ....8 C2
High St E15 ....27 B4
High St
Brentford TW8 ....44 A4
High Street Harlesden
NW10 ....21 B3
High Street Kensington
Sta 11 W8 ....128 A3
High The SW16 ....74 A1
High Timber St
EC4 ....122 C4
High Trees SW2 ......74 C3
High View Prim Sch
SW11 ....59 C3
Highbridge Ct 8
SE14 ....50 B3
Highbury & Islington Sta
N1 ....15 A1
Highbury (Arsenal FC)
N5 ....6 A1
Highbury Cnr N5 ....5 C1
Highbury Corner
N5 ....15 A2
Highbury Cres N5 ...14 C3
Highbury Fields Sch
N5 ....15 A2
Highbury Grange
N5 ....15 B4
Highbury Grove Ct
N5 ....15 A2
Highbury Grove Sch
N5 ....15 A2
Highbury Hill N5 .....15 A4

Highbury New Pk
N5 ....15 B4
Highbury Pk N5 ......15 A4
Highbury Pl N5 ......15 A3
Highbury Quadrant
N5 ....6 B1
Highbury Quadrant Prim
Sch N5 ....15 B4
Highbury Station Rd
N1 ....14 C2
Highbury Terr N1 ....15 A2
Highbury Terrace Mews
N5 ....15 A3
Highcliffe Dr SW15 .56 B1
Highcroft Rd N19 ....5 A4
Highcross Way 4
SW15 ....68 C3
Highdown Rd SW15 .56 C2
Highenden Ho NW15 .90 A2
Highfield Ave NW11 .1 A4
Highfield Cl SE13 ....67 C1
Highfield Gr N6 ....3 B3
Highfield Rd W3 ....28 B4
Highfield Sch SE8 ..72 A4
Highgate Archway
N19 ....4 B3
Highgate Ave N6 ......4 A4
Highgate Cemetery★
N19 ....3 C2
Highgate Ho 10
SE26 ....76 C1
Highgate Jun Sch N6 .3 B4
Highgate Rd NW5 ..13 A4
Highgate Sch N6 ......3 C4
Highgate West Hill
N6 ....3 C2
Highgrove Point 5
NW3 ....11 B4
Highlands Ave W3 ..28 B2
Highlands Cl N4 ......5 A4
Highlands Heath
SW15 ....69 B4
Highlever Rd W10 ..30 C4
Highmore Rd SE3 ..53 A3
Highshore Rd SE15 .49 B1
Highshore Sch SE15 .49 B2
Highstone Mans 13
NW1 ....13 B1
Hightrees Ho SW12 .60 C1
Highview N6 ....5 A4
Highview 17
SW19 ....70 A3
Highway Bsns Pk The 7
E1 ....32 C2
Highway The E1 ......32 B2
Highway Trad Ctr The 6
E1 ....32 C2
Highwood Rd N19 ....5 A1
Highworth St NW1 .102 B4
Hilary Cl SW6 ....156 A2
Hilary Rd W12 ....29 B2
Hilborough Ct 1
E8 ....24 B4
Hilborough Rd 1
E8 ....16 B1
Hilda Terr SW9 ......173 C2
Hildith Ho 7

Hildreth Street Mews 2
SW12 ....73 A3
Hildyard Rd SW6 ...155 C4
Riley Rd NW10 ......22 B2
Hilgrove Rd NW6 ....11 B1
Hill Burgess NW2 ....10 C4
Hill Ct NW3 ....12 A4
Hill St SW1 ....57 C2
Hill Farm Rd W10 ..30 C4
Hill House Int Jun Sch
SW1 ....131 A1
Hill Lo SW11 ....59 C3
Hill Rd NW8 ....79 A1
Hill Top NW11 ....1 A2
Hill St W1 ....118 A2
Hill Wood Ho W1 ....83 B1
Hillary Ho E14 ....34 B4
Hillbeck Cl SE15 ....50 B3

Hillbrook Rd SW17 .72 B1
Hillbrow 7 TW10 ..54 A1
Hillbury Rd SW17 ..73 A1
Hillcourt Rd SE22 ..65 A1
Hillcrest W11 ....112 C3
N6 ....3 C4
SE24 ....63 C3
Hillcrest Cl NW2 ....10 A3
Hillcrest Rd W3 .....28 A1
Hilldrop Cres N7 ....13 C3
Hilldrop Est 4 N7 ..13 C3
Hilldrop La N7 ....13 C3
Hilldrop Rd N7 ....13 C3

Hillersdon Ave
SW13 ....46 C1
Hillersdon Ho
SW1 ....146 A2
Hillery Cl SE17 ......151 C3
Hillfield Ct NW3 ....12 A3
Hillfield Ho N5 ....15 B3
Hillfield Mans NW3 .12 A3
Hillfield Rd NW6 ....10 C3

Hillgate Pl
W8 ....31 C1 113 B2
SW12 ....73 A4
Hillgate St W8 ....113 B2
Hilliard Ho 15 E1 ....32 A1
Hilliard's Ct E1 ....32 B1
Hillier Ho NW1 ......13 C1
Hillier Rd SW11 ....60 B1
Hillingdon St SE17 .48 A4
Hillman St E8 ....17 A2
Hillmarton Rd N7 ..14 A3
Hillmead Dr SW9 ..63 A3
Hillmead Prim Sch
SW9 ....63 A3
Hillmore Ct SE13 ...67 C4
Hillrise Mans N19 ...5 A4
Hillrise Rd N19 ....5 A4
Hills Pl W1 ....104 C1
Hillsboro Rd SE22 .64 A2
Hillsborough Ct

NW6 ....78 A3
Hillside NW10 ....20 C4
Hillside Cl NW8 .....78 B2
Hillside Ct NW3 .....11 A3
Hillside Gdns SW2 .74 C2
Hillsleigh Rd
W14 ....31 B1 113 A2
Hillstone Ct 5 E3 ...27 A1
Hilltop Ct NW8 ......11 B1
Hilltop Ho 6 N6 ......4 C4
Hilltop Rd NW6 .....10 C1
Hillway N6 ....3 C2
Hillworth Rd SW2 ..74 C4

Hilly Fields Cres
SE4 ....66 C4
Hillyard St SW9 ....173 B3
Hilsea Point 7
SW15 ....69 A3
Hilsea St E5 ....17 B4
Hilton Ho N7 ....14 A4
Hinde Ho W1 ....103 C2
Hinde Mews W1 ...103 C2
Hinde St W1 ....103 C2
Hindhead Point 8
SW15 ....69 A3
Hinckley Rd SE15 ..64 C3
Hind Ct EC4 ....107 C1
Hind Gr E14 ....33 C3
Hind Ho N7 ....14 C4
Hinde St E14 ....50 C4
Hindle Ho E8 ....16 B3
Hindley Ho N7 ....5 B1
Hindlip Ho SW8 ...171 B3
Hindmans Rd SE22 .64 C2
Hindmarsh Cl E1 ..125 C4
Hindrey Rd E5 ....17 A3
Hinstock Ho E14 ...34 A4
Hinton Rd SE24 ......63 A3
Hippodrome Mews
W11 ....112 A3
Hippodrome Pl
W11 ....112 A3
Hitchin Sq E3 ....26 A3
Hither Green Hospl
SE13 ....67 C1
Hither Green La
SE13 ....67 C1
Hither Green Sch
SE13 ....67 C2
Hitherfield Prim Sch
SW16 ....74 B1
Hitherfield Rd
SW16 ....74 C1
HM Prison Wormwood
Scrubs W12 ....29 C3
HMS Belfast★ SE1 .124 B2
Hoadly Rd SW16 ...73 C2
Hobart Pl SW1 ......132 A2
8 TW10 ....54 B1
Hobbs Ct SE1 ....139 A4
Hobbs Wlk SW15 ..57 A2
Hobbs' Pl N1 ....24 A4
Hobday St E14 ....34 A3
Hobson's Pl E1 ......111 B4
Hobury St SW10 ...157 B3
Hocker St E2 ....98 C3
Hockley Ho E19 ....17 C2
Hockworth Ho 7

Hockley Ho W10 ..30 B4
Hockney Ct SE16 ...40 A1
Hockworth Ho 7
SW9 ....7 A3
Hocroft Ave NW2 ...1 B1
Hocroft Ct NW2 ......1 B1
Hocroft Rd NW2 .....1 B1
Hocroft Wlk NW2 ...1 B1
Hodford Rd NW11 ...1 B3
Hodister Cl 26 SE5 ..48 B3
Hodnet Grove SE16 .40 C2
Hofland Rd W14 ...126 A2
Hogan Mews W2 ..101 B4
Hogan Way E5 ....7 C2
Hogarth Bsns Pk

W4 ....46 A4
Hogarth Ct E1 ....111 C1
16 ....124 B4
61 NW1 ....13 B1

Hogarth Ho SW1 ...147 C3
Hogarth Ind Est
SW9 ....163 A1
Hogarth La W4 ......46 A4
Hogarth Pl SW5 ...142 A3
Hogarth Prim Sch
W4 ....38 A1
Hogarth Rd SW5 ..142 A3
Hogarth Roundabout
W4 ....46 A4
Holbeach Mews 1
SW12 ....73 A3
Holbeach Row SE15 .49 C3
Holbein Ho SW1 ...145 B2
Holbein Mews
SW1 ....145 B2
Holbein Pl SW1 ....145 B3
Holberton Gdns
NW10 ....22 A2
Holborn EC1 ....107 C3
Holborn Cir EC1 ...107 C2
Holborn Coll SE14 154 B4
Holborn Sta WC1 ..106 C3
Holbrook Cl N19 .....4 A3
Holbrook Ho W3 ...28 C4
Holburn 3 N1 ....24 A4
Holborn Viaduct
EC1 ....108 A3
Holcombe Ho SW9 .62 A4
Holcombe St W6 ...39 A2
Holcroft Ct W1 .....104 C4
Holcroft Ho SW11 .59 C4
SW13 ....47 A4
Holcroft Rd E9 ....17 B1
Holden Ho N1 ....86 C3
8 SE8 ....51 C3
Holden St SW11 ...169 B1
Holdenby Rd SE4 ..66 A2
Holderness Ho SE5 .64 A4
Holfernesse Rd 8
SW17 ....72 C2
Holdsworth Ho 5
SW2 ....74 C4
Holford Ho 6 SE16 .40 A2
Holford Pl WC1 ....95 A4
Holford Rd NW3 .....2 C1
Holford St WC1 ......95 A4
Holgate Ave SW11 .59 C4
Holland Gdns W14 126 B2
Holland Gr SW9 ...163 C1
Holland Park
W11 ....31 B1 112 B1
Holland Park Ave
W11 ....31 B1 112 B1
Holland Park Ct
W14 ....126 B4
Holland Park Gdns
W14 ....126 A4
Holland Park Mews
W11 ....31 B1 112 B1
Holland Park Rd
W14 ....127 A1
Holland Park Rdbt
W11 ....39 C4
Holland Park Sta
W11 ....31 B1 112 B1
Holland Pl W8 ......128 A4
Holland Rd W14 ...126 B2
NW10 ....22 A3

Holland Rise Ho
SW9 ....163 A1
Holland St SE1 ......122 B2
8 W8 ....127 C4
Holland Villas Rd
W14 ....126 A4
Holland Wlk W14 ...127 A3
8 N19 ....4 C3
Hollar Rd N16 ....7 B1
Hollen St W9 ....173 B2
Holles St W1 ....104 B2
Holley Rd W3 ....38 A4
Holliday Sq 7
SW11 ....59 C4
Hollies Way 1
SW12 ....72 C4
Hollingbourne Rd
SE24 ....63 B2
Hollins Ho N7 ....14 A4
Hollisfield WC1 ......94 B3
Holloway Rd N19 ....4 C2
N7 ....14 B2
Holloway Road Sta
N7 ....14 B3
Holly Berry La 8
NW3 ....11 B4
Holly Bush Vale 9
NW3 ....11 B4
Holly Bush Wlk
SW9 ....63 A3
Holly Cl NW10 ....8 A1
Holly Dale Prim Sch
SE15 ....50 B1
Holly Gr SE15 ....49 C1
Holly Hedge Terr
SE13 ....67 C2
Holly Hill NW3 ....11 B4
Holly Lo SE13 ....67 C3
Holly Lodge Gdns N6 .3 C2
Holly Lodge Mans
N6 ....3 C2
Holly Mews SW10 .143 A1
Holly Mount NW3 ..11 B4
Holly Park Est N4 ....5 B4
Holly Pk N4 ....5 B4
Holly Rd W4 ....37 C2
Holly St E8 ....16 B1
Holly Terr N6 ....3 C2
Holly Tree Ho SE4 ..66 B4
Holly Village N6 ......4 A2
Holly Wlk NW3 ......11 B4
Hollybush Gdns E2 .25 A2
Hollybush Ho 22 E2 .25 A2
Hollybush Pl E2 .....25 A2
Hollycroft Ave NW3 .1 C1
Hollydale Rd SE15 .50 B1
Hollydene SE15 ......50 A2
SE13 ....67 C4
Hollymount Cl 8
SE10 ....52 B2
Hollytree Cl SW19 .69 C3
Hollywell Row
EC2 ....24 A1 98 A1
Hollywood Mews
SW10 ....156 C4
Hollywood Rd
SW10 ....156 C4
Holm Oak Cl SW15 .58 B1
Holm Wlk SE3 ....53 C1
Holman Ho 2 E2 ....25 C2
Holman Hunt Ho
W14 ....140 A1
Holman Rd SW11 ..167 B1
Holmbury Ct SW17 .72 B1

Holmbury Ho SW9 . . . . . . .63 A2
Holmbush Rd SW15 . . . . .58 A1
Holmcote Gdns N5 . . . . . .15 B3
Holmdale Rd NW6 . . . . . .10 C3
Holmdene Ave SE24 .63 B2
Holmead Rd SW6 . . . . .156 B1
Holmefield Ho W10 . .23 A1
Holmes Ct ■ SW4 . . . . .172 A2
  ■ SW4 . . . . .37 B3
Holmes PI SW10 . . . . . .157 A4
Holmes Rd NW5 . . . . . . .13 A3
Holmes Terr SE1 . . . . .135 B4
Holmesdale Ave
  SW14 . . . . .55 A3
Holmesdale Ho
  NW6 . . . . .23 C4
Holmesdale Rd N6 . . . . . .4 A4
  Richmond TW9 . . . . . . .44 C2
Holmesley Rd SE23 . . .66 A1
Holmewood Gdns
  SW2 . . . . .74 B4
Holmewood Rd
  SW2 . . . . .74 B4
Holmfield Ct ■
  NW3 . . . . .12 A2
Holmhurst SE13 . . . . . . .67 C1
Holmleigh JMI Sch
  N16 . . . . .7 A3
Holmleigh Rd N16 . . . . .7 A3
Holmsbury Ho ■
  N7 . . . . .13 C3
Holmsdale Ho ■
  E14 . . . . .34 A2
Holmside Ct SW12 . . . .60 C1
Holmside Rd SW12 . . . .60 C1
Holmsley Ho SW15 . . . .68 B4
Holmwood Ct ■ N16 .7 B4
Holroyd Rd SW15 . . . . . .57 B3
Holsgrove Ct W3 . . . . . . .29 A1
Holst Mans SW13 . . . . . .47 B3
Holsworthy Ho ■
  E3 .26 B3
Holsworthy Sq WC1 .95 A1
Holt Ct SE10 . . . . .52 B4
Holt Ho SW2 . . . . .62 C1
Holton St E1 . . . . .25 C1
Holwood PI ■ SW4 .61 C3
Holy Cross RC Prim Sch
  SW6 . . . . .165 B4
Holy Family RC JMI Sch
  E14 . . . . .34 A3
Holy Ghost & St Stephen
  RC Prim Sch The
  W12 . . . . .38 B4
Holy Ghost RC Prim Sch
  SW12 . . . . .72 C4
Holy Trinity CE Inf Sch
  SW17 . . . . .72 B2
Holy Trinity CE Jun Sch
  TW10 . . . . .54 C3
Holy Trinity CE Prim Sch
  SW1 . . . . .145 A4
  SW1 . . . . .145 B4
  NW3 . . . . .12 A1
  NW1 . . . . .13 A1
  SW2 . . . . .74 B4
Holy Trinity Dalston CE
  JMI Sch E8 . . . . .16 B2
Holybourne Ave
  SW15 . . . . .68 C4
Holyhead CI E3 . . . . .26 C2
Holyoak Rd SE11 . . . .150 B3
Holyoake Ct SE16 . . . . .41 B4
Holyport Rd SW6 . . . . . .47 C3
Holyrood Ho N4 . . . . .6 B3

Holyrood Mews ■
  E16 . . . . .35 C1
Holyrood St SE1 . . . .124 A1
Holywell CI ■ SE16 .40 A1
  ■ SE3 . . . . .53 C4
Holywell La EC2 . . . . . . .98 B2
Homan Ho ■ SW4 .73 C4
Home Office SW1 . . . .133 C3
Home Park Rd
  SW19 . . . . .70 B1
Homecroft Rd SE26 .76 C1
Homefield Rd W4 . . . . . .38 B1
Homefield St N1 ■ .24 A3
Homeleigh Ct ■
  SW16 . . . . .74 A1
Homeleigh Rd SE15 .65 C2
Homemead SW12 . . . .73 A2
Homer Dr E14 . . . . .41 C2
Homer Rd E9 . . . . .18 A2
Homer Row W1 . . . .102 B3
Homer St W1 . . . . .102 B3
Homerton Coll of
  Technology E9 . . . . .17 B3
Homerton Gr E9 . . . . . . .17 C3
Homerton High St
  E9 .17 C3
Homerton Hospl E9 . .17 C2
Homerton Row E9 . . . . .17 B3
Homerton Sta E9 . . . . . .17 C2
Homerton Terr E9 . . . . .17 C2
Homestead Rd SE22 .65 B2
Homestead Rd
  SW6 . . . . .155 A1
Homewoods ■
  SW12 . . . . .73 C4
Homildon Ho ■
  SE26 . . . . .76 C1
Honduras St EC1 . . . . . .96 C2
Honey La EC2 . . . . . .109 A1
Honeybourne Rd
  NW6 . . . . .11 A3
Honeybrook Rd
  SW12,SW4 . . . . .73 B4
Honeyfield N4 . . . . .5 C2
Honeyman CI NW6 . . . .9 C1
Honeywell Jun & Inf
  Schs SW11 . . . . .60 B1
Honeywell Rd SW11 .60 B1
Honeywood Ho ■
  SE15 . . . . .49 C2
Honeywood Rd
  NW10 . . . . .21 B3
Honiton Gdns ■
  SE15 . . . . .50 B1
Honiton Ho ■ SES .48 B1
Honiton Rd NW6 . . . . . .23 B3
Honor Oak Park Sta
  SE23 . . . . .65 C1
Honor Oak Rd SE23 .65 B1
Honor Oak Rise
  SE23 . . . . .65 B1
Honwell Ho ■ W2 .31 C4
Hood Ave SW14 . . . . . . .55 B2
Hood Ct N7 . . . . .5 B1
Hood Ho ■ SE5 . . . . . . .48 C3
Hooke Ct SE10 . . . . .52 B2
Hooke Ho ■ E3 . . . . . . .26 A3
Hookham Ct SW8 .171 B4
Hooks CI SE15 . . . . .50 A2
Hoop La NW11 . . . . .1 C4
Hooper Ho ■ SW18 .58 B2
Hooper Rd E16 . . . . .35 C3
Hooper St E1 . . . . .111 B1
Hooper's Ct SW1 . . . .130 C3

Hooper's Mews ■
  W3 . . . . .28 B1
Hop Gdns WC2 . . . . . .120 A3
Hope CI N1 . . . . .15 B2
  ■ Brentford TW8 . . . . . .36 A1
Hope St SW11 . . . . .59 C4
Hopefield Ave NW6 .23 A3
Hopetown St E1 . . . . .111 A3
Hopewell St SE5 . . . . .48 C3
Hopgood St W12 . . . . . .30 B1
Hopkins Ho ■ E14 .33 C3
Hopkins St W1 . . . . . .105 B1
Hopkinson Ho
  SW11 . . . . .169 B2
Hopkinson's PI
  NW1 . . . . .81 B4
Hopping La N1 . . . . .15 A2
Hopton Ho ■ SW9 .48 A1
Hopton St SE1 . . . . . .122 B2
Hopton's Gdns
  SE1 . . . . .122 B2
Hopwood CI SW17 .71 B1
Hopwood Rd SE17 .48 C4
Hopwood Wlk E8 . . . . . .16 C1
Horatio Ho ■ E2 .24 B3
Horatio PI E14 . . . . .34 B1
Horatio St ■ E2 . . . . . . .24 B3
Horbury Cres
  W11 . . . . .31 C2 113 B3
Horbury Mews
  W11 . . . . .31 C2 113 A3
Horder Rd SW6 . . . . .164 B3
Hordle Promenade E ■
  SE15 . . . . .49 B3
Hordle Promenade N ■
  SE15 . . . . .49 B3
Hordle Promenade S ■
  SE15 . . . . .49 A3
Hordle Promenade W ■
  SE15 . . . . .49 A3
Horizon Sch N16 . . . . . .16 A4
Horle Wlk SE5 . . . . .48 A1
Hormead Rd W9 . . . . . . .23 B1
Horn La W3 . . . . .28 B3
  SE10 . . . . .43 C2
Hornbeam CI SE11 .149 B4
Hornbeam Ho ■
  NW3 . . . . .12 B2
Hornblower St ■
  SE16 . . . . .41 A2
Hornby CI NW3 . . . . .11 C1
Hornby Ho ■ SE11 .163 C4
Horndean CI ■
  SW15 . . . . .68 C3
Horne Way SW15 . . . . . .47 B1
Horner Hos ■ N1 . . . . .24 A4
Hornsey La N6 . . . . .4 B4
Hornsey Lane Gdns
  N6 . . . . .4 B4
Hornsey Rd N7,N19 . . .5 B2
Hornsey Rise Gdns
  N19 . . . . .5 A4
Hornsey Rd N7 . . . . .14 B3
Hornshay St SE15 . . . . .50 B4
HorNton Ct W8 . . . .127 C3
Hornton PI W8 . . . . . .127 C3
Hornton St W8 . . . . . .127 C3
Horrocks Ho SW15 .57 A2
Horse & Dolphin Yd
  W1 . . . . .119 C4
Horse Guards Par*
  SW1 . . . . .119 C1
Horse Guards Rd
  SW1 . . . . .133 C4
Horse Shoe Yd W1 .118 B4
Horse Yd ■ N1 . . . . .86 B4

Horseferry PI SE10 .52 B4
Horseferry Rd
  SW1 . . . . .147 C4
  E14 . . . . .33 A2
Horseferry Road Est
  SW1 . . . . .133 B1
Horseguards Ave
  SW1 . . . . .120 A1
Horsell Rd N5 . . . . .14 C3
Horselydown La
  SE1 . . . . .124 C1
Horselydown Mans ■
  SE1 . . . . .138 C4
Horsendon Ho ■
  N7 . . . . .13 C3
Horseshoe CI E14 . . . . .42 B1
Horsfield Ho ■ N1 .15 B1
Horsford Rd SW2 . . . . . .62 B2
Horsley Ho ■ SE4 . . . . .65 C3
Horsley St SE17 . . . . . . .48 C4
Horsman Ho SE5 . . . . . .48 B4
Horsman St SE5 . . . . . . .48 B4
Horsmonden Rd
  SE4 . . . . .66 B1
Horston Ho N4 . . . . .6 B4
Hortensia Ho ■
  SW10 . . . . .156 C2
Hortensia Rd
  SW10 . . . . .156 C2
Horticultural PI ■
  W4 . . . . .37 C1
Horton Ave NW2 . . . . . .10 A4
Horton Ho SW10 . . . .157 A2
  ■ SW8 . . . . .162 C2
  SE15 . . . . .50 B4
  ■ W6 . . . . .154 A4
Horton Rd E8 . . . . .17 A2
Horton St SE13 . . . . .67 A4
Horwood Ho NW8 . . . .90 B2
  ■ E2 . . . . .25 A2
Hosack Rd SW12,
  SW17 . . . . .72 C2
Hosier La EC1 . . . . .108 B3
Hoskins St SE10 . . . . . .42 C1
Hospital Way SE13 . . . .67 C1
Hospl for Tropical
  Diseases NW1 . . . . .83 B3
Hospl of St John and St
  Elizabeth NW8 . . . .79 B1
Hotham Prim Sch
  SW15 . . . . .57 C3
Hotham Rd SW15 . . . . .57 B4
Hothfield PI SE16 . . . . .40 B3
Hotspur St SE11 . . . .149 B2
Houblon Rd TW10 . . . .54 A2
Houghton CI ■ E8 .16 B2
Houghton St WC2 . .107 A1
Houndsditch EC3 . . . .110 B2
Houses of Parliament*
  SW1 . . . . .134 B2
Housman Way ■
  SE5 . . . . .48 C3
Hoveden Rd NW2 . . . . .10 A3
Hove's St E2 . . . . .24 B3
How Rd NW7 . . . . .10 A4
  W3 . . . . .28 A3
Howard CI SE15 . . . . . . .64 C4
Howard Ho ■ W1 .92 B1
  ■ SE8 . . . . .51 B4
  ■ SW9 . . . . .62 C4
Howard's La SW15 . . . .57 B3
Howard Rd NW2 . . . . . .9 C4
Howbury Rd SE15 . . . . .65 B4
Howcroft Ho ■ E3 .26 B2
Howden St SE15 . . . . . .64 C4
Howell Ho ■ N7 . . . . . .13 C3

Howell Wlk SE1 . . . .150 B3
Howgate Rd SW14 . . . .55 C4
Howick PI SW1 . . . . . .133 A1
Howie St SW11 . . . . . .158 A1
Howitt CI ■ NW3 . . . . . .12 A2
Howitt Rd NW3 . . . . .12 A2
Howland Ho ■
  SW16 . . . . .74 A1
Howland Mews E
  W1 . . . . .105 A4
Howland St W1 . . . . . .105 A4
Howland Way SE16 .41 A4
Howletts Rd SE24 . . . . .63 B1
Howley PI W2 . . . . . . .101 A4
Howsman Rd SW13 .46 C4
Howson Rd SE4 . . . . . . .66 A3
Howson Terr TW10 . . . .54 A1
Hoxton Mkt N1 . . . . .98 A3
Hoxton Sq N1 . . . . .98 A3
Hoxton St N1 . . . . .98 B4
  N1 .24 A3
Hoylake Rd W3 . . . . .29 A3
Hoyland CI ■ SE15 .50 A3
Huberd Ho SE1 . . . . . .137 C2
Hubert Gr SW9 . . . . .62 A4
Hubert Ho NW8 . . . . . . .90 A1
Hucknall Ct NW8 . . . . . .89 B2
Huddart St ■ E3 . . . . . .33 B4
Huddleston CI E2 . . . . .25 B3
Huddleston Rd N7 . . . .13 B4
Huddlestone Rd NW2 .9 A2
Hudson CI ■ W12 .30 A2
Hudson Ct SW10 . . . .156 C2
  ■ W11 . . . . .31 A3
Hudson's PI SW1 . . . .146 C4
Hudsons Ho ■ N1 .97 C3
Huggin Ct EC4 . . . . . .123 A4
Huggin Hill EC4 . . . . .123 A4
Huggins Ho ■ E3 . . . . .26 C2
Huggins PI SW2 . . . . . . .74 B3
Hugh Astor Ct SE1 .136 B2
Hugh Gaitskell CI
  SW6 . . . . .154 C3
Hugh Gaitskell Ho
  N16 . . . . .7 B2
  NW10 . . . . .8 B1
Hugh Mews SW1 . . . .146 B3
Hugh Morgan Ho ■
  SW4 . . . . .61 C4
Hugh Myddelton Prim
  Sch EC1 . . . . .95 C3
Hugh Platt Ho ■
  E2 .25 A3
Hugh St SW1 . . . . .146 B3
Hughan Rd E15 . . . . . . .19 C3
Hughendon Terr
  E15 . . . . .76 B4
Hughes Fields Prim Sch
  SE8 . . . . .51 C4
Hughes Ho ■ SE17 .150 B3
  ■ SE5 . . . . .48 B2
  ■ SE8 . . . . .51 C4
  SE5 . . . . .48 B2
  ■ E2 . . . . .25 B2
Hughes Mans
  E1 . . . . .24 C1 99 C1
Hughes Terr ■ E16 .35 B2
Hugo Ho SW1 . . . . . . .131 A2
Hugo Rd N19 . . . . .13 B4
Hugon Rd SW6 . . . . .59 A4
Huguenot PI SW18 . . . .59 B2
Huguenot Sq SE15 . . . .65 A4
Hull CI SE16 . . . . .32 C1

Hull Ct SE5 ....48 C1
Hull St EC1 ....96 C3
Hullbridge Mews
N1 ....87 B4
Hulme Pl SE1 ....137 A3
Humber Dr W10 ....22 C1
Humber Rd SE3 ....53 B4
Humberstone Rd E13 ....18 A3
Humbolt Rd W6 ....154 A3
Hume Ct E2 ....15 A1
Hume Ho E2 ....99 B3
14 W11 ....30 C1
Humphrey Ct
SW11 ....167 C3
Humphrey St SE1 ....152 C2
Humphry Ho **10**
SW15 ....57 C2
Hungerford Bridge
WC2 ....120 C2
Hungerford Ho
SW1 ....161 A4
Hungerford Inf Sch
N7 ....14 A2
Hungerford Jun & Inf
Schs N7 ....13 C2
Hungerford La
WC2 ....120 B2
Hungerford Prim Sch
N7 ....14 A2
Hungerford Rd
4 N7 ....13 C2
N7 ....14 A3
Hungerford St **24**
E1 ....32 A3
Hunsdon Rd SE14 ....50 C3
Hunslett St **27** 25 B3
Hunstanton Ho
NW1 ....102 B4
Hunt St W11 ....30 C1
Hunt's Ct WC2 ....119 C3
Hunt's La E15 ....27 B3
Hunter Cl SE1 ....137 C1
SW12 ....72 C3
Hunter Ct **8** SE5 ....63 C3
Hunter Ho WC1 ....94 B2
SE1 ....136 B3
SW5 ....141 C1
SW8 ....161 C1
8 N19 ....4 B1
Hunter Lo **3** W9 ....31 C4
Hunter St WC1 ....94 B2
Huntingdon Ct
SW14 ....55 B4
Huntingdon Gdns
W4 ....45 B3
Huntingdon Ho
SW5 ....141 C4
Huntingdon St N1 ....14 B1
E16 ....35 B1
Huntingfield Rd
SW15 ....56 C2
Huntingford Ho
SW15 ....47 B1
Huntley St WC1 ....93 B1
Hunton St E1 ....111 B4
Hunts Cl SE3 ....53 C1
Hunts Slip Rd SE21 ....76 A2
Huntshaw Ho **37** E3 ....27 A2
Huntsman St SE17 ....152 A3
Huntspill St SW17 ....71 B1
Huntsworth Mews
NW1 ....90 C1
Hurdwick Ho NW1 ....82 C2

Hurleston Ho **11**
SE8 ....41 B1
Hurley Cres SE16 ....40 C4
Hurley Ho E2 ....98 C3
SE11 ....149 C3
Hurley Lo SE22 ....65 B1
Hurlingham & Chelsea
Sch SW6 ....58 C4
Hurlingham Bsns Pk
SW6 ....165 B1
Hurlingham Ct SW6 ....58 B4
Hurlingham Gdns
SW6 ....58 B4
Hurlingham Rd
SW6 ....165 A1
Hurlock Ho N5 ....6 A1
Hurlock St N5 ....6 A1
Huron Rd SW17 ....72 C1
Hurst Ho N1 ....85 A1
Hurst St SE24 ....63 A1
SW11 ....56 B1
Hurstbourne Ho **9**
SW15 ....58 A2
Hurstdene Gdns N15 ....7 A4
Hurstway Wlk **2** 30 C2
Husborne Ho **8**
SE8 ....41 A2
Huson Cl NW3 ....12 A1
Hutching's St E14 ....41 C4
Hutchins Cl E15 ....76 B1
Hutchins Ho **3**
SW4 ....73 C4
Hutchinson Ho **8**
SE14 ....50 B3
Hutton Ct **3** N4 ....5 B3
Hutton Ho E2 ....99 B3
Hutton St EC4 ....107 C1
Huxbear St SE4 ....66 B2
Huxley Ho NW8 ....89 C1
SW9 ....172 C2
Huxley St W10 ....23 A2
Hyacinth Rd SW15 ....68 C3
Hyde Farm Sch
SW12 ....73 C3
Hyde La SW11 ....168 A4
Hyde Park* W2 ....116 C2
Hyde Park Cnr
SW1 ....131 C4
Hyde Park Cres
W2 ....102 A1
Hyde Park Gate
SW7 ....129 A3
Hyde Park Gate Mews
SW7 ....129 A3
Hyde Park Gdns
W2 ....115 C4
Hyde Park Gdns Mews
W2 ....116 A4
Hyde Park Mans
NW1 ....102 A4
Hyde Park Pl W2 ....116 B4
Hyde Park Sq W2 ....102 A1
Hyde Park Sq Mews
W2 ....102 A1
Hyde Park Twrs
W2 ....114 C3
Hyde Rd N1 ....24 A4
Richmond TW10 ....54 B2
Hyde St SE8 ....51 C4

Hyde Vale SE10 ....52 B3
Hyde's Pl **12** N1 ....15 A1
Hydethorpe Rd
SW12 ....73 B3
Hylda Ct NW5 ....3 C1
Hyndman Ho **5** ....
Hyndman St SE15 ....50 A4
Hyperion Ho **22** E3 ....26 A3
Hyson Rd SE16 ....40 A1
Hythe Ho **16** SE16 ....40 B4
Hythe Rd NW10 ....21 C1
Hythe Road Ind Est
NW10 ....21 C1

I

Ibberton Ho SW8 ....162 C2
Ibbotson Ave E16 ....35 B3
Ibbott St **2** E1 ....25 B1
Iberia Ho N19 ....4 C4
Ibis Cl **10** SE8 ....51 B4
Ibis La W4 ....45 B2
Ibsley Gdns SW15 ....68 C3
Icarus Ho **2** E3 ....26 B2
Iceland Rd E3 ....26 C4
Ickburgh Rd E5 ....17 A4
Idmiston Rd SE21,
....75 C2
Idol La EC3 ....124 A3
Idonia St SE8 ....51 C3
Iffley Ho E2 ....99 A3
Iffley Rd W6 ....39 A3
Ifield Ho SE17 ....152 B2
Ifield Rd SW10 ....156 B4
Ifor Evans Pl E1 ....25 C1
Ightham Ho SE17 ....152 A3
Ilbert St W10 ....23 A2
Ilchester Gdns W2 ....114 A4
Ilchester Mans W8 ....127 C1
Ilchester Pl W14 ....127 A2
Ildersly Gr SE21 ....75 C2
Ilderton Jun & Inf Sch
SE16 ....40 B1
Ilderton Rd SE15,
SE16 ....50 B4
Ilex Rd NW10 ....8 B2
Ilford Ho **1** N1 ....15 C2
Iliffe St SE17 ....150 B2
Iliffe Yd SE17 ....150 B2
Ilkeston Ct **5** E5 ....17 C4
Ilminster Gdns
SW11 ....60 A3
Ilsley Ct SW8 ....170 C1
Imber St N1 ....87 B3
Imperial Ave **5** N16 ....16 A4
Imperial Coll of Science
& Technology
SW7 ....129 B2
Imperial College Rd
SW7 ....129 B2
Imperial Cres NW8 ....80 B2
Imperial Ho E14 ....33 B2
2 E14 ....26 A2
Imperial Rd SW6 ....166 B3
Imperial Sq SW6 ....166 B4
Imperial St E3 ....27 B2
Imperial Twrs **3**
NW3 ....11 B2
Imperial War Mus*
SE1,SE11 ....135 C1
Independant Pl E8 ....16 B3
Indescon Ct E14 ....42 A4

India St EC3 ....110 C1
India Way W12 ....30 A2
Indigo Mews N16 ....6 C1
Indus Ct SE15 ....49 B3
Ingate Pl SW8 ....170 B3
Ingelow Ho W8 ....128 A4
Ingelow St SW8 ....170 A1
Ingersoll Rd W12 ....30 A1
Ingestre Pl W1 ....105 A1
Ingestre Rd NW5 ....13 A4
Ingham Rd NW6 ....10 C4
Ingle Ho **3** SW12 ....73 C3
Inglebert St EC1 ....95 B4
Ingleborough St
SW9 ....173 B2
Ingleby Rd N7 ....5 A1
Inglefield Sq **12** E1 ....32 A1
Ingleshaw Wlk E9 ....18 B2
Ingleside Gr SE3 ....53 B4
Inglethorpe Ho **6** E5 ....17 C4
Inglethorpe St SW6 ....47 C2
Ingleton St SW9 ....173 B2
Inglewood Cl E14 ....41 C2
Inglewood Mans **2**
NW6 ....10 C3
Inglewood Rd NW6 ....10 C3
Inglis Ho **1** SW15 ....57 B2
Inglis St SE5 ....48 A2
Ingram Ave NW11 ....2 B4
Ingram Cl SE11 ....149 A4
Ingram Ho **2** E3 ....26 A4
Ingram Lo **3** SW4 ....61 C1
Ingrave St SW11 ....60 A4
Ingrebourne Ho
NW8 ....101 C4
Ingress St **4** W4 ....38 A1
Inigo Pl WC2 ....120 A4
Inkerman Rd NW5 ....13 A2
Inkerman Terr W8 ....127 C1
Inkster Ho **8** SW11 ....60 A4
Inman Rd NW10 ....21 A4
SW18 ....71 B4
Inner Circ NW1 ....91 B3
Inner Park Rd SW19 ....69 C2
Inner Temple La
EC4 ....107 B1
Innes Gdns SW15 ....57 A1
Innis Ho SE17 ....152 A2
Insley Ho **13** E3 ....27 A2
Inst for Child Health
WC1 ....94 C1
Institute Pl **3** E8 ....17 A3
Interchange The
NW5 ....13 A3
International Sch of
London W3 ....36 C2
Inveagh Cl E9 ....25 C4
Inver Ct W2 ....100 B1
Inverforth Cl NW3 ....2 B2
Inverforth House Hospl
NW3 ....2 B2
Invergarry Ho NW6 ....78 A1
Inverness Gdns
W8 ....114 A1
Inverness Mews
W2 ....114 B4
Inverness Pl W2 ....114 B4
Inverness St NW1 ....82 B4
Inverness Terr W2 ....114 B4
Inverton Rd SE15 ....65 C3
Invicta Plaza SE1 ....122 A2
Invicta Prim Sch
SE3 ....53 C3
Invicta Rd SE3,SE7 ....53 C4
Inville Rd SE17 ....151 C1

Inwen Ct SE8 ....41 A1
Inwood Ct **3** NW1 ....13 B1
Inwood Ho **10** SE22 ....64 A4
Inworth St SW11 ....168 B2
Inworth Wlk N1 ....86 C4
Ion Sq **8** E2 ....24 C3
Ionian Ho **22** E1 ....25 C1
Ipsden Bldgs SE1 ....135 C4
Ipswich Ho SE4 ....65 C2
Irby Ho SW2 ....62 C1
Ireland Yd EC4 ....108 B1
Irene Rd SW6 ....165 C3
Ireton Ho SW9 ....173 C1
Ireton St **7** E3 ....26 C1
Iroko Ho **7** NW3 ....11 A2
Iron Bridge Cl NW10 ....8 A3
Iron Bridge Ho NW3 ....12 B1
Iron Mill Pl SW18 ....59 A1
Iron Mill Rd SW18 ....59 A1
Ironmonger La
EC2 ....109 B1
Ironmonger Pas
EC1 ....97 A3
Ironmonger Row
EC1 ....97 A3
Ironmonger's Pl **13**
E14 ....41 C2
Ironside Cl SE16 ....40 C4
Ironside Ho E9 ....18 A4
Irvine Cl N20 ....9 C2
Irvine Ct W1 ....93 A1
Irvine Ho N7 ....14 B2
3 E14 ....34 A4
Irving Gr SW9 ....172 C1
Irving Ho SE17 ....150 A1
Irving Mews N1 ....15 B2
Irving Rd W14 ....39 C3
Irving St WC2 ....119 C3
Irwell Est **20** SE16 ....40 B4
Irwin Gdns NW10 ....22 A4
Isaac Newton Ctr
....
Isabel St SW9 ....173 A4
Isabella Cl **8** TW10 ....54 B1
Isabella Ho SE1 ....150 A2
19 W6 ....39 B1
Isabella Rd E9 ....17 B3
Isabella St SE1 ....122 A1
Isambard Mews E14 ....42 B3
Isambard Pl SE16 ....32 B1
Isel Way **4** SE22 ....64 A2
Iseldon Ct N7 ....14 A4
Isis Cl SW15 ....57 B3
Isis Ct W4 ....45 A3
Isis Ho NW8 ....89 C1
Isis St SW18 ....71 B2
Islamia Sch Ctr
NW6 ....23 A4
Islamic Coll for
Advanced Studies
NW10 ....9 A2
Island Gardens Sta
E14 ....42 B1
Island Row E14 ....33 B3
Isleden Ho N1 ....86 C4
Isledon Rd N4,N7 ....5 C1
Islington Est N1 ....86 C4
Islington Gn N1 ....86 A3
Islington Green Sch
N1 ....86 A2
Islington High St
N1 ....86 A2
Islington Park Mews **1**
N1 ....15 A1
Islington Park St
N1 ....15 A1

Islington Sixth Form Ctr N7 . . . . . 14 C4
Islip St NW5 . . . . . 13 B3
Isokon Flats 3 NW3 . . . . . 12 B3
Ivanhoe Ho 32 E3 . . . 26 A3
11 SW12 . . . . . 73 A4
Ivanhoe Rd SE5 . . . . . 64 B4
Ivatt Pl W14 . . . . . 141 A1
Iveagh Ct EC3 . . . . . 110 C1
Iveagh Ho SW10 . . . 157 A2
2 SW9 . . . . . 48 A1
Ivebury Ct W10 . . . . . 30 B3
Iveley Rd SW4 . . . . . 170 C1
Iver Ct N1 . . . . . 15 B2
Iverna Ct W8 . . . . . 127 C2
Iverna Gdns W8 . . . 127 C2
Iverson Rd NW6 . . . . 10 C2
Ives Rd E16 . . . . . 35 A4
Ives St SW3 . . . . . 144 B4
Ivimey St E2 . . 24 C2 99 C4
Ivinghoe Ho 14 N7 . . 13 C3
Ivor Ct NW1 . . . . . 90 C2
Ivor Pl NW1 . . . . . 90 C1
Ivor St NW1 . . . . . 13 B1
Ivories The N1 . . . . . 15 B1
Ivory Ho E1 . . . . . 125 A2
9 SW11 . . . . . 59 B4
Ivy Church La SE1, SE17 . . . . . 152 C2
Ivy Cres W4 . . . . . 37 B2
Ivy Ct SE16 . . . . . 153 C1
SE13 . . . . . 66 C2
Ivy Lodge W8 . . . . . 113 B2
Ivy Rd NW2 . . . . . 9 B4
E16 . . . . . 35 C3
SE4 . . . . . 66 C3
Ivy St N1 . . . . . 24 A3
Ivybridge Ho 18 SE22 . . . . . 64 A4
Ivybridge La WC2 . . 120 B3
Ivydale Jun & Inf Sch SE15 . . . . . 65 C3
Ivydale Rd SE15 . . . . . 65 C3
Ivyday Gr SW16 . . . . . 74 B1
Ivymount Rd SE27 . . 74 C1
Ixworth Pl SW3 . . . . 144 A3

J

Jack Taylor Sch NW8 . . . . . 78 C4
Jack Tizard Sch SW6 . . . . . 47 C2
Jack Walker Ct N5 . . 15 A4
Jackman Ho 24 E1 . . 32 A1
Jackman St E8 . . . . . 25 A4
Jackson Cl E9 . . . . . 17 C1
Jackson Ho 16 SW11 . . . . . 59 C4
Jackson Rd N7 . . . . . 14 B4
Jackson's La N6 . . . . . 4 A4
Jacob Mans 1 E1 . . 32 A3
Jacob St SE1 . . . . . 139 A4
SE1 . . . . . 139 B4
Jacob's Well Mews W1 . . . . . 103 C2
Jacobin Lo N7 . . . . . 14 A3
Jacobson Ct SW11 . 168 B3
Jacobson Ho E1 . . . 110 C2
Jacotts Ho W10 . . . . 22 B1
Jaggard Way SW12 . 72 B4
Jagger Ho SW11 . . 168 C4
Jamahirya Sch SW3 . . . . . 158 A4
Jamaica Rd SE1,SE16 . . . . . 139 B2
SE16 . . . . . 40 A3
Jamaica St E1 . . . . . 32 B4
James Allen's Girls' Sch SE22 . . . . . 64 A2
James Allen's Prep Sch SE21 . . . . . 63 C1
James Anderson Ct 29 E2 . . . . . 24 A3
James Ave NW2 . . . . . 9 B3
James Brine Ho E2 . 99 A4
James Campbell Ho 2 E2 . . . . . 25 B3
James Collins Cl W9 . . . . . 23 B1
James Docherty Ho 4 E2 . . . . . 25 B3
James Hammett Ho 9 E2 . . . . . 24 B3
James Ho E1 . . . . . 26 A1
33 SE16 . . . . . 40 C4
James Joyes Wlk 7 SE24 . . . . . 63 A3
James Leicester Hall of Residence N7 . . . . . 14 A2
James Lind Ho 5 SE8 . . . . . 41 B2
James Middleton Ho 20 E2 . . . . . 25 A2
James St W1 . . . . . 103 C1
WC2 . . . . . 120 B4
James Stewart Ho NW6 . . . . . 10 B1
James Stroud Ho SE17 . . . . . 151 A1
James Wolfe Jun & Inf Sch SE10 . . . . . 52 B3
Jameson Ct 6 E2 . . 25 B3
Jameson Ho SE11 . 148 C2
Jameson St W8 . . . 113 C2
Jamestown Rd NW1 82 A4
Jamestown Way E14 . . . . . 34 C2
Jane St E1 . . . . . 32 A3
Janet St E14 . . . . . 41 C3
Janeway Pl 2 SE16 . 40 A4
Janeway St SE16 . . 139 C3
Jansen Wlk SW11 . . . 59 C3
Japan Cres N4 . . . . . 5 B3
Jardine Rd E1 . . . . . 32 C2
Jarman Ho 13 E1 . . . 32 B4
SE16 . . . . . 40 C2
Jarret Ho 1 E3 . . . . . 26 C2
Jarrett Cl SW2 . . . . . 75 A3
Jarrow Rd SE16 . . . . . 40 B1
Jarrow Way E9 . . . . . 18 A4
Jarvis Ct 2 SE10 . . . 52 B2
Jarvis Ho 3 SE15 . . . 49 C2
Jarvis Rd SE22 . . . . . 64 A3
Jasmin SE1 . . . . . 125 A1
Jasmin Ho SE4 . . . . . 66 B4
Jasmin Lo 17 SE16 . . 40 A1
Jason Ct W1 . . . . . 103 C2
SW9 . . . . . 173 B4
Jasper Wlk N1 . . . . . 97 B4
Java Wharf SE1 . . . 139 A4
Jay Ho SW15 . . . . . 47 B1
Jay Mews SW7 . . . . 129 A3
Jean Darling Ho SW10 . . . . . 157 B3
Jean Pardies Ho 21 E1 . . . . . 32 B4
Jebb Ave SW2 . . . . . 62 A1
Jebb St E3 . . . . . 26 C3
Jedburgh St SW11 . . 60 C3
Jeddo Mews W12 . . . 38 B4
Jeddo Rd W12 . . . . . 38 B4
Jeffrey's Ct SW4 . . 172 A2
Jeffrey's Pl NW1 . . . 13 B1
Jeffrey's Rd SW4 . . 172 A2
Jeffrey's St NW1 . . . . 13 B1
Jeger Ave E2 . . . . . 24 B4
Jelf Rd SW2 . . . . . 62 C2
Jellicoe Ho 5 E2 . . . 24 C3
11 SW15 . . . . . 57 C2
Jemotts Ct 9 SE14 . 50 C4
Jenkins Ho SW8 . . . 171 B4
Jenkinson Ho 12 E2 25 C2
Jenner Ave W3 . . . . . 28 C4
Jenner Ho SE3 . . . . . 53 A4
Jenner Pl SW13 . . . . 47 A4
Jenner Rd N16 . . . . . 7 B1
Jennifer Ho SE11 . . 149 C3
Jennings Ho SE10 . . 42 C1
Jennings Rd SE22 . . . 64 B1
Jensen Ho 10 E3 . . . 26 C1
Jephson Ho SW4 . . 172 B2
6 SE17 . . . . . 48 A4
Jephson St SE5 . . . . . 48 C2
Jephtha Rd SW18 . . . 58 C1
Jepson Ho SW6 . . . 166 B3
Jerdan Pl SW6 . . . . 155 B2
Jeremiah St 11 E14 . 34 A3
Jeremy Bentham Ho E2 . . . . . 99 C3
Jermyn St SW1 . . . . 119 A2
Jerningham Ct SE14 . . . . . 51 A2
Jerningham Rd SE14 . . . . . 51 A2
Jerome Cres NW8 . . 90 A2
Jerome Ho NW1 . . . 102 B4
8 E14 . . . . . 33 A3
Jerome St E1 . 24 B1 98 C1
Jerome Twr 5 W3 . . 37 A4
Jerrard St SE13 . . . . . 67 A4
Jerrold Lo SW15 . . . . 57 B4
Jerrold St 24 N1 . . . . 24 A3
Jersey Ho 12 N1 . . . . 15 B2
Jersey Rd N1 . . . . . 15 B2
Jersey St E2 . . . . . 25 A2
Jerusalem Pas EC1 . 96 A1
Jervis Bay Ho 8 E14 . . . . . 34 C3
Jervis Ct W1 . . . . . 104 B1
Jessel Ho WC1 . . . . . 94 A3
SW1 . . . . . 147 C4
Jessica Rd SW18 . . . . 59 B2
Jessie Blythe La 2 N19 . . . . . 5 A4
Jesson Ho SE17 . . . 151 B3
Jessop Ct N1 . . . . . 86 B1
Jessop Prim Sch SE24 . . . . . 63 B3
Jessop Sq E14 . . . . . 33 C1
Jeston Ho 10 SE27 . . 75 A1
Jethou Ho 13 N1 . . . . 15 B2
Jevons Ho 9 NW8 . . 11 C1
Jewell Ho 3 SW12 . 73 B4
Jewry St EC3 . . . . . 110 C1
Jews Free Sch NW1 13 C2
Jews Row SW18 . . . . 59 B3
Jeymer Ave NW2 . . . . . 9 B3
Jeypore Rd SW18 . . . 59 B1
Jim Griffiths Ho SW6 . . . . . 155 A3
Joan St SE1 . . . . . 122 A1
Joanna Ho 7 W6 . . . 39 B1
Jocelin Ho N1 . . . . . 85 A3
Jocelyn Rd TW9 . . . . 54 A4
Jocelyn St SE15 . . . . 49 C2
Jockey's Fields WC1 . . . . . 107 A4
Jodane Rd SE8 . . . . . 41 B2
Jodrell Rd E3 . . . . . 18 B1
Johanna Prim Sch SE1 . . . . . 135 B3
Johanna St SE1 . . . 135 B3
John Adam St WC2 . . . . . 120 B3
John Aird Ct W2 . . 101 A4
John Archer Way SW18 . . . . . 59 C1
John Ashby Cl SW2 . 62 A1
John Ball Prim Sch SE3 . . . . . 53 A1
John Barker Ct NW6 . . . . . 10 A1
John Betts' Ho W12 . 38 C3
John Bond Ho 2 E3 . . . . . 26 B3
John Brent Ho 8 SE8 . . . . . 40 C2
John Buck Ho NW10 . . . . . 21 B4
John Burns Prim Sch SW11 . . . . . 169 C1
John Campbell Rd 26 N16 . . . . . 16 A3
John Carpenter St EC4 . . . . . 122 A4
John Cartwright Ho 7 E2 . . . . . 25 A2
John Dee Ho 3 SW14 . . . . . 55 C4
John Donne Jun & Inf Sch SE15 . . . . . 50 A2
John Dwight Ho SW6 . . . . . 59 A4
John F. Kennedy Sch E15 . . . . . 27 C4
John Felton Rd SE16 . . . . . 139 B3
John Fielden Ho 10 E2 . . . . . 25 A2
John Fisher St E1 . 125 B4
John Glynes Ct SW15 . . . . . 57 A3
John Harris Ho SE15 . . . . . 64 C4
John Islip St SW1 . 148 A3
John Keall Ho SW15 . . . . . 57 C4
John Keats Sec & Prim Sch NW8 . . . . . 11 C1
John Keble CE Prim Sch NW10 . . . . . 21 B4
John Kennedy Ct 1 N1 . . . . . 15 C2
John Kennedy Ho 1 SE16 . . . . . 40 C2
John Kennedy Lo 2 N1 . . . . . 15 C2
John King Ct 4 N19 . 4 C2
John Kirk Ho 22 SW11 . . . . . 59 C4
5 SW16 . . . . . 74 A1
John Knight Lo SW6 . . . . . 155 C2
John Maurice Cl SE17 . . . . . 151 B4
John McDonald Ho 3 E14 . . . . . 42 B3
John McKenna Wlk SE16 . . . . . 139 C2
John Milton Prim Sch SW8 . . . . . 160 C1
John Nettleford Ho 14 E2 . . . . . 25 A2
John Orwell Sports Ctr E1 . . . . . 32 A1
John Parker Sq 8 SW11 . . . . . 59 C4
John Parry Ct 28 N1 . . . . . 24 A3
John Paul II RC Sec Sch SW19 . . . . . 69 C4
John Penn St SE13 . 52 A2
John Perryn Prim Sch W3 . . . . . 29 A3
John Prince's St W1 . . . . . 104 B2
John Pritchard Ho E1 . . . . . 99 C1
John Ratcliffe Ho 5 NW6 . . . . . 23 C2
John Rennie Wlk 1 E1 . . . . . 32 B1
John Roan Sec Sch (Lower) The SE3 . . 53 B3
John Roan Sec Sch (Upper) The SE3 . . 53 A3
John Roll Way SE16 . . . . . 139 C2
John Ruskin Jun & Inf Sch SE5 . . . . . 48 B4
John Ruskin St SE5 . 48 B4
John Scurr Ho 20 E14 . . . . . 33 A3
John Scurr JMI Sch E1 . . . . . 25 B1
John Silkin La SE8 . . 40 C1
John Smith Ave SW6 . . . . . 154 C2
John Spencer Sq N1 . . . . . 15 A2
John St WC1 . . . . . 95 A1
John Steiner Jun Sch SE4 . . . . . 66 A4
John Strachey Ho SW6 . . . . . 155 A3
John Trundle Ct EC2 . . . . . 108 C4
John Tucker Ho 2 E14 . . . . . 41 C3
John Wesley's House & Mus★ EC1 . . . . . 97 C2
John Wheatley Ho SW6 . . . . . 155 A3
14 N19 . . . . . 4 C4
John Williams Cl SE14 . . . . . 50 C4
John's Mews WC1 . . 95 A1
John's Pl E1 . . . . . 32 A3
Johnson Cl E8 . . . . . 24 C4
Johnson Ct 10 SW18 . . . . . 59 C3
Johnson Ho NW1 . . . 83 A1
E2 . . . . . 99 C3
SW1 . . . . . 145 C3
SW8 . . . . . 161 C1
Johnson Lo 12 W9 . . 31 C4
Johnson St E1 . . . . . 32 B3
Johnson's Pl SW1 . . . . . 146 C1
Johnsons Ct EC4 . . 107 C1
Johnsons Way NW10 . . . . . 20 A1
Johnston Cl SW9 . . 173 A3
Johnstone Ho SE13 . 67 C4

Johsen Ho **5** SW15 . .56 C2
Joiner St SE1 . . . . . .123 C1
Joiners Arms Yd **1**
SE8 . . . . .48 C2
Jolles Ho **9** E3 . . . . . .27 A2
Jonathan Ct W4 . . . .38 A2
Jonathan St SE11 . .148 C2
Jones Ho N16 . . . . . . .7 A3
  1 E14 . . . . .34 C3
Jones St W1 . . . . . . .118 A3
Jones Wlk **6** TW10 . .54 B1
Jonson Ho SE1 . . . . .137 C1
  16 N16 . . . . .15 C4
Jordan Ct SW15 . . . .57 C3
Jordan Ho N1 . . . . . .87 C3
  2 SE4 . . . . .65 C3
Jordans Ho NW8 . . . .90 A1
Joscoyne Ho **14** E1 . .32 A3
Joseph Ave W3 . . . . .28 C3
Joseph Conrad Ho
  SW1 . . . . .147 A3
Joseph Ct N16 . . . . . . .7 A4
Joseph Irwin Ho **11**
  E14 . . . . .33 B2
Joseph Lancaster Jun &
  Inf Sch SE1 . . . . . .137 B1
Joseph Powell Cl **1**
  SW12 . . . . .61 B1
Joseph Priestley Ho **19**
  E2 . . . . .25 A2
Joseph St E3 . . . . . . .26 B1
Joseph Tritton Prim Sch
  SW18 . . . . .59 B2
Joseph Trotter Cl
  EC1 . . . . .95 C3
Josephine Ave SW2 . .62 B2
Joshua St E14 . . . . . . .34 B3
Josseline Ct **8** E3 . . .26 A3
Joubert Mans SW3 .144 B2
Joubert St SW11 . . .169 A2
Jowett St SW9 . . . . .172 B1
Jowett St SE1 . . . . . .49 B3
Jubet Ho **9** E14 . . . . . .15 C4
Jubilee Bldgs NW8 . .79 B2
Jubilee Cres E14 . . . .42 B3
Jubilee Ho SE11 . . . .149 C3
Jubilee Mans **10** E1 . .32 B3
Jubilee Mkt WC2 . . .120 B4
Jubilee Pl SW3 . . . . .144 B2
Jubilee St E1 . . . . . . .32 B4
Jubilee The **2** SE10 . .52 A3
Jubilee Yd SE1 . . . . .138 C4
Judd St WC1 . . . . . . .94 A3
Jude St E16 . . . . .35 B1
Judges' Wlk NW3 . . . .2 B1
Juer St SW11 . . . . . .158 A2
Julia St NW5 . . . . . . .12 C3
Julian Ave W3 . . . . . .28 A2
Julian Pl E14 . . . . . . .42 A1
Juliet Ho **11** N1 . . . . .24 A3
Julius Ct TW8 . . . . . .44 A3
Junction App SW11 . .60 A4
  SE13 . . . . .67 B4
Junction Mews
  W2 . . . . .102 A2
Junction Pl W2 . . . . .101 C2
Junction Rd N19 . . . . .4 B1
Juniper Cres NW1 . . .12 C1
Juniper Ct N16 . . . . . .6 C2
Juniper Dr SW18 . . . .59 B4
Juniper Ho **3** SE14 . .50 B3
Juno Ct SW9 . . . . . .163 B1
Juno Way SE14 . . . . .50 C4

Juno Way Ind Est
  SE14 . . . . .50 C4
Jupiter Ct SW9 . . . . .163 B1
Jupiter Way N7 . . . . .14 B2
Jupp Rd E15 . . . . . . .19 C1
Jupp Rd W E15 . . . . .27 C4
Jura Ho SE16 . . . . . . .41 A2
Jurston Ct SE1 . . . . .135 C3
Justice Wlk SW3 . . . .158 A3
Jutland Cl N19 . . . . . . .5 A3
Jutland Ho **4** SE5 . . .48 B1
Juxon St SE11 . . . . . .149 A4

K

Kambala Rd SW11 . . .59 C4
Karen Ct **2** SE5 . . . . .64 A4
Karen Ho **7** N16 . . . .15 C4
Kasmin Ct NW10 . . . . .8 C1
Kassala Rd SW11 . . .169 A3
Katherine Cl **3**
  SE16 . . . . .32 C1
Katherine Ho **18**
  W10 . . . . .23 A1
Katherine Sq W11 . . .112 A2
Katherine's Wlk **1**
  W11 . . . . .30 C1
Kathleen Ave W3 . . . .28 B4
Kathleen Rd SW11 . . .60 B4
Kay Rd SW9 . . . . . . .172 C1
Kay St E15 . . . . .19 C1
  E2 . . . . .24 C3
Kean St WC2 . . . . . .106 C1
Kean Ho **5** SE17 . . . .48 A4
Kean St **1** WC2 . . . .106 C1
Keates Est N16 . . . . . .7 B2
Keates St **5** E1 . . . . .32 A4
Keats Cl SE1 . . . . . . .152 C3
Keats Ho NW1 . . . . . .12 A4
  1 E2 . . . . .25 B2
  6 SE5 . . . . .48 B3
Keats Pl EC2 . . . . . . .109 B3
Keble Ho **4** SW15 . . .57 C1
Keble Pl SW13 . . . . . .47 A4
Kedge Ho **10** E14 . . .41 C3
Kedleston Ct E5 . . . . .18 A4
Kedleston Wlk **21**
  E2 . . . . .25 A2
Keel Cl SE16 . . . . . . .32 C1
Keeley St WC2 . . . . .106 C1
Keen's Yd N1 . . . . . . .15 A2
Keep The SE3 . . . . . . .53 C1
Keeper Wharf E1 . . . .32 C2
Keeton's Rd SE16 . . . .40 A3
Keevil Dr SW19 . . . . .70 A4
Keighley Cl N7 . . . . . .14 A4
Keildon Rd SW11 . . . .60 B3
Keir Hardie Ho
  1 N19 . . . . .4 C4
  W6 . . . . .47 C4
Keith Connor Cl **5**
  SW8 . . . . .61 A4
Keith Gr W12 . . . . . . .29 C1
Keith Ho NW6 . . . . . .78 A1
Kelby Ho N7 . . . . .14 B2
Kelfield Ct **1** W10 . . .30 C3
Kelfield Gdns W10 . . .30 C3
Kell St SE1 . . . . .136 B2
Kellett Ho N1 . . . . . . .87 C3
Kellett Rd SW2 . . . . . .62 C3
Kellow Ho SE1 . . . . .137 B4
Kelly Ave SE15 . . . . . .49 B3
Kelly Ct **13** E14 . . . . .33 C2
Kelly Mews **3** W9 . . .23 B1
Kelman Cl SW4 . . . . .171 C1
Kelmore Gr SE22 . . . .64 C3

Kelmscott Gdns
  W12 . . . . .38 C3
Kelmscott Rd SW11 . .60 B2
Kelross Rd N5 . . . . . . .15 B4
Kelsey St E2 . . . . .24 C1 99 B2
Kelshall Ct N4 . . . . . . .6 B2
Kelso Pl W8 . . . . . . .128 B2
Kelson Ho E14 . . . . . .42 B3
Kelvedon Ho SW8 . . .172 B4
Kelvedon Rd SW6 . . .155 A1
Kelvin Ct W11 . . . . . .113 B3
  W4 . . . . .45 B3
Kelvington Rd SE15 . .65 C2
Kelway Ho **20** SW2 . .74 C4
Kember St N1 . . . . . . .14 B1
Kemble Ho SW9 . . . . .63 A4
Kemble Rd SE23 . . . . .65 C1
Kemerton Rd SE5 . . . .63 B4
Kemey's St E9 . . . . . .18 A3
Kemp Ho **1** E2 . . . . . .25 C3
  W1 . . . . .105 B1
Kemp's Ct W1 . . . . . .105 B1
Kempe Ho SE1 . . . . .137 C1
Kempe Rd NW6 . . . . .22 C3
Kempis Way **5**
  SE22 . . . . .64 A2
Kemplay Rd NW3 . . . .11 C4
Kemps Dr E14 . . . . . .33 C2
Kempsford Gdns
  SW5 . . . . .141 C1
Kempsford Rd
  SE11 . . . . .149 C3
Kempson Rd SW6 . . .155 C1
Kempthorne Rd SE8 . .41 B2
Kempton Ct E1 . . . . . .32 A4
Kempton Ho **18** N1 . .24 A4
Kemsford Rd SE11 . . .150 A3
Kemsing Ho SE1 . . . .137 C3
Kemsing Rd SE10 . . . .43 C1
Kemsley SE13 . . . . . .67 A2
Ken Wilson Ho **17**
  E2 . . . . .24 C3
Kenbrook Ho W14 . . .127 A1
  5 NW5 . . . . .13 B3
Kenbury Gdns **10**
  SE5 . . . . .48 B1
Kenbury Mans **18**
  SE5 . . . . .48 B1
Kenbury St SE5 . . . . .48 B1
Kenchester Cl
  SW8 . . . . .162 B1
Kendal Ho N1 . . . . . . .84 C1
  2 E9 . . . . .25 B4
Kendal Ave W3 . . . . . .28 A4
Kendal Cl SE5 . . . . . .48 A3
Kendal Ho N1 . . . . . . .85 A2
  32 E9 . . . . .25 B4
Kendal Pl SW15 . . . . .58 B2
Kendal Rd NW10 . . . . .8 C4
Kendal St W2 . . . . . .102 B1
Kendal Steps W2 . . .102 B1
Kendall Ct **8** SE22 . . .64 C2
Kendall Pl W1 . . . . . .103 B3
Kender Prim Sch
  SE14 . . . . .50 B2
Kender St SE14 . . . . .50 B2
Kendoa Rd **4** SW4 . . .61 C3
Kendrick Mews
  SW7 . . . . .143 B3
Kendrick Pl SW7 . . . .143 B3
Kenilford Rd SW12 . . .73 A4
Kenilworth Ct SW6 . . .58 A4
Kenilworth Rd NW6 . .23 B4
  E3 . . . . .26 A3

Kenley Wlk W11 . . . .112 A3
Kenmare Mans
  NW6 . . . . .10 B3
Kenmont Gdns
  NW10 . . . . .22 B2
Kenmont Prim Sch
  NW10 . . . . .22 B2
Kenmore Cl TW9 . . . .44 C3
Kenmore Rd N6 . . . . .16 C1
Kenmure Rd E8 . . . . .17 A3
Kenmure Yd E8 . . . . .17 A3
Kennacraig Cl **7**
  E16 . . . . .35 C1
Kennard Ho SW11 . . .169 C3
Kennard Rd E15 . . . . .19 C1
Kennard St SW11 . . .169 C3
Kennedy Cox Ho **9**
  E16 . . . . .35 B2
Kennedy Ho SE11 . . .148 C2
Kennedy Wlk SE17 . .151 C3
Kennet Cl SW11 . . . . .59 C3
Kennet Ho NW8 . . . . .89 C1
Kennet Rd W9 . . . . . .23 B1
Kennet St E1 . . . . . . .125 C2
Kennet Wharf La
  EC4 . . . . .123 A4
Kenneth Campbell Ho
  NW8 . . . . .89 C2
Kenneth Cres NW2 . . .9 A3
Kenneth Ct SE11 . . . .149 C4
Kenneth Younger Ho
  SW6 . . . . .155 A3
Kenning Ho **6** N1 . . . .24 A4
Kenning St **12** SE16 . .40 B4
Kennings Way
  SE11 . . . . .149 C2
Kennington Gr
  SE11 . . . . .163 A4
Kennington La
  SE11 . . . . .149 B1
Kennington Oval
  SE11 . . . . .163 A3
Kennington Palace Ct
  SE11 . . . . .149 B2
Kennington Park Gdns
  SE17 . . . . .149 A1
Kennington Park Ho
  SE11 . . . . .150 A2
Kennington Park Pl
  SE11 . . . . .150 A2
Kennington Park Rd
  SE11 . . . . .150 A2
Kennington Rd
  SE1 . . . . .149 B4
  SE11 . . . . .149 B4
Kennington Sta
  SE17 . . . . .150 A2
Kennolds SE21 . . . . . .75 C2
Kenrick Pl W1 . . . . . .103 B3
Kensal Green Cemetery
  (All Souls) * NW10 . .22 B2
Kensal Green Sta
  NW10 . . . . .22 B2
Kensal Ho W10 . . . . . .22 C1
Kensal Rd W10 . . . . . .23 A1
Kensal Rise Prim Sch
  NW6 . . . . .22 C3
Kensal Rise Sta
  NW10 . . . . .22 C3
Kensington & Chelsea
  Coll
  SW7 . . . . .156 C2
  SW10 . . . . .156 C2
  W10 . . . . .31 A4
Kensington Church Ct
  W8 . . . . .128 A3

Kensington Church St
  W8 . . . . .31 C1 113 C2
Kensington Church Wlk
  W8 . . . . .128 A3
Kensington Court Mans
  W8 . . . . .128 B3
Kensington Court Mews
  W8 . . . . .128 C3
Kensington Court Pl
  W8 . . . . .128 B2
Kensington Ct W8 . . .128 B3
Kensington Ct Gdns
  W8 . . . . .128 B2
Kensington Gardens
  W2 . . . . .115 A1
Kensington Gardens Sq
  W2 . . . . .100 A1
Kensington Gate
  W8 . . . . .128 C2
Kensington Hall Gdns
  W14 . . . . .140 C2
Kensington High St
  W8 . . . . .127 C2
Kensington Ho **3**
  NW5 . . . . .13 B3
Kensington Hts
  W8 . . . . .113 B2
Kensington Mall
  W8 . . . . .113 C2
Kensington Mans
  SW5 . . . . .141 C2
Kensington Olympia Sta
  W14 . . . . .126 A2
Kensington Palace *
  W8 . . . . .114 A1
Kensington Palace Gdns
  W8 . . . . .114 A2
Kensington Park Gdns
  W11 . . . . .31 B2 113 A3
Kensington Park Mews
  W11 . . . . .31 B3
Kensington Park Rd
  W11 . . . . .31 B2 113 A4
Kensington Pl
  W8 . . . . .31 C1 113 B2
Kensington Prep Sch
  SW6 . . . . .165 A4
Kensington Rd
  SW7 . . . . .129 A3
  W8 . . . . .128 C3
  W11 . . . . .128 C3
Kensington Sq W8 . . .128 A3
Kensington Village
  W14 . . . . .141 A3
Kensington W
  W14 . . . . .140 A4
Kensworth Ho EC1 . . .97 C3
Kent Ct **3** E2 . . . . . . .24 B3
Kent Ho No1 . . . . . . .142 A1
  SE1 . . . . .153 A1
  13 W4 . . . . .38 A1
  Richmond TW10 . . . .54 C2
Kent Lo **9** SW19 . . . .69 C3
Kent Pas NW1 . . . . . . .90 C2
Kent Rd W4 . . . . .37 B3
  Richmond TW9 . . . . .44 C3
Kent St E2 . . . . .24 B3
Kent Terr NW1 . . . . . .90 B2
Kent Wlk SW9 . . . . . .63 A3
Kent Yard SW7 . . . . .130 B3
Kentish Bldgs SE1 . . .123 B1

Kentish Town CE Prim Sch NW5 .... 13 B3
Kentish Town Rd
NW1 .... 82 B4
NW1 .... 13 A2
Kentish Town Sta
NW5 .... 13 B3
Kentish Town West Sta
NW5 .... 13 A2
Kentmere Ho SE15 .. 50 B4
Kenton Ct W14 .... 126 C1
Kenton Ho N5 .... 5 C1
21 E1 .... 25 B1
Kenton Rd E9 ...... 17 C2
Kenton St WC1 .... 94 A2
Kentwell Cl SE4 .... 66 A3
Kentwode Gn SW13 . 46 C3
Kenway Rd SW5 ... 142 A3
Kenwood Cl NW3 .... 2 C3
Kenwood Ho* NW3 .. 3 A3
15 SW9 .... 63 A3
Kenworthy Rd E9 ... 18 A2
Kenwrick Ho N1 .... 85 A3
Kenwyn Rd SW4 .... 61 C3
Kenyon Ho 31 SE5 .. 48 B3
Kenyon St SW6 ..... 47 C2
Kepler Ho 9 SE10 .. 43 B1
Kepler Rd SW2,SW4 . 62 A3
Keppel Ho SW3 ... 144 A3
5 SE8 .... 41 B1
Keppel Row SE1 .. 122 C1
Keppel St WC1 .... 105 C4
Kerbela St E2 ...... 99 B2
Kerbey St E14 ...... 34 A3
Kerfield Cres SE5 .. 48 C2
Kerfield Pl SE5 ..... 48 C2
Kerridge Ct N1 ..... 16 A2
Kerrier Ho SW10 .. 157 A1
Kerrin Point SE11 . 149 B2
Kerrington Ct 7
W12 .... 39 B4
Kerrison Rd E15 .... 27 C4
SW11 .... 60 A4
Kerry N7 .... 14 A2
Kerry Ho 5 E1 ..... 32 B3
Kerry Path SE8 ..... 51 B4
Kerry Rd SE8 .... 51 B4
Kerscott Ho 30 E3 .. 27 A2
Kersfield Ho SW15 .. 57 C1
Kersfield Rd SW15 .. 57 C1
Kershaw Cl SW18 ... 59 C1
Kershaw Ho 7
SE27 .... 75 A1
Kersley Mews
SW11 .... 168 C3
Kersley Rd N16 ...... 7 A1
Kersley St SW11 .. 168 C2
Kerwick Cl 1 N7 ... 14 B1
Keslake Mans
NW10 .... 22 C3
Keslake Rd NW6 .... 22 C3
Keston Ho SE17 ... 152 B2
Keston Rd SE15 ..... 64 C4
Kestral Ho EC1 ..... 96 C4
Kestrel Ave SE24 ... 63 B2
Kestrel Ct 27 SE8 .. 51 B4
Kestrel Ho 4 SW11 . 60 A4
Kestrel Pl SE14 ..... 51 A4
Keswick Ct 2 SE22 . 64 C2
Keswick Ho 8 SE5 .. 48 B2
Keswick Hts 9
SW15 .... 58 A2
Keswick Lo E8 ...... 16 B2
Keswick Rd SW15 ... 58 A2
Ketley Ho SE15 ..... 49 C2
Kett Gdns SW2 ..... 62 B2
Kettleby Ho SW9 ... 63 A4
Ketton Ho W10 ..... 22 B1
Kevan Ho SE5 ...... 48 B3
Kew Bridge TW8 .... 36 B1
Kew Bridge Ct 8
W4 .... 36 C1
Kew Bridge Rd TW8 36 B1
Kew Bridge Sta
TW8 .... 36 B1
Kew Bridge Steam Mus
TW8 .... 36 B1
Kew Foot Rd TW9 .. 54 A4
Kew Gardens Rd
TW9 .... 44 C2
Kew Gardens Sta
TW9 .... 44 C2
Kew Gardens(Royal Botanic)* TW9 .... 44 A2
Kew Gn TW9 .... 44 B4
Kew Green TW9 .... 44 C3
Kew Lo 11 TW9 ..... 44 B2
Kew Palace TW9 .... 44 A3
Kew Pier TW9 ...... 44 C4
Kew Rd TW9,W4 .... 44 B2
Kew Ret Pk TW9 .... 45 A2
Key Cl E1 .... 25 A1
Key Ho SE11 ...... 163 B4
Keyes Ct SE22 ...... 64 C2
Keyes Rd NW2 .... 9 C3
Keyham Ho 31 W2 .. 31 C4
Keymer Rd SW2 .... 74 B2
Keynsham Ho 2 N4 .. 6 B4
Keyse Rd SE1 ...... 138 C1
Keystone Cres N1 ... 84 B1
Keyworth Cl E5 ..... 18 A4
Keyworth Jun & Inf Sch
SE17 .... 150 A1
Keyworth Pl SE1 .. 136 B2
Keyworth St SE1 .. 136 B2
Kezia St SE8 .... 41 A1
Khyber Rd SW11 .. 168 A1
Kibworth St SW8 .. 162 C1
Kidbrooke Gdns
SE3 .... 53 C2
Kidbrooke Gr SE3 ... 53 C2
Kidbrooke Park Rd
SE3 .... 53 C2
Kidderpore Ave
NW3 .... 10 C4
Kidderpore Gdns
NW3 .... 10 C4
Kidron Way 18 E9 ... 25 B4
Kiffen St EC2 .... 97 C2
Kilbrennan Ho 5
E14 .... 34 B3
Kilburn Bridge 14
NW6 .... 23 C4
Kilburn Gate NW6 .. 78 A2
Kilburn High Rd
NW6 .... 23 C4
Kilburn High Road Sta
NW6 .... 78 A3
Kilburn Ho 13 W9 ... 23 B2
Kilburn La W10 ..... 23 A3
Kilburn Park Jun Sch
NW6 .... 23 B3
Kilburn Park Rd
NW6 .... 23 C2
Kilburn Park Sta
NW6 .... 23 C3
Kilburn Pl NW6 ..... 23 C4
Kilburn Priory NW6 78 A3
Kilburn Sq NW6 .... 23 C4
Kilburn Sta NW2 .... 10 B2
Kilburn Vale NW6 .. 78 A3
Kilburn Vale Est 13
NW6 .... 23 C4
Kildare Ct W2 ...... 31 C3
Kildare Gdns W2 ... 31 C3
Kildare Rd E16 ..... 35 C4
Kildare Terr W2 ..... 31 C3
Kildare Wlk E14 .... 33 C3
Kildoran Rd SW2 ... 62 A2
Kilgour Rd SE23 .... 66 A1
Kilkie St SW6 ..... 166 C1
Killarney Rd SW18 .. 59 B1
Killick St N1 .... 84 C1
Killieser Ave SW2 ... 74 A2
Killip Cl E16 .... 35 B1
Killowen Rd E9 ..... 17 C2
Killyon Rd SW8 ... 171 B1
Kilmaine Rd SW6 .. 154 B1
Kilmarsh Rd W6 .... 39 B2
Kilmington Rd
SW13 .... 46 C4
Kilmore Ho 17 E14 .. 34 A3
Kilmuir Ho SW1 ... 145 C3
Kiln Ct E14 .... 33 B2
Kiln Pl NW5 .... 12 C3
Kilner Ho SE11 .... 163 B4
Kilner St E14 .... 33 C4
Kiloh Ct 1 SW11 .... 60 A4
Kilpatrick Ct N16 ..... 7 B3
Kilpeck Ho 3 N4 ..... 6 B4
Kilravock St W10 ... 23 A2
Kilronan 5 W3 ..... 28 C3
Kimbell Gdns SW6 164 A3
Kimber Ctr The
SW18 .... 70 C4
Kimber Rd SW18 .... 71 A4
Kimberley Ave SE15 . 65 B4
Kimberley Ho 7
E14 .... 42 B3
Kimberley Rd NW6 .23 A4
SW9 .... 62 A4
Kimble Ho NW8 ..... 90 B2
1 N7 .... 14 A3
Kimbolton Row
SW3 .... 144 A3
Kimpton Ct 12 SE5 .. 48 C2
Kimpton Ho SW15 .. 68 C4
Kimpton Rd SE5 .... 48 C2
Kinburn St SE16 .... 40 C4
Kincaid Rd SE15 .... 50 A3
Kincardine Gdns
W9 .... 23 C1
Kindell Ho 4 SW14 . 55 C4
Kinder Ho N1 .... 87 C2
Kinder St 9 E1 ..... 32 A3
Kindersley Ho E1 .. 111 C1
Kinefold Ho N7 ..... 14 A2
Kinfauns Rd SW2 ... 74 C2
King & Queen St
SE17 .... 151 A2
King Alfred Sch
NW11 .... 2 A3
King Arthur Cl SE15 . 50 B3
King Charles Ho
SW6 .... 156 B2
King Charles St
SW1 .... 134 A4
King Charles Wlk 6
SW19 .... 70 A3
King David La E1 ... 32 B2
King Edward Mans 12
E8 .... 25 A4
King Edward Mews
SW13 .... 46 C2
King Edward St
EC1 .... 108 C2
King Edward The Third Mews 8 SE16 ..... 40 A4
King Edward Wlk
SE1 .... 135 C2
King Edward's Rd
E9 .... 25 B4
King Edwards Mans
SW6 .... 155 B1
King Fahed Acad The
W3 .... 29 B2
King Frederick IX Ct
SE16 .... 41 B3
King George Sq
TW10 .... 54 B1
King George St
SE10 .... 52 B3
King Henry St N16 .. 16 A3
King Henry's Rd
NW3 .... 12 A1
King Henry's Wlk
N1 .... 16 A2
King Henry's Yd 5
N16 .... 16 A3
King Ho W12 .... 30 A3
King James St SE1 136 B3
King John Ct EC2 ... 98 B2
King John St E1 .... 32 C4
King Sq EC1 .... 96 C3
King St EC2 .... 109 A1
SW1 .... 119 A2
WC2 .... 120 A4
W3 .... 28 B1
W6 .... 38 C2
King Stairs Cl SE16 . 40 A4
King Street Cloisters 8
W6 .... 39 A2
King William La 3
SE10 .... 43 A1
King William St
EC4 .... 123 C4
King William Wlk
SE10 .... 52 B4
King's Arms Ct
E1 .... 111 B3
King's Arms Yd
EC2 .... 109 B2
King's Bench St
SE1 .... 136 B4
King's Bench Wlk
EC4 .... 107 C1
King's Coll SE24 .... 63 C1
King's Coll WC2 .. 121 A4
King's College Hospl
SE5 .... 48 C1
King's College London
NW3 .... 10 C4
King's Court N
SW3 .... 144 A1
King's Court S
SW3 .... 144 A1
King's Cres N4,N5 .... 6 B1
King's Cross WC1 ... 94 B4
King's Cross (Midland City) Sta WC1 .... 94 B4
King's Cross (Thames Link) Sta WC1 .... 94 B4
King's Cross Bridge
WC1 .... 94 B4
King's Cross Rd
WC1 .... 95 A3
King's Cross Sta
N1 .... 84 B1
King's Cross, St Pancras Sta WC1 .. 94 A4
King's Gdns 6 NW6 10 C1
King's Gr SE15 ...... 50 A2
King's Gr *continued*
SE15 .... 50 A3
King's Head Yd
SE1 .... 123 B1
King's House Jun Sch
TW10 .... 54 B2
King's House Sch
TW10 .... 54 B2
King's Keep 6
SW15 .... 57 C2
King's Mansions
SW3 .... 158 A3
King's Mead Way
E5,E9 .... 18 A4
King's Mews 1
SW4 .... 62 A2
King's Mews WC1 .. 95 A1
King's Par NW10 .... 22 B4
W12 .... 38 C3
King's Pl SE1 ..... 136 C3
King's Quay
SW10 .... 167 A4
King's Rd SW14 ..... 55 C4
King's Rd SW3 .... 144 A1
SW10 .... 156 B1
King's Scholars' Pas
SW1 .... 146 C4
King's Terr NW1 .... 82 C3
Kingdon Ho 8 E14 .42 B3
Kingdon Rd NW6 ... 10 C2
Kingfield St E14 .... 42 B2
Kingfisher Ct
12 E14 .... 42 B4
11 SW11 .... 60 A4
SW19 .... 70 A2
Kingfisher Ho
W14 .... 126 C2
SE15 .... 49 B2
Kingfisher Mews
SE13 .... 67 A2
Kingfisher Sq 19
SE8 .... 51 B4
Kingham Cl 3 W11 . 39 C4
SW18 .... 71 B4
Kinghorn St EC1 .. 108 C3
Kinglake St SE17 .. 152 B2
Kingley St W1 ..... 104 C1
Kingly Ct W1 ...... 119 A4
Kingly St W1 ...... 118 C4
Kings Acre Prim Sch
SW4 .... 62 A2
Kings Ave SW4 ..... 62 A1
Kings Coll Chelsea Campus (Univ of London) SW10 ... 156 B2
Kings Coll London (Chelsea Campus)
SW3 .... 144 A1
Kings College Ct
NW3 .... 12 A1
Kings College London
W8 .... 127 B4
Kings Ct NW8 .... 80 C3
6 N7 .... 14 B1
W6 .... 38 C2
SE22 .... 64 C3
10 SW15 .... 68 C4
Kings Farm Ave
TW10 .... 54 C3
Kings Hall Mews
SE13 .... 67 B4
Kings Ho SW8 ..... 162 B2
Kings Mall W6 ...... 39 B2

Kings Pl W4 . . . . .37 B2
Kings Rd NW10 . . . . .9 A1
Richmond TW10,TW9 . . . .54 B2
Kings Ride Gate
TW10 . . . . .54 C3
Kings Wood Ct 4
NW6 . . . . .10 C1
Kingsbridge N16 . . . . .6 C3
Kingsbridge Ave
W3 . . . . .36 B4
Kingsbridge Ct E14 . . .41 C2
Kingsbridge Rd
W10 . . . . .30 B3
Kingsbury Rd N1 . . . .16 A2
Kingsbury Terr N1 . . .16 A2
Kingsclere Cl SW8 . . .68 C4
Kingscliffe Gdns
SW19 . . . . .70 B3
Kingscote NW11 . . . . .1 B3
Kingscote Rd W4 . . . .37 C3
Kingscote St EC4 . . .122 A4
Kingscourt Rd
SW16 . . . . .74 A1
Kingscroft SW4 . . . . .62 A1
Kingscroft Rd NW2 . . .10 B2
Kingsdale Gdns
W11 . . . . .30 C1
Kingsdale Sch SE21 . .76 A1
Kingsdown Ave W3 . . .29 A2
Kingsdown Cl W10 . . .30 C3
11 W11 . . . . .31 A3
28 SE16 . . . . .40 A1
Kingsdown Cl SW11 . . .60 A1
Kingsdown Ho 1
E8 . . . . .16 C3
Kingsdown Rd 3
N19 . . . . .5 A2
Kingsfield Ho 16 N16 .7 A4
Kingsford St NW5 . . .12 B3
Kingsgate Est N1 . . . .16 A2
Kingsgate Ho SW9 .173 C4
Kingsgate Jun & Inf Sch
NW6 . . . . .10 C1
Kingsgate Ho NW6 . . .10 C1
Kingsgate Rd NW6 . . .10 C1
Kingshill SE17 . . . . . .151 A4
Kingshold Rd E9 . . . .17 B1
Kingshold Rd 8 . . . . .80 B3
Kingsland Gn 1 E8,
N1 . . . . .16 A2
Kingsland High St
E8 . . . . .16 B3
Kingsland Pas 2
E8 . . . . .16 A2
Kingsland Rd E2 . . . .24 A3
Kingsland Sch E8 . . . .16 B3
Kingsland Sh Ctr E8 . .16 B3
Kingslawn Cl SW15 . . .57 A2
Kingsley Ct NW2 . . . . . .9 A2
Kingsley Flats SE1 . . .152 B3
Kingsley Ho SW3 . .157 C3
SW4 . . . . .171 C2
Kingsley Mews
W8 . . . . .128 B1
Kingsley Pl N6 . . . . .3 C4
Kingsley Rd NW6 . . . . .23 B4
Kingsley St SW11 . . . . .60 B4
Kingsmead TW10 . . . . .54 B1
Kingsmead Ho E9 . . .18 A4
Kingsmead JMI Sch
E9 . . . . .18 A4
Kingsmead Rd SW2 .74 C2

Kingsmere Cl SW15 .57 C4
Kingsmere Pl N16 . . . . .6 C3
Kingsmere Rd
SW19 . . . . .69 C2
Kingsmill NW8 . . . . . .79 C2
Kingsmill Terr NW8 . .79 C2
Kingsnorth Ho 12
W10 . . . . .30 C3
Kingsridge SW19 . . . . .70 A2
Kingston Ho 2
NW6 . . . . .10 A1
Kingston Ho E
SW7 . . . . .130 A3
Kingston Ho N
SW7 . . . . .130 A3
Kingston Ho S
SW7 . . . . .130 A3
Kingston Univ
Roehampton Vale Ctr
SW15 . . . . .68 B1
Kingston Vale SW15 . .68 A2
Kingstown St SW1 . . .81 B4
Kingswater Pl
SW11 . . . . .158 A1
Kingsway WC2 . . . . . .106 C2
Kingsway SW14,TW9 . . . .55 A4
Kingsway Coll WC1 .94 C3
NW5 . . . . .13 A2
Kingswear Rd NW5 . . . .4 A1
Kingswood 32 E2 . . . .25 B3
Kingswood Ave
NW6 . . . . .23 A3
Kingswood Cl SW8 .162 B2
Kingswood Ct 7
TW10 . . . . .54 B2
Kingswood Rd W4 . . . .37 B3
Kingswood Rd SW2 . . .74 B4
Kingswood Terr W4 . . .37 B3
Kingston Ho NW6 . . . .78 B3
Kingward Ho E1 . . . .111 B4
Kingwood Rd SW6 .154 A1
Kinloch St N7 . . . . .5 B1
Kinnaird Ave W4 . . . . .45 B3
Kinnear Rd W12 . . . . .38 B4
Kinnerton Pl N
SW1 . . . . .131 A3
Kinnerton Pl S
SW1 . . . . .131 A3
Kinnerton St SW1 . . .131 B3
Kinnerton Yd SW1 . .131 B3
Kinnoul Rd W6 . . . . .154 A4
Kinnoull Mans 10
E5 .7 A2
Kinross Ho N1 . . . . . .84 C4
Kinsale Rd SE15 . . . . .64 C4
Kinsham Ho E2 . . . . .99 B2
Kintore Way SE1 . . . .152 C4
Kintyre Ct 8 SW2 . . .74 A4
Kinver Ho N4 . . . . .6 C4
Kipling Ho 20 SE5 . . .48 B3
Kipling St SE1 . . . . . .137 C4
Kipling Twr 3 W3 . . . .37 B3
Kirby Est SE16 . . . . . .40 A3
Kirby Gr SE1 . . . . . . .138 A4
Kirby St EC1 . . . . . . .107 C4
Kirk's Pl E3 . . . . .33 B4
Kirkeby Ho EC1 . . . .107 B4
Kirkland Wlk 4 E8 . . . .16 B2
Kirkley Ho N16 . . . . . . .7 A3
Kirkman Pl W1 . . . . . .105 B3
Kirkmichael Rd E14 . .34 B3
Kirkside Rd SE3 . . . . .53 C4
Kirkstall Gdns SW2 . .74 A3

Kirkstall Ho SW1 . . .146 A2
Kirkstall Rd SW2 . . . .74 A3
Kirkstead Ct E5 . . . . .18 A4
Kirkstone NW1 . . . . . .92 C4
Kirkton Lo SW18 . . . .59 A1
Kirkwall Pl E2 . . . . . . .25 B2
Kirkwood Rd SE15 . . .50 A1
Kirtley Ho SW8 . . . . .171 A4
Kirtling St SW8 . . . . .160 C2
Kirton Cl W4 . . . . . . .37 C2
Kirton Gdns E2 . . . . . .99 A3
Kirwin Way SE5 . . . . .48 A3
Kitcat Terr E3 . . . . . . .26 C2
Kite Ho 5 SW11 . . . . .60 A4
Kite Pl E2 . . . . .99 C4
Kitson Rd SW13 . . . . .46 C2
SE5 . . . . .48 B3
Kittiwake Ct 20 SE8 . .51 B4
Kitto Rd SE14 . . . . . . .50 C1
Kiver Rd N19 . . . . .5 A2
Klea Ave SW4 . . . . . . .61 B1
Kleffens Ct 2 SE3 . . . .53 B3
Knapp Cl NW10 . . . . . .8 A2
Knapp Rd E3 . . . . . . .26 C1
Knaresborough Dr
SW18 . . . . .71 A3
Knaresborough Ho 4
N4 .6 B4
Knaresborough Pl
SW5 . . . . .142 A4
Knatchbull Rd
NW10 . . . . .20 C4
SE5 . . . . .48 A2
Knebworth Ho
SW8 . . . . .171 C3
2 N16 . . . . .16 A4
Knebworth Rd 3
N16 . . . . .16 A4
Kneller Ho SW8 . . . .171 C2
Kneller Rd SE4 . . . . . .66 A3
Knight Ho SE17 . . . .152 A3
Knight's Ave W5 . . . . .36 A4
Knight's Ho SW10 .156 C2
Knight's Wlk
SE11 . . . . .150 A3
Knighten St E1 . . . . .32 A1
Knighthead Point
E14 . . . . .41 C4
Knightleas Ct NW2 . . .9 B2
Knightrider Ct EC4 . .122 C4
Knightrider St EC4 . .122 C4
Knights Arc SW1 . . . .130 C3
Knights Cl E9 . . . . . . .17 B3
Knights Ho SE1 . . . . .138 C4
SW10 . . . . .156 C2
SW8 . . . . .162 B1
Knights Rd E16 . . . . . .43 C4
Knightsbridge
SW1,SW7 . . . . .130 C3
Knightsbridge Ct
SW1 . . . . .131 A3
Knightsbridge Gn
SW1 . . . . .130 C3
Knightsbridge Sta
SW1 . . . . .130 C3
Knightswood Ct N6 . . .4 C4
Knivett Rd SW6 . . . . .155 B3
Knobs Hill Rd E15 . . .27 A4
Knoll Ho NW8 . . . . . . .78 C2
Knoll Rd SW18 . . . . . .59 B2
Knolly's Cl SW27,
SW16 . . . . .74 C1
Knolly's Rd SW27,
SW16 . . . . .74 C1
Knot Ho SE1 . . . . . . .124 C1

Knottisford St E2 . . . .25 B2
Knowlden Ho 4 E1 . .32 B2
Knowle Cl SW9 . . . . . .62 C4
Knowles Hill Cres
SE13 . . . . .67 C2
Knowles Ho NW10 . . .21 C4
SW18 . . . . .59 A1
Knowles Wlk SW4 . . . .61 B4
Knowlton Ho NW9 .173 C4
Knowsley Rd
SW11 . . . . .168 C1
Knox Ct SW4 . . . . . . .172 B2
Knox Ho SW15 . . . . . .47 B1
Knox St W1 . . . . .102 C4
Knoyle St SE14 . . . . . .51 A4
Kobi Nazrul Prim Sch
E1 . . . . .111 C2
Kossuth St SE10 . . . .43 A1
Kramer Mews
SW5 . . . . .142 A1
Kreedman Wlk 8
E8 . . . . .16 C3
Kreisel Wlk TW9 . . . . .44 B4
Kylemore Ct 4
W12 . . . . .38 C4
Kylemore Rd NW6 . . .10 C1
Kylestrome Ho
SW1 . . . . .145 C3
Kynance Mews
SW7 . . . . .128 B1
Kynance Pl SW7 . . . .128 C1
Kynaston Ho 7
SW2 . . . . .74 B3
Kynaston Rd N16 . . . . .7 A1
Kyrle Rd SW11 . . . . . .60 C1
Kyverdale Rd N16 . . . .7 B3

Ladbroke Sq
W11 . . . . .31 B2 113 A3
Ladbroke Terr
W11 . . . . .31 B1 113 A4
Ladbroke Wlk
W11 . . . . .31 B1 113 A3
Ladlands SE22 . . . . . .76 C4
Lady Elizabeth Ho
SW14 . . . . .55 B4
Lady Margaret Rd
NW5 . . . . .13 B3
Lady Margaret Sch
SW6 . . . . .165 B3
Lady Somerset Rd
NW5 . . . . .13 A4
Ladybower Ct 6 E5 .17 C4
Ladycroft Rd SE13 . . .67 A4
Ladywell Cl SE4 . . . . .66 C3
Ladywell Hts SE4 . . . .66 B1
Ladywell Rd SE13 . . . .67 A2
Ladywell Sta SE13 . . .67 A2
Lafitte Ho 22 N19 . . . . .5 A3
Lafone Ho 10 SW2 . . .74 A4
Lafone St SE1 . . . . . .138 C4
Lagado Mews SE16 . .32 C1
Lagan Ho 5 SE15 . . . .49 C2
SE15 . . . . .49 C3
Lagonda Ho 11 E3 . . .26 C1
Lagonier Ho EC1 . . . . .97 A3
Laindon Ho 6 N16 . . . .7 B3
Laird Ho SE5 . . . . . . .48 B3
Lairdale Cl SE21 . . . . .75 B4
Lairs Cl N7 . . . . .14 A2
Laitwood Rd SW12 . . .73 A3
Lakanal 16 SE5 . . . . .49 A2
Lake Ho SE1 . . . . . . .136 C3
Lake View Ct SW1 . . .132 B2
Laker Ct SW4 . . . . . .172 B2
Laker Pl SW15 . . . . . .58 A1
Lakeside Ct N4 . . . . . . .6 B3
Lakeside Rd W14 . . . .39 C3
Lakeview 23 E3 . . . . .25 C3
Lakis Cl NW3 . . . . . . .11 B4
Laleham Ho E2 . . . . . .98 C2
Lalor St SW6 . . . . . . .164 B2
Lamb Ho 20 SE5 . . . . .48 B3
11 SE5 . . . . .48 C2
SE10 . . . . .52 B4
Lamb La E8 . . . . .17 A1
Lamb St E1 . . . . .110 C4
Lamb Wlk SE1 . . . . . .138 A3
Lamb's Bldgs EC1 . . . .97 B1
Lamb's Conduit Pas
WC1 . . . . .106 C4
Lamb's Conduit St
WC1 . . . . .94 C1
Lamb's Mews N1 . . . . .86 A3
Lamb's Pas EC1 . . . . .97 B1
Lamberhurst Ho
SE15 . . . . .50 B4
Lambert Ave TW9 . . . .55 A4
Lambert Ho N19 . . . .173 B1
10 N19 . . . . .4 C4
Lambert Rd SW2 . . . .62 B2
Lambert St N1 . . . . . . .14 C1
Lambeth Coll SW2 . . .62 B2
Lambeth Coll (Clapham
Ctr) SW4 . . . . .61 B2
Lambeth Coll (Tower
Bridge Ctr) SE1 . . . .124 B1
Lambeth Coll (Vauxhall
Ctr) SW8 . . . . .171 B4
Lambeth Ct 8
SW18 . . . . .58 C2

Lambeth High St
SE1 ....148 C4
Lambeth Hill EC4 .122 C4
Lambeth Inst Strand Ctr
SW2 ....74 B4
Lambeth North Sta
SE1 ....135 B2
Lambeth Palace *
SE1 ....134 C1
Lambeth Palace Rd
SE1 ....134 C2
Lambeth Pier SE1 .134 B1
Lambeth Rd SE1 ..135 B1
Lambeth Twrs
SE11 ....135 B1
Lambeth Wlk SE11 .149 A4
Lambfold Ho N7 ...14 A2
Lamble St NW5 ....12 C2
Lambolle Pl NW3 ..12 A2
Lambolle Rd NW3 .12 A2
Lambourn Cl 9
NW5 ....13 B4
Lambourn Rd SW4 .61 A4
Lamborne Ho
NW8 ....101 C4
SE16 ....40 C2
Lambrook Terr
SW6 ....164 A4
Lamb's Ct 2 N19 ..5 A3
Lambton Pl W11 ...113 A4
Lambton Rd N19 ...5 A3
Lamerton Lo 10
TW9 ....44 B2
Lamerton St 8 SE8 .51 C4
Lamington St 3
W6 ....39 A2
Lamlash St SE11 ..150 A4
Lamley Ho SE10 ...52 A3
Lammas Rd E9 ......17 C1
Lammermoor Rd
SW12 ....73 A4
Lamont Rd SW10 .157 B3
Lamont Rd Pas
SW10 ....157 B3
Lampard Gr N16 ...7 B3
Lampern Sq 22 ...99 C4
Lampeter Sq W6 ..154 A3
Lamplighter Cl 8
E1 ....25 B1
Lampson Ho 6 N19 .13 B4
Lanark Ho SE1 ....153 B1
Lanark Mans 89 A2
6 W12 ....39 B4
Lanark Pl W9 ....89 A2
Lanark Rd W9 ......88 C3
Lanark Sq E14 .....42 A3
Lanbury Rd SE15 ..65 C3
Lancashire Ct W1 .118 B4
Lancaster Ave SE21, ..
SE27 ....75 C2
Lancaster Cl W2 ..114 A3
N1 ....16 A1
Lancaster Cotts 1
TW10 ....54 A1
Lancaster Ct W1 ..115 A4
SW6 ....155 A1
SE27 ....75 A2
E14 ....34 B1
Lancaster Dr NW3 .12 A2
Lancaster Gate
W2 ....115 A3
Lancaster Gate Sta

Lancaster Gr NW3 ..12 A2
Lancaster Ho SW1 .132 C4
SW15 ....47 B1
SW18 ....71 A4
Lancaster Lo 2 ...
W11 ....31 A3
Lancaster Mews
W2 ....115 A4
2 Richmond TW10 .54 A1
3 SW18 ....59 A2
Lancaster Pk TW10 .54 A2
Lancaster Pl WC2 .120 C3
Lancaster Rd N4 ...5 C4
NW10 ....8 C3
W11 ....31 A3
Lancaster St 1
SE1 ....136 B3
Lancaster Stables 10
NW3 ....12 A2
Lancaster Terr W2 .115 B4
Lancaster Wlk W2 .115 A2
Lancefield Ct 1
N19 ....23 A3
Lancefield Ho SE15 .65 A4
Lancefield St W10 .23 B2
Lancell St N16 .....7 B2
Lancelot Pl SW7 ..130 C3
Lancer Sq 4 W8 ..128 A4
Lanchester Ct W2 .102 C1
Lancing St NW1 ....93 B3
Lancresse Ct N1 ...24 A4
Landale Ho 1 SE16 .40 B3
Landcroft Rd SE22 .64 C1
Landells Rd SE22 ..64 C1
Landford Rd SW15 .57 B4
Landin Ho 1 E14 ..33 C3
Landleys Field 21
N7 ....13 C3
Landmann Ho 18
SE16 ....40 A2
Landmann Way
SE14 ....50 C4
Landon Pl SW1 ...130 C2
Landon Wlk E14 ...34 A2
Landons Cl E14 ...34 B1
Landor Ct N16 .....16 A3
Landor Ho 7 SE5 ..48 C3
Landor Rd SW9 ...62 A4
Landor Wlk 11 W12 .38 C4
Landrake NW1 .....83 A1
Landridge Rd SW6 .164 C2
Landseer Ho NW8 .89 C2
SW1 ....147 C3
SW11 ....169 C3
Landseer Rd N19 ..5 A2
Landulph Ho SE11 .149 C2
Landward Ct W1 ..102 B2
Lane Ct SW11 ......72 B4
Lane The NW8 .....78 C1
Lanercost Cl SW2 .74 C2
Lanercost Rd SW2 .74 C2
Laneway SW15 ....57 A2
Laney Ho EC1 .....107 B4
Lanfranc Rd E3 ....26 A3
Lanfrey Pl W14 ...140 C1
Lang Ho SW8 .....162 A1
3 N19 ....4 B1
Lang St E1 ....25 B1
Langbourne Ave N6 .3 C2
Langbourne Ho 7
SW2 ....62 C2
Langbourne Mans
N6 ....3 C2
Langbourne Prim Sch

Langdale Cl continued
SW14 ....55 A3
Langdale Ho SW1 .146 C1
Langdale Rd SE10 .52 B3
Langdale St 3 E1 ..32 A3
Langdon Ct 86 B1
Langdon Ho 11 E14 .34 B3
Langdon Park Rd N6 .4 B4
Langdon Park Sec Sch
E14 ....34 B3
Langdon Way 5 ...153 C3
SE1 ....153 C3
Langford Cl NW8 ..79 A2
E8 ....16 C3
Langford Ct NW8 ..79 A1
Langford Gn SE5 ..64 A4
Langford Ho 6 SE8 .51 C4
Langford Prim Sch
SW6 ....166 B2
Langford Rd SW6 .166 B2
Langham Ct SW15 .57 C2
5 SW15 ....57 C1
Langham Ho SW4 .61 B2
Langham Mans
SW5 ....142 A1
Langham Pl W1 ...104 B3
W4 ....46 A4
Langham St W1 ...104 B3
Langholm Cl SW12 .73 C4
Langhorne Ct 8
NW8 ....11 C1
Langhurst Ho 169 B2
3 SW11 ....169 B2
Langland Gdns
NW3 ....11 A3
Langland Ho 10 SE5 .48 C3
Langler Rd NW10 ..22 B3
Langley Ct WC2 ...120 A4
SE9 ....172 A4
Langley Dr W3 .....37 A4
Langley Ho 11 E5 ..17 A3
Langley La SW8 ..162 B4
Langley Mans SW8 .162 B4
Langley St WC2 ..106 A1
Langmead Ho 24 E3 .27 A2
Langmore Ho 5 E1 .111 C1
Langport Ho 5
SW9 ....48 A1
Langridge 13 NW5 .12 C2
Langroyd Rd SW17 .72 B2
Langside Ave SW15 .56 C3
Langston Hughes Cl 3
SE24 ....63 A3
Langthorn Ct EC2 .109 C2
Langthorne St SW6 .47 C3
Langton Cl WC1 ...95 A2
Langton Ho SE11 ..149 A4
Langton Pl SW18 ..70 C3
Langton Rd SW9 ..48 A3
Langton St SW10 .157 A3
Langton Way SE3 .53 C3
Langtry Pl SW6 ...155 C4
Langtry Rd NW8 ..78 A3
Langtry Wlk NW8 ..78 C4
Lanhill Rd W9 .....23 C1
Lanier Rd SE13 ....67 C1
Lanner Ho 2 SW11 .60 A4
Lannoy Point SW6 .154 B2
Lanrick Rd E14 ....35 A3
Lansbury Gdns 1
E14 ....34 C3
Lanscombe Wlk
SW8 ....162 A1

Lansdown Ho 28 ...
SE5 ....48 B1
Lansdowne SW15 ..58 A2
Lansdowne Cres
W11 ....112 A3
Lansdowne Dr E8 .16 C1
Lansdowne Gdns
SW8 ....172 A4
Lansdowne Ho 9 ...
W11 ....112 A3
Lansdowne Hill
SE27 ....75 A1
Lansdowne Ho
W11 ....112 C3
Lansdowne Mews
W11 ....112 C3
Lansdowne Pl SE1 .137 C2
Lansdowne Rd ......
W11 ....112 C3
E8 ....16 C1
Lansdowne Rise
W11 ....112 A3
Lansdowne Row
W1 ....118 C2
Lansdowne Sch
SW9 ....62 B4
Lansdowne Terr
WC1 ....94 B1
Lansdowne Way
SW4,SW8 ....172 B3
Lansdowne Wlk
W11 ....112 C3
Lansdowne Wood Cl 1
SE27 ....75 A1
Lant Ho SE1 ....136 C3
Lant St SE1 ....137 A3
Lantern Cl SW15 ..56 C3
Lantern Ho E14 ...41 C4
Lanterns Ct E14 ..41 C3
Lanthorn Ho E14 ..41 A4
Lanvanor Rd SE15 .50 B1
Lanyard Ho 8 SE8 .41 B2
Lapford Cl W9 .....23 B1
Lapsang SE1 ......125 A1
Lapwing Twr 8 SE8 .51 B4
Lapworth Ct W2 ...100 A4
Lara Cl SE13 ....67 B1
Larch Ave W3 .....29 A1
Larch Cl 7 N19 ....4 B2
15 SE8 ....51 B4
SW12 ....73 A2
Larch Ct 5 W9 ....23 B2
Larch Ho 16 SE16 .40 B4
Larch Rd NW2 .....9 B4
Larches Ave SW14 .55 C3
Larchfield Ho 2 N5 .15 B3
Larchmore Ct N19 .5 A2
Larcom St SE17 ...151 A3
Larden Rd W3 .....38 A4
Larissa St SE17 ...151 C3
Lark Hall Inf Sch
SW4 ....171 C1
Lark Hall Jun & Inf Sch
SW4 ....172 A4
Lark Row 2 E2 ....25 B4
Larkfield Rd TW9 ..54 A3
Larkhall La SW4 ..171 C2
Larkhall Rise SW4 .171 B1
Larmenier RC Inf Sch

Lam – Lav   223

Latchmere Rd
SW11 ....168 C1
Latchmere St
SW11 ....168 C2
Latham Ho E1 .....32 C3
Latimer SE17 ......152 A1
Latimer Ho E11 ...113 A3
11 E9 ....17 C2
W4 ....46 A4
Latimer Pl W10 ...30 B3
Latimer Rd W10 ...30 B3
Latimer Road Sta

W10 ....30 C2
Latona Rd SE15 ...49 C4
Latymer Ct W6 ....39 C2
Latymer Upper Sch
W6 ....38 C1
Laud St SE11 .....148 C2
Lauderdale Mans

W9 ....88 B3
Lauderdale Rd W9 .88 C3
Lauderdale Twr
EC2 ....108 C4
Laughton Ho 11 ...
SW2 ....62 C1
Launcelot St SE1 .135 B3
Launceston Pl W8 .128 C1
Launch St E14 .....42 B3
Laundress La N16 .7 C1
Laundry Rd W6 ...154 A3
Laura Pl E5 ....17 B4
Laurel Bank Gdns

SW6 ....165 A2
Laurel Cl 5 N19 ...4 B2
Laurel Ct E8 ....16 B2
5 SW15 ....57 C2
Laurel Rd 3 SW13 .46 C1
Laurel St E8 ....16 B2
Laurel Way N20 ...4 B4
Laurence Mews 12
W12 ....38 C4
Laurence Pountney Hill
EC4 ....123 B4
Laurence Pountney La
EC4 ....123 B4
Laurie Gr SE14 ...51 A2
Laurie Ho SE1 ....136 B1
SE1 ....136 B1
Laurier Rd NW5 ...4 A1
Lauriston Ho 6 E9 .17 C1
Lauriston JMI Sch

E9 ....25 C4
Lauriston Lo 10 ...82
E9 ....82 A1
Lauriston Rd E9 ..17 C1
Lausanne Rd SE15 .50 B2
Lavell St N16 ......15 C4
Lavender Cl 3
SW3 ....157 C3
Lavender Ct SW4 .172 B3
Lavender Gdns
SW11 ....60 B3
Lavender Gr E8 ...16 C1
Lavender Hill SW11 .60 C4
Lavender Ho 14 ...
SE16 ....32 C1
Lavender Rd SE16 .33 A1
SW11 ....59 C4
Lavender Sweep
SW11 ....60 B3
Lavender Terr 12 ...
SW11 ....60 A4
Lavender Wlk SW11 .60 B3

Lavendon Ho NW8 ....**90** B2
Lavengro Rd SE27 ..**75** B2
Lavenham Rd SW18 ..**70** C3
Lavers Rd N16 ....**7** A1
Laverstoke Gdns
SW15 ....**68** C4
Laverton Mews
SW5 ....**142** B3
Laverton Pl SW5 ..**142** B3
Lavina Gr N1 ....**84** C2
Lavington Cl E9 ......**18** B2
Lavington St SE1 ..**122** B1
Law St SE1 ....**137** C2
Lawdale Jun Sch
E2 ....**24** C2 99 C4
Lawford Rd NW5 ....**13** B2
N1 ....**16** A1
W4 ....**45** B3
Lawless Ho ▣ E14 ..**34** B2
Lawless St ▣ E14 ..**34** A2
Lawley St E5 ....**17** A4
Lawman Ct ▣ TW9 ..**44** B2
Lawn Cres TW9 ......**44** C1
Lawn House Cl E14 ..**42** B4
Lawn La SW8 ....**162** C4
Lawn Rd NW3 ....**12** B3
Lawnfield NW6 ......**22** C4
Lawns The N16 ......**16** A3
Lawrence Cl E3 ......**26** C3
  ▣ W12 ....**30** A2
Lawrence Ct N16 ....**7** A1
  ▣ W3 ....**37** B4
Lawrence Ho SW1 ..**147** C3
Lawrence La EC2 ..**109** A2
Lawrence Mans
SW3 ....**158** A3
Lawrence Pl N1 ......**84** B4
Lawrence St SW3 ..**158** A3
E16 ....**35** B2
Lawrence Trad Est
SE10 ....**43** A2
Lawrence's Bldgs ▣
N16 ....**7** B2
Lawson Cl SW19 ....**69** C1
Lawson Ct ▣ N4 ....**5** B3
Lawson Ho ▣ W12 ..**30** A2
Lawton Rd E3 ....**26** A2
Laxfield Ct E8 ......**24** C4
Laxley Cl SE5 ....**48** A3
Laxton Path ▣ SE4 ..**65** C3
Laxton Pl NW1 ......**92** B2
Layard Rd SE16 ......**40** A2
Layard Sq SE16 ......**40** A2
Laycock Prim Sch
N1 ....**15** A2
Laycock St N1 ......**14** C2
Layfield Ho ▣ SE10 ..**43** C1
Laystall Ct EC1 ......**95** B1
Laystall St EC1 ......**95** B1
Layton Ho ▣ E9 ....**25** B4
Layton Pl TW9 ......**44** C2
Layton Rd N1 ....**85** C2
Lazar Wlk ▣ N7 ....**5** B2
Le Moal Ho ▣ E1 ..**32** B4
Lea Ct ▣ W12 ......**38** A4
Lea Ho NW8 ....**90** A1
Lea Int E9 ....**18** C2
Leabank Sq E9 ......**18** C2
Leabourne Rd N16 ..**7** C4
Leacroft Ave SW12 ..**72** B4
Leadenhall Mkt
EC3 ....**110** A1
Leadenhall Pl EC3 ..**110** A1
Leadenhall St EC3 ..**110** A1

Leadenham Ct ▣
E3 ....**26** C1
Leake St SE1 ....**135** A4
SE1 ....**135** B3
Leamington Ct W3 ..**28** C4
  ▣ SE26 ....**76** C1
Leamington Ho
  ▣ W11 ....**31** B4
Leamington Pk W3 ..**28** C4
Leamington Rd Villas
W11 ....**31** B4
Leamore St W6 ......**39** B2
Leamouth Rd E14 ..**34** C3
Leander Ct ▣ E9 ..**17** B1
SE8 ....**51** C2
Leander Rd SW2 ....**62** C1
Leary Ho SE11 ......**149** A1
Leather La EC1 ......**107** C4
Leatherdale St ▣
E1 ....**25** B1
Leatherhead Cl N16 ..**7** B3
Leathermarket Ct
SE1 ....**138** A3
Leathermarket St
SE1 ....**138** A3
Leathwaite Rd
SW11 ....**60** B2
Leathwell Rd SE8 ..**52** A1
Lebanon Gdns
SW18 ....**58** C1
Lebanon Rd SW18 ..**58** C2
Lebus Ho NW8 ......**80** A1
Lechmere Rd NW2 ..**9** A2
Leckford Rd SW18 ..**71** B3
Leckhampton Pl ▣
SW2 ....**74** C4
Lecky St SW7 ....**143** B2
Leconfield Ave
SW13;SW15 ....**56** B4
Leconfield Ho SE5 ..**64** A4
Leconfield Rd N5 ..**15** C4
Leda Ct SW9 ....**163** B1
Ledam Ho EC1 ......**107** B4
Ledbury Ho ▣ SE22 ..**64** A4
Ledbury Mews N
W11 ....**31** C3
Ledbury Mews W
W11 ....**113** B4
Ledbury Rd W11 ....**113** B4
Ledbury St SE15 ....**49** C3
Ledo Ho N1 ....**15** C4
Lee Conservancy Rd
E9 ....**18** B3
Lee High Rd SE13 ..**67** C3
Lee St E8 ....**24** B4
Lee St ▣ N19 ....**13** C3
Lee Valley Sp Ctr
E15 ....**19** A4
Leeke St WC1 ....**94** C4
Leeland Way NW10 ..**8** B4
Leerdam Dr E14 ....**42** B3
Lees Ct W1 ....**117** B4
Lees Ho SE17 ......**151** C1
Lees Pl W1 ....**117** B4
Leeson Rd ▣ SE24 ..**62** C3
Lees Rd E14 ....**15** C4
Leeve Ho ▣ W9 ....**23** B2
Leeward Ct E1 ......**125** C2
Leeway SE8 ....**41** B1
Lefevre Wlk E3 ......**26** C4
Leff Ho ▣ NW6 ....**10** A1
Leffern Rd W12 ......**38** C4
Lefroy Ho SE1 ......**136** C3
Lefroy Rd W12 ......**38** B4
Legard Rd N5 ....**6** A1

Leggatt Rd E15 ......**27** B3
Legge St SE13 ....**67** B2
Legion Cl N1 ....**14** C1
Legion Ct ▣ **119** C4
Leicester Ct WC2 ..**119** C4
Leicester Ho
  ▣ SW9 ....**63** A4
Leicester Ho
  ▣ SW15 ....**69** B4
Leicester Pl WC2 ..**119** C4
Leicester Sq WC2 ..**119** C4
Leicester Square Sta
WC2 ....**119** C4
Leicester St WC2 ..**119** C4
Leigh Ct ▣ SW2 ....**62** C2
Leigh Ho ▣ SW15 ..**56** C2
Leigh Orchard Cl
SW16 ....**74** B1
Leigh Pl EC1 ....**107** B4
Leigh Rd N5 ....**15** A4
  ▣ NW10 ....**22** B1
Leigh St WC1 ....**94** A3
Leigham Ave SW16 ..**74** A1
Leigham Hall ▣
SW16 ....**74** A1
Leigham Hall Par ▣
SW16 ....**74** A1
Leigham Vale SW27,
SW16 ....**74** C2
Leighfield Ho ▣ N4 ..**6** B4
Leighton Cres NW5 ..**13** B3
NW10 ....**22** B3
Leighton Gr NW5 ..**13** B3
Leighton House (Art
Gall & Mus) W14 ..**127** A2
Leighton Pl NW5 ....**13** B3
Leighton Rd NW5 ....**13** B3
Leinster Ave SW14 ..**55** B3
Leinster Ct NW6 ....**23** C2
Leinster Gdns W2 ..**100** C1
W2 ....**114** C4
Leinster Mews W2 ..**114** C4
Leinster Pl W2 ......**100** C1
Leinster Sq W2 ......**100** A1
W2 ....**100** A4
Leinster Terr W2 ..**114** C4
Leitch Ho ▣ NW8 ..**11** C1
Leith Ho ▣ N7 ......**13** C3
  ▣ SW2 ....**74** B4
Leith Mews W9 ......**88** A3
Leith Yd ▣ NW6 ....**23** C4
Leithcote Path
SW16 ....**74** B1
Lelitia Cl E8 ....**24** C4
Leman St E1 ....**111** A1
Lemmon Rd SE10 ..**53** A4
Lemsford Cl N4 ......**6** B2
Len Freeman Pl
SW6 ....**154** C3
Len Williams Ct
NW6 ....**23** C3
Lena Gardens Prim Sch
W6 ....**39** B3
Lena Gdns W6 ......**39** B3
Lendal Terr ▣ SW4 ..**61** C4
Lenham ▣ NW5 ......**12** C2
Lenham Ho SE1 ....**137** C3
Lennard Rd NW2 ....**9** B2
Lennon Rd NW2 ......**9** B2
Lennox Gdns SW1 ..**130** C1
Lennox Gdns Mews
SW1 ....**144** C4
Lennox Ho ▣ E9 ....**17** B2
Lennox Rd N4,N7 ....**5** C2

Lenton Rise TW9 ....**54** A4
Leo St SE15 ....**50** A3
Leo Yd EC1 ....**96** B1
Leonard Ct WC1 ....**94** A2
W8 ....**127** B2
Leonard Day Ho ▣
NW5 ....**13** A2
Leonard Pl ▣ N16 ..**16** A4
Leonard St EC2 ....**97** C2
Leontine Cl SE15 ....**49** C3
Leopards Ct EC1 ..**107** B4
Leopold Bldgs E2 ..**98** C4
Leopold Mews E9 ..**25** B4
Leopold Prim Sch
NW10 ....**8** B1
Leopold Rd NW10 ....**8** B1
  ▣ SW19 ....**69** C1
Leopold St E3 ....**33** B4
Leopold Wlk SE11 ..**148** C1
Leppoc Rd SW4 ....**61** C2
Leroy St SE1 ....**152** A4
Lerwick Ho SW18 ..**59** B3
Lessar Ave SW4 ....**61** B1
Lessar Ct SW4 ......**61** B1
Lessing St SE23 ....**66** A1
Lester Ct ▣ E3 ......**27** A2
Leswin Pl N16 ....**7** B1
Leswin Rd N16 ......**7** B1
Letchford Gdns
NW10 ....**21** C2
Letchford Mews
NW10 ....**21** C2
Letchmore Ho W10 ..**22** B1
Lethbridge Cl SE13 ..**52** B1
Lett Rd E15 ....**19** C1
Letterstone Rd
SW6 ....**154** C1
Lettice St SW6 ......**165** A3
Lettsom St SE5 ......**49** A1
Levana Cl SW19 ....**70** A3
Levant Ho ▣ E1 ....**25** C1
Levehurst Way
SW4,SW9 ....**172** B2
Leven Rd E14 ....**34** C3
Lever Ct ▣ E9 ......**17** C2
Lever St EC1 ....**96** C3
Leverett St SW3 ..**144** B4
Leverington Pl N1 ..**97** C3
Leverstock Ho
SW3 ....**144** B2
Leverton Pl NW5 ....**13** B3
Leverton St NW5 ....**13** B3
Levison Way ▣ N19 ..**4** C3
Levita Ho NW1 ......**93** C4
Levyne Ct EC1 ......**95** B2
Lewes Ho SE1 ......**138** B4
SE15 ....**49** C4
Lewesdon Cl ▣
SW19 ....**69** C3
Leweston Pl N16 ....**7** B4
Lewey Ho E3 ....**26** B1
Lewin Rd SW14 ......**55** C4
Lewis Cl N6 ....**4** A4
Lewis Ct ▣ SE16 ....**40** A1
Lewis Gr SE13 ......**67** B4
Lewis Pl E8 ....**16** C3
Lewis Silkin Ho ▣
SE15 ....**50** B4
Lewis St NW1 ....**13** A2
Lewisham Bridge Prim
Sch SE13 ....**67** A4
Lewisham Bsns Ctr
SE14 ....**50** C4
Lewisham Coll SE4 ..**51** C1
Lewisham Ctr SE13 ..**67** B4

Lewisham High St
SE13 ....**67** A2
SE13 ....**67** B4
Lewisham Hill SE13 ..**52** B1
Lewisham Hospl
SE13 ....**67** A1
Lewisham Pk SE13 ..**67** B1
Lewisham Rd SE13 ..**52** B1
Lewisham St SW1 ..**133** C3
Lewisham Sta SE13 ..**67** B4
Lewisham Way SE4,
SE14 ....**51** B3
Lexden Rd W3 ....**28** A1
Lexfield Ho N5 ......**15** B4
Lexham Gardens Mews
W8 ....**128** B1
Lexham Gdns W8 ..**142** A4
Lexham Mews W8 ..**141** C4
Lexham Wlk W8 ....**128** B1
Lexington St W1 ....**105** A1
Lexton Gdns SW12 ..**73** C3
Ley Ho SE1 ....**136** C3
Leybourne Ho ▣
E14 ....**33** B3
  ▣ SE15 ....**50** B4
Leybourne Rd ▣
NW1 ....**13** A1
Leybourne St ▣
NW1 ....**13** A1
Leyden Mans ▣ N19 ..**5** A4
Leyden St E1 ....**110** C3
Leydon Cl SE16 ....**32** C1
Leyland Ho ▣ E14 ..**34** A2
Leylands SW18 ......**58** B1
Leylang Rd SE14 ....**50** C3
Leys Ct ▣ SW9 ....**173** B1
Leysdown ▣ NW5 ..**12** C2
Leysdown Ho SE17 ..**152** B2
Leysfield Rd W12 ..**38** C4
Leythe Rd W3 ....**37** B4
Leyton Rd E15 ......**19** C2
Leyton Sixth Form Coll
E10 ....**19** C4
Liardet St SE14 ......**51** A4
Liberia Rd N5 ....**15** A2
Liberty Mews SW12 ..**61** A1
Liberty St SW9 ....**173** A4
Libra Rd ▣ E3 ......**26** B3
Library Mans ▣
W12 ....**39** B4
Library Par NW10 ..**21** A4
Library Pl E1 ....**32** A2
Library St SE1 ......**136** B3
Lichfield Ct TW9 ....**54** A3
Lichfield Gdns
TW10,TW9 ....**54** A2
Lichfield Ho ▣ SE5 ..**48** B1
E3 ....**26** B2
  Richmond TW9 ......**44** B2
Lichfield Terr ▣
TW9 ....**54** A2
Lichport Ct N4 ......**6** A3
Lickey Ho W14 ......**155** A4
Lidcote Gdns SW9 ..**173** A1
Liddell Gdns NW10 ..**22** B3
Liddell Rd NW6 ......**10** C2
Lidfield Rd N16 ......**15** C4
Lidgate Rd ▣ SE15 ..**49** B3
Lidiard Rd SW18 ....**71** B2
Lidlington Pl NW1 ..**83** A1
Lidyard Rd N19 ......**4** B3
Liffey Ct NW10 ......**8** C1
Liford Rd SW15 ......**57** C3
Lighter Cl ▣ SE16 ..**41** A2
Lighterman Mews ▣
E1 ....**32** C3

Lighterman's Rd E14 .... 42 A4
Lighterman's Wlk SW18 .... 58 C3
Ligonier St E2 .... 98 C2
Lilac Ho SE4 .... 66 B4
Lilac Pl SE11 .... 148 C3
Lilac St W12 .... 29 C2
Lilburn Ct SW15 .... 57 C4
Lilestone Est NW8 .... 89 C1
Lilestone Ho NW8 .... 89 C2
Lilestone St NW8 .... 90 A2
Lilford Ho 21 SE5 .... 48 C1
Lilford Rd SE5 .... 48 B1
Lilian Baylis Ho N1 .... 15 B2
Lilian Baylis Sch SE11 .... 149 A3
Lilian Baylis Sec Sch SE11 .... 149 A2
Lilley Cl E1 .... 125 C1
Lilian Ave W3 .... 36 C4
Lilian Cl 4 N16 .... 7 A1
Lilian Rd SW13 .... 47 A4
Lillie Ho N5 .... 14 C3
Lillie Rd SW6 .... 156 C2
Lillie Yd SW6 .... 155 B4
Lillieshall Rd SW4 .... 61 B4
Lillingston Ho N1 .... 14 C1
Lily Cl W14 .... 39 C2
Lily Pl EC1 .... 107 C4
Lilyville Rd SW6 .... 164 C4
Limberg Ho SE8 .... 41 B2
Limborough Ho 5 E14 .... 33 C4
Limburg Rd SW11 .... 60 A3
Lime Cl E1 .... 125 C2
Lime Ct SW15 .... 57 A4
Lime Gr W12 .... 39 B4
Lime St EC3 .... 110 A1
Lime St Pas EC3 .... 124 A4
Limeburner La EC4 .... 108 A2
Limeharbour E14 .... 42 A4
Limehouse Cswy E14 .... 33 B2
Limehouse Cut 5 E14 .... 34 A4
Limehouse Fields Est E14 .... 33 A4
Limehouse Link (Tunnel) E14 .... 33 B2
Limehouse Sta E14 .... 33 A3
Limerick Cl 1 SW12 .... 73 B4
Limerston St SW10 .... 157 A3
Limes Ave NW11 .... 1 A4
SW13 .... 46 B1
Limes Ct NW6 .... 9 C1
Limes Field Rd SW14 .... 56 A4
Limes Gdns SW18 .... 58 C1
Limes Gr SE13 .... 67 B3
Limes The W2 .... 113 C3
SE5 .... 64 A4
Limes Wlk SE15 .... 65 B3
Limesford Rd SE15 .... 65 C3
Limetree Cl SW2 .... 74 B3
Limpsfield Ave SW19 .... 69 C2
Linacre Cl SE15 .... 65 B4
Linacre Ct W6 .... 39 C1
Linacre Rd NW2 .... 9 A2
Linale Ho N1 .... 87 C1
Linberry Wlk 2 SE8 .... 41 B2

Lincoln Ave SW19 .... 69 C1
Lincoln Ct N16 .... 6 C4
Lincoln Ho SW1 .... 130 C3
10 SW15 .... 58 A2
Lincoln Mews NW6 .... 23 B4
Lincoln St SW3 .... 144 C3
Lincoln's Inn* WC2 .... 107 A2
Lincoln's Inn Fields WC2 .... 107 A2
Lind St SE8 .... 52 A1
Lindal Rd SE4 .... 66 B2
Lindale SW19 .... 70 A3
Linden Ave NW10 .... 22 C2
Linden Ct 2 W12 .... 30 B1
8 SW18 .... 59 C3
Linden Gdns W2 .... 31 C2
W4 .... 37 C1
Linden Gr SE15 .... 65 B4
Linden Ho 10 SE8 .... 51 B4
8 SE15 .... 65 A4
Linden Lodge Sch SW19 .... 70 A3
Linden Mans N6 .... 4 A3
Linden Mews N1 .... 15 B1
W2 .... 113 C3
Lindens The W4 .... 45 B2
Lindfield Gdns NW3 .... 11 B3
Lindfield Ho NW3 .... 11 B3
Lindfield St E14 .... 33 C3
Lindisfarne Mead E9 .... 18 A4
Lindley Ho E1 .... 32 B4
5 SE15 .... 49 C3
Lindley Pl TW9 .... 44 C2
Lindley St E1 .... 32 B4
Lindo Ho 7 SE15 .... 50 B1
Lindore Rd SW11 .... 60 B3
Lindrop St SW6 .... 166 C2
Lindsay Ct SW11 .... 167 C3
Lindsay Sq SW1 .... 147 C2
Lindsell St 6 SE10 .... 52 B2
Lindsey Ho SW10 .... 157 C2
Lindsey Mews 13 N1 .... 15 B1
Lindsey St EC1 .... 108 B4
Linford Ho 17 E2 .... 24 C4
Linford St SW8 .... 170 C3
Ling Rd E16 .... 35 C4
Ling's Coppice SE21 .... 75 C2
Lingard Ho 8 E14 .... 42 B3
Lingards Rd SE13 .... 67 B3
Lingfield Ho SE1 .... 136 B3
W4 .... 37 B1
Lingham St SW9 .... 172 C1
Lingwell Rd SW17 .... 72 A1
Lingwood Rd E5 .... 7 C4
Linhope St NW1 .... 90 C1
Link St E9 .... 17 B2
Linkenholt Mans W6 .... 38 B2
Links Yd E1 .... 111 A4
Linkway N4 .... 6 B4
Linkwood Wlk NW1 .... 13 C1
Linnell Ho NW8 .... 78 C4
E1 .... 111 A4
Linnell Rd SE5 .... 49 A1
Linnet Mews SW12 .... 72 C4
Linom Rd SW4 .... 62 A3
Linscott Rd E5 .... 17 B4
Linsey St SE16 .... 153 B4
SE16 .... 153 C3
Linslade Ho NW8 .... 90 B2

Linslade Ho *continued*
10 E2 .... 24 C4
Linstead St 6 NW6 .... 10 C1
Linstead Way SW18, SW19 .... 70 A4
Lintaine Cl W6 .... 154 B3
Linthorpe Rd N16 .... 7 A4
Linton Ho 2 E3 .... 33 C4
Linton St N1 .... 87 A3
Linver Rd SW6 .... 166 A2
Linwood Cl SE5 .... 49 B1
Lion Gate Gdns TW9 .... 54 B4
Lion Mills 8 E2 .... 24 C3
Lionel Ho 10 W10 .... 31 A4
Lionel Mans W14 .... 39 C3
Lionel Mews 16 W10 .... 31 A4
Lionel Rd N TW8 .... 36 B1
Lionel Road N TW8 .... 36 A2
Lionel Road Prim Sch TW8 .... 36 A2
Lionel Rd S TW8 .... 36 A2
Lipton Rd E1 .... 32 C3
Lisburne Rd NW3 .... 12 B4
Lisford St SE15 .... 49 B2
Lisgar Terr W14 .... 140 C4
Liskeard Gdns SE3 .... 53 C2
Liskeard Ho SE11 .... 149 C2
Lisle Ct NW2 .... 1 A1
Lisle St WC2 .... 119 C4
Lismore Wlk 4 N1 .... 15 B2
Lissenden Gdns NW5 .... 12 C4
Lissenden Mans NW5 .... 12 C4
Lisson Cotts NW1 .... 102 B4
Lisson Gr NW1,NW8 .... 90 B2
Lisson Ho NW1 .... 102 A4
Lisson St NW1 .... 102 A4
Lister Cl W3 .... 28 C4
Lister Ct N16 .... 7 A2
Lister Ho E1 .... 111 C4
SE3 .... 53 A4
Lister Hospl SW1 .... 146 A1
Lister Mews N7 .... 14 B4
Liston Rd SW4 .... 61 B4
Listowel Cl SW9 .... 163 C2
Listria Lo N16 .... 7 A2
Listria Pk N16 .... 7 A2
Litcham Ho 2 E1 .... 25 C2
Litchfield Gdns NW10 .... 8 C2
Litchfield St WC2 .... 119 C4
Lithos Rd NW3 .... 11 B2
Little Albany St NW1 .... 92 B2
Little Argyll St W1 .... 104 C1
Little Boltons The SW10,SW5 .... 142 B1
Little Britain EC1 .... 108 C3
Little Chelsea Ho SW10 .... 157 A3
Little Chester St SW1 .... 132 A2
Little College St SW1 .... 134 A2
Little Combe Cl 13 SW15 .... 57 C1
Little Dimocks SW12 .... 73 A2
Little Dorrit Ct SE1 .... 137 A4
Little Essex St WC2 .... 121 B4
Little George St SW1 .... 134 A3

Little Green St NW5 .... 13 A4
Little Marlborough St W1 .... 104 C1
Little New St EC4 .... 107 C2
Little Newport St WC2 .... 119 C4
Little Portland St W1 .... 104 C2
Little Road Mans SW6 .... 154 B3
Little Russell St WC1 .... 106 A3
Little Sanctuary SW1 .... 134 A3
Little Smith St SW1 .... 133 C2
Little Somerset St E1 .... 110 C1
Little St James's St SW1 .... 118 C1
Little St Leonards SW14 .... 55 B4
Little Titchfield St W1 .... 104 C3
Little Trinity La EC4 .... 123 A4
*Little Venice** W9 .... 88 C1
Littlebury Rd SW4 .... 61 C4
Littlecote Cl SW19 .... 70 A4
Littlefield Cl N19 .... 13 B4
Littleton St SW18 .... 71 B2
Littlewood SE13 .... 67 B1
Livermere Ct 8 E8 .... 24 B4
Livermere Rd E8 .... 24 B4
Liverpool Gr SE17 .... 151 B1
Liverpool Ho N7 .... 14 C2
Liverpool Rd N1 .... 85 C3
N1,N7 .... 14 C2
E16 .... 35 A4
Liverpool Street Sta EC2 .... 110 A3
Livesey Mus SE15 .... 50 A4
Livesey Pl SE15 .... 49 C4
Livingstone Ho 18 SE5 .... 48 B3
Livingstone Lo 13 W9 .... 31 C4
Livingstone Pl E14 .... 42 B1
Livingstone Rd E15 .... 27 B4
8 SW11 .... 59 C4
Livonia St W1 .... 105 A1
Lizard St EC1 .... 97 A3
Llandovery Ho 1 E14 .... 42 B4
Llanelly Rd NW2 .... 1 B2
Llanvanor Rd NW2 .... 1 B2
Llewellyn St SE16 .... 139 C3
Lloyd Baker St WC1 .... 95 B3
Lloyd Ct SE13 .... 67 A2
Lloyd Ho N16 .... 6 C4
Lloyd Sq WC1 .... 95 B4
Lloyd Villas SE4 .... 51 C1
Lloyd's Ave EC3 .... 110 B1
Lloyd's Bldg* EC3 .... 110 A1
Lloyd's Pl SE3 .... 53 A1
Lloyd's Row EC1 .... 96 A3
Loampit Hill SE13 .... 52 A1
Loampit Vale SE13 .... 67 B4
Loanda Cl 17 E8 .... 24 B4
Loanda Ho SE15 .... 65 B3
Loats Rd SW2 .... 62 A1
Locarno Rd 6 W3 .... 28 B1

Lochaline St W6 .... 47 B4
Lochbie 5 N4 .... 5 A4
Lochinvar St SW12 .... 73 A4
Lochmore Ho SW1 .... 145 C3
Lochnagar St E14 .... 34 B4
Lock Ho N16 .... 7 B3
Lock View Ct 8 E14 .... 33 A2
Lockbridge Ct 8 W9 .... 31 C4
Locke Ho SW8 .... 170 C4
Lockesfield Pl E14 .... 42 A1
Lockgate Cl E9 .... 18 B3
Lockhart Cl N7 .... 14 B2
Lockhart St E3 .... 26 B1
Lockington Rd SW8 .... 170 B4
Lockmead Rd SE13 .... 67 B4
Locksley St E14 .... 33 B4
Lockwood Ho SE11 .... 163 B3
Lockwood Sq SE16 .... 40 A3
Lockyer Est SE1 .... 137 C3
Lockyer Ho SW8 .... 162 A2
2 SE10 .... 43 B1
SW15 .... 57 C4
Lockyer St SE1 .... 137 C3
Locton Gn 2 E3 .... 26 B4
Loddiges Ho 5 E9 .... 17 B1
Loddiges Rd E9 .... 17 B1
Loddon Ho NW8 .... 89 C1
Loder St SE15 .... 50 B3
Lodge Rd NW8 .... 90 A3
Lodore St E14 .... 34 B3
Lodsworth Ho SW11 .... 169 B3
Loftie St SE16 .... 139 C3
Lofting Rd N1 .... 14 C1
Loftus Rd W12 .... 30 A1
Loftus Rd (Queens Park Rangers FC) W12 .... 30 A1
Logan Mews W8 .... 141 B4
Logan Pl W8 .... 141 B4
Loggetts SE21 .... 76 A2
Lohmann Ho 1 SE11 .... 163 B4
Lolesworth Cl E1 .... 111 A3
Lollard St SE11 .... 149 B3
Loman St SE1 .... 136 B4
Lomas St E1 .... 111 C4
Lombard Ct EC3 .... 123 C4
Lombard Ho 4 SE10 .... 52 B3
Lombard La EC4 .... 107 C1
Lombard Rd SW11 .... 167 B2
Lombard St EC3 .... 109 C1
Lombardy Pl W2 .... 114 B3
Lomley Ho 10 SW2 .... 62 C1
Lomond Gr SE5 .... 48 C3
Lomond Ho 10 SE5 .... 48 C2
Loncroft Rd SE5 .... 49 A4
Londale Ct SE10 .... 52 B2
Londesborough Ho N16 .... 16 A4
Londesborough Rd N16 .... 16 A4
London Acad The E14 .... 61 B4
London Aquarium* SE1 .... 134 C3
London Arena E14 .... 42 B3
London Bridge EC4,SE1 .... 123 C3

London Bridge City Pier
SE1 . . . . **124** A2
London Bridge Hospl
SE1 . . . . **123** C2
London Bridge St
SE1 . . . . **123** C2
London Bridge Sta
SE1 . . . . **123** C2
London Business Sch
NW1 . . . .**90** C2
London Canal Mus ★
N1 . . . .**84** B2
London Central
Mosque ★ NW1 . . . . **90** C3
London Chest Hospl
E2 . . . .**25** B3
London Clinic NW1 . .**91** C1
London Coll of Fashion
EC2 . . . . **24** A1 **98** B1
London Coll of Fashion
The W1 . . . .**103** C1
London Coll of Printing
SE1 . . . .**136** B1
London Docklands
Visitor Ctr E14 . . . . .**42** B4
London Dungeon The ★
SE1 . . . . **123** C2
London Eye (Millennium
Wheel) ★ SE1 . . . . .**134** C4
London Fields East Side
E8 . . . .**17** A1
London Fields JMI Sch
E8 . . . .**25** A4
London Fields Sta
E8 . . . .**17** A1
London Fields West Side
E8 . . . .**16** C1
London Foot Hospl
W1 . . . .**93** A1
London Gas Mus The
E3,E16 . . . .**27** C1
London Guildhall Univ
EC2 . . . .**109** B3
E1 . . . .**111** A2
EC3 . . . .**111** A2
E14 . . . .**33** C3
London Guildhall Univ
(Coll of Tech & Design)
E1 . . . .**111** B2
London Ho NW8 . . . . . .**79** C3
London Hospital Dental
Inst E1 . . . .**32** A4
London Hospital
Medical Coll E1 . . . . .**32** A4
London Hospl (Mile
End) The E2 . . . .**25** C2
London Hospl (St
Clements) The E3 . . .**26** B2
London Independent
Hospl The E1 . . . .**32** C4
London Inst The
EC1 . . . .**95** C1
EC1 . . . .**96** C1
W1 . . . .**104** A1
EC1 . . . .**96** B2
London La E8 . . . .**17** B1
London Mews W2 . . .**101** C2
London Nautical Sch
The SE1 . . . .**121** C2
London Oratory Sch The
SW6 . . . .**155** C2

London Peace Pagoda ★
SW3 . . . .**159** A2
Longstone Ave
NW10 . . . .**21** B4
Longthorne Ho 5
E3 . . . .**26** B2
Longton Ave SE26 . . . .**76** C1
Longville Rd SE11 . . .**150** B4
Longwood Dr SW15 . . .**56** B1
Lonsdale Ho 6
SW6 . . . .**58** C4
Lonsdale Mews
W11 . . . .**31** B3
  4 Richmond TW9 . . . .**44** C2
Lonsdale Pl N1 . . . . . .**14** C1
Lonsdale Rd NW6 . . . .**23** B3
W11 . . . .**31** B3
W4 . . . .**38** B2
SW13 . . . .**46** C3
Lonsdale Sq. **6** **85** C4
London Stile 6 W4 . . .**36** C1
London Terr 1 E2 . . . .**24** C3
London Toy & Model
Mus w2 . . . .**114** C4
London Transport Mus ★
WC2 . . . .**120** B4
London Wall EC2 . . . . .**109** B3
London Wharf 4
E2 . . . .**25** A4
London Zoo★ NW1 . . .**81** C2
Long Dr W3 . . . .**29** A3
Long La EC1 . . . .**108** B4
SE1 . . . .**137** C4
Long Meadow 20
N7 . . . .**13** C3
Long Pond Rd SE3 . . . .**53** A2
Long Rd SW4 . . . .**61** B3
Long St E2 . . . .**98** C4
Long Wlk SE1 . . . .**138** B2
Long Yd WC1 . . . .**94** C1
Long's Ct 1 W1 . . . . .**119** C3
Longbeach Rd
SW11 . . . .**60** B4
Longberrys Nr2 . . . . . .**10** B4
Longbow Ho 20 N1 . . .**24** A4
Longbridge Way
SE13 . . . .**67** B2
Longcliffe Ho W1 . . . . .**95** A4
Longfellow Way
SE1 . . . .**153** A3
Longfield Dr SW14 . . . .**55** A2
Longfield Est SE1 . . .**153** A3
Longfield St SW18 . . . .**70** C4
Longford Ct 2 E5 . . . .**18** A3
  1 W12 . . . .**38** A4
Longford Ho 7 E1 . . . .**32** B3
Longford St NW1 . . . . .**92** B2
Longford Wlk 9
SW2 . . . .**74** C4
Longhedge St
SW11 . . . .**169** C2
Longhope Cl SE15 . . . .**49** B4
Longhurst Ho 4
W9 . . . .**23** B2
Longland Ct 1 SE1 . .**153** B2
E9 . . . .**18** A3
Longlands Ct 1 W11 . .**113** A4
Longleat Ho 3 SW1 . .**147** B2
Longleigh Ho 6
SE5 . . . .**49** A2
Longlents Ho 2
NW10 . . . .**20** C4
Longley Ho 5 N19 . . . .**13** B4
Longley St SE1 . . . . .**153** B4
Longman Ho 10 E8 . . . .**24** B4
  9 E2 . . . .**25** C3
Longmoor Point 14
SW15 . . . .**69** A3
Longmore St SW1 . . .**146** C3
Longnor Rd E1 . . . .**25** C2
Longridge Ho SE1 . . .**137** A1
Longridge Rd SW5 . .**141** C3
Longs Ct 2 TW9 . . . . .**54** B3
Longshore SE8 . . . . . .**41** B2
Longstaff Cres
SW18 . . . .**70** C4

Longstaff Rd SW18 . . .**58** C1
Loughborough Ct 7
SW9 . . . .**63** A4
Loughborough Jun & Inf
Schs SW9 . . . .**48** A1
Loughborough Junction
Sta SW9 . . . .**63** A4
Loughborough Pk
SW9 . . . .**63** A3
Loughborough Rd
SE5,SW9 . . . .**48** A1
Loughborough St
SE11 . . . .**149** A1
Louisa Gdns 1 E1 . . . .**25** C1
Louisa Ho SW15 . . . . .**56** B3
Louisa St E1 . . . .**25** C1
Louise Bennett Cl 9
SE24 . . . .**63** A3
Louise De Marillac Ho
1 E1 . . . .**32** B4
Louise White Ho 3
N19 . . . .**4** C3
Louisville Rd SW17 . . .**72** C1
Louvaine Rd SW11 . . . .**59** C3
Lovat La EC3 . . . .**124** A3
Lovatt Ct SW12 . . . . . .**73** A3
Love La EC2 . . . .**109** A2
Love Wlk SE5 . . . .**48** C1
Loveday Ho 2 SW2 . . .**74** C3
Lovegrove St SE1 . . . .**49** C4
Lovegrove Wlk E14 . . .**34** B1
Lovelace Ho 8 E8 . . . .**24** B4
Lovelace Rd SE21 . . . .**75** B3
Lovelinch Cl SE15 . . . .**50** B4
Lovell Ho E8 . . . .**24** C4
Lovell Pl SE16 . . . .**41** A3
Lover's Wlk W1 . . . . .**117** B1
Loveridge Mews
NW6 . . . .**10** B2
Loveridge Rd NW6 . . . .**10** B2
Lovette Ho 3 E3 . . . . .**26** C2
Low Cross Wood La
SE21 . . . .**76** B1
Lowden Rd SE24 . . . . .**63** B3
Lowder Ho 6 E1 . . . . .**32** A1
Lowe Ave E16 . . . .**35** C4
Lowell Ho 5 SE5 . . . . .**48** B3
Lowell St E14 . . . .**33** A3
Lower Addison Gdns
W14 . . . .**126** A3
Lower Belgrave St
SW1 . . . .**132** A1
Lower Clapton Rd
E5 . . . .**17** B4
Lower Comm S
SW15 . . . .**57** A4
Lower Grosvenor Pl
SW1 . . . .**132** B2
Lower Grove Rd
TW10 . . . .**54** B2
Lower James St
W1 . . . .**119** A4
Lower John St W1 . . .**119** A4
Lower Lea Crossing
E14,E16 . . . .**35** A1
Lower Mall w6 . . . .**39** A1
Lower Marsh SE1 . . . .**135** B3
Lower Merton Rise
NW3 . . . .**12** A1
Lower Mortlake Rd
TW9 . . . .**54** B4
Lower Pk Rd 5 SW5 . .**57** C2
Lower Place Bsns Ctr
NW10 . . . .**20** B3
Lower Rd SE1 . . . .**135** B4
SE8 . . . .**40** B4
SE16 . . . .**40** B4

Lower Richmond Rd
SW14,TW9 . . . .**55** A4
SW15 . . . .**57** B4
Lower Robert St
WC2 . . . .**120** B3
Lower Sloane St
SW1 . . . .**145** B2
Lower Terr NW3 . . . .**2** B1
Lower Thames St
EC3 . . . .**124** A3
Lowerwood Ct W11 . . .**31** A3
Loweswater Ho E3 . . . .**26** B2
Lowfield Rd NW6 . . . . .**10** C1
W3 . . . .**28** B4
Lowlands SW6 . . . . . .**166** A2
NW3 . . . .**12** A2
Lowman Rd N7 . . . .**14** B4
Lowndes Cl SW1 . . . .**131** C1
Lowndes Ct W1 . . . . .**131** A2
Lowndes Pl SW1 . . . .**131** B1
Lowndes Sq. SW1 . . .**131** A3
Lowndes St SW1 . . . .**131** B2
Lowood Ho 1 E1 . . . . . .**32** B2
Lowood St E1 . . . .**32** A2
Lowry Ct 8 SE16 . . . . .**40** A1
Lowth Rd SE5 . . . .**48** B1
Lowther Ho NW6 . . . .**147** A1
E8 . . . .**24** B4
Lowther Jun & Inf Sch
SW13 . . . .**46** C4
Lowther Rd N7 . . . .**14** C3
SW13 . . . .**46** B2
Loxford Ho SW1 . . . . .**145** C3
Loxham St WC1 . . . . . .**94** B3
Loxley Rd SW18 . . . . .**71** C3
Lubbock Ho 16 E14 . . .**34** A2
Lubbock St SE14 . . . . .**50** B3
Lucan Ho N1 . . . .**87** C3
Lucan Pl SW3 . . . .**144** B3
Lucas Ct SW11 . . . . . .**169** C3
Lucas Ho SW8 . . . . . .**171** A2
Lucas St SE4,SE8 . . . .**51** C2
Lucas Vale Prim Sch
SE8 . . . .**51** C2
Lucerne Mews W8 . . .**113** C2
Lucerne Rd N5 . . . .**15** A4
Lucey Rd SE16 . . . . . .**139** B1
Lucey Way SE16 . . . . .**153** C4
Lucien Rd SW18 . . . . . .**71** A2
Lucraft Ho 12 SW2 . . .**74** A4
Lucy Ashe Rd SE17 . .**150** B3
Lucy Brown Ho
SE1 . . . .**123** A1
Ludgate Broadway
EC4 . . . .**108** B1
Ludgate Cir EC4 . . . . .**108** A1
Ludgate Hill EC4 . . . .**108** B1
Ludgate Sq. EC4 . . . .**108** B1
Ludham NW5 . . . .**12** B3
Ludlow Ct W3 . . . .**37** B4
Ludlow St EC1 . . . .**96** C2
Ludovick Wlk SW15 . . .**56** A3
Ludwick Mews
SE14 . . . .**51** A3
Lugard Ho 12 W12 . . . .**30** A1
Lugard Rd SE15 . . . . . .**50** A2
Luke Ho 31 E1 . . . .**32** A3
Luke St EC2 . . . .**24** A1 **98** A2
Lukin St E1 . . . .**32** B3
Lullingstone Ho 2
SE15 . . . .**50** B4
Lullingstone La
SE13 . . . .**67** C1
Lulot Gdns N19 . . . .**4** A2
Lulworth SE17 . . . . . .**151** B2
NW1 . . . .**13** C1

Lulworth Ho SW8 .....162 C1
Lulworth Rd SE15 .....50 A1
Lumley Ct WC2 .....120 B3
Lumley Flats SW1 .....145 B2
Lumley St W1 .....103 C1
Lumsden Ho 78 B3
Lunan Ho 12 E3 .....26 B3
Lund Point E15 .....27 B4
Lupin Cl SW2 .....75 A2
Lupin Point SE1 .....139 A3
Lupton St NW5 .....13 B4
Lupus St SW1 .....147 A1
Luralda Gdns E14 .....42 C1
Lurgan Ave W6 .....47 C4
Lurline Gdns
   SW11 .....169 C4
Luscombe Ho SW18 .....58 B2
Luscombe Way
   SW8 .....162 A2
Lusher Ho SW15 .....57 C1
Lushington Rd
   NW10 .....22 A3
Lushington Terr
   E8 .....16 C3
Luton Pl SE10 .....52 B3
Luton St NW8 .....89 C1
Luttrell Ave SW15 .....57 A2
Lutyens Ho SW1 .....146 C1
Luxborough Ho
   W1 .....103 B4
Luxborough St W1 .....103 B4
Luxborough Twr
   W1 .....103 B4
Luxemburg Gdns
   W6 .....39 C2
Luxford St SE16 .....40 C2
Luxmore St SE4 .....51 B2
Luxor St SE5 .....63 B4
Lyal Rd E3 .....26 A3
Lyall Ave SE21 .....76 A1
Lyall Mews SW1 .....131 B1
Lyall Mews W SW1 .....131 B1
Lyall St SW1 .....131 B1
Lycee Francais Charles
   de Gaulle (French Univ
   Coll) SW7 .....143 B4
LyceThe SE11 .....149 C1
Lycett Ho 10 SW2 .....74 A4
Lycett Pl 8 W12 .....38 C4
Lydden Gr SW18 .....71 A4
Lydden Rd SW18 .....71 A4
Lydford NW1 .....83 A3
Lydford Cl 22 N16 .....16 A3
Lydford Rd NW2 .....9 C2
   W9 .....23 B1
Lydgate Ho 8 N16 .....16 A3
Lydhurst Ave SW2 .....74 B2
Lydney Cl SE15 .....49 A3
   SW19 .....70 A2
Lydon Rd SW4 .....61 B4
Lydwell Ho SW8 .....171 B1
Lyford Rd SW18 .....72 A3
Lygoe Ho 10 N6 .....4 C4
Lygon Ho E2 .....99 B4
Lygon Pl SW1 .....132 A1
Lyham Cl SW2 .....62 A1
Lyham Rd SW2 .....62 A1
Lyly Ho SE1 .....137 C1
Lyme Gr E9 .....17 B1
Lyme Grove Ho 2
   E9 .....17 B1
Lyme St NW1 .....82 C4
Lyminge Gdns
   SW17,SW18 .....72 A3
Lymington Lo E14 .....42 C3

Lymington Mans
   NW6 .....11 A2
Lymington Rd NW6 .....11 A2
Lympstone Gdns
   SE15 .....49 C3
Lynbrook Cl SE15 .....49 A3
Lynch Cl SE3 .....53 B3
Lynch Wlk 2 SE8 .....51 B4
Lyncott Cres SW4 .....61 A3
Lyncourt SE3 .....52 C1
Lyncroft Mans 4
   NW6 .....10 C3
Lyndale NW2 .....1 B1
Lyndale Ave NW2 .....1 B1
Lyndale Cl SE3 .....53 B4
Lynde Ho 2 SW4 .....61 C4
Lynden Gate SW15 .....69 A3
Lyndhurst Gdns
   NW3 .....11 C3
Lyndhurst Gr SE5 .....49 B1
   SE15 .....49 B1
Lyndhurst Ho 2
   SW15 .....68 C4
Lyndhurst Lo 8
   E14 .....42 C2
Lyndhurst Rd NW3 .....11 C3
Lyndhurst Sch SE5 .....49 B1
Lyndhurst Terr
   NW3 .....11 C3
Lyndhurst Way SE15 .....49 B1
Lyneham Wlk E5 .....18 A3
Lynette Ave SW4 .....61 B1
Lynford French Ho
   SE17 .....150 C2
Lynmouth Rd N16 .....7 B3
Lynn Ho SE15 .....49 C4
Lynn Rd SW12 .....73 A4
Lynne Way NW10 .....8 A2
Lynnett Ct E9 .....18 A2
Lynton Cl NW10 .....8 B3
Lynton Est 1 SE1 .....153 B3
Lynton Ho W2 .....100 B1
Lynton Lo N5 .....15 A3
Lynton Mans SE1 .....135 B1
Lynton Rd N8 .....5 C4
   NW6 .....23 B3
   W3 .....28 A2
Lynton Terr 4 W3 .....28 B3
Lynwood Rd SW17 .....72 B1
Lyon Ho NW8 .....90 A1
Lyon St N1 .....14 B1
Lyons PI NW8 .....89 B1
Lyons Wlk W14 .....140 A4
Lyric Rd SW13 .....46 B2
Lysander Ho 10 E2 .....25 A3
Lysander Rd NW10 .....21 A1
Lysia St SW6 .....47 C3
Lysias Rd SW12 .....61 A1
Lytcott Gr SE22 .....64 B2
Lytham St SE17 .....151 B1
Lyttelton Cl NW3 .....12 A1
Lyttelton Ho 13 E9 .....17 B1
Lyttleton Ho 11 E9 .....17 B1
Lytton Ct WC1 .....106 B3
Lytton Gr SW15 .....58 A1

M

Mabel Thornton Ho 12
   N16 .....15 C4
Mableton Pl NW1,
   WC1 .....93 C3
Mablethorpe Rd
   SW6 .....154 A1
Mabley St E9 .....18 A3
Mac's End E14 .....107 C2
MacArthur Ho 4
   SW2 .....74 A4
Macaulay CE Prim Sch
   SW4 .....61 A3
Macaulay Ct SW4 .....61 A4
Macaulay Ho 3 W6 .....N16 .....7 A1
   2 W10 .....31 A4
Macaulay Rd SW4 .....61 A3
Macaulay Sq SW4 .....61 A3
Macbeth Ho N1 .....24 A3
Macbeth St W6 .....39 A1
Macclesfield Rd
   EC1 .....96 C4
Macclesfield St
   W1 .....119 C4
Macdonald Ho 7
Macdonald Rd N19 .....4 B2
Macduff Rd SW11 .....169 B4
Mace Cl E1 .....32 A1
Mace St E2 .....25 C3
Macey Ho 3 SW11 .....168 A3
   8 SE10 .....52 B4
Macfarlane Rd W12 .....30 B1
Macfarren Ho 6
   W10 .....23 A2
MacFarren Pl NW1 .....91 C1
MacGregor Ho 2
   SW12 .....73 B3
Machell Rd SE15 .....65 B4
Mackay Ho 33 W12 .....30 A2
Mackay Rd SW4 .....61 A4
Mackennal St NW8 .....80 B2
Mackenzie Cl 7
   W12 .....30 A2
Mackenzie Rd N7 .....14 B2
Mackenzie Wlk E14 .....33 C1
Mackeson Rd NW3 .....12 B4
Mackie Ho 9 SW2 .....74 C4
Mackie Rd SW2 .....74 C4
Mackintosh La E9 .....17 C3
Macklin St WC2 .....106 B2
Mackonochie Ho
   EC1 .....107 B4
Mackrow Wlk 11
   E14 .....34 B2
Macks Rd SE16 .....153 C4
Mackworth Ho NW1 .....92 C4
Mackworth St NW1 .....92 C4
Maclean Rd SE23 .....66 A1
Macleod St SE17 .....151 A1
Maclise Rd W14 .....126 A1
Macmillan Ho NW4 .....9 A4
   NW8 .....90 B3
Macnamara Ho
   SW10 .....157 B2
Maconochies Rd
   E14 .....42 A1
Macquarie Way E14 .....42 A2
Macready Ho W1 .....102 B3
Macready Pl 2 N7 .....14 A4
Mackworth St NW1 .....92 C4
Macroom Ho W9 .....23 B2
Macroom Rd W9 .....23 B2
Madame Tussaud's &
   Planetarium*
   NW1 .....91 B1
Maddams St E3 .....27 A1

Maddock Way SE17 .....48 A4
Maddocks Ho 3 E1 .....32 A2
Maddox St W1 .....104 C1
   W1 .....118 C4
Madinah Rd E8 .....16 C3
Madison Cl 6 E3 .....27 A2
Madison Ho E3 .....27 A2
Madras Pl N7 .....14 C2
Madrid Rd SW13 .....46 C3
Madron St SE17 .....152 B2
Mafeking Ave 8 E6 .....N44 .....A4
Magdala Ave N19 .....4 B2
Magdalen Pas E1 .....125 A4
Magdalen Rd SW18 .....71 C3
Magdalen St SE1 .....124 A1
Magdalene Cl 7
   SE15 .....50 A1
Magdalene Ho 7
   SW15 .....57 C1
Magee St SE11 .....163 C4
Magellan Ho 16 E1 .....25 C1
Magellan Pl 10 E14 .....41 C2
Magnin Pl 5 SE8 .....51 A4
Magnolia Ct
   Richmond TW9 .....45 A2
   SW11 .....60 B1
Magnolia Ho 18 SE8 .....51 B4
Magnolia Pl SW4 .....62 A2
Magnolia Rd W4 .....45 A4
Magnolia Wharf
   W4 .....45 A4
Magpie Alley EC4 .....107 C1
Magpie Pl SE14 .....51 A4
Maguire St SE1 .....139 A4
Mahatma Ganhi Ind Est
   11 SE24 .....63 A3
Mahogany Cl SE16 .....33 A1
Mahoney Ho SE14 .....51 B2
Maida Ave W2 .....89 A1
Maida Vale W9 .....88 C3
Maida Vale Psychiatric
   Hospl W9 .....23 C2
Maida Vale Sta W9 .....88 B4
Maiden La WC2 .....120 B4
   SE1 .....123 A2
   NW1 .....13 C1
Maidenstone Hill
   SE10 .....52 B2
Maidstone Bldgs
   SE1 .....123 B1
Maidstone Ho 4
   E14 .....34 A3
Mail Coach Yd E2 .....98 B4
Maismore St SE15 .....49 C4
Maitland Cl 5 SE10 .....52 A3
Maitland Ct W2 .....115 B4
Maitland Ho SW1 .....160 C4
   17 E2 .....25 B3
Maitland Park Rd
   NW3 .....12 B2
Maitland Park Villas
   NW3 .....12 B2
Maitland Pl E5 .....17 B4
Majestic Ct N4 .....6 A3
Major Rd SE16 .....139 C2
   E15 .....19 C3
Makepeace Ave N6 .....3 C2
Makepeace Mans N6 .....3 C2
Makins St SW3 .....144 B3
Malabar Ct 12 W12 .....30 A2
Malabar St E14 .....41 C4
Malacca Ho E1 .....33 A4
Malam Ct SE11 .....149 B3
Malam Gdns 3 E14 .....34 A2
Malay Ho 2 E1 .....32 B1
Malbrook Rd SW15 .....57 A3

Maddox Way SE17 .....48 A4
Malcolm Ho 13 N1 .....24 A3
Malcolm Pl E2 .....25 B1
Malcolm Rd E1 .....25 B1
Malcolmson Ho
   SW1 .....147 C1
Malden Cres NW1 .....12 C2
Malden Pl NW5 .....12 C3
Malden Rd NW5 .....12 C2
Maldon Cl N1 .....87 A4
   E15 .....19 C3
   SE5 .....64 A4
Maldon Rd W3 .....28 B2
Malet Pl WC1 .....93 B1
Malet St WC1 .....105 C4
Maley Ave SE27 .....75 A2
Malfort Rd SE5 .....64 A4
Mall Rd W6 .....39 A1
Mall Studios 9
   NW3 .....12 B3
Mall The SW1 .....119 B1
   SW14 .....55 B2
Mallams Mews 2
   SW9 .....63 A4
Mallard Cl 5 E9 .....18 B2
   NW6 .....23 C4
Mallard Ho NW8 .....80 A1
   7 SE15 .....49 B2
Mallard Point 5 E3 .....26 C2
Mallet Ho 16 SW15 .....56 C2
Mallet Rd SE13 .....67 C1
Malling SE13 .....67 A2
Mallinson Rd SW11 .....60 B2
Mallon Gdns E1 .....111 A3
Mallord St SW3 .....157 C4
Mallory Bldgs EC1 .....96 A1
Mallory Cl SE4 .....66 A3
Mallory Ho E14 .....34 B4
Mallory St NW8 .....90 B2
Mallow Ct E14 .....42 B4
Mallow St EC1 .....97 B2
Malmesbury 33 E2 .....25 B3
Malmesbury Inf Sch
   E2 .....25 B3
Malmesbury Rd 26 E3 .....26 B3
   E16 .....35 A4
Malmesbury Terr
   E16 .....35 B4
Malmsey Ho SE11 .....149 A2
Malmsmead Ho E9 .....18 A3
Malorees Jun & Inf Schs
   NW6 .....9 C1
Malpas Rd E8 .....17 A2
   SE4 .....51 B1
Malt Mill SE1 .....124 C1
Malt St SE1 .....49 C4
Malta St EC1 .....96 B2
Maltby St SE1 .....138 C2
Malthouse Dr W4 .....46 B4
Malthouse Pas
   SW13 .....46 A1
Malting Ho E14 .....33 B2
Maltings W4 .....36 C1
Maltings Cl SW13 .....46 A1
Maltings Lo W4 .....46 A3
Maltings Pl SW6 .....166 B3
Malton Mews W10 .....31 A3
Malton Rd W10 .....31 A3
Maltravers St WC2 .....121 B4
Malva Cl SW18 .....59 A2
Malvern Cl W10 .....31 B4
Malvern Ct SW7 .....143 C4
Malvern Gdns NW2 .....1 A2
Malvern Ho N16 .....7 B3

Malvern Mews NW6 ...23 C2
Malvern Pl NW6 ...23 B2
Malvern Rd N19 ...4 C3
  E8 ...16 C1
  NW6 ...23 C2
Malvern Terr N1 ...85 B4
Malwood Rd SW12 ...61 A1
Malyons Rd SE13 ...67 A2
Malyons Terr SE13 ...67 A2
Managers St E14 ...34 B1
Manaton Cl SE15 ...65 A4
Manbre Rd W6 ...47 B4
Manchester Dr W10 ...23 A1
Manchester Gr E14 ...42 B1
Manchester Ho
  SE17 ...151 A2
Manchester Mans
  N19 ...4 C4
Manchester Mews
  W1 ...103 B3
Manchester Rd E14 ...42 B3
Manchester Sq
  W1 ...103 C2
Manchester St W1 ...103 B3
Manchuria Rd
  SW11 ...60 C1
Manciple St SE1 ...137 C2
Mandalay Ho N16 ...16 C4
Mandalay Rd SW4 ...61 B2
Mandarin Ct **6** SE8 ...51 C4
Mandela Cl **9** W12 ...30 A2
Mandela Ho E2 ...98 C4
Mandela Rd E16 ...35 C3
Mandela St NW1 ...83 A4
  SW9 ...163 B1
Mandela Way SE1 ...152 B4
Manderville Ho
  SE1 ...153 A2
Mandeville Cl **5**
  SE3 ...53 B3
Mandeville Ctyd
  SW11 ...169 B3
Mandeville Ho **6**
  SW4 ...61 B2
Mandeville Pl W1 ...103 C2
Mandrake Rd SW17 ...72 B1
Mandrell Rd SW2 ...62 A2
Manette St W1 ...105 C1
Manfred Ct **8**
  SW15 ...58 B2
Manfred Rd SW15 ...58 B2
Manger Rd N7 ...14 A2
Manilla St E14 ...41 C4
Manitoba Ct **23**
  SE16 ...40 B4
Manley Ct N16 ...7 B1
Manley Ho SE11 ...149 B2
Manley St NW1 ...81 B4
Mannebury Prior
  N1 ...85 A1
Mannering Ho **7** E9 ...25 B4
Mannering Ho **16**
  SW2 ...62 B2
Manning Ho **3**
  W11 ...31 A3
Manning Pl TW10 ...54 B1
Manningford Cl EC1 ...96 A4
Manningtree Cl
  SW19 ...70 A3
Manningtree St E1 ...111 B2

Manny Shinwell Ho
  SW6 ...155 A3
Manor Ave SE4 ...51 B1
Manor Circus TW9 ...54 C4
Manor Ct SW6 ...166 B3
  W3 ...36 C2
  SE15 ...49 B2
  7 SW2 ...62 B2
  SW16 ...74 A1
Manor Gdns SW4 ...171 A1
  N7 ...14 A4
  W3 ...36 C2
  Richmond TW10,TW9 ...54 B3
Manor Gr SE15 ...50 B4
  Richmond TW9 ...54 C4
Manor Ho E15 ...27 C4
Manor House NW1 ...102 B4
Manor House Ct
  W9 ...88 C1
Manor House Dr
  NW6 ...9 C1
Manor Mans **7** N7 ...5 A1
Manor Mews NW6 ...23 C3
  SE4 ...51 B1
Manor Oak Mans
  SE22 ...65 A1
Manor Par N16 ...7 B2
Manor Park Rd
  NW10 ...21 B4
Manor Pk
  Richmond TW9 ...54 B3
  SE13 ...67 C2
Manor Rd N16 ...7 A3
  N16 ...7 A2
  Richmond TW9 ...54 B4
Manor Sch NW6 ...10 A1
Manor Street Est
  SW3 ...158 B4
Manor The W1 ...118 A3
Manor Way W3 ...36 C2
Manorfield Cl **8**
  N19 ...13 B4
Manorfield JMI Sch
  E14 ...34 A4
Manresa Rd SW3 ...144 A1
Manse Rd N16 ...7 B1
Mansel Ct SW11 ...168 B3
Mansel St E1 ...111 A1
Mansell Ho SW8 ...171 A4
Mansell Rd W3 ...37 C4
Mansell Ct **13** E2 ...24 B4
Mansfield Ho SW15 ...57 C1
Mansfield Mews
  W1 ...104 A3
Mansfield Pl **11**
  NW3 ...11 B4
Mansfield Rd NW3 ...12 B4
  W3 ...20 A1
Mansfield St W1 ...104 A3
Mansford St E2 ...25 A2
Mansion Cl SW9 ...173 C4
Mansion Gdns NW3 ...2 A1
Mansion House ★
  EC4 ...109 B1
Mansion House Pl
  EC3,EC4 ...109 B1
Mansion House St
  EC2 ...109 B1
Mansion House Sta
  EC4 ...123 A4
Mansions The NW6 ...10 B3
Manson Mews
  SW7 ...143 B3

Manson Pl SW7 ...143 B3
Manston NW1 ...13 A1
Manstone Rd NW2 ...10 A3
Mantell Ho NW5 ...12 C2
Mantle Rd SE4 ...66 A4
Manton Ho N16 ...6 C1
Mantua St **20** SW11 ...59 C4
Mantus Cl E1 ...25 B1
Mantus Rd E1 ...25 B1
Manville Gdns
  SW17 ...73 A1
Manville Rd SW17 ...73 A1
Manwood Rd SE4 ...66 B1
Many Gates SW12 ...73 A2
Mape St E2 ...25 A1
Mapes Ho **5** NW6 ...10 A1
Mapesbury Ct NW2 ...10 A3
Mapesbury Rd NW2 ...10 A2
Mapeshill Pl NW2 ...9 B2
Maple Ave W3 ...29 A1
Maple Cl SW4 ...61 C1
Maple Ho **8** NW3 ...12 B2
Maple Ho **7** SE8 ...51 B3
Maple Leaf Sq **27**
  SE16 ...40 C4
Maple Lo SW15 ...58 A1
Maple Mews NW6 ...78 A2
Maple Pl W1 ...93 A1
Maple St W1 ...93 A1
Maple Wlk W10 ...22 C1
Mapledene E8 ...16 C1
Mapledene Rd E8 ...16 C1
Maples Pl E1 ...32 A4
Maplestead Rd SW2 ...74 B4
Mapleton Cres
  SW18 ...59 A1
Mapleton Rd SW18 ...59 A1
Maplin St E3 ...26 B2
Marada Ho NW6 ...10 A1
Marais W4 ...45 B3
Marban Rd W9 ...23 B2
Marble Arch W1 ...103 A1
Marble Arch **17**
  W1 ...117 A4
Marble Arch Sta
  W1 ...103 A1
Marble Cl W3 ...28 A1
Marble Ho W9 ...23 B1
Marbleford Ct **4** N6 ...4 C4
March Ct SW15 ...57 A3
Marchant Ct SE1 ...153 A2
Marchant Ho **13**
  SW2 ...62 B2
Marchbank Rd
  W14 ...155 A4
Marchmont Rd
  TW10 ...54 B2
Marchmont St WC1 ...94 A2
Marchwood Cl **17**
  SE5 ...49 A3
Marcia Rd SE1 ...152 B3
Marcilly Rd SW18 ...59 C2
Marco Rd W6 ...39 B3
Marcon Ct **8** E8 ...17 A3
Marcon Pl E8 ...17 A3
Marcus Ct **7** E15 ...27 C4
Marcus Garvey Mews
  SE22 ...65 A2
Marcus Garvey Way **6**
  SE24 ...62 C3
Marcus Ho **13** SE15 ...49 B2
Marcus St SW18 ...59 A1
Marcus Terr SW18 ...59 A1
Marden Ho **6** E8 ...17 A3
Marden Sq SE16 ...40 A3
Mardyke Ho SE17 ...151 C4

Mare St E8 ...17 A2
  E8,E2 ...25 A4
Maresfield Gdns
  NW3 ...11 B2
Margaret Bondfield Ho
  22 N7 ...13 C3
  E3 ...26 A3
Margaret Ct W1 ...104 C2
Margaret Herbison Ho
  SW6 ...155 A3
Margaret Ho **10** W6 ...39 B1
Margaret Ingram Cl
  SW6 ...154 C3
Margaret Mcmillan Ho
  10 N19 ...4 C4
Margaret Rd N16 ...7 B3
Margaret St W1 ...104 C2
Margaret's Ct
  SE1 ...123 B1
Margaretta Terr
  SW3 ...158 B4
Margate Rd SW2 ...62 A2
Margery Fry Ct N7 ...5 A1
Margery St WC1 ...95 B3
Margravine Gdns
  W6 ...140 A2
  W14 ...39 C1
Margravine Rd
  W6 ...154 A4
Marham Gdns SW17,
  SW18 ...72 A3
Maria Cl SE1 ...153 A3
Maria Fidelis Convent
  Sch
  NW1 ...93 A3
  NW1 ...93 B4
Maria Terr E1 ...25 C1
Marian Ct E9 ...17 B3
Marian Pl E2 ...25 A3
Marian Sq E2 ...25 A3
Marian St **8** E2 ...25 A3
Marian Way NW10 ...8 B1
Marie Curie SE5 ...49 A2
Marie Lloyd Ct **13**
  SW9 ...173 B4
Marie Lloyd Gdns **1**
  N19 ...5 A4
Marie Lloyd Ho N1 ...87 B1
Marigold St SE16 ...40 A4
Marina Ct **11** E3 ...26 C2
Marine Ct SE16 ...33 B1
Marine Twr **20** SE8 ...51 B4
Marinefield Rd
  SW6 ...166 B2
Marinel Ho **25** SE5 ...48 B3
Mariners Mews E14 ...42 C2
Marion Richardson JMI
  Sch E1 ...32 C3
Marischal Rd SE13 ...67 C4
Maritime Ho **5**
  SW4 ...61 B4
Maritime St E3 ...26 B1
Marius Mans **8**
  SW17 ...72 C2
Marius Rd SW17 ...72 C2
Marjorie Gr SW11 ...60 B3
Mark Ho **8** E2 ...25 C3
Mark La EC3 ...124 B4
Mark Mans W12 ...38 C4
Mark Sq EC2 ...98 A2
Mark St EC2 ...98 A2
Market Ct W1 ...104 C2
Market Mews W1 ...118 A1
Market Pl W1 ...104 C2
  8 W3 ...28 B1

Market Pl continued
  1 SE16 ...40 A2
Market Rd N7 ...14 A2
  Mortlake TW9 ...54 C4
Market Sq E14 ...34 A3
Market Way E14 ...34 A3
Markham Sq SW3 ...144 C2
Markham St SW3 ...144 B2
Markland Ho W10 ...30 C2
Marksbury Ave TW9 ...54 C4
Markstone Ho SE1 ...136 A3
Markyate Ho W10 ...22 B1
Marl Rd SW18 ...59 B3
Marland Ho SW1 ...131 A2
Marlborough
  W9 ...88 C4
Marlborough **11**
  SW19 ...69 C3
Marlborough Ave **3**
  E8 ...24 C4
Marlborough Cl
  SE17 ...150 B3
Marlborough Cres
  W4 ...38 A3
Marlborough Ct
  W8 ...141 B4
Marlborough Day Hospl
  NW8 ...78 C2
Marlborough Flats
  SW3 ...144 B4
Marlborough Gr
  SE1 ...153 B1
Marlborough Hill
  NW8 ...79 A3
Marlborough Ho
  NW8 ...78 C1
  N4 ...6 B3
  Richmond TW10 ...54 C2
  SW19 ...69 C1
Marlborough House ★
  SW1 ...119 A1
Marlborough Mans **5**
  NW6 ...10 C3
Marlborough Prim Sch
  SW3 ...144 B3
Marlborough Rd
  SW1 ...119 A1
  N19 ...4 C2
  W4 ...37 B1
  Richmond TW10 ...54 B1
Marlborough St
  SW3 ...144 B3
Marlborough Trad Est
  TW9 ...45 A2
Marlborough Yd N19 ...4 C2
Marlbury NW8 ...78 B3
Marley Ho **14** W11 ...30 C2
Marley Wlk NW2 ...9 B3
Marlin Ho SW15 ...58 A2
Marloes Rd W8 ...128 A1
Marlow Ct NW6 ...9 C1
Marlow Ho E2 ...98 C3
  SE1 ...138 C2
  12 W2 ...100 B1
Marlow Studio
  Workshops E2 ...98 C3
Marlow Way SE16 ...40 C4
Marlowe Bsns Ctr **2**
  SE14 ...51 A3
Marlowe Ct SW3 ...144 B3
Marlowe Ho **15** N16 ...16 A4
  SE8 ...41 B1
Marlowes The NW8 ...79 B4
Marlston NW1 ...92 B3
Marlton St SE10 ...43 B1

Marmion Ho 13 SW12 ...73 A4
Marmion Mews 4 SW11 ...60 C3
Marmion Rd SW11 ...60 C3
Marmont Rd SE15 ...49 C3
Marmora Ho E1 ...33 A4
Marmora Rd SE22 ...65 B1
Marne St W10 ...23 A2
Marner Prim Sch E3 ...27 A1
Marney Rd SW11 ...60 C3
Marnham Cres Gr W3 ...37 A4
Marnham Ave NW2 ...10 A4
Marnock Ho SE17 ...151 B2
Marnock Rd SE4 ...66 B2
Maroon Ho 16 E14 ...33 A4
Maroon St E14 ...33 A4
Marquess Rd N N1 ...15 C2
Marquess Rd N1 ...15 C2
Marquess Rd S 17 N1 ...15 B2
Marquis Ct N4 ...5 C3
Marquis Rd N4 ...5 C3
NW1 ...13 C2
Marrayat Sq SW6 ...164 A4
Marrick Cl SW15 ...56 C3
Marrick Ho NW6 ...78 B3
Marriott Rd N4 ...5 B3
Marryat Ct 12 W6 ...39 A2
Marryat Ho 1 SW1 ...146 C1
Marsala Rd SE13 ...67 A3
Marsalis Ho 3 E3 ...26 C2
Marsden Rd SE15 ...64 B4
Marsden St NW5 ...12 C2
Marsh Ct E8 ...16 C2
Marsh Hill E9 ...18 A3
Marsh Ho SW1 ...147 C1
SW8 ...171 A4
Marsh St E14 ...42 A2
Marsh Wall E14 ...42 A2
Marshall Cl SW18 ...59 B1
Marshall Ho N1 ...87 C2
SE17 ...151 B2
NW6 ...23 B3
Marshall St W1 ...105 A1
Marshall's Pl SE16 ...139 A1
Marshalsea Rd SE1 ...137 A4
Marsham Ct SW1 ...147 C4
19 SW19 ...69 C3
Marsham St SW1 ...147 C4
Marshfield St E14 ...42 B3
Marshgate Bsns Ctr E15 ...27 B3
Marshgate La E15 ...19 A1
Marshwood Ho 10 NW6 ...23 C4
Marsland Cl SE17 ...150 B1
Marsom Ho N1 ...87 B1
Marston SE17 ...151 A1
Marston Cl NW6 ...11 B1
Marston Ho 8 SW9 ...173 C1
Marsworth Ho 8 E2 ...24 C4
Martaban Rd N16 ...7 B2
Martel Pl E8 ...16 B2
Martell Rd SE21 ...75 C1
Martello St E8 ...17 A1
Martello Terr E8 ...17 A1
Martha St 1 E1 ...32 B3
Martin Ct 10 E14 ...42 B4
Martin Ho SW8 ...162 A2

Martin La EC4 ...123 C4
Martindale SW14 ...55 B2
Martindale Ave 5 E16 ...35 C2
Martindale Ho 20 E14 ...34 A2
Martindale Rd SW12 ...73 A4
Martineau Ho SW1 ...146 C1
Martineau Mews N5 ...15 A4
Martineau Rd N5 ...15 A4
Martlett Ct WC2 ...106 B1
Martlett Lo NW3 ...11 A4
Martley Ho SW8 ...171 A4
Martock Ct 10 SE15 ...50 A2
Marton Rd 2 N16 ...7 A1
Marvel Ho 5 SE5 ...48 C3
Marville Ho SW18 ...72 A4
Marville Rd SW6 ...154 C1
Marvin St 8 E8 ...17 A2
Mary Adelaide Cl SW15 ...68 A1
Mary Ann Bldgs SE8 ...51 C4
Mary Datchelor Cl SE5 ...48 C2
Mary Dine St SW8 ...163 A1
Mary Gn NW8 ...78 B4
Mary Ho SW9 ...172 C1
6 W6 ...39 B1
Mary James Ho 29 E2 ...24 C3
Mary Lawrenson Pl 1 SE3 ...53 C3
Mary Macarthur Ho 15 E2 ...25 C2
W14 ...154 A4
Mary McArthur Ho 4 N19 ...
Mary Pl W11 ...31 A2 112 A3
Mary Secole Cl 2 E8 ...24 B4
Mary St 1 N1 ...87 A3
6 E16 ...35 B2
Mary Terr NW1 ...82 C3
Mary Wharrie Ho 4 NW3 ...12 B1
Maryland Rd E15 ...19 C3
W9 ...23 C1
Maryland Wlk N1 ...86 C4
Marylands Rd W9 ...88 A1
Marylebone Flyover NW1,W1 ...102 A3
Marylebone High St W1 ...103 C4
Marylebone La W1 ...104 A3
Marylebone Mews W1 ...104 A3
Marylebone Pas W1 ...105 A2
Marylebone Rd NW1 ...103 A4
Marylebone St W1 ...103 C3
Marylebone Sta NW1 ...90 C1
Marylee Way SW11 ...149 A3
Maryon Mews NW3 ...12 A4
Masbro' Rd W14 ...39 C3
Masbro' Rd W14 ...126 A2
Mascotte Rd 2 SW15 ...57 C3

Masefield Ct N5 ...15 C3
Masefield Ho 1 NW6 ...23 C2
Mashie Rd W3 ...29 A3
Maskall Cl SW2 ...74 C3
Maskell Rd SW17 ...71 B1
Maskelyne Cl SW11 ...168 B4
Mason Bradbear Ct 5 N1 ...15 C2
Mason Cl SE16 ...153 C2
E16 ...35 C2
Mason Ho SE1 ...153 A3
16 E9 ...17 B1
Mason St SE17 ...151 C4
Mason's Arms Mews W1 ...104 B1
Mason's Arms Mews W1 ...118 B4
Mason's Ave EC2 ...109 B2
Mason's Pl EC1 ...96 C4
Mason's Yd SW1 ...119 A2
Massie Rd E8 ...16 C2
Massinger St SE1 ...
Massingham St E1 ...25 C1
Mast Ct 17 SE16 ...41 A2
Mast House Terr E14 ...41 C2
Master's St 14 E1 ...32 C4
Masterman Ho 1 SE5 ...48 C3
Masters Dr SE16 ...40 A1
Masters Lo 20 E1 ...32 B3
Mastin Ho SW18 ...70 C3
Mastmaker Rd E14 ...41 C4
Matching Ct 13 E3 ...26 C2
Matham Gr SE22 ...64 B3
Matheson Lang Ho SE1 ...135 B3
Matheson Rd W14 ...140 C3
Mathieson Ct SE1 ...136 B3
Matilda Ho 1 E1 ...125 B2
Matilda St N1 ...85 A4
Matlock Cl SE24 ...63 B3
Matlock Ct NW8 ...78 C2
7 SE5 ...63 C3
Matlock St E14 ...33 A3
Maton Ho SW6 ...154 C2
Matson Ho 17 9 SE16 ...40 A3
Matthew Cl W10 ...22 C1
Matthew Parker St SW1 ...133 C3
Matthews Ct N5 ...15 B4
Matthews Ho 5 E14 ...33 C4
Matthews St SW11 ...168 C2
Matthias Ho 2 N16 ...16 A3
Matthias Rd N16 ...16 A3
Mattingly Way 4 SE5 ...49 B3
Maud St E16 ...35 B2
Maude Ho 8 E2 ...24 C3
Maude Rd SE5 ...49 A2
Maudlins Gn E1 ...125 B2
Maudsley Ho TW8 ...36 A1
Maudslay Hospl The SE5 ...48 C1
Maugham Ct 13 W3 ...37 B3
Mauleverer Rd SW2 ...62 A2
Maundeby Wlk NW10 ...8 A2
Maunsel St SW1 ...147 B4

Mauretania Bldg 11 E1 ...32 C2
Maurice Ho SW9 ...172 C2
Maurice St W12 ...30 A3
Mauritius Rd SE10 ...43 A2
Maverton Rd E3 ...26 C4
Mawbey Ho SE1 ...153 A1
Mawbey Pl SE1 ...153 A1
Mawbey Rd SE1 ...153 A1
Mawbey St SW8 ...162 A1
Mawdley Ho SE1 ...135 C3
Mawson Ct N1 ...87 C3
Mawson Ho EC1 ...107 B4
Mawson La W4 ...46 B4
Maxden Ct SE15 ...64 C4
Maxted Rd SE15 ...64 B4
Maxwell Ct SE21 ...76 C3
Maxwell Rd SW6 ...156 B1
May St W14 ...140 C1
W14 ...141 A1
May Tree Ho SE4 ...66 B4
May's Buildings Mews SE10 ...52 C3
May's Ct SE10 ...52 C3
Maybury Ct W1 ...103 C3
Maybury Gdns NW10 ...9 A2
Maybury Mews N6 ...4 B4
Maydew Ho SE16 ...40 B2
Maydwell Ho 6 E14 ...33 C4
Mayfair Pl W1 ...118 C2
Mayfield Ave W4 ...38 A2
Mayfield Cl E8 ...16 B2
SW4 ...61 C2
4 SW4 ...
Mayfield Ho N16 ...7 A4
20 E2 ...25 A3
Mayfield Mans SW15 ...58 B2
Mayfield Rd E8 ...16 B1
W3 ...28 A2
W12 ...38 B4
Mayflower Cl SE16 ...40 C2
Mayflower Prim Sch E14 ...34 A3
Mayflower Rd SW9 ...62 A4
Mayflower St 1 SE16 ...40 B4
Mayford NW1 ...83 A2
Mayford Cl SW12 ...72 B4
Mayford Rd SW12 ...72 C4
Maygood Ho N1 ...85 B2
Maygood St N1 ...85 B2
Maygrove Rd NW6 ...10 B2
Mayhew Ct 5 SE5 ...63 C3
Maylands Ho SW3 ...144 B3
Maynard Cl SW6 ...156 B1
Maynard Ho E1 ...26 A2
Maynards Quay E1 ...32 B2
Mayo Ho NW10 ...4 A2
Mayo Ho 17 E1 ...32 B4
Mayola Rd E5 ...17 B4
Mays Ct WC2 ...120 A3
Maysoule Rd SW11 ...59 C3
Mayston Mews 3 SE10 ...43 C1
Maythorne Cotts SE13 ...67 C1
Mayton St N7 ...5 B1
Maytree Wlk SW2 ...74 C2
Mayward Ho 7 SE5 ...49 A2
Maze Hill SE10,SE3 ...53 A4
Maze Hill Ho 8 SE10 ...53 A4
Maze Hill Sch SE10 ...53 A4

Maze Hill Specl Sch SE10 ...52 B3
Maze Hill Sta SE10 ...53 A4
Maze Rd TW9 ...44 C3
Mazenod Ave NW6 ...10 C1
McAuley Cl SE1 ...135 B2
McBride Ho 5 E3 ...26 B3
McCall Cl SW4 ...172 A2
McCall Ho N7 ...14 A4
McCarthy Ct SW11 ...168 B3
McCoid Way SE1 ...136 C3
Mcconnell Ho SW8 ...171 B3
McCormick Ho 8 SW2 ...74 C3
McCrone Mews 3 NW3 ...11 C2
McCullum Rd E3 ...26 B4
McDermott Cl SW11 ...60 A4
McDermott Rd SE15 ...64 C4
McDougall Ct TW9 ...44 C1
McDougall Ho E2 ...99 B3
McDowall Cl E16 ...35 B2
McDowall Rd SE5 ...48 B2
McEwan Way E15 ...27 C4
McGlashon Ho E1 ...99 B1
McGregor Ct N1 ...98 B4
McGregor Rd W11 ...31 B4
McIndoe Ct N1 ...87 B4
McIntosh Ho 11 SE16 ...40 B2
McKay Trad Est W10 ...23 A3
McKenna Ho 3 E3 ...26 B3
McKerrell Rd SE15 ...49 C2
McKiernan Ct SW11 ...168 A2
McKinnon Wood Ho E2 ...99 B3
Mcleod Ct SE21 ...76 C3
McLeod's Mews SW7 ...142 B4
McManus Ho 3 SW11 ...59 C4
Mcmillan Ho SE4 ...66 A4
McMillan St SE8 ...51 C4
Mcmorran Ho N7 ...14 A4
Mcneil Rd SE5 ...49 A1
McNicol Dr NW10 ...20 B3
Mead Ho N1 ...112 C3
Mead Lo W4 ...37 C4
Mead Pl E9 ...17 B2
Mead Row SE1 ...135 B2
Meadcroft Rd SE17 ...48 A4
Meade Cl W4 ...44 C4
Meader Ct SE14 ...50 C3
Meadow Bank 5 SE3 ...53 B2
Meadow Mews SW8 ...162 C3
Meadow Pl SW8 ...162 B2
W4 ...46 A3
Meadow Rd SW8 ...162 C2
Meadow Row SE1 ...136 C1
Meadowbank NW3 ...12 B1
Meadowbank Cl SW6 ...47 B3
Meadowcroft W4 ...36 C1

Meadowgate Sch SE4 ......66 A4
Meadway The SE3 .52 C1
Meakin Est SE1 ...138 A2
Meakin Ho N7 ......14 B3
Meard St W1 .....105 B1
Meath Ho SE24 ....63 A1
Meath St SW11 ...170 A4
Mecklenburgh Pl WC1 ......94 C2
Mecklenburgh Sq WC1 ......94 C2
Medburn St NW1 .83 B2
Medcroft Gdns SW14 ......55 B3
Medfield St SW15 ..69 A4
Medhurst Cl 17 E3 ..26 A3
Median Rd E5 ......17 B3
Medical Coll of St Bartholomew's Hospl The EC1 ......96 B1
Medina Ct N7 ......5 C1
Medina Gr N7 ......5 C1
Medina Ho SE15 ..65 B3
Medina Rd N7 ......5 C1
Medlar St SE5 ....48 B2
Medley Rd NW6 ...10 C2
Medora Rd SW2 ...74 B4
Medresco Ho NW3 .11 C3
Medusa Rd SE6,SE13 67 A1
Medway Bldgs 6 E3 .26 A3
Medway Ct WC1 ...94 A3
Medway Ho NW8 .102 A4
SE1 ......137 C3
N16 ......15 C4
Medway Rd E3 ....26 A3
Medway St SW1 ..133 C1
Medwin St SW4 ...62 B3
Meecham Ct SW11 168 A2
Meeson St E5 ......17 C4
Meeting House Alley 7 E1 ......32 A1
Meeting House La SE15 ......50 A3
Mehetabel Rd E9 .17 B3
Melaris Mews 1 NW6 ......10 C3
Melba Ct E8 ......16 B1
Melbourne Ct W9 .89 A2
E5 ......18 A4
Melbourne Gr SE22 64 B3
Melbourne Ho W8 113 B1
Melbourne Mews SW9 ......173 B3
Melbourne Pl WC2 107 A1
Melbourne Sq SW9 ......173 B3
Melbourne Ho 11 SE22 ......64 A4
Melbury Ct W8 ...127 A2
Melbury Dr SE5 ...49 A3
Melbury Ho SW8 162 C2
Melbury Rd W14 .127 A2
Melchester 3 W11 .31 B3
Melchester Ho 1 N19 ......4 C1
Melcombe Ct NW1 102 C4
Melcombe Ho SW8 ......162 C1
Melcombe Pl NW1 102 C4
Melcombe Prim Sch W6 ......47 C4
Melcombe St NW1 .91 A1

Meldon Cl SW6 ..166 B4
Melford Ct SE22 ..76 C4
Melford Rd SE21,SE22 ......76 C3
SE22 ......76 C4
Melgund Rd N5 ...14 C3
Melina Ct NW8 ...89 B3
SW15 ......56 C4
Melina Pl NW8 ...89 B3
Melina Rd W12 ...39 A4
Melior Pl SE1 ....138 A4
Melior St SE1 ....138 A4
Melisa Ct N6 ......4 C4
Mell St 6 SE10 ...43 A1
Mellington Ct 12 N16 7 C1
Mellish Ho 12 E1 ..32 A3
Mellish St E14 ....41 C3
Mellitus St W12 ...29 B3
Melody Rd SW18 ..59 B2
Melon Ho SE15 ..127 C4
Melon Rd SE15 ...49 C2
Melrose Ave SW2 ..9 B3
SW16 ......74 A1
Melrose Cl SE14 ..51 B1
Melrose Gdns W6 .39 B3
Melrose Ho SW1 .146 B2
NW6 ......23 C2
Melrose Rd SW13 ......46 B1
SW18 ......58 B1
Melrose Terr W6 ..39 B3
Melton Ct SW7 ..143 C3
Melton Ho E5 ......7 C2
Melton St NW1 ...93 B3
Melville Court Flats W12 ......39 A4
Melville Ct 8 W4 ..36 C1
Melville Pl 4 N1 ..15 B1
Melville Rd SW13 .46 C2
Melville Villas Rd W3 ......28 C1
Melvin Ct 11 TW9 ..44 C2
Melwood Ho 22 E1 .32 A3
Melyn Cl N7 ......13 B4
Memel Ct EC1 ....96 C1
Memel St EC1 ....96 C1
Mendham Ho SE1 138 A2
Mendip Ct SE14 ..50 B4
12 SW11 ......59 B4
Mendip Dr NW2,
13 Ho 12 E14 ...42 A3
Mendip Ho 12 E1 .25 B2
Mendip Rd SW11 .59 B4
Mendora Rd SW6 154 C2
Menelik Rd NW2 ..10 B4
Menorah Gram Sch NW11 ......1 A4
Menorah Prim Sch NW11 ......1 A4
Menotti St 12 E2 ..99 B2
Menteath Ho 5 E14 ......33 C3
Mentmore Terr E8 .17 A1
Mentone Ct SW8 172 B4
Meon Rd W3 ......37 B4
Mepham St SE1 ..121 B1
Merbury Cl SE13 ..67 C2
Mercator Pl E14 ..41 C1
Mercator Rd SE13 .67 C3
Mercer St WC2 ..106 A1
Mercer's Cotts 33 E3 ......33 A3
Merceron Ho 3 E2 .25 B2

Merceron St E1 ...25 A1
Mercers Cl SE10 ..43 B2
Mercers Pl W6 ....39 C2
Mercers Rd N19 ....4 C1
Merchant St E3 ...26 B2
Merchant Taylors Hall EC2 ......109 C1
Merchon Ho N7 ...13 B4
Mercia Gr SE13 ...67 B3
Mercia Ho SE5 ...48 B1
Mercier Rd SW15 .58 A2
Mercury Ct SW9 .173 B4
11 E14 ......41 C2
Mercury Way SE14 .50 C4
Mercy Terr SE13 ..67 A2
Mere Cl SW15,SW19 69 C4
Meredith Ave NW2 .9 B3
Meredith Ho 17 N16 16 A3
Meredith Mews SE4 66 B3
Meredith St EC1 ..96 A3
Meredyth Rd SW13 46 C1
Meretone Cl SE4 ..66 A3
Mereworth Ho 4 SE15 ......50 B4
Merganser Ct 17 SE8 ......51 B4
Meridan Ct SE13 ..67 C3
Meriden Ct SW3 .144 A1
Meriden Ho 23 N1 .24 A4
Meridian Building SE10 ......52 C3
Meridian Ho SE10 .43 A2
Meridian Pl E14 ..42 B4
Meridian Prim Sch SE10 ......52 C4
Merivale Rd SW15 58 A3
Merlin Ho NW3 ...11 A4
7 W4 ......37 C1
Merlin St EC1 ....95 B3
Mermaid Ct SE1 .137 B4
SE16 ......33 B1
Mermaid Ho 8 E14 34 B2
Mermaid Twr 22 SE8 ......51 B4
Meroe Ct N16 ......7 A2
Merredene St SW2 62 B1
Merrick Sq SE1 ..137 B2
Merricks Ct 5 SW14 ......55 A3
Merrington Rd SW6 ......155 C4
Merritt Rd SE4 ...66 B2
Merrivale NW1 ...83 A3
Merrow St SE17 .151 C2
Merrow Wlk SE17 151 C2
Merryfield SE3 ...53 B1
Mersey Ho 10 N7 ..14 C3
Merston Ho SW18 .59 A1
Merthyr Terr SW13 .47 A4
Merton Road Ind Est SW18 ......70 C4
Merton Ave W4 ...38 B2
Merton La N6 ......3 B2
Merton Ho SW18 .70 C3
Merton Rd SW18 .59 A1
Merton Rise NW3 .12 A1
Merttins Rd SE15 .65 C2
Mervan Rd SW2 ..62 C3
Messaline Ave W3 .28 B3
Messina Ave NW6 .10 C1
Metcalfe Ho 15 SW8 ......171 B2
Meteor St SW11 ..60 C3

Methley Ho 8 N7 ..5 B2
Methley St SE11 .149 C1
Methodist Central Hall* SW1 ......133 C3
Methwold Rd W10 .30 C4
Metropolitan Benefit Societies Almshouses 6 E8 ......16 C1
Mews St E1 ......125 B2
Mexborough NW1 .82 C3
Mexfield Rd SW15 58 B2
Meyer Ho 1 SW12 73 A4
Meymott St SE1 .122 A1
Meynell Cres E9 ..17 C1
Meynell Gdns E9 ..17 C1
Meynell Rd E9 ....17 C1
Meyrick Ho 4 E14 33 C4
Meyrick Rd NW10 .8 C2
SW11 ......60 A4
Miah Terr 1 E1 ..125 C1
Micawber Ct N1 ...97 A4
Micawber Ho SE16 139 C3
Micawber St N1 ...97 A4
Michael Cliffe Ho EC1 ......95 C3
Michael Faraday Ho SE17 ......151 C1
Michael Faraday Prim Sch SE17 ......151 C1
Michel's Row 3 TW9 ......54 A3
Michelangelo Ct 14 SE16 ......40 A1
Michelle Ct W3 ...28 C2
Michels Almshouses 11 TW10 ......54 A2
Micklethwaite Rd SW6 ......155 C3
Mickleton Ho 30 W2 ......31 C4
Middle Row Prim Sch W10 ......23 A1
Middle St EC1 ...108 C4
Middle Temple EC4 ......121 B4
Middle Temple La EC4 ......121 B4
Middlefield NW8 ..79 B4
Middlesex Ct 8 W4 38 B2
Middlesex Hospl W1 ......105 A3
Middlesex Hospl Annexe W1 ......105 A3
Middlesex Pas EC1 108 B3
Middlesex Pl 16 E9 17 B2
Middleton Bldgs W1 ......104 C3
Middleton Dr SE16 40 C4
Middleton Gr N7 ..14 A3
Middleton Ho E8 ..16 B1
SE1 ......137 B1
15 ......16 B1
Middleton Mews N7 ......14 A3
Middleton Pl W1 .104 C3
Middleton Rd NW11 1 C4
E8 ......16 B1
Middleton St E2 ..25 A2

Middleton Way SE13 ......67 C3
Midford Pl W1 ....93 A1
Midhope Ho WC1 ..94 B3
Midhope St WC1 ..94 B3
Midhurst Ct N8 ....5 A4
Midhurst Ho 6 E14 33 B3
Midland Pl E14 ...42 B1
Midland Rd NW1 ..84 A1
Midland Terr NW10 21 A1
Midlothian Rd 2 E3 26 B1
Midmoor Rd SW12 73 B3
Midship Cl SE16 ..32 C1
Midship Point E14 .41 C4
Midstrath Rd NW10 .8 A4
Midway Ho EC1 ...96 B4
Milborne Gr SW10 143 A1
Milborne Ho 11 E9 17 B2
Milborne St E9 ...17 B2
Milcote St SE1 ...136 B3
Mildmay Ave N1 ..15 C2
Mildmay Ct N1 ...15 C3
Mildmay Gr N N1 .15 C3
Mildmay Gr S N1 .15 C3
Mildmay Ho 6 SW15 ......57 B2
Mildmay Mission Hospl E2 ......98 C3
Mildmay Pk N1 ...15 C3
Mildmay Rd N1 ...16 A3
Mildmay St N1 ...15 C3
Mile End Pl E1 ...25 C1
Mile End Rd E1,E3 25 C1
Mile End Sta E3 ..26 B2
Miles Bldgs NW1 .102 A4
Miles Coverdale Prim Sch W12 ......39 B4
Miles Ct E1 ......32 A3
Miles Ho 5 SE10 .43 A1
Miles Lo E15 ......19 C3
Miles Pl NW8 ....101 C4
Miles St SW8 ....162 B3
Milestone Green SW14 ......55 C3
Milfoil St W12 ....29 C2
Milford Ct 3 N16 ..7 A3
Milford La WC2 ..121 B4
Milford Mews SW16 74 B1
Milk St EC2 ......109 A2
Milk Yd E1 ......32 B2
Milkwell Yd SE5 ..48 B2
Milkwood Rd SE24 63 A3
Mill Hill SW13 ....56 C4
Mill Hill Gr 3 W3 .37 A4
Mill Hill Rd W3 ...37 A4
SW13 ......46 C1
Mill Hill Terr 9 W3 28 A1
Mill La NW6 ......10 B3
Mill Pl E14 ......33 A3
Mill Row N1 ......24 A4
SE1 ......139 A4
Mill Trad Est The NW10 ......20 B2
Mill Yd E1 ......125 B4
Millais Rd E11 ....19 C4
Milland Ho 1 SW15 68 C3
Millard Cl 13 N16 ..16 A3
Millard Ho SE8 ...41 B1
Millbank SW1 ....148 A3
Millbank Prim Sch SW1 ......147 C3
Millbrook Ho 4 SE15 ......49 C4
Millbrook Rd SW9 .63 A4
Millbrooke Ct 7 SW15 ......58 A2
Millender Wlk SE16 40 B2

Millennium Bridge ★
SE1,EC4 .... 122 C3
Millennium Dome ★
SE10 .... 35 A1
Millennium Dr E14 ..42 A4
Millennium Pl 27
E2 .... 25 A3
Millennium Sq
SE1 .... 139 A4
Miller Ho 2 SW2 ...74 A4
Miller St NW1 ....82 C2
Miller Wlk SE1 .....121 C1
Miller's Ave E8,N16 .16 C4
Miller's Ct 1 W4 ...38 B1
Miller's Terr 8 E8 ..16 B3
Miller's Way W6 ....39 B4
Millers Wharf Ho
E1 .... 125 B1
Millfield 5 C2
Millfield La N6 ......3 B2
Millfield Pl N6 ......3 C2
Millfields JMI Sch
E5 .... 17 B4
Millgrove St SW11 .169 B2
Millharbour E14 ....42 A4
Milligan St E14 .....33 B2
Millington Ho N16 ...6 C1
Millman Ct W.C1 .....94 C1
Millman Mews
W.C1 .... 94 C1
Millman Pl W.C1 ....95 A1
Millman St W.C1 ....94 C1
Millmark Gr SE14 ..51 A1
Millner Ct SE4 ......51 B1
Millpond Est SE16 ..40 A4
Mills Ct EC2 ....98 A3
Mills Gr E14 ....34 B1
Mills Ho SW8 ......171 A4
Mills Row 2 W4 ....37 C2
Millshot Cl SW6 ....47 C2
Millstream Rd SE1 .138 C3
Millwall Dock Rd
E14 .... 41 C3
Millwood St 10 W10 31 A4
Milman Rd NW6 ....23 A3
Milman's Ho
SW10 .... 157 B3
Milman's St SW10 .157 B3
Milner Ho 2 SW11 .59 C4
Milner Pl N1 ....85 C4
Milner Sq N1 ....15 A1
Milner St SW3 .....144 C4
Milnthorpe Rd W4 .45 C4
Milo Rd SE22 ......64 B1
Milrood Ho E1 .....32 C4
Milroy Wlk SE1 ....122 A2
Milson Rd W14 ....126 A2
Milstead Ho 22 E5 ..17 A3
Milton Ave N6 ......4 B4
NW10 .... 20 C4
Milton Cl SE1 .....152 C3
Milton Court Rd
SE14 .... 51 A4
Milton Ct EC2 .....109 B4
SW6 .... 58 A4
9 SW18 .... 58 C2
Milton Ho 8 E2 ....25 B2
2 SE5 .... 48 C3
Milton House Mans
E8 .... 16 B4
Milton Pk N6 ....4 B4
Milton Rd N6 ....4 B4
W3 .... 28 C1
SW14 .... 55 C4

Milton Rd continued
SE24 .... 63 A2
Milton St EC1,EC2 .109 B4
Milverton NW5 ......12 C3
Milverton Rd NW6 ..9 B1
Milverton St SE11 .149 C1
Milward St E1 ....32 A4
Mimosa 4 SW4 ....172 B3
Mimosa St SW6 ...165 A3
Mina Rd SE17 .....152 B2
Minchin Ho 6 E14 ..33 C3
Mincing La EC3 ....124 A4
Minera Mews SW1 .145 C4
Minerva Cl SW9 ...163 C2
Minerva Rd NW10 ..20 C2
Minerva St E2 ......25 A3
Minet Ave NW10 ...21 A3
Minet Gdns NW10 ..21 A3
Minet Rd SE5,SW9 .48 A1
Minford Gdns W14 .39 C4
Ming St E14 ....33 C2
Mingard Wlk N7 ....5 B1
Minnow Wlk SE17 .152 B3
Minories EC3 ......124 C4
Minshull St SW8 ..171 B3
Minson Rd E9 ......25 C4
Minstead Gdns
SW15 .... 68 B4
Minster Rd NW2 ...10 A3
Mint Bsns Pk 23
E16 .... 35 C4
Mint St SE1 ....137 A4
Mintern St N1 ......87 C2
Minton Ho SE11 ...149 B4
Minton Mews 3
NW6 .... 11 A2
Mirabel Rd SW6 ..155 A2
Miranda Cl 16 E1 ..32 B4
Miranda Ho 6 N1 ..24 A3
Miranda Rd N19 ....4 B3
Missenden SE17 ...151 C1
Missenden Ho NW8 .90 A2
Mission Sq 13 TW8 .44 A4
Mission St SE15 ...49 C2
Misterton Ct SW11 167 C4
Mistral SE5 ....49 A2
Mitali Pas E1 ......111 B1
Mitcham Ho 8 SE5 .48 B2
Mitcheldean Ct
SE15 .... 49 A4
Mitchell Brook Prim Sch
NW10 .... 8 A2
Mitchell Ho 5 W12 30 A2
W4 .... 37 A1
Mitchell St EC1 ....97 A2
Mitchell's Pl N1 ...12 C1
Mitford Rd N19 ....5 A2
Mitre Bridge Ind Pk
W10 .... 22 A1
Mitre Ct EC2 ......109 A2
Mitre Rd SE1 ......135 C4
Mitre Sq 2 EC3 ...110 B1
Mitre St EC3 ......110 B1
Mitre The 9 E14 ...33 B2
Mitre Way W10 ....30 A4
Moat Pl 3 W3 .....28 A3
SW9 .... 62 B4
Moatfield NW6 .....10 A1
Moberly Rd SW4 ..73 C4
Mobey Ct SW4 ....172 A3
Mocatta Ho 9 E1 ..25 A1
Modbury Gdns NW5 12 C2
Modder Pl SW15 ...57 C3
Model Cotts SW14 .55 B4
Modling Ho 8 E2 ..25 C3

Moelwyn Hughes Ct
N7 .... 13 C3
Moffat Ho 24 SE5 ..48 B3
Mohawk Ho 51 E3 ..26 A3
Moiety Rd E14 .....41 C4
Moira Ct SW17 ....72 C2
Moira Ho SW9 ....173 B4
Moland Mead SE16 .40 C1
Molasses Ho 1
SW11 .... 59 B4
Molasses Row 2
SW11 .... 59 B4
Mole Ct 2 W12 ....38 A4
Mole Ho NW8 .....89 C1
Molesey Ho E2 ....98 C2
Molesford Rd SW6 165 B3
Molesworth Ho 8
SE17 .... 48 A4
Molly Huggins Cl
SW12 .... 73 B4
Molton Ho N1 .....85 A3
Moncey Ho N1 .....97 B4
Mona Rd SE15 .....50 B1
Mona St E16 ....35 B2
Monck St SW1 ....133 C1
Monck's Row SW18 58 B1
Monclar Rd SE5 ...63 C3
Moncorvo Cl SW7 .130 A3
Moncrieff St SE15 .49 C1
Mondragon Ho
SW8 .... 172 B4
Monier Rd 2 E3 ...18 C1
Monk Ct W12 ......29 C1
Monk Dr E16 ......35 C2
Monkbretton Ho E2 99 B3
Monksfield N4 .....5 C2
Monkswell Ho 22 E2 99 C3
Monkton Ho E5 ....17 A3
Monkton St SE11 .149 C4
Monkwell Sq 22 EC2 109 A3
Monmouth Cl W4 ..37 C3
Monmouth Gr TW8 .36 A2
Monmouth Ho
5 NW5 .... 12 C2
SW18 .... 58 C1
Monmouth Pl W2 ..100 A1
Monmouth Rd W2 .100 A1
Monmouth St WC2 .106 A1
Monnery Rd N19 ...4 B1
Monnow Rd SE1 ..153 B3
Monro Ho 9 NW3 ..11 B4
SW15 .... 57 A2
Monroe Dr SW14 ..55 A2
Monroe Ho 10 N4 ..6 B4
Monsal Ct E5 ......18 A4
Monsell Rd N4,N5 ..6 A1
Monson Prim Sch
SE14 .... 50 C3
Monson Rd NW10 .22 A3
SE14 .... 50 C3
Montagu Ct W1 ...103 A3
Montagu Mans
W1 .... 103 A3
Montagu Mews N
W1 .... 103 A3
Montagu Mews S
W1 .... 103 A3

Montagu Mews W
W1 .... 103 A3
Montagu Pl W1 ....103 A3
Montagu Row W1 ..103 A3
Montagu Sq W1 ...103 A3
Montagu St W1 ....103 A3
Montague Ave SE4 .66 C3
Montague Cl SE1 ..123 B2
Montague Pl WC1 .105 C4
Montague Rd E8 ...16 C3
Richmond TW10 ....54 A1
Montague Sq SE15 50 B3
Montague St EC1 .108 C3
WC1 .... 106 A4
Montana Rd SW17 .72 C1
Montcalm Ho E14 ..41 C2
Montclare St
E2 .... 24 B1 98 C2
Monteagle Ct 2 N1 24 A3
Monteagle Way E5 ..7 C1
SW15 .... 65 A4
Montefiore 2 N16 ..7 B3
Montefiore St
SW8 .... 170 B1
Montem Prim Sch
N7 .... 5 B1
Montem St N4 .....5 B3
Montenotte Rd N8 ..4 C4
Montesquieu Terr 3
E16 .... 35 B1
Montford Pl SE11 .149 B1
Montfort Ho 4 E2 ..25 B2
2 E14 .... 42 B3
Montfort Pl SW19 .69 C3
Montgo Cl 11 SW2 ..62 B3
Montgomery Ho 8
SW14 .... 55 C4
Montgomery Lo 34
E1 .... 25 B1
Montgomery Rd W4 37 B2
Montholme Rd
SW11 .... 60 B1
Monthope Rd E1 ..111 B3
Montolieu Gdns
SW15 .... 57 A3
Montpelier Gr NW5 13 B3
Montpelier Mews
SW7 .... 130 B2
Montpelier Pl 21
E1 .... 32 B3
SW7 .... 130 B2
Montpelier Rd SE15 50 A2
Montpelier Rise
NW11 .... 1 A4
Montpelier Row
SE3 .... 53 B1
Montpelier Sq
SW7 .... 130 B3
Montpelier St
SW7 .... 130 B2
Montpelier Terr
SW7 .... 130 B3
Montpelier Vale
SE3 .... 53 B1
Montpelier Way
NW11 .... 1 A4
Montpelier Wlk
SW7 .... 130 B2
Montreal Pl WC2 ..120 C4
Montrell Rd SW2 ..74 A3
Montrose Ave NW6 23 A3
Montrose Ct SW7 .130 A3
Montrose Ho
E14 .... 41 C3
SW1 .... 131 C3
Montrose Pl SW1 .131 C3
Montrose Villas W6 38 C1
Montserrat Rd
SW15 .... 58 A3

Monument Gdns
SE13 .... 67 B2
Monument St EC3 .124 A3
Monument Sta
EC3 .... 123 C4
Monument The ★
EC3 .... 123 C4
Monza St E1 ....32 B2
Moodkee St SE16 ..40 B3
Moody St E1 ....25 C2
Moon St N1 ....86 A4
Moor La EC2 ......109 B3
Moor Pl EC2 ......109 B3
Moor St W1 ....105 C1
Moorcroft Rd SW16 74 A1
Moore Cl SW14 ....55 B4
Moore Ho 16 E2 ...25 B2
6 E1 .... 32 B2
5 SE10 .... 43 B1
SW17 .... 71 C1
Moore Park Ct
SW6 .... 156 B2
Moore Park Rd
SW6 .... 156 A1
Moore St SW3 ....144 C4
Moore's Yd W4 ....38 A1
Moorfields EC2 ...109 B3
Moorfields Eye Hospl
EC1 .... 97 B3
Moorfields Highwalk
EC2 .... 109 B3
Moorfields Prim Sch
EC1 .... 97 B2
Moorgate EC2 ....109 B3
Moorgate Pl EC2 .109 B2
Moorgate Sta EC2 109 B3
Moorgreen Ho EC1 96 A4
Moorhen Ct 55 SE8 51 B4
Moorhouse Rd W2 31 C3
Moorland Rd SW9 .63 A3
Mora Prim Sch NW2 9 B4
Mora Rd NW2 ......9 B4
Mora St EC1 ....97 A3
Morant St E14 ....33 C2
Morant St SW9 ...172 C2
Morat St SW9 .....173 a4
Moravian Cl SW3 .157 C3
Moravian Pl SW10 157 D3
Moravian St 19 E2 ..25 B2
Moray Ho 4 E1 ....26 A1
Moray Mews N4,N7 ..5 B2
Moray Rd N4,N7 ...5 B2
Mordaunt Ho SW8 171 B1
4 NW10 .... 20 C4
Mordaunt Rd NW10 20 C4
Mordaunt St SW9 ..62 B4
Morden Hill SE13 ..52 B1
Morden La SE13 ...52 B2
Morden Mount Prim Sch
SE13 .... 52 A1
Morden Rd SE3 ...53 C1
Morden Road Mews
SE3 .... 53 C1
Morden St SE13 ...52 A2
Morden Wharf Rd
SE10 .... 43 A3
Mordern Ho NW1 ..90 B1
More Cl W14 ......140 A3
E16 .... 35 B1
More House Sch
SW1 .... 131 A1
More's Gdn 3 SW3 157 C3
Morecambe Cl 2
E1 .... 32 C4

Morecambe St
SE17 ....**151** A2
Moredown Ho **3**
SE8 ....16 C3
Moreland Ct **5** SE1 ....23 C3
Moreland Prim Sch
EC1 ....96 A4
Moreland St EC1 ....96 B4
Morell Ho SW9 ....172 C1
Morella Rd SW11,
SW12 ....72 B4
Moresby Wlk SW8 ......170 B1
Moreton Ho SE16 ....40 A3
Moreton Pl **1**
SW1 ....147 A2
Moreton Pl SW1 ....147 A2
Moreton St SW1 ....147 B2
Moreton Terr SW1 ......147 A2
Moreton Terr Mews N
SW1 ....147 A2
Moreton Terr Mews S
SW1 ....147 A2
Moreton Twr **3** W3 ....28 A1
Morgan Ct SW11 ....167 C2
Morgan Ho SW1 ....171 A4
Morgan Rd N7 ....14 C3
W10 ....31 B4
Morgan St E3 ....26 A2
E16 ....35 B4
Morgan's Wlk
SW11 ....158 A1
Moriatry Cl N7 ....14 A4
Morie St SW18 ....59 A2
Morkyns Wlk SE21 ......76 A1
Morland Cl NW11 ....2 A4
Morland Ct W12 ....39 A4
Morland Est SE8 ....51 C3
Morland Ho NW1 ....83 A1
SW1 ....148 A4
NW6 ....23 C4
W11 ....31 A3
Morley Coll SE1 ....135 C2
Morley Ho N16 ....7 C2
SW2 ....74 A4
Morley Rd SE13 ....135 C3
Morley St SE1 ....135 C3
Morna Rd SE5 ....48 C1
Morning La E9 ....17 B2
Morningside JMI Sch
E9 ....17 B2
Mornington Ave
W14 ....140 C3
Mornington Ave
Mans W14 ....140 C3
Mornington Cres
NW1 ....82 C2
Mornington Crescent
Sta NW1 ....82 C2
Mornington Ct NW1 .....82 C2
Mornington Gr E3 ....26 C2
Mornington Mews **2**
SE5 ....48 B2
Mornington PI NW1 .....82 C2
SE8 ....51 B3
Mornington Rd
SE14,SE8 ....51 B3
Mornington St NW1 .....82 B2
Mornington Terr
NW1 ....82 B2
Morocco St SE1 ....138 A3
Morpeth Gr E9 ....25 C4

Morpeth Rd E9 ....25 C4
Morpeth Sec Sch
E2 ....25 B2
Morpeth St E2 ....25 C2
Morpeth Terr SW1 .....146 C4
Morrel Ct E2 ....24 C3
Morris Blitz Ct **1**
N16 ....16 B3
Morris Ct **3** SE5 ....63 C3
Morris Gdns SW18 ......70 C4
Morris Ho NW8 ....90 A1
10 N19 ....13 B4
17 E2 ....25 B2
5 SW4 ....62 A3
Morris Pl N4 ....5 C2
Morrish Rd SW2 ....74 A4
Morrison Bldgs E1 .....111 B2
Morrison Ho SW2 ....74 C3
Morrison St SW11 ....60 C4
Morris St **7** SE16 ....40 A4
Morshead Mans W9 ....23 C2
Morshead Rd W9 ....23 C2
Mortain Ho **9** SE16 .....40 A2
Morten CI SW4 ....61 C1
Mortimer CI **1** NW2 ....1 B1
SW16 ....73 C2
Mortimer Cres NW6 ....78 B3
Mortimer Ct NW8 ....79 A1
Mortimer Est NW6 ....78 A3
Mortimer Ho **1**
6 W11 ....30 C1
Mortimer Lo **11**
SW19 ....70 A3
Mortimer Market
WC1 ....93 A1
Mortimer PI NW6 ....78 A3
Mortimer Rd N1 ....16 A1
NW10 ....22 B2
Mortimer Sq W11 ....30 C2
Mortimer St W1 ....105 A3
Mortimer Terr NW5 .....13 A4
Mortlake High St
SW14 ....55 C4
Mortlake Rd SW14,
TW9 ....44 C2
Mortlock CI SE15 ....50 A2
Morton Ho SE17 ....48 A4
Morton Mews
SW5 ....142 A3
Morton PI SE1 ....135 B1
Morton Rd N1 ....15 B1
Morval Rd SW2 ....62 C2
Morven Rd SW17 ....72 B1
Morville Ho SW18 ....72 B4
Morville St E3 ....26 C3
Morwell St WC1 ....105 C3
Moscow PI W2 ....114 A4
Moscow Rd W2 ....114 A4
Mosedale NW1 ....92 B3
Moss CI E1 ....111 C4
Mossbury Rd SW11 .....60 A4
Mossford St E3 ....26 B1
Mossington Gdns
SE16 ....40 B2
Mostyn Gr **5** E3 ....26 C3
Mostyn Gdns NW10 ....22 C3
Mostyn Gr E3 ....26 C3
Mostyn Lo **5** 15 B4
Mostyn Rd SW9 ....173 C3
Motcomb St SW1 ....131 B2

Mothers Sq The **13**
E5 ....17 A4
Motley Ave EC2 ....98 A2
Motley St SW8 ....170 C2
Moules Ct SE5 ....48 B3
Moulins Rd E9 ....17 C1
Moulsford Ho
5 N7 ....14 A3
2 W2 ....31 C4
Mounsey Ho **10**
W10 ....23 A2
Mount Adon Pk
SE21,SE22 ....76 C4
Mount Angelus Rd
SW15 ....68 B4
Mount Ararat Rd
TW10 ....54 A2
Mount Carmel RC Sec
Sch
N19 ....4 B3
N7 ....14 B3
Mount Ephraim La
SW16 ....73 C1
Mount Ephraim Rd
SW16 ....73 C1
Mount Ford St E1 ....111 B2
Mount Mills EC1 ....96 B3
Mount Nod Rd
SW16,SW2 ....74 B1
Mount PI **9** W3 ....28 A1
Mount Pleasant
WC1 ....95 B1
Mount Pleasant Cres
N4 ....5 B4
Mount Pleasant Rd
NW10 ....22 B4
SE13 ....67 B1
Mount Pleasant Villas
N4 ....5 B4
Mount Rd SW18,
SW19 ....71 A2
Mount Row **8** W1 .....118 A3
Mount Sq The NW3 .....2 B1
Mount St W1 ....117 C3
Mount Terr E1 ....32 A4
Mount The **8**
SW16,SW2 ....74 B1
NW3 ....2 C1
Mount Tyndal NW3 ......2 C3
Mount Vernon NW3 .....11 B4
Mount Villas SE27 ....75 A1
Montague PI **2**
E14 ....34 B2
Mountain Ho SE1 ....148 C2
Mountbatten Ho **6**
N6 ....3 C4
Mountbatten Mews
SW18 ....71 B3
Mountcarl Gdns
SW16,SW2 ....74 B1
Mountfield NW2 ....1 A2
Mountfield CI SE13 ......67 C1
Mountfort Cres N1 ....14 C1
Mountfort Terr **1**
N1 ....14 C1
Mountgrove Rd N5 ......6 B1
Mountjoy Ho EC2 ....24 A1
Mounts Pond Rd
SE3,SE13 ....52 C1
Mountview **5** SW16 ...74 B1
Mourne Ho NW3 ....11 B2
Mowatt CI N19 ....4 C3
Mowbray Rd NW6 ....10 A1
Moxon CI E3 ....26 A3
Moxon St W1 ....103 B3

Moye CI **9** E2 ....24 C3
Moylan Rd W6 ....154 B3
Moyle Ho SW1 ....161 A4
Moyne Ho **10** SW9 .....63 A3
Mozart St W10 ....23 B2
Mozart Terr SW1 ....145 C3
Mudchute Sta E14 ....42 A2
Mudie Ho **3** SW2 ....74 A4
Muir Rd E5 ....7 C1
Muirdown Ave
SW14 ....55 C3
Muirfield W3 ....29 A3
Muirfield CI **22**
SE16 ....40 A1
Muirfield Cres E14 ....42 A3
Mulberry Bsns Ctr
SE16 ....40 C4
Mulberry Cl **3** SE3 ....53 C3
NW3 ....11 C4
SE22 ....64 C1
Mulberry Ct **1** 96 B3
N5 ....15 A3
1 E11 ....19 C4
10 W9 ....23 B2
Mulberry Ho **1** E2 .....25 B2
8 SE8 ....51 B4
Mulberry Mews
SE14 ....51 B2
Mulberry PI W6 ....38 C1
Mulberry Rd E8 ....16 B1
Mulberry Sch for Girls
E1 ....32 A2
Mulberry Sec Sch
Mulberry St **1** 111 B2
Mulberry Wlk SW3 .....157 C4
Mulgrave Rd W14 ......154 C4
NW10 ....8 B4
Mulkern Rd N19 ....4 C3
Mull Ho **19** E3 ....26 B3
Mull Wlk N1 ....15 C2
Mullard Ho WC1 ....105 B4
Mullen Twr EC1 ....95 B1
Mullens Ho **7**
SW15 ....57 B2
Mullet Gdns E2 ....24 C2
Mulletsfield WC1 ....94 B3
Mullins Path SW14 ......55 C4
Mulready St NW8 ....90 A1
Multi Way W3 ....38 A4
Multon Rd SW18 ....17 B1
Mulvaney Way SE1 ....137 C3
Mumford Ct EC2 ....109 A2
Mumford Rd SE24 ....63 A2
Muncaster Rd SW11 ....60 C2
Mund St W14 ....141 A1
Mundania Ct SE22 ....65 B1
Mundania Rd SE22 ......65 B1
Munday Ho SE1 ....137 B1
Munday Rd E16 ....35 C2
Munden Ho **5** E3 ......27 A2
Munden St W14 ....140 A4
Mundy Ho **8** W10 ......23 A2
Mundy St N1 ....98 B4
Munro Ho SE1 ....135 B3
SE1 ....121 C1
Munro Mews W10 ....31 A4
Munster Ct SW6 ....164 C2
Munster Rd SW6 ....154 B2
SW6 ....164 B4
Munster Sq NW1 ....92 B2
Munton Rd SE1,
SE17 ....151 A4
Murchison Ho **1**
W10 ....31 A4

Murdoch Ho **4**
SE16 ....40 B3
Murdock CI E16 ....35 B1
Murdock St SE15 ....50 A4
Muriel St N1 ....85 A2
Murillo Rd SE13 ....67 C3
Murphy Ho SE1 ....136 B2
Murphy St SE1 ....135 B3
Murray Gr N1 ....87 B1
Murray Mews NW1 ......13 C1
Murray St NW1 ....13 C1
Murray Terr NW3 ....11 C4
Mus of Garden History

SE1 ....134 C1
Mus of London *
EC2 ....108 C3

Mus of the Moving
Image SE1 ....121 A2
Musard Rd W6 ....154 B4
Musbury St E1 ....32 B3
Muscal W6 ....154 A4
Muscatel PI SE5 ....49 A2
Muschamp Rd SE15 ....64 B4
Muscott Ho **3** E2 ....24 C4
Muscovy St EC3 ....124 B4
Museum Ho **3** E2 .....25 B2
Museum St WC1 ....106 A2

Musgrave Cres

SW6 ....165 C4
Musgrave Ct SW11 ....168 A4
Musgrove Ho **9**
E9 ....17 C2
Musgrove Rd SE14 .....51 A2
Musical Mus The

TW8 ....44 A4
Musjid Rd SW11 ....167 C1
Mustow PI SW6 ....165 A2
Mutrix Rd NW6 ....23 C4
Mutton PI NW1 ....12 C2
Myatt Ct SE4 ....51 B1
Myatt Garden Prim Sch

SE4 ....51 B1
Myatt Ho SE5 ....48 A1
Myers La SE14 ....50 C4
Mylius CI SE14 ....50 B2
Mylne CI W6 ....38 C1
Mylne St EC1 ....85 B1
Mynterne Ct **18**

SW19 ....69 C3
Myrdle Ct E1 ....111 C2
Myrdle St E1 ....111 C2
Myron PI SE13 ....67 B4
Myrtle Ave E14 ....50 C2
Myrtle Rd W3 ....28 B1
Myrtle Wlk **20** N1 ......24 A3
Mysore Rd SW11 ....60 B3
Myton Rd SE21 ....75 C1
Mytton Ho SW8 ....162 C1

N

Nags Head N7 ....14 B4
Nags Head Ct EC1 ....97 A1
Nailsworth St E9

SE15 ....49 A4
Nainby Ho SE11 ....149 B3
Nairn St E14 ....34 B4
Nairne Gr SE5,SE24 ....63 C3

Naish Ct N1 ....84 B4
Nalton Ho 4 NW6 ...11 B1
Nankin St E14 ....33 C3
Nansen Rd SW11 .....60 C4
Nant Ct NW2 ....1 B2
Nant Rd NW2 ....1 B2
Nant St E2 ....25 A2
Nantes Cl SW18 ....59 B3
Naoroji St WC1 ....95 B3
Napier Ave E14 ...41 C1
SW6 ....58 B4
Napier Cl W14 ......126 C1
SE14,SE8 ....51 B3
Napier Ct SW6 ....58 B4
SE12 ....87 B2
Napier Gr N1 ....87 A2
Napier Pl W14 .....126 C1
Napier Rd W14 .....126 C1
NW10 ....22 A2
Napier Terr N1 ......15 A1
Narbonne Ave SW4 .61 B2
Narborough St
SW6 ....166 A1
Narcissus Rd NW6 ..10 C3
Narford Rd E5 ....7 C2
Narrow St 6 W3 .....28 A1
E14 ....33 A2
Nascot St W12 ....30 B3
Naseby Cl NW6 ......11 B1
Naseby Twr SE14 ....51 A3
Nash Ho 5 SW1 ....146 B1
Nash Rd SE4 ....66 A2
Nashe Ho 5 SE1 ....137 B1
Nasmyth St W6 ......39 A3
Nassau Rd SW13 .....46 B2
Nassau St W1 ....104 C3
Nassington Rd NW3 .12 B4
Nat West Tower *
EC2 ....110 A2
Nat West Twr *
EC2 ....110 A2
Nathan Ho SE11 ...149 C3
Nathaniel Cl E1 ....111 A3
National Army Mus *
SW3 ....159 A4
National Fan Mus
SE10 ....52 B3
National Film Theatre *
SE1 ....121 A2
National Gallery *
W1 ....119 C3
National Hospl The
WC1 ....94 B1
National Maritime
Mus * SE10 ....52 C4
National Portrait
Gallery * W1 ......119 C3
National Portrait
Gallery (Annexe) *
SW1 ....119 C2
National Postal Mus *
EC1 ....108 C2
National Theatre *
SE1 ....121 A2
Natural History Mus *
SW7 ....129 B1
Naval Row E14 ....34 B2
Navarino Gr E8 ....16 C2
Navarino Mans E8 ..16 C2
Navarre St E2 ....24 B1 B2
Navenby Wlk 13 E3 .26 C1
Navy St SW4 ....61 C4
Naylor Ho SE17 ....151 C2
5 W10 ....23 B2
Naylor Rd SE15 ......50 A3

Nazareth Cl SE15 ....50 A1
Neal St WC2 ....106 A1
Neal's Yd WC2 ......106 A1
Nealden St SW9 ......62 B3
Neasden Cl NW10 ....8 A3
Neasden Junc NW10 .8 A4
Neasden La NW10 ....8 A3
Neasden La N NW10 ..8 A2
Neate St SE5 ....49 A4
SE5 ....49 A3
Neathouse Pl SW1 .146 C4
Nebraska St SE1 ....137 B3
Neckinger SE16 .....139 A2
Neckinger Est
SE16 ....139 A2
Neckinger St SE1 ..139 A3
Nectarine Way SE13 .52 A1
Nedahall Ct 4 NW11 ..1 B4
Needham Ho SE11 .149 B3
Needham Rd W11 ...31 C3
Needleman St SE16 .40 C4
Needwood Ho N4 .....6 B3
Nevill Cl NW1 ....8 A1
Nevill Ct SW10 ....156 C2
Nevill Rd N16 ....7 A1
Neville Cl NW1 ....83 C1
NW6 ....23 B3
W3 ....37 B4
SE15 ....49 C2
17 SE15 ....49 C3
Neville Ct 7 NW6 ...78 B4
10 SW12 ....73 B4
Neville Gill Cl SW18 .59 C1
Neville Rd NW6 ......23 B3
Neville St SW7 ......143 B2
Neville Terr SW7 ...143 B2
Nevinson Cl SW18 ..59 C1
Nevis Rd SW17 ....72 C2
Nevitt Ho N1 ....87 C1
New Bentham Ct 1
N1 ....15 B1
New Bond St W1 ...104 B1
W1 ....118 B4
New Bridge St
EC4 ....108 A1
New Broad St EC2 .110 A3
New Burlington Mews
W1 ....118 C4
New Burlington Pl
W1 ....118 C4
New Burlington St
W1 ....118 C4
New Butt La SE8 ....51 C3
New Caledonian Wharf
SE16 ....41 B3
New Campden Ct 7
NW3 ....11 B4
New Cavendish St
W1 ....104 A3
New Change EC4 ...108 C1
New Charles St EC1 .96 B4
New Church Rd
32 SE5 ....48 B3
SE5 ....48 C3
New College Ct 6
NW3 ....11 B2
New College Par 1
NW3 ....11 B2
New Compton St
WC2 ....106 A1
New Concordia Wharf
SE1 ....139 A4
New Covent Garden
Flower Market
SW8 ....162 A3

Netherwood Rd
W14 ....39 C4
Netherwood St
NW6 ....10 C2
Netley 15 SE5 ....49 A2
Netley Prim Sch
SW1 ....92 C3
Netley Rd NW8 ......44 A4
Netley St NW1 ....92 C3
Nettlecombe NW1 ..13 C1
Nettleden Ho SW3 .144 B3
Nettlefold Pl SE27 ..75 A1
Nettleton Rd SE14 ..50 C2
Nevada St SE10 .....52 B4
Nevena Ct 3 SW2 ...62 C2
Nevern Mans SW5 .141 B2
Nevern Pl SW5 ......141 C3
Nevern Rd SW5 .....141 B3
Nevern Sq SW5 .....141 C3
Nevil Ho 7 SW9 ......48 A1
New Den The(Millwall
FC) SE16 ....40 B1
New End NW3 ....2 B1
New End Prim Sch
NW3 ....2 B1
New End Sq NW3 .....11 C4
New Fetter La EC4 ..107 C2
New Furness Prim Sch
The NW10 ....21 C3
New Globe Wlk
SE1 ....122 C2
New Goulston St
E1 ....110 C2
New Inn Broadway
EC2 ....98 B2
New Inn Pas WC2 ..107 A1
New Inn Sq EC2 ......98 B2
New Inn St EC2 ....98 B2
New Inn Yd
EC2 ....24 A1 98 B2
New James Ct SE15 .65 A4
New Kent Rd SE1 ...151 C4
New King St SE8 .....51 C4
New King's Rd
SW6 ....165 C3
New King's Rd
SW6 ....165 B2
New Kings Sch
SW6 ....164 C2
New London St
EC3 ....124 B4
New Mount St E15 ..19 C1
New North Pl EC2 ....98 A2
New North Rd N1 ....87 B3
New North St WC1 .106 C4
New Oxford St WC1 .106 A2
New Palace Yd
SW1 ....134 A3
New Park Ct 28
SW2 ....74 A4
New Park Par 14
SW2 ....74 A4
New Park Rd SW2 ...74 A4
New Place Sq SE16 .40 A3
New Priory Ct 9
NW6 ....10 C1
New Quebec St
W1 ....103 A1
New Rd E1 ....32 A4
New Ride SW7 ....130 B4
New River Ct N5 .....15 C4
New River Way N4 ...6 C4
New Row WC2 ......120 A4
New Royal Horticultural
Society Hall SW1 ..133 B1
New Scotland Yard *
SW1 ....133 B2
New Spring Gardens
Wlk SE11 ....148 B1

New Covent Garden
Fruit & Vegetable
MarketMarket
SW8 ....161 B1
New Cross SE14 .....51 B3
New Cross Gate
SE14 ....50 C2
New Cross Gate Sta
SE14 ....51 A3
New Cross Hospl
SE14 ....50 B3
New Cross Rd SE14 .51 B3
New Cross Sta SE14 .51 B3
New Ct EC4 ....107 B1
N16 ....6 C3
19 NW3 ....11 B4
New Den The(Millwall
FC) SE16 ....40 B1
New Goulston St
E1 ....110 C2
Newall Ho SE1 ......137 A2
Newark Cres NW10 .20 C2
Newark Ho 3 SW9 .48 A1
Newark St E1 ....32 A4
Newbery Ho N1 .....15 B1
Newbold Cotts 4
E1 ....32 B3
Newburgh Rd W3 ..28 B1
Newburgh St W1 ...105 A1
Newburn Ho SE11 .149 A2
Newburn St SE11 ..149 A2
Newbury Ct E5 ....18 A3
Newbury Ho W2 ...100 B1
SW9 ....173 C1
SW9 ....48 A1
Newbury Mews
NW5 ....12 C2
Newby St SE11 .....108 C4
Newby St SW8 ....61 A4
Newcastle Cl EC4 ..108 A2
Newcastle Ct EC4 ..123 A4
Newcastle Ho W1 ..103 B4
Newcastle Pl W2 ...101 C4
Newcastle Row EC1 .95 C1
Newcombe Ho N5 ..15 B3
Newcombe St W8 ..113 C2
Newcomen Ho 5
N1 ....13 A4
Newcomen Rd
SW11 ....59 C4
Newcourt Ho 26 E2 .25 A2
Newcourt St NW8 ...80 A1
Newdigate Ho 5
E14 ....33 B3
Newell St E14 ....33 B3
Newent Cl SE15 .....49 A3
Newfield Prim Sch
NW10 ....8 B1
Newgate St EC1 ....108 B2
Newham Sch of Nursing
E13 ....27 B1
Newham's Row
SE1 ....138 B3
Newhaven La 5
E16 ....35 C4
New Spring Gardens
Wlk SE11 ....148 B1
Newington Barrow Way
SE7 ....150 C3

New Sq WC2 ....107 A2
New Sq Pas SE17 ..107 B2
New St EC2 ....110 B3
New St E4 ....107 C2
New Tower Bldgs 27
E1 ....32 A1
New Union Cl E14 ..42 B3
New Union St EC2 .109 B3
New Wharf Rd N1 ...84 B2
Newall Ho SE1 ......137 A2
Newark Cres NW10 .20 C2
Newark Ho 3 SW9 .48 A1
Newark St E1 ....32 A4
Newbery Ho N1 .....15 B1
Newbold Cotts 4
E1 ....32 B3
Newburgh Rd W3 ..28 B1
Newburgh St W1 ...105 A1
Newburn Ho SE11 .149 A2
Newburn St SE11 ..149 A2
Newbury Ct E5 ....18 A3
Newbury Ho W2 ...100 B1
SW9 ....173 C1
SW9 ....48 A1
Newbury Mews
NW5 ....12 C2
Newby Pl E14 ....34 B2
Newby St SW8 ....61 A4
Newcastle Cl EC4 ..108 A2
Newcastle Ct EC4 ..123 A4
Newcastle Ho W1 ..103 B4
Newcastle Pl W2 ...101 C4
Newcastle Row EC1 .95 C1
Newcombe Ho N5 ..15 B3
Newcombe St W8 ..113 C2
Newcomen Ho 5
N1 ....13 A4
Newcomen Rd
SW11 ....59 C4
Newcourt Ho 26 E2 .25 A2
Newcourt St NW8 ...80 A1
Newdigate Ho 5
E14 ....33 B3
Newell St E14 ....33 B3
Newent Cl SE15 .....49 A3
Newfield Prim Sch
NW10 ....8 B1
Newgate St EC1 ....108 B2
Newham Sch of Nursing
E13 ....27 B1
Newham's Row
SE1 ....138 B3
Newhaven La 5
E16 ....35 C4
Newington Barrow Way
SE7 ....150 C3
Newington Butts
SE1,SE11 ....150 B3
Newington Cswy
SE1 ....136 C2
Newington Green Mans
N16 ....15 C3
Newington Green Rd
Sch N16 ....15 C3
Newington Green Rd
N1 ....15 C3
Newington Ind Est
SE17 ....150 C3
Newland Ct EC1 .....97 B2

Newland Ho **17**
SE14 ....50 C4

Newlands NW1 ....92 C4
Newlands Quay E1 ..32 B2
Newlyn NW1 ....83 A3
Newman Pas W1 ..105 A3
Newman St W1 ......105 A3
Newman's Ct E3 ...109 C1
Newman's Row
WC2 ....107 A3

Newmill Ho E3 ....27 B1
Newmount NW3 ......11 C3
Newnes Path SW5 ..57 A3
Newnham Ho **9**
SW15 ....57 C1

Newnham Terr
SE1 ....135 B2

Newton CI N4 ....6 C4
Newton Ave E14 ......34 C2
Newport Ct WC2 ....119 C4
Newport Ho E3 ....26 A2
Newport PI WC2 ....119 C4
Newport Rd SW13 ...46 C2
Newport St SE11 ...149 A4
Nerquay Ho SE11 ..109 B2
Newton Ave W3 ......37 B4
Newton Gr W4 ....38 A2
Newton Ho NW8 ......78 B4
1 E1 ....32 A2

Newton Point **1**
E16 ....35 B1

Newton Prep Sch
SW8 ....170 B4
Newton Rd W2 ......100 A1
E15 ....19 C3
Newton St WC2 .....106 B2
Newton's Yd **14**
SW18 ....58 C2
Newtown Ct SW11 170 A3
SW4 ....61 A2
Newtown St SW11 170 A3
Niagara CI N1 ....87 A2
Niagara Ct E6 ....40 B3
Nicholas Ct W4 ......46 A3
Nicholas Ho **2**
SW15 ....56 C2
Nicholas La EC2,
EC4 ....123 C4
Nicholas Pas EC3 ..123 C4
Nicholas Rd E1 ....25 B1
Nicholay Rd N19 ......4 C3
Nicholl Ho N4 ....6 B3
Nicholl St E2 ....24 C4
Nichols Ct N1 ....24 A3
Nicholson Ho SE17 151 B2
Nicholson St SE1 ...122 A1
Nicklebly Ho SE1 ...139 B3
7 W11 ....30 C1
Nicoll Ct NW10 ....21 A4
Nicoll Rd NW10 ......21 A4
Nicosia Rd SW18 ....72 A4
Nigel Ho EC1 ....107 B4
Nigel Playfair Ave
W6 ....39 A1
Nigel Rd SE15 ....64 C4
Nightingale CI W4 ...45 B4
Nightingale Ct
SW6 ....166 B3
N4 ....5 B2
2 E14 ....42 B3
Nightingale Gr SE13 67 C2
Nightingale Ho **1** ..125 B2

Nightingale Ho continued
21 E1 ....24 A4
W12 ....30 B3
Nightingale La
SW11,SW12 ....60 C1
Nightingale Lo **5**
W9 ....31 C4
Nightingale Rd
NW10 ....21 B3
Nightingale Sq
SW12 ....72 C4
Nightingale Wlk
SW18,SW4 ....61 A1
Nile CI N16 ....7 B1
Nile Ho N1 ....97 B4
Nile St N1 ....97 B4
Nile Terr SE1,SE15 .153 A1
Ninnegen Way **13**
SE22 ....64 A2
Nimrod Pas **1** N1 ....16 A2
Nine Elms La SW8 ..161 B3
Nisbet Ho E9 ....17 C3
Niton Rd TW9 ....54 C4
Niton St SW6 ....47 C3
Nobel Ho **8** SE5 ......48 B1
Noble Ct **2**
SW2 ....108 C2
E1 ....32 A2
Noel Coward Ho
SW1 ....147 A3
Noel Ho **3** NW3 ....11 C1
Noel Rd N1 ....86 B2
W3 ....28 A3
Nolan Way E5 ....16 C4
Noll Ho N7 ....5 B2
Norbiton Rd E14 .....33 B3
Norbroke St W12 ....29 B2
Norburn St W10 ......31 A4
Norcombe Ho **2** N19 4 C1
Norcott Rd N16 ....7 C1
Norcroft Gdns SE22 .76 C4
Norden Ho **28** E2 ....25 A2
Nore Ct NW10 ....8 C1
Norfolk Cres W2 ....102 B2
Norfolk Ho EC4 ......122 C4
SW1 ....147 C4
E8 ....16 B4
SE3 ....53 A4
Richmond TW10 ......54 C2
SW16 ....74 A1
Norfolk Mans
SW11 ....169 A3
10 SW18 ....58 C2
Norfolk PI W2 ....101 C2
Norfolk Rd NW8 ......79 C3
NW10 ....21 A4
Norfolk Row SE1,
SE11 ....148 C4
Norfolk Sq W2 ....101 C2
Norfolk Sq Mews
W2 ....101 C1
Norgrove St SW12 ..72 C4
Norland PI
W11 ....31 A1 113 A1
Norland Place Sch
W11 ....31 A1 112 A1
Norland Rd W11 .....30 C1
Norland Sq
W11 ....31 A1 112 B1
Norley Vale SW15 ...68 C3

Norman Butler Ho **10**
W10 ....23 A1
Norman Ct N4 ....5 C4
NW10 ....8 C1
SE22 ....76 C4
Norman Gr E3 ....26 A3
Norman Ho **9** 162 A2
Norman Rd SE10 ....52 A3
Norman St EC1 ....97 A3
Norman Way W3 ....28 A3
Normanby CI SW15 .58 B2
Normanby Rd NW10 .8 B4
Normand Mews
W14 ....154 B4
Normand Park Prim Sch
W14 ....154 C4
Normand Rd W14 ...154 C4
Normandy Rd SW9 173 B3
Normanhurst Rd
SW2 ....74 C2
Normanton Ave
SW18,SW19 ....70 C2
Normanton Ho **6**
SW4 ....61 B1
Norris Ho **12** N1 ....24 A4
22 E9 ....25 B4
Norris St SW1 ....119 B3
Norroy Rd SW15 ....57 C3
Norse Ho **15** SE5 ...48 B1
Norstead PI SW15 ..68 C2
North Acton Rd
NW10 ....20 C2
North Acton Sta
NW10 ....22 B2
North Audley St
W1 ....103 B1
North Ave **13** TW9 ..44 C2
North Bank NW8 .....90 A3
North Block **18** E1 ..32 B2
North Branch Ave
NW10 ....22 B2
North Carriage Dr
W2 ....116 B3
North Church Ho **8**
E2 ....24 C4
North Circular Rd
NW10 ....8 A3
North Colonnade
E14 ....101 A1
North Cres E4 ....11 C1
E16 ....27 C1
North Cross Rd
SE22 ....64 C2
North Ct **1** SW1 ....134 A1
North Dulwich Sta
SE21 ....63 C2
North End NW3 ....2 B2
North End Ave NW3 ..2 B2
North End Cres
W14 ....140 C3
North End Ho **14** ...140 B3
North End Par
W14 ....140 B3
North End Rd W14 141 A1
NW11 ....1 C3
NW11 ....1 C3
North Eyot Gdns **5**
W6 ....38 B1
North Flower Wlk
W2 ....115 B3
North Gate NW8 .....80 A1
North Gower St
NW1 ....93 A3
North Gr N6 ....3 C4

North Greenwich Sta
SE10 ....43 A4
North Hill Ct N6 ....3 C4
North Ho **3** SE8 ....41 B1
North Lodge CI
SW15 ....57 C2
North London Bsns
Pk N11 ....95 A1
North Mews WC1 ....95 A1
North Pas SW18 ......58 C2
North Pole Rd W10 ..30 B4
North Rd N6 ....3 C4
N7 ....14 A2
Brentford TW8 ....44 A4
Richmond TW9 ....44 C1
North Ride W2 ....116 A3
North Rise W2 ....102 B1
North Row W1 ......117 B4
W1 ....117 B4
North Sheen Sta
TW10 ....54 C3
North Side Wandsworth
Comm SW18 ....59 C2
North St SW4 ....61 B4
North Tenter St
E1 ....111 A1
North Terr SW3 ......130 A1
North Verbena Gdns
W6 ....38 C1
North Villas NW1 ....13 C2
North West...

North Westminster Com
Sch
NW1 ....102 A4
W9 ....23 C1
North Westminster Com
Sch (Upper) **2** W2 101 B3
North Wharf Rd
W2 ....101 B3
North Wik W2 ....114 C3
North Wood Lo
NW3 ....11 A4
North Worple Way
SW14 ....55 C4
Northampton Gr N1 15 C3
Northampton Pk
N1 ....15 C2
Northampton Rd
EC1 ....95 C2
Northampton Sq
EC1 ....96 A3
Northampton St N1 15 B1
Northaw Ho W10 ....22 B1
Northbourne Ho **21**
E5 ....17 A3
Northbourne Rd
SW4 ....61 C2
Northbrook Rd
SE13 ....67 C2
Northburgh St EC1 ..96 B2
Northchurch SE17 ..151 C2
Northchurch Rd N1 15 C1
Northchurch Terr
N1 ....16 A1
Northcote Rd NW10 .8 A1
SW11 ....60 B2
Northcourt W1 ....105 A4
Northcroft Ct **3**
W12 ....38 C4
Northdown St N1 ....84 C1
Northern Ho **6** E2 ..24 C3
Northesk Ho **6** E1 ..25 A1
Northey St E14 ....33 A2
Northfield Hall N6 ....3 C4
Northfield Ho **3**
SE15 ....49 C4
Northfield Rd N16 ....7 A4

Northfields SW18 ....58 C3
Northfields Prospect
SW18 ....58 C3
Northfields Rd W3 ..28 B4
Northfleet Ho SE1 ..137 B4
Northgate Ct **19**
SW9 ....62 C4
Northiam WC1 ....94 B3
Northiam St E9 ....25 B4
Northington St WC1 95 A1
Northlands St SE5 ...48 B1
Northleach Ct **2**
SE15 ....49 A4
Northleigh Ho **36**
E3 ....27 A2
Northolme Rd N5 ....15 B4
Northport St N1 ....87 C3
Northstead Rd SW2 74 C2
Northumberland Alley
EC3 ....110 B1
Northumberland Ave
WC2 ....120 A2
Northumberland Ho
NW5 ....13 B2
Northumberland Mans
E5 ....17 B4
Northumberland PI
W2 ....31 C3
Northumberland St
WC2 ....120 A2
Northumbria Ct **14**
TW9 ....54 A3
Northumbria St
E14 ....33 C3
Northview **1** N7 ......5 A1
Northview Cres
NW10 ....8 B4
Northview Prim Sch
NW10 ....8 B4
Northway Rd SE5 ....63 B4
Northways Par **2**
NW3 ....11 C1
Northwest PI N1 ......85 C2
Northwick CI NW8 ..89 B2
Northwick Ho NW8 .89 A2
Northwick Terr
NW8 ....89 B2
Northwold JMI Sch
E5 ....7 C2
Northwold Rd E5,N16 7 C2
Northwood Ho **6** ...44 A4
Norton Folgate E1 ..110 B4
Norton Ho SW9 ......173 A1
4 E2 ....25 C3
55 E1 ....32 A3
Norval Gn SW9 .....173 C2
Norvic Ho **5** SE5 ...48 B1
Norway Gate SE16 ..41 A3
Norway PI E14 ....33 B3
Norway St SE10 ......52 A4
Norwich Ho **8** E14 ..34 A3
Norwich St EC4 ......107 B2
Norwood High St
SE27 ....75 A1
Norwood Ho **22** E14 34 A2
Norwood Rd SE24,
SE27 ....75 A3
Notley St SE5 ....48 C3
Notre Dame RC Sec Sch
SE1 ....136 A2

Notting Barn Rd
W10 ....22 C1
Notting Hill Gate
W11 ....31 C1 113 B2
Notting Hill Gate Sta
W11 ....31 C1 113 A2
Nottingdale Sq
W11 ....112 A2

Nottingham Ct
WC2 ....**106** A1
Nottingham Ho N4 ....6 B3
34 SE5 ....48 B1
Nottingham PI W1 **103** B4
Nottingham Ho
SW17 ....72 B3
Nottingham St W1 **103** B4
Nottingham Terr
NW1 ....**91** B1
Nottingwood Ho
W11 ....**112** A4
Novello Ho **6** W10 ..23 B2
Novello St SW6 .....**165** B4
Nowell Rd SW13 .....46 C4
Noyna Rd SW17 .....72 B1
Nuding Cl SE13 ......**66** C4
Nuffield Lo **4** W9 ...31 C4
Nugent Rd N19 ....5 A3
Nugent Terr NW8 ....79 A1
Nun Ct EC2 ....**109** B2
Nunhead Cres SE15 .65 A4
Nunhead Gr SE15 ....65 A4
Nunhead La SE15 ....65 A4
Nunhead Sch SE15 ..50 B1
Nursery Cl SE4 ....51 B1
SW15 ....57 C3
Nursery La E2 ....24 B4
W10 ....30 B4
Nursery Rd E9 ....17 B2
SW9 ....62 B3
Nutbourne St W10 .23 A2
Nutbrook St SE15 ...64 C4
Nutcroft Rd SE15 ....50 A3
Nutfield Rd SE22 ....64 B3
E15 ....76 B4
Nutford PI W1 ......**102** C2
Nuthurst Ave SW2 ..74 B2
Nutley Terr NW3 .....11 C2
Nutmeg La E14 ....34 C3
Nutt St SE15 ....49 B3
Nuttall St N1 ....24 A3
NW London Jewish Day
Prim Sch NW6 ....10 A1
Nye Bevan Ho
SW6 ....**154** C2
Nye's Wharf SE1 ....49 C4
Nylands Ave TW9 ...44 C1
Nynehead St SE14 ..51 A3
Nyton Ct N19 ....5 A3

O

O'Brian Ho **16** E1 ....25 C2
O'Donnell Ct WC1 ...**94** B2
O'Driscoll Ho W12 ..30 A3
O'Gorman Ho
SW10 ....**157** A2
O'Leary Sq E1 ....32 B4
O'Neill Ho NW8 .....**79** C1
O'Shea Gr E3 ....26 B4
Oak Cres E16 ....35 A4
Oak Gr NW2 ....10 A4
Oak Hill Lo W11 .....11 A4
Oak Hill Park Mews
NW3 ....11 A4
Oak Hill Pk NW3 .....11 A4
Oak Hill Way NW3 ..11 A4
Oak Ho N16 ....6 C2
8 W3 ....12 B2
E14 ....42 B4
Oak La E14 ....33 B2
Oak Lodge Sch
SW12 ....72 C4
Oak Park Gdns
SW19 ....69 C3

Oak Park Mews N16 .7 B1
Oak Tree Ct W3 ....28 A2
Oak Tree Ho W9 .....**88** A2
Oak Tree Rd NW8 ...**90** A3
Oak Village NW5 ....12 C4
Oakbank Gr SE24 ...63 B3
Oakbury Rd SW6 ..**166** B1
Oakcourt **8** SW15 ..49 B3
Oakcroft Rd SE13 ...52 C1
Oakdale Ct N19 ....5 A2
Oakdale Rd N4 ....5 C4
SE15 ....65 B4
Oakden St SE11 ....**149** C4
Oakdene **3** SE5 .....50 A2
Oakdene Ho N16 ......7 A3
Oake Ct SW15 ....58 A2
Oakend Ho **6** N4 ......6 C4
Oakeshott Ave N6 ....3 C2
Oakey La SE1 ....**135** B2
Oakfield Ct N8 ....5 A4
N16 ....6 C4
SW4 ....62 A1
Oakfield Rd N4 ....5 C4
SW19 ....69 C1
Oakfield Sch SE21 ..75 C3
Oakfield St SW10 ..**156** C4
Oakford Rd NW5 ....13 B4
Oakham Ho W10 .....22 B1
Oakhill Ave NW3 ....11 A4
Oakhill Ct SW15 .....58 B2
SE23 ....65 B1
Oakhill PI SW15 .....58 C2
Oakhill Rd SW15 ....58 B2
Oakhurst Gr SE22 ..64 C3
Oakington Rd W9 ...23 C1
Oakington Way N8 ...5 A4
Oaklands NW10 ......21 A4
Oaklands Ct NW10 ..21 A4
W12 ....29 C1
Oaklands Ho SE4 ....66 B4
Oaklands Mews NW2 9 C4
Oaklands Pas NW2 ...9 C4
Oaklands PI **8** SW4 61 C3
Oaklands Rd NW2 ....9 C4
SW14 ....55 C4

Oaklands Sec Sch
E2 ....25 A2
Oakley Cres EC1 ....**86** B1
Oakley Dr SE13 ......67 C1
Oakley Gdns SW3 .**158** B4
Oakley Ho SW1 ....**145** A4
Oakley PI SE1 ....**152** C1
Oakley Rd N1 ....15 C1
Oakley Sq NW1 ......**83** A2
Oakley St SW3 .....**158** A4
Oakley Wlk W6 ....47 C4
Oakman Ho **29**
SW19 ....69 C3
Oakmead Rd SW12 .73 A3
Oaks Sh Ctr The
W3 ....28 B1
Oaks The W10 ....9 A1
NW6 ....9 C1
Oakshaw Rd SW18 .71 A4
Oakshott Ct NW1 ....**83** B1
Oakwell Ho SW8 ..**171** B1
Oakwood Ct W14 ..**126** C2
Oakwood La W14 ..**126** C2
Oakworth Rd W10 ..30 C4
Oast Ct **3** E14 ....33 B2
Oat La EC2 ....**109** A2
Oatlands Ct **3**
SW19 ....69 C3
Oatwell Ho SW3 ...**144** B3
Oban Ho E14 ....34 C3
Oban St E14 ....34 C3

Oberon Ho **5** N1 ...24 A3
Oberstein Rd **15**
SW11 ....59 C3
Oborne Cl SE24 ......63 A2
Observatory Gdns
W8 ....**127** C4
Observatory Rd
SW14 ....55 B3
Occupation Rd
SE17 ....**150** C2
Ocean St E1 ....32 C4
Ockbrook **3** E1 .....32 B4
Ockendon Rd N1 ....15 C2
Ockley Rd SW16 ....74 A1
Octagon Arc EC2 ..**110** A3
Octagon The W10 ..30 C4
Octavia Ho W10 .....23 A1
Octavia St SW11 ..**168** B3
Octavius St SE8 .....51 C3
Odeon Ct NW10 .....21 A4
E16 ....35 C4
Odessa Rd NW10 ...21 C3
E7 ....19 C4
Odessa St SE16 .....41 B3
Odette Duval Ho **24**
E1 ....32 B4
Odger St SW11 ....**169** A2
Odhams Wlk WC2 .**106** B1
Offa's Mead E9 ....18 A4
Offenbach Ho **12** E2 25 C3
Offerton Rd SW4 ....61 B4
Offham Ho SE17 ..**152** A3
Offley Ho **10** E9 ....17 C2
Offley Rd SW9 ....**163** B2
Offord Rd N1 ....14 B1
Offord St N1 ....14 B1
Ogilvie Ho **11** E1 ..32 C3
Oglander Rd SE15 ..64 B4
Ogle St W1 ....**104** C4
Oil Mill La W6 ....38 C1
Okehampton Rd
NW10 ....22 C4
Okeover Manor
SW4 ....61 A3
Olaf St W11 ....30 C2
Old Bailey EC4 .....**108** B1
Old Barrack Yd
SW1 ....**131** B3
Old Bellgate Wharf
E14 ....41 C3
Old Bethnal Green Rd
E2 ....25 A2
Old Bldgs WC2 ....**107** B2
Old Bond St W1 ....**118** C3
Old Brewery Mews
NW3 ....11 C4
Old Broad St EC2 .**109** C2
Old Brompton Rd
SW7 ....**143** A3
SW5 ....**142** C3
Old Burlington St
W1 ....**118** C3
Old Castle St E1 ...**111** A3
Old Cavendish St
W1 ....**104** A1
Old Change Ct
EC4 ....**108** C1
Old Church Rd E1 ..32 C3
Old Church St
SW3 ....**143** B1
Old Compton St
W1 ....**105** B1
Old County Hall
SE1 ....**134** C4
Old Court Ho W8 ..**128** A3
Old Court PI W8 ...**128** A3

Old Covent Garden
WC2 ....**120** A4
Old Dairy Mews **4**
NW5 ....13 A2
Old Deer Park Gdns
TW9 ....54 A4
Old Devonshire Rd
SW12 ....73 A4
Old Dock Cl TW9 ....44 C4
Old Dover Rd SE3 ..53 C3
Old Fish St Hill
EC4 ....**122** C4
Old Fleet La EC4 ..**108** A2
Old Ford Rd E3 ......26 B3
Old Ford Jun Sch
E3 ....26 B3
Old Ford Rd E2,E3 ..25 C3
Old Ford Trad Ctr
E3 ....26 C4
Old Forge Mews
W12 ....39 A4
Old Gloucester St
WC1 ....**106** B4
Old Hospital Cl
SW12,SW17 ....72 B3
Old Jamaica Rd
SE16 ....**139** B2
Old James St SE15 .65 A4
Old Jewry EC2 .....**109** B1
Old Kent Rd SE1 ..**152** B2
SE15 ....**152** B2
Old Laundry The **14**
SW18 ....59 C3
Old Manor Yd
SW5 ....**142** A3
Old Market Sq E2 ..24 B3
Old Marylebone Rd
NW1 ....**102** B3
Old Mitre Ct EC4 ..**107** C1
Old Montague St
E1 ....**111** B3
Old Nichol St
E2 ....24 B1 **98** C2
Old North St WC1 .**106** C4
Old Oak Common La
NW10 ....21 A1
Old Oak La NW10 ..21 B2
Old Oak Prim Sch
W3 ....28 B3
Old Oak Rd W3 ......29 B2
Old Orch The NW3 ..12 B3
Old Palace JMI Sch
E3 ....27 A2
Old Paradise St
SE11 ....**148** C4
Old Park Ave SW12 .60 C1
Old Park La W1 .....**118** A1
Old Pye St SW1 ...**133** B1
Old Pye Street Est
SW1 ....**133** B1
Old Quebec St W1 .**103** A1
Old Queen St SW1 **133** C3
Old Royal Free PI
N1 ....**85** C3
Old Royal Free Sq
N1 ....**85** C3
Old Royal Horticultural
Society SW1 ....**147** B4
Old Royal Observatory
Greenwich (National
Maritime Mus
Annex)* SE10 ....52 C3
Old Seacoal La
EC4 ....**108** A1
Old South Lambeth Rd
SW8 ....**162** B1

Not - Ons 235

Old Sq WC2 ....**107** A2
Old St EC1 ....**97** B2
EC1 ....**97** B3
Old Stable Mews N5 .6 B1
Old Street Sta EC1 .**97** C2
Old Sun Wharf E14 .33 A2
Old Swan Wharf
SW11 ....**167** A4
Old Theatre Ct
SE1 ....**123** A2
Old Town SW4 ....61 B4
Old Woolwich Rd
SE10 ....52 C4
Old York Rd SW18 ..59 A2
Oldbury Ct E9 ....18 A3
Oldbury PI W1 ......**103** C4
Oldfield Gr SE16 .....40 C2
Oldfield Ho **14** W4 .38 A1
Oldfield Mews N6 ....4 B4
Oldfield Rd N16 ....7 A1
N8 ....5 A4
W3,W12 ....38 C4
Oldham Terr W3 .....28 B1
Oldhill St N16 ....7 C3
Olding Ho **6** SW12 .73 B4
Oldridge Rd SW12 ..73 A4
Olga St **26** E3 ....26 A3
Olga St **8** E3 ....26 A3
Oliphant St W10 .....23 A2
Olive Blythe Ho **14**
W10 ....23 A1
Olive Rd NW2 ....9 B4
Olive Tree Ho **7**
SE15 ....50 B4
Olive Waite Ho
NW6 ....11 A1
Oliver Goldsmith Prim
Schs SE5 ....49 B2
Oliver Ho SE16 ....**139** B3
SW8 ....**162** A2
Oliver's Yd EC1 ......**97** C2
Olivette St **1** SW15 .57 C3
Ollerton Gn E3 ......26 B4
Ollgar Cl W12 ....29 B1
Olliffe St E14 ....42 B3
Olmar St SE1 ....49 C4
Olney Ho NW8 ....**90** B2
Olney Rd SE7 ....**158** A4
Olympia Ex Hall*
W14 ....**126** B1
Olympia Way W14 .**126** B1
Olympia Yd W2 ....**114** B3
Olympian Ct **1** E14 .41 C2
Olympic Ho W10 ....30 B3
Olympus Sq E5 ....7 C1
Oman Ave NW2 ....9 B4
Oman Ct NW4 ....9 A4
Ombersley Ho N4 ....6 B4
Omeara St SE1 ....**123** A1
Omega Cl E14 ....42 A3
Omega Ho SW10 ..**157** A2
Omega PI N1 ....**84** B1
Omega St SE14 ......51 C2
Ommaney Rd SE14 .51 A2
Ondine Rd SE15 .....64 B3
Onega Gate SE16 ...41 A3
Ongar Ho **1** N1 .....15 C2
Ongar Rd SW6 .....**155** B3
Onslow Ave TW10 ..54 A2

Onslow Avenue Mans **18**
TW10 .... 54 A2
Onslow Ct SW11 ...... 143 B2
Onslow Gdns SW7 .... 143 B3
Onslow Ho **10** W10 ... 23 A2
Onslow Mews E
SW7 .... 143 B3
Onslow Mews W
SW7 .... 143 B3
Onslow Rd TW10 ...... 54 A1
Onslow Sq SW7 .... 143 C3
Onslow St EC1 .... 95 C1
Ontario St SE1 .... 136 B2
Ontario Way E14 ...... 33 C2
Opal St SE11 .... 150 A2
Open Air Theatre,
Regent's Park
NW1 .... 91 B3
Openview SW17,
SW18 .... 71 C2
Operating Theatre Mus
& Herb Garret
SE1 .... 123 C1
Ophelia Gdns NW2 **1** ... 1 A1
Ophir Terr SE15 .... 49 C2
Opie Ho NW8 .... 80 B2
Oppenheim Rd SE13 .. 52 B1
Oppidans Rd NW3 .... 12 B1
Orange PI SE16 .... 40 B3
Orange St WC2 .... 119 C3
Orange Yd W1 .... 105 C1
Oratory La SW3 .... 143 C2
Oratory RC Prim Sch
SW3 .... 144 A2
Oratory The **7**
SW7 .... 130 A1
Orb St SE17 .... 151 B3
Orbain Rd SW6 .... 154 B1
Orbel St SW11 .... 168 A3
Orchard CI N1 .... 15 B1
W10 .... 31 A4
SE23 .... 65 B1
Orchard Ct **11**
TW10 .... 54 B2
Orchard Dr SE3 .... 53 A1
Orchard Hill SE13 .... 52 A2
Orchard Ho W12 ..... 29 C1
11 SE16 .... 40 B3
SE5 .... 48 B2
Orchard JMI Sch E9 ... 17 B1
Orchard Mead House
NW11 .... 1 C2
Orchard Mews N1 ..... 15 C1
Orchard PI E14 .... 35 A1
Orchard Rd N6 .... 4 A4
Mortlake TW9 .... 54 C4
Orchard Rise SW15 ... 55 A3
Orchard Sq W14 ...... 140 C1
Orchard St W1 .... 103 C2
Orchard The W4 ...... 37 C2
SE3 .... 52 C1
Orchardson Ho
NW8 .... 89 C1
Orchardson St NW8 **8** 89 C1
Orchid St W12 .... 29 C2
Orde Hall St WC1 ..... 106 C4
Orde Ho **10** E3 .... 26 B1
Ordell Ct E3 .... 26 B3
Ordell Rd E3 .... 26 B3
Ordnance Cres
SE10 .... 43 A4
Ordnance Hill NW8 .. 79 C3

Ordnance Mews
NW8 .... 79 C2
Ordnance Rd E16 ..... 35 B2
Oregano Dr E14 .... 34 C3
Orford Ct SE27 .... 75 A2
Oriana Ho **1** E14 ..... 33 B2
Oriel Ct NW3 .... 11 B4
Oriel Dr SW13 .... 47 B4
Oriel Rd E9 .... 17 C2
Orient St SE11 .... 150 A4
Orion Bsns Ctr SE14 40 C1
Orion Ho **20** E1 .... 25 A1
Orkney Ho N1 .... 84 C4
Orkney St SW11 ...... 169 B2
Orlando Rd SW4 ...... 61 C3
Orleston Mews N7 .... 14 C2
Orleston Rd N7 .... 14 C2
Orlop St SE10 .... 43 A1
Orme Ct W2 .... 114 A3
Orme Ct Mews W2 **1** 114 B3
Orme Ho **8** E8 .... 24 B4
Orme La W2 .... 114 A3
Orme Sq W2 .... 114 A3
Ormeley Rd SW12 .... 73 A3
Ormiston Gr W12 ..... 30 A1
Ormiston Rd SE10 .... 43 C1
Ormond CI WC1 ...... 106 B4
Ormond Ho **7** N16 ... 6 C2
Ormond Mans WC1 **4** 94 B1
Ormond Rd N4,N19 .... 5 A3
Ormond Yd SW1 ..... 119 A2
Ormonde Ct SW15 ... 57 B3
Ormonde Gate
SW3 .... 145 A1
Ormonde PI SW1 .... 145 C3
Ormonde Terr NW8 .. 80 C3
Ormrod Ct W11 .... 31 B3
Ormsby Lo **1** W4 .... 38 A3
Ormsby PI N16 .... 7 B1
Ormside St SE15 ...... 50 B4
Ornan Rd NW3 .... 12 A3
Oronsay Wlk **15** N1 .. 15 B2
Orpheus Ho **25** N19 4 C4
Orpheus St SE5 .... 48 C2
Orpheus Twr **6**
SE14 .... 51 A3
Orsett Mews W2 .... 100 B2
W2 .... 100 C2
Orsett St SE11 .... 149 A2
Orsett Terr W2 ...... 100 C2
Orsman Rd N1 .... 24 A4
Orton St E1 .... 125 B1
Orville Rd SW11 ..... 167 C2
Orwell Ct N5 .... 15 B4
N16 .... 24 C4
Orwell Ho W12 .... 29 C2
Osbaldeston Rd N16 .. 7 C3
Osbert St SW1 .... 147 B3
Osborn Cl E8 .... 24 C4
Osborn St E1 .... 111 A3
Osborne Rd N4 .... 5 C3
Osborne Rd E9 .... 18 B2
E7 .... 37 A4
N4 .... 5 C3
Osbourne Ho **10** TW10 54 C2
Oscar Faber PI **8**
N1 .... 16 A1
Oscar St SE8 .... 51 C2
Oseney Cres NW5 .... 13 C2
Osier Ct E1 .... 25 C1
Osier Mews W4 .... 46 B4
Osier St E1 .... 25 B1
Osiers Rd SW18 ...... 58 C3
Oslo Ct NW8 .... 80 A1

Oslo Ho **2** SE5 ...... 48 B1
Oslo Sq SE16 .... 41 A3
Osman Rd W6 .... 39 B3
Osmani JMI Sch
E1 .... 111 C4
Osmington Ho
SW8 .... 163 A1
Osmund St W12 ...... 29 B4
Osnaburgh St NW1 .. 92 B2
Osnaburgh Terr
NW1 .... 92 B2
Osprey Ct SW3 .... 11 A3
Osprey Ho **3** E14 ... 33 A2
SE15 .... 49 B2
Ospringe Ho SE1 .... 121 C1
Ospringe Rd NW5 .... 13 B4
Osram Ct W6 .... 39 B3
Osric Path **8** N1 ..... 24 A3
Ossian Rd N4 .... 5 B4
Ossington Bldgs
W1 .... 103 B3
Ossington Cl W2 **3** . 113 C3
Ossington St W2 .... 114 A3
Ossory Rd SE1 .... 49 C4
Ossulston St NW1 .... 93 C4
Ostade Rd SW2 ...... 74 B4
Osten Mews SW7 ... 128 B1
Osterley Ho **5** E14 . 34 A3
Osterley Rd N16 ...... 16 A4
Oswald's Mead **1** E9 18 A4
Osward Rd SW12,
SW17 .... 72 B2
Oswell Ho **9** E1 ..... 32 A1
Oswin St SE11 .... 150 B4
Osward Rd SW17 ... 150 B4
Otford Cres SE4 ...... 66 B1
Otford Ho SE1 .... 137 C2
6 SE15 .... 50 B4
Otha Ho SW9 .... 172 B2
Othello Cl SE11 ..... 150 A2
Otis St E3 .... 27 B2
Otley Ho N5 .... 6 A1
Ottaway Ct E5 .... 7 C1
Ottaway St E5 .... 7 C1
Otterburn Ho **18**
SE5 .... 48 B3
Otto St SE17 .... 148 A4
Our Lady & St Josephs
RC JMI Sch N1 ...... 16 A2
Our Lady of Dolours RC
Prim Sch W2 .... 100 A4
Our Lady of Lourdes
Prim Sch NW10 ..... 20 B4
Our Lady of Lourdes RC
Prim Sch SE13 ..... 67 C4
Our Lady of the
Assumption RC Inf Sch
E2 .... 25 B3
Our Lady of the Sacred
Heart RC Prim Sch
(Annex) N7 .... 14 A2
Our Lady of the Sacred
Heart RC Sch N7 .. 14 A3
Our Lady of Victories RC
Prim Sch
SW7 .... 143 A3
SW15 .... 57 C3
Our Lady Queen of
Heaven RC Prim Sch
SW19 .... 69 C4
Our Lady RC JMI Sch
E14 .... 33 B3
Our Lady's Convent High
Sch N15,N16 .... 7 A4
Ouseley Rd SW12 .... 72 B3
Outer Circ NW1 ...... 80 B1

Outgate Rd NW10 ..... 8 B1
Outram PI N1 .... 84 B4
Outram Rd N1 .... 84 B4
Outwich St EC3 ..... 110 B2
Outwood Ho **3**
SW2 .... 74 B4
Oval Mans SE11 ..... 163 A4
Oval PI SW8 .... 163 A2
Oval Rd NW1 .... 82 A4
Oval Sta SE11 .... 163 B3
Oval The E2 .... 25 A3
Oval The (Surrey Cnty
Crkt Gd) SE11 ..... 163 A4
Oval Way SE11 ...... 149 A1
Overbury Ho **5** E5 17 C4
Overbury St E5 .... 17 C4
Overcliff Rd SE13 ... 66 C4
Overhill Rd SE21,
SE22 .... 76 C4
Overlea Rd E5 .... 7 C4
Oversley Ho **17** W2 . 31 C4
Overstone Ho **17**
E14 .... 33 C3
Overstone Rd W6 .... 39 B2
Overstrand Mans
SW11 .... 169 B3
Overton Ho SW15 ... 68 B4
Overton Rd SW9 ... 173 C1
Overy Ho SE1 .... 136 A3
Ovex Cl E14 .... 42 B4
Ovington Ct SW3 ... 130 B1
Ovington Gdns
SW3 .... 130 B1
Ovington Mews
SW3 .... 130 B1
Ovington Sq SW3 .. 130 B1
Ovington St SW3 ... 144 B4
Owen Ho **6** N19 ... 13 B4
Owen St EC1 .... 86 A1
Owen's Ct EC1 .... 96 A4
Owen's Row EC1 ..... 96 A4
Owgan Cl SE5 .... 48 C3
Oxberry Ave SW6 .. 164 B2
Oxbridge Ct **4** W4 .. 37 A1
Oxenden St
W1 .... 119 B3
Oxenford St SE15 .... 64 B4
Oxenham Ho **18** SE1 C4
Oxenholme NW1 ..... 83 A1
Oxestalls Rd SE8 ..... 41 A1
Oxford & Cambridge
Mans NW1 .... 102 B3
Oxford Ave NW10 ... 22 B2
Oxford Cir W1 .... 104 C1
Oxford Circus Ave
W1 .... 104 C1
Oxford Circus Sta
W1 .... 104 C1
Oxford Ct EC4 .... 123 B4
Oxford Dr SE1 .... 124 A1
W4 .... 37 A1
Oxford Gardens Prim
Sch W10 .... 30 C3
Oxford Gate W6 ..... 39 C2
Oxford Gdns W10 ... 30 C3
W4 .... 44 C4
Oxford Rd N4 .... 5 C3
NW6 .... 23 C3
SW15 .... 58 A3
Oxford Rd N4 .... 37 A1
Oxford Rd W5 .... 37 A1
Oxford Sq W2 .... 102 B1
Oxford St W1 .... 104 B1
Oxley Cl SE1 .... 153 A2
Oxo Tower SE1 ...... 122 A3
Oxo Tower Wharf
SE1 .... 121 C3

Oxonian St SE22 ..... 64 B3
Oxted Ct N16 .... 7 A3
Oyster Row E1 .... 32 B3
Ozolins Way E16 ...... 35 C3

P

Pablo Neruda CI **4**
SE24 .... 63 A3
Pace PI E1 .... 32 A3
Pacific Ho **15** E1 ... 25 C1
Pacific Rd E16 .... 35 C3
Packenham Ho **2** .. 99 A4
24 N19 .... 4 C4
Packington Ho
SW1 .... 172 B2
Packington Sq N1 .... 86 C4
Packington St N1 .... 86 B3
Padbury SE17 .... 152 B1
Padbury Ct E2 .... 99 A3
Padbury Ho NW8 ..... 90 B2
Paddenswick Ct
W6 .... 39 A3
Paddenswick Rd
W6 .... 38 C3
Paddington Com Hospl
W10 .... 31 C4
Paddington Gn
W2 .... 101 B4
Paddington Green Prim
Sch NW8 .... 89 B1
Paddington St W1 .. 103 B4
Paddington Sta
W2 .... 101 B2
Paddock CI SE3 ...... 53 C1
Paddock Sch SW15 . 56 B3
Padfield Rd SE5 ...... 63 B4
Padstow Ho **11** E14 33 B2
Padua Rd SE20 .... 75 C4
Pagden St SW8 ..... 170 B4
Page Ho SE10 .... 52 B4
Page St SW1 .... 147 C4
Page's Wlk SE1 ..... 138 B1
Page's Yd W4 .... 46 A4
Pageant Cres SE16 .. 33 B1
Pageantmaster Ct
EC4 .... 108 A1
Paget Ho **12** E2 ..... 25 B3
Paget Rd N16 .... 6 C3
Paget St EC1 .... 96 A4
Pagham Ho W10 ..... 22 B1
Pagnell St SE14 ...... 51 B3
Pagoda Ave TW9 .... 54 B4
Pagoda Gdns SE3 ... 52 C1
Paine Ct SE3 .... 53 B4
Painsthorpe Rd **5**
N16 .... 7 A1
Painswick Ct **7**
SE15 .... 49 B3
Pakeman Ho SE1 ... 136 B4
Pakeman Prim Sch
N7 .... 5 B1
Pakeman St N7 .... 5 B1
Pakenham CI SW12 .. 72 C3
Pakenham St WC1 ... 95 A2
Palace Ave W8 ..... 128 B4
Palace Ct W2 .... 114 A3
NW3 .... 11 A3
SW2 .... 74 C2
Palace Garden Mews
W8 .... 114 A3
Palace Gate W8 ... 128 C3
Palace Gdns Mews
W8 .... 114 B3
Palace Mans W14 .. 140 B4
Palace Mews SW1 . 145 C3

Palace Mews continued	
SW6	155 A2
Palace Pl SW1	132 C2
Palace Rd SE27,	
SW16,SW2	74 C2
Palace St SW1	132 C2
Palamon Ct SE1	153 A2
Palatine Ave N16	16 A4
Palatine Rd N16	16 A4
Palermo Rd NW10	21 C3
Palewell Common Dr	
SW14	55 C2
Palewell Pk SW14	55 C2
Palfrey Pl SW8	163 A2
Palgrave Ho	
NW3	12 B3
SE5	48 B3
Palgrave Rd W12	38 B3
Palissy St E2	98 C3
Pall Mall SW1	119 B1
Pall Mall E SW1	119 C2
Pall Mall Pl SW1	119 A1
Pallant Ho SE1	137 C2
Palliser Ct W14	140 A1
Palliser Ho ☐ E1	25 C1
SE10	52 C4
Palliser Rd W14	140 A1
Palm Ct N16	6 C2
17 SE15	49 B3
Palm Gr W5	36 A3
Palm Tree Ho	
SE14	50 C3
Palmer Ct NW10	20 C4
Palmer Ho 5 N19	4 B1
8 NW5	13 B4
SE14	50 C3
Palmer Pl N7	14 C3
Palmers Rd E2	25 C3
SW14	55 B4
Palmerston Ct 22	
E3	25 C3
Palmerston Ho	
W8	113 B1
SW11	169 C3
Palmerston Rd NW6	10 B1
W3	37 B3
SW14	55 B3
Palmerston Way	
SW8	160 B1
Pamela Ct NW10	8 C1
Pamela Ho 16 E8	24 B4
Pamlion Ct N4	5 A4
Panama Ho 5 E1	32 C4
Pancras La EC2	109 B1
Pancras Rd NW1	83 C2
Pandora Rd NW6	10 C2
Pangbourne NW1	92 C3
Pangbourne Ave	
W10	30 B4
Pangbourne Ho 4	
N7	14 A3
Pankhurst Cl 7	
SE14	50 C3
Panmure Cl N5	15 A4
Pansy Gdns W12	29 C2
Panton St SW1	119 B3
Panyer Alley EC2	108 C2
Panyer Alley Steps	
EC4	108 C2
Paper Mill Wharf	
E14	33 A2
Papillons Walk SE3	53 C1
Papworth Gdns N7	14 B3
Papworth Way SW2	74 C4
Parade Mans 19	
SE5	48 B1
Parade Mews SE27,	
SW2	75 A2
Parade The SW11	159 A2
Paradise Pas N7	14 C3
Paradise Rd SW4	172 A2
Richmond TW9	54 A2
Paradise Row E2	25 A2
Paradise St SE16	40 A4
Paradise Wlk SW3	159 A4
Paragon Cl E16	35 C3
Paragon Mews	
SE1	151 C4
Paragon Pl SE3	53 B1
Paragon Rd E9	17 B2
Paragon The SE3	53 C1
Paramount Bldg	
EC1	96 A2
Paramount Ct WC1	93 A1
Parbury Rd SE23	66 A1
Pardon St EC1	96 B2
Pardoner St SE1	137 C2
Parfett St E1	111 C2
Parfitt Cl NW3	2 B3
Parfrey St W6	47 B4
Paris Gdns SE1	122 A2
Paris Ho 12 E2	25 A3
Park Ave NW11	2 A3
NW2	9 B2
SW14	55 C3
Park Ave N NW10	9 A3
Park Bsns Ctr 4	
NW6	23 C2
Park Cl W14	127 A2
SW1	130 C3
32 E9	25 B4
Park Cres W1	92 A1
Park Cres Mews E	
W1	92 B1
Park Cres Mews W	92 A1
Park Ct SW11	170 A4
SW4	61 C2
SE21	72 C3
SE21	75 C1
Park Dr NW11	2 A3
SW14	55 C3
Park Dwellings 7	
NW3	12 B3
Park End NW3	12 A4
Park Flats N6	3 A4
Park Hall Rd SE21	75 C1
Park Hall Road Trad Est	
SE21	75 C1
Park Hill	
Richmond TW10	54 B1
SW4	61 C2
Park Hill Ct SW17	72 B1
Park Hill Wlk 10	
NW3	12 B3
Park Ho N4	6 A2
SE9	17 B1
8 SE5	48 C2
Park La E14	33 B2
Park Lea Ct N16	7 A4
Park Lo NW2	9 B4
13 NW8	11 C1
10 E1	32 A1
Park Lorne NW8	90 B3
Park Mans NW8	80 A1
SW1	130 C3
SW8	162 B4
SW6	164 B3
Park Mans continued	
SW11	168 C3
W6	38 B3
Park Mews W10	23 A3
Park Par NW10	21 B3
W3	36 C4
Park Pl W3	118 C2
E14	33 C1
W3	36 C2
Park Place Dr W3	36 C3
Park Place Villas	
W2	101 A4
Park Rd NW1,NW8	90 B2
NW10	21 A4
W4	45 C4
Richmond TW10	54 B1
Park Rd E W3	37 B4
Park Rd N W3	37 A4
W4	37 C1
Park Row SE10	52 C4
Park Royal Rd NW10	20 A4
Park Royal Bsns Ctr	
NW10	20 B1
Park Royal Metro Ctr	
NW10	20 A1
Park Royal Rd	
NW10,W3	20 B1
Park S SW11	169 B3
Park Sheen 3	
SW14	55 A3
Park Sq E NW1	92 B2
Park Sq Mews NW1	92 A1
Park Sq W NW1	92 A1
Park St W1	117 B3
Park St James SE8	80 C3
Park Steps W2	116 B4
Park The NW11	2 A3
Park Twrs W1	118 A1
Park View N5	15 B4
W3	28 B4
Park View Ct SW18	58 C1
Park View Ho SE24	63 A1
Park View Mews 2	
SW9	172 C2
Park View Rd NW10	8 B4
Park Village E 1	82 B1
Park Village W	
NW1	82 A2
Park Vista SE10	52 C4
Park Walk Prim Sch	
SW10	157 B3
Park Way W3	36 C2
Park West W2	102 B1
Park West Pl W1	
W2	102 B2
Park Wood Ho SW4	157 B4
Park Wood Mews W3	80 C3
Parke Rd SW13	46 C2
Parker Ct N1	87 A4
SW4	172 A3
Parker St WC2	106 B2
Parker St W2	106 B2
Parker's Row SE1	139 A3
Parkers Row SE16	139 B3
Parkfield Ave SW14	56 A3
Parkfield Ind Est	
SW11	169 C2
Parkfield Rd NW10	9 A1
SE14	51 B2
Parkfield St N1	85 C2
Parkfields SW15	57 B3
Parkgate Gdns	
SW14	55 C2
Parkgate Mews N6	4 B4
Parkgate Rd SW11	158 B1
Parkham St SW11	168 A3
Parkhill Rd NW3	12 B3
Parkholme Rd E8	16 C2
Parkhouse St SE5	48 C3
Parkhurst Ct N7	14 A4
Parkhurst Rd N7	14 A4
Parkinson Ct N1	97 C3
Parkinson Ho 6 E9	17 B1
Parkland Ct E14	126 A4
Parkland Gdns 12	
SW19	69 C3
Parkland Wlk N4,N8	5 B4
SW22	65 A2
Parklands Cl SW14	55 B2
Parkmead SW15	57 A1
Parkshot TW9	54 A3
Parkside W3	29 A1
SE3	53 B3
SW19	69 C1
Parkside Cres N7	5 C1
Parkside Est E9	25 C4
Parkside St SW11	169 B3
Parkstead Rd SW15	57 A2
Parkstone Rd 8	
SE15	49 C1
Parkthorne Rd	
SW12	73 C4
Parkview Ct SW6	164 B1
Parkville Rd SW6	154 C1
Parkway NW1	82 A3
Parkwood Prim Sch	
N4	6 B3
Parliament Ct NW3	12 A4
Parliament Hill	
NW3	12 A4
Parliament Hill Mans	
NW5	12 C4
Parliament Hill Sch	
NW5	12 C4
Parliament Mews	
SW14	45 B1
Parliament Sq	
SW1	134 A3
Parliament St	
SW1	134 A4
Parma Cres SW11	60 B3
Parmiter Ind Est 3	
E2	25 A3
Parmiter St E2	25 A3
Parmoor Ct EC1	96 C2
Parnell Cl W12	39 A3
Parnell Rd E3	26 B4
Parnham St E14	33 A3
Parolles Rd N19	4 B3
Parr Ct N1	87 B2
Parr St N1	87 B2
Parrington Ho 1	
SW4	61 C1
Parry Ho 32 E1	32 A1
Parry Rd W10	23 A2
Parry St SW8	162 B4
Parsifal Coll NW3	10 C4
Parsifal Ho NW3	10 C4
Parsifal Rd NW6	10 C3
Parson Ct SE13	67 A4
Parsonage St E14	42 B2
Parsons Gn SW6	165 B3
Parsons Green La	
SW6	165 B4
Parsons Green Sta	
SW6	165 B3
Parsons Ho 2	
SW2	89 B1
21 SW12	74 A4
Parsons Lo NW6	11 A1
Parthenia Rd SW6	165 C3
Partington Cl N19	4 C3
Parton Lo 4 E8	96 C4
Partridge Ct EC1	96 A2
Partridge Ho 28 E3	26 B3
Pascal St SW8	161 C2
Pascall Ho SE17	48 B4
Pascoe Rd SE13	67 C2
Pasley Cl SE17	150 C2
Passfield Dr E14	34 A4
Passfields W14	140 C1
Passing Alley EC1	96 B1
Passmore St SW1	145 B2
Pat Shaw Ho 2 E1	25 C1
Patcham Terr SW8	170 B4
Patchway Ct 2	
SE15	49 A4
Patent Ho E14	34 A4
Paternoster La	
EC4	108 B2
Paternoster Row	
EC2,EC4	108 C1
Paternoster Sq	
EC4	108 B2
Patience Rd SW11	168 A1
Patio Cl SW4	61 C1
Patmore Ho 6 N16	16 A3
Patmore St SW8	171 A4
Paton Cl 3 E3	26 C2
Paton Ho SW9	172 C2
Paton St EC1	96 C3
Patrick Coman Ho	
EC1	96 A3
Patrick Connolly Gdns	
3 E3	27 A2
Patriot Sq E2	25 A3
Patrol Pl SE6	67 A1
Patshull Pl NW5	13 B2
Patshull Rd NW5	13 B2
Patten Ho N4	6 B3
Patten Rd SW18	72 A4
Patterdale NW1	92 B3
Patterdale Rd SE15	50 B3
Pattina Wlk SE16	33 A1
Pattinson Point 10	
E16	35 C4
Pattison Ho 1	137 A4
1 E1	32 C3
Paul Ho 19 W10	23 A1
Paul Julius Cl E14	34 C2
Pauls Ho E3	33 B4
Paulet Rd SE5	48 A2
Paul's Ho E3	33 B4
Paulton Ho 1	111 C4
Paultons Ho SW3	157 C4
Paultons Sq SW3	157 C4
Paultons St SW3	157 C3
Pauntley Ho 6 N19	4 B3
Pauntley St 4 N19	4 B3
Pavan Ct 2 E2	25 B2
Paveley Dr SW11	158 A1
Paveley Ho N1	84 C1
11 E9	25 B4
Paveley St NW8	90 B2
Pavement The W5	36 A3
SW4	61 B3
Pavilion Ct 5 NW3	11 B4
NW6	23 C3
Pavilion Mans 10	
SW9	62 B3
Pavilion Rd SW1	131 A1
Pavilion St SW1	131 A1

Pavilion Terr W12 ...30 B3
Paxton Cl TW9 ...44 B2
Paxton Ho SE17 ...151 A2
Paxton Terr SW1 ...160 B4
Payens Wk W6 ...154 A3
Paymal Ho 20 E1 ...32 B4
Payne Ho N1 ...85 A3
Payne Rd E3 ...27 A3
Payne St SE8 ...51 B4
Paynesfield Ave
SW14 ...55 C4
Peabody Ave SW1 ...146 B3
Peabody Bldgs
SE17 ...151 B3
8 SE5 ...48 C2
Peabody Cl SW1 ...160 B4
Peabody Cl EC1 ...97 A1
9 SE5 ...48 C2
Peabody Est EC1 ...95 C1
EC1 ...97 A1
WC2 ...106 C1
SE1 ...121 C1
SE1 ...122 C1
E1 ...125 B4
SW1 ...147 A4
SW6 ...155 A4
18 E2 ...25 A3
W10 ...30 B4
4 E1 ...32 C2
17 W6 ...39 B1
SE24 ...75 B4
Peabody Hill SE21 ...75 B3
Peabody Sq SE1 ...136 A3
Peabody Twr EC1 ...97 A1
Peabody Yd N1 ...86 C4
Peach Rd W10 ...23 A2
Peachum Rd SE3 ...53 B4
Peacock St SE17 ...150 B3
Peacock Yd SE17 ...150 B3
Peak Ho N4 ...6 B3
Pear Cl SE14 ...51 A3
Pear Ct 20 SE15 ...49 B3
Pear Pl SE1 ...135 B4
Pear Tree Cl 22 E2 ...24 B4
Pear Tree Ct EC1 ...95 C1
SW15 ...57 A3
Pear Tree Ho SE4 ...66 B3
Pearce Ho N19 ...4 B1
7 SW2 ...74 A4
Peardon St SW8 ...170 B1
Pearfield Ho 1 N5 ...15 B3
Pearl St E1 ...32 A1
Pearman St SE1 ...135 C3
Pearscroft Ct SW6 ...166 B3
Pearscroft Rd SW6 ...166 B3
Pearson Ho SW15 ...47 B1
Pearson St E2 ...24 B3
Pearson's Ave SE8,
SE14 ...51 C2
Peartree Ave SW17 ...71 B1
Peartree La E1 ...32 B2
Peartree St EC1 ...96 C2
Peary Pl E2 ...25 B2
Peckarmans Wood
SE21,SE26 ...76 C1
Peckett Sq 3 N5 ...15 A4
Peckford Pl SW9 ...173 C1
Peckham Gr SE15 ...49 A3
Peckham High St
SE15 ...49 C2
Peckham Hill St
SE15 ...49 C3

Peckham Park Prim
Schs SE15 ...49 C3
Peckham Park Rd
SE15 ...49 C3
Peckham Rye SE22 ...64 C3
Peckham Rye
SE15,SE22 ...65 A3
Peckham Rye Jun & Inf
Sch SE15 ...65 A4
Peckham Rye Sta
SE15 ...49 C1
Peckwater St NW5 ...13 B3
Pedlars Wlk N7 ...14 A3
Pedley St E1 ...24 C1 99 B1
Pedro St E5 ...17 C4
Pedworth Gdns 4
SE16 ...40 B2
Peel Gr E2 ...25 B3
Peel Pass W8 ...113 B1
Peel Prec NW6 ...23 C3
Peel Rd NW6 ...23 C3
Peel St W8 ...31 C1 113 B1
Peerless St EC1 ...97 B3
Pegasus Cl N16 ...15 C4
Pegasus Ct
Brentford TW8 ...36 B1
Pegasus Ho 8 E1 ...25 C1
Pegasus Pl SE11 ...163 B4
Pegwell Ho 15 E5 ...17 A3
Pekin St E14 ...33 C3
Pekoe SE1 ...125 A1
Peldon Ct TW10 ...54 B2
Pelham Cl SE5 ...64 A4
Pelham Cres SW7 ...144 A3
Pelham Ho W14 ...140 C3
Pelham Pl SW7 ...144 A3
Pelham St SW7 ...143 C4
Pelican Ho 7 SE8 ...41 B2
Pelican Wlk SW9 ...63 A3
Pelier St SE17 ...48 B4
Pella Ho SE11 ...149 A2
Pellant Rd SW6 ...154 B2
Pellatt Rd SE22 ...64 B2
Pellerin Rd N16 ...16 A3
Pellew Ho 11 E1 ...25 A1
Pelling St E14 ...33 C3
Pelter St E2 ...98 C4
Pelton Rd SE10 ...43 A1
Pember Rd NW10 ...22 C2
Pemberton Ct 18
E1 ...25 C2
Pemberton Gdns N19 ...4 B1
Pemberton Pl 2 E8 ...17 A1
Pemberton Row
EC4 ...107 C2
Pemberton Terr N19 ...4 B1
Pembridge Cres
W11 ...31 C2 113 B4
Pembridge Gdns
W2 ...31 C2 113 B3
Pembridge Mews
W11 ...31 C2 113 B4
Pembridge Pl
W2 ...31 C2 113 C4
1 SW15 ...58 C2
Pembridge Rd
W11 ...31 C2 113 B3
Pembridge Sq
W2 ...31 C2 113 C3
Pembridge Villas
W11 ...31 C2 113 B4
Pembroke Bldgs
NW10 ...21 C2
Pembroke Cl SW1 ...131 C3
Pembroke Gdns
W8 ...141 A4

Pembroke Gdns Cl
W8 ...127 B1
Pembroke Ho W3 ...37 B4
SW15 ...56 C2
W2 ...100 B1
Pembroke Mews
W8 ...127 B1
Pembroke Pl W8 ...127 B1
Pembroke Rd W8 ...141 B4
Pembroke Sq W8 ...127 B1
Pembroke St N1 ...84 B4
Pembroke Studios
W8 ...127 A1
Pembroke Terr
NW8 ...79 B3
Pembroke Villas
W8 ...141 B4
Pembroke Wlk W8 ...141 B4
Pembrook Lo 2
SW16 ...74 B1
Pembury Cl 1 E5 ...17 A3
Pembury Ho SE5 ...49 A1
Pembury Pl 15 E5, ...17 A3
E8 ...17 A3
Pembury Rd E5 ...17 A3
Pemell Cl 1 E1 ...25 B1
Pemell Ho 2 E1 ...25 B1
Penally Pl N1 ...87 C4
Penang St E1 ...32 A1
Penarth St SE15 ...50 B4
Pencombe Mews
W11 ...113 A4
Pencraig Way SE15 ...50 A4
Penda's Mead E9 ...18 A4
Pendennis Ho 15
SE8 ...41 A2
Penderyn Way N7 ...13 C4
Pendle Ho 15 SE26 ...76 C1
Pendley Ho 15 E2 ...24 C4
Pendrell Rd SE4 ...51 A1
Pendrell St SW18 ...71 B4
Penfield Lo 7 W9 ...31 C4
Penfields Ho 5 N7 ...14 A2
Penfold Pl NW1 ...102 A3
Penfold Rd NW1 ...102 A4
Penfold St NW1 ...89 C1
Penford St SE5 ...48 A1
Penge Ho SW11 ...167 C1
Penhurst Mans
SW6 ...164 C4
Peninsula Ct E14 ...42 A3
Peninsular Park Rd
SE7 ...43 C2
Penmayne Ho
SE11 ...149 C2
Penn Almshouse 1
SE10 ...52 B3
Penn Ho NW8 ...90 A1
Penn Rd N7 ...14 A4
Penn St N1 ...87 C3
Pennack Rd SE15 ...49 B4
Pennant Mews
W8 ...142 A4
Pennard Mans 5
W12 ...39 B4
Pennine Ct E14 ...42 B2
Pennine Ct SW9 ...173 B3
Pennethorne Cl E9 ...25 B4
Pennethorne Ho
SW11 ...59 C4
Pennethorne Rd
SE15 ...50 A3
Pennine Mans NW2 ...1 A2
Pennine Par NW2 ...1 A2

Pennington Ct E1 ...125 C3
SE16 ...33 A1
Pennington St E1 ...32 A2
Penn Rd SW10 ...157 A4
Penny Mews SW12 ...73 A4
Penny Rd NW10 ...20 A2
Pennyfields E14 ...33 C2
Pennyford Ct NW8 ...89 B1
Pennymore Wk W9 ...23 B1
Penpoll Rd E8 ...17 A2
Penrhyn Cres SW14 ...55 B3
Penrith Cl SW15 ...58 A2
Penrith Pl SE27 ...75 A2
Penrose Gr SE17 ...150 C1
Penrose Ho SE17 ...150 C1
Penrose St SE17 ...150 C1
Penry St SE1 ...152 B3
Penryn Ho SE11 ...150 A2
Penryn St NW1 ...83 B2
Pensbury Pl SW8 ...171 A2
Pensbury St SW8 ...171 A2
Pensford Ave TW9 ...44 C1
Penshurst 2 NW5 ...12 C2
Penshurst Ho 1
SE15 ...50 B4
Penshurst Rd E9 ...17 C1
Pentland Cl NW11 ...1 A2
Pentland Ho 2 N16 ...7 B3
17 NW5 ...12 C2
Pentland St SW18 ...59 B1
Pentlow St SW15 ...57 B4
Pentney Rd SW12 ...73 B3
Penton Gr N1 ...85 B1
Penton Ho N1 ...85 B1
Penton Pl SE17 ...150 B2
Penton Rise WC1 ...95 A4
Penton St N1 ...85 B1
Pentonville Rd N1 ...84 C1
Pentridge St SE15 ...49 B3
Penwith Rd SW18 ...71 A2
Penwood Ho 4
SW15 ...56 B1
Penywern Rd SW5 ...141 C2
Penzance Ho SE11 ...149 C2
Penzance Pl
W11 ...31 A1 112 B2
Penzance St
W11 ...31 A1 112 A2
Peony Gdns W12 ...29 C2
Peperfield WC1 ...94 C3
Pepler Ho 17 W10 ...23 A1
Peploe Rd NW6 ...22 C3
Pepper St SE1 ...136 C4
E14 ...42 A3
Peppermead Sq
SE13 ...66 C2
Pepys Ct N16 ...7 A2
Pepys Cres 2 E16 ...35 C1
Pepys Ho 14 E2 ...25 B2
SW4 ...61 C2
Pepys Rd SE14 ...50 C1
Pepys St EC3 ...124 B4
Perceval Ave NW3 ...12 A3
Perch St E8 ...16 B4
Percival Rd SW14 ...55 B3
Percival St EC1 ...96 B3
Percy Cir WC1 ...95 A4
Percy Mews W1 ...105 B3
Percy Pass W1 ...105 B3
Percy Rd E16 ...35 A4
W12 ...38 C4
Percy St W1 ...105 B3
Peregrine Ct 7 SE8 ...51 C4
Peregrine Ho EC1 ...96 B4

Peregrine Ho continued
6 SW11 ...60 A4
Perham Rd W14 ...140 B1
Perifield SE21 ...75 B3
Perkins Ho 13 E14 ...33 B4
Perkins Rents
SW1 ...133 B1
Perkins Sq SE1 ...123 A2
Perks Cl SE3 ...53 A1
Perley Ho 10 E3 ...33 B4
Perotti Ho SW6 ...59 A4
Perran Rd SE24,SW2 ...75 A3
Perran Wlk TW8 ...36 A1
Perren St NW5 ...13 A2
Perrers Rd W6 ...39 A2
Perrin's Ct 21 NW3 ...11 B4
Perrin's La NW3 ...11 B4
Perrin's Wlk NW3 ...11 B4
Perring Est E3 ...33 C4
Perronet Ho SE1 ...136 B1
Perry Ave W3 ...28 C3
Perry Ho 52 SW2 ...74 A4
Perry's Pl W1 ...105 B2
Perrymead St SW6 ...166 A3
Perryn Ho W3 ...29 A2
Perryn Rd SW2 ...28 C2
SE16 ...40 A3
Perrywood Ho 17
E5 ...17 A3
Perseverance Works
E2 ...98 B4
Perseverance Pl
SW9 ...163 C1
Perth Ct 5 SE5 ...63 C3
Perth Ho N1 ...14 B1
Perth Rd N4 ...5 C3
Peter Ave NW10 ...9 A1
Peter Best Ho 6 E1 ...32 A3
Peter Butler Ho
SE1 ...139 B3
Peter Hills Ho
SE16 ...153 B4
Peter Hills with St
Mary's & St Paul's CE
Prim Sch SE16 ...32 C1
Peter Ho SW8 ...162 A2
Peter St W1 ...119 B4
Peter's Ct SW4 ...62 A1
Peter's La EC1 ...108 B4
Peterboat Cl SE10 ...43 A2
Peterborough Ct
EC4 ...107 C1
Peterborough Mews
SW6 ...165 B2
Peterborough Prim Sch
SW6 ...166 C1
Peterborough Rd
SW6 ...58 C4
Peterborough Villas
SW6 ...166 A4
Peterchurch Ho
SE15 ...50 A4
Petergate SW11 ...59 B3
Peterley Bsns Ctr 69
E2 ...25 A3
Peters Ct W2 ...100 B2
Petersfield Rd W3 ...37 B4
Petersfield Rise
SW15 ...69 A3
Petersham Ho
SW7 ...143 B4
Petersham La
SW7 ...128 C2
Petersham Mews
SW7 ...129 A1
Petersham Pl SW7 ...129 A1

Petersham Rd
TW10 ....54 A1
Peterstow Cl SW19 ....70 A2
Petherton Cl SW10 .....5 C1
Petherton Ho N4 ....6 B3
Petherton Rd N5 ......15 B3
Petiver Cl 28 E9 ......17 B1
Petley Rd W6 ....47 C3
Peto Pl NW1 ....92 B2
Peto St N E16 ....35 B1
Petrel Ct 7 SE21 .....75 C2
Petrie Cl NW2 ....10 A2
Petros Gdns 1
NW3 ....11 B2
Petticoat Lane Mkt*
EC2 ....110 C3
Petticoat Sq E1 .....110 C2
Petticoat Twr E1 ....110 C2
Pettiward Cl SW15 ....57 B3
Petty France SW1 ....133 B2
Petworth Ho 15
SE22 ....64 A4
Petworth St SW11 ...168 B4
Petyt Pl SW3 ....158 A3
Petyward SW3 ....144 B3
Pevensey Ct 4 W3 ....37 A4
SW16 ....74 C1
Pevensey Ho 5 E1 ....33 A4
Peveril Ho SE1 ......137 C1
Pewsham Ho N4 ....6 B3
Peyton Pl SE10 ......52 B3
Pharamond NW2 ....9 C2
Phelp St SE17 ....48 C4
Phelps Ho SW15 .....57 C4
Phene St SW3 ....158 B4
Phil Brown Pl 3
SW8 ....170 B1
Philadelphia Ct
SW10 ....157 A1
Philbeach Gdns
SW5 ....141 B2
Philchurch Pl E1 ....111 C1
Philia Ho 2 NW1 .....13 B1
Philip Cl W2 ....101 A4
Philip Ct W2 ....101 B4
Philip Ho 5 NW6 .....78 A3
Philip Rd SE15 ......64 C4
Philip Turner Est 28
E9 ....17 B1
Philip Wlk SE15 .....65 A4
Phillimore Ct W8 ....127 B3
Phillimore Gardens Cl
W8 ....127 B2
Phillimore Gdns
W8 ....127 B3
NW10 ....22 B4
Phillimore Pl W8 ....127 B3
Phillimore Terr
W8 ....127 C2
Phillimore Wlk
W8 ....127 C2
Phillip Ho E1 ....111 A3
Phillipp St N1 ....24 A4
Philpot La EC3 ......124 A4
Philpot Sq SW6 .....59 A4
Philpot St E1 ....32 A3
Phipp St EC2 ..24 A1 98 A2
Phipps Ho 10 W12 ....30 A2
Phoebeth Rd SE4 ....66 C2
Phoenix Cl 18 E8 ....24 B4
Phoenix Ct
4 Brentford TW8 ...36 A1
2 E14 ....41 C2
5 SE14 ....51 A4
Phoenix High Sch
W12 ....29 C2

Phoenix Lodge Mans 1
W6 ....39 B2
Phoenix Pl WC1 .....95 A2
Phoenix Rd NW1 ....93 B4
Phoenix Sch E3 ......26 B2
Phoenix St WC2 ....105 C1
Phoenix Wharf Rd
SE1 ....139 A3
Physic Pl SW3 ......158 C4
Piccadilly W1 ....118 C2
Piccadilly Arc
SW1 ....118 C2
Piccadilly Circ W1 ..119 B3
Piccadilly Circus Sta
SW1 ....119 B3
Piccadilly Pl W1 .....119 A3
Pickard St EC1 ....96 B4
Pickering Ho N4 ......6 C4
W2 ....100 B1
Pickering Pl SW1 ...119 A1
Pickering St N1 ......86 B4
Pickets St SW12 .....73 A4
Pickfords Wharf N1 ..86 C1
Pickwick Ho 16
1 SE16 ....139 B3
3 W11 ....30 C1
Pickwick Rd SE21 ...76 A4
Pickwick St SE1 ....136 C3
Pickworth Cl SW8 ...162 B1
Picton Ho 1 SW4 ....74 A4
Picton Pl W1 ....103 C1
Picton St SE5 ....48 C3
Pied Bull Ct WC1 ...106 B3
Pied Bull Yd WC1 ...106 B3
Pier Ho SW3 ....158 B3
Pier St E14 ....42 B2
Pier Terr SW18 ......59 B3
Pierhead Wharf 37
E1 ....32 A1
Piermont Rd SE22 ...65 A2
Pierrepoint Rd W3 ...28 A2
Piggott St E14 ......33 C3
Pigott St E14 ....33 C3
Pilgrim Ho SE1 .....137 C1
Pilgrim St EC4 ......108 A1
Pilgrim's La NW3 ....11 C4
Pilgrimage St SE1 ..137 B3
Pilgrims Cloisters 18
SE5 ....49 A3
Pilgrims Ct SE3 .....53 C2
Pilgrims Mews E14 ..34 C2
Pilgrims Way N19 ....4 C3
Pilgrims Way Prim Sch
SE15 ....50 B4
Pilkington Rd 4
SE15 ....50 A1
Pilot Ind Ctr NW10 ..21 A1
Pilsden Cl SW19 ....69 C3
Pilton Pl SE17 ......151 A2
Pimlico Rd SW1 ....145 C2
Pimlico Sch SW1 ....147 A1
Pimlico Sta SW1 ....147 B2
Pimlico Wlk N1 ......98 A4
Pinchin St E1 ....125 C4
Pincombe Ho 17 ....151 B2
Pincott Pl SE4 ......65 C4
Pindar St EC2 ....110 A4
Pindock Mews W9 ...88 B1
Pine Apple Ct
SW1 ....132 C2
Pine Ave E15 ....19 C3
Pine Cl E8 ....16 B1
Pine Gr N4,N19 ......5 B2
Pine Ho 16 SE16 ....40 B4
Pine Lo SW15 ....58 A1
Pine Rd NW2 ....9 C4

Pine St EC1 ....95 B2
Pine Tree Ho 14 SE14 .50 C3
Pinedene 2 SE15 ....50 A2
Pinefield Cl E14 .....33 C2
Pinehurst Ct 6
W11 ....31 B3
Pinelands 1 E14 ....41 C4
Pines Ct 14 SW19 ...69 C3
Pinewood Ct SW4 ...61 C1
Pinkham Mans W4 ..36 C1
Pinnacle Ho E14 ....42 B3
Pinner Ho 11 SE5 ...48 B1
Pintail Ct 28 SE8 ....51 B4
Pinter Ho 10 SW9 ..172 B1
Pioneer Cl W12 .....30 A3
Pioneer St SE15 .....49 C2
Pioneer Way W12 ...30 B3
Piper Cl N7 ....14 B2
Pippins Ct 5 SW6 ..162 C4
Pirbright Rd SW18 ..70 C3
Pitcairn Ho 1 E9 ....17 B1
Pitfield Ho N5 ....15 B3
Pitfield St N1 ....24 A3
N1 ....24 A3 98 B4
Pitman Ho 4 SE8 ...51 C2
Pitman St SE5 ......48 B3
Pitmaston Ho 2
SE13 ....52 B1
Pitsea Pl E1 ....32 C3
Pitsea St E1 ....32 C3
Pitt Ho 4 SW11 .....59 C3
Pitt St W8 ....127 C4
Pitt's Head Mews
W1 ....117 C1
Pixley St E14 ....33 B3
Plane Tree Ho 11 SE8 .51 A4
Planetree Ct W6 ....39 C2
Plantain Pl SE1 .....137 B4
Plantation The SE3 ..53 C1
Plantation Wharf
SW11 ....59 C4
Plato Pl 16 SW6 ....165 A2
Plato Rd SW2 ....62 A3
Platt's La NW3 ....1 C1
Platt's La NW3 ....1 C1
Plaxdale Ho SE17 ..152 A3
Playfair St W6 ....39 B1
Playfield Cres SE22 ..64 B2
Playford Rd N4 ......5 B2
N4 ....5 C2
Playhouse Yd EC4 ..108 A1
Pleasance Rd SW15 ..57 A2
Pleasance The
SW15 ....57 A3
Pleasant Pl N1 ......15 A1
Pleasant Row NW1 ..82 B3
Plender Ct NW1 .....83 A3
Plender St NW1 .....83 A3
Pleshey Rd N7 ......13 C4
Plevna St E14 ....42 B3
Pleydell Ave W6 ....38 B2
Pleydell Ct EC4 .....107 C1
Pleydell St EC4 .....107 C1
Plimsoll Cl E14 .....34 A3
Plimsoll Rd N4 ......6 A1
Plough Ct EC3 ......123 C4
Plough La SE22 .....64 B1
Plough Pl EC4 ....107 C2
Plough Rd SW11 ....59 C3
Plough St 11 E1 ....111 B2
Plough Ter SW11 ....59 C3
Plough Way SE16 ...41 A2
Plough Yd EC2 ......98 C1
Ploughmans Cl
NW1 ....83 B4
Plover Ho 57 SE8 ....51 B4
Plover Ho SW9 ......163 B2

Plover Way SE16 ....41 A3
Plowman Ho SW19 ..69 C3
Plumbers Row 1 E1 ..111 C2
Plumbridge St
SE10 ....52 B2
Plume Ho SE10 .....52 A4
Plummer Ho SE13 ..67 A1
Plummer Rd SW4 ...73 C4
Plumtree Ct EC4 ...108 A2
Plymouth Rd E16 ...35 C4
Plymouth Wharf
E14 ....42 C2
Plympton Ave NW6 ..10 B1
Plympton Pl NW1 ...90 A1
Plympton Rd NW6 ..10 B1
Plympton St NW8 ...90 A1
Pocklington Ct
SW15 ....68 C3
Pocock St SE1 ......136 B4
Podmore Rd SW18 ..59 B3
Poet's Corner SW1 ..134 A2
Poet's Rd N5 ....15 C3
Point Hill SE10 .....52 B2
Point Pleasant
SW18 ....58 C3
Pointer Sch The 53 C3
Pointers Cl E14 .....42 A1
Poland St W1 ....105 A1
Polesworth Ho 10
W2 ....31 C4
Pollard Cl N7 ....14 B4
E16 ....35 C2
Pollard Ho N1 ....84 C1
Pollard Row E2 ..24 C2 99 C4
Pollard St E2 ....24 C2 99 C4
Pollen St W1 ....104 B1
Pollitt Dr NW8 ......89 C2
Pollock Ho 10 W10 ..23 A1
Polperro Mans 3
NW6 ....10 C3
Polygon Rd NW1 ....83 C2
Polygon The NW8 ...79 C4
1 SW4 ....61 B3
Pomell Way E1 .....111 A2
Pomeroy Ct 11 W11 ..31 A3
Pomeroy Ho 5 E2 ...25 C3
Pomeroy St SE14 ...50 B2
Pomfret Rd SE5 .....63 A4
Pomoja La N19 ......5 A2
Pond Cl SE3 ....53 C1
Pond Cotts SE21 ....76 A3
Pond Ho SW3 ....144 A3
Pond Mead SE21 ....63 C1
Pond Pl SW3 ....144 A3
Pond Rd SE3 ....53 B1
Pond Sq N6 ....3 C3
Pond St NW3 ....12 A3
Ponder St 3 N7 .....14 B1
Ponler St E1 ....32 A3
Ponsard Rd NW10 ..22 A2
Ponsford St E9 ......17 B2
Ponsonby Ho 13 E2 ..25 B3
Ponsonby Pl SW1 ..147 C2
Ponsonby Rd SW15 ..69 A4
Ponsonby Terr
SW1 ....147 C2
Pont St Mews
SW1 ....130 C1
Ponton Ho SW2 .....74 C3

Ponton Rd SW8 .....161 C3
Pontypool Pl SE1 ...136 A4
Pool Ho NW8 ....101 C4
Poole Ct N1 ....16 A1
Poole Ho SE11 .....135 A1
Poole Rd E9 ....17 C2
Pooles Bldgs EC1 ...95 B1
Pooles La SW10 ....156 C1
Pooles Park Prim Sch
N4 ....5 B2
Pooles Pk N4 ....5 C2
Poolmans St SE16 ..40 C4
Poonah St E1 ....32 B3
Pope Ho 7 SE16 ....40 A2
3 SE5 ....48 C3
Pope John RC Prim Sch
W12 ....30 A2
Pope's La W5 ....36 A3
Pope's Rd SW9 .....62 C4
Popham Ct N16 .....7 A1
Popham Gdns TW9 ..55 A4
Popham Rd N1 ......86 C4
Popham St N1 ......86 B4
N1 ....86 C4
Poplar Bath St 10
E14 ....34 A2
Poplar Bsns Pk E14 ..34 B2
Poplar Cl E9 ....18 B3
Poplar Ct 4 SW16 ..74 B1
Poplar Gr W6 ....39 B4
Poplar High St E14 ..34 A2
Poplar Ho 18 SE16 ..40 C4
SE4 ....66 B3
Poplar Mews W12 ..30 B1
Poplar Pl W2 ....114 B4
Poplar Rd SE24 ....63 B3
Poplar Sta E14 .....34 A2
Poplar Wlk SE24 ...63 B3
Poplars The NW5 ...13 B3
Poppins Ct EC4 ....108 A1
Porchester Ct 2 W2 ..114 B4
Porchester Garden
Mews W2 ....114 C4
Porchester Gate
W2 ....114 C3
Porchester Gdns
W2 ....114 B4
Porchester Mews
W2 ....100 B2
Porchester Pl W2 ...102 B1
Porchester Rd W2 ..100 B2
Porchester Sq W2 ..100 B2
Porchester Terr
W2 ....114 C4
Porchester Terrace N
W2 ....100 B2
Porden Rd SW2 ....62 B3
Porlock Ho 5 SE26 ..76 C1
Porlock St SE1 .....137 C4
Port Ho 6 SW11 ...158 A4
Port Royal Pl 3
N16 ....16 A3
Portal Cl SE27 .....74 C1
Portbury Cl 16 SE15 ..49 C2
Porchester Cl SE14 ..51 A4
Portelet Ct 1 N1 ....24 A4
Portelet Rd E1 ......25 C2
Porten Hos W14 ...126 A1
Porten Rd W14 ....126 A1

Porter Sq N19 ...5 A3
Porter St W1 ...103 A4
SE1 ...123 A2
Porteus Rd W2 ...101 A4
Portgate Cl W9 ...23 B1
Portia Way E3 ...26 B1
Porticos The SW3 ...157 B3
Portinscale Rd
SW15 ...58 B2
Portishead Ho 28
W2 ...31 C4
Portland Ave N16 ...7 B4
Portland Ct 7 N1 ...16 A1
1 SE14 ...51 A4
Portland Gr SW8 ...172 C4
Portland Ho 80 SW2 ...74 C3
Portland Hospl for
Women & Children The
W1 ...92 B1
Portland Mews
W1 ...105 A1
Portland Pl W1 ...104 B3
Portland Rd W11 ...31 A3
W11 ...31 A1 112 B2
Portland Rise N4 ...6 B3
Portland Sq 4 E1 ...32 A1
Portland St SE17 ...151 B1
Portland Village
W6 ...39 B3
Portman Ave SW14 ...55 C4
Portman Cl W1 ...103 B2
Portman Gate NW1 ...90 B1
Portman Hts 11 NW3 ...1 C1
Portman Mews S
W1 ...103 B1
Portman Pl E2 ...25 B2
Portman Sq W1 ...103 B2
Portman St W1 ...103 B1
Portman Twrs W1 ...103 A1
Portnall Rd W9 ...23 B2
Portobello Ct Est
W11 ...31 B3
Portobello Mews
W11 ...113 B3
Portobello Rd
W11 ...31 A4 113 A4
Portobello Road Mkt*
W10 ...31 A4
Portpool La E1 ...107 B4
Portree St E14 ...34 C3
Portsea Hall W2 ...102 B1
Portsea Ho 8
SW15 ...69 A3
Portsea Mews W2 ...102 B1
Portsea Pl W2 ...102 B1
Portslade Rd SW8 ...170 C2
Portsmouth Rd
SW15 ...69 B4
Portsmouth St
WC2 ...107 A1
Portsoken St E1,
EC3 ...124 C4
Portswood Pl 30
SW15 ...56 B1
Portugal St WC2 ...107 A1
Poseidon Ct 8 E14 ...41 C2
Post Office Way
SW8 ...161 B2
Postern The E2 ...109 A3
Pott St E2 ...25 A2

Potterne Cl 5
SW19 ...69 C4
Potters Fields SE1 ...124 B1
Potters Lo E14 ...42 B1
Potters Rd SW6 ...166 C1
Pottery La
W11 ...31 A1 112 B2
Pottery Rd TW8 ...44 A4
Pottery St SE16 ...40 A4
Poullett Ho SW2 ...75 A3
Poulton Cl E8 ...17 A2
Poultry EC2 ...109 B1
Pound La NW10 ...8 C2
Pountney Rd SW11 ...60 C4
Povey Ho 37 SW2 ...152 A3
SW2 ...62 C1
Powell's Wlk W4 ...46 B4
Power Ho 7 TW9 ...44 C2
Power Ho The W4 ...38 B2
Power Rd W4 ...36 C2
Powerscroft Rd E5 ...17 B4
Powis Gdns NW11 ...1 B4
W11 ...31 B3
Powis Mews W11 ...31 B3
Powis Pl WC1 ...94 B1
Powis Rd E3 ...27 A2
Powis Sq W11 ...31 B3
Powis Terr W11 ...31 B3
Powlett Ho NW1 ...13 A2
Powlett Pl NW1 ...13 A1
Pownall Rd E8 ...24 C4
Powrie Ho 6 SW11 ...167 C2
Poynder Ct 3 N7 ...14 A3
Poynders Gdns
SW12 ...73 B4
Poynders Rd SW12,
SW4 ...73 C4
Poynings Rd N19 ...4 B1
Poynter Ho NW8 ...89 B2
10 W11 ...30 C1
Poyntz Rd SW11 ...168 C1
Poyser St E2 ...25 A3
Praed Mews W2 ...101 C2
Praed St W2 ...101 C2
Prague Pl SW2 ...62 A2
Prah Rd N4 ...5 C2
Prairie St SW8 ...170 A1
Pratt Mews NW1 ...82 C3
Pratt St NW1 ...82 C4
Pratt Wlk SE11 ...149 A4
Prebend Gdns W4,
W6 ...38 B2
Prebend Mans 4
W4 ...38 B2
Prebend St N1 ...86 C4
Precinct The N1 ...86 C3
NS ...15 B2
Preedy Ho N1 ...85 A2
Premier Park Rd
NW10 ...20 A3
Premier Pl E14 ...33 C2
Prendergast Ho 7
SW4 ...73 C3
Prendergast Sch
SE4 ...66 C3
Prescot St E1 ...125 A4
Prescott Ho 15
SE17 ...48 A4
Prescott Pl SW4 ...61 C3
Presentation Mews
SW2 ...74 B3
President Dr E1 ...32 A1
President Ho EC1 ...96 B3
President St EC1 ...96 C4

Prestage Way E14 ...34 B2
Prested Rd SW11 ...60 A3
Preston Cl SE1 ...152 A4
Preston Gdns NW10 ...8 A2
Preston Ho SE1 ...138 C2
SE1 ...152 A4
Preston Pl NW2 ...8 C2
Richmond TW10 ...54 A2
Preston's Rd E14 ...34 B1
Prestwich Terr SW4 ...61 C2
Prestwood Ho 3
SE16 ...40 A3
Prestwood St N1 ...87 A1
Priam Ho 17 E2 ...25 A3
Price Cl SW17 ...72 B1
Price Ho N1 ...86 C3
Price's St SE1 ...122 B2
Price's Yd N1 ...85 A3
Prichard Ct N1 ...167 C3
N7 ...14 B3
Prideaux Ho WC1 ...95 A4
Prideaux Pl WC1 ...95 A4
W3 ...28 C3
Priestfield Rd SE23 ...66 A2
Priest's Ct EC2 ...108 C2
Priestley Cl N16 ...7 B4
Priestley Ho EC1 ...97 A2
2 NW5 ...13 A4
Priestman Point 25
E3 ...27 A2
Priests Bridge
SW14 ...56 A4
Prima Road SW9 ...163 B2
Primrose Ct 11
SW12 ...73 C4
Primrose Gdns
NW3 ...12 A2
Primrose Hill EC4 ...107 C1
Primrose Hill Ct
NW3 ...12 B1
Primrose Hill Prim Sch
NW1 ...81 C4
Primrose Hill Rd
NW1,NW3 ...80 C4
Primrose Hill Sta
NW3 ...12 C1
Primrose Hill Studios
NW1 ...81 B4
Primrose Ho 2
Richmond TW9 ...44 B2
17 SE15 ...49 C2
Primrose Mans
SW11 ...169 B4
Primrose Mews 9
NW1 ...12 B1
Primrose Sq E9 ...25 B4
Primrose St EC2 ...110 B4
Primula St W12 ...29 C3
Prince Albert Ct
NW8 ...80 C3
Prince Albert Rd
NW8 ...80 C3
Prince Arthur Ct 19
NW3 ...11 B4
Prince Arthur Mews 20
NW3 ...11 B4
Prince Arthur Rd
NW3 ...11 C3
Prince Charles Rd
SE3 ...53 B2
Prince Consort Rd
SW7 ...129 C2
Prince Edward Mans
W2 ...113 C4
Prince Edward Rd
E9 ...18 B2

Prince George Rd
N16 ...16 A4
Prince of Orange La S
SE10 ...52 B3
Prince of Wales Dr
SW11 ...169 B4
Prince of Wales Mans
SW11 ...169 C4
SW4 ...61 A2
Prince of Wales Pas
NW1 ...92 C3
Prince Of Wales Rd
SE3 ...53 B2
NW5 ...12 C2
Prince of Wales Terr
W8 ...128 B3
W4 ...38 A1
Prince Regent Ct
SE16 ...33 A1
Prince Regent Mews
NW1 ...92 C3
Prince St SE8 ...51 B4
Prince's Ct SE16 ...41 B3
Prince's Gate
SW7 ...130 A3
Prince's Mews W6 ...39 A1
Prince's Mews
W2 ...114 A4
Prince's Rd SW14 ...55 C4
Prince's Sq W2 ...114 A4
Prince's St TW10,
TW9 ...54 A2
Prince's St EC2 ...109 B1
Princedale Rd
W11 ...31 A1 112 B2
Princelet St E1 ...111 A4
Princes Arc SW1 ...119 A2
Princes Ave W3 ...36 C3
Princes Cir WC2 ...106 A2
Princes Cl N4 ...6 A3
Princes Ct NW2 ...10 A3
NW3 ...11 C4
E1 ...32 A2
Princes Gate SW7 ...129 C3
Princes Gate Ct
SW7 ...129 C3
Princes Gate Mews
SW7 ...129 C2
Princes Ho W11 ...113 B3
Princes Pl
W11 ...31 A1 112 B2
SW1 ...119 A2
Princes Rd
Richmond TW10 ...54 B2
Princes Rise SE13 ...52 B1
Princes Riverside Rd 5
SE16 ...32 C1
Princes St W1 ...104 B1
Princes Way W3 ...36 C3
SW15,SW19 ...70 A3
Princes Yd W11 ...112 B1

Princess Frederica CE
Prim Sch NW10 ...22 B3
Princess Grace Hospl
The W1 ...91 B1
Princess Louise Hospl
W10 ...30 A4
Princess Mary Ho
SW1 ...147 C3
Princess May JMI Sch
N16 ...16 B4
Princess May Rd
N16 ...16 A4
Princess Mews
NW3 ...11 C2
Princess Rd NW1 ...81 C4
NW6 ...23 C3
Princess St SE1 ...136 B1
Princethorpe Ho
W2 ...100 A4
Princeton Ct SW15 ...57 C4
Princeton Mans
WC1 ...106 C3
Princeton St WC1 ...106 C4
Print Village Ind Est
SW15 ...49 B1
Printer St EC4 ...107 C2
Printing House Yd
E2 ...98 B3
Printon Ho 12 E3 ...33 B4
Prior Bolton St N1 ...15 A2
Prior St SE10 ...52 B3
Prior Weston Prim Sch
EC1 ...97 A1
Prioress Ho 2 E3 ...27 A2
Prioress Rd SE27 ...75 A1
Priors Lo 4 TW10 ...54 A1
Priory Ave CE4 ...38 A3
Priory Ct EC4 ...108 B1
SW8 ...171 C4
E9 ...17 C3
SW15 ...56 B3
Priory Gdns 6 W4 ...38 A3
SW13 ...56 B4
Priory Gn N1 ...84 C2
Priory Gr SW8 ...172 A3
Priory Ho EC1 ...96 A2
E1 ...110 C4
SW1 ...147 B2
Priory Hospl The
SW15 ...56 B3
Priory Lo 6 W4 ...36 C1
Priory Mans NW3 ...11 B2
SW10 ...143 A1
Priory Park Rd NW6 ...23 B4
Priory Rd NW6 ...78 A4
NW6 ...11 A1
W4 ...37 C3
Richmond TW9 ...44 C3
Priory St 16 E3 ...27 A2
Priory Terr NW6 ...78 A4
Priory The SE1 ...136 A3
Priory Wlk SW10 ...143 A1
Pritchard Ho 82 E2 ...24 C3
Pritchard's Rd E2 ...24 C4
Priter Rd SE16 ...139 C1
SE16 ...153 C4
Priter Road Hostel
SE16 ...139 C1
Probert Rd SW2 ...62 C2
Probyn Ho SW1 ...147 C4
Probyn Rd SW2 ...75 A2
Procter Ho 15 SE5 ...48 C3
SE16 ...153 B1
Procter St WC1 ...106 C3
Proctor Ho SE1 ...153 B1

Prome Ho 3 N16 ...15 C4
Promenade Approach Rd W4 ....46 A3
Promenade The W4 .46 A2
Prospect Cotts SW18 ....58 C3
Prospect Ho N1 ...85 B1
SE1 ....136 B1
1 E8 ....16 B2
14 W10 ....30 C3
Prospect Pl 4 NW2 ..1 B1
E1 ....32 B1
2 W4 ....37 C1
6 SE8 ....51 B4
Prospect Rd NW2 ....1 C1
Prospect St SE16 ..40 A4
Prospect Wharf E1 .32 B2
Prospero Rd N19 ....4 C3
Prothero Rd SW6 ..154 C2
Prout Gr NW10 ....8 B4
Provence St N1 ....86 C2
Providence Ct W1 .117 C4
Providence Ho E9 ..25 C4
Providence Pl N1 ..86 A3
Providence Row N1 84 C1
Providence Sq SE1 139 B4
Providence Twr SE16 ....139 B4
Provost Ct NW3 ....12 B2
Provost Rd NW3 ....12 B1
Provost St N1 ....97 B4
Prowse Pl NW1 ....13 B1
Prudent Pas EC2 ..109 A1
Prusom St E1 ....32 A1
Prusom's Island 8 E1 ....32 B1
Pryors The NW3 ....2 C1
Public Record Office EC4,WC2 ....107 B2
Richmond TW9 ....45 A3
Pudding La EC3 ...123 C4
Pudding Mill La E15 ....27 A4
Pudding Mill Lane Sta E15 ....27 A4
Puddle Dock EC4 ..122 B4
Pugin Ct N1 ....14 C1
Pulborough Rd SW18 ....70 B4
Pulham Ho SW8 ...162 C1
Pullman Ct SW2 ....74 B3
Pullman Gdns SW15 57 B1
Pulross Rd SW9 ....62 B4
Pulteney Cl 13 E3 ...26 B4
Pulteney Terr N1 ..85 A4
Pulton Ho SE4 ....66 A3
Pulton Pl SW6 ....155 B1
Puma Ct E1 ....110 C4
Pump Ct EC4 ....107 B1
Pump La SE14 ....50 B3
Pumping Station Rd W4 ....46 A4
Punderson's Gdns E2 ....25 A2
Purbeck Ho SW8 ..162 C1
Purbrook Est SE1 ..138 B3
Purbrook Ho 2 SW15 ....69 A3
Purbrook St SE1 ...138 B2
Purcell Cres SW6 ..154 A2
Purcell Ho SW10 ..157 B3
Purcell Mews NW10 ..8 A1
Purcell St N1 ....24 A3
Purchese St NW1 ...83 C1
Purday Ho 4 W10 ..23 B2
Purdon Ho 10 SE15 .49 C2
Purdy St E3 ....27 A1
Purley Ave NW2 ....1 A2
Purley Pl N1 ....15 A1
Purser Ho 3 SW2 ..62 C1
Pursers Cross Rd SW6 ....165 A4
Purves Rd NW10 ...22 B3
Pusey Ho 16 E14 ...33 C3
Puteaux Ho 6 E2 ...25 C3
Putney Bridge App SW6 ....58 A4
Putney Bridge Rd SW15 ....58 B3
Putney Bridge Sta SW6 ....58 B4
Putney Comm SW15 57 B4
Putney Heath SW15 .57 B1
Putney Heath La SW15 ....57 C1
Putney High Sch SW15 ....57 C2
Putney High St SW15 ....58 A3
Putney Hill SW15 ..57 C2
Putney Hospl SW15 .57 B4
Putney Park Ave SW15 ....56 C3
Putney Park La SW15 ....57 A2
Putney Pier SW15 ..58 A4
Putney School of Art & Design SW15 ....58 A3
Putney Sta SW15 ....58 A3
Pylon Trad Est E16 ..34 C4
Pym Ho SW9 ....173 C1
Pymers Mead SE21 .75 B3
Pynfolds SE16 ....40 A4
Pynnersmead SE24 .63 B2
Pyrford Ho 12 SW9 .63 A3
Pyrland Rd N5 ....15 C3
Richmond TW10 ....54 B1
Pyrmont Gr SE27 ..75 A1
Pyrmont Rd W4 ....44 C4
Pytchley Rd SE22 ..64 A4

Q

Quadrangle Cl SE1 152 A4
Quadrangle The W2 ....102 A2
SW6 ....154 A1
SW10 ....167 A4
W12 ....30 B3
SE24 ....63 B2
Quadrant Arc W1 .119 A3
Quadrant Gr NW5 ..12 B3
Quadrant The 4 W10 ....22 C2
Richmond TW9 ....54 A3
Quaker Ct EC1 ....97 A2
Quaker St E1 24 B1 98 C1
Quality Ct WC2 ...107 B2
Quantock Ho N16 ...7 B3
Quarley Way 6 SE15 ....49 B3
Quarrendon St SW6 ....165 C2
Quarry Rd SW18 ...59 B1
Quarterdeck The E14 ....41 C4
Quartermile La E10, E15 ....19 A4
Quayside Ct 6 SE16 ....32 C1
Quebec & Crown Wharves E14 ....33 B3
Quebec Mews W1 .103 A1
Quebec Way SE16 ..41 A4
Quebeck Ind Est SE16 ....41 A3
Quedgeley Ct 3 SE15 ....49 B4
Queen Alexandra Mans WC1 ....94 A3
Queen Anne Mews W1 ....104 B3
Queen Anne Rd E9 .17 C2
Queen Anne St W1 ....104 A3
Queen Anne's Gate SW1 ....133 B3
Queen Anne's Gdns W5 ....36 A4
W4 ....38 A3
Queen Anne's Gr W5 ....36 A4
W4 ....38 A3
Queen Caroline St W6 ....39 B1
Queen Charlotte's Maternity Hospl W6 ....38 C2
Queen Elizabeth Hall & Purcell Room* SE1 ....121 A2
Queen Elizabeth Hospital for Children The E2 ....24 C3
Queen Elizabeth II Con Ctr SW1 ....133 C3
Queen Elizabeth II Pier SE10 ....35 B1
Queen Elizabeth II Sch W9 ....23 B1
Queen Elizabeth St SE1 ....138 C4
Queen Elizabeth Wlk SW13 ....47 A2
Queen Elizabeth's Cl N16 ....6 C2
Queen Elizabeth's Coll SE10 ....52 B3
Queen Elizabeth's Wlk N16 ....6 C2
Queen Margaret Flats 22 E2 ....25 A2
Queen Margaret's Gr N1 ....16 A3
Queen Margarets Ct N1 ....16 A3
Queen Mary's Gdns NW1 ....91 B3
Queen Mary's Hospl NW3 ....2 B1
Queen Mary's Univ Hospl SW15 ....56 C1
Queen of Denmark Ct SE16 ....41 B3
Queen Sq WC1 ....106 B4
Queen Sq Pl WC1 ...94 B1
Queen St W1 ....118 A2
EC4 ....123 A4
Queen St Pl EC4 ...123 A4
Queen Victoria Mon* SW1 ....132 C4
Queen Victoria St EC4 ....122 C4
Queen's CE Jun Mix Sch The TW9 ....44 C3
Queen's CE Jun Sch The TW9 ....44 C3
Queen's Cir SW11 .160 A1
Queen's Club Gdns W14 ....154 B4
Queen's Club The W14 ....140 B1
Queen's Coll W1 ..104 A3
Queen's Cres NW5 ..12 C2
Queen's Ct NW8 ...79 B2
3 Richmond TW10 ...54 B1
SW13 ....56 C4
Queen's Ct W2 ...114 B3
Queen's Dr N4 ....6 A2
Queen's Elm Sq SW3 ....143 C1
Queen's Gallery The* SW1 ....132 B3
Queen's Gate SW7 ....129 A1
Queen's Gate Gdns SW7 ....129 A1
Queen's Gate Mews SW7 ....129 A2
Queen's Gate Pl SW7 ....129 A1
Queen's Gate Pl Mews SW7 ....129 A1
Queen's Gate Terr SW7 ....129 A2
Queen's Gdns W2 .100 C1
Queen's Gdns W2 .114 C4
Queen's Gr NW8 ...79 C3
Queen's Head St N1 ....86 B3
Queen's Head Yd SE1 ....123 B1
Queen's House The SE10 ....52 C4
Queen's Mans W6 ..39 C2
Queen's Mews W2 ....114 A4
Queen's Park Prim Sch W10 ....23 A1
Queen's Park Sta NW6 ....23 B3
Queen's Quay EC4 ....123 A4
Queen's Rd SE14,SE15 ....50 B2
Richmond TW10 ....54 B1
SW14 ....55 C4
Queen's Ride SW13 .57 A4
Queen's Rise TW10 .54 B1
Queen's Road Sta SE15 ....50 B2
Queen's Row SE17 .48 C4
Queen's Wlk SW1 .118 C1
Queen's Yd W1 ....93 A1
Queenhithe EC4 ...123 A4
Queens Cres TW10 ..54 B2
Queens Ct SW11 ...170 A4
4 E14 ....33 B2
SE5 ....49 A1
Queens Down Rd E5 ....17 A4
Queens Ho 1 SE17 .48 C4
Queens Manor Prim Sch SW6 ....47 C3
Queens Mans NW6 .11 A3
Queens Par NW2 ....9 B2
Queens Park Com Sch NW6 ....22 C4
Queens Park Ct 5 W10 ....22 C2
Queens Terr NW8 ...79 B2
Queens Yd E9 ....18 C2
Queensberry Mews W SW7 ....143 B4
Queensberry Pl SW7 ....143 B4
Queensberry Way SW7 ....143 B4
Queensborough Mews W2 ....114 C4
Queensborough Pas W2 ....114 C4
Queensborough Terr W2 ....114 B4
Queensbridge Ct 1 E2 ....24 B3
Queensbridge Inf Sch E8 ....16 B1
Queensbridge Rd E8 ....16 B1
E2,E8 ....24 B4
Queensbury St N1 ..15 B1
Queensdale Cres W11 ....30 C1
Queensdale Pl W11 ....112 A1
Queensdale Rd W11 ....31 A1 112 A1
Queensdale Wlk W11 ....112 A1
Queensgate Gdns SW15 ....57 A3
Queensgate Pl 10 NW6 ....10 C1
Queensland Pl N7 ..14 C4
Queensland Rd N7 ..14 C4
Queensmead NW8 ..79 C4
Queensmere (Southlands Coll) SW19 ....69 C2
Queensmere Cl SW19 ....69 C2
Queensmere Ct SW13 ....46 C4
Queensmere Rd SW19 ....69 C2
Queensmill Rd SW6 .47 C3
Queensmill Sch SW6 ....166 B1
Queenstown Rd SW8 ....160 A2
Queenstown Road Sta SW8 ....170 B4
Queensville Rd SW12,SW4 ....73 C4
Queensway W2 ...100 B2
W2 ....114 B4
Queensway Sta W2 ....114 B3
Queenswood Ct 5 SW4 ....62 A2
Quelch Ho 2 N19 ..13 C3
Quemerford Rd N7 .14 B3
Quendon Ho W10 ..22 B1
Quenington Ct 5 SE15 ....49 B4
Quennel Ho 7 SW12 ....73 B4
Quentington Mans SW6 ....164 C4
Querrin St SW6 ...166 C1
Quested Ct 27 E8 ..17 A3
Quex Mews NW6 ..23 C4
Quex Rd NW6 ....23 C4
Quick Rd W4 ....38 A1
Quick St N1 ....86 B1
Quickswood NW3 ..12 A1

Quill La SW15 ....57 C3
Quill St N4 ....5 C1
Quilp St SE1 ....136 C4
Quilter Ho 11 W9 ....23 B2
Quilter St E2 ..24 C2 99 B4
Quilting Ct 23 SE16 ..40 C4
Quintin Ct W4 ....44 C4
Quintock Ho 2
TW9 ....44 C2
Quinton Ho 10 SW8 .162 A2
Quinton Kynaston Sch
NW8 ....79 B3
Quinton St SW18 .....71 B2
Quixley St E14 ......34 C2
Quorn Rd SE22 ....64 A4

R

Rabbit Row W8 .....113 C2
Raby St E14 ....33 A3
Rachel McMillan Coll
(Annexe) E14 .....137 C1
Rachel Point E5 .....16 C4
Racine SE5 ....49 A2
Racton Rd W6 ......155 B3
Radbourne Cl E5 .....17 C4
Radbourne Rd
SW12 ....73 C3
Radcliff Ho EC1 ...107 B4
Radcliffe Ave NW10 .21 C3
Radcliffe Ho 9
SE16 ....40 A2
Radcliffe Path
SW8 ....170 B1
Radcliffe Rd SE1 ...138 B2
Radcliffe Sq SW15 ...57 C1
Radcot St SE11 .....149 C1
Raddington Rd W10 ..31 A4
Radford Ho N7 ....14 B3
14 E14 ....34 A4
Radford Rd SE13 .....67 B1
Radipole Rd SW6 ...164 C4
Radland Rd E16 ......35 C3
Radlett Pl NW8 ......80 A4
Radley Ct 23 SE16 ...40 C4
Radley Ho NW1 ......90 C2
Radley Lo 10 SW9 ...69 C3
Radley Mews W8 ...127 C1
Radley Terr 1 E16 ...35 B2
Radnor Lo W2 ......101 C1
Radnor Mews W2 ...101 C1
Radnor Pl W2 ....102 A1
Radnor Rd NW6 ......23 A4
SE15 ....49 C3
Radnor St EC1 ....97 A3
Radnor Terr W14 ...140 C4
Radnor Way NW10 ...20 A1
Radnor Wlk SW3 ...144 C1
14 E14 ....41 C2
Radstock St SW11 ..158 A1
Raeburn Cl NW11 ...2 A4
Raeburn St SW2 .....62 A3
Ragate Ho E5 ....7 C1
Ragged School Mus The
E3 ....33 A4
Raglan Ct SW9 ......62 C4
Raglan St NW5 ......13 A2
Ragley Cl W3 ....37 B4
Rahere Ho EC1 ......96 C4
Railey Mews NW5 ...13 B3
Railton Rd SE24 .....63 A2

Railway App SE1 ...123 C2
Railway Ave SE16 ...40 B4
Railway Cotts 66 ...39 B4
Railway Gr SE14 .....51 B3
Railway Side SW13 ..56 A4
Railway St N1 ....84 B1
Railway Terr SE13 ...67 A2
Rainbow Ave E14 ....42 A1
Rainbow Ct 33 ......51 B3
Rainbow Quay SE16 ..41 A3
Rainbow St SE5 ......49 A3
Raine St E1 ....32 A1
Raine's Foundation Sch
E2 ....25 B3
Raine's Foundation Sec
E2 ....25 B3
Rainford Ho 9 N7 ...5 B2
Rainham Cl SW11 ....60 A1
Rainham Ho NW1 ....83 A3
Rainham Rd NW10 ...22 C2
Rainhill Way E3 .....26 C2
Rainsborough Ave
SE8 ....41 A2
Rainsford Ct NW10 ..20 A3
Rainsford Ho 14
SW2 ....62 B2
Rainsford Rd NW10 ..20 A3
Rainsford St W2 ...102 A2
Rainville Rd W6 .....47 C4
Raleigh Ct 2 SE16 ...32 C1
Raleigh Gdns SW2 ...62 B2
5 SW2 ....171 B2
Raleigh Ho 8
14 E14 ....42 A3
Raleigh Mews N1 ....86 B3
Raleigh St N1 ....86 B3
Ralph Ct 5 W2 .....100 B2
Ralston St SW3 .....144 C1
Ram St SW18 ....59 A2
Ramar Ho E1 ....111 B4
Ramilies Cl SW2 .....62 A1
Ramillies Pl W1 ....104 C1
Ramillies Rd W4 ....37 C3
Ramillies St W1 ....104 C1
Rampart St E1 ....32 A3
Rampayne St SW1 ..147 B2
Ramsay Ho NW8 .....80 A2
Ramsay Rd W3 ......37 B4
Ramsdean Ho 1
SW15 ....69 A3
Ramsden Rd SW12 ..72 C4
Ramsey Ho SW9 ....163 C1
Ramsey St 24 C1 99 C2
Ramsfort Ho 6
SE16 ....40 A2
Ramsgate St E8 .....16 B2
Randal Cremer JMI Sch
E2 ....24 B3
Randall Cl SW11 ...168 A4
Randall Pl SE10 .....52 B3
Randall Rd SE11 ...148 C3
Randall Row SE11 ..148 C3
Randell's Rd N1 .....84 B4
Randolph Ave W9 ...88 C3
Randolph Cres W9 ...88 C2
Randolph Gdns
NW6 ....78 A1
Randolph Mews W9 ..89 A1
Randolph Rd W9 .....89 A1
Randolph St NW1 ...13 B1
Ranelagh Ave SW13 .46 C1

Ranelagh Ave continued
SW6 ....58 B4
Ranelagh Bridge
W2 ....100 B3
Ranelagh Gardens (site
of Chelsea Flower
Show)* SW1 .....145 C1
Ranelagh Gardens Mans
SW6 ....58 A4
Ranelagh Gdns 38 B3
4 ....45 B3
W6 ....38 B3
Ranelagh Gr SW1 ..145 C2
5 SW3 ....144 C2
Ranelagh Mans
SW6 ....165 A2
Ranelagh Rd 11
NW10 ....21 B3
Rangdon St EC3 ....110 C1
Rangers Sq SE10 ....52 C2
Rangoon Ho 5 N16 .15 C4
Rankine Ho SE1 ....136 C1
Ranmere St SW12 ...73 A3
Rann House 1
SW14 ....55 C4
Rannoch Rd W6 .....47 C4
Ranston St NW1 ...102 A4
Ranulf Rd NW2 ......10 B4
Ranwell Cl 11 E3 ...26 B4
Ranwell Ho 10 E3 ..26 B4
Raphael Ct 3 SE16 .40 A1
Raphael St SW7 ...130 D3
Rapley Ho 2 ....99 C3
Rashleigh Ct 3
SW8 ....61 A4
Rashleigh Ho NW1 ..93 C4
Rastell Ave SW12 ...73 B3
Ratcliffe Cross St
E1 ....32 C3
Ratcliffe Ho 10 E14 .33 A3
Ratcliffe La 15 E14 ..33 A3
Ratcliffe Orch 3
E1 ....32 C3
Rathbone Ho 6 ......23 C4
E16 ....35 B3
Rathbone Mkt 2
E16 ....35 B4
Rathbone Pl W1 ...105 B2
Rathbone Point E5 ...16 C4
Rathbone St W1 ....105 A3
E16 ....35 B4
Rathgar Rd SW9 ....63 A4
Rathmell Dr SW4 ...61 C1
Rattray Rd SW2 .....62 C2
Raul Rd SE15 ....49 C2
Rav Pinter Cl N16 ...7 A4
Raveley St NW5 .....13 B4
Raven Ho 10 SE16 ..40 C2
Raven Row E1 ....32 A4
Ravenet St SW11 ..170 A3
SW4 ....61 A2
Ravenfield Rd SW17 .72 B1
Ravenna Rd SW15 ..57 C2
Ravensbourne Ho
NW8 ....102 A4
Ravensbourne Pk
SE4 ....66 C4
Ravensbourne Pl
SE13 ....52 A1
Ravensbury Rd
SW18 ....71 A2
Ravensbury Terr
SW18 ....71 A2
Ravenscar NW1 .....82 C3

Ravenscourt 1 N16 .7 C1
Ravenscourt Ave
W6 ....38 C2
Ravenscourt Gdns
W6 ....38 C2
Ravenscourt Park Mans
W6 ....39 A3
Ravenscourt Park Prep
Sch W6 ....38 C2
Ravenscourt Park Sta
W6 ....39 A2
Ravenscourt Pk W6 .39 A3
Ravenscourt Pl W6 ..39 A2
Ravenscourt Rd W6 .39 A2
Ravenscourt Sq W6 .38 C3
Ravenscroft Ave
NW11 ....1 B4
Ravenscroft Cl 4
E16 ....35 C4
Ravenscroft Ct NW11 1 B4
Ravenscroft Rd E16 .35 C4
W4 ....37 B2
Ravenscroft St E2 ...99 A4
Ravensdon St
SE11 ....149 C1
Ravenshaw St NW6 .10 B3
Ravenslea Rd SW11,
SW12 ....72 B4
Ravensmede Way
W4 ....38 B2
Ravenstone SE17 ..152 B1
Ravenstone Jun & Inf
Schs SW12 ....72 C3
Ravenstone St
SW12 ....72 C3
Ravenswood Rd
SW12 ....73 A4
Ravensworth Ct
SW6 ....155 B1
Ravensworth Rd
NW10 ....22 A2
Raven Rd E11 ....19 C4
Ravey St EC2 ..24 A1 98 A2
Rawlings St SW3 ...144 C4
Rawlinson Ho SE13 .67 C3
Rawlinson Point 8
E16 ....35 B2
Rawreth Wlk (off Basire
St) N1 ....87 A4
Rawson Ct SW11 ..169 C3
Rawson St SW11 ...170 A3
Rawstone St EC1 ....96 A4
Rawstorne Pl EC1 ...96 A4
Ray Ho W10 ....30 C3
Ray St EC1 ....95 C1
Ray Wlk N7 ....5 B2
Rayburne Ct W14 ..126 A2
Raydon St N19 ......4 A2
Raymede Twr W10 ..30 C4
Raymouth Rd SE16 ..40 A2
Raynald Ho 15
SW16 ....74 A1
Rayne Ct 10 W12 ...38 C4
Rayne Ho W9 ....88 A2
1 SW12 ....60 C1
Rayner Ct 10 W12 ..39 B4
Rayner's Rd SW15 ..58 A2
Raynes St NW2 .....10 A4
Raynham E1 ....102 A2
Raynham Ho 1 E1 ...25 C1
Raynham Rd W6 ....39 A2
Raynor Pl N1 ....87 A4
Re Sassoon Ho
SE5 ....50 B2
Reachview Cl 14
NW1 ....13 B1

Read Ho SE11 ......163 B4
Reade Ct 6 W3 .....37 B3
Reade Ho 7 SE10 ...52 C4
Reade Wlk NW10 ....8 A1
Reading Ho W2 ....100 C1
SE15 ....49 C4
Reading La E8 ......17 A2
Reapers Cl NW1 ....83 B4
Reardon Ho 5 E1 ...32 A1
Reardon Path 11 E1 32 A1
Reardon St E1 ......32 A1
Reaston St SE14 ....50 C3
Reay Prim Sch
SW9 ....163 A1
Reckitt Rd W4 ......38 A1
Record St SE15 .....50 B4
Rector St N1 ....86 C3
Rectory Gdns 4 SW4 61 B4
Rectory Gr SW4 ....61 B4
Rectory Rd N16 .....7 B1
SW13 ....46 C1
1 W3 ....28 B1
Rectory Road Sta
N16 ....7 B1
Rectory Sq E1 ......32 C4
Reculver Ho 2
SE15 ....50 B4
Reculver Rd SE16 ..40 C1
Red Anchor Cl
SW3 ....158 A3
Red Lion Cl 9 SE17 48 C4
Red Lion Ct EC4 ...107 C1
Red Lion Row SE17 .48 C4
Red Lion Sq WC1 ..106 C3
Red Lion St WC1 ...106 C3
Red Lion Yd W1 ....117 C2
Red Pl W1 ....117 B4
Red Post Hill SE21,
SE24 ....63 C2
Red Rover SW13 ....56 C4
Redan Pl W2 ....100 A1
Redan St W14 ......39 C3
Redan Terr SE5 .....48 A1
Redbourn Ho W10 ..22 B1
Redbourne Ho 7
E14 ....33 B3
Redbridge Gdns
SE5 ....49 A3
Redburn St SW3 ...158 C4
Redcar St SE5 ......48 B3
Redcastle Cl E1 .....32 B2
Redchurch St
E2 ....24 B1 98 C2
Redcliffe Cl SW5 ..142 A1
Redcliffe Gdns
SW10 ....156 B4
Redcliffe Mews
SW10 ....142 B1
Redcliffe Missionary
Training Coll W4 ...45 A3
Redcliffe Pl SW10 ..156 C3
Redcliffe Rd SW10 .157 A3
Redcliffe Sch SW10 156 B4
Redclyf Ho 12 E1 ...25 B1
Redcroft 5 NW6 ....10 C2
Redcross Way SE1 ..123 A1
Reddins Rd SE15 ...49 C4
Rede Pl W2 ..31 A2 113 C4
Redesdale St SW3 ..158 C4
Redfern Rd NW10 ...8 A1
Redfield La SW5 ...142 A4
Redfield Mews
SW5 ....141 C4
Rediff Est SE16 .....41 B3
Redford Wlk N1 .....86 C4

Redgate Terr SW15 .57 C1
Redgrave Rd SW15 .57 C1
Redhill Ct SW2 ...74 C2
Redhill St NW1 ...92 C4
Redington Gdns
NW3 ...11 A4
Redington Ho NW3 .85 A2
Redington Rd NW3 .11 A4
Redlands JMI Sch
E1 ...32 B4
Redlands Way SW7 .74 B4
Redlynch Ct W14 .126 B3
Redlynch Ho SW9 .173 C4
Redman Ho EC1 .107 B4
SE1 ...137 A3
Redman's Rd E1 ...32 B4
Redmayne Ho
SW9 ...173 A2
Redmead La E1 .125 B1
Redmill Ho 24 E1 ...25 A1
Redmond Ho N1 .85 A3
Redmore Rd W6 .39 A2
Redriff Prim Sch
SE16 ...41 A4
Redriff Rd 20 SE16 ...40 C3
Redrup Ho 2 SE14 .50 C4
Redruth Rd E9 .25 B4
Redstart Ho SE14 .51 A3
Redvers St E2 ...98 B4
Redwood Cl SE16 .33 A1
Redwood Ct N19 ...4 C4
NW6 ...10 A1
Redwood Mews 2
SW4 ...61 A4
Redwoods SW15 .68 C3
Reece Mews SW7 .143 B4
Reed Cl E16 ...35 C4
Reed Ho SW15 ...56 C1
Reed's Pl NW1 .13 B1
Reedham St SE15 .64 C1
Reedholm Villas
N16 ...15 C4
Reedworth St
SE11 ...149 C3
Reef Ho E14 ...42 B3
Rees St N1 ...87 A3
Reeves Ho W1 ...117 B3
SE1 ...135 B3
Reeves Mews W1 .117 C3
Reeves Rd E3 ...27 A1
Reform St SW11 .169 A2
SW11 ...169 A2
Regal Cl E1 ...111 C4
Regal La NW1 ...81 C4
Regal Pl SW6 .156 B1
E3 ...26 B2
Regan Way N1 ...24 A3
Regency Ct 21 E9 .18 A2
Regency Lo NW5 ...11 C1
Regency Mews 1
NW10 ...8 C2
Regency St SW1 .147 C3
Regency Wlk 6
TW10 ...54 A2
Regent Ct NW8 ...90 A3
N16 ...7 B4
Regent Ho W14 .140 A4
Regent Lo 9 SW2 .74 B3
Regent Pl W1 ...119 A4
Regent Rd SE24 ...63 A2
Regent Sq WC1 ...94 B3
23 E3 ...27 A2
Regent St SW1 ...104 C1
W1 ...118 C4
Regent's Coll NW1 .91 B2

Regent's Park
NW1 ...81 B1
Regent's Park Barracks
NW1 ...92 B4
Regent's Park Rd
NW1 ...81 B4
Regent's Park Sta
NW1 ...92 A1
Regent's Park Terr
NW1 ...82 A4
Regent's Pl 12
SE3 ...53 C1
Regent's Row E8 .24 C4
Regents Bridge Gdns
SW8 ...162 B2
Regents Canal Ho 5
E14 ...33 B3
Regents Ct E8 ...24 C4
Regents Mews NW8 .78 C2
Regents Plaza NW6 .78 A2
Regents Wharf 3
E2 ...25 A4
N1 ...84 C3
Regina Point SE16 .40 B3
Regina Rd N4 ...5 B3
Reginald Rd SE8 .51 C3
Reginald Sq SE8 .51 C3
Regis Ct NW1 ...102 C4
Regis Rd NW5 ...13 A3
Regnart Bldgs NW1 .93 A3
Reid Ct SW14 ...45 B1
Reighton Rd E5 ...7 C2
Relay Rd W12 ...30 B1
Relf Rd SE15 ...64 C4
Relton Mews SW7 .130 B2
Rembrandt Cl E14 .42 C3
Rembrandt Ct 10
SE16 ...40 A1
Remington St N1 .86 B1
Remnant St WC2 .106 C2
Remsted Ho W6 .78 A3
Remus Rd E3 ...26 C4
Renbold Ho 12 SE8 52 B2
Rendlesham Ho 8
E5,N16 ...7 C1
Rendlesham Rd E5 .7 C1
Renforth St SE16 ...40 B4
Renfrew Ho NW6 .78 A1
Renfrew Rd SE11 .150 A3
Rennell Ho 18 E9 .17 C2
Rennell St SE13 ...67 B4
Rennie Cotts 24 E1 .25 B1
Rennie Ct SE1 ...122 A2
Rennie Ho SE1 ...136 C1
Rennie St SE1 ...122 A2
Renoir Ct 8 SE16 .40 A1
Renton Cl SW2 ...62 B1
Rephidim St SE1 .138 A1
Replingham Rd
SW18 ...70 C3
Reporton Rd SW6 .154 B1
Repton Ho SW1 .147 A3
E14 2 ...33 A3
Repton St E14 ...33 A3
Reservoir Rd SE4 .51 A1
Restell Cl SE3 ...53 A4
Reston Pl SW7 .128 C3
Retcar Pl N19 ...4 A2
Retford St N1 ...24 A3
Retreat Ho E9 ...17 B2
Retreat Pl E9 ...17 B2
Retreat The SW14 .56 A4
Reunion Row E1 .32 A2
Reveley Sq SE16 .41 A4
Revelon Rd SE4 ...66 A4
Revelstoke Rd
SW18,SW19 ...70 C2

Reverdy Rd SE1 .153 B3
Rewell St SW6 ...156 C1
Rex Pl W1 ...117 C2
Reynard Cl 5 SE4 ...66 A4
Reynard Pl SE14 ...51 A4
Reynolds Ho NW8 .79 C1
N4 ...6 B3
SE1 10 ...152 C3
Reynolds Pl 12
TW10 ...54 B1
Reynolds Rd W4 ...37 B3
Rheidol Mews N1 .86 C2
Rheidol Terr N1 ...86 C3
Rhoda St E2 ...24 A1 99 A2
Rhodes Ho N1 ...97 B4
W12 ...30 A1
Rhodes St N7 ...14 B3
Rhodesia Rd SW9 .172 B1
Rhodeswell Rd E14 .33 B3
Rhondda Gr E3 ...26 B2
Rhyl Prim Sch NW5 .12 C2
Rhyl St NW5 ...12 C2
Ribblesdale Ho 11
...23 C4
Ribbon Dance Mews
SE5 ...48 C2
Ribstone Ho 4 E9 .17 C2
Ricardo St E14 ...34 A3
Riceyman Ho WC1 .95 B3
Rich La SW5 ...142 A2
Rich St E14 ...33 B2
Richard Anderson Ct 1
SE14 ...50 C3
Richard Atkins Prim Sch
SW2 ...74 A4
Richard Cloudesley Sch
EC1 ...96 C1
Richard Cobden Prim
Sch NW1 ...83 A3
Richard Fox Ho N4 .6 B1
Richard Ho 8 SE16 .40 B2
Richard Knight Ho
SW6 ...165 C4
Richard Neale Ho 2
E1 ...32 A2
Richard St 10 E1 ...32 A3
Richard's Pl SW3 .144 B4
Richardson Cl 19 E8 24 B4
Richardson Ct
SW4 ...172 B2
Richardson's Mews
W1 ...92 C1
Richbell Pl WC1 .106 C4
Richborne Terr
SW8 ...163 A2
Richborough Ho
E14 5 ...17 A4
SE15 ...50 B4
Richborough Rd
NW2 ...10 A3
Richford Gate W6 .39 B3
Richford St W6 ...39 B3
Richland Ho 4
...49 C2
Richman Ho 10 SE8 41 B1
Richmond Adult Coll 6
TW9 ...54 A3
Richmond Ave N1 ...85 A4
NW10 ...9 B2
Richmond Bldgs
W1 ...105 B1
Richmond Circus
TW9 ...54 A3
Richmond Coll W8 .128 B2

Richmond Cres N1 ...85 B4
Richmond Ct SW1 .131 A3
Richmond Gr N1 ...15 A1
Richmond Hill
TW10 ...54 A1
Richmond Hill Ct 5
TW10 ...54 A1
Richmond Ho NW1 .82 B1
SE17 ...151 B2
TW10 12 ...54 A1
SE26 ...76 C1
Richmond Mans
W12 ...142 A2
SW5 ...142 A2
SW15 ...58 A4
Richmond Mews
W1 ...105 B1
Richmond Park Rd
SW14 ...55 C3
Richmond Rd E8 ...16 C1
W5 ...36 A4
Richmond Sta TW9 .54 A3
Richmond Terr
SW1 ...134 A4
Richmond Way
W12,W14 ...39 C4
Rickard Cl SW2 ...74 C3
Rickett St SW6 ...155 C4
Rickman Ho 22 E1 .25 B1
Rickman St 21 E1 .25 B1
Rickthorne Rd 6
N19 ...5 A2
Riddell Ct SE1 ...152 C2
Ridgdale St E3 ...27 A3
Ridge Hill NW11 ...1 A3
Ridge Rd NW2 ...1 B1
Ridgeway 9 TW10 .54 A1
Ridgeway Dr W3 ...36 C3
Ridgeway Gdns N6 ...4 B4
Ridgeway The NW11 .1 B3
W3 ...36 C3
Ridgewell Cl N1 ...87 A4
Ridgmount Gdns
WC1 ...105 B4
Ridgmount Pl WC1 105 B4
Ridgmount Rd
SW18 ...59 A2
Ridgmount St WC1 105 B4
Ridgway Rd SW9 .63 A4
Riding House St
W1 ...104 C3
Riding The NW11 ...1 B4
Ridings Cl N6 ...4 B4
Ridley Ho 8 SW11 .60 A4
Ridley Rd E8 ...16 B3
NW10 ...21 C3
Ridley Road Mkt E8 16 B2
Riffel Rd NW2 ...9 B3
Rifle Court SE11 .163 C4
Rifle Pl W11 ...30 C1
Rifle St E14 ...34 A4
Rigault Rd SW6 .164 B1
Rigden St E14 ...34 A3
Rigeley Rd NW10 .21 C2
Rigg Ho 2 SW4 ...74 A4
Rigge Pl SW4 ...61 C3
Rignold Ho 6 SE5 .49 A1
Rigo Ho 8 E1 ...32 C4
Riley Ho SW10 .157 B3
SW11 ...169 B1
8 E3 ...26 C1
1 SW4 ...73 C4
Riley Rd SE1 ...138 C2
Riley St SW10 ...157 B2
Rill Ho 5 SE5 ...49 A3
Rinaldo Rd SW12 ...73 A4
Ring Cross Prim Sch
N7 ...14 B3
Ring Ho 14 E1 ...32 B2

Ringcroft St N7 ...14 C3
Ringford Ho SW18 .58 B3
Ringford Rd SW18 .58 C1
Ringmer Ave SW6 .164 B3
Ringmer Gdns 2
N19 ...5 A2
Ringmer Ho 15
SE22 ...64 A4
Ringsfield Ho
SE17 ...151 A1
Ringwood Gdns
E14 ...41 C2
SW15 ...68 C3
Ripley Gdns SW14 .55 C4
Ripley Ho SW1 ...160 C4
Ripley House SW14 .56 A4
Riplington Ct SW9 .62 B4
Ripplevale Gr N1 ...14 B1
Risborough 3 SE17 .150 C4
Risborough Ho
NW8 ...90 B2
Risdon Ho 20 SE16 .40 B4
Risdon St 21 SE16 .40 B4
Riseholme Ho 14
SE22 ...76 C4
Riseldine Rd SE23 .66 A1
Rising Sun Ct EC1 .108 B3
Risinghill St N1 ...85 B2
Risley Ho 9 E9 ...17 C2
Rita Rd SW8 ...162 C2
Ritchie Ho N19 ...4 C4
11 E14 ...34 C3
10 SE16 ...40 B3
Ritchie St N1 ...85 C2
Ritherdon Rd SW17 .73 A2
Ritson Ho N1 ...84 C3
Ritson Rd E8 ...16 C2
Rivaz Pl E9 ...17 B2
River Barge Cl E14 .42 B4
River Ct SW1 ...122 A3
River Ho SW13 ...46 A1
River Pl N1 ...15 B1
River St EC1 ...95 B4
River Terr W6 ...39 B1
River Way SE10 ...43 B3
Riverains The
SW11 ...167 B3
Rivercourt Rd W6 .39 A1
Riverdale Dr SW18 .71 A3
Riverfleet WC1 ...94 B4
Riverford Ho 20 W2 31 C4
Rivermead Ct SW6 .58 B4
Rivermead Ho E9 ...18 A3
Riverside SW18 ...70 C3
Riverside Bsns Ctr
SW18 ...71 A3
Riverside Cl N5 ...6 B1
Riversdale Rd N5 ...6 B1
Riverside 4 W4 ...46 A2
Riverside Gdns W6 .39 A1
Riverside Ind Est
SE10 ...43 B3
Riverside Mans 4
E1 ...32 B1
Riverside Prim Sch
SE16 ...139 C3
Riverside Rd E15 ...27 B3
SW17 ...71 A1

Riverside Rd continued
SW17,SW19 . . . .**71** B1
Riverside Workshops
SE1 . . . .**123** A2
Riverton Cl W9 . . . .**23** B2
Riverview Gdns
SW13 . . . .**47** A4
Riverview Gr W4 . . . . . .**45** A4
Riverview Rd W4 . . . . . .**45** A4
Rivet Ho SE1 . . . .**153** A2
Rivington Pl EC2 . . . . . .**98** B3
Rivington St EC2 . . . . . .**98** A3
Rivington Wlk 4
E8 . . . .**24** C4
Rixon St N7 . . . .**5** C1
Roach Rd E3 . . . .**18** C1
Roads Pl N19 . . . .**5** A2
Roan St SE10 . . . .**52** B4
Robert Adam St
W1 . . . .**103** B2
Robert Bell Ho
SE16 . . . .**153** B4
Robert Blair Prim Sch
N7 . . . .**14** A2
*Robert Browning Prim
Sch* SE17 . . . .**151** B2
Robert Cl W9 . . . .**89** A1
Robert Dashwood Way
SE17 . . . .**150** C3
Robert Gentry Ho
W14 . . . .**140** B1
Robert Jones Ho
SE16 . . . .**153** B4
Robert Keen Cl 7
SE15 . . . .**49** C2
Robert Lowe Cl
SE14 . . . .**50** C3
Robert Owen Ho E2 .**99** A4
SW6 . . . .**47** C2
Robert Owen Lo 5
E5 . . . .**17** A4
Robert St NW1 . . . .**92** B3
WC2 . . . .**120** B3
Robert Sutton Ho 20
E1 . . . .**32** B3
Robert's Pl EC1 . .**24** 95 C12
Roberta St
E2 . . . .**24** C2 **99** C3
Roberts Ho 5 SE27 .**75** A1
Roberts Mews
SW1 . . . .**131** B1
Robertson Ho 11
SE10 . . . .**52** B2
Robertson Rd E15 . .**27** B4
Robertson St SW8 .**170** B1
Robeson St 8 E3 . . . .**33** B4
Robin Ct E14 . . . .**153** B4
13 E14 . . . .**42** B3
Robin Gr N6 . . . .**3** C2
Robin Ho NW8 . . . .**80** A1
Robin Hood Gdns 12
E14 . . . .**34** B2
Robin Hood La E14 .**34** B2
SW15 . . . .**68** A1
Robin's Ct SW4 . . . . . .**62** A1
Robins Ct TW10 . . . . . .**54** A1
Robinscroft Mews
SE10 . . . .**52** A2

Robinsfield Inf Sch
NW8 . . . .**80** A2
Robinson Cl N1 . . . . . .**86** B4
4 Richmond TW9 . . . .**54** B3
Robinson Ho
4 W10 . . . .**30** C3
5 E14 . . . .**33** C4
Robinson Rd E2 . . . . . .**25** B3
Robinson St SW3 . . .**158** C4
Robsart St SW9 . . . . .**173** B2
Robson Ave NW10 . . .**8** C1
Robson Rd SE21, ...
SE27 . . . .**75** B1
Roby Ho EC1 . . . .**96** C2
Rochdale Way 4
SE8 . . . .**51** C3
Roche Ho 10 E14 . . . .**33** B2
Rochelle Cl SW11 . . . .**59** C3
Rochelle Ct 14 E1 . . .**32** B3
Rochelle St E2 . . . .**98** C3
Rochemont Wlk 2
E8 . . . .**24** C4
Rochester Ct
7 NW1 . . . .**13** B2
6 E2 . . . .**25** A1
Rochester Ho SE1 .**137** C3
18 SE15 . . . .**50** B4
Rochester Mews
NW1 . . . .**13** B1
Rochester Pl NW1 . . .**13** B1
Rochester Rd NW1 . .**13** B2
Rochester Row
SW1 . . . .**147** A4
Rochester Sq NW1 . .**13** B1
Rochester St SW1 .**133** B1
Rochester Terr
NW1 . . . .**13** B2
Rochester Wlk
SE1 . . . .**123** B2
Rochford Wlk 8 E8 .**16** C1
Rochfort Ho 8 SE8 .**41** B1
Rock Ave 14 SW14 . . .**55** C4
Rock St N4 . . . .**5** C2
Rockell's Pl SE22 . . . .**65** A1
Rockfield Ho SE10 . .**52** B4
Rockhall Rd NW2 . . . . .**9** C4
Rockingham Cl
SW15 . . . .**56** B3
Rockingham St
SE1 . . . .**136** C1
Rockland Rd SW15 .**58** A3
Rockley Ct 9 W14 . . .**39** C4
Rockley Rd W14 . . . . . .**39** C4
Rocks La SW13 . . . .**56** C4
Rockstraw Ho 5
NW3 . . . .**12** B1
Rockwood Ct N16 . . . . .**7** C4
Rockcliffe St N1 . . . . . .**86** B1
Rocque Ho SW6 . . . .**154** C2
Rodborough Rd
NW11 . . . .**1** C3
Roden St N7 . . . .**5** B1
Rodenhurst Ct SW4 .**61** C2
Rodenhurst Rd SW4 .**61** C1
Roderick Ho 3
SE16 . . . .**40** B2
Roderick Rd NW3 . . .**12** B4
Rodgers Ho 4 SW4 .**73** C4
Roding Ct 6 W12 . . . .**38** A4
Roding Ho N1 . . . .**85** B3
Roding Mews E1 . . .**125** C2
Roding Rd E5 . . . .**18** A3
Rodmarton St WC1 .**103** A3
Rodmell WC1 . . . .**94** B3

Rodmere St SE10 . . . .**43** A1
Rodmill La SW2 . . . . . .**74** A4
Rodney Ct NW8 . . . . . .**89** A2
Rodney Ho N1 . . . .**85** A1
W11 . . . .**113** B4
4 E14 . . . .**42** A2
Rodney Pl SE17 . . . .**151** A4
Rodney Rd SE17 . . . .**151** B3
Rodney St N1 . . . .**85** A1
Rodway Rd SW15 . . . .**68** C4
Rodwell Rd SE22 . . . . .**64** B1
Roebuck Ho WC1 . . .**132** C2
Roedean Cres SW15 .**56** A2
*Roehampton CE Prim
Sch* SW15 . . . .**69** A4
Roehampton Cl
SW15 . . . .**56** C3
Roehampton Ct
SW13 . . . .**56** C4
Roehampton Gate
SW15 . . . .**56** A1
*Roehampton Gate City
Prim Sch* SW15 . . . . .**56** A1
Roehampton High St
SW15 . . . .**68** C4
Roehampton La
SW15 . . . .**56** C1
Roehampton Vale
SW15 . . . .**68** B2
Roffey St E14 . . . .**42** B4
Roger Dowley Ct 8
E2 . . . .**25** B3
Roger St WC1 . . . .**95** A1
Roger's Almshouses 7
SW9 . . . .**62** B3
Rogers Est 28 E2 . . . .**25** B2
Rogers Rd E16 . . . .**35** B3
Rokeby Ho WC1 . . . . . .**94** C1
9 SW12 . . . .**73** A4
Rokeby Rd SE4 . . . .**51** B1
Rokeby Sch E15 . . . . . .**19** C1
Rokeland Ho SE4 . . . .**66** A3
Roland Gdns SW7 .**143** A2
Roland Mews 1 E1 .**32** C4
Roland Way SW7 . . .**143** A2
SE17 . . . .**151** C1
Rollins St SE15 . . . .**50** B4
Rollit Ho N7 . . . .**14** C3
Rollit St N7 . . . .**14** C3
Rollo Ct SW11 . . . .**73** A4
Rolls Bldgs EC4 . . . .**107** C2
Rolls Pas EC4 . . . .**107** B2
Rolls Rd SW1 . . . .**147** C3
SE1 . . . .**153** A2
Rollscourt Ave SE24 .**63** B2
Rolt St SE8 . . . .**51** A4
Roma Read Cl . . . .
SW15 . . . .**69** A4
Roman Cl W3 . . . .**37** A4
Roman Rd E2,E3 . . . . . .**25** C3
E3 . . . .**26** A4
W4 . . . .**38** B2
Roman Square Mkt 11
E3 . . . .**26** B3
Roman Way N7 . . . .**14** B2
SE15 . . . .**50** B3
Romanfield Rd SW2 .**74** B4
Romayne Ho SW4 . . .**61** C4
Romberg Rd SW17 . .**72** C1
Romborough Gdns
SE13 . . . .**67** B2
Romborough Way
SE13 . . . .**67** B2

Romer Ho 12 SW2 . . .**23** B2
9 SW2 . . . .**62** B2
Romero Cl SW9 . . . . . .**62** B4
Romey Mews W1 . .**103** B4
Romeyn Rd SW16 . . . .**74** B1
Romford Ho 17 N1 . . .**15** C2
Romford St E1 . . . .**32** A4
Romilly Pl E14 . . . .**42** A4
Romilly Rd N4 . . . .**6** A2
Romilly St W1 . . . . . .**105** C1
W1 . . . .**119** C4
Romily Ct SW6 . . . . . .**164** B2
Romney Cl NW11 . . . . . .**2** B3
4 N17 . . . .
Romney Ct 8 NW3 . .**12** A2
9 W12 . . . .**39** B4
Romney Rd SE10 . . . .**52** C4
Romney St SW1 . . . .**134** A1
Romola Rd SE24, ...
SW2 . . . .**75** A3
Romsey Ho 5 . . . .
SW11 . . . .**59** C3
Rona Rd NW3 . . . .**12** C4
Rona Wlk 26 N1 . . . . . .**15** C2
Ronald Ross Prim Sch
SW19 . . . .**70** A4
Ronald St E1 . . . .**32** B3
Ronalds Rd N5 . . . .**14** C3
Ronaldshay N4 . . . .**5** C3
Rondu Rd NW2 . . . .**10** A3
Rood La EC3 . . . .**124** A4
Rooke Way SE10 . . . . .**43** B1
Rookery Rd SW4 . . . . .**61** B3
Rookwood Rd N16 . . . . .**7** C4
Rootes Dr W10 . . . .**30** C4
Rope St SE16 . . . .**41** A3
Ropemaker Rd . . . .
SE16 . . . .**41** A3
Ropemaker St EC2 .**109** B4
Ropemaker's Fields 9
E14 . . . .**33** B2
Roper La SE1 . . . .**138** B3
Roper's Orchard . . . .
SW3 . . . .**158** A3
Ropers Wlk 18 SE24 .**74** C4
Ropery St E3 . . . .**26** B1
Ropewalk Gdns 1 E1 **111** C2
Ropley St E2 . . . .**24** C3
Rosa Alba Mews N5 .**15** B4
Rosa Parks Ho . . . .
SW9 . . . .**172** C1
Rosalind Ho 25 N1 . .**24** A3
Rosaline Rd SW6 . . . .**154** B1
Rosaline Terr SW6 .**154** B1
Rosary Gdns SW7 . .**143** A3
Rosary RC Prim Sch
NW3 . . . .**12** B3
Rosaville Rd SW6 . . .**154** C1
Rosbury SW15 . . . .**58** A1
Roscoe St EC1 . . . .**97** A1
Roscommon Ho 2
NW3 . . . .**11** C3
Rose & Crown Ct
EC2 . . . .**108** C2
Rose & Crown Yd
SW1 . . . .**119** A1
Rose Alley EC2 . . . . . .**110** B3
SE1 . . . .**123** A2
Rose Bruford Coll
SE8 . . . .**51** C4
Rose Bush Ct NW3 . .**12** B3
Rose Ct E1 . . . .**111** A3
Rose St WC2 . . . .**120** A4
Rosebank 3 W3 . . . . . .**28** C3
Rosebank Gdns E3 . .**26** B3
3 W3 . . . .**28** C3

Rosebank Way W3 . .**28** C3
Rosebank Wlk NW1 .**13** C1
Roseberry Pl E8 . . . . . .**16** B2
Roseberry St SE16 . .**40** A2
Rosebery Ave EC1 . . .**95** C3
Rosebery Ct EC1 . . . . .**95** C3
W1 . . . .**118** A2
Rosebery Ho 2 E2 . . .**25** B3
Rosebery Rd SW2 . . .**62** A1
Rosebery Sq EC1 . . . . .**95** B1
Rosebery Wd SW6 .**166** B1
Rosecroft Ave NW3 . . .**1** C1
Rosedale Ct N5 . . . .**15** A4
Rosedale Ho N16 . . . . . .**6** C3
Rosedale Rd TW9 . . . .**54** A3
Rosedale Terr W6 . . .**39** A3
Rosedene NW6 . . . .**22** C4
Rosedene Ave . . . .
SW16 . . . .**74** B1
Rosedew Rd W6 . . . . . .**47** C4
Rosefield Gdns E14 .**33** C2
Roseford Ct 16 . . . .
W12 . . . .**39** C4
Rosehart Mews 8 . . . .
W11 . . . .**31** C3
Rosehill Rd SW18 . . .**59** B2
Roseland Ho NW6 . . .**58** A4
Roseleigh Ave N5 . . . .**15** A4
Rosemary Dr 15 . . . .
E14 . . . .**34** C3
Rosemary Gdns . . . .
SW14 . . . .**55** B4
Rosemary Ho N1 . . . .**87** C3
Rosemary La SW14 .**55** B4
Rosemary Mews N1 .**87** C4
Rosemary Rd SE15 .**49** B3
SW17 . . . .**71** B1
Rosemary Sch N1 . . .**87** A4
EC1 . . . .**96** A2
Rosemead SE27 **75** B2 . . . .
Rosemont Mans 11 . . . .
NW3 . . . .**11** A3
Rosemont Rd NW3 . .**11** B2
W3 . . . .**28** A2
Richmond TW10 . . . . . .**54** A1
Rosemoor St SW3 . .**144** C3
Rosemount Ct 2 . . . .
W3 . . . .**28** A1
Rosemount Lo W3 . . .**28** A2
Rosenau Cres . . . .
SW11 . . . .**168** C3
Rosenau Rd SW11 . .**168** C4
Rosendale Inf Sch
SE21 . . . .**75** B4
Rosendale Jun Sch
SE21 . . . .**75** B4
Rosendale Rd SE21, ...
SE24 . . . .**75** B4
Roseneath Rd SW11 .**60** C1
Rosenthal Rd SE6 . . .**67** B1
Rosenthorpe Rd . . . .
SE15 . . . .**65** C2
Roserton St E14 . . . . .**42** B4
Rosethorn Cl SW12 .**73** C4
Rosetta Cl SW8 . . . .**162** B1
Roseway SE21 . . . .**63** C1
E1 . . . .**19** C4
Rosewood Ho 8 . . . .
NW3 . . . .**11** A2
Rosewood Sq W12 . .**29** C3
Rosher Cl E15 . . . .**19** C1
Rosina St E9 . . . .**17** C3
Roskell Rd SW15 . . . . .**57** C4
Roslin Ho 2 E1 . . . .**32** C2
Roslin Rd W3 . . . .**37** A3
Rosmead Rd . . . .
W11 . . . .**31** A2 **112** B4

Rosoman Pl EC1 ....95 C2
Ross Ct 4 SW15 ......69 C4
Ross Ho 10 E1 ....32 A1
Rossdale Rd SW15 ....57 B3
Rossendale Way
NW1 ....83 A4
Rossetti Gdns Mans
SW3 ....158 C4
Rossetti Ho SW1 ....147 C3
Rossetti Mews SW3 ..79 C3
Rossetti Rd SE16 .....40 A1
Rossington St E5 .....7 C2
Rossiter Rd SW12 ....73 A3
Rosslyn Ave SW13 ....56 B4
Rosslyn Hill NW3 .....12 A3
Rosslyn Ct NW3 ......12 A3
Rosslyn Ho 8 TW9 ...44 B2
Rosslyn Mans NW6 ...11 B2
Rosslyn Park Mews
NW3 ....11 C3
Rossmore Ct NW1 .....90 C2
Rossmore Rd NW1 ....90 B2
Roston St 5 ....5 B2
Rostrevor Mans
SW6 ....164 C4
Rostrevor Rd SW6 ...164 C4
Rotary St SE1 ....136 B2
Roth Wlk N7 ....5 B2
Rothay NW1 ....92 B4
Rothbury Rd E9 ......18 C1
Rother Ho SE15 ......65 A3
Rotherfield Ct N1 ....87 B4
Rotherfield Prim Sch
N1 ....87 A4
Rotherfield St N1 .....87 A4
Rotherham Wlk
SE1 ....122 A1
Rotherhithe SE16 .....33 B1
Rotherhithe Holiday Inn
Pier(River Bus)
SE16 ....33 A1
Rotherhithe New Rd
SE16 ....40 A1
Rotherhithe Old Rd
SE16 ....40 C2
Rotherhithe Prim Sch
SE16 ....40 C3
Rotherhithe St
10 SE16 ....40 A4
SE16 ....40 B4
Rotherhithe Sta
SE16 ....40 B4
Rotherhithe Tunnel
SE16 ....32 C1
Rotherwick Rd NW11 1 C4
Rotherwood Rd
SW15 ....57 C4
Rothery St N1 ....86 B4
Rothesay Ave SW14,
TW10 ....55 A3
Rothesay Ct SE11 ...163 B3
Rothley St NW8 ......89 B2
Rothsay St SE1 ......138 A1
Rothsay Wlk 10 E14 .41 C2
Rothschild Rd W4 ....37 B3
Rothwell St NW1 .....81 A4
10 NW1 ....12 B1
Rotten Row SW1 ....130 C4
Rotterdam Dr E14 ....42 B3
Rouel Rd SE16 ......139 B1
SE1 ....153 B4
Roundacre SW19 .....69 C2
Roundel Cl SE4 ......66 B3
Roundwood Rd
NW10 ....8 B1
Rounton Rd E3 ....26 C1
Roupell Rd SW2 .....74 B3

Roupell St SE1 ......121 C1
Rousden St NW1 .....13 B1
Routh Rd SW18 ......72 A4
Rover Ho 22 N1 ......24 A4
Rowallan Rd SW6 ...154 A1
Rowan Cl W5 ....36 A4
Rowan Ct 18 SE15 ...49 B3
SW11 ....60 B1
Rowan Ho 5 NW3 ....12 B2
NW10 ....8 C1
Rowan Rd W6 ....39 C2
Rowan Wlk N19 ......4 B2
W10 ....23 A1
Rowans Close SW6 ..47 B3
Rowcross St 5 ....153 A2
Rowditch La SW11 ..169 B2
Rowdon Ave NW10 ...9 A1
Rowe La E9 ....17 B3
Rowena Cres
SW11 ....168 B1
Rowfant Rd SW12,
SW17 ....72 C2
Rowhill Mans 6 E5 ..17 A4
Rowhill Rd E5 ....17 A4
Rowington Cl W2 ...100 A4
Rowland Hill Ho
SE1 ....136 A4
Rowland Hill St
NW3 ....12 A3
Rowley Gdns N4 .....6 B4
Rowley Ho SE8 ......51 C4
Rowley Ind Pk W3 ..37 A3
Rowley Way NW8 ....78 C4
NW8 ....79 A4
Rowntree Cl NW6 ...10 C2
Rowse Cl E15 ....27 B4
Rowstock 1 NW5 ....13 C2
Rowstock Gdns N7 ..13 C3
Roxby Pl SW6 ......155 C4
Roxford Ho 2 E3 ....27 A1
Roxley Rd SE13 .....67 A1
Roxwell 10 NW1 .....13 A2
Roxwell Rd W12 ......38 C4
Roy Ho N1 ....87 C3
Roy Ridley Ho 6
SW4 ....61 C4
Roy Sq 14 ....33 A2
Royal Acad of Arts*
W1 ....118 C3
Royal Acad of Dancing
SW11 ....167 C3
Royal Acad of Music
NW1 ....91 C1
Royal Albert Hall*
SW7 ....129 B3
Royal Arc W1 ....118 C3
Royal Army Medical Coll
SW1 ....148 A2
Royal Ave SW3 .....144 C2
Royal Avenue Ho
SW3 ....144 C2
Royal Ballet Sch
W14 ....140 A2
Royal Brompton & Nat
Heart Hospl The
SW3 ....144 A2
Royal Cir SE27 ......75 A1
Royal Cl N16 ....7 A3
N1 ....87 A4
Royal Coll of Art
SW7 ....129 B3
SW7 ....129 C3
Royal Coll of Art
Sculpture Sch
SW11 ....158 B1
Royal Coll of Midwives
W1 ....104 B3

Royal Coll of Music
SW7 ....129 B2
Royal Coll of
Obstetricians &
Gynaecologists
NW1 ....90 C2
Royal Coll of Organists
SW7 ....129 B3
Royal Coll of Physicians
NW1 ....92 B2
Royal Coll of Science
SW7 ....129 B2
Royal Coll of Surgeons
WC2 ....107 A2
Royal College St
NW1 ....83 A4
Royal Courts of Justice
WC2 ....107 B1
Royal Cres
W11 ....31 A1 112 A1
Royal Crescent Mews
W11 ....30 C1
Royal Ct SE16 ....41 B3
Royal Duchess Mews
SW12 ....73 A4
Royal Ear Hospl
WC1 ....93 B1
Royal Exchange
EC3 ....109 C1
Royal Exchange Ave
EC3 ....109 C1
Royal Exchange Bldgs
EC3 ....109 C1
Royal Festival Hall*
SE1 ....121 A1
Royal Free Hospl
NW3 ....12 A3
Royal Geographical
Society SW7 ....129 C3
Royal Hill SE10 .....52 B3
Royal Hospital (Army
Pensioners) SW1 ..145 B1
Royal Hospital Rd
SW3 ....145 A1
Royal Hospl SW15 ..58 A1
Royal Langford
NW6 ....78 A2
Royal London Est The
NW10 ....20 C3
Royal London
Homeopathic
Hospl The WC1 ....106 B4
Royal London Hospl
(Whitechapel) The
E1 ....32 A4
Royal Marsden Hospl
SW3 ....143 C2
Royal Masonic Hospl
W6 ....38 C2
Royal Mews The*
SW1 ....132 B2
Royal National
Orthopaedic Hospl
W1 ....92 B1
Royal National TNE
Hospl The WC1 .....94 C4
Royal Naval Coll
Buildings SE10 ....52 C4
Royal Naval Pl SE14 .51 B3
Royal Oak Ct 5 N1 ..98 A4
Royal Oak Pl SE22 ..65 A1
Royal Oak Rd 8 E8 .17 A2
Royal Oak Sta W2 ..100 B3

Royal Opera Arc
SW1 ....119 B2
Royal Opera House,
Covent Garden*
WC2 ....106 B1
Royal Orchard Cl
SW18 ....70 A4
Royal Par SW6 .....154 A2
SE3 ....53 B1
Royal Pl 11 SE10 ....52 B3
Royal Rd SE17 ......48 A4
Royal Sch The NW3 .11 C4
Royal St SE1 ....135 A2
Royal United Services
Mus SW1 ....120 A1
Royal Veterinary Coll
NW1 ....83 B3
Royal Victor Pl E13 .25 C3
Royal Victoria Sta
E16 ....35 C2
Royalty Studios
W11 ....31 A3
Roycroft Cl SW2 .....74 C3
Roydon Cl SW11 ...168 C2
Royston Ct 3 TW9 ..44 B2
Royston Ho 11 SE15 .49 C4
Royston Rd TW10 ...54 A2
Royston St 22 E2 ....25 B3
Rozel Ct 3 N1 ....24 A4
Rozel Rd SW4 ....61 B4
Ruby St SE15 ....50 A4
Ruby Triangle SE15 .50 A4
Rucklidge Ave
NW10 ....21 C3
Rudall Cres NW3 ....11 C4
Rudbeck Ho 10
SE15 ....49 C3
Ruddington Cl E5 ...18 A4
Rudge Ho SE16 ....139 C2
Rudgwick Terr NW8 .80 B3
Rudhall Ho 4 SW2 ..62 C1
Rudloe Rd SW12 ....73 B4
Rudolf Pl SW8 ......162 B3
Rudolph Rd NW6 ....23 C3
Rudstone Ho 10 E3 .27 A2
Rudyard Ct SE1 ....137 C3
Rufford St N1 ....84 B4
Rufford Twr 5 W3 ...28 A1
Rufus Bsns Ctr
SW18 ....71 A2
Rufus Ho SE1 ......139 A2
Rufus St N1 ....98 A3
Rugby Mans W14 ...140 B4
Rugby Rd W4 ....38 A4
Rugby St WC1 ....94 C1
Rugg St E14 ....33 C2
Rugless Ho 2 E14 ..42 B4
Rugmere 4 NW1 ....12 C1
Rum Cl E1 ....32 B2
Rumball Ho 22 SE5 .49 A3
Rumbold Rd SW6 ..156 B1
Rumford Ho SE1 ...136 C1
Rumsey Rd SW9 ....62 B4
Runacres Ct SE17 ..150 C1
Runcorn Pl W11 ....112 A4
Rundell Tower
SW8 ....172 C4
Running Horse Yd 1
TW8 ....44 A4
Runnymead Ho
TW10 ....54 C2
Runnymede Ho E9 ..18 A4
Rupack St 3 SE16 ..40 B4
Rupert Ct W1 ......119 B4
Rupert Gdns SW9 ...48 A1
Rupert Ho SE11 ....149 C3

Rupert Rd N19 ....4 C2
NW6 ....23 B3
W4 ....38 A3
Rupert St W1 ....119 B4
Ruscoe Rd E16 .....35 B3
Rush Hill Mews 3
SW11 ....60 C4
Rush Hill Rd SW11 ..60 C4
Rusham Rd SW12 ..72 B4
Rushbrook Ho
SW8 ....171 B2
Rushby Ct SW4 ....172 A3
Rushcroft Rd SW2,
SW9 ....62 C3
Rushcutters Ct 18
SE16 ....41 A2
Rushey Gn SE13 ....67 A1
Rushey Mead SE4 ..66 C2
Rushford Rd SE4 ....66 B1
Rushgrove St SE18 169 B2
Rushmead 5 E2 .....25 A2
Rushmere Ho 2
SW15 ....68 C3
Rushmon Gdns
SW15 ....57 C1
Rushmore Cres 9
E5 ....17 C4
Rushmore Ho N7 13 C3
W14 ....126 B1
Rushmore Prim Sch
E5 ....17 C4
Rushmore Rd
18 E5 ....18 A4
E5 ....17 C4
Rusholme Rd SW15 58 A1
Rushton Ho SW8 ...171 B1
Rushton St N1 ....87 C2
Rushworth St SE1 ..136 B3
Ruskin Ave TW9 ....44 C1
Ruskin Ho SW1 ....147 C3
Ruskin Park Ho SE5 .63 C4
Ruskin Wlk SE24 ....63 B2
Rusper Ct SW9 ....172 B1
Russell Ct SW1 ....119 A1
SE15 ....50 A1
Russell Gdns W14 .126 A2
Russell Gdns Mews
W14 ....126 A2
Russell Gr SW9 ....173 C4
Russell Ho SW1 ....146 C2
5 E14 ....33 C3
Russell Kerr Cl W4 .45 B3
Russell Pickering Ho 8
SW4 ....62 A4
Russell Pl NW3 .....12 A3
SE16 ....41 A3
Russell Rd W14 ....126 B1
Russell Sq WC1 ....94 A1
Russell Square Sta
WC1 ....94 A1
Russell St WC2 ....120 B4
Russell Wlk 4
TW10 ....54 B1
Russet Cres N7 .....14 B3
Russet Way SE13 ...52 A1
Russia Ct EC2 ......109 A2
Russia Dock Rd
SE16 ....33 A1
Russia La E2 ....25 B3
Russia Row EC2 ....109 A1
Rust Sq SE5 ....48 C3
Rusthall Ave W4 ....37 C3
Rusthall Mans W4 ...37 C2
Ruston Mews W11 ..31 A3

Ruston St E3 . . . . .26 B4
Ruth Cl E14 . . . . .26 A3
Ruth Ho SW1 . . . . .23 A1
Rutherford Ho **12**
E1 . . . . .25 A1
Rutherford St SW1 .**147** B4
Ruthin Rd SE5 . . . . .53 C4
Ruthven St E5 . . . . .25 C4
Rutland Cl SW14 . . . . . .55 A4
Rutland Ct SW7 . . . . .**130** B3
SE5 . . . . .63 C3
Rutland Gate SW7 .**130** B3
Rutland Gate Mews
SW7 . . . .**130** A2
Rutland Gdns SW7 .**130** B3
Rutland Gdns Mews
SW7 . . . .**130** A2
Rutland Gr W6 . . . . .39 A1
Rutland Ho W8 . . . . . .**128** A1
10 SW15 . . . . .57 C2
Rutland Mews E
SW7 . . . .**130** B2
Rutland Mews S
SW7 . . . .**130** A2
Rutland Mews W
SW7 . . . .**130** A2
Rutland Park Gdns
NW2 . . . . .9 B2
Rutland Park Mans
NW2 . . . . .9 B2
Rutland Ph NW2 . . . . .9 B2
Rutland Pl EC1 . . . .**108** B4
Rutland Rd E9 . . . . .25 C4
Rutland St SW7 . . . . . .**130** B2
Rutland Studios
NW10 . . . . .21 C2
Rutley Cl SE11 . . . . .48 A4
Rutt's Terr SE14 . . . . . . .50 C2
Ruvigny Gdns SW15 .57 C4
Ruvigny Mans SW15 . .57 C4
Rycott Path SE22 . . . . . .76 C4
Ryculff Sq SE3 . . . . .53 B1
Rydal Ho SW8 . . . .**171** B1
Rydal Water NW1 . . . .**92** C3
Ryde Ho NW6 . . . . .23 C4
Ryde Vale Rd SW12 .73 B2
Ryder Ct SW1 . . . .**119** A2
Ryder Dr SE16 . . . . .40 A1
Ryder St SW1 . . . .**119** A2
Ryder Yd SW1 . . . .**119** A2
Ryder's Terr NW8 . . . . . .78 C2
Rydon St N1 . . . . .87 A4
Rydston Cl **2** N7 . . . . . .14 B1
Rye Hill Pk SE15 . . . . . .65 B3
Rye Ho **10** SE16 . . . . . . .40 B4
Rye La SE15 . . . . .49 C1
Rye Rd SE15 . . . . .65 C3
Rye Wlk SW15 . . . . .57 C2
Ryecotes Mead
SE21 . . . . .76 A3
Ryecroft Rd SE13 . . . . .67 B2
Ryecroft St SW6 . . . . .**166** A3
Ryedale SE22 . . . . .65 A1
Ryefield Path **7**
SW15 . . . . .68 C3
Ryegates **2** SE15 . . . . .50 A1
Ryfold Rd SW19 . . . . . . .70 C1
Ryland Rd NW5 . . . . .13 A2
Rylett Cres W12 . . . . . . .38 B3
Rylett Rd W12 . . . . .38 B3
Rylston Rd SW6 . . . . .**154** C3
Rymer St SE24 . . . . .63 A1

Rysbrack St SW1 . . .**130** C2

S

Sabella Ct E3 . . . . .26 B3
Sabine Rd SW11 . . . . . . .60 C4
Sable St N1 . . . . .15 A1
Sacketts Ho SW9 . . . .**173** C4
Sackville Ho **18**
SW16 . . . . .74 A1
Sackville St W1 . . . . . .**119** A3
Sacred Heart High Sch
W6 . . . . .39 B2
Sacred Heart Jun Sch
W6 . . . . .39 C2
Sacred Heart Prim Sch
SW15 . . . . .56 C2
**Sacred Heart RC Jun &
Inf Schs** SW11 . . .**168** B3
**Sacred Heart RC Sch
The** SE5 . . . . .48 B2
Saddlers Mews
SW8 . . . .**172** A4
Sadler Ho **5**
17 E3 . . . . .27 A2
Saffron Ave E14 . . . . . . .34 C2
Saffron Ct **15** N1 . . . . . .15 C2
Saffron Hill EC1 . . . . .**107** C4
Saffron St EC1 . . . .**107** C4
Saffron Wharf SE1 . .**139** A4
Sage St E1 . . . . .32 B2
Sage Way WC1 . . . .**94** C3
Sailmakers Ct SW6 . . .60 A4
Sainfoin Rd SW17 . . . . .72 C2
Salamanca Pl SE1 .**148** C3
Salamanca St SE1,
SE11 . . . .**148** C3
Salcombe Gdns
SW4 . . . . .61 A3
Salcombe Lo NW5 . . . .12 C4
Salcombe Rd **22**
N16 . . . . .16 A3
Salcot N4 . . . . .5 B2
Salcott Rd SW11 . . . . . .60 B2
Sale Pl W2 . . . .**102** A2
Sale St E2 . . . . .24 C1
Salehurst Rd SE4 . . . . . .66 B1
Salem Ho **19** E9 . . . . . . .17 C2
Salem Rd W2 . . . .**114** B4
Salesian Coll
SW11 . . . .**168** A3
Salford Ho **4** E14 . . . . .42 B2
Salford Rd SW12,
SW2 . . . . .73 C3
Salisbury Cl SE17 .**151** B4
Salisbury Ct EC4 . . . .**108** A1
SE16 . . . .**139** C1
E9 . . . . .18 A3
W4 . . . . .38 A2
Salisbury Ho N1 . . . . . .**86** A4
10 E14 . . . .**147** C2
3 E14 . . . . .34 A3
SW1 . . . .**146** A2
Salisbury Mews
SW6 . . . .**154** C1
Salisbury Pl W1 . . . .**103** A4
SW9 . . . .**48** A3
Salisbury Rd NW8 . . . .**90** A1
10 W3 . . . . .37 A4
Salisbury Sq EC4 . . . .**107** C1
Salisbury St NW8 . . . . .**90** A1
Salisbury Terr SE15 .65 B4
Salisbury Wlk N19 . . . . .4 B2
Salmon La E14 . . . . .33 A3
Saltash Ho SE11 . . . .**150** A2

Saltcoats Rd W4 . . . . . . .38 A4
Saltdene N4 . . . . .5 B3
Salter Rd SE16 . . . . .33 A1
Salter St **10** 21 C2
Salters Rd W10 . . . . .22 C1
Salters' Hall Ct
EC4 . . . .**123** B4
Salterton Rd N7 . . . . .5 B1
Saltoun Rd SW2,
SW9 . . . . .62 C3
Saltram Cres W9 . . . . . .23 C2
Saltwell St E14 . . . . .33 C2
Saltwood Gr SE17 .**151** B1
Salusbury Prim Sch
NW6 . . . . .23 B4
Salusbury Rd NW6 . . . .23 A4
Salvin Rd SW15 . . . . . . .57 C4
Salway Ho SW8 . . . . .**172** B4
Salway Rd E15 . . . . .19 C2
Salween Ho **2** N16 . . . .15 C4
Sam Manners Ho 5
SE10 . . . . .43 A1
Sam March Ho **5**
E14 . . . . .34 C3
**Samaritan Hospl for
Women** NW1 . . . .**102** C4
Sambrook Ho **19** E1 .32 B4
Samels Ct W6 . . . . .38 C1
Samford Ho N1 . . . . .85 B3
Samford St NW8 . . . . .**90** A1
Sampson St **1** **125** C1
Samuel Cl E8 . . . . .24 B4
SE14 . . . . .50 C4
Samuel Jones Ind Est 5
SE15 . . . . .49 A3
Samuel Lewis Bldgs
N1 . . . .**14** C2
**Samuel Lewis Trust
Dwellings**
W14 . . . .**140** B4
SW3 . . . .**144** A3
SW6 . . . .**155** C2
E8 . . . . .16 C4
6 SE5 . . . . .48 B2
Samuel Rhodes Sch
N1 . . . . .85 B4
Samuel Richardson Ho
W14 . . . .**140** C3
Samuel's Cl 2 W6 . .39 B2
Sancroft St SE11 . . . .**149** A2
Sanctuary St SE1 . . .**137** A4
Sanctuary The
SW1 . . . .**133** C2
3 E1 . . . . .32 A1
Sandale Cl N16 . . . . .6 C1
Sandall Ho **6** E3 . . . . . . .26 A3
Sandall Rd NW5 . . . . . . .13 B2
Sandalwood Cl **11**
E1 . . . . .26 A1
Sandalwood Ho **8**
NW3 . . . . .11 A2
Sandbourne **8** W11 .31 C3
Sandbourne Rd SE4 .51 A1
Sandbrook Rd N16 . . . . .7 A1
Sandby Ho **6** NW6 . . . .23 C4
11 SE5 . . . . .49 A2
Sandcroft Ho SE11 .**149** A2
Sandell St SE1 . . . .**135** B4
Sanderling **20**
SE8 . . . . .51 B4
Sanders Ho WC1 . . . . .**95** B4
Sanders Way **3** N19 . . .4 C3

Sanderson Cl NW5 . . . .13 A4
Sanderson Ho **7**
SE8 . . . . .41 B1
Sanderstead Ave
NW2 . . . . .1 A2
Sanderstead Cl
SW12 . . . . .73 B4
Sandfield WC1 . . . . .94 B3
Sandford Ct N16 . . . . . . .7 A3
Sandford Row
SE17 . . . .**151** C2
Sandford St SW6 . . . .**156** B1
Sandford Wlk **4** N16 .7 B2
SE14 . . . . .51 A4
Sandgate Ho **15** E5 . .17 A4
Sandgate La SW17,
SW18 . . . . .72 A3
Sandgate St **5**
SE15 . . . . .50 A4
Sandgate Trad Est
SE15 . . . . .50 A4
Sandham Ct SW4 . .**172** B3
Sandhills The
SW10 . . . .**157** A4
Sandhurst Ct SW2 . . . .62 A3
Sandhurst Ho **10** E1 .32 B4
Sandilands Rd
SW6 . . . .**166** A3
Sandison St SE15 . . . . .64 C4
Sandland St **1** WC1 .**107** A3
Sandlings Cl SE15 . . . . .50 A1
Sandmere Rd SW4 . . . .62 A3
Sandon Ho **5** SW2 . . . .74 A4
Sandown Ho **2** W4 .37 B1
Sandpiper Cl SE16 . . . . .41 B4
Sandpiper Ct
11 E14 . . . . .42 B3
7 SE8 . . . . .51 C3
Sandridge Ct N4 . . . . . . .6 B2
Sandridge St **2** N19 .4 B2
Sandringham Cl 1
SW19 . . . . .69 C3
Sandringham Ct
W9 . . . .**89** A3
10 W1 . . . .**105** A1
18 SE16 . . . . .32 C1
SW15 . . . . .57 C1
Sandringham Flats
WC2 . . . .**119** C4
Sandringham Ho
W14 . . . .**140** A4
Richmond TW10 . . . .54 C2
Sandringham Rd
NW11 . . . . .1 A4
NW2 . . . . .9 A2
E8 . . . . .16 B3
Sandrock Rd SE13 . . . .66 C4
Sands End La SW6 . .**166** B4
Sandstone TW9 . . . . . . .44 C3
Sandstone Pl N19 . . . . . .4 A2
Sandways **3** TW9 . . . . .44 C2
Sandwell Cres **2**
NW6 . . . . .10 C2
Sandwell Mans **3**
NW6 . . . . .10 C2
Sandwich Ho WC1 . .**94** A3
10 SE16 . . . . .40 B4
Sandwich St WC1 . . . .**94** A3
Sandy Lo N6 . . . . .4 B4
Sandy Rd NW3 . . . . .2 A2
Sandy's Row E1 . . . . .**110** B3
Sandycombe Rd
TW9 . . . . .44 C1
Sanford La **3** SE14,SE8 .51 A4
Sanford St SE14,SE8 .51 A4
Sanford Terr N16 . . . . . . .7 B1

Sangora Rd **17**
SW11 . . . . .59 C3
Sankey Ho **22** E2 . . . . . .25 B3
Sans Wlk EC1 . . . .**96** A2
Sansom Rd E11 . . . . .19 C4
Sansom St SE5 . . . . .48 C2
20 SE5 . . . . .48 C3
Santley Ho SE1 . . . . .**135** C3
Santley St SW4 . . . . .62 B3
Santos Rd SW18 . . . . . .58 C2
Sapcote Trad Ctr
NW10 . . . . .8 B2
Saperton Wlk
SE11 . . . .**149** A4
Sapperton Ct EC1 . . .**96** C2
Sapphire Ct **1** E1 . . .**125** B4
Sapphire Rd SE8 . . . . .**41** A2
Sara Lane Ct **31** N1 .24 A3
Saracen St E14 . . . . .33 C3
Sarah Ho **11** E1 . . . . . . .32 A3
SW15 . . . . .56 B3
Sarah Swift Ho
SE1 . . . .**137** C4
Saratoga Rd E5 . . . . .17 B4
Sardinia St WC2 . . . .**106** C2
Sarjant Path SW19 . . . .69 C2
Sarjant Path N1 . . . . .15 B2
Sarnesfield Ho
SE15 . . . . .50 A4
Sarratt Ho W10 . . . . .30 B4
Sarre Rd NW2 . . . . .10 B3
Sarsden Bldgs W1 .**103** C1
Sarsfeld Rd SW12 . . . . .72 B3
Sartor Rd SE15 . . . . .65 C3
Sarum Hall Sch
NW3 . . . . .12 A1
Sarum Ho W11 . . . . . .**113** A3
Satchwell Rd **2** E2 .**99** B3
Saul Ct **4** SE15 . . . . .49 B4
Saunders Cl **14** E14 .33 B2
Saunders Ho
18 SW2 . . . . .74 C3
6 W11 . . . . .30 C1
Saunders Ness Rd
E14 . . . . .42 C2
Saunders St SE11 . . .**149** B4
Savage Gdns EC3 . . .**124** B4
Savanna N16 . . . . .7 A2
Savernake Ho N4 . . . . . . .6 C4
Savernake Rd NW3 . . .12 B4
Savill Ho **2** SW4 . . . . . .61 C1
Saville Row W4 . . . . .37 B2
Saville Row **1** W1 .**118** C4
Savona St SW8 . . . . . .**160** C1
Savoy Bldgs WC2 . . . .**29** B2
Savoy Circus W3 . . . . . .29 B2
Savoy Ct WC2 . . . .**120** B3
SW5 . . . .**141** C4
Savoy Hill WC2 . . . . . .**120** C3
Savoy Pier WC2 . . . . .**120** C3
Savoy Row WC2 . . . . .**120** C4
Savoy St WC2 . . . .**120** C3
Savoy Steps WC2 . . .**120** C3
Savoy Way WC2 . . . . .**120** C3
Sawkins Cl SW19 . . . . . .70 A2
Sawley Rd W12 . . . . .29 C1
Sawyer St SE1 . . . .**136** C4
Saxby Rd SW2 . . . . .74 A4
Saxon Ho **4** SW4 . . . . .61 C3
Saxon Hall W2 . . . . . .**114** A3
Saxon Rd E3 . . . . .26 B3
Saxonbury Ct **10** N7 .13 C3
2 N7 . . . . .14 A3
Saxonfield Cl SW2 . . . .74 B4

Saxton Cl SE13 .....67 C4
Sayer Ho SE4 ....66 A3
Sayes Court St SE8 .51 B4
Sayes Ct SE8 ....51 B4
Scafell NW1 ....92 C4
Scala St W1 ....105 A4
Scampston Mews 5
W10 ....30 C3
Scandrett St 38 E1 ..32 A1
Scarba Wlk N1 .....15 C2
Scarborough Rd N4 ..5 C3
Scarborough St
E1 ....111 A1
Scarlette Manor Wlk 10
SE24 ....74 C4
Scarsbrook Ho 2
SW2 ....62 C1
Scarsdale Pl W8 ..128 A2
Scarsdale Villas
W8 ....127 C1
Scarth Rd SW13 ....56 B4
Scawen Rd SE8 .....41 A1
Scawfell St E2 ......24 B3
Sceptre Ho 9 E1 ...25 B1
Sceptre Rd E2 ......25 B2
Sch of Nursing
W1 ....104 C4
Sch of Pharmacy
WC1 ....94 B2
Schofield Wlk SE3 ..53 C3
Scholars Rd SW12 ..73 B3
Scholefield Rd N19 ..4 C2
Scholey Ho SW11 ...60 A4
Schomberg Ho
SW1 ....147 C4
Schonfeld Sq N16 ....6 C3
School App E2 ......98 B4
School Bell Cloisters 15
E3 ....26 A3
School Flats SW8 ..172 A3
School Ho SE1 ....152 A4
School of Finance &
Management N7 ...14 B2
School Rd NW10 ....20 C1
Schoolbell Mews 16
E3 ....26 A3
Schoolhouse La E1 .32 C2
Schooner Cl
1 SE16 ....40 C4
E14 ....42 C3
Schubert Rd SW15 ..58 B2
Science Mus★
SW7 ....129 B1
Sclater St E1 ......99 A2
Scoles Cres SW2 ...74 C3
Scoresby St SE1 ..122 A1
Scorton Ho 2 N1 ...24 A3
Scotch House
SW1 ....130 C3
Scoter Ct 23 SE8 ....51 B4
Scotia Bldg 10 E1 ...32 C2
Scotia Ct 3 SE16 ....40 B3
Scotia Rd 24 SW2 ...74 C4
Scotland Pl SW1 ...120 A1
Scotney Ho E9 ......17 B2
Scotson Ho SE11 ..149 B3
Scotswood St EC1 ..95 C2
Scott Ct SW11 .....170 B1
17 N16 ....7 A1
W4 ....37 C4
Scott Ellis Gdns
NW8 ....89 B3
Scott Ho N1 ....87 B4
NW8 ....90 A1
N7 ....14 B2

Scott Lidgett Cres
SE16 ....139 C3
Scott St E1 ....25 A1
Scott's Rd W12 .....39 A4
Scott's Sufferance
Wharf SE1 ....139 A3
Scott's Yd EC4 ....123 B4
Scotts Ct 6 W12 ...39 A4
Scoulding Ho 6
E14 ....41 C3
Scoulding Rd E16 ...35 C3
Scouler St E14 .....34 C2
Scout App NW10 .....8 A4
Scovell Cres SE1 ..136 C3
Scovell Rd SE1 ....136 C3
Scriven Ct 2 E8 ....24 B4
Scriven St E8 ....24 B4
Scrooby St SE6 .....67 A1
Scrope Ho EC1 ....107 B4
Scrubs La NW10,
W10,W12 ....22 A2
Scrutton Cl SW12 ...73 C4
Scrutton St
EC2 ....24 A1 98 A1
Scutari Rd SE22 ....65 B2
Scylla Rd SE15 ......65 A4
Seabright St 27 E2 ..25 A2
Seacole Cl W3 ......28 C4
Seaford Ho 8 SE16 .40 B4
Seaford St WC1 .....94 B3
Seaforth Cres N5 ...15 B3
Seaforth Lo 2
SW13 ....46 B1
Seaforth Pl SW1 ...133 A2
Seager Pl E3 ....33 B4
Seagrave Lodge
SW6 ....155 C4
Seagrave Rd SW6 .155 C4
Seagrove Cl E1 .....32 C4
Seal Ho SE1 ....137 C2
Seal St E8 ....16 B4
Searle Ct N4 ....5 B3
Searle Ho 15 E1 ....32 C4
Searles Cl SW11 ...158 B1
Searles Rd SE1 ....151 C4
Sears St SE5 ....48 C3
Searson Ho SE17 ..150 B3
Seasalter Ho SW9 .173 B4
Seaton Cl SE11 ....150 A2
SW15 ....69 A3
Seaton Point E5 ....16 C4
Seavington Ho 3
SE5 ....64 A4
Sebastian Ho 22 N1 .24 A3
Sebastion St EC1 ...96 B3
Sebbon St N1 ....15 A1
Sebright Ho 21 E2 ..24 C3
Sebright JMI Sch
E2 ....24 C3
Secker Ho SW9 .....48 A1
Secker St SE1 .....121 B1
Second Ave W10 ...23 A1
W3 ....29 B1
SW14 ....56 A4
Sedan Way SE17 ..152 A2
Sedding St SW1 ...145 B4
Seddon Ho EC2 ....108 C4
Seddon St WC1 .....95 A3
Sedgeford Rd W12 ..29 B1
Sedgewick Ho
SW19 ....69 C2
Sedgley Ho N4 ....5 B2
Sedgmoor Pl SE5 ...49 A3
Sedgwick St E9 .....17 C3
Sedleigh Rd SW18 ..58 B1

Sedlescombe Rd
SW6 ....155 B4
Sedley Ho SE11 ....149 A2
Sedley Pl W1 ......104 A1
Seething La EC3 ...124 B4
Sefton St SW15 .....57 B4
Sekforde St EC1 ....96 A2
Selbie Ave NW10 .....8 B3
Selborne 2 SW11 ..60 C4
Selborne Ho SE1 ..137 B3
Selborne Rd 1 SE5 .48 C1
Selby Ho 6 W10 ....23 A2
10 SW4 ....61 B1
Selby St E1 ...24 C1 99 C1
Selden Ho 2 SE15 ..50 B1
Selden Rd SE15 .....50 B1
Selden Wlk N7 ....5 B2
Seldon Ho SW1 ....146 C1
SW8 ....160 C1
Selfridges W1 .....103 C1
Selhurst Cl SW19 ...69 C3
Selina Ho NW8 .....89 C2
Selkirk Ho N1 ......84 C4
4 N16 ....7 A1
Sellons Ave NW10 ..21 B4
Selma Ho W12 ......30 A3
Selman Ho 3 E9 ...18 A2
Selsdon Rd SE27 ....75 A1
Selsdon Way E14 ....42 A3
Selsea Pl N16 ......16 A3
Selsey St E14 ....33 C4
Selwood Ho 1 N4 ...6 C4
Selwood Pl SW7 ...143 B2
Selwood Terr SW7 .143 B2
Selworthy Ho
SW11 ....167 C4
Selwyn Ave TW9 ....54 B4
Selwyn Ct 8 TW10 .54 B2
Selwyn Ho 3 SW15 .57 C1
Selwyn Rd NW10 .....8 A1
E3 ....26 B3
Semley Ho SW1 ...146 A3
Semley Pl SW1 ....146 A3
Senate St SE15 .....50 B1
Senators Lo 29 E3 ..26 A3
Sendall Ct 13 SW11 .59 C4
Senior St W2 ......100 A4
Senrab St E1 ....32 C3
Seraph Ct EC1 ......96 C4
Sergeant Ind Est The
SW18 ....59 A1
Serica Ct 14 SE10 ...52 B3
Serjeants' Inn
EC4 ....107 C1
Serlby Ct W14 ....126 C2
Serle St WC2 ......107 A2
Sermon La EC4 ....108 C1
Serpentine Br W2 .115 C1
Serpentine Ct 10
SE16 ....40 C4
Serpentine Gallery★
W2 ....129 C4
Serpentine Rd W2 .116 C1
Serpentine The★
W2 ....116 B1
Service Route No 1
E15 ....19 C1
Service Route No 2
E15 ....19 C1
Service Route No 3
E15 ....19 C1
Servite Ho SE13 ....52 A2
Servite RC Prim Sch
SW10 ....156 C4
Setchell Rd SE1 ...152 C4
Setchell Way SE1 ..152 C4

Seth St 18 SE16 .....40 B4
Settles St E1 ......111 C2
Settrington Rd
SW6 ....166 A1
Seven Dials WC2 ..106 A1
Seven Mills JMI Sch
E14 ....41 C4
Seven Sisters Rd N4,
N7,N15 ....6 B4
Seven Stars Cnr
W12 ....38 C3
Sevenoaks Rd SE4 ..66 B1
Severn Ho 7 W10 ...23 A2
Severn Way NW10 ....8 B3
Severnake Cl E14 ...41 C2
Severus Rd SW11 ...60 A3
Seville Ho E1 ......125 C1
Seville Mews N1 ....16 A1
Seville St SW1 ....131 A3
Sevington St W9 ....88 A1
Seward St EC1 .....96 C3
Sewardstone Rd E2 .25 B3
Sewell Ho 7 N16 ...16 A3
Sextant Ave E14 ....42 C2
Sexton's Ho 4 SE13 52 B4
Seymour Ct N16 .....7 C3
SW15 ....57 A3
Seymour Gdns SE4 .66 A4
Seymour Ho NW1 ...93 C3
WC1 ....94 A2
SW8 ....171 A2
Seymour Mews
W1 ....103 B2
Seymour Pl W1 ...102 C2
Seymour Rd W4 ....37 B2
SW18 ....58 B1
SW19 ....69 C1
Seymour St W1 ...103 A1
Seymour Wlk
SW10 ....156 C4
Seyssel St E14 ......42 B2
Shaa Rd W3 ....28 C2
Shackleton Ct
4 W12 ....39 A4
2 SE21 ....75 C2
Shackleton Ho 5
E1 ....32 B1
Shacklewell Ho 3
E8 ....16 B4
Shacklewell JMI Sch
E8 ....16 B4
Shacklewell La E8 ..16 B3
Shacklewell Rd N16 16 B4
Shacklewell Row
E8 ....16 B4
Shacklewell St E2 ..99 A3
Shad Thames SE1 .139 A4
Shadwell Gdns E1 ..32 B2
Shadwell Pierhead
E1 ....32 B2
Shadwell Sta E1 ....32 A2
Shaftesbury Ave
WC2 ....105 C1
W1 ....119 C4
Shaftesbury Ct N1 ..87 B1
1 SE5 ....63 C3
Shaftesbury Gdns
NW10 ....21 A1
Shaftesbury Ho
W2 ....114 B4
13 N16 ....7 A1
Shaftesbury Lo 9
E14 ....34 A3
Shaftesbury Mews
W8 ....127 C1

Shaftesbury Park
Chambers 1
SW11 ....60 C4
Shaftesbury Rd
N4,N19 ....5 A3
Richmond TW9 ......54 A4
Shaftesbury St N1 ..87 B1
Shafteswood Ct
SW17 ....72 B1
Shafto Mews SW1 .131 A1
Shafton Rd E9 ......25 C4
Shafts Ct EC3 .....110 A1
Shaftsbury Ct SW6 166 B3
Shaftsbury Mews 2
SW4 ....61 B2
Shaftsbury Park Prim
Sch SW11 ....169 B1
Shahjalal Ho 18 E2 .24 C3
Shakespeare Ave
NW10 ....20 C4
Shakespeare Cres
NW10 ....20 C4
Shakespeare Ho 3
E9 ....17 B1
Shakespeare Rd
W3 ....28 B1
SE24 ....63 A3
Shakespeare Twr
EC2 ....109 A4
Shakespeare's Globe
Theatre (site of)
SE1 ....123 A2
Shakspeare Mews 7
N16 ....16 A4
Shakspeare Wlk
N16 ....16 A4
Shalcomb St SW10 157 A3
Shalden Ho 6
SW15 ....56 B1
Shalfleet Dr W10 ...30 C2
Shalford NW10 .....21 C4
Shalford Ct N1 .....86 A2
Shalford Ho SE1 ..137 C2
Shalimar Gdns W3 ..28 B2
Shalimar Lo W3 ....28 B2
Shalimar Rd W3 ....28 B2
Shalstone Rd SW14,
TW9 ....55 A4
Shamrock St SW4 ..61 C4
Shand St SE1 ......138 B4
Shandon Rd SW4 ...61 B1
Shandy St E1 ....25 C1
Shannon Ct N16 .....7 A1
NW10 ....8 C2
9 SE15 ....49 B3
Shannon Gr SW9 ...62 B3
Shannon Pl NW8 ...80 B2
Shanti Ct SW18 .....70 C3
Shapla JMI Sch E1 125 B4
Shard's Sq SE15 ....49 C4
Shardcroft Ave
SE24 ....63 A2
Shardeloes Rd SE14 .51 B1
Sharebourne Ho
SW2 ....62 C2
Sharnbrook Ho
W6 ....155 B4
Sharon Gdns E9 ...25 B4
Sharon Rd W4 ......37 C1
Sharp Ho SW8 ......61 A4
Sharples Hall St 8
NW1 ....12 B1

Sharpness Ct 2 SE15 ...49 B3
Sharratt St SE15 ...50 B4
Sharstead St SE17 ...150 A1
Sharwell Ho SW18 ...59 A1
Sharwood WC1 ...85 A1
Shaver's Pl SW1 ...119 B3
Shaw Ct SW11 ...5 A2
8 W3 ...37 B3
12 SW11 ...59 C4
Shaw Ho E14 ...33 A3
Shaw Rd SE22 ...64 A3
Shawbury Ct SE22 ...64 B2
Shawbury Rd SE22 ...64 B2
Shawfield St SW3 ...144 B1
Shawford Ct 8 SW15 ...68 C4
Shearling Way N7 ...14 A2
Shearsmith Ho E1 ...125 C4
Shearwater Ct 3 SE8 ...51 B4
Sheen Common Dr SW14,TW10 ...54 C3
Sheen Court Rd TW10 ...54 C3
Sheen Ct TW10 ...54 C3
Sheen Gate Gdns SW14 ...55 B3
Sheen Gr N1 ...85 B3
Sheen La SW14 ...55 B3
Sheen Mount JMI Sch SW14 ...55 A2
Sheen Pk TW10,TW9 ...54 B3
Sheen Rd TW10,TW9 ...54 A3
Sheen Wood SW14 ...55 B2
Sheendale Rd TW9 ...54 B3
Sheep La E8 ...25 A4
Sheepcote La SW11 ...169 A1
Sheffield Ho 14 SE15 ...49 B2
Sheffield Sq 2 E3 ...26 B2
Sheffield St WC2 ...106 C1
Sheffield Terr W8 ...31 C1 113 C4
Shelburne Ho 20 N19 ...4 C4
Shelburne Ct SW15 ...57 C2
Shelburne Rd N7 ...14 B4
Shelburne Rd SE22 ...65 A2
Sheldon Ct SW8 ...162 A1
Sheldon Ho 9 E9 ...17 C2
Sheldon Rd NW2 ...9 C4
Sheldrake Ho 15 SE16 ...40 C2
Sheldrake Pl W8 ...127 B4
Shelduck Ct 30 SE8 ...51 B4
Shelford Pl N16 ...6 C1
Shelgate Rd SW11 ...60 B2
Shelgrove Rd N16 ...16 A4
Shell Ctr SE1 ...121 A1
Shell Rd SE13 ...67 A4
Shelley Cl SE15 ...50 A1
Shelley Ct SW3 ...159 A4
N4 ...5 B3
Shelley Ho SE17 ...151 A2
5 N16 ...16 A4
21 E2 ...25 B2
Shelley Sch SE11 ...149 C3
Shellness Rd E5 ...17 A3
Shellwood Rd SW11 ...168 C1

Shelmerdine Cl E3 ...33 C4
Shelton St WC2 ...106 A1
Shene Ho EC1 ...107 B4
Shene Sec Sch SW14 ...56 A3
Shenfield St N1 ...24 A3
Shenley Rd SE5 ...49 A2
Shepherd Cl W1 ...117 B4
Shepherd Ho N7 ...14 A2
10 E14 ...34 A3
Shepherd Mkt W1 ...118 A1
Shepherd St W1 ...118 A1
Shepherd's Bush Gn W12 ...39 B4
Shepherd's Bush Market W12 ...39 B4
Shepherd's Bush Pl W12 ...39 C4
Shepherd's Bush Rd W6 ...39 B3
Shepherd's Bush Sta W12 ...30 B1
Shepherd's La E9 ...17 C2
Shepherd's Wlk NW3 ...11 C4
Shepherdess Pl N1 ...97 A4
Shepherds Wlk N1 ...87 A1
Shepherds Pl W1 ...117 B4
W12 ...39 C4
Sheppard Ho 5 N1 ...87 B4
20 E2 ...24 C3
18 SW2 ...74 C3
Shepperton Rd N1 ...87 B4
Sheppey Ho 16 E5 ...17 A4
Sheppey Wlk N1 ...15 B1
Shepton Ct SW1 ...167 C4
Shepton Hos 11 E2 ...25 B2
Sherard Ct N19 ...5 A1
Sherard Ho 20 E9 ...17 B1
Sheraton Ho SW1 ...160 B4
Sheraton St W1 ...105 B1
Sherborne Ho SW1 ...146 B2
SW8 ...162 B2
Sherborne La EC4 ...123 C4
Sherborne St N1 ...87 B4
Sherbrooke Ho 9 E2 ...25 B3
Sherbrooke Rd SW6 ...154 B1
Sherborne Terr SW6 ...154 B1
Sherfield Gdns SW15 ...56 B1
Sheridan Bldgs WC2 ...106 B1
Sheridan Ct NW6 ...11 B1
Sheridan Ho SE11 ...149 C3
7 N16 ...16 A4
1 E1 ...32 B3
Sheridan Pl SW13 ...56 B4
Sheridan St 20 E1 ...32 A3
Sheridan Ct SW5 ...142 A3
Sheringdale Prim Sch SW18 ...70 B3
Sheringham NW8 ...79 C4
Sheringham Ho NW1 ...102 B4
Sheringham Rd N7 ...14 C2
Sherlock Holmes Mus * NW1 ...91 A1

Sherlock Mews W1 ...103 B4
Sherrick Green Rd NW10 ...9 A3
Sherriff Ct NW6 ...10 C2
Sherriff Rd NW6 ...10 C2
Sherrin Rd E10 ...19 A4
Sherston Ct WC1 ...95 B3
SE1 ...150 B4
Sherwin Ho SE11 ...163 B4
Sherwin Rd SE14 ...50 C2
Sherwood NW6 ...10 A1
Sherwood Cl SW13 ...57 A4
Sherwood Ct W1 ...102 C3
SE16 ...40 A1
SE13 ...52 A1
Sherwood Gdns SE16 ...40 A1
E14 ...41 C2
Sherwood Ho N4 ...6 B4
Sherwood St W1 ...119 A4
Shetland Rd E3 ...26 B3
Shillaker Ct 3 W3 ...29 B1
Shillibeer Pl W1 ...102 B3
Shillingford Ho 28 E3 ...27 A2
Shillingford St 22 N1 ...15 A1
Shinfield St W12 ...30 B3
Ship and Mermaid Row SE1 ...138 A4
Ship La SW14 ...45 B1
Ship St SE8 ...51 C2
Ship Tavern Pas EC3 ...124 A4
Shipka Rd SW12 ...73 A3
Shiplake Ho 2 E2 ...98 C3
Shipley Ho SW8 ...171 B1
Shipton Ho 7 NW5 ...12 C2
E2 ...24 B3
Shipton St E2 ...24 B3
Shipwright Rd SE16 ...41 A4
Shipwright Yd SE1 ...124 A1
Shire Pl SW18 ...71 B4
Shirland Mews W9 ...23 B2
Shirland Rd W9 ...23 C1
Shirley Gr SW11 ...60 C4
Shirley Ho 13 SE5 ...48 C3
Shirley Rd W4 ...37 C4
Shirley St E16 ...35 B1
Shirlock Rd NW3 ...12 B4
Shoe La EC4 ...107 C2
Shooters Hill Rd SE3,SE10 ...53 A2
Shore Bsns Ctr 17 E9 ...17 B1
Shore Ho SW8 ...61 A4
Shore Mews 3 E9 ...17 B1
Shore Pl E9 ...17 B1
Shore Rd E9 ...17 B1
Shoreditch Ct 2 E8 ...16 B1
Shoreditch High St E1 ...24 A1 98 B2
Shoreditch Sta E1 ...24 B1 99 A2
Shoreham Cl SW18 ...59 A2
Shorncliffe Rd SE1 ...152 C2
Shorrolds Rd SW6 ...155 A2
Short Rd E15 ...27 C4
Short St SE1 ...135 C4
Short Rd W4 ...46 A4
Shorter St EC3 ...125 A4

Shortlands W6 ...39 C2
Shorts Gdns WC2 ...106 A1
Shottendale Rd SW6 ...165 B3
Shottfield Ave SW14 ...56 A3
Shottsford 1 W11 ...31 C3
Shoulder of Mutton Alley 10 E14 ...33 A2
Shouldham St W1 ...102 B3
Shreveport Ho 20 N19 ...4 C4
Shrewsbury Ave SW14 ...55 C3
Shrewsbury Cres NW10 ...20 C4
Shrewsbury Ho SW3 ...158 A3
SE11 ...163 A3
Shrewsbury Mews 33 W2 ...31 C4
Shrewsbury Rd W2 ...31 C3
Shrewsbury St W10 ...22 B1
Shropshire Pl WC1 ...93 A1
Shroton St NW1 ...102 B4
Shrubland Rd E8 ...25 A4
Shrubs Ho SW1 ...147 C3
Shubbery Cl N1 ...87 A3
Shurland Gdns SE15 ...49 B3
Shuters Sq W14 ...140 C1
Shuttle St E1 ...24 C1 99 B1
Shuttleworth Rd SW11 ...168 A2
Sibella Rd SW4 ...171 C1
Sicilian Ave WC1 ...106 B3
Sidbury St SW6 ...164 A4
Siddons Ct WC2 ...106 C1
Siddons Ho W2 ...101 C3
8 NW3 ...12 B2
Siddons La NW1 ...91 A1
Sidford Ho SE1 ...135 A1
Sidford Pl SE1 ...135 A1
Sidgwick Ho SW9 ...172 B1
Sidings Mews N7 ...14 C4
Sidlaw Ho N16 ...7 B3
Sidmouth Ho W11 ...102 B2
10 SE15 ...49 C3
Sidmouth Par NW2 ...9 B1
Sidmouth Rd NW2 ...9 B1
Sidmouth St WC1 ...94 C3
Sidney Boyd Ct NW6 ...10 C1
Sidney Godley (VC) Ho 2 E2 ...25 B2
Sidney Gr EC1 ...86 A1
Sidney Ho 4 E2 ...25 B3
Sidney Miller Ct 8 W3 ...37 A4
Sidney Rd SW9 ...173 A1
Sidney Sq E1 ...32 B4
Sidney St E1 ...32 B4
Sidworth St 6 E8 ...17 A1
Siebert Rd SE3 ...53 C4
Siege Ho 22 E1 ...32 A3
Sigdon Rd E8 ...16 C3
Signmakers Yd NW1 ...82 C3
Silbury Ho 9 SE26 ...76 C1
Silbury St N1 ...97 B4
Silchester Rd W10 ...30 C3
Silesia Bldgs E8 ...17 A1
Silex St SE1 ...136 B3

Silsoe Ho NW1 ...82 B1
Silver Cl SE14 ...51 A3
Silver Cres W4 ...37 A2
Silver Ct N19 ...4 B3
Silver Pl W1 ...119 A4
Silver Rd W12 ...30 C2
Silver Wlk SE16 ...33 B1
Silverbirch Cl SE8 ...16 B1
Silverbirch Wlk 1 NW3 ...12 C2
Silverburn Ho 4 SW9 ...48 A2
Silverdale NW1 ...92 C4
Silvermere Rd SE6 ...67 A1
Silverthorn 9 NW8 ...78 B3
Silverthorne Rd SW8 ...170 A3
SW8 ...170 B1
Silverton Rd W6 ...47 C4
Silvertown Way E16 ...35 C1
Silvester Ho 27 E2 ...25 B2
17 E1 ...32 B3
Silvester Rd SE22 ...64 B2
Silvester St SE1 ...137 B3
Silwood St SE16 ...40 B1
Simla Cl SE14 ...51 A4
Simla Ho 1 SE1 ...137 C3
Simmons Ho 2 N7 ...5 B2
E2 ...99 B3
Simms Rd SE1 ...153 C3
Simon Cl W11 ...31 A2 113 A4
Simon Ct W9 ...23 C2
Simon Marks (Jewish) JMI Sch N16 ...7 B2
Simons Wlk E15 ...19 C3
Simpson Dr W3 ...28 C3
Simpson Ho NW8 ...90 A3
SE11 ...148 C1
Simpson St SW11 ...168 A1
Simpsons Rd E14 ...34 A2
Sinclair Ct N5 ...15 B2
Sinclair Gdns W14 ...39 C4
Sinclair Ho 1 WC1 ...73 C2
SW12 ...73 C2
Sinclair Mans 13 W12 ...30 A3
Sinclair Pl W14 ...126 A2
Sinclairs Ho 14 E3 ...26 B3
Singer St EC2 ...97 C3
Sion-Manning Sch for Girls W10 ...30 C4
Sion-Manning Sec Sch W10 ...30 C4
Sir Abraham Dawes Cotts SW11 ...58 A3
Sir Alexander Cl W3 ...29 B1
Sir Alexander Rd W3 ...29 B1
Sir Francis Drake Prim Sch SE8 ...41 A1
Sir James Barrie Prim Sch SW8 ...171 A3
Sir John Cass's Foundation & Redcoat CE Sec Sch E1 ...32 C4
Sir John Cass's Foundation CE Prim Sch EC3 ...110 B1
Sir John Lillie Prim Sch SW6 ...154 B3

Sir Oswald Stoll Foundation The SW6 ...156 A2
Sir Thomas Abney JMI Sch N16 ...6 C3
Sir Thomas More Est SW3 ...157 C3
Sir William Burrough JMI Sch E14 ...33 A3
Sir William Powell's Almshos SW6 ...4 C2
Sirdar Rd W11 ...31 A2 112 A3
Sirinham Point SW8 ...163 A3
Sirius Bldg E1 ...22 C2
Sise La EC4 ...109 B1
Siskin Ho SE16 ...40 C2
Sispara Gdns SW18 ...58 B1
Sissinghurst Ho E5 ...5 B2
Sister Mabel's Way E4 ...20 C2
Sisters Ave SW11 ...69 C3
Sistova Rd SW12 ...73 A3
Sisulu Pl SW9 ...62 C4
Site of Changing of the Guard* SW1 ...132 C3
Sivill Ho E2 ...99 A4
Siward Rd SW17 ...71 B1
Six Bridges Ind Est SE1 ...153 C1
Sixth Ave W10 ...23 A2
Skardu Rd NW2 ...10 A3
Skeena Hill SW18, SW19 ...70 A4
Skeggs Ho E14 ...42 B3
Skegness Ho N7 ...14 B4
Skelbrook St SW18 ...71 B2
Skelgill Rd SW15 ...58 B3
Skelton Cl E8 ...16 B2
Skelton Ho N16 ...16 A3
Skelwith Rd W6 ...47 B4
Skenfrith Ho SE15 ...50 A4
Sketchley Gdns SE16 ...40 C1
Skiffington Cl SW2 ...74 C3
Skinner Pl SW1 ...145 B3
Skinner St EC1 ...95 C2
Skinners Company Sch (Upper) N16 ...7 B4
Skinners La EC4 ...123 A4
Skipsea Ho SW18 ...59 C1
Skipton Ho SE4 ...66 A3
Skipwith Ho EC1 ...107 B4
Skipworth Rd E9 ...25 B4
Skomer Wlk N1 ...15 B2
Skua Ct SE8 ...51 B4
Skylines E14 ...42 B4
Slade Ct NW2 ...10 A3
Slade Wlk SE17 ...48 B4
Sladen Pl E5 ...17 A4
Slagrove Pl SE13 ...67 A2
Slaidburn St SW10 ...157 A3
Slaithwaite Rd SE13 ...67 B3
Slaney Ct NW10 ...9 B1
Sleaford Ho E3 ...26 C1
Sleaford Ind Est SW8 ...161 A1
Sleaford St SW8 ...161 A1
Sleat Ho E3 ...26 B3
Slievemore Ct E8 ...61 C4
Sligo Ho E1 ...25 C1
Slingsby Pl WC2 ...120 A4
Slippers Pl SE16 ...40 A3

Sloane Ave SW3 ...144 B3
Sloane Avenue Mans SW3 ...144 C3
Sloane Ct E SW3 ...145 B2
Sloane Ct W SW3 ...145 B2
Sloane Gate Mans SW1 ...145 B4
Sloane Gdns SW1 ...145 B3
Sloane Ho E9 ...17 B1
Sloane Sq SW1 ...145 A3
Sloane Square Sta SW1 ...145 B3
Sloane St SW1 ...131 A1
Sloane Terr SW1 ...145 B4
Sloane Terr Mans SW1 ...145 B4
Slomon Ho W10 ...23 A2
Sly St E1 ...32 A3
Smallbrook Mews W2 ...101 B1
Smalley Cl N16 ...7 B1
Smart St E2 ...25 C2
Smart's Pl WC1, WC2 ...106 B2
Smeaton Ct SE1 ...136 C1
Smeaton Rd SW18 ...70 C4
Smeaton St E1 ...32 A1
Smedley St SW4 ...171 C2
Smeed Rd E3 ...18 C1
Smetherton Ho E2 ...25 A3
Smiles Pl SE13 ...52 B1
Smith Cl SE16 ...32 C1
Smith Sq SW1 ...134 A1
Smith St SW3 ...144 C1
Smith Terr SW3 ...144 C1
Smith's Ct W1 ...119 B4
Smith's Yd SW18 ...71 B2
Smithfield Mkt* EC1 ...108 B3
Smithfield St EC1 ...108 A3
Smithies Ct E15 ...76 A3
Smithwood Cl SW19 ...70 A3
Smithy JMI Sch E1 ...32 B4
Smithy St E1 ...32 B4
Smugglers Way SW18 ...59 A3
Smyrk's Rd SE17 ...152 B1
Smyrna Mans NW6 ...10 C1
Smyrna Rd NW6 ...10 C1
Smythe St E14 ...34 A2
Snarsgate St W10 ...30 B4
Sneath Ave NW11 ...1 B4
Sneyd Rd NW2 ...9 B4
Snipe Ct SE8 ...51 A4
Snow Hill EC1 ...108 A3
Snow Ho SE27 ...75 A1
Snowberry Cl E11 ...19 C4
Snowbury Rd SW6 ...166 B1
Snowden St EC2 ...24 A1 98 A1
Snowman Ho NW6 ...78 B4
Snowsfields Prim Sch SE1 ...138 A4
Snowsfields SE1 ...64 B4
Soames St SE15 ...64 B4
Soane Ct E1 ...32 B3
Soane Ho SE17 ...151 C1
Soane Mus* WC2 ...106 C2
Soho Parish CE Prim Sch W1 ...119 B4
Soho Sq W1 ...105 B2
Soho St W1 ...105 B2

Sojourner-Truth Cl E8 ...17 A2
Solander Gdns E1 ...32 B2
  E1 ...32 A2
Soldene Ct N7 ...14 B2
Solebay St E1 ...26 A1
Solent Ho E1 ...33 A4
Solent Rd NW6 ...10 C3
Soley Mews WC1 ...95 B4
Solna Ave SW15 ...57 B2
Solomon's Pas SE15 ...65 A3
Solon New Rd SW4 ...62 A3
Solon Rd SW2 ...62 A3
Solway Ho E1 ...25 C1
Solway Rd SE22 ...64 C3
Somali Rd NW2 ...10 B3
Somborne Ho SW15 ...68 C4
Sombrook Ho SE11 ...149 B3
Somer Cl SW6 ...155 B3
Somerfield Ho SE16 ...40 C1
Somerfield Rd N4 ...6 A2
Somerford Gr N16 ...16 B4
Somerford Grove Est N16 ...16 B4
Somerford St E1 ...25 A1
Somerford Way SE16 ...41 A4
Somerleyton Rd SW9 ...62 C3
Somers Cl NW1 ...83 B2
Somers Cres W2 ...102 A1
Somers Pl SW2 ...74 B4
Somers Rd SW2 ...62 B1
Somers Town Est NW1 ...83 A1
Somerset Gdns N6 ...3 C4
  SE13 ...52 A1
Somerset Ho SW19 ...70 A1
Somerset House* WC2 ...121 A4
Somerset Lo SW15 ...57 B3
Somerset Rd W4 ...37 C3
Somerset Sq W14 ...126 C3
Somerton Ave TW9 ...55 A4
Somerton Rd NW2 ...1 A1
  SE15 ...65 A3
Somerville Ho SW15 ...57 C1
Sonderburg Rd N7 ...5 B2
Sondes St SE17 ...48 C4
Sonia Gdns NW10 ...8 B4
Sonning Ho E2 ...98 C3
Sophia Cl N7 ...14 B2
Sophia Ho W6 ...39 B1
Sophia Sq SE16 ...33 A2
Sopwith Way SW11 ...160 A2
Sorrel La E14 ...34 C3
Sorrell Cl SW9 ...173 C2
  SE14 ...51 A3
Sotheby Rd N5 ...15 B4
Sotheran Cl E8 ...24 C4
Sotheron Pl SW6 ...156 B1
Soudan Rd SW11 ...168 C3
Souldern Rd W14 ...39 C3
South Acton Sta W3,W4 ...37 A3
South Africa Rd W12 ...30 A2
South Audley St W1 ...117 C2
South Ave TW9 ...44 C1

South Bank Bsns Ctr SW8 ...161 C3
South Bank Univ SE1 ...171 C4
  SE1 ...136 C4
South Bermondsey Sta SE16 ...40 B1
South Black Lion La W6 ...38 C1
South Block E1 ...32 B2
South Bolton Gdns SW5 ...142 B2
South Building SE10 ...52 C3
South Camden Com Sch NW1 ...83 B2
South Carriage Dr SW1,SW7 ...130 C4
South Colonnade E14 ...33 C1
South Cres WC1 ...105 B3
South Ct SW15 ...57 C1
South Eaton Pl SW1 ...145 C4
South Edwardes Sq W8 ...127 B1
South End W8 ...128 B2
South End Cl NW3 ...12 A4
South End Gn NW3 ...12 A4
South End Rd NW3 ...12 A4
South End Row W8 ...128 B2
South Gr N6 ...3 C3
South Grove Ho N6 ...3 C3
South Hampstead High Sch (Jun Dept) NW3 ...11 B2
South Hampstead High Sch for Girls NW3 ...11 C1
South Hampstead Sta NW6 ...11 B1
South Hill Pk NW3 ...12 A4
South Hill Pk Gdns NW3 ...12 A4
South Island Pl SW9 ...163 A1
South Kensington Sta SW7 ...143 C4
South Lambeth Pl SW8 ...162 B4
South Lambeth Rd SW8 ...162 B2
South Lo NW8 ...89 B4
South London Montessori Sch The SW11 ...168 A3
South Molton La W1 ...104 A1
South Molton Rd E16 ...35 C3
South Molton St W1 ...104 A1
South Par W4 ...37 C2
South Parade SW3 ...143 C2
South Park Mews SW6 ...59 A4
South Pl EC2 ...109 C3
South Pl Mews EC2 ...109 C3
South Quay Plaza E14 ...42 B4
South Quay Sta E14 ...42 A4
South Rise W2 ...116 B4
South Row SE3 ...53 B1
South Sea St SE16 ...41 B3

South Side W6 ...38 B3
South Sq WC1 ...107 B3
South St W1 ...117 C2
South Tenter St E1 ...111 A1
South Terr SW7 ...144 A4
South Thames Coll SW15 ...57 C2
  SW18 ...59 A2
South Thames Coll (Roehampton Centre) SW15 ...56 C1
South Villas NW1 ...13 C2
South West London Coll SW16 ...74 A1
South Western Hospl SW9 ...62 B4
South Wharf Rd W2 ...101 C2
South Worple Way SW14 ...55 C4
Southall Pl SE1 ...137 B3
Southam Ho W10 ...23 A1
Southam St W10 ...23 A1
Southampton Bldgs WC2 ...107 B3
Southampton Pl WC1 ...106 B3
Southampton Rd NW5 ...12 B3
Southampton Row WC1 ...106 B4
Southampton Way SE5 ...49 A3
Southborough Ho SE17 ...152 B2
Southborough Rd E9 ...25 C4
Southbury NW8 ...79 A4
Southcombe St W14 ...140 A4
Southcote Rd N19 ...13 B4
Southcott Ho W9 ...89 A1
  E3 ...27 A2
Southdean Gdns SW19 ...70 B2
Southdown N7 ...14 A2
Southern Gr E3 ...26 B1
Southern Row W10 ...23 A1
Southern St N1 ...84 C2
Southerngate Way SE14 ...51 A3
Southerton Rd W6 ...39 B2
Southey Ho SE17 ...151 A2
Southey Rd SW9 ...173 B4
Southfield JMI Sch W4 ...38 A4
Southfield Rd W4 ...37 C4
Southfields SW18 ...58 C1
Southfields Sch SW18 ...58 C1
Southfields Sta SW18 ...70 C3
Southgate Ct N1 ...15 C1
Southgate Gr N1 ...15 C1
Southgate Rd N1 ...87 C4
Southill St E14 ...34 A3

Southlands Coll
  SW15 ....56 C2
Southlands Dr
  SW19 ....69 C2
Southmead Jun & Inf
  Sch SW19 ....70 A4
Southmead Rd
  SW19 ....70 A3
Southmoor Way E9 .18 B3
Southolm St SW11 .170 B3
Southside N7 ....13 C4
Southside Ind Est
  SW8 ....170 C4
Southside Quarter
  SW11 ....170 A4
Southvale Rd SE3 ...53 A1
Southview Ave NW10 .8 B3
Southville SW8 .....171 C3
Southwark Bridge
  SE1,EC4 ....123 A3
Southwark Bridge Office
  Village SE1 ....123 A2
Southwark Bridge Rd
  SE1 ....123 A2
Southwark Cath ★
  SE1 ....123 B2
Southwark Coll
  SE1 ....136 A4
  SE15 ....50 A3
  SE15 ....50 B2
Southwark Coll
  (Blackfriars Ctr)
  SE1 ....122 A1
Southwark Coll
  (Camberwell Centre)
  SE5 ....49 A3
Southwark Coll (Surrey
  Docks Ctr) SE16 ...40 A3
Southwark Park Est
  SE16 ....40 A2
Southwark Park Prim
  Sch SE16 ....153 A4
Southwark Park Rd
  SE16 ....153 A4
  SE16 ....153 B4
Southwark St SE1 ..122 C1
Southwater Cl 🔟
  E14 ....33 B2
Southwell Gdns
  SW7 ....142 C3
Southwell Ho
  🖪 N16 ....16 A3
  🔟 SE16 ....40 A2
Southwell Rd SE5 ...63 B4
Southwick Mews
  W2 ....101 C2
Southwick Pl W2 ..102 A1
Southwick St W2 ...102 A2
Southwick Yd W2 ..102 A1
Southwold Mans
  W9 ....23 C2
Southwood Ave N6 ...4 B4
Southwood Ct EC1 ..96 A3
Southwood Ho
  W11 ....112 A4
Southwood Hts N6 ...4 A4
Southwood La N6 .....4 A4
Southwood Lawn Rd
  N6 ....4 A4

Southwood Park N6 ...3 C4
Southwood Smith Ho 🖪
  E2 ....25 A2
Southwood Smith St
  N1 ....86 A3
Southwyck Ho SW9 .62 C3
Sovereign Cl E1 ......32 A2
Sovereign Cres
  SE16 ....33 A2
Sovereign Ct E1 .....32 A2
  🖪 Richmond TW9 ..54 B3
Sovereign Ho 🖪 E1 .25 A1
Sovereign Mews 🖪
  E2 ....24 B3
Sovereign Pk NW10 .20 A1
Spa Ct SE16 ....139 B1
Spa Rd SE16 ....139 A1
Spa Sch SE1 ....153 B4
Spa View 🔟 SW16 ..74 B1
Spade Wlk NW3 .....11 A3
Spafield St EC1 ......95 B2
Spalding Ho SE4 .....66 A2
Spanby Rd E3 ....26 C1
Spaniards Cl NW11 ...2 C3
Spaniards End NW3 ..2 C3
Spaniards Rd NW3 ...2 B2
Spanish Bilingual Sch
  W10 ....31 A4
Spanish Pl W1 ......103 C2
Spanish Rd SW18 ...59 B2
Sparke Terr 🔟 E16 .35 B1
Sparkford Ho
  SW11 ....167 C4
Sparks Cl W3 ....28 C3
Sparsholt Rd N19 ....5 B3
Sparta St SE10 .....152 B2
Speakers' Corner ★
  W1 ....117 A4
Speakman Ho SE4 ..66 A4
Spear Mews SW5 ..141 C3
Spears Rd N19 ....5 A3
Spectrum Ho NW5 ..12 C4
Spedan Cl NW3 ......2 B1
Speed Ho EC2 .....109 A4
Speedwell St 🖪
  SE8 ....51 C3
Speedy Pl WC1 .....94 A3
Speldhurst Rd E9 ...17 C1
  W4 ....37 C3
Spellbrook Wlk (off
  Basire St) N1 ....87 A4
Spelman Ho E1 .....111 B3
Spelman St E1 ......111 B3
  E1 ....111 B4
Spence Cl SE16 .....41 B4
Spencer Gdns SW14 .55 B2
Spencer Ho SW8 ...171 B1
  NW3 ....2 C1
  SW19 ....69 C1
  🟪 SW19 ....69 C1
Spencer Mews W6 .154 A4
Spencer Park Ct
  SW18 ....59 C2
Spencer Pk SW18 ..59 C2
Spencer Pl SW1 ....133 A1
  🔟 N1 ....15 A1
Spencer Rd W3 .....28 B1
  W4 ....45 B3
  SW18 ....59 B2
  🟪 SW19 ....69 C1
Spencer Rise NW5 ...4 A1
Spencer St EC1 ......96 A3
Spencer Wlk
  🟪 NW3 ....11 C4
  SW15 ....57 C3
Spenlow Ho SE16 ..139 C2
Spens Ho WC1 ......94 C1

Spenser Gr N16 .....16 A4
Spenser Mews SE21 .75 C3
Spenser Rd SE24 ....63 A2
Spenser St SW1 ....133 A2
Spensley Wlk N16 ...6 C1
Spert St E14 ....33 A2
Spey St E14 ....34 A4
Spezia Rd NW10 ....21 C3
Spice Ct E1 ....125 C2
  🟪 SW11 ....59 B4
Spicer Cl SE5,SW9 ..48 A1
Spicer Ho E2 ....24 C2
Spindrift Ave E14 ...42 A2
Spinnaker Ho E14 ...41 C4
Spinney The SW13 ..47 A4
Spire Ct 🔟 E1 ....32 A1
Spire Ho 🔟 W2 ....115 A4
Spirit Quay E1 .....125 C2
  E1 ....32 A1
Spital Sq E1 ....110 B4
Spital St E1 ....99 B1
Spitalfields Mkt
  E1 ....110 C4
Splendour Wlk
  SE16 ....40 B1
Spode Ho SE11 ....135 B1
Sporle Ct 🖪 SW11 .59 C4
Sprewell SW15 ......58 A1
Spriggs Ho N1 ....15 A1
Sprimont Pl SW3 ..144 C2
Spring Cott 🔟 W12 .38 C4
Spring Gdns SW1 ..120 A2
  N5 ....15 B3
Spring Gr W4 ....44 C4
Spring Grove Rd
  TW10 ....54 B2
Spring Hill E5 ....7 C4
Spring Ho WC1 ......95 B3
Spring Mews W1 ...103 A4
Spring Pl NW5 ....13 A3
Spring St W2 ....101 B1
Spring Terr TW10 ...54 A2
Spring Wlk E1 ....111 C4
Springall St 🟪 SE15 .50 A3
Springalls Wharf
  SE16 ....139 B4
Springbank Wlk
  NW1 ....13 C1
Springdale Rd N16 .15 C4
Springett Ho 🔟
  SW2 ....62 B2
Springfield Ct
  SW4 ....171 C2
  NW3 ....12 A1
  🖪 W3 ....28 B3
  🟪 SE5 ....49 A1
Springfield Hospl
  SW17 ....72 A1
Springfield La NW6 .78 A3
Springfield Rd NW8 .79 A3
  🖪 E15 ....27 C4
Springhill Cl SE5 ....63 C4
Springpark Dr N4 ....6 B3
Springrice Rd SE13 .67 C1
Springvale Ave TW8 .36 A1
Springvale Terr 🖪
  W14 ....139 C4
Springwater WC1 ..106 C4
Springwell Ave
  NW10 ....21 B4
Spruce Ct W5 ....36 A3
Spruce Ho 🔟 SE16 .40 C4

Sprules Rd SE4 .....51 A1
Spur Rd SE1 ....135 C4
Spur Rd SE1 ....137 B2
Spurgeon St SE1 ...137 B2
Spurling Rd SE22 ...64 B3
Spurstowe Rd E8 ...17 A2
Spurstowe Terr E8 .17 A3
Square Rigger Row 🔟
  SW11 ....59 B4
Square The SW6 ...165 B3
  W6 ....39 B1
Squarey St SW17 ...71 B1
Squire Gdns NW8 ...89 B3
Squire's Mount NW3 .2 C1
Squires Ct SW4 ...172 B3
Squire's The SE13 ..67 C4
Squirrels St
  E2 ....24 C2,99 C3
St Agnes Cl E9 .....25 B4
St Agnes Pl SE11 ...48 A4
St Agnes RC Prim Sch
  NW2 ....1 A1
St Agnes' RC JMI Sch
  E3 ....27 A2
St Aidan's Prim Sch
  N4 ....5 C2
St Aidan's Rd SE22 .65 A2
St Alban's CE Prim Sch
  EC1 ....107 B4
St Alban's Gr 🖪 W8 .128 B2
St Alban's Pl N1 ....86 A3
St Alban's RC Prim Sch
  SE15 ....49 B2
St Alban's St SW1 .119 B3
St Alban's Villas NW5 .3 C1
St Albans Ave W4 ...37 C3
St Albans La NW11 ...1 C3
St Albans Mans
  W8 ....128 B2
St Albans Studios
  W8 ....128 B2
St Albans Terr W6 ..154 A4
St Alfege Pas SE10 .52 B4
St Alfege with St Peter's
  CE Prim Sch SE10 .52 C4
St Aloysius' R C Jun &
  Inf Sch NW1 ....93 A3
St Aloysius' RC Coll
  N6 ....4 B3
St Alphage Gdn
  EC2 ....109 A3
St Alphage Highwalk
  EC2 ....109 A3
St Alphonsus Rd
  SW4 ....61 C3
St Andrew & St Francis
  CE Prim Sch NW2 ...8 C2
St Andrew St EC4 ..107 C3
St Andrew's CE Prim
  Sch
  N16 ....85 A4
  SW9 ....172 B1
St Andrew's Ct
  SW18 ....71 B2
St Andrew's Gr N16 .6 C3
St Andrew's Greek Sch
  NW1 ....13 B1
St Andrew's Hill
  EC4 ....108 B1
St Andrew's Mans
  W1 ....103 B3

St Andrew's Mews
  N16 ....7 A3
St Andrew's Pl
  NW1 ....92 B2
St Andrew's Rd NW2 .9 A2
  W3 ....29 A3
St Andrew's Rd
  W14 ....154 B4
St Andrew's Sq
  W11 ....31 A3
St Andrew's Wharf
  SE1 ....139 A4
St Andrews Cl 🟪
  SE16 ....40 A1
St Andrews Ct W4 ..45 B2
St Andrews Mews
  SE3 ....53 C3
St Andrews Way E3 .27 A1
St Ann's Cres SW18 .59 B1
St Ann's Gdns NW5 .12 C2
St Ann's Hill SW18 .59 B1
St Ann's Ho WC1 ...95 B3
St Ann's La SW1 ...133 C1
St Ann's Park Rd
  SW18 ....59 B1
St Ann's Rd W11 ...30 C2
St Ann's St SW1 ...133 C2
St Ann's Terr NW8 ..79 C2
St Ann's Villas
  W11 ....112 A1
St Anne St E14 ......33 B3
St Anne's CE Prim Sch
  SW18 ....71 A3
St Anne's Cl N6 .....3 C1
St Anne's Ct NW6 ..23 A4
St Anne's Ct W1 ...105 B1
St Anne's Flats
  NW1 ....93 B4
St Anne's Pas E14 ..33 B3
St Anne's RC JMI Sch
  E1 ....24 C1,99 B1
St Anne's RC Prim Sch
  SE11 ....162 C4
St Anne's Row E14 .33 B3
St Anne's Trad Est
  E14 ....33 B3
St Anns Rd SW13 ...46 B2
St Anselm's Pl W1 .104 A1
St Anselm's Pl
  W1 ....118 A4
St Anselm's RC Prim Sch
  SW17 ....72 C1
St Anthony's Cl E1 .125 B2
St Anthony's Ct
  🟪 SW17 ....72 C2
St Anthony's Flats
  NW1 ....83 B1
St Anthony's RC Prim
  Sch SE22 ....64 C1
St Anthonys Cl
  SW17 ....72 A2
St Asaph Ct SE4 ....65 C4
St Asaph Rd SE4 ...65 C4
St Aubins Ct N1 .....87 C4
St Augustine's CE Prim
  & Sec Schs NW6 ...23 C3
St Augustine's CE Prim
  & Sec Schs NW6 ...78 A2
St Augustine's RC Prim
  Sch W6 ....154 B3
St Augustine's Rd
  NW1 ....13 C1
St Austell Rd SE13 .67 B4
St Barnabas & St Philip
  CE Prim Sch W8 ..127 B1

St Barnabas CE Prim Sch SW1 .... 145 C2
St Barnabas St SW1 .... 145 C2
St Barnabas Terr E9 .... 17 C3
St Barnabas Villas SW8 .... 172 B4
St Bartholomew's Hospl EC1 .... 108 B3
St Bede's RC Inf Sch SW12 .... 173 C3
St Benet's Pl EC3 .... 123 C4
St Benets Cl SW17 .... 72 B4
St Bernadette RC Jun Mix Sch SW12 .... 73 B4
St Bernard Ho E6 .... 42 B3
St Botolph St E1, EC3 .... 110 C2
St Brelades Cl N1 .... 87 C4
St Briavel's Ct ❷ SE15 .... 49 C3
St Bride St EC4 .... 108 A2
St Bride's Ave EC4 .... 108 A1
St Bride's Pas EC4 .... 108 A1
St Catherine's Ct ❽ W4 .... 38 A3
St Catherine's Dr SE14 .... 50 C1
St Catherines Cl SW17 .... 72 A2
St Catherines Mews SW3 .... 144 C4
St Chad's Pl WC1 .... 94 C4
St Chad's St WC1 .... 94 C4
St Charles Pl W10 .... 31 A4
St Charles RC Prim Sch W10 .... 30 C4
St Charles RC Sixth Form Coll W10 .... 30 C4
St Charles Sq W10 .... 30 C4
St Charles' Hospl W10 .... 30 C4
St Christina's RC Sch NW8 .... 80 B2
St Christopher's Ho NW1 .... 83 B1
St Christopher's Pl W1 .... 103 C2
St Christopher's Sch NW3 .... 11 C3
St Clair Ho ❶⓸ E3 .... 26 B2
St Clare St EC3 .... 110 C1
St Clement Danes CE Prim Sch WC2 .... 106 C1
St Clement's Ct EC3 .... 123 C4
St Clement's La WC2 .... 107 A1
St Clements & St James CE Prim Sch W11 .... 31 A1
St Clements Ct N7 .... 14 B2
❽ W11 .... 31 A1
❼ SE14 .... 50 C4
St Clements Mans SW6 .... 47 C4
St Clements St N7 .... 14 C1
St Columb's Ho ❶ W10 .... 31 A4
St Crispins Cl NW3 .... 12 A4
St Cross St EC1 .... 107 C4

St Cuthbert with St Matthias Prim Sch SW5 .... 142 A2
St Cuthbert's Rd NW2 .... 10 B2
St David's Sq E14 .... 42 A1
St Davids Cl ⓳ 27
St Dionis Rd SW6 .... 165 A2
St Dominic's RC JMI Schs E9 .... 18 A2
St Dominic's RC Prim Sch NW5 .... 12 B3
St Donatt's Rd SE14 .... 51 B2
St Dunstan's Alley EC3 .... 124 A3
St Dunstan's Ave W3 .... 28 C2
St Dunstan's Ct EC4 .... 107 C1
St Dunstan's Gdns W3 .... 28 C2
St Dunstan's Hill EC3 .... 124 A3
St Dunstan's La EC3 .... 124 A3
St Dunstan's Rd W6 .... 39 C1
St Edmund's Cl NW8 .... 80 C3
St Edmund's Ct NW8 .... 80 C3
St Edmund's RC JMI Sch E14 .... 41 C2
St Edmund's Terr NW8 .... 80 C3
St Edmunds Cl SW17 .... 72 A2
St Edward's RC Prim Sch NW1 .... 90 B1
St Elizabeth's RC Prim Sch N16 .... 7 A3
St Elmo Rd W12 .... 38 B4
St Elmos Rd SE16 .... 41 A4
St Ermin's Hill SW1 .... 133 B2
St Ervan's Rd W10 .... 31 B4
St Eugene of Mazenod RC Prim Sch NW6 .... 10 C1
St Faith's CE Prim Sch SW18 .... 59 B3
St Faith's Rd SE24 .... 75 A3
St Francesca Cabrini Prim Sch SE23 .... 65 B1
St Francis RC Jun & Inf Sch SE15 .... 49 C3
St Francis RC Prim Sch W11 .... 30 C2
St Francis Xavier Sixth Form Coll SW12 .... 61 A1
St Francis' Ho NW1 .... 83 B1
St Gabriel's CE Prim Sch SW1 .... 146 C1
St Gabriel's Rd NW2 .... 9 C3
St George Ho SW11 .... 169 C3
St George St W1 .... 118 B4
St George the Martyr CE Prim Sch WC1 .... 95 A1
St George's Ave N7 .... 13 C4
St George's Battersea CE Prim Sch SW8 .... 161 A1
St George's Cath NW1 .... 92 B4
SE1 .... 135 C2

St George's Cath RC Jun & Inf Sch SE1 .... 136 A2
St George's CE Jun & Inf Sch SE5 .... 48 A3
St George's Circ SE1 .... 136 A2
St George's Ct SW7 .... 128 C1
SW1 .... 136 A1
SW3 .... 144 A4
St George's Dr SW1 .... 146 B2
St George's Field W2 .... 102 B1
St George's Gr SW17 .... 71 C1
St George's Ho NW1 .... 83 A1
St George's La EC3 .... 124 A4
St George's Mews NW1 .... 12 C1
St George's Mews SE1 .... 135 C2
St George's RC Sec Sch W9 .... 78 B1
St George's Rd TW9 .... 54 B4
St George's Rd SE1 .... 136 A1
St George's Residences ❹ SW2 .... 62 C2
St George's Sq SW1 .... 147 B1
St George's Square Mews SW1 .... 147 B1
St George's Way SE15 .... 49 A4
St Georges Ct SW15 .... 58 B3
St Georges Cl SW15 .... 58 B3
St Georges Hanover Sq Sch W1 .... 117 C3
St Georges Rd W4 .... 37 C4
St Georges Sq ❶ E14 .... 33 A2
St George's Ct EC4 .... 108 A2
St Gerards Cl SW4 .... 61 B2
St German's Pl SE3 .... 53 C2
St Giles Cir WC1 .... 105 C2
St Giles Coll WC1 .... 106 B4
St Giles Ct WC2 .... 106 A2
St Giles High St WC2 .... 105 C2
St Giles Pas WC2 .... 105 C1
St Giles Rd SE5 .... 49 A2
St Giles Twr ❸ SE5 .... 49 A2
St Gilles Ho ❶ E2 .... 25 C3
St Gothard Rd SE21 .... 75 C1
St Helen's Gdns W10 .... 30 C3
St Helen's Pl EC3 .... 110 A2
St Helen's RC Prim Sch SW9 .... 62 C4
St Helen's RC Prim Sch (Annexe) SW9 .... 173 A2
St Helena Ho WC1 .... 95 B3
St Helena Rd SE16 .... 40 C2
St Helena St WC1 .... 95 B3
St Helier Ct ❶ N1 .... 24 A4
St Hilda's Cl NW6 .... 9 C1
St Hilda's Rd SW13 .... 47 A4
St Hildas Wharf E1 .... 32 B1
St Hubert's Ho ❶ E14 .... 41 C3

St Hughes Cl SW17 .... 72 A2
St James Ct E2 .... 99 C3
❿ W4 .... 37 C1
St James Hatcham CE Prim Sch SE14 .... 51 A3
St James Ind Mews SE1 .... 153 C1
St James Mews E14 .... 42 B3
St James School Flats ❽ N7 .... 14 C3
St James St W6 .... 39 B1
St James the Less Prim Sch SW1 .... 147 B2
St James' & St Michaels CE Sch W2 .... 115 A4
St James' Ct W4 .... 37 C3
St James' Ct SW1 .... 133 A2
St James' Mans NW6 .... 10 C1
St James' App EC2 .... 98 A1
St James' Ave E3 .... 25 B3
St James' CE Jun & Inf Sch SE16 .... 139 B2
St James' Cl SW17 .... 72 C2
St James' Cl NW8 .... 80 C2
St James' Cloisters ❷ SE22 .... 64 B3
St James' Cres SW9 .... 62 C4
St James' Dr SW17 .... 72 A2
SW12,SW17 .... 72 A2
St James' Gdns W11 .... 31 A1 112 A2
St James' Gr SW11 .... 169 A2
St James' Market SW1 .... 119 B3
St James' Palace* SW1 .... 119 A1
St James' Park SW1 .... 133 B3
St James' Park Sta SW1 .... 133 B2
St James' Pas EC3 .... 110 B1
St James' Pl SW1 .... 118 C1
St James' Rd SE1, SE16 .... 153 C4
St James' Sq SW1 .... 119 A2
St James' St SW1 .... 118 C2
St James' Terr ❷ SW12 .... 72 C3
St James' Terr NW8 .... 80 C3
St James' Terrace Mews NW8 .... 80 C3
St James' Wlk EC1 .... 96 A2
St Joan of Arc RC Prim Sch N5 .... 15 B4
St John Angell Town CE Prim Sch SW9 .... 173 C1
St John CE Prim Sch SE17 .... 151 A3
St John CE Sch SW11 .... 155 B2
St John Evangelist RC Prim Sch N1 .... 86 A2
St John of Jerusalem CE JMI Sch E9 .... 17 B1
St John St EC1 .... 96 A2

St John the Baptist JMI Sch N1 .... 24 A3
St John the Baptist RC Jun Sch E2 .... 25 B3
St John the Divine CE Prim Sch SE5 .... 48 A3
St John's & St Clements CE Prim Sch SE15 .... 64 C4
St John's (Highbury Vale) CE Prim Sch N5 .... 6 A1
St John's (Upper Holloway) Prim Sch N19 .... 4 C2
St John's CE JMI Sch SW15 .... 57 C2
St John's CE JMI Sch E2 .... 25 B3
St John's Church Rd E9 .... 17 B3
St John's Cres SW2 .... 62 C4
❻ NW3 .... 11 B2
St John's Ct N4 .... 6 A2
❹ NW3 .... 11 B2
W6 .... 39 A2
SE13 .... 52 B1
St John's Dr SW18 .... 71 A3
St John's Est SE1 .... 138 C3
St John's Gdns W11 .... 31 B2 112 C3
St John's Gr N19 .... 4 B2
❸ SW13 .... 46 B1
❶ Richmond TW9 .... 54 A3
St John's Hill SW11 .... 59 C3
St John's Hill Gr SW11 .... 59 C3
St John's La EC1 .... 108 B4
St John's Mans E5 .... 17 B3
St John's Park Mans N19 .... 4 B1
St John's Path EC1 .... 96 A1
St John's Pk SE3 .... 53 C3
St John's Pl EC1 .... 96 A1
St John's RC Jun & Inf Sch SE16 .... 41 A4
St John's Rd E16 .... 35 C3
Richmond TW9 .... 54 A3
SW11 .... 60 A3
St John's Sq EC1 .... 164 B4
St John's Sta SE8 .... 51 C1
St John's Terr W10 .... 22 C1
St John's Vale SE8 .... 51 C1
St John's Villas N19 .... 4 C2
St John's Villas W8 .... 128 B1
St John's Way N19 .... 4 C2
St John's Wood Ct NW8 .... 89 C3
St John's Wood High St NW8 .... 80 A1
St John's Wood Jun Prep Sch NW8 .... 90 A4
St John's Wood Pk NW8 .... 79 B4
St John's Wood Rd NW8 .... 89 C3
St John's Wood Sta NW8 .... 79 B2
St John's Wood Terr NW8 .... 80 A1
St Johns Concert Hall SW1 .... 134 A1

St Johns Ho �</br>
SE17 ....48 C4
St Joseph's CI W10 .31 A4
St Joseph's Flats
NW1 ....93 B4
St Joseph's Ho W6 .39 C2
St Joseph's Hospice
E9,E8 ....25 A4
St Joseph's RC Jun & Inf
Sch
SE16 ....40 B3
SE5 ....48 B3
St Joseph's RC Jun &
Inf Sch
SE1 ....137 A4
SE16 ....139 B3
St Joseph's RC Jun & Inf
Schs NW10 ....4 A3
St Joseph's RC Prim Sch
N19 ....4 A3
SE10 ....43 A1
SE8 ....51 C3
St Joseph's RC Prim
Sch
W9 ....88 C3
WC2 ....106 B2
SW3 ....144 C3
St Joseph's St
SW8 ....170 A4
St Joseph's Vale
SE3 ....67 C4
St Josephs RC Prim Sch
SW18 ....58 C2
St Jude St N16 .....16 A3
St Jude's St 58 C2
St Jude's RC Prim Sch
SE24 ....75 A4
St Jude's CE Prim Sch
SE1 ....136 A1
St Jude's Rd E2 ....25 A3
St Julian's Rd NW6 .23 C4
St Katharine's Ho
N1 ....85 B2
St Katharine's Way
E1 ....125 B1
St Katharine's Dock★
St Katherine's Dock
(East Dock)★ E1 .125 B2
St Katharine's Pier
E1 ....125 A2
St Katharine's Prec
NW1 ....82 A2
St Katharine's Row
EC3 ....110 B1
St Katharine's Way
E1 ....125 B1
St Kilda's Rd N16 ....7 A3
St Laurence's CI
NW6 ....22 C4
St Lawrence Ct N1 .87 C4
St Lawrence Ho
SE1 ....138 B2
St Lawrence St E14 .34 B1
St Lawrence Terr
W10 ....31 A4
St Lawrence Way
SW9 ....173 C2
St Leonard's Ct N1 .97 C4
St Leonard's Hospl
N1 ....24 A3

St Leonard's Rd
NW10 ....20 C1
E14 ....34 B4
St Leonard's Sq
NW5 ....12 C2
St Leonard's St E3 .27 A2
St Leonard's Terr
SW3 ....145 A1
St Leonards Ct
SW14 ....55 B4
St Leonards Rd
SW14 ....55 B4
St Loo Ave SW3 ...158 B4
St Loo Ct SW3 .....158 B4
St Luke's Ave SW4 .61 C3
St Luke's CE JMI Sch
E14 ....42 C2
St Luke's CE Prim Sch
W9 ....23 B2
E16 ....35 B1
Richmond TW9 .....44 C2
St Luke's Ct EC1 ....97 A2
St Luke's Ct W11 ...31 B3
St Luke's Hospl
W1 ....92 C1
St Luke's Mews
W11 ....31 B3
St Luke's Prim Sch
EC1 ....97 A3
St Luke's Rd W11 ..31 B4
St Luke's Sq E16 ...35 B1
St Luke's St SW3 ..144 B2
St Margaret St
SW1 ....134 A3
St Margaret's Cres
SW15 ....57 A2
St Margaret's Ct
SW15 ....57 A3
St Margaret's La
W8 ....128 A1
St Margaret's Rd
NW10 ....22 B2
SE4 ....66 B3
St Margaret's Sch
NW3 ....11 A4
St Margarets Lo
W3 ....37 A4
St Mark St E1 .....111 A1
St Mark's CE Prim Sch
SW1 ....163 A4
St Mark's Cres
NW1 ....81 C4
St Mark's Gr
SW10 ....156 C2
St Mark's Hospl
EC1 ....96 B4
St Mark's Pl W11 ...31 A3
St Mark's Rd W10 ..30 C4
W11 ....31 A3
St Mark's Rise E8 ..16 B3
St Marks Cl 🄳 SE10 .52 B3
St Marks Gate E9 ..18 B1
St Marks Ho 🄶
SE17 ....48 C4
St Martin's Almshouses
NW1 ....82 C4
St Martin's Cl NW1 .82 C4
St Martin's Ct SE27 .75 A2
St Martin's Ct
WC2 ....120 A4
St Martin's La
WC2 ....120 A4

St Martin's Le Grand
EC1 ....108 C2
St Martin's Pl
WC2 ....120 A3
St Martin's Rd
SW9 ....172 C2
St Martin's St
WC2 ....119 C3
St Martin's Way
SW17 ....71 B1
St Martin-in-the-Fields
High Sch SW2 .....74 C3
St Martins Ct N1 ....24 A4
St Mary & St Michael
Prim Sch E1 ....32 B3
St Mary & St Pancras CE
Prim Sch NW1 ......83 B1
St Mary Abbot's Ct
W14 ....126 C1
St Mary Abbot's Pl
W8 ....127 A1
St Mary Abbots CE Prim
Sch W8 ....128 A4
St Mary Abbots Terr
W14 ....127 A1
St Mary at Hill
EC3 ....124 A3
St Mary Axe EC3 ...110 B2
St Mary Graces Ct
E1 ....125 A4
St Mary Magdalene CE
Prim Sch N7 ....14 C2
St Mary Magdalene CE
Sec Sch TW10 ......54 C2
St Mary Magdalene's
CE Prim Sch SE15 .65 A4
St Mary Magdalens CE
Prim Sch W2 ....100 A4
St Mary Magdalens RC
Prim Sch SE4 ....66 A3
St Mary Magdelen's RC
Jun Sch NW2 ....9 A2
St Mary Newington CE
SE17 ....152 B2
St Mary of the Angels
Cath Prim Sch W2 .31 C3
St Mary's Bryanston
Square CE Sch
W1 ....102 C4
St Mary's CE Prim Sch
NW10 ....8 A4
SW15 ....57 C2
SE13 ....67 A2
N1 ....86 B4
St Mary's Ct W6 .....38 B3
SE16 ....40 B4
St Mary's Flats
NW1 ....93 B4
St Mary's Gate
W8 ....128 A1
St Mary's Gdns
SE11 ....149 C4
St Mary's Gr N1 .....15 A2
W4 ....45 A4
Richmond TW10,TW9 .54 B3
St Mary's Ho N1 .....86 B4
St Mary's Hospl
W2 ....101 C2
St Mary's Kilburn CE
Prim Sch NW6 ......23 C4
St Mary's Mans
NW10 ....21 A4

St Mary's Mans
W2 ....101 B4
St Mary's Medical Sch
W2 ....101 C2
St Mary's Mews
NW6 ....11 A1
St Mary's Path N1 ..86 B4
St Mary's Pl W8 ....128 A1
St Mary's Rd NW10 ..21 A4
NW6 ....23 A1
W14 ....39 C3
W4 ....46 A4
SW4 ....61 B2
St Mary's Rd NW11 ...1 A4
NW10 ....21 A4
SE15 ....50 B1
St Mary's Sch
Hampstead NW3 ...11 C3
St Mary's Sq W2 ..101 B4
St Mary's Stoke
Newington JMI Sch
N16 ....7 A2
St Mary's Terr
W2 ....101 B4
St Mary's Twr EC1 ..97 A1
St Mary's Wlk
SE11 ....149 C4
St Mary-le-Park Ct
SW11 ....158 B1
St Marychurch St
SE16 ....40 B4
St Marylebone CE Sch
W1 ....103 C4
St Matthew St
SW1 ....133 B1
St Matthew's Ho 🄱
SE17 ....48 C4
St Matthew's Lo
NW1 ....83 A2
St Matthew's Rd
SW2 ....62 B2
St Matthew's Row
E2 ....24 C1
St Matthews CE Prim
Sch SW1 ....133 C2
St Matthew's Ct
SE1 ....136 C1
St Matthias CE Sch
E2 ....24 B1
St Matthias's CE Prim
Sch N16 ....16 A4
St Maur Rd SW6 ...165 A3
St Michael's Alley
EC3 ....109 C1
St Michael's CE Prim
Sch N6 ....3 C4
St Michael's CE NW11 ..1 B4
St Michael's Flats
NW1 ....83 B1
St Michael's Gdns
W10 ....31 A4
St Michael's Prim Sch
SW18 ....70 B4
St Michael's RC Sec
SE16 ....139 B3
St Michael's Rd
SW9 ....172 C2
St Michael's St
W2 ....102 A2

St Michaels Camden
Town CE Prim Sch &
Our Lady's RC Prim
Sch NW1 ....82 C4
St Michels Ct E14 ..34 B4
St Mildred's Ct
EC2 ....109 B1
St Monica's JMI Sch
N1 ....98 A4
St Nicholas Ho SE8 .51 C2
St Nicholas St SE8 .51 C2
St Nicholas' Flats
NW1 ....83 B1
St Norbert Grn SE4 .66 A3
St Norbert Rd SE4 .66 A3
St Olaf's Rd SW6 ..154 B1
St Olave's Ct EC2 ..109 B1
St Olave's Est SE1 .138 B4
St Olave's Gdns
SE11 ....149 B4
St Olave's Mans
SE11 ....149 B4
St Olaves Ct W2 ...114 A3
St Osmund's RC Prim
Sch SW13 ....46 B2
St Oswald's Pl
SE11 ....148 C1
St Oswulf St SW1 ..147 C3
St Owen Ho SE1 ...138 B2
St Pancras Almshouses
🄽 NW5 ....12 B3
St Pancras Commercial
Ctr NW1 ....83 A4
St Pancras Hospl
NW1 ....83 B3
St Pancras Way
NW1 ....83 B4
St Pancras Sta WC1 .94 A4
St Patrick's RC Inf Sch
E1 ....32 A1
St Patrick's RC Jun Sch
E1 ....32 A1
St Patrick's RC Prim Sch
NW5 ....13 A3
St Paul St N1 ....87 A3
St Paul's Ave NW2 ..9 B2
SE16 ....32 C2
St Paul's Cath★
EC4 ....108 C1
St Paul's Cath Sch
EC4 ....108 C1
St Paul's CE JMI Sch
E1 ....125 C4
St Paul's CE Jun & Inf
Sch SE17 ....150 C1
St Paul's Church Yd
EC4 ....108 C1
St Paul's Ct 🄵 SW19 ...5 A2
St Paul's Dr E15 ....19 C2
St Paul's Girls' Sch
W6 ....39 C2
St Paul's Pl N1 ......15 C2
St Paul's Rd N1 .....15 B2
St Paul's Sch SW13 .38 C1
St Paul's Terr SE17 .48 A4
St Paul's Way E3 ...33 C4
St Paul's Way Sec Sch
E3 ....33 C4
St Paul's with Lukes JMI
Sch E3 ....33 C4
St Pauls Ct W5 ......36 B4
St Pauls Cres NW1 ..14 A1
St Pauls Mews NW1 .13 C1

St Pauls Rd TW9 . . . . 54 B4
St Pauls View WC1 . . . 95 B3
St Pauls with St
  Michaels Haggerston
  CE JMI Sch E8 . . . . 24 C4
St Peter's Alley
  EC3 . . . . 109 C1
St Peter's CE Prim Sch
  W9 . . . . 23 C1
  W6 . . . . 38 C1
St Peter's Cl E2 . . . . . 24 C3
St Peter's Eaton Square
  CE Sch SW1 . . . . . 132 B1
St Peter's Gdns
  SE27 . . . . 74 C1
St Peter's Gr W6 . . . . 38 C2
St Peter's Ho N16 . . . . 7 A4
  ■ SE17 . . . . 48 C4
St Peter's Pl ■ W9 . . 88 A1
St Peter's Prim Sch
  SE17 . . . . 151 B1
St Peter's Rd W6 . . . . 38 C1
St Peter's Sch E1 . . . . 32 B1
  W6 . . . . 38 B1
St Peter's Sq W6 . . . . 24 C3
St Peter's St N1 . . . . . 86 B3
St Peter's Street Mews
  N1 . . . . 86 B2
St Peter's Terr
  SW6 . . . . 154 B1
St Peter's Villas
  W6 . . . . 38 C2
St Peter's Way N1 . . . . 24 A1
St Peters & St Pauls RC
  Prim Sch EC1 . . . . 96 B2
St Peters Cl SW17 . . . 72 A2
St Peters Cl SE4 . . . . 51 B1
St Peters Rd N1 . . . . . 94 B3
St Petersburgh Mews
  W2 . . . . 114 A4
St Petersburgh Pl
  W2 . . . . 114 A3
St Philip Ho WC1 . . . . 95 B3
St Philip Sq SW8 . . . 170 A1
St Philip St SW8 . . . 170 A1
St Philip's Rd E8 . . . . 16 C2
St Philip's Way N1 . . . 87 A3
St Quentin Ho
  SW18 . . . . 59 C1
St Quintin Ave W10 . . 30 C4
St Quintin Gdns
  W10 . . . . 30 B4
St Regis Hts NW3 . . . . 2 A1
St Richard of Chichester
  RC Sec Sch NW1 . . 13 A1
St Rule St SW8 . . . . 170 C1
St Saviour's CE JMI Sch
  E14 . . . . 34 A4
St Saviour's CE Prim
  SE24 . . . . 63 B4
St Saviour's CE Prim
  Sch W9 . . . . 88 B1
St Saviour's RC Prim
  Sch SE13 . . . . 67 B3
St Saviour's Wharf
  SE1 . . . . 139 A4
St Saviours SW8 . . . . 61 A3
St Saviours & St Olaves
  CE Sch SE1 . . . . . 137 C1
St Scholastica's RC JMI
  Sch E5 . . . . 7 C1
St Silas Pl NW5 . . . . 12 C2
St Simon's Ave
  SW15 . . . . 57 B2

St Stephen CE Prim Sch
  W12 . . . . 39 B4
St Stephen's Ave
  W12 . . . . 39 A4
St Stephen's CE Prim
  Sch
  W2 . . . . 31 C4
  SW8 . . . . 162 C2
St Stephen's CE Prim
  Sch SW8 . . . . 162 C2
St Stephen's Cl
  NW5 . . . . 12 B3
St Stephen's Cl
  NW8 . . . . 80 B3
St Stephen's Cres
  W2 . . . . 31 C3
St Stephen's Gdns
  W2 . . . . 31 C3
  ■ SW15 . . . . 58 B2
St Stephen's Gr
  SE13 . . . . 67 B4
St Stephen's Mews ■
  W2 . . . . 31 C4
St Stephen's Rd E3 . . 26 B3
St Stephen's Row
  EC4 . . . . 109 B1
St Stephen's Terr
  SW8 . . . . 162 C1
St Stephens Ho ■
  SE17 . . . . 48 C4
St Swithin's La
  EC4 . . . . 109 B1
St Swithun's Rd
  SE13 . . . . 67 C2
St Thomas Ho ■
  E1 . . . . 32 C3
St Thomas of
  Canterbury RC Prim
  Sch SW6 . . . . . . 154 C2
St Thomas Rd E16 . . . 35 C3
St Thomas St SE1 . . 123 C1
St Thomas the Apostle
  Coll The SE15 . . . . 50 B2
St Thomas' CE JMI Sch
  N16 . . . . 7 C3
St Thomas' Gdns
  NW5 . . . . 12 C2
St Thomas' Hospl
  SE1 . . . . 134 C2
St Thomas's CE Prim
  Sch W10 . . . . 23 A1
St Thomas's Hospital
  Medical Sch SE1 . . 134 C1
St Thomas's Pas ■
  E17 . . . . 19 B1
St Thomas's Rd
  N4,N5 . . . . 5 C1
  NW10 . . . . 21 A4
St Thomas's Sq E9 . . . 17 B1
St Thomas's Way
  SW6 . . . . 155 A2
St Ursula's Convent Sch
  SE10 . . . . 52 C3
St Vincent De Paul Ho
  ■ E1 . . . . 32 B4
St Vincent Ho SE1 . . 138 C2
St Vincent St W1 . . . 103 C3
St Vincent's RC Prim
  Sch W1 . . . . 103 C3

St William of York RC
  Sec Boys Sch (Upper)
  N1 . . . . 14 A1
St. Paul's Sta EC2 . . 108 C2
Stable Way W10 . . . . 30 B3
Stable Yd Rd SW1 . . 133 A4
Stables Way SE11 . . 149 B2
Stacey St WC2 . . . . . 105 C1
  N7 . . . . 5 B1
Stack Ho SW1 . . . . . 145 C3
Stackhouse St
  SW1 . . . . 130 C2
Stacy Path ■ SE5 . . . 49 A3
Stadium St SW10 . . 157 A1
Stafford Cl NW6 . . . . 23 C2
Stafford Cripps Ho
  SW6 . . . . 155 A3
  ■ E2 . . . . 25 B2
Stafford Ct W8 . . . . 127 C2
  SW8 . . . . 172 A4
Stafford Ho SE1 . . . 153 A2
Stafford Mans
  SW11 . . . . 158 C1
  ■ W14 . . . . 39 C3
Stafford Pl SW1 . . . 132 C2
Stafford Rd NW6 . . . . 23 C2
Standard . . . .
Stafford St W1 . . . . 118 C2
Stafford Terr W8 . . . 127 B2
Staffordshire St
  SE15 . . . . 49 C2
Stag La SW15 . . . . . . 68 B2
Stag Pl SW1 . . . . . . 132 C2
Stagshaw Ho ■
  SE22 . . . . 64 A4
Stainer St SE1 . . . . . 123 C1
Stainsby La E12 . . . 109 A2
Stainsby St ■ E14 . . 33 C3
Stainsby Pl E14 . . . . 33 C3
Stainton Rd SE13 . . . 67 C1
Stalbridge Ho NW1 . . 82 C1
Stalbridge St NW1 . . 102 B4
Stalham St SE16 . . . . 40 A3
Stambourne Ho
  SW8 . . . . 172 B4
Stamford Bridge
  Stadium (Chelsea FC)
  SW6 . . . . 156 A2
Stamford Brook Ave
  W6 . . . . 38 B3
Stamford Brook Gdns
  ■ W6 . . . . 38 B3
Stamford Brook Mans ■
  W6 . . . . 38 B3
Stamford Brook Rd
  W6 . . . . 38 B3
Stamford Brook Sta
  W6 . . . . 38 B3
Stamford Ct W6 . . . . 38 C2
Stamford Grove E ■
  N16 . . . . 7 C3
Stamford Grove W ■
  N16 . . . . 7 C3
Stamford Hill N16 . . . . 7 B3
Stamford Hill Mans ■
  N16 . . . . 7 B3
Stamford Hill Sta
  N16 . . . . 7 A3
Stamford Lo ■ N2 . . . . 2 C4
Stamford Mans ■
  N16 . . . . 7 C3
Stamford Rd N1 . . . . 16 A2
Stamford St SE1 . . . 121 C2
Stanard Cl N16 . . . . . 7 A4

Stanborough Ho ■
  E3 . . . . 27 A1
Stanborough Pas
  E8 . . . . 16 B2
Stanbridge Mans
  SW15 . . . . 57 B4
Stanbridge Rd
  SW15 . . . . 57 B4
Stanbrook Ct W1 . . . 118 C2
Stanbury Ct ■ NW3 . . 12 B2
Stanbury Rd SE15 . . . 50 A1
  SE15 . . . . 50 B1
Standard Pl EC2 . . . . 98 B3
Standard Rd NW10 . . 20 C1
Standen Rd SW18 . . . 70 C4
Standish Ho ■ W6 . . . 38 C2
Standish Rd W6 . . . . 38 C2
Stanesgate Ho ■
  SE15 . . . . 49 C3
Stanfield Ho NW8 . . . 89 C2
Stanfield Rd ■ E3 . . . 26 A3
Stanford Ct W8 . . . . 128 B1
  SW6 . . . . 166 B3
Stanford Pl SE1 . . . 152 A3
Stanford Rd W8 . . . 128 B2
Stanford St SW1 . . . 147 B3
Stanhope Cl ■
  SE16 . . . . 40 C4
Stanhope Gate
  W1 . . . . 117 C2
Stanhope Gdns
  SW7 . . . . 143 A4
Stanhope Ho SE8 . . . 51 B3
  ■ SW15 . . . . 57 B2
Stanhope Mews E
  SW7 . . . . 143 A4
Stanhope Mews S
  SW7 . . . . 143 A3
Stanhope Mews W
  SW7 . . . . 143 A3
Stanhope Pl W2 . . . 102 C1
Stanhope Rd N6 . . . . 4 B4
Stanhope Row W1 . . 118 A1
Stanhope St NW1 . . . 92 C3
Stanhope Terr W2 . . 115 C4
Stanier Cl SW5 . . . . 141 A1
Stanlake Rd W12 . . . 30 B1
Stanlake Villas W12 . . 30 B1
Stanley Bldgs NW1 . . 84 A1
Stanley Cl SW8 . . . . 162 C3
Stanley Cres
  W11 . . . . 31 B2 112 C4
Stanley Gdns W11 . . 112 C4
  NW2 . . . . 9 B3
  W3 . . . . 38 A4
Stanley Gr SW11 . . . 169 C1
Stanley Ho SW8 . . . 171 B1
  ■ E14 . . . . 33 C3
Stanley Mans
  SW10 . . . . 157 A4
Stanley Pas NW1 . . . 84 A1
Stanley Rd E15 . . . . . 27 C4
  W3 . . . . 37 A3
Stanley St SE14,SE8 . 51 B3
Stanley Studios
  SW10 . . . . 157 A4
Stanley Terr ■ N7 . . . . 5 C2
Stanmer St SW11 . . . 168 B2
Stanmore Gdns
  TW9 . . . . 54 B4
Stanmore Ho ■ SW8 . 171 C2
Stanmore Pl NW1 . . . 82 B4
Stanmore Rd TW9 . . . 54 B4
Stanmore St N1 . . . . 84 C4

Stannard Cotts ■
  E1 . . . . 25 B1
Stannard Mews E8 . . 16 C2
Stannard Rd E8 . . . . 16 C2
Stannary Pl SE11 . . . 149 C1
Stannary St SE11 . . . 149 C1
Stansbury Ho ■
  W10 . . . . 23 A2
Stansfield Ho SE1 . . 153 A3
Stansfield Rd SW9 . . 62 B4
Stanstead Ho ■ E3 . . 27 A1
Stanswood Gdns
  SE5 . . . . 49 A3
Stanton Ct N16 . . . . . 6 C4
Stanton Ho ■ SE10 . . 52 B4
Stanton Rd SW13 . . . 46 B1
Stanway Ct ■ N1 . . . . 24 A3
Stanway St N1 . . . . . 24 A3
Stanwick Rd W14 . . . 140 C3
Stanworth St SE1 . . 139 A3
Stapelhurst Ho ■
  E5 . . . . 17 A3
Staple Inn WC2 . . . . 107 B3
Staple Inn Bldgs
  WC2 . . . . 107 B3
Staple St SE1 . . . . . 137 C3
Staplefield Cl ■
  SW2 . . . . 74 A3
Stapleford Cl SW19 . . 70 A4
Staplehurst St
  SW11 . . . . 60 B1
Staples Cl SE16 . . . . 33 A1
Stapleton Hall N4 . . . . 5 B4
Stapleton Hall Rd N4 . 5 B4
Stapleton Ho ■ E2 . . 25 A2
Stapleton Rd SW17 . . 72 C1
Star & Garter Mans
  SW15 . . . . 57 C4
Star Alley EC3 . . . . . 124 B4
Star Rd W14 . . . . . . 140 C1
Star St W2 . . . . 102 A2
Star Works NW10 . . . 21 C2
Starboard Way E14 . . 41 C3
Starcross St NW1 . . . 93 A3
Starfield Rd W12 . . . . 38 C4
Starliner Ct N7 . . . . . 14 C2
Starling Ho NW8 . . . . 80 A2
Statham Gr N16 . . . . . 6 C1
Statham Ho SW8 . . . 170 C4
Stathard Ho ■ E1 . . . 25 B1
Station App NW10 . . . 21 B2
Station Cres SE3 . . . . 53 C4
  TW9 . . . . 44 C3
Richmond TW9 . . . . . 44 C2
Station Approach Rd
  SE1 . . . . 135 B4
  W4 . . . . 45 B3
Station Ave SW9 . . . . 63 A4
Station Cres SE3 . . . . 43 C1
Station Ct ■ SE15 . . . 50 B1
Station Gdns W4 . . . . 45 B3
Station Par NW2 . . . . 9 B2
Richmond TW9 . . . . . 44 C2
Station Pas SE15 . . . . 50 B2
Station Pl N4 . . . . 5 C2
Station Rd N19 . . . . . 4 B1
  NW10 . . . . 21 B3
  SW13 . . . . 46 B1
  SE13 . . . . 67 B4
Station Rise SE27 . . . 75 A2
Station St E15 . . . . . 19 C1
Station Terr NW10 . . . 22 C3

Station Terr continued
SE5 ....48 B2
Stationers Hall Ct
EC4 ....108 B1
Staunton Ho SE17 ....152 A3
Staunton St SE8 ....51 A4
Stave Yard Rd SE16 ....33 A1
Staveley NW1 ....92 C4
Staveley Cl N7 ....14 A3
E9 ....17 B3
8 SE15 ....50 A2
SE15 ....50 B2
Staveley Gdns W4 ....45 C2
Staveley Rd W4 ....45 C3
Stavers Ho 8 E3 ....26 B3
Staverton Rd NW2 ....9 B1
Stavordale Rd N5 ....15 A4
Stayner's Rd E1 ....25 C1
Stead St SE17 ....151 B3
Steadman Ct EC1 ....97 A2
Stean St E8 ....24 B4
Stebbing Ho 8
W11 ....30 C1
Stebon JMI Sch
E14 ....33 C4
Stebondale St E14 .....42 B2
Stedham Pl WC1 ....106 A2
Steedman St SE17 .....150 C3
Steel's La 2 E1 ....32 B3
Steele Rd NW10 ....20 B3
W4 ....37 B3
Steele's Mews N
NW3 ....12 B2
Steele's Mews S
NW3 ....12 B2
Steele's Rd NW3 ....12 B2
Steen Way 7 SE22 .....64 A2
Steep Hill SW16 ....73 C1
Steeple Cl SW6 ....164 B1
Steeple Ct 10 E1 ....25 A1
Steeple Wlk (off Maldon
Cl) N1 ....87 A4
Steerforth St SW18 ....71 B2
Steers Way SE16 ....41 A4
Stelfax Ho WC1 ....95 A4
Stellman Cl E5 ....7 C1
Stephan Cl E8 ....24 C4
Stephen Ct 18 SW19 ..69 C3
Stephen Fox Ho 7
W4 ....38 A1
Stephen Hawking Sch
E14 ....33 A3
Stephen Mews W1 .....105 B3
Stephen Pl SW4 ....61 B4
Stephen Saunders Ct
SW11 ....60 A2
Stephen St W1 ....105 B3
Stephendale Rd
SW6 ....166 C1
Stephens Ct SE4 ....66 A4
Stephenson Ho
SE1 ....136 C2
1 NW3 ....12 B3
2 NW5 ....13 A4
Stephenson St
NW10 ....21 B2
E16 ....35 A4
Stephenson Way
NW1 ....93 A3
Stepney Cswy E1 ....32 C3
Stepney Day Hospl
E1 ....32 B3

Stepney Gn E1 ....32 C4
**Stepney Green Boys Sec
Sch** E1 ....25 C1
Stepney Green Ct 8
E1 ....32 C4
Stepney Green Sta
E1 ....25 C1
Stepney Greencoat Ct
JMI Sch E14 ....33 B3
Stepney High St E1 .....32 C4
Stepney Way E1 ....32 B4
Sterling Cl NW10 ....8 C1
Sterling Gdns SE14 .....51 A4
Sterling Pl W5 ....36 A3
Sterling St SW7 ....130 B2
Sterndale Rd W14 ......39 C3
Sterne St W12 ....39 C4
Sternhall La SE15 ......64 C4
Sternhold Ave
SW2,SW12 ....73 C2
Sterry St SE1 ....137 B3
Steve Biko Ct W10 .....22 C1
Steve Biko Rd N7 ....5 C1
Stevedore St 8 E1 .....32 A1
Stevenage Rd SW6 .....47 C2
Stevens Ave E9 ....17 B2
Stevens St SE1 ....138 B2
Stevenson Cres
SE16 ....40 A1
Stevenson Ho NW8 .....78 C4
SW11 ....168 C1
Steventon Rd W12 .....29 B2
Stew La EC4 ....122 C4
Steward St E1 ....110 C4
Stewart Headlam JMI
Sch E1 ....25 A1
Stewart Ho SE1 ....138 A1
Stewart Rd E15 ....19 C4
Stewart St E14 ....42 B4
Stewart's Gr SW3 ......144 A2
Stewart's Rd SW8 ......170 A4
Steyne Rd W3 ....28 A1
Stifford Ho E1 ....32 B4
Stile Hall Gdns W4 .....36 C1
Stile Hall Par 6
W4 ....36 C1
Stileman Ho 2 E3 ....33 B4
Stillingfleet Rd
SW13 ....46 C4
Stillington St SW1 .....147 A4
Stillness Prim Sch
SE23 ....66 A1
Stillness Rd SE23 ....66 B1
Stirling Ct WC2 ....106 C1
Stirling Mans NW6 .....11 B2
Stirling Rd SW9 ....172 B1
W3 ....37 A3
Stoatley Ho 10
SW15 ....68 C3
Stock Exchange
EC2 ....109 C1
Stock Orchard Cres
N7 ....14 B3
Stock Orchard St
N7 ....14 B3
Stockbeck NW1 ....83 A1
Stockfield Rd SW16 ...74 B1
Stockholm Ho 8 E1 ....125 C4
Stockholm Rd SE16 ...40 B1
Stockholm Way 1 E1 .125 B2
Stockhurst Cl SW15 ...57 C4
Stockleigh Hall
NW8 ....80 B2
Stocks Ct 5 E1 ....25 C1
Stocks Pl 16 E14 ....33 B2
Stockton Ho 16 E2 .....25 A2

Stockwell Ave SW9 .....62 B4
Stockwell Gdns
SW9 ....172 C3
Stockwell Gn SW9 .....172 C1
Stockwell Jun & Inf Sch
SW9 ....172 C1
Stockwell Park Cres
SW9 ....173 A2
Stockwell Park Rd
SW9 ....173 A3
Stockwell Park Sch
SW9 ....173 A3
Stockwell Park Wlk
SW9 ....173 A1
Stockwell Prim Sch
SW9 ....173 A1
Stockwell Rd SW9 .....173 A1
Stockwell St SE10 .....52 B4
Stockwell Sta SW4 ....172 B2
Stockwell Terr
SW9 ....172 C3
Stoddart Ho SW8 ....163 A3
Stodmarsh Ho 5
SW9 ....173 C4
Stoford Cl SW19 ....70 A4
Stoke Newington
Church St N16 ....7 A2
Stoke Newington Comm
N16 ....7 B3
Stoke Newington High
St N16 ....7 B1
Stoke Newington Rd
N16 ....16 B4
Stoke Newington Sch
N16 ....6 C1
Stoke Newington Sta
N16 ....7 A3
Stoke Pl NW10 ....21 B2
Stokenchurch St
SW6 ....166 A3
Stokesley St W12 ....29 B3
Stondon Pk SE23 ....66 A1
Stone Bldgs WC2 ....107 A3
Stone Cl SW4 ....171 A1
Stone Gate 6 NW5 .....12 C2
Stonebridge Prim Sch
The NW10 ....20 C4
Stonecutter St
EC4 ....108 A2
Stonefield N4 ....5 B2
Stonefield Mans N1 ...85 B3
Stonefield St N1 ....85 C4
Stonehill Cl SW14 ....55 C2
Stonehill Rd SW14 .....56 A3
W4 ....44 C1
Stonehill's Mans 3
SW16 ....74 A2
Stonehills Ct SE21 .....76 A1
Stonehouse NW1 ....83 A3
Stonehouse Ct
EC2 ....110 B2
Stonehouse Ho 27
W2 ....31 C4
Stoneleigh Lo 13
TW9 ....44 B2
Stoneleigh Pl W11 .....30 C2
Stoneleigh St W11 .....30 C2
Stoneleigh Terr N19 ....4 A2
Stonenest St N4 ....5 B3
Stones End St SE1 ....136 C3
Stoney La E1 ....110 B2
Stoney St SE1 ....123 B2
Stoneyard La E14 ....34 A2
Stonhouse St SW4 .....61 C3
Stonnell's Rd SW11 ....60 B2
Stonor Rd W14 ....140 C3
Stopes St SE15 ....49 B3

Stopford Rd SE17 ......150 B1
Stopher Ho SE1 ....136 B3
Storace Ho 6 SW4 .....62 A3
Store St WC1 ....105 B4
Storers Quay E14 ......42 C2
Storey Ct NW8 ....89 B3
Storey Ho 12 E14 ....34 A2
Storey's Gate
SW1 ....133 C3
Stories Rd SE5 ....64 A4
Storks Rd SE16 ....139 C1
Stormont House Sch
E5 ....17 A4
Stormont Rd N6 ....3 B4
SW11 ....60 C3
Storrington WC1 ....94 B3
Story St N1 ....14 B1
Stothard Pl E1 ....110 B4
Stothard St 11 E1 ....25 B1
Stoughton Cl SE11 ....149 A3
SW15 ....68 C3
Stour Rd E3 ....18 C1
Stourcliffe Cl W1 ....102 C2
Stourcliffe St W1 ....102 C1
Stourhead Cl 6
SW19 ....69 C4
Stowage SE8 ....52 A4
Stowe Ho 11 N16 ....7 A1
Stowe Rd W12 ....30 A1
Stracey Rd NW10 ....20 C4
Stradbroke Rd N5 ....15 B4
Stradella Rd SE24 ......63 B1
Straffan Lo 3 NW3 .....12 A2
Strafford Ho 9 SE8 .....41 B1
Strafford Rd W3 ....37 B4
Strafford St E14 ....41 C4
Strahan Rd E3 ....26 A2
Straightsmouth
SE10 ....52 B3
Straker's Rd SE15 ......65 A3
Strale Ho 17 N1 ....24 A4
Strand WC2 ....120 C4
Strand La WC2 ....121 A4
**Strand on the Green Inf
Sch** W4 ....44 C4
**Strand on the Green Jun
Sch** W4 ....44 C4
Strand-on-the-Green
W4 ....44 C4
Strang Ho N1 ....86 C3
Strangways Terr
W14 ....126 C1
Stranraer Way N1 ......14 B1
Strasburg Rd
SW11 ....169 C3
Stratford Bus Sta
E15 ....19 C1
Stratford Gr SW15 .....57 C3
Stratford Pl W1 ....104 A1
Stratford Rd W8 ....127 C1
Stratford Sta E15 ....19 C1
Stratford Studios
W8 ....128 A1
Stratford Villas
NW1 ....13 C1
Strath Terr SW11 ....60 A3
Strathan Cl SW18 ......58 A1
Strathblaine Rd
SW11 ....59 C3
Strathdon Dr SW17 ....71 C1
Strathearn Ho W2 .....116 A4
Strathearn Pl W2 ....116 A4
W2 ....116 A4
Strathearn Par SE3 ....53 C1

Stratheden Rd SE3 .....53 C3
Strathleven Rd SW2 ...62 A2
Strathmore Ct NW8 .....90 A4
Strathmore Gdns
W8 ....113 C2
Strathmore Rd
SW19 ....70 C1
Strathnairn St SE1 ....153 C3
Strathray Gdns
NW3 ....12 A2
Strathville Rd SW18 ...71 A2
Stratton Cl SW19 ....79 C4
Stratton St W1 ....118 B2
Strattondale St E14 ....42 B3
Strauss Rd W4 ....37 C4
Streatham & Tooting
Adult Inst SW16 ....74 B2
Streatham Cl SW16 ....74 B2
Streatham Ct SW16 ....74 A1
Streatham Hill SW2 ....74 A3
**Streatham Hill &
Clapham High Sch**
SW2 ....74 B3
Streatham Hill Sta
SW2 ....74 B3
Streatham Pl SW2 ......74 A4
Streatham St WC1 ....106 A2
Streathbourne Rd
SW17 ....72 C1
**Streatham Wells Prim
Sch** SW2 ....74 C2
Streatley Par 4
SW16 ....74 A2
Streatley Pl 12 NW3 ..11 B4
Streatley Rd NW6 ....10 B1
Streimer Rd E15 ....27 B3
Strelley Way W3 ....29 A2
Strickland Ct SE15 .....64 C4
Strickland Ho 2
E2 ....99 A3
Strickland Row
SW18 ....71 C4
Strickland St SE8 ....51 C2
Stringer Hos 8 N1 ......24 A4
Strode Ho 3 SW2 ....74 C3
Strode Rd SW6 ....154 A2
NW10 ....8 C2
Strome Ho NW6 ....78 A1
Stronsa Rd W12 ....38 B4
Strood Ho SE1 ....137 C3
Stroud Cres SW15 ......68 C1
Stroud Green Prim Sch
N4 ....5 C3
Stroud Green Rd N4 ...5 C3
Stroud Rd SW19 ....70 C1
Stroudley Ho SW8 ......171 A4
Stroudley Wlk E3 ....27 A2
Strout's Pl 2 E2 ....98 C4
Strudwick Ct SW4 .....172 B3
Strutton Ground
SW1 ....133 B1
Strype St E1 ....110 C3
Stuart Ave W5 ....36 A4
Stuart Ho W14 ....140 A4
1 E9 ....17 C1
5 SW4 ....62 A3
Stuart Mill Ho N1 ....84 C1
Stuart Rd NW6 ....23 C2
W3 ....28 B1
SW19 ....70 C1
Stubbs Dr SE16 ....40 A1
Stubbs Ho N1 ....5 B3
1 E2 ....25 C2
Stucley Pl 8 NW1 ....13 A1
Studd St N1 ....86 A4

Studdridge St SW6 165 C2
Studholme Ct NW3 10 C4
Studholme St SE15 50 A3
Studio Pl SW1 131 A3
Studios The SW8 171 C3
4 SW4 61 B3
Studland SE17 151 B2
Studland Ho E14 33 A3
Studland St W6 39 A2
Studley Cl E5 18 A3
Studley Rd SW4 172 B2
Stukeley St WC2 106 B2
Stunnell Ho 23 SE14 50 C4
Sturdee Ho 2 E2 24 C3
Sturdy Ho 26 E3 26 A3
Sturdy Rd SE15 50 A1
Sturge St SE1 136 C4
Sturgeon Rd SE17 150 C1
Sturmer Way N7 14 B3
Sturminster Ho SW8 163 A1
Sturry St E14 34 A3
Sturt St N1 87 A1
Stutfield St E1 111 C1
Stuttle Ho E1 99 B1
Styles Gdns SW9 63 A4
Styles Ho SE1 122 A1
Sudbourne Prim Sch SW2 62 B2
Sudbourne Rd SW2 62 B2
Sudbrooke Rd SW12 60 C1
Sudbury Ct SW8 171 C4
E5 18 A4
Sudbury Ho SW18 59 A2
Sudeley St N1 86 B1
Sudlow Rd SW18 58 C2
Sudrey St SE1 136 C3
Suffield Ho SE17 150 B2
Suffolk La EC4 123 B4
Suffolk Pl SW1 119 C2
Suffolk Rd NW10 8 A1
SW13 46 C3
Suffolk St SW1 119 C2
Sugar House La E15 27 B3
Sugar Loaf Wlk 6 E2 25 B2
Sugden Ho SE11 149 A4
Sugden Rd SW11 60 C3
Sulby Ho SE4 66 A3
Sulgrave Gdns 11 W6 39 B4
Sulgrave Rd W6 39 B3
Sulina Rd SW2 74 A4
Sulivan Ct SW6 165 B1
Sulivan Ent Ctr SW6 58 C4
Sulivan Prim Sch SW6 165 C1
Sulivan Rd SW6 58 C4
Sulkin Ho 11 E2 25 C2
Sullivan Cl SW11 60 A4
Sullivan Ct SW5 141 C4
N16 7 B3
Sullivan Ho SE11 149 A3
SW1 160 B4
Sullivan Rd SE11 149 C4
Sultan St SE5 48 B3
Sumatra Rd NW6 10 C2
Sumburgh Rd SW12 60 C1
Summer Ho SE13 67 C3
Summercourt Rd E1 32 B3
Summerfield Ave NW6 23 A3
Summerhouse Rd N16 7 A2
Summerlands Ave W3 28 B2
Summerley St SW18 71 A2
Summers St EC1 95 B1
Summerstown SW17 71 B1
Summit Ct NW2 10 A3
Summit Est N16 7 C4
Sumner Ave SE15 49 B2
Sumner Bldgs SE1 122 C2
Sumner Ct SW8 172 A4
Sumner Ho 1 E3 34 A4
Sumner Pl SW7 143 C3
Sumner Place Mews SW7 143 C3
Sumner Rd SE15 49 B3
Sumner St SE1 122 C2
Sumpter Cl NW3 11 B2
Sun Alley 6 TW9 54 A3
Sun Ct EC3 109 C1
Sun Pas SE16 139 B2
Sun Rd W14 140 C1
Sun St EC2 109 C4
Sun St Pas EC2 110 A3
Sunbeam Cres W10 22 B1
Sunbeam Rd NW10 20 C1
Sunbury Ave SW14 55 C3
Sunbury Ct 3 SE14 50 C4
Sunbury Ho E2 98 C3
Sunbury La SW11 167 C4
Sunbury Workshops E2 98 C3
Sunderland Ct SE22 76 C4
Sunderland Ho 26 W2 31 C4
Sunderland Terr W2 100 A2
Sundew Ave W12 29 C2
Sundridge Ho 4 E9 17 C1
Sunningdale Ave W3 29 A2
Sunningdale Cl 22 SE16 40 A1
Sunningdale Gdns W8 127 C1
Sunninghill Ct 9 W3 37 B4
Sunninghill Rd SE13 52 A1
Sunnyhill Cl E5 18 A4
Sunnymead Rd SW15 57 A2
Sunnyside 3 NW2 1 B1
Sunnyside Ho 2 NW2 1 B1
Sunnyside Rd N19 4 C4
Sunray Ave SE5, SE24 63 C3
Sunset Rd SE5 63 C3
Sunwell Cl SE15 50 A2
Surcot Ho SW4 171 C1
Surma Cl E1 24 C1 99 C1
Surr St N7 14 A3
Surrendale Pl W9 23 C1
Surrey Canal Rd SE14,SE16,SE8 50 C4
Surrey Commercial Wharf SE16 32 C1
Surrey Cres 1 W4 36 C1
Surrey Gr SE17 152 A1
Surrey Ho 8 SE16 32 C1
Surrey La SW11 168 B3
Surrey Quays Rd SE16 40 C4
Surrey Quays Sh Ctr SE16 40 C3
Surrey Quays Sta SE16 40 C2
Surrey Rd SE15 65 C2
Surrey Row SE1 136 B4
Surrey Sq SE17 152 B2
Surrey Square Inf Sch SE17 152 A2
Surrey Square Jun Sch SE17 152 A2
Surrey St WC2 121 A4
Surrey Terr SE17 152 B2
Surrey Water Rd SE16 32 C1
Surrey Wharf SE1 49 C4
Surridge Ct SW9 172 B2
Susan Lawrence Jun & Inf Schs E14 34 A3
Susannah St E14 34 B3
Sussex Cl N19 5 A2
Sussex Ct W2 101 B1
4 SW13 46 B1
SE10 52 B4
Sussex Gdns W2 101 C1
W2 115 B4
Sussex Ho NW3 12 A2
Richmond TW9 44 B1
Sussex Lo W2 101 C1
Sussex Mans WC2 120 B4
SW7 143 B3
Sussex Mews E W2 101 C1
Sussex Mews W W2 115 C4
Sussex Pl NW1 90 C2
W2 101 C1
Sussex Sq W2 115 C4
Sussex St SW1 146 B2
Sussex Way N19 4 C3
N7,N19 5 A2
Sussex Wlk 18 SW9 63 A3
Sutherland Ave W9 88 B2
Sutherland Ct N16 6 C1
2 W9 23 C1
Sutherland Gdns SW14 56 A4
Sutherland Gr SW18, SW19 70 B4
Sutherland Ho W8 128 A1
7 SW15 69 B4
Sutherland Pl W2 31 C3
Sutherland Point 1 E5 17 A4
Sutherland Rd E3 26 B3
W4 46 A4
Sutherland Row SW1 146 B2
Sutherland Sq SE17 150 C1
Sutherland St SW1 146 B2
Sutherland Wlk SE17 151 A1
Sutterton St N7 14 B2
Sutton Court Rd W4 45 B4
Sutton Ct 9 E5 17 A4
W4 45 B4
Sutton Est SW3 144 B2
Sutton Est The W10 30 B4
Sutton La N W4 37 B1
Sutton La S W4 45 B4
Sutton Pl E9 17 B3
Sutton Row W1 105 C2
Sutton Sq E9 17 B3
Sutton St E1 32 B3
Sutton Way W10 30 B4
Suttons Way EC1 97 A1
Swaby Rd SW17, SW18 71 B2
Swaffield Prim Sch SW18 71 B4
Swaffield Rd SW18 71 B4
Swain's La N6 4 A2
Swainson Ho N7 14 C4
Swainson Rd W3 38 B4
Swallow Cl SE14 50 C2
Swallow Ct 4 W9 31 C4
Swallow Ho NW8 80 A2
Swallow Pl W1 104 B1
Swallow St W1 119 A3
Swallowfield NW1 92 B3
Swan Ct SW3 144 B1
SW6 155 B1
E14 33 B3
Swan Ctr SW17 71 B1
Swan Ho N1 15 C1
Swan La EC4 123 C3
Swan Lane Pier EC4 123 C3
Swan Mead SE1 138 A1
Swan Mews SW9 172 C2
Swan Pas E1 125 B3
Swan Pl SW13 46 B1
Swan Rd SE16 40 B4
Swan St SE1 137 A3
Swan Wlk SW3 158 C4
Swan Yd N1 15 A2
Swanage Ct 5 N1 16 A1
Swanage Ho SW8 162 C1
Swanage Rd SW18 59 B1
Swanbourne SE17 150 C3
Swanbourne Ho NW8 90 A2
Swandon Way SW18 59 A3
Swanfield St E2 99 A2
E2 99 A3
Swanlea Sec Sch E1 25 A1
Swanley Ho SE17 152 B2
Swanmore Ct SW18 59 B1
Swanne Ho 12 SE10 52 B3
Swanscombe Ho 11 W11 30 C1
Swanscombe Point 7 E16 35 B2
Swanscombe Rd W11 30 C1
5 W4 38 A1
Swanton Gdns SW19 69 C3
Swanwick Cl SW15 68 B4
Swaton Rd E3 26 C1
Swaythling Ho 2 SW15 56 B1
Sweden Gate SE16 41 A2
Swedenborg Gdns E1 32 A2
Swedish Sch SW13 46 B4
Sweeney Cres SE1 139 A3
Sweyn Pl SE3 53 C1
Swift Ho SW9 163 C2
15 N16 7 A1
Swift St SW6 164 C4
Swinbrook Rd W10 31 A4
Swinburne Ct 4 SE5 63 C3
Swinburne Ho 15 E2 25 B2
Swinburne Rd SW15 56 C3
Swindon St W12 30 B1
Swinford Gdns SW9 63 A4
Swingfield Ho 5 E9 25 B4
Swinley Ho NW1 92 B4
Swinnerton St E9 18 A3
Swinton Ho E2 99 B3
Swinton Pl WC1 94 C4
Swinton St WC1 94 C4
Swiss Cottage NW3 11 C1
Swiss Cottage Sch NW8 79 C4
Swiss Cottage Sta NW3 11 C1
Swiss Terr 7 NW3 11 C1
Sybil Phoenix Cl SE8 40 C1
Sybil Thorndike Casson Ho SW5 141 C1
Sybil Thorndike Ho 7 N1 15 B2
Sycamore Cl W3 29 A1
Sycamore Ct N19 4 C1
NW6 23 C4
4 SE5 48 B2
Sycamore Gdns W6, W12 39 A3
Sycamore Gr SE6 67 B1
Sycamore Ho 2 N16 6 C2
10 NW3 12 B2
3 W6 39 A4
17 SE16 40 C4
Sycamore Lo SW15 57 A4
Sycamore Mews 4 SW4 61 B4
Sycamore St EC1 96 C1
Sycamore Wlk 1 W10 23 A1
Sydenham Hill SE21, SE22,SE23,SE26,SE19 76 C1
Sydenham Hill Sta SE21 76 B1
Sydner Mews N16 16 B4
Sydner Rd N16 16 B4
Sydney Cl SW3 143 C3
Sydney Ho 4 W4 38 A2
Sydney Mews SW3 143 C3
Sydney Pl SW7 143 C3
Sydney Rd TW10, TW9 54 A3
Sydney St SW3 144 A2
Sylva Ct 3 SW15 69 C4
Sylvan Gr NW2 9 C4
SE15 50 A4
Sylvester Ho 7 E8 17 A2
Sylvester Path 8 E8 17 A2
Sylvester Rd E8 17 A2
Sylvia Cotts 3 SE8 51 C2
Sylvia Ct N1 87 B1
Sylvia Pankhurst Ho 14 E2 25 C2
Symes Mews NW1 82 C2
Symington Ho SE1 137 B1
Symons St SW3 145 A3
Syringa Ho SE4 66 B4

T

Tabard Ct 3 E14 34 B3
Tabard Ho SE1 137 C2

Tabard St SE1 .... **137** B2
Tabernacle St EC2 .... **97** C2
Tableer Ave SW4 .... **61** C2
Tabley Rd N7 .... **14** A4
Tabley Rd W6 .... **39** A3
Tachbrook Est
SW1 .... **147** C1
Tachbrook Mews
SW1 .... **146** C4
Tachbrook St SW1 .... **147** A3
Tack Mews SE4 .... **66** B1
Tadema Ho NW8 .... **89** C1
Tadema Rd SW10 .... **157** A1
Tadmor St W12 .... **30** C1
Tadworth Ho SE1 ... **136** A3
Taeping St E14 .... **42** A2
Taft Way E3 .... **27** A2
Tait Ct SW8 .... **171** C4
  9 E3 .... **26** A4
Tait Ho SE1 .... **121** C1
  N19 .... **5** A2
Talacre Rd NW5 .... **12** C2
Talbot Ct EC3 .... **123** C4
Talbot Grove Ho 9
W11 .... **31** A3
Talbot Ho E14 .... **34** A3
  E14 .... **19** C1
Talbot Pl SE3 .... **53** A1
Talbot Rd W11 .... **31** B3
  W2 .... **31** C3
  SE22 .... **64** A3
Talbot Sq W2 .... **101** B1
Talbot Wlk NW10 .... **8** A2
  W11 .... **31** A3
Talcott Path **12**
SW2 .... **74** C3
Talfourd Pl SE15 .... **49** B2
Talfourd Rd SE15 .... **49** B2
Talgarth Rd W14 .... **140** B2
  W6 .... **39** C1
Talia Ho E14 .... **42** B3
Talina Ctr SW6 .... **166** C3
Talleyrand Ho SE5 ...... **48** B1
Tallis St EC4 .... **121** C4
Talma Ho **2** E2 .... **25** B3
Talma Rd SW2 .... **62** C3
Talmud Torah Sch
N16 .... **7** A4
Talmudical Coll N16 .... **6** C4
Talwin St E3 .... **27** A2
Tamar Cl E3 .... **26** B4
Tamar Ho SE11 .... **149** C2
Tamarind Ct **8** W3 ... **28** B3
Tamarind Ho 4
SE15 .... **49** C3
Tamarind Yd E1 .... **125** C2
Tamarisk Sq W12 .... **29** B2
Tamworth N7 .... **14** A2
Tamworth St SW6 ...... **155** B3
Tangier Rd TW10 .... **55** A4
Tangley Gr SW15 .... **68** B4
Tangmere WC1 .... **94** C3
Tanhurst Ho 27
SW2 .... **74** A4
Tankerton St WC1 ...... **94** B3
Tanner Cl **5** E2 .... **24** C3
Tanner St SE1 .... **138** B3
Tanner's Hill SE8 ...... **51** C2
Tannington Terr N5 ... **5** C1
Tanswell St SE1 .... **135** B3
Tant Ave E16 .... **35** B1

Tantallon Rd SW12 ..... **72** C3
Tanza Rd NW3 .... **12** B4
Taplow NW3 .... **11** C1
Taplow Ho **2** **98** C3
Taplow St N1 .... **87** A1
Tapp St E1 .... **25** A1
Tappesfield Rd
SE15 .... **65** B4
Taranto Ho **11** E1 ... **32** B4
Tarbert Rd SE22 .... **64** A2
Tarbert Wlk E1 .... **32** B2
Tarling Ho **22** E1 ... **32** A3
Tarling Rd E16 .... **35** B1
Tarling St E1 .... **32** B3
Tarn St SE1 .... **136** C1
Tarnbrook Ct SW1 .... **145** B3
Tarns The NW1 .... **92** C4
Tarplett Ho **22** SE14 **50** C4
Tarragon Cl SE14 ...... **51** A3
Tarranbrane Ho **25** B2
Tarrant Ho E2 .... **25** B2
Tarrant Pl W1 .... **102** C3
Tarriff Cres SE8 .... **41** B2
Tarrington Cl SW16 ... **73** C1
Tartan Ho **3** E14 ..... **34** B3
Tarver Rd SE17 .... **150** B2
Tarves Way SE10 ...... **52** A3
Tasker Ho **3** E14 .... **33** B4
Tasker Rd NW3 .... **12** B3
Tasman Ho **17** E1 ... **32** A1
Tasman Rd SW9 .... **62** A4
Tasso Rd W6 .... **154** A4
Tasso Yd W6 .... **154** A3
Tatchbury Ho 3
SW15 .... **56** B1
Tate Gallery
(Britain)The★
SW1 .... **148** A3
**Tate Gallery of Modern
Art★** SE1 .... **122** B3
Tate Ho **10** E2 .... **25** C3
Tatnell Rd SE23 .... **66** A1
Tatton Cres E5,N16 ... **7** A4
Tatum St SE17 .... **151** C3
Tauheed Cl N4 .... **6** B2
Taunton Ho W2 .... **100** C1
Taunton Mews NW1 ... **90** C1
Taunton Pl NW1 .... **90** C2
Tavern La SW9 .... **173** C2
Taverner Ho N16 ...... **6** C1
Taverner Sq **4** N5 ... **15** B4
Taverners Cl W11 ..... **112** A1
Tavistock Cl N16 ...... **16** A3
Tavistock Cres W11 ... **31** B4
Tavistock Ho WC1 ..... **93** C2
Tavistock Ho **31** B4
Tavistock Mews 1
W11 .... **31** B4
Tavistock Pl WC1 ...... **94** A2
Tavistock Rd NW10 ... **21** B3
  W11 .... **31** B4
Tavistock Sq WC1 ..... **93** C2
Tavistock St WC2 ..... **120** B4
Tavistock Terr N19 ... **4** C1
Taviton St WC1 .... **93** B2
Tay Cl SE11 .... **149** C2
Tay Way SE10 .... **40** C2
Tay Ho **2** E3 .... **26** B3
Taybridge Rd SW11 ... **60** C3
Tayburn Cl E14 .... **34** B3
Tayler Ct NW8 .... **79** B4
Taylor Ave TW9 .... **45** A1
Taylor Ct E15 .... **76** B3

Taylor Ho **10** SW2 ... **74** C3
Taylor's Gn W3 .... **29** A3
Taylor's La NW10 ..... **8** A1
Tayport Cl N1 .... **14** A1
Tayside Ct **5** SE5 ... **63** C3
Teak Cl SE16 .... **33** A1
Teal Ct **30** SE8 ...... **51** B4
Tealby Ct N7 .... **14** B2
Teale St E2 .... **24** C3
Teather St **20** SE5 ... **49** A3
Tebbs Ho **7** SW2 ... **74** C4
Ted Roberts Ho **24**
E2 .... **25** A3
Tedworth Gdns
SW3 .... **144** C1
Tedworth Sq SW3 .... **144** C1
Tee The W3 .... **29** A3
Teesdale Cl E2 .... **25** A3
Teesdale St E2 .... **25** A3
Teignmouth Cl 6
SW4 .... **61** C3
Teignmouth Rd NW2 ... **9** C2
Telegraph Hill NW3 ... **2** A1
Telegraph Pl E14 ..... **42** A2
Telegraph Rd SW15 ... **69** B4
Telegraph St EC2 ... **109** B2
Telfer Cl **3** W3 ...... **37** B4
Telfer Ho EC1 .... **96** B3
Telferscroft JMI Sch
SW12 .... **73** A3
Telferscroft Rd SW12 **73** C3
Telford Ave SW12, ... **73** C3
  SW2 .... **74** A3
Telford Ho SE1 .... **136** C2
  8 W10 .... **31** A4
Telford Parade Mans 8
SW2 .... **74** A3
Telford Rd W10 ...... **31** A4
Telford Terr SW1 ..... **146** B1
Telford Way W3 ...... **29** A4
Tell Gr SE22 .... **64** B3
Telscombe Ho **169** B3
Temair Ho **1** SE10 ... **52** B3
Temeraire St SE16 ... **40** B4
Temperley Rd SW12 .. **72** C4
Templar Ho NW2 ..... **10** B2
Templar St SE5 ...... **48** A1
Templars Ho E15 ..... **19** A3
Temple Ave EC4 ..... **121** C4
Temple Ct SW8 ...... **162** A1
Temple Dwellings 7
E2 .... **25** A3
Temple Ho **6** N7 ... **4** B1
  13 SW11 .... **60** A4
Temple La EC4 .... **107** C1
Temple Mills La **E10**,E15
   .... **76** B4
Temple Mills Rd E9 .. **18** C4
Temple Pl WC2 ...... **121** A4
Temple Rd W4 .... **37** B3
   Richmond TW9 ..... **54** B4
Temple Sheen
SW14 .... **55** B2
Temple Sheen Rd
SW14 .... **55** A3
Temple St E2 .... **25** A3
Temple West Mews
SE11 .... **136** A1
Templecombe Rd
E9 .... **25** B4
Templemead Cl W3 .. **29** A3
Templemead Ho E9 .. **18** A4

Thames Quay
SW10 .... **167** A3
  E14 .... **42** A4
Thames Rd W4 .... **45** A4
Thames Reach W6 ... **47** B4
Thames St SE10 ..... **52** A4
Thames Village W4 ... **45** B2
Thames Wlk SW11 ... **158** A2
Thameside Ctr TW8 .. **44** B4
Thane Mans N7 ...... **5** B1
Thane Villas N7 ..... **5** B1
Thane Works N7 ..... **5** B1
Thanet Ho WC1 ...... **94** A3
  1 SE27 .... **75** A1
Thanet Lo NW2 ...... **10** A2
Thanet St WC1 ...... **94** A3
Thavie's Inn EC4 ... **107** C2
Thaxted Ct N1 ...... **87** C1
Thaxted Ho SE16 .... **40** B2
Thaxton Rd W14 ... **155** A4
Thayer St W1 .... **103** C2
Theatre Mus★ WC2 . **120** B4
Theatre St SW11 .... **60** B4
Theberton St N1 .... **86** A4
Theed St SE1 .... **121** C1
Thelbridge Ho
23 .... **27** A2
Theobald St SE1 .... **137** B1
Theobald's Rd
WC1 .... **106** C4
Theobalds Ct N4 .... **6** B2
Theodore Ho **1**
SW15 .... **56** C2
Theodore Rd SE13 .. **67** C1
Therapia Rd SE22 ... **65** B1
Theresa Rd W6 ...... **38** C2
Therfield Ct N4 ...... **6** B2
Thermopylae Gate
E14 .... **42** A2
Theseus Wlk N1 .... **86** B1
Thessaly Ho SW8 .. **160** C1
Thessaly Rd SW8 .. **171** A4
Thesus Ho **2** E14 . **34** C3
Thetford Ho SE1 ... **138** C2
Thetis Terr TW9 .... **44** C4
Third Ave W10 ...... **23** A2
  W3 .... **29** B1
Thirleby Rd SW1 ... **133** A1
Thirlmere NW1 ...... **92** B4
Thirlmere Ho
N16 .... **15** C4
Thirsk Rd SW11 .... **60** C3
Thistle Gr SW7 .... **143** A1
Thistle Ho **6** E14 . **34** B3
Thistlewood Cl **3** N7 **5** B2
Thomas Baines Rd
SW11 .... **59** C4
Thomas Burt Ho **9**
E2 .... **25** A2
Thomas Buxton Jun &
Inf Sch E1 .... **99** C1
Thomas Doyle St
SE1 .... **136** B2
Thomas Fairchild JMI
Sch N1 .... **87** A2
Thomas Ho **8** E9 .. **17** B2
  4 SW4 .... **62** A3
Thomas Hollywood Ho
2 E2 .... **25** B3
Thomas Jones Prim Sch
W11 .... **31** A3
Thomas More Ho
EC2 .... **108** C3
Thomas More Sq
E1 .... **125** B3

Thomas More St
E1 ....125 B2
Thomas North Terr
E16 ....35 C2
Thomas Rd E14 ....33 C4
Thomas Road Ind Est
E14 ....33 C3
Thomas's Prep Sch
SW11 ....167 C3
Thomas's Prep Sch
SW11 ....167 C3
Thompson Ave TW9 ...54 C4
Thompson Ho
☑ W10 ....23 A1
SE14 ....50 C4
Thompson Rd SE22 ....64 B1
Thompson's Ave ☑
SE5 ....48 B3
Thomson Ho SW1 ......147 C1
SE17 ....152 A3
Thorburn Ho SW1 ......131 B3
Thorburn Sq SE1 ....153 B3
Thoresby Ho N16 ....6 C1
Thoresby St N1 ....97 A4
Thorn Ham Ho
SE1 ....137 C2
Thornaby Ho ☑☑
SE15 ....49 C3
Thornbill Ho ☑
SE15 ....49 C3
Thornbury Cl N16 ..16 A4
Thornbury Ct W11 ....113 B4
Thornbury Ho N6 ....4 B3
Thornbury Rd SW2 ....62 A1
Thornbury Sq N6 ....4 B3
Thorncliffe Ct SW2 ....62 A1
Thorncliffe Rd SW2 ....62 A1
Thorncombe Rd
SE22 ....64 A2
Thorncroft St SW8 ....162 A1
Thorndale Ho N16 ....7 A3
Thorndean St SW18 ...71 B2
Thorndike Cl
SW10 ....156 C2
Thorndike Ho SW1 ....147 B2
Thorndike St SW1 ....147 B3
Thorne Cl E16 ....35 C3
Thorne Ho ☑☑ E2 .....25 B2
☑ E14 ....42 B3
Thorne Pas ☑
SW13 ....46 B1
Thorne Rd SW8 ....162 B1
Thorne St SW13,
SW14 ....56 A4
Thorness Ct SW18 .....59 B1
Thornewill Ho ☑
E1 ....32 B2
Thorney Cres
SW11 ....157 C1
Thorney Ct ☑
SW7 ....128 C3
Thorney Hedge Rd
W4 ....37 A2
Thorney St SW1 ....148 A4
Thorneycroft Ho ☑
W4 ....38 A1
Thornfield Ho ☑
E14 ....33 C2
Thornfield Rd W12 ...39 A4
Thornford Rd SE13 .....67 B2
Thorngate Rd W9 ......23 C1
Thornham Gr E15 ......19 C3
Thornham St SE10 .....52 A4
Thornhaugh St
WC1 ....93 C1
Thornhill Bridge Wharf
N1 ....84 C3
Thornhill Cres N1 ...14 B1
Thornhill Gr N1 ....14 C1
Thornhill Ho N1 ....14 C1
☑ W4 ....38 A1
Thornhill Prim Sch
N1 ....14 B1
Thornhill Rd N1 ....85 B4
Thornhill Sq N1 ....14 B1
N1 ....14 B1
Thornicroft Ho
SW9 ....173 A1
Thornley Pl ☑ SW19 ..14 C1
Thornsett Rd SW18 ...71 A3
Thornton Ave W4 ......38 A2
SW2 ....73 C3
Thornton Ct N7 ....13 C3
Thornton Gdns
SW12 ....73 C3
Thornton Ho SE17 ...152 A3
Thornton Pl W1 ....103 A4
Thornton Rd SW14 ....55 C4
SW12,SW2 ....73 C3
Thornton St SW9 .....173 B2
Thornville St SE8 ......51 C2
Thornycroft Ct TW9 ...44 B1
Thorold Ho SE1 ....136 C4
☑ SW2 ....74 A4
Thorparch Rd
SW8 ....161 C1
Thorpe Cl W10 ....31 A3
Thorpe Ho N1 ....85 A3
Thorpebank Rd
W12 ....29 C1
Thorpedale Rd N4 ....5 B3
Thorverton Rd NW2 ...1 A1
Thoydon Rd E3 ....26 A3
Thrale St SE1 ....123 A1
Thrasher Cl ☑ E8 ......24 B4
Thrawl St E1 ....111 A3
Thrayle Ho ☑ SW9 ...62 B4
Threadgold Ho ☑
N1 ....15 C2
Threadneedle St
EC2,EC3 ....109 C1
Three Colt St E14 ....33 B2
Three Colts La E2 ......25 A1
Three Cups Yd
WC1 ....107 A3
Three Kings Yd
W1 ....118 A4
Three Mill La E3 ....27 B2
Three Nun Ct EC2 ....109 B2
Three Oak La SE1 ....138 C4
Threshers Pl W11 ....112 A4
Thring Ho SW9 ....172 C2
Throgmorton Ave
EC2 ....109 C2
Throgmorton St
EC2 ....109 C2
Thrush St SE17 ....150 C2
Thurland Ho ☑
SE16 ....40 A2
Thurland Rd SE16 ...139 B2
Thurleigh Ave
SW12 ....60 C1
Thurleigh Ct SW12 ...60 C1
Thurleigh Rd SW12 ...60 C1
Thurloe Cl SW7 ....144 A3
Thurloe Ct SW3 ....144 A3
Thurloe Pl SW7 ....143 C4
Thurloe Place Mews
SW7 ....143 C4
Thurloe Sq SW7 ....144 A4
Thurloe St SW7 ....143 C4
Thurlow Hill SE21 .....75 B2
Thurlow Ho ☑
SW16 ....74 A1
Thurlow Park Rd
SE21,SE24 ....75 B2
Thurlow Park Sch
SE27 ....75 A2
Thurlow Rd NW3 ....11 C3
Thurlow St SE17 ......152 A1
Thurlow Terr NW5 ......12 C3
Thurlow Twrs SE27 ...74 C1
Thurnscoe NW1 ....82 C3
Thursley Gdns
SW19 ....69 C2
Thursley Ho ☑
SW2 ....74 B4
Thurso Ho NW6 ....78 A1
Thurston Ind Est
SE13 ....67 A4
Thurston Rd SE8,
SE13 ....51 C3
Thurtle Rd E2 ....24 B3
Tibbatts Rd E3 ....27 A1
Tibbet's Corner
SW19 ....69 C2
Tibbet's Ride SW19 ...69 C4
Tibbets Cl SW19 ....69 C2
Tiber Gdns N1 ....84 B3
Tickford Ho NW8 ....90 A3
Tidal Basin Rd E16 ....35 B2
Tidbury Ct SW8 ....160 C1
Tidemill Prim Sch
SE8 ....51 C3
Tideswell ☑☑ NW5 ...13 A4
Tideswell Rd SW15 ...57 B3
Tideway Ct ☑ SE16 ...32 C1
Tideway Ho E14 ....41 C4
Tideway Ind Est
SW8 ....161 A3
Tideway Wharf
SW13 ....46 A1
Tideway Yd SW13 ......46 A1
Tidey St E3 ....33 C4
Tidworth Ho ☑☑
SE22 ....64 A4
Tidworth Rd E3 ....26 C1
Tierney Rd SW2 ....74 A3
Tierney Terr SW2 ......74 A3
Tiger Way E5 ....17 A4
Tilbury Cl ☑ SE15 .....49 B3
Tilbury Ho ☑ SE14 ....50 C4
Tildesley Rd SW15 ....57 B1
Tile Kiln La N6 ....4 B3
Tilehurst NW1 ....92 B3
Tilehurst Rd SW17,
SW18 ....71 C3
Tileyard Rd N7 ....14 A1
Tilford Gdns SW19 ....69 C2
Tilford Ho ☑ SW2 .....74 B4
Tilia Rd E5 ....17 A4
Tilleard Ho ☑ W10 ....23 A2
Tiller Ho ☑ N1 ....24 A4
Tiller Rd E14 ....41 C3
Tillet Sq SE16 ....41 A4
Tillet Way ☑ E2 ....99 B4
Tilling Ho ☑ SE15 .....65 A4
Tillman Ho ☑ SW2 ....74 B3
Tillman St E1 ....32 A3
Tilloch St ☑ N1 ....14 B1
Tilney Ct EC1 ....97 A2
Tilney Gdns ☑ N1 .....15 C2
Tilney St W1 ....117 C2
Tilson Gdns SW2,
....................................74 A4
Tilson Ho SW2 ....74 A4
Tilton St SW6 ....154 B3
Tiltwood The W3 ....28 B2
Timber Mill Way
SW4 ....61 C4
Timber Pond Rd
SE16 ....40 C4
Timberland Cl ☑
SE15 ....49 C3
Timberland Rd E1 ....32 A3
Time Sq E8 ....16 B3
Timothy Cl ☑ SW4 ...61 B2
Timothy Rd E3 ....33 B4
Timsbury Wlk ☑
SW15 ....68 C3
Tina Ct SW16 ....74 C1
Tindal St SW9 ....48 A2
Tinniswood Cl N5 .....14 C3
Tinsley Rd E1 ....32 B4
Tintagel Cres SE22 ....64 B3
Tintern Cl SW15 ....58 A2
Intern Ho NW1 ....82 B1
Tintern St SW4 ....62 A3
Tinworth St SE11 .....148 B2
Tiptorpe Rd SW11 .....60 C4
Tiptree ☑ NW1 ....13 A1
Tisbury Ct W1 ....119 B4
Tisdall Pl SE17 ....151 C3
Tissington Ct ☑
SE16 ....40 C2
Titan Bsns Est ☑
..................................51 C3
Titan Ct TW8 ....36 B1
Titchborne Row
W2 ....102 B1
Titchfield Rd NW8 .....80 C3
Titchwell Rd SW18 ...71 C3
Tite St SW3 ....158 C4
Titmuss St ☑ W12 ....39 B4
Tiverton Rd NW10,
NW10 ....22 C5
Tiverton St SE1 ....136 C2
Tivoli Ct SE16 ....33 B1
Tobago St ☑ E14 ....41 C4
Tobin Cl NW3 ....12 A1
Toby La E1 ....26 A1
Todds Wlk N7 ....5 B2
Tokenhouse Yd
EC2 ....109 B2
Toland Sq SW15 ....56 C2
Tolchurch ☑ W11 .....31 A3
Tolhurst Ho ☑ W10 ...23 A2
Tollbridge Cl W10 ....23 A1
Tollet St E1 ....25 C1
Tollgate Dr SE21 ....76 A2
Tollgate Ho NW6 ......78 A2
Tollgate Rd E6,E16 ....35 C4
Tollhouse Way N19 ....4 B2
Tollington Ho ☑ N19 ..4 B1
Tollington Pk N4 ....5 B2
Tollington Pl N4 ....5 B2
Tollington Rd N7 ....14 B4
Tollington Way N7 ......5 A1
Tolmers Sq NW1 ....93 A3
Tolpaide Ho SE11 ....149 B3
Tolpuddle St N1 ....85 B2
Tolsford Rd E5 ....17 A3
Tom Groves Cl E15 ...19 C3
Tom Hood Cl E15 ......19 C3
Tom Jenkinson Rd ☑
E16 ....35 C1
Tom Smith Cl SE10 ...53 A4
Tom Williams Ho
SW6 ....154 C3
Tomkyns Ho SE11 ....149 B3
Tomlin's Gr E3 ....26 C2
Tomlin's Terr E14 ......33 A3
Tomline Ho SE1 ....122 C1
Tomlins Wlk ☑ N7 .....5 B2
Tomlinson Cl E2 ....99 A3
☑ W4 ....37 A1
Tompion Ho EC1 ....96 B2
Tompion St EC1 ....96 B3
Tomson Ho SE1 ....138 C2
Tonbridge Ho SE6 .....67 A1
Tonbridge St WC1 .....94 A3
Tonbridge Wlk 94 A3
Toneborough NW8 ....78 B3
Tonsley Hill SW18 ....59 A2
Tonsley Pl SW18 ......59 A2
Tonsley Rd SW18 .....59 A2
Tonsley St SW18 ......59 A2
Took's Ct EC4 ....107 B2
Tooley St SE1 ....124 A1
Tooting Bec SW17 .....72 C1
Tooting Bec Sta
SW17 ....72 C3
Topham Ho ☑ SE10 ...52 B3
Topham St EC1 ....95 B2
Topiary Sq TW9 ....54 B4
Topmast Point E14 ...41 C4
Topsham Rd SW17 ....72 C1
Tor Ct W8 ....127 C4
Tor Gdns W8 ....127 B4
Torbay Ct ☑ NW1 ......13 A1
Torbay Mans NW6 ....23 B4
Torbay Rd NW6 ....10 B1
Torbay St ☑ NW1 ......13 A1
Tornay Ho N1 ....84 C2
....................................17 B1
Toronto Rd E11 ....19 C4
Torquay St W2 ....100 A3
Torrens Ct SE5 ....63 C4
Torrens Rd SW2 ....62 B2
Torrens St EC1 ....86 A1
Torres Sq E14 ....41 C1
Torriano Ave NW5 ....13 C3
Torriano Cotts NW5 ..13 B3
Torriano Jun & Inf Schs
NW5 ....13 C3
Torridge Gdns SE15 ..65 B3
Torridon Ho NW6 ......78 A1
Torrington Pl WC1 ...105 B4
E1 ....125 C2
Torrington Sq WC1 ...93 C1
Tortington Ho ☑
SE15 ....50 A3
Torwood Rd SW15 ....56 C2
Tothill Ho SW1 ....147 C4
Tothill St SW1 ....133 C3
Totland Ho SW18 ......59 A1
Tottan Terr E1 ....32 C3
Tottenhall ☑ NW1 .....12 C1
Tottenham Court Road
Sta W1 ....105 C2
Tottenham Mews
W1 ....105 A4
Tottenham Rd N1 ......16 A2
Tottenham St W1 .....105 A4
Totteridge Ho
SW11 ....167 C2
Touchard Ho N1 ....97 C3
Toulmin St SE1 ....136 C3
Toulon St SE5 ....48 B3
Toulouse Ct ☑
SE16 ....40 A1
Tournay Rd SW6 ......155 A2
Toussaint Wlk
SE16 ....139 C2
Tovy Ho SE1 ....153 B1

Towcester Rd E3 ....27 B1
Tower Bldgs 22 E1 ...32 A1
Tower Br App E1,
EC3 ....124 C3
Tower Br Piazza
SE1 ....124 C1
Tower Bridge★
E1,EC3,SE1 ....124 C2
Tower Bridge Bsns
Complex E1 ....40 A3
Tower Bridge Bsns Sq
SE16 ....40 A2
Tower Bridge Sch
SE1 ....138 C4
Tower Bridge Rd
EC3,SE1 ....124 C1
Tower Bridge Sq
SE1 ....138 C4
Tower Ct NW8 ....80 B2
WC2 ....7 B4
E5 ....7 B4
Tower Gateway Sta
EC3 ....124 C4
Tower Hamlets Coll
E1 ....32 B4
E3 ....26 C2
E14 ....34 A3
E14 ....34 A3
Tower Hill EC3 ...124 C3
Tower Hill Sta EC3 124 C4
Tower Hill Terr
EC3 ....124 C3
Tower Mans SE1 ..138 C1
Tower Mews E5 ...18 A3
Tower Millennium Pier
EC3 ....124 B3
Tower Pl EC3 ....124 B3
Tower Rd NW10 ...8 C1
Tower Rise TW9 ..54 A4
Tower Royal EC4 .123 B4
Tower St WC2 ....106 A1
The Tower★ EC3 ..124 C3
Tower Wharf SE1 .138 C4
Tower Wlk SE1 ...152 A4
Towergate SE1 ...152 A4
Towers Pl TW10 ..54 A2
Towers The NW5 ...4 A1
1 Richmond TW9 ..54 A3
Town Hall Rd SW11 60 B4
Towncourt Path N4 ..6 B3
Townhall Ave 3
W4 ....37 C1
Townley Rd SE22 ..64 A2
Townley St 1 SE17 152 B2
Townmead Bsns Ctr
SW6 ....59 B4
Townmead Rd
SW6 ....166 C1
SW6 ....166 C3
Richmond TW9 ...45 A1
Towns Ho 4 SW4 ..62 A3
Townsend Ho SE1 153 C3
Townsend Ind Est
NW10 ....21 A2
Townsend Prim Sch
SE17 ....152 A4
Townsend St SE1,
SE17 ....152 A4
Townsend Yd N6 ...4 A3
Townshend Ct NW8 .80 B2
Townshend Est
NW8 ....80 B2

Townshend Rd
NW8 ....80 A3
Richmond TW9 ...54 B3
Townshend Terr
TW9 ....54 B3
Towton Rd SE27 ..75 B2
Toxteth Ho N4 ....6 B4
Toynbee St E1 ...110 C3
Tracey Ave NW2 ...9 B3
Tracy Ho 12 E3 ...26 B2
Trade Twr 8 SW11 .59 B4
Trade Winds Ct E1 125 C2
Tradescant Ho 15
E9 ....17 B1
Tradescant Rd
SW8 ....162 B1
Trading Estate Rd
NW10 ....20 B1
Traemore Ct SW16 74 A1
Trafalgar Ave SE15 .49 B4
Trafalgar Cl 1
SE16 ....41 A2
Trafalgar Gdns
E1 ....32 C4
W8 ....128 B2
Trafalgar Gr SE10 ..52 C4
Trafalgar Ho SE17 151 A2
Trafalgar Rd SE10 ..43 A1
Trafalgar Sq SW1 .119 C2
Trafalgar St SE17 151 C2
Trafalgar Way E14 .34 B1
Trafford Cl E15 ...19 A3
Trafford Ho N1 ...87 C2
Tragail SW15 ....58 A2
Traitors Gate EC3 ..124 C3
Tralee Ct 15 SE16 ...40 A1
Tramway Ave E15 ..19 C1
Trance Way W4 ....45 B3
Tranmere Ho 7 N7 .14 C3
Tranmere Rd SW17,
SW18 ....71 B2
Tranquil Pass SE3 ..53 B1
Tranquil Vale SE3 ..53 A1
Transept St NW1 ..102 B3
Transom Cl SE16 ..41 A2
Transom Sq E14 ..42 A1
Tranton Rd SE16 ..139 C2
Trappes Ho 2 SE16 .40 A2
Travel Clinic, Hospl for
Tropical Diseases
WC1 ....93 A1
Travers Ho 8 SE10 .52 C4
Travers Rd N7 ....5 C1
Travis Ho SE10 ...52 B2
Treadgold Ho W11 112 A4
7 W11 ....30 C2
Treadgold St W11 .112 A4
W11 ....30 C2
Treadway St E2 ...25 A3
Treasury Buildings
SW1 ....134 A4
Treaty St N1 ....84 C3
Trebeck St W1 ...118 A1
Treborough Ho
W1 ....103 B4
Trebovir Rd SW5 .141 C3
Treby St E3 ......26 B1
Trecastle Way 3
N7 ....13 C4
Tredegar Rd E3 ...26 B3
Tredegar Sq E3 ...26 B2
Tredegar Terr E3 ..26 B2
Trederwen Rd E8 ..24 C4
Treen Ave SW13 ..56 B4
Trees The N16 .....6 C4

Trefil Wlk N7 ....14 A4
Trefoil Rd SW18 ..59 B2
Tregarvon Rd SW11 60 C3
Trego Rd E9 ......18 C1
Tregothnan Rd SW9 62 A4
Tregunter Rd
SW10 ....142 C1
Trehern Rd 1
SW14 ....55 C4
Treherne Ct SW9 ..48 A2
Trehurst St E5 ...18 A3
Trelawn Rd E9 ....17 B2
Trelawney Est E9 ..17 B2
Trelawney Ho SE1 136 C4
Trellis Sq 1 E3 ...26 B2
Tremadoc Rd SW4 .61 C3
Tremaine Cl SE4 ..51 C1
Trematon Ho SE11 149 C2
Tremlett Gr N19 ...4 B1
Tremlett Mews N19 .4 B1
Trenchard St SE10 ..43 A1
Trenchold St SW8 162 A3
Trendell Ho 7 E14 .33 C3
Trenmar Gdns
NW10 ....22 A2
Trenmar Ho NW10 ..22 A2
Trent Ho SE15 ...65 B3
Trent Rd SW2 ....62 B2
Trentham St SW18 .70 C3
Treport St SW18 ..71 A4
Tresco Ho SE11 ..149 B2
Tresco Rd SE15 ...65 A3
Tresham Cres NW8 90 A2
Tresham Wlk E9 ...17 B3
Tresidder Ho 10
SW4 ....73 C4
Tressel Cl 20 N1 ..15 A1
Tressillian Cres SE4 66 C4
Tressillian Rd SE4 ..66 C4
Trevanion Rd W14 140 B2
Trevelyan Gdns
NW10 ....22 B4
Trevelyan Ho 16 E2 .25 C2
SE5 ....48 A3
Treveris St SE1 ..122 B1
Treverton St W10 ..30 C4
Treverton Twr 1
W10 ....30 C4
Treves Ho E1 ....24 C1 99 C1
Treville St SW15 ..69 A4
Trevithick Ho SW8 171 B4
3 NW5 ....12 C2
13 SE16 ....40 A2
Trevithick St SE8 ..51 C4
Trevor Pl SW7 ...130 B3
Trevor Sq SW7 ...130 B3
Trevose Ho SE11 ..149 A2
Trewint St SW18 ..71 B2
Triangle Pl SW4 ..61 C3
Triangle Rd 7 E8 ..25 A4
The Triangle E8 ...25 A4
N19 ....4 C3
E8 ....25 A4
Trident Ho 9 E14 ..34 B3
Trident St SE16 ...40 C2
Trigon Rd SW8 ...163 A2
Trim St SE14 .....51 B4
Trimdon NW1 .....83 A3
Trimmer Wlk 10
TW8 ....44 A4
Trinder Rd N4,N19 ..5 A3
Trinidad Ho 17 E14 .33 B2
Trinidad St E14 ...33 B2
Trinity Church Rd
SW13 ....47 A4

Trinity Church Sq
SE1 ....137 A2
Trinity Cl 3 SW4 ..61 B3
SE13 ....67 C3
Trinity Coll of Music
W1 ....103 C2
Trinity Cotts 1 TW9 54 B4
Trinity Cres SW17 ..72 C2
Trinity Ct WC1 ...94 C2
2 N1 ....24 A4
SE16 ....41 A4
Trinity Gdns E16 ..35 B2
SW2,SW9 ......62 B3
Trinity Gn 1 E1 ...32 B4
Trinity Gr 12 SE10 .52 B2
Trinity Ho SE1 ...137 A2
SW2 ....62 B3
Trinity Homes 14
SW2 ....62 B3
Trinity Pl EC3 ...124 C3
Trinity Rd
Richmond TW9 ...54 B4
SW18 ....72 A3
Trinity Rise SE24,
SW2 ....75 A3
Trinity Sq EC3 ...124 B4
Trinity St 1 E16 ..35 C4
3 E16 ....35 C4
Trinity St Mary's CE
Prim Sch SW12 72 C3
Trinity Way W3 ...29 B2
Trinity Wharf Bsns Ctr
SE16 ....41 B4
Trio Pl SE1 .....137 A3
Tristan Ct 4 SE8 ..51 B4
Triton Ct EC2 ....97 C1
Triton Ho 6 E14 ..42 A2
Triton Sq NW1 ...92 C2
Tritton Rd SE21,
SE27 ....75 C1
Trocette Mans 1 SE1 138 B2
Trojan Ct NW6 ...10 A1
Trojan Ind Est NW10 8 B2
Troon Cl 6 SE16 ..40 A1
Troon Ho 11 E14 ..33 A3
Troon St E1 ......33 A3
Tropical Ct 2 W10 ..22 C2
Trossachs Rd SE22 64 A2
Trothy Rd SE1 ...153 C3
Trotman Ho SE14 ..50 B2
Trott St SW11 ...168 A3
Trotwood Ho 3
SE16 ....40 A4
Troubeck Rd SE14 .51 B2
Troutbeck 6 NW1 ..92 B3
Troutbeck Rd SE14 .51 C2
Trouville Rd SW4 ..61 B1
Trowbridge Est 6
E9 ....18 B2
Trower Ho 5 E9 ...18 A2
Troy Ct W8 ......127 B2
Troy Town SE15 ..64 C4
Troy Town Flats
SE15 ....64 C4
Troyes Ho NW3 ...12 B3
Truman's Rd 22 N16 16 A3
Trump St EC2 ....109 A1
Trundle St SE1 ...136 C4
Trundleys Rd SE8 ..40 C1
Trundleys Terr SE8 .40 C2
Trundleys Rd SE8 ..51 A4
Truro Ho 22 W2 ..31 C4
Truro St NW5 ....12 C2
Trussley Rd W6 ...39 B3
Trust Wlk SE21 ...75 A3
Tryon St SW3 ....144 C2
Tubbs Rd NW10 ..21 B3
Tudor Cl N6 .....4 B4
NW3 ....12 A2

Tudor Cl continued
SW2 ....62 B1
Tudor Ct N1 .....16 A2
SE16 ....32 C1
W5 ....36 C4
Tudor Est NW10 ...20 A3
Tudor Gdns SW14 ..56 A4
Tudor Gr E9 .....17 B1
Tudor Ho E9 .....17 B1
W14 ....39 C2
Tudor Mews 2
NW10 ....8 C2
Tudor Rd E9 .....25 A4
Tudor St EC4 ....121 C4
Tudor Way W3 ...36 C4
Tufnell Ct 12 E3 ..26 B4
Tufnell Park Mans 2
N7 ....5 A1
Tufnell Park Prim Sch
N7 ....13 C4
Tufnell Park Rd
N19,N7 ....13 C4
Tufnell Rd N7 ....14 A3
Tufton St SW1 ...134 A1
Tufton St SW1 ...134 A1
Tuke Sch SE15 ...50 A2
Tullis Ho 12 E9 ..17 B1
Tulse Hill SW2,SE24 74 C4
SW2 ....74 C3
Tulse Hill Sta SE27 75 A2
Tulse Ho SW2 ....62 C1
Tulsemere Rd SE21,
SE27 ....76 A1
Tunbridge Ct 1
SE26 ....76 C1
Tunbridge Ho EC1 .96 A4
Tunis Ho 3 W11 ..33 A4
Tunis Rd W12 ....30 A1
Tunley Grn 16 E14 .33 B4
Tunley Rd NW10 ..21 A4
SW12,SW17 .....72 C2
Tunnel Ave SE10 ..42 C4
SE10 ....43 B2
Tunnel Rd SE16 ...40 B4
Tunstall Ct 14 SW9 44 A2
Tunstall Rd SW9 ..62 B3
Tunstall Wlk 10
TW8 ....44 A4
Tunworth Cres
SW15 ....56 B1
Tupman Ho SE16 139 B3
Turberville Ho
SW9 ....62 B4
Turene Cl SW18 ..59 B3
Turin St 2 ....24 C2 99 C3
Turk's Head Yd
EC1 ....108 A4
Turks Row SW3 ...145 A2
Turle Rd N4 .....5 B2
Turlewray Cl N4 ...5 B3
Turnagain La EC4 ..108 A2
Turnberry Cl
SE16 ....40 A1
Turnbull Ho N1 ...86 B4
Turnchapel Mews 1
SW4 ....61 A4
Turner Cl 7 SW9 ..48 A2
13 SE16 ....40 A4
9 SE5 ....63 C3
Turner Ho NW8 ...80 A2
WC2 ....120 B3
SW1 ....147 C3
N4 ....5 A4

Turner Lo 10 SW19 ..69 C3
Turner St E1 ....32 A4
  E16 ....35 B1
Turner's Rd E3 ....33 B4
Turneville Rd W14 .154 C4
Turney Rd SE21 ......75 C4
Turney Sch SE21 ....75 C4
Turnham Green Sta
  W4 ....38 A2
Turnham Green Terr
  W4 ....38 A2
Turnham Ho SE4 ....66 A3
Turnham Prim Sch
  SE4 ....66 A3
Turnham Rd SE4 ....66 A3
Turnmill Ho 8 SW2 .62 C2
Turnmill St EC1 ....108 A4
Turnour Ho 12 E1 ...32 A3
Turnpike Cl SE8 .....51 B3
Turnpike Ho EC1 ....96 B3
Turnpin La 13 SE10 .52 B4
Turnstone Ct 17
  SE8 ....51 B4
Turpentine La
  SW1 ....146 B1
Turpin Ho SW11 ...170 A4
Turpin Way N19 ......4 C3
Turquand St SE17 .151 A3
Turret Gr SW4 ....61 B4
Turville Ho NW8 ....90 A2
Turville St E2 ....98 C2
Tuscan Ho 58 E2 ...25 B2
Tuskar St SE10 ......43 A1
Tutshill Ct SE25 .....49 A3
Tuttle Ho SW1 .....147 C1
Tweed Ho E14 ....27 B1
Tweedale Ct E15 ....76 B3
Tweezer's Alley
  WC2 ....121 B4
Twelvetrees Cres
  E3 ....27 A2
Twig Folly Cl E2 ....25 C3
Twilley St SW18 .....71 A4
Twine Ct E1 ....32 B2
Twisden Rd NW5 ...13 A4
Twyford CE High Sch
  W3 ....28 A1
Twyford Ho N5 ....6 A1
Twyford Pl WC2 ....106 C2
Twyford St N1 ....84 C4
Twynholm Mans
  SW6 ....154 A2
Tyburn RC Inf Sch
  NW8 ....89 C2
Tyburn Tree (site of)
  W2 ....116 C3
Tyburn Way W1 ....117 A4
Tyer's Est SE1 ......138 A4
Tyers Gate SE1 ....138 A3
Tyers St SE11 ......148 C2
Tyers Terr SE11 ....149 A1
Tyler Cl E2 ....24 B3
Tyler St SE10 ....43 A1
Tylney Ho 10 E1 ....32 A3
Tymperley St SW19 .70 A3
Tyndale La N1 ....15 A1
Tyndale Mans N1 ...15 A1
Tyndale Terr 13 N1 .15 A1
Tyne St E1 ....111 A2
Tynedale Ct E14 ....42 A1
Tynemouth Cl 16
  SW11 ....60 C4
Tyneham Cl 10
  SW11 ....60 C4
Tyneham Rd SW11 .60 C4
Tynemouth St
  SW6 ....166 C2
Tynte Ct E9 ....18 A3

Tynwald Ho 14 SE26 76 C1
Type St E2 ....25 C3
Tyrawley Rd SW6 .166 A4
Tyrrell Ho SW1 .....161 A4
Tyrrell Rd SE22 .....64 C3
Tyrwhitt Rd SE4 ....66 C4
Tysoe St EC1 ....95 C3
Tyssen JMI Sch N16 .7 C3
Tyssen Rd N16 ......7 B1
Tyssen St E8 ....16 B2
  N1 ....24 A3
Tytherton 30 E2 .....25 B3
Tytherton Rd N19 ...4 C1

U

Uamvar St E14 .....34 A4
Udall St SW1 ....147 A3
Udimore Ho W10 ...30 B4
Uffington Rd NW10 .22 A4
Ufford St SE1 ....135 C4
Ufton Gr N1 ....16 A1
Ufton Rd N1 ....16 A1
Uhura Sq 18 N16 ...7 A1
Ujima Ct N19 ....5 A3
Ullin St E14 ....34 B4
Ullswater SW15 ....57 C1
Ullswater Ho SE15 .50 B4
Ullswater Rd SW13 .46 C3
Ulster Pl NW1 ......92 A1
Ulundi Rd SE3 ......53 A4
Ulva Rd SW15 ....57 C3
Ulverscroft Rd SE22 64 C2
Ulverstone Rd SE27 .75 A2
Ulysses Rd NW6 ....10 B3
Umberston St E1 ...32 A3
Umbria St SW15 ....56 C1
Una Ho 7 NW5 ......13 A2
Under Cliff SE10 ....52 B2
Undercliff Rd SE13 .67 A4
Underhill Ho 7 E14 .33 C4
Underhill Pas NW1 .82 B4
Underhill Rd SE22 ..65 A2
Underhill St NW1 ...82 B3
Undershaft EC3 ....110 A1
Underwood Ho W6 .39 A3
Underwood Rd
  E1 ....24 C1 99 C1
Underwood Row
  N1 ....97 A4
Underwood St N1 ..97 A4
Undine Rd E14 ......42 A2
Unicorn Bldg 14 E1 .32 C2
Unicorn Sch TW9 ..44 B2
Union Ct 12 SW4 ..172 A1
  2 Richmond TW10 .54 A2
Union Dr E1 ....26 A1
Union Gr SW8 ......171 C2
Union Mews SW9 ..172 A1
Union Rd SW8 .....171 B1
Union Sq N1 ....87 A3
Union St SE1 ....122 C1
  E15 ....27 C4
Union Wlk E2 ....98 C4
Union Yd W1 ....104 B1
Unity Cl NW10 ......8 C2
Unity Mews NW1 ...83 A2
Univ Coll Hospl
  WC1 ....93 A1
Univ Coll Jun Sch
  NW3 ....11 B4
Univ Coll London
  WC1 ....93 B1
  WC1 ....93 C1
  NW3 ....11 B4

Univ Coll London
continued
  W1 ....105 A1
Univ College Hospl
  (Annexe) W1 .....103 C1
Univ of East London
  E15 ....76 A3
Univ of Greenwich
  Maritime Campus
  SE10 ....52 C4
Univ of Greenwich
  Rachel Mcmillan
  Campus SE8 ......51 C4
Univ of Greenwich The
  SW15 ....68 C4
Univ of London
  WC1 ....94 A3
Univ of London (King's
  Coll Hall) SE5 ....64 A4
Univ of London (Queen
  Mary & Westfield Coll)
  E1 ....26 A1
Univ of London
  (Raymont Hall)
  SE4 ....66 A3
Univ of London
  Goldsmith's Coll
  SE14 ....51 A2
Univ of North London
  N7 ....14 A3
Univ of North London
  (Carleton Grange Hall)
  2 N7 ....13 B4
Univ of Westminster
  NW8 ....90 A1
  W1 ....92 C2
  W1 ....103 B4
  W1 ....104 B2
  W1 ....104 C3
  W1 ....104 C4
University College Sch
  NW3 ....11 B3
University Mans
  SW15 ....57 C4
University of North
  London (Tufnel Park
  Hall) N7 ....13 C4
Unwin Cl SE15 .....49 C4
Unwin Rd SW7 ....129 C2
Upbrook Mews
  W2 ....101 A1
Upcerne Rd SW10 .157 A1
Upcott Ho E9 ......17 B1
  3 E3 ....27 A2
Upgrove Manor Way 3
  SE24 ....74 C4
Upham Park Rd W4 .38 A3
Upland Rd SE22 ....64 C1
Uplands Cl SW14 ..55 A2
Upnall Ho 16 SE15 .50 B4
Upnor Way SE17 ..152 B2
Upper Addison Gdns
  W14 ....126 A4
Upper Belgrave St
  SW1 ....131 C2
Upper Berkeley St
  W1 ....103 A1
Upper Brockley Rd
  SE4 ....51 B1
Upper Brook St
  W1 ....117 B4
Upper Caldy Wlk 14
  N1 ....15 B2

Upper Cheyne Row
  SW3 ....158 A4
Upper Dengie Wlk (off
  Maldon Cl) N1 ...86 C4
Upper Grosvenor St
  W1 ....117 B3
Upper Ground SE1 .121 B2
Upper Gulland Wlk 19
  N1 ....15 B2
Upper Harley St
  NW1 ....91 C1
Upper Hawkwell Ho
  (off Maldon Cl) N1 .87 A4
Upper Holloway Sta
  N19 ....4 C2
Upper James St
  W1 ....119 A4
Upper John St W1 .119 A4
Upper Mall W6 ......39 A1
Upper Marsh SE1 ..135 A2
Upper Montague St
  W1 ....102 C3
Upper North St
  E14 ....33 C4
Upper Park Rd NW3 12 B3
Upper Phillimore Gdns
  W8 ....127 B3
Upper Rawreth Wlk (off
  Basire St) N1 ......87 A4
Upper Richmond Rd
  SW15 ....57 B3
Upper Richmond Rd W
  TW10,SW14,SW15 .55 B3
Upper St N1 ....86 A3
Upper St Martin's La
  WC2 ....120 A4
Upper Tachbrook St
  SW1 ....147 A4
Upper Terr NW3 ....2 B1
Upper Thames St
  EC4 ....123 A4
Upper Tollington Pk
  N4 ....5 C3
Upper Tooting
  Independent High Sch
  SW17 ....72 B2
Upper Tooting Park
  Mans 1 SW17 ....72 C2
Upper Tooting Pk
  SW17 ....72 B2
Upper Tooting Rd
  SW17 ....72 B1
Upper Tulse Hill
  SW2 ....74 B3
Upper Wimpole St
  W1 ....103 C4
Upper Woburn Pl
  NW1,WC1 ....93 C2
Upstall St SE5 ......48 A2
Urlwin St SE5 ....48 B4
Urlwin Wlk SW9 ....48 A2
Urmston Dr SW19 ..70 A3
Urmston Ho 8 E14 .42 B2
Ursula Mews N4 ....6 B3
Ursula St SW11 ...168 A3
Urswick Rd E5,E9 ..17 B3
Usborne Mews
  SW8 ....163 A2
Usher Rd E3 ....26 B3
Usk Rd SW11 ....59 B3
Usk St E2 ....25 C2
Utopia Village NW1 .81 B4
Uverdale Rd SW10 .157 A1
Uxbridge Rd W12 ..30 A1
Uxbridge St
  W8 ....31 C1 113 B2

V

Vaine Ho 4 E9 ......18 A2
Vale Cl W9 ....88 C3
Vale Cres SW15 ....68 A1
Vale End SE22 ......64 B3
Vale Est The W3 ...29 A1
Vale Gr N4 ....6 B4
  W3 ....28 C1
Vale of Health NW3 .2 C1
Vale Rd N4 ....6 B4
Vale Rise NW11 .....1 B3
Vale Row N5 ....6 A1
Vale Royal N7 ......14 A1
Vale Sch The SW3 .129 B2
  NW11 ....1 A2
  W3 ....29 A1
Valens Ho 1 SW2 ..74 C3
Valentia Pl SW9 ....62 C3
Valentine Ho 11
  SW4 ....61 B1
Valentine Pl SE1 ..136 A4
Valentine Rd E9 ....17 C2
Valentine Row
  SE1 ....136 A3
Valetta Rd W3 ......38 B4
Valette Ho E9 ....17 B2
Valette St E8 ....17 A2
Valiant Ho SW11 ..167 C3
Vallance Rd
  E1 ....24 C1 99 C1
Valliere Rd NW10 ..21 C2
Valmar Rd SE5 .....48 B2
Valmar Trad Est 7
  SE5 ....48 B2
Valois Ho SE1 .....138 C2
Valonia Gdns SW18 58 B1
Van Gogh Ct E14 ..42 C3
Vanbern Ho NW5 ..12 C2
Vanbrugh Ct SE11 .149 C3
Vanbrugh Fields
  SE3 ....53 B3
Vanbrugh Hill SE10,
  SE3 ....53 B3
Vanbrugh Ho 8 E9 .17 B1
Vanbrugh Park Rd
  SE3 ....53 B3
Vanbrugh Park Rd W
  SE3 ....53 B3
Vanbrugh Pk SE3 ..53 B3
Vanbrugh Rd W4 ..37 C3
Vanbrugh Terr SE3 .53 B2
Vanburgh Ho E1 ..110 C4
Vancover Ho 33 E1 .32 A1
Vanderbilt Rd SW18 71 B3
Vanderbilt Villas 1
  W12 ....39 C4
Vandon Ct SW1 ...133 A2
Vandon Pas SW1 .133 A2
Vandon St SW1 ...133 A2
Vandy St EC2 ....98 A1
Vandyke Cl SW15 ..57 C4
Vane Cl NW3 ....11 C4
Vane St SW1 ......147 A4
Vange Ho W10 .....30 B4
Vanguard Ho E8 ...17 A1
Vanneck Sq SW15 .56 C2
Vansittart St 7
  SE14 ....51 A3
Vanston Pl SW6 ..155 C2

Vantage Mews E14 .....34 B1
Vantrey Ho SE11 ....149 B3
Varcoe Rd SE16 .....40 B1
Varden St E1 ....32 A3
Vardens Rd SW11 ....59 C3
Varden Ct W3 ......28 C2
Vardon Ho SE10 ......52 B2
Varey Ho E1 ....26 A2
Varley Ho 5 NW6 ....23 C4
Varna Rd SW6 ......154 C1
Varndell St NW1 .....92 C4
Varsity Row SW14 ....45 B1
Vassal Rd SE5 ......26 A2
Vassall Rd SW9 ....163 C1
Vat Ho SW8 ....162 B2
Vauban Est SE16 ...139 A1
Vauban St SE16 ....139 A1
Vaudeville Ct N4 .....5 C2
Vaughan Ave W6 ....38 B2
Vaughan Est E2 .....98 C4
Vaughan Rd SE5 .....63 B4
Vaughan St SE16 ....41 B4
Vaughan Way E1 ...125 C2
Vaughan Williams Cl
  ....51 C3
Vauxhall Bridge Rd
  SW1 ....147 A3
Vauxhall Cross
  SE1,SW8 ....148 B1
Vauxhall Gr SW8 ...162 C4
Vauxhall Prim Sch
  ....149 A2
Vauxhall St SE11 ...149 A2
Vauxhall Sta SE11 ..148 B1
Vauxhall Wlk SE11 .149 A2
Vawdrey Cl E1 ......25 B1
Vaynor Ho N7 ....14 A4
Vectis Ct SW18 .....59 A1
Veda Rd SE13 ......66 C3
Velde Way 7 SE22 ...64 A2
Vellacott Ho W12 ....30 A3
Velletri Ho 1 E2 .....25 C3
Venables St NW8 ...101 C4
Vencourt Pl W6 .....38 C2
Venetian Rd SE5 .....48 B1
Venice Ct 15 SE5 ....48 B3
Venn Ho N1 ....85 A3
Venn St SW4 ....61 B3
Ventnor Rd SE14 ....50 C3
Venue St E14 ....34 B4
Vera Ct W2 ....100 A2
Vera Rd SW6 ......164 B4
Verbena Gdns W6 ...38 C1
Verdi Ho 2 W10 .....23 A3
Verdun Rd SW13 ....46 C3
Vere Bank SW19 ....70 B3
Vere St W1 ....104 A1
Vereker Rd W14 ....140 B1
Verity Cl W11 ....112 A4
  W11 ....31 A3
Verity Ho 15 E3 .....26 B2
Vermeer Ct E14 ......42 C3
Vermont Rd SW18 ....59 A1
Verne Ct 2 W3 ......37 B3
Verney Ho NW8 ......90 A2
Verney Rd SE16 ......40 A4
Verney Way SE16 ....40 A1
Vernon Ct NW2 ......1 B1
Vernon Ho SE11 ....149 A1
Vernon Mews W14 ..140 B3
Vernon Pl WC1 .....106 B3
Vernon Rd E3 ....26 B3

Vernon Rd continued
  SW14 ....55 C4
Vernon Rise WC1 .....95 A4
Vernon Sq WC1 ......95 A4
Vernon St W14 .....140 B3
Vernon Yd
  W11 ....31 B2 112 C4
Verona Ct 10 SE14 ...50 C4
Veronica Ho SE4 .....66 B4
Veronica Rd SW17 ...73 A2
Verran Rd SW12 .....73 A4
Verulam Ho 1 W6 ....39 B4
Verulam St EC1 ....107 B4
Vervain Ho 2 SE15 ..49 C3
Verwood Ho SW8 ...163 A1
Verwood Lo 1 E14 ...42 C2
Vesage Ct EC1 .....107 C3
Vesey Path 11 E14 ...34 A3
Vesta Rd SE4,SE14 ...51 A1
Vestry Mews 15 SE5 .49 A2
Vestry Rd SE5 ......49 A2
Vestry St N1 ....97 B4
Viaduct Pl 28 E2 ....25 A2
Viaduct St E2 ......25 A2
Vian St SE13 ....67 A4
Vibart Gdns SW2 ....74 B4
Vibart Wlk N1 ......84 B4
Vic Johnson Ho 18
  E3 ....26 B4
Vicar's Ct E1 ......125 B4
Vicar's Rd NW5 .....12 C3
Vicarage Ave SE3 ...53 C3
Vicarage Cres
  SW11 ....167 B3
  SW11 ....167 C2
Vicarage Ct 18 W8 ..128 A4
  7 SW15 ....68 C4
Vicarage Dr SW14 ...55 C2
Vicarage Gate W8 ..114 A1
Vicarage Gdns W8 ..113 C1
  SW14 ....55 C3
Vicarage Gr SE5 ....48 C2
Vicarage Mans
  ....170 A1
Vicarage Rd SW14 ...55 C3
Vicarage Wlk
  SW11 ....167 C4
Vicars Hill SE13 .....67 A3
Vicars Oth W12 .....80 B2
Viceroy Rd SW8 ....172 A4
Vickery Ct EC1 ......97 A2
Victor Cazalet Ho
  N1 ....86 A4
Victor Rd NW10 .....22 A2
Victoria & Albert Mus*
  SW7 ....129 C1
Victoria Arc SW1 ...132 B1
Victoria Ave EC2 ...110 B3
Victoria Bldgs 18
  E8 ....25 A4
Victoria Coach Sta
  SW1 ....146 A3
Victoria Cotts E1 ...111 B4
  7 Richmond TW9 ...44 C2
Victoria Ct E1 .....125 B3
  W3 ....36 C4
  5 SW4 ....61 C3
Victoria Dr SW19 ....69 C3
Victoria Emb SW1 ..120 B2
Victoria Gdns
  W11 ......31 C1 113 B2
Victoria Gr 4 W8 ...128 C2
Victoria Gr Mews
  W2 ....114 A3
Victoria Ho SW1 ...146 A2

Victoria Ho continued
  2 W12 ....30 A3
  6 SW4 ....61 C1
Victoria Ind Est W3 ..29 A4
Victoria Mans NW10 .9 A1
  8 N7 ....14 B3
Victoria Mews NW6 ..23 C4
  SW4 ....73 B3
Victoria Park Ct 11
  E9 ....17 B1
Victoria Park Ind Ctr
  E3 ....27 A2
Victoria Park Rd E9 .17 C1
Victoria Park Sq E2 ..25 B2
Victoria Pas NW8 ....89 B2
Victoria Rd 11 E14 ..34 A2
  N4 ....5 B3
  NW10 ....21 A1
  NW6 ....23 B3
  SW14 ....55 C4
Victoria Rise SW4 ...61 A4
Victoria Sq SW1 ...132 B2
Victoria St SW1 ....133 A1
Victoria Sta SW1 ...146 B4
Victoria Terr N4 .....5 C3
  NW10 ....21 A1
Victoria Villas TW9 ..54 B3
Victorian Gr N16 .....7 A1
Victorian Rd N16 .....7 B1
Victory Pl SE17 ....151 B4
  2 E14 ....33 A2
Victory Prim Sch
  SE17 ....151 A4
Victory Way SE16 ...41 A4
Victory Wharf E14 ...33 A2
Victory Wlk SE8 ....51 C2
Video Ct N4 ....5 A4
View Cl N6 ....3 B4
Viewfield Rd SW18 ..58 B1
Viking Cl 22 E3 .....26 A3
Viking Ho 8 SE5 .....48 B1
Villa Rd SW9 ......62 C4
Villa St SE17 ......151 C1
Village Cl NW3 .....11 C3
Village Mount 18
  NW3 ....11 B4
Village Sch The
  ....12 B2
Village The SW11 ...60 B4
Village Way SE21 ...63 C1
Villiers Ct SW11 ...168 B4
Villiers Ho 15 E9 ....25 B4
Villiers Rd NW2 .....8 C2
Villiers St WC2 ....120 B2
Vince St N1 ....97 C3
Vincent Cl SE16 .....41 A4
Vincent Ct N4 ....5 A3
  SW9 ....173 A3
Vincent Rd W3 ......37 B3
Vincent Sq SW1 ...147 C4
Vincent St SW1 ....147 C4
  E16 ....35 B4
Vincent Terr N1 .....86 B2
Vincents Cl SE16 ....41 A4
Vine Ct E1 ....111 C3
Vine Hill EC1 ....95 B1
Vine La SE1 ....124 B1
Vine Rd SW13 ....56 B4
Vine Sq W14 ......141 A1
Vine St EC3 ....110 C1
  W1 ....119 A3
Vine St Bridge EC1 ..95 C1
Vine Yd SE1 ....137 A4
Vinegar St E1 ......32 A1

Vinegar Yd SE1 ....138 A4
Vines Prim Sch The
  ....60 C3
Viney Ct 9 SW4 ....61 C1
Viney Rd SE13 ......67 A4
Vineyard Hill Rd
  SW19 ....70 C1
Vineyard Path
  SW14 ....55 C4
Vineyard The TW10 .54 A2
Vineyard Wlk EC1 ...95 B2
Vining St SW2,SW9 .62 C3
Vinson Ho N1 ......87 C1
Vintners Ct EC4 ...123 A4
Viola Sq W12 ......29 B2
Violet Hill NW8 .....78 C1
Violet Hill Ho NW8 ..78 C1
Violet Rd E3 ....27 A1
Violet St E2 ....25 A1
Virgil Pl W1 ....102 C3
Virgil St SE1 ......135 A2
Virginia Ct 23 SE16 .40 C4
Virginia Ho 3 E14 ...34 B2
Virginia Rd 22 E2 ...98 C3
Virginia St E1 .....125 C3
Virginia Wlk SW2 ...62 B1
Viscount Ct 9 W11 .31 C3
Viscount St EC1 ...108 C4
Vittoria Ho N1 .....85 A3
Vittoria Prim Sch
  ....85 B2
Vivian Ct NW6 .....78 A2
Vivian Ho N4 ......6 C4
Vivian Rd E3 ......26 A3
Vivian Sq SE15 .....65 A4
Vogans Mill SE1 ...139 A4
Vogler Ho 2 E1 .....32 B2
Vollasky Ho E1 ....111 B4
Voltaire
  5 Richmond TW9 ..44 B2
  2 SE5 ....49 B2
Voltaire Ct SW11 ..169 C2
Voltaire Rd SW4 ....61 C4
Vorley Rd N19 ......4 B2
Voss St E2 ....24 C2 99
Voyager Bsns Est
  SE16 ....139 B2
Vulcan Rd SE4 ......51 B1
Vulcan Sq E14 ......41 C2
Vulcan Terr SE4 ....51 B1
Vulcan Way N7 .....14 B2
Vyner Ct E5 ....7 C2
Vyner Rd W3 ......28 C2
Vyner St E2 ....25 A4

Waite St SE15 ......49 B4
Waithman St EC4 ...108 A1
Wakefield Ho 8
  SE15 ....49 C2
Wakefield Mews
  WC1 ....94 B3
Wakefield St WC1 ...94 B3
Wakeham St 9 N1 ..15 C2
Wakehurst Rd SW11 60 B2
Wakelin Ho 10 N1 ..15 A1
Wakeling Ho 8
  SE27 ....75 A1
Wakeling St 13 E14 .33 A3
Wakelyn Ho E3 .....25 B4
Wakeman Rd NW10 22 C2
Wakley St EC1 .....96 A4
Walberswick St
  SW8 ....162 B1
Walbrook EC4 .....123 B4
Walburgh St 1 E1 ...32 A3
Walcorde Ave
  SE17 ....151 A3
Walcot Gdns SE11 .149 B4
Walcot Ho 6 SE22 ..64 A4
Walcot Sq SE11 ...149 C4
Walcott St SW1 ....147 A4
Waldeck Gr SE27 ...75 A1
Waldeck Rd W4 ....44 C4
  SW14 ....55 B4
Waldeck Terr SW14 .55 B4
Waldegrave Ho 5
  SW5 ....141 C2
Waldemar Ave
  SW6 ....164 B2
Waldemar Avenue Mans
  SW6 ....164 A3
Walden Ct SW8 ....171 C4
Walden Ho SW1 ...145 C3
  SW11 ....169 B2
Walden St E1 ......32 A3
Waldo Cl SW4 .....61 B2
Waldo Rd NW10 ....22 A2
Waldron Ho 25 SW2 62 B2
Waldron Mews
  SW3 ....157 C4
Waldron Rd SW18 ..71 B1
Waleran Flats 1 SE1 152 A4
Wales Farm Rd W3 .28 C4
Waley St 1 E1 ......33 A4
Walford Ct E1 .....138 B2
Walford Ho 2 E1 ...32 A3
Walford Rd N16 .....16 A4
Walham Ct 18 NW3 .12 B3
Walham Gr SW6 ...155 B2
Walham Yd SW6 ...155 B2
Walker Ho NW1 ....83 B1
Walker's Ct 1 W1 ..119 B4
Walker's PI SW15 ...58 A3
Walkerscroft Mead
  ....75 B1
Walkinshaw Ct 14
  N1 ....15 B1
Walkynscroft 5
  SE15 ....50 A1
Wall Ct N4 ....5 B3
Wall St N1 ....15 C2
Wallace Collection*
  ....103 B3
Wallace Ho N7 ......14 B2
Wallace Rd N1,N5 ..15 B2
Wallbutton Rd SE4 .51 A1
Waller Rd SE14 .....50 C1
Wallett Ct 9 NW1 ..13 B1

Wallflower St E14 .29 B2
Wallgrave Rd SW5 142 A3
Wallingford Ave
 W10 ....30 C3
Wallis Alley SE1 .137 A4
Wallis Cl SW11 ....59 C4
Wallis Rd E9 ......18 C2
Wallorton Gdns
 SW14 ....55 C3
Wallside EC2 .....109 A3
Wallwood St E14 ..33 B4
Walm La NW2 ......9 B2
Walmer Ho 6 W10 .30 C3
Walmer Pl W1 ....102 C4
Walmer Rd
 W11 .....31 A2 112 A3
 W10 ....30 C3
Walmer St NW1 ...102 C4
Walnut Cl SE8 ....51 B4
Walnut Tree Cl
 SW13 ....46 B2
Walnut Tree Ho
 SW10 ....156 B4
Walnut Tree Rd
 SE10 ....43 A1
 Brentford TW8 ....36 A1
Walnut Tree Walk Prim
 Sch SE11 ....149 B4
Walnut Tree Wlk
 SE11 ....149 B4
Walpole Ave TW9 ..44 B1
Walpole Ct NW6 ...11 B1
 7 W14 ....39 C3
Walpole Gdns W4 ..37 B1
Walpole Mews NW8 79 B3
Walpole St SW3 ..145 A2
Walsham Cl N16 ....7 C3
Walsham Ho SE17 151 B2
 SE14 ....50 C1
Walsham Rd SE14 .50 C1
Walsingham NW8 ..79 C4
Walsingham Lo
 SW13 ....46 C2
Walsingham Mans
 SW6 ....156 B2
Walsingham Pl
 SW4,SW11 ....60 C1
Walsingham Rd E5 .7 C2
Walt Whitman Cl 6
 SE24 ....63 A3
Walter Besant Ho 20
 E1 ....25 C2
Walter Ct 5 W3 ...28 B3
Walter Green Ho
 SE15 ....50 B2
Walter Ho SW10 ..157 B2
Walter Northcott Ho 2
 NW6 ....10 C3
Walter St E2 ......25 C2
Walter Terr E1 .....32 C3
Waters Cl SE17 ...151 A3
Walters Ho SE17 ..48 A4
 8 SE5 ....49 A1
Walters Way SE23 .65 C1
Walterton Rd W9 ..23 C1
Waltham Green Ct
 SW6 ....156 A1
Waltham Ho NW8 ..78 C4
 SW9 ....173 A1
Walton Cl SW8 ...162 B2
Walton Gdns W3 ..28 A4
Walton Ho E2 ......99 A3
 SW18 ....58 C1
Walton Pl SW3 ...130 C2
Walton St SW3 ...130 B1

Walton Way W3 ....28 A4
Walworth Lower Sch
 SE17 ....151 C2
Walworth Pl SE17 151 A1
Walworth Rd SE17 151 A2
Walworth Sch
 SE17 ....152 B1
Walworth Upper Sch
 SE17 ....152 B1
Wanborough Dr
 SW15 ....69 A3
Wandle Ct 1 W12 .38 A4
Wandle Ho NW8 ..102 A4
 SW18 ....71 A4
Wandle Prim Sch
 SW18 ....71 A3
Wandle Rd SW17 ..72 A2
Wandle Way SW18 71 A3
Wandon Rd SW6 ..156 B1
Wandsworth Bridge Rd
 SW6 ....166 A2
Wandsworth Common
 Sta SW12 ....72 B4
Wandsworth Common
 West Side SW18 ..59 B2
Wandsworth Gyratory
 SW18 ....59 A2
Wandsworth High St
 SW18 ....59 A1
Wandsworth Mus
 SW18 ....58 A3
Wandsworth Plain
 SW18 ....59 A2
Wandsworth Rd
 SW8 ....162 A3
Wandsworth Road Sta
 SW4 ....171 A1
Wandsworth Town Sta
 SW18 ....59 B3
Wangford Ho 8
 SW9 ....63 A3
Wanless Rd SE24 ..63 B3
Wanley Rd SE5 ....63 C3
Wansbeck Rd E3,E9 18 B1
Wansdown Pl SW6 156 A2
Wansey St SE17 ..151 A3
Wapping Dock St 19
 E1 ....32 A1
Wapping High St
 E1 ....32 A1
Wapping La E1 .....32 A1
Wapping Sta E1 ...32 B1
Wapping Wall E1 ..32 B1
War Memorial Homes
 W4 ....45 B3
Warbeck Rd W12 ..39 B3
Warburg Ho E2 ....99 B3
Warburton Cl SE15 64 C4
Warburton Ho 6
 E8 ....25 A4
Warburton Rd 6
 E8 ....25 A4
Warburton St 6 E8 25 A4
Ward Point SE11 ..149 B3
Ward Rd N19 ....4 B1
 E15 ....27 C4
Wardalls Ho 12 SE8 51 B4
Wardell Ho 6 SE10 52 B4
Warden Rd NW5 ...12 C2
Wardens Gr SE1 ..122 C1
Wardle St E9 ......17 C3
Wardley St SW18 ..71 A4
Wardlow 3 N7 .....14 B2
Wardo Ave SW6 ..164 A4
Wardour Mews
 W1 ....105 A1

Wardour St W1 ...105 B1
Wardrobe Pl EC4 .108 B1
Wardrobe Terr
 EC4 ....122 B4
Wareham Ct 11 N1 16 A1
Wareham Ho SW8 162 C2
Warfield Rd NW10 22 C2
Warfield Yd 8
 NW10 ....22 C2
Wargrave Ho 12 ...98 C3
Warham Rd N4 .....5 C4
Warham St SE5 ...48 A3
Waring Ho 2 ....99 C3
Warley Ho N1 .....15 C2
Warley St E2 ......25 C2
Warlock Rd W9 ...23 C1
Warlters Cl N7 ....14 A4
Warlters Rd N7 ...14 A4
Warltersville Mans
 N19 ....5 A4
Warltersville Rd N4,
 N8,N19 ....5 A4
Warmington Rd
 SE24 ....63 B1
Warmley Ct 3 SE15 49 B4
Warmsworth NW1 .82 C4
Warncliffe Ho 8
 SW15 ....57 B2
Warndon St SE16 .40 B2
Warneford St E9 ..25 A4
Warner Ho NW8 ...88 C4
 SE13 ....52 A1
Warner Pl E2 ......99 C4
Warner Rd SE5 ....48 B2
Warner St EC1 ....95 B1
Warner Yd EC1 ....95 B1
Warnford Ho SW15 56 A1
Warnham WC1 .....94 C3
Warnham Ho 6
 SW2 ....74 B4
Warple Mews W3 ..38 A4
Warple Way W3,
 W12 ....38 A4
Warren Ave SW14,
 TW10 ....55 A3
Warren Cl SE21 ...75 B4
Warren Ct N1 .....85 B2
Warren Gdns E15 .19 C3
Warren Ho 2 E3 ...27 A2
Warren Mews W1 ..92 C1
Warren St W1 .....92 C1
Warren Street Sta
 NW1 ....93 A2
Warrender Rd N19 13 B4
Warriner Gdns
 SW11 ....169 B3
Warrington Cres
 W9 ....88 C2
Warrington Gdns
 W9 ....88 C1
Warton Rd E15 ....27 B4
Warwick W14 .....141 A4
Warwick Ave W9 ..88 C1
Warwick Avenue Sta
 W9 ....88 C2
Warwick Chambers
 W8 ....127 B2
Warwick Cres W2 100 C4
Warwick Ct WC1 ..107 A3
Warwick Dr SW15 ..57 A4
Warwick Gdns
 W14 ....141 A4
 N4 ....6 B3

Warwick Ho continued
 6 SW5 ....69 B4
Warwick House St
 SW1 ....119 B2
Warwick La EC4 ..108 B1
Warwick Mans
 SW5 ....141 B4
Warwick Park Sch
 SE15 ....50 A1
Warwick Pl EC4 ..108 B2
 W5 ....129 C4
 N1 ....86 C3
Warwick Pl N SW1 146 C3
Warwick Rd SW5 .141 C4
 W14 ....141 A4
Warwick Row SW1 132 B2
Warwick Sq EC4 ..108 B2
 SW1 ....146 C2
Warwick Sq Mews
 SW1 ....146 C3
Warwick St W1 ...119 A4
Warwick Way SW1 146 B3
Warwick Yd EC1 ...97 A1
Warwickshire Path
 SE8 ....51 B3
Warwickshire Rd
 N16 ....16 A4
Wasdale NW1 .....92 C3
Washbrook Ho SW2 62 C1
Washington Ho
 SW1 ....130 C3
Washington Rd
 SW13 ....46 C3
Wat Tyler Rd SE10 52 C2
Watchfield Ct 7
 W4 ....37 B1
Watcombe Cotts
 TW9 ....44 C4
Water Gdns The
 W2 ....102 B2
Water La EC3 .....124 A4
Water Mews SE15 .65 B3
Water St WC2 .....121 B4
Water Tower Ho
 W8 ....113 B1
Water Tower Pl N1 86 A3
Watercress Pl N1 ..16 A1
Waterden Rd E15 ..18 C2
Waterford Ho W11 113 A4
Waterford Rd SW6 156 A1
Watergate EC4 ...122 A4
Watergate Sch
 SE13 ....67 A3
Watergate St SE8 ..51 C4
Watergate Wlk
 WC2 ....120 B2
Waterhead NW1 ..92 C4
Waterhouse Cl
 NW3 ....11 C3
 W6 ....39 C1
Wateridge Cl E14 ..41 C3
Waterloo Bridge
 SE1,WC2 ....121 A3
Waterloo Cl E9 ....17 B3
Waterloo East Sta
 SE1 ....121 C1
Waterloo Gdns E2 25 B3
Waterloo Int Sta
 SE1 ....135 A4
Waterloo Pier SE1 134 C4
Waterloo Pl SW1 .119 B2
 Richmond TW9 ...54 B3
Waterloo Rd SE1 .135 C4
Waterloo Sta SE1 135 B4
Waterloo Terr N1 ..15 A1
Waterlow Ct NW11 .2 A4
Waterlow Rd N19 ...4 B3
Waterman St SW15 57 C4

Watermead Way E1 32 A4
Watermead Ho E9 .18 A3
Watermeadow La
 SW6 ....166 C1
Watermint Quay N16 7 C4
Waters Pl SW15 ...47 B1
Waterside Cl SE16 139 C3
 E3 ....26 B4
Waterside Pl NW1 .81 C4
Waterside Point
 SW11 ....158 B2
Waterson St E2 ...98 C4
Waterview Ho E14 33 A4
Waterworks Rd
 SW2 ....62 B1
Watford Cl SW11 .168 B4
Watford Rd E16 ...35 C4
Watkin Ho N16 .....7 B3
Watkinson Rd N7 .14 B2
Watling Ct EC4 ...109 A1
Watling Gdns NW2 10 A2
Watling St EC4 ...109 A1
Watney Cotts SW14 55 B4
Watney Mkt E1 ....32 A3
Watney Rd SW14 ..55 B4
Watney St E1 ......32 A3
Watson Cl N16 ....15 C3
Watson Ho 8 SW2 74 A4
Watson's Mews
 W1 ....102 B3
Watson's St SE8 ..51 C3
Watts Gr E3 ....34 A4
Watts Ho 6 W10 ..31 A4
Watts St E1 ....32 A1
 SE15 ....49 B2
Wavel Ct 7 E1 ....32 B1
 SW16 ....74 B1
Wavel Mews NW6 .11 A1
Wavendon Ave W4 37 C1
Waveney Ave SE15 65 A3
Waveney Cl E1 ...125 C2
Waverley Ct NW3 .11 A3
 8 NW6 ....10 A1
Waverley Pl N4 ...79 B2
Waverley Rd N8 ....5 A4
Waverley Sch (Upper)
 SE15 ....65 B3
Waverton Ho 2 E3 26 B4
Waverton Rd SW18 71 B4
Waverton St W1 ..118 A2
Wavertree Ct 9
 SW2 ....74 A3
Wavertree Rd SW2 74 B3
Waxham NW5 .....12 B3
Waxlow Rd NW10 .20 C3
Wayford St SW11 .168 B1
Wayland Ave E8 ...16 C3
Wayland Ho SW9 .173 B2
Waylett Ho SE11 .149 B1
Waylett Pl SE27 ...75 A1
Wayman Ct E8 ....17 A2
Waynflete Sq 18
 W10 ....30 C3
Waynflete St SW18 71 B2
Wayside NW11 .....1 A3
 SW14 ....55 B2
Weald Cl 10 SE16 .40 A1
Wear Pl 9 E2 ......25 A2
Weardale Ho N4 ...6 B4
Weardale Rd SE13 67 C3

Wearmouth Ho 🏽 1
E3 ....33 B4
Wearside Rd SE13 ...67 A3
Weatherbury 🖪 W2 31 C3
Weatherbury Ho 🏽 3
N19 ....4 C1
Weatherley Cl E3 ....33 B4
Weaver Cl 🏽 2 E2 ....25 A1
Weaver Ho 🏽 1 ....99 B1
Weaver St E1 24 C1 99 B1
Weaver's Field Sch
E2 ....99 B1
Weaver's La SE1 ...124 B1
Weavers Way NW1 ...83 A4
🖪 NW1 ....13 C1
Webb Ct W3 ....37 A4
Webb Ho NW8 .....161 C1
Webb Pl NW10 ....21 B2
Webb Rd SE3 ....53 B4
Webb St SE1 ....138 A1
Webb's Rd SW11 ....60 B2
Webber Row SE1 ...136 A3
Webber St SE1 ......136 A3
Webheath 🖪 NW6 ...10 B1
Webster Ho 🏽 N16 N16 16 A3
Webster Rd SE16 ....139 C1
Weddell Ho 🏽 E1 ...25 C1
Wedderburn Rd
NW3 ....11 C3
Wedgewood Ho
SW1 ....146 C1
Wedgewood Mews
W1 ....105 C1
Wedgwood Ho
SE11 ....135 B1
🖪 E2 ....25 C2
Wedlake St W10 .....23 A1
Wedmore Gdns N19 ..4 C2
Wedmore Rd N19 ....4 C1
Weech Rd NW6 ....10 C4
Weedington Rd
NW5 ....12 C3
Weedon Ho W12 .....29 C3
Weekley Sq SW11 ...59 C4
Weighhouse St
W1 ....103 C1
Weimar St SW15 .....58 A4
Weir Ho 🏽 SW12 ....73 B4
Weir Rd SW18,SW17 71 A1
SW12 ....73 B4
Weir's Pas NW1 ......93 C4
Weiss Rd SW15 ....57 C4
Welbeck Ct W14 ....140 C4
Welbeck Mans 🔟
NW6 ....10 C3
Welbeck St W1 .....104 A2
Welbeck Way W1 ...104 A2
Welby Ho N19 ....4 C4
Welby St SE5 ....48 A2
Weldon Ct SE21 .....75 B3
🖪 NW1 ....13 A1
Well Ct EC4 ....109 A1
Well La SW14 ....55 B2
Well Rd NW3 ....2 C1
Well St E9 ....17 B1
Well Wlk NW3 ....2 C1
Welland Ho SE15 ....65 B3
Welland Mews E1 ..125 C2
Welland St SE10 ....52 B4
Wellclose Sq E1 ...125 C4
Wellclose St 🏽 E1 125 C3
Wellday Ho 🏽 E9 ...18 A2

Weller Ho SE16 .....139 B3
Weller St SE1 ....136 C4
Wellers Ct NW1 ......84 A1
Wellesley Ave W6 ...39 A3
Wellesley Ct W9 .....88 C4
Wellesley Ho NW1 ...93 B3
Wellesley Pl NW1 ...93 B3
Wellesley Rd NW5 ..12 C3
W4 ....37 A1
Wellesley St E1 ......32 C4
Wellesley Terr N1 ...97 A4
Wellfit St 🖪 SE24 ...63 A4
Wellgarth Rd NW11 ..2 A3
Wellington Arch ★
SW1 ....131 C4
Wellington Bldgs
SW1 ....145 C1
🖪 E3 ....26 C2
Wellington Cl W11 .31 C3
SE14 ....50 C2
Wellington Ct NW8 ..79 C1
WC2 ....120 A4
SW1 ....130 C3
SW6 ....166 B3
SW18 ....60 A2
Wellington Gr SE10 .52 C3
Wellington Ho 🏽
NW3 ....12 B3
Wellington Hospl
(North) NW8 ....79 C1
Wellington Hospl
(South) NW8 ....79 C1
Wellington JMI Sch
E3 ....26 C2
Wellington Mans
N16 ....16 B4
Wellington Mews
SE22 ....64 C3
🖪 N7 ....14 B2
Wellington Mus (Apsley
Ho) SW1 ....131 C4
Wellington Pl NW8 ..79 C1
Wellington Rd NW8 ..79 C1
NW10 ....22 C2
SW19 ....70 C2
Wellington Row
E2 ....24 C2 99 B4
Wellington Sq
SW3 ....144 C2
Wellington St
WC2 ....120 C4
Wellington Terr 🏽
E1 ....32 A1
Wellington Way E3 .26 C2
Wells Ct 🖪 NW6 ....11 B4
N1 ....16 A3
🔳 NW6 ....23 C3
Wells Ho EC1 ....96 A4
🖪 W10 ....23 A2
🖪 SE16 ....40 B3
Wells Ho The NW3 ..11 C4
Wells House Rd
NW10 ....21 A1
Wells Park Rd SE26 76 C1
Wells Rd W12 ....39 B4
Wells Rise NW8 ......80 C3
Wells Sq WC1 ....95 A3
Wells St W1 ....105 A2
Wells Terr N4 ....5 C2
Wells Way SW7 ....129 B2
SE5 ....49 A4
Wells Yd 🖪 N7 ......14 C3
Wellside Gdns

Welsh Ho 🔟 E1 ......32 A1
Welshpool Ho 🔟
E8 ....24 C4
Welshpool St 🖪 E8 .25 A4
Welstead Ho 🖪 E1 ...32 A3
Welstead Way W4 ...38 B2
Weltje Rd W6 ....38 C2
Welton Ho E1 ....32 C4
SE5 ....49 A2
Welwyn St E2 ....25 B2
Wembury Rd N6 ....4 A4
Wemyss Rd SE3 ......53 B1
Wendell Park Prim Sch
W12 ....38 B4
Wendell Rd W12 .....38 B4
Wendle Ct SW8 .....162 A3
Wendling NW5 ....12 B3
Wendon St E3 ....26 B4
Wendover SE17 .....152 A1
Wendover Ct W1 ...103 B3
🖪 W2 ....1 C1
W3 ....20 B1
Wendover Ho W1 ...103 B3
Wendover Rd NW10 21 B3
Wengham Ho W12 ..29 C2
Wenham Ho SW8 ..170 C4
Wenlake Ho EC1 .....96 C2
Wenlock Ct N1 ....87 C1
Wenlock Rd N1 ....87 A1
Wenlock St N1 ....87 B1
Wennington Rd E3 ..25 C3
Wensdale Ho E5 ....7 C2
Wensleydale Ho 🖪
N6 ....4 B4
Wentworth Cres
SE15 ....49 C3
Wentworth Ct W6 .154 A1
SW18 ....59 A1
Wentworth Dwellings
E1 ....110 C2
Wentworth Mews
E3 ....26 B2
Wentworth St E1 ...111 A3
Werington St NW1 ..83 A1
Werter Rd SW15 ....58 A3
Wesley Ave NW10 ...20 C2
Wesley Cl SE17 ....150 B3
N7 ....5 B2
Wesley Ho SE24 .....63 C1
Wesley Rd NW10 ....20 B4
Wesley Sq W11 ....31 A3
Wesley St W1 ....103 C3
Wesleyan Pl NW5 ...13 A4
Wessex Ct SW11 ....57 C2
Wessex Gardens Prim
Sch NW11 ....1 A3
Wessex Gdns NW11 ..1 A3
Wessex Ho SE1 ....153 A1
🖪 N19 ....4 C1
Wessex St E2 ....25 B2
Wessex Way NW11 ...1 A4
West Acton Prim Sch
W3 ....28 A3
West Arbour St E1 ..32 C3
West Bank N16 ....7 A4
West Block 🔟 E1 ...32 B2
West Brompton Sta
SW5 ....141 C1
West Carriage Dr
W2 ....116 A2
West Central Ave
NW10 ....22 B2
West Central St
WC1 ....106 A2
West Cotts NW6 .....10 C3

Welsh Cromwell Rd
W14 ....141 A2
West Cross Route
W10,W11 ....30 C2
West Dulwich Sta
SE21 ....75 C3
West Eaton Pl
SW1 ....145 B4
West Eaton Pl Mews
SW1 ....145 B4
West Ella Rd NW10 ..8 A1
West End Ct NW6 ...11 A1
West End La NW6 ...78 A4
NW6 ....10 C2
West Garden Pl
W2 ....102 B1
West Gdns E1 ....32 A2
West Gr SE10 ....52 C2
West Halkin St
SW1 ....131 B2
West Hall Rd TW9 ..45 A2
West Hampstead Mews
NW6 ....11 A2
West Hampstead Sta
NW6 ....10 C2
West Hampstead
Thameslink Sta
NW6 ....10 C2
West Harding St
EC4 ....107 C2
West Heath Ave
NW11 ....1 C3
West Heath Cl NW3 ..1 C1
West Heath Ct NW11 .1 C3
West Heath Dr NW11 1 C3
West Heath Gdns
NW3 ....1 C1
West Heath Rd NW3 ..2 A1
West Hill N6 ....3 C4
West Hill Ct N6 ....3 C1
West Hill Prim Sch
SW18 ....58 C2
West Hill Rd SW18 ..58 B1
West Ho 🖪 SW12 ...73 B4
West House Cl
SW19 ....70 A3
West India Ave E14 .33 C1
West India Dock Rd
E14 ....33 C2
West India Ho 🔟
E14 ....33 C2
West India Quay Sta
E14 ....33 C2
West Kensington Ct
W14 ....140 C2
West Kensington Mans
W14 ....140 C1
West Kensington Sta
W14 ....140 C2
West La SE16 ....40 A4
West London Sta The
W3 ....37 A4
West Mall W11 ......113 C2
West Mews SW1 ...146 C3
West Norwood Sta
SE27 ....75 A1
West Park Ave TW9 .45 A2
West Park Rd TW9 ..44 C2
West Point SE1 .....153 B2
West Poultry Ave
EC1 ....108 A3
West Quarters W12 .29 C3
West Rd SW3 ....159 A4
SW4 ....61 C2
West Row W10 ....23 A1

West Sheen Vale
TW9 ....54 B3
West Smithfield
EC1 ....108 B3
West Sq SE11 ....136 A1
West St WC2 ....105 C1
🖪 E2 ....25 A3
West Temple Sheen
SW14 ....55 A2
West Tenter St E1 ..111 A1
West Warwick Pl
SW1 ....146 C3
Westacott Cl N19 ....4 C3
Westbere Rd NW2 ..10 A3
Westbourne Ave
W3 ....28 C3
Westbourne Br
W2 ....100 C3
Westbourne Cres
W2 ....115 B4
Westbourne Ct
W2 ....100 C2
Westbourne Gdns
W2 ....100 A2
Westbourne Gr
W2 ....100 A1
W2,W11 ......31 C3 113 A4
Westbourne Gr Mews 🔟
W11 ....31 C3
Westbourne Grove Terr
W2 ....100 A1
Westbourne Ho
SW1 ....146 A2
Westbourne Park Rd
W11 ....31 B3
W2 ....100 C3
Westbourne Park Sta
W11 ....31 B4
Westbourne Park Villas
W2 ....100 A3
W11 ....31 B4
Westbourne Rd N7 .14 B2
W2 ....100 C3
Westbourne St
W2 ....115 B4
Westbourne Terr
W2 ....101 A2
Westbourne Terr Mews
W2 ....100 C2
Westbourne Terr Rd
W2 ....100 C2
Westbridge Cl W12 .29 C1
Westbridge Rd
SW11 ....168 A4
Westbrook Ho
🖪 E2 ....25 B2
🖪 SW4 ....61 B2
Westbury Ct SW4 ...61 A1
Westbush Ct 🔟
W12 ....39 A4
Westchester Ct
W2 ....102 C1
Westcliffe Ho 🔟 N1 ..15 C2
Westcombe Hill
SE3 ....53 B3
Westcombe Hill
SE3,SE10 ....53 C4
Westcombe Park Rd
SE3 ....53 B3
Westcombe Park Sta
SE3 ....43 C1
Westcott Ho 🔟 E14 .34 A2
Westcott Rd SE17 ...48 A4
Westcott Road
SE17 ....150 B1
Westcroft Cl NW2 ...10 A4
Westcroft 🔟 W6 ....38 C2

Westcroft Sq W6 ....38 C2
Westcroft Way NW2 10 A4
Westdean Cl SW18 ...59 A1
Westdown Rd E15 ...76 B4
Westerdale Ct N5 ...15 B4
Westerdale Rd **2**
SE16 ....43 C1
Westerham NW1 ....82 C3
Westerham Ho
SE1 ....**137** C2
Western Ave W3 ....28 C3
Western Ct W3 .....33 B3
4 W3 ....28 C1
Western Eye Hospl The
NW1 ....**102** C4
Western La SW12 ...72 C4
Western Mews W9 .23 B1
Western Pl **15** SE16 .46 A4
Western Rd NW10 ..20 A4
Western Terr W6 ...38 C2
Western Wharf **2**
SE15 ....50 A4
Westferry Cir E14 ..33 C1
Westferry Rd E14 ..41 C3
Westferry Sta E14 .33 C2
Westfield Cl SW10 .**156** C1
Westfield Ct **1**
W10 ....22 C2
Westfield Ho **6**
SE16 ....40 C2
Westfield Way E1 ...26 A1
Westfields SW13 ...56 B4
Westfields Ave
SW13 ....56 A4
Westfields Rd W3 ..28 A4
Westfields Sch
SW13 ....56 B4
Westgate Bsns Ctr
W10 ....22 C1
2 W10 ....30 C3
Westgate Ct **16**
SW9 ....62 C4
Westgate St E8 ....25 A4
Westgate Terr
SW10 ....**156** C4
Westgrove La SE10 .52 B2
Westhay Gdns
SW14 ....55 A2
Westhill Ct W11 ...**113** A4
Westhill Pk N6 ....3 C2
Westhope Ho E2 ...**99** C3
Westhorpe Rd
SW13 ....46 C3
Westland PI N1 ....**97** B4
Westlands Terr **3**
SW12 ....61 B1
Westleigh Ave
SW15 ....57 A2
Westly Ct NW2 ....9 C2
Westmacott Ho
NW8 ....**89** C1
Westmark Point **9**
SW15 ....69 A3
Westmead SW15 ..57 A1
Westmill Ct N4 ....6 B2
Westminster Abbey*
SW1 ....**134** A2
Westminster Abbey
  Choir Sch SW1 ...**133** C2
Westminster Boating
  Base SW1 ....**161** B4
Westminster Bridge
SE1,SW1 ....**134** B3

Westminster Bridge Rd
SE1 ....**135** B2
Westminster Cath *
SW1 ....**132** C1
Westminster Cath Choir
  Sch SW1 ....**133** A1
Westminster Cath RC
  Prim Sch SW1 ....**147** C2
Westminster City CE Sch
W1 ....**110** C1
Westminster City Hall
SW1 ....**133** A2
Westminster Coll
W1 ....**119** B4
SW1 ....**133** A2
SW1 ....**147** B3
SW1 ....**169** C4
Westminster Ct
22 SE16 ....32 C1
5 SW18 ....58 C2
Westminster Gdns
SW1 ....**148** A4
Westminster Sch
SW1 ....**134** A2
Westminster Sta
SW1 ....**134** A3
Westmore Ct SW15 58 A2
Westmoreland Ho
NW10 ....21 C2
Westmoreland PI
SW1 ....**146** B1
Westmoreland Rd
SE17 ....48 C2
SW13 ....46 C3
Westmoreland St
W1 ....**103** C3
Westmoreland Terr
SW1 ....**146** B1
Weston Ct N4 ....6 B1
Weston Ed Ctr The
SE5 ....48 B1
Weston Ho **4** NW6 10 A1
E9 ....25 B4
Weston Rd W4 .....37 B3
Weston Rise WC1 ..95 A4
Weston St SE1 .....**137** C4
Weston Wlk **3** E8, E9 17 A1
Westonbirt Ct **6**
SE15 ....49 B4
Westover Hill NW3 1 C2
Westover Rd SW18 59 B1
Westpoint SW15 ...57 C1
Westpoint Trad Est
W3 ....28 A4
Westport St E1 .....32 C3
Westrow SW15 ....57 B1
Westside Ct **9**
W9 ....23 C1
Westview CI NW10 .22 B2
Westville Rd W12 ..38 C4
Westway W2 ....**100** C3
W10,W12 ....29 C2
Westway (Elevated Rd)
W10 ....30 A3
Westwell **4** NW5 ...12 C2
Westwick Gdns
W14 ....39 C4
Westwood Gdns
SW13 ....56 B4
Westwood Ho **5** N4 6 C4
W12 ....30 B1
Westwood Rd SW13 56 B4
Wetherby Gdns
SW5 ....142 C3

Wetherby Mans **2**
SW5 ....142 A2
Wetherby Mews
SW5 ....142 A2
Wetherby Pl SW5 ..**143** A3
Wetherell Rd E9 ...25 C4
Wetland Centre The
SW13 ....47 A4
Wevco Wharf SE15 .50 A4
Wexford Ho **8** E1 ...32 B4
Wexford Rd SW12 .72 B4
Wey Ho NW8 ....**89** C1
Weybourne St
SW18 ....71 B2
Weybridge Ct **18**
SE16 ....40 A1
Weybridge Ho N4 ..6 B4
Weybridge Point
SW11 ....**169** A2
Weydown Cl SW19 .70 A3
Weyhill Ho **27** SE5 .48 B1
Weyhill Rd E1 ......**111** C2
Weymouth Ct **5** E2 24 B3
15 SW2 ....74 B4
Weymouth Ho
SW8 ....**162** C1
Weymouth Mews
W1 ....**104** A4
Weymouth St W1 ..**104** A4
Weymouth Terr E2 .24 B3
Whadcoat St N4 ....5 C2
Whadden Ho **10**
SE5
Whaddon Ho SW1 .**131** A3
Wharf Pl E2 ....25 A4
Wharf Rd NW1 .....**83** C3
N1 ....**86** C1
E15 ....27 C4
Wharf St E16 ....35 A4
Wharfdale Ho **3**
N1 ....**85** A2
Wharfdale Rd N1 ..**84** B2
Wharfedale Ct **5**
E5 ....17 C4
Wharfedale St
SW10 ....142 A1
Wharfside Rd E16 .35 A4
Wharton Cl NW10 ..8 A2
Wharton Ho SE1 ..**138** C2
Wharton St WC1 ...95 A3
Whateley Rd SE22 .64 B2
Wheat Sheaf Cl E14 42 A2
Wheatland Ho **7**
SE22 ....64 A4
Wheatlands Rd
SW17 ....72 C1
Wheatley Ho NW5 .13 A4
3 SW15 ....68 C4
Wheatley St W1 ...**103** C3
Wheatsheaf La
SW8 ....**162** B2
SW6 ....47 B3
Wheatsheaf Terr
SW6 ....**155** A1
Wheatstone Ho **7**
W10 ....31 A4
Wheatstone Rd
W10 ....31 A4
Wheeler Ct **5**
SW11 ....59 C4
Wheeler Gdns N1 ..**84** B4
Wheeler La E1 ......110 C4
Wheelwright St N7 .14 B1
Wheldon Ct SE1 ...**138** C4
Wheler Ho **4**
E1 ....24 B1 C1
Wheler St E1 ....24 B1
Whellock Rd W4 ...38 A3

Whetstone Pk
WC2 ....**106** C2
Whewell Rd N19 ....**5** A2
Whichcote St SE1 ..121 B1
Whidborne Bldgs
WC1 ....94 A3
Whidborne Cl SE8 .51 C1
Whidborne St WC1 .94 A3
Whippingham Ho **17**
E3 ....26 B2
Whiskin St EC1 .....**96** A3
Whistler Mews **20**
SE8 ....51 A4
Whistler St N5 .....15 A3
Whistler Twr
SW10 ....156 C1
Whistler Wlk
SW10 ....**157** A2
Whistlers Ave
SW11 ....**157** C1
Whiston Ho **18** N1 .15 A1
Whiston Rd E2 .....24 C4
Whitbread Ctr EC1 .97 A1
Whitbread Rd SE4 .66 B3
Whitburn Rd SE13 .67 B3
White Ave NW10 ...20 A2
Whitby Ct N7 ......14 A4
Whitby Ho NW8 ....**78** C3
Whitby St E1 ....**98** C2
Whitcher Cl SE14 ..51 A4
Whitcher Pl NW1 ..13 B2
Whitchurch Ho **18**
W10 ....30 C3
Whitchurch Rd W11 30 C2
Whitcomb St WC2 .**119** C3
White Bear Pl NW3 11 C4
White Bear Yd EC1 .95 B1
White City W10 ....30 B3
White City Cl W12 .30 B2
White City Rd W12 .30 B2
White City Sta W12 30 B2
White Conduit St
N1 ....**85** C2
White Hart Ct EC2 .110 A3
White Hart La NW10 8 B2
SW13 ....56 A4
White Hart St
SE11 ....**149** C2
White Hart Yd SE1 .123 B1
White Horse La E1 .**167** C2
3 SW4 ....73 C4
White Ho The NW1 .**92** B2
White Horse La E1 .32 C4
White Horse Rd E1 .33 A3
White Horse St
W1 ....**118** B1
White Horse Yd
EC2 ....**109** B2
White Kennett St
E1 ....110 B2
White Lion Ct EC3 .110 A1
White Lion Hill
EC4 ....122 B4
White Lion St N1 ...**85** C1
White Lion Yd W1 ..118 A4
White Post La E9 ...18 C2
White Post St SE14,
SE15 ....50 B3
White's Grounds
SE1 ....**138** B4
White's Grounds Est
SE1 ....**138** B4
White's Row E1 ....110 C3
White's Sq SW4 ...61 C3
Whiteadder Way
E14 ....42 A2
Whitear Wlk E15 ...19 C2

Whitebeam Cl
SW9 ....**163** A1
Whitebeam Ho **3**
NW3 ....12 B2
Whitechapel High St
E1 ....**111** A2
Whitechapel Rd
E1 ....**111** B3
E1 ....32 A4
Whitechapel Sta E1 32 A4
Whitecliff Ho SW18 59 A1
Whitecross Pl EC2 .**109** C4
Whitecross St EC1 .**97** A1
Whitefield Cl SW15 58 A1
Whitefriars St EC4 .**107** C1
Whitehall SW1 .....**134** A4
Whitehall Ct SW1 ..**120** B1
Whitehall Gdns
SW1 ....**120** A1
W3 ....28 A1
SW14 ....55 B3
Whitehall Mans **3**
N19 ....4 B3
Whitehall Park Rd
W4 ....45 A4
Whitehall Pk N19 ...4 B3
Whitehall Pl SW1, WC2,
SW1 ....**120** A1
Whitehaven NW8 ...**90** A1
Whitehead Cl SW18 71 B4
Whitehead Ho **8**
SW5 ....57 C2
Whitehead's Gr
SW3 ....**144** B3
Whitehorn Ho E1 ...32 B1
Whitehorse Mews
SE1 ....**136** A2
Whitehorse Rd E1 .33 A4
Whitelands Coll,
  Roehampton Inst
SW18 ....70 A4
Whitelands Ho
SW3 ....**145** A2
Whiteley Ho **9**
SW4 ....73 C4
Whitelock Ho **21** E9 17 B2
Whiteness Ho **9**
SW9 ....**173** B4
Whitestone La NW3 2 B1
Whitestone Wlk NW3 2 B1
Whitethorn St E3 ..33 C4
Whitfield Ct SW4 ..**172** A3
Whitfield Gdns
W1 ....**105** A4
Whitfield Ho NW8 .**90** A1
Whitfield Pl W1 ....**93** A1
Whitfield Rd SE10,
SE13 ....52 C2
Whitfield St W1 ....**105** A4
Whitgift Ho SE11 ..**148** C4
SW11 ....**168** A4
Whitgift St SE11 ...**148** C4
Whitington Ave
EC3 ....110 A1
Whitley Ho SW1 ...**161** A4
Whitlock Dr SW19 .70 A3
Whitman Ho **20** E2 .25 B2
Whitman Rd E3 ....26 A1
Whitmore Gdns
NW10 ....22 B3
Whitmore Ho **29** E8 24 B4
Whitmore Jun & Inf Sch
N1 ....**87** C3
Whitmore Rd N1 ...24 A4

Whitnell Ct **7**
Whitnell Way SW15 ....57 C2
Whitney Ho **6** SE22 ..64 A4
Whitstable Ho **11**
  W10 ....30 C3
Whitsters Ho SE1 ....138 C4
Whittaker Ct SW4 ......172 B3
Whittaker St SW1 ......145 B3
Whittingham Ct W4 ..46 A3
Whittingstall Mans
  SW6 ....165 A3
Whittingstall Rd
  SW6 ....165 A3
Whittington Hospl The
  N19 ....4 B2
Whittlebury Ho N4 ....6 B4
Whittlesey St SE1 ....121 C1
Whitton NW3 ....12 B1
Whitton Wlk E3 ....26 C2
Whitworth Ho SE1 ..137 A1
Whitworth St SE10 ....43 A1
Whorlton Rd SE15 ....65 A4
Whytlaw Ho **11** **8** ..33 B4
Wick La E3 ....18 B1
Wick Mews **1** E9 ....18 A2
Wick Rd E9 ....18 B2
Wick Sq E9 ....18 C1
Wicker St **2** E1 ......32 A3
Wickersley Rd
  SW11 ....169 C1
Wickfield Ho SE16 ..139 C3
Wickford Ho **4** E1 ..25 B1
Wickford St E1 ....25 B1
Wickham Gdns SE4 ..66 B4
Wickham Ho E1 ......32 B4
  SW15 ....57 C1
Wickham Mews SE4 ..51 B1
Wickham Rd SE4 ......66 B3
Wickham St SE11 ....148 C2
Wicklow Ho N16 ......7 B3
Wickstead Ho TW8 ..36 B1
Wicksteed Ho SE1 ..137 A1
Wickway Ct **7** SE15 49 B4
Wickwood St SE5 ....48 A1
Widdenham Rd N7 ....14 B4
Widecombe Ho **53**
  SE5 ....48 B1
Widegate St E1 ......110 B3
Widford NW1 ....13 A2
Widford Ho N1 ....86 A1
Widley Rd W9 ....23 C1
Widnes Ho **6** N7 ....14 C3
Wigmore Hall W1 ....104 A2
Wigmore Pl W1 ......104 A2
Wigmore St W1 ......103 C2
Wigram Ct SW11 ....168 A4
Wigram Ho **6** E14 ..34 A2
Wigton Pl SE11 ......149 C1
Wilberforce Ho **4**
  SW11 ....59 C4
Wilberforce Prim Sch
  W10 ....22 B1
Wilberforce Rd N4 ..6 A2
  N4,N5 ....6 B1
Wilbraham Ho
  SW8 ....162 A1
Wilby Mews
  W11 ....31 B1 113 A2

Wilcox Cl SW8 ....162 B2
Wilcox Ho **6** E3 ......33 B4
Wilcox Pl SW1 ....133 A1
Wilcox Rd SW8 ......162 A2
Wild Ct WC2 ....106 C2
Wild Goose Dr SE14 50 B2
Wild St WC2 ....106 C1
Wild's Rents SE1 ....138 A2
Wildcroft Manor
  SW15 ....69 B4
Wildcroft Rd SW15 ..69 B4
Wilde Cl E8 ....24 C4
Wilde Pl SW18 ....71 C4
Wilderton Rd N16 ..7 A4
Wilding Ho **6** E9 ..17 C2
Wildwood Gr NW3 ..2 B3
Wildwood Rd NW11 ..2 B4
Wildwood Rise NW11 2 B3
Wildwood Terr NW3 2 B3
Wilfred Fienburgh Ho
  N7 ....13 C4
Wilfred St SW1 ......132 C2
Wilfrid Gdns W3 ......28 B4
Wilkes Rd **3** TW8 ..44 A4
Wilkie Ho SW1 ......147 C2
Wilkin St Mews NW5 13 A2
Wilkins Ho SW1 ....160 C4
Wilkinson Ho N1 ....87 C1
  17 E14 ....33 A4
Wilkinson St SW8 ..162 C1
Wilkinson Way W4 ..37 C4
Wilks Pl N1 ....24 A3
Willan Wall E16 ......35 B2
Willard St SW8 ....61 A4
Willbury Ho **6** N7 ..13 C3
Willcott Rd W3 ......28 A1
Willenfield Rd
  NW10 ....20 B3
Willes Rd NW5 ......13 A2
Willesden Community
  Hospl The NW10 ..8 C1
Willesden Green Sta
  NW2 ....9 B2
Willesden High Sch
  NW10 ....22 A4
Willesden Junction Sta
  NW10 ....21 B2
Willesden La NW2,
  NW6 ....9 C1
Willett Ho SW9 ......62 A4
William Banfield Ho
  SW6 ....164 C2
William Booth Meml
  Training Coll SE5 48 C1
William Brown Ct
  SE27 ....75 A2
William Caslon Ho **5**
  E2 ....25 A3
William Channing Ho **6**
  E2 ....25 A2
William Cl SE13 ......67 B4
William Davis Prim Sch
  E2 ....24 C1 99 B2
William Dromey Ct
  NW6 ....10 B1
William Dunbar Ho
  NW6 ....23 B3
William Ellis Sch
  NW5 ....3 C1
William Ellis Way
  SE16 ....139 C1
William Evans Ho **9**
  SE8 ....40 C2
William Gdns SW15 57 A2

William Guy Gdns **4**
  E3 ....27 A2
William Harvey Ho **3**
  SW19 ....70 A3
William IV St WC2 ..120 A3
William Margrie Cl **1**
  SE15 ....49 C1
William Mews
  SW1 ....131 A3
William Morris Acad
  W6 ....39 C1
William Morris Ho
  W6 ....47 C4
William Morris Way
  SW6 ....59 B4
William Patten JMI Sch
  N16 ....7 B2
William Rathbone Ho **8**
  E2 ....25 A2
William Rd NW1 ......92 C3
William Rushbrooke Ho
  SE16 ....153 B4
William Saville Ho **6**
  NW6 ....23 B3
Williams Ho **9** E9 ..25 A4
  9 E3 ....26 C2
  7 E14 ....33 A3
  14 SW2 ....74 C3
Williams La SW14 ....45 B1
Williamson Cl SE10 ..43 B1
Williamson Ct
  SE17 ....150 C1
Williamson St N7 ....14 A4
Willingham Cl **4**
  NW5 ....13 B3
Willingham Terr
  NW5 ....13 B3
Willington Rd SW9 ..62 A4
Willis Ho **6** E14 ....34 A2
Willis St E14 ....34 A3
Willoughby Ho
  EC2 ....109 B3
Willoughby Rd NW3 11 C4
Willoughby St
  WC1 ....106 A3
Willoughbys The
  SW14 ....56 A3
Willow Ave SW13 ....46 B1
Willow Bridge Rd
  N1 ....15 B2
Willow Cotts TW9 ....44 C4
Willow Ct EC2 ....98 A2
  SW9 ....173 B4
  N7 ....14 B3
  W4 ....46 A3
  3 SW16 ....74 A1
Willow Farm La
  SW15 ....57 A4
Willow Hall NW3 ....11 C4
Willow Ho **3** W10 ..23 B2
  W10 ....30 C3
Willow Lo SW6 ....47 C2
Willow Pl SW1 ......147 A4
Willow Rd NW3 ......11 C4
  W5 ....36 A4
Willow St
  EC2 ....24 A1 98 A2
Willow Tree Cl E3 ..26 B4

Willow Tree Cl *continued*
  SW18 ....71 A3
Willow Vale W12 ....29 C1
Willow Way W11 ....30 C1
Willow Wlk SE1 ....152 C4
Willowbank SW6 ....58 A4
Willowbank Rd
  SE15 ....49 B4
Willowbrook Rd
  1 SE5 ....50 A2
  8 SE15 ....50 A3
Willowdene N6 ......3 B4
  2 SE15 ....50 A3
Willows Terr NW10 21 B3
Willsbridge Ct **1**
  SE15 ....49 B4
Wilman Gr E8 ....16 C1
Wilmcote Ho W2 ..100 A4
Wilmer Gdns N1 ....24 A4
Wilmer Ho **6** E3 ..26 A3
Wilmer Lea Cl E15 ..19 C1
Wilmer Pl N16 ......7 B2
Wilmers Ct **5**
  NW10 ....20 C4
Wilmington Ave W4 45 C3
Wilmington Sq WC1 95 B3
Wilmington St WC1 95 B3
Wilmot Cl SE15 ......49 C3
Wilmot Pl NW1 ......13 B1
Wilmot St E2 ....25 A1
Wilna Rd SW18 ......71 B4
Wilsham St
  W11 ..31 A1 112 A2
Wilshaw Ho **10** SE8 51 C3
Wilson Gr SE16 ....40 A4
Wilson Ho **9** SW8 171 B1
Wilson Rd SE5 ......49 A2
Wilson St EC2 ......109 C4
Wilson's Pl E14 ....33 B3
Wilson's Rd W6 ....39 C1
Wilston Ct SW6 ....164 C2
Wiltern Ct NW2 ......10 A2
Wilton Ave W4 ......38 A1
Wilton Cres SW1 ..131 B3
Wilton Ct **1** E1 ......32 A3
  8 Richmond TW10 54 A2
Wilton Est E8 ....16 C2
Wilton Ho **3** SE22 64 A4
Wilton Mews SW1 ..131 C2
Wilton Pl SW1 ......131 B3
Wilton Rd SW1 ......146 C4
Wilton Row SW1 ..131 B3
Wilton Sq N1 ....87 B4
Wilton St SW1 ......132 A2
Wilton Terr SW1 ..131 B2
Wilton Villas N1 ......87 B3
Wilton Way E8 ......16 C2
Wiltshire Cl SW3 ..144 C3
Wiltshire Ct **2** N4 ..5 B3
Wiltshire Rd SW9 ..62 C4
Wiltshire Row N1 ..87 C3
Wimbart Rd SW2 ..74 B4
Wimbledon Common
  SW19 ....69 A1
Wimbledon Lawn Tennis
  Mus SW19 ....70 A3
Wimbledon Park Prim
  Sch SW19 ....71 A2
Wimbledon Park Rd
  SW18,SW19 ....70 C3
Wimbledon Park Side
  SW19 ....69 C1
Wimbledon Park Sta
  SW19 ....70 C1

Wimbledon Stadium
  Bsns Ctr SW17 ....71 A1
Wimbledon Windmill
  Mus SW19 ....69 B1
Wimbolt St
  E2 ....24 C2 99 B4
Wimborne Ho NW1 ..90 B1
  SW8 ....163 A1
  13 E16 ....76 A1
Wimbourne St N1 ..87 B2
Wimbourne St N1 ..87 B2
Wimpole Mews
  W1 ....104 A3
Wimpole St W1 ......104 A2
Winans Wlk SW9 ..173 B1
Winant Ho **17** E14 ..34 A2
Wincanton Rd
  SW18 ....70 B4
Winch Ho SW10 ..157 A2
Winchcombe Ct **6**
  SE15 ....49 A4
Winchelsea Cl
  SW15 ....57 C2
Winchelsea Ho **11**
  SE16 ....40 B4
Winchelsea Rd
  NW10 ....20 C4
Winchendon Rd
  SW6 ....165 A4
Winchester Ave
  NW6 ....10 A1
Winchester Cl
  SE17 ....150 B3
Winchester Ct **8** W8 128 A4
Winchester Ho
  W2 ....100 C1
  SW3 ....157 C3
  13 E14 ....26 B2
Winchester Pl N6 ....4 A3
  6 E8 ....16 B3
Winchester Rd N6 ..4 A3
  NW3 ....11 C1
Winchester Sq
  SE1 ....123 B2
Winchester St
  SW1 ....146 B2
  W3 ....37 B4
Winchester Wlk
  SE1 ....123 B2
Winchfield Ho
  SW15 ....56 B1
Winchilsea Ho NW8 89 C3
Wincott St SE11 ....149 C3
Windermere NW1 ..92 B4
  2 SW15 ....57 C1
Windermere Ave
  NW6 ....23 A4
Windermere Ct
  SW13 ....46 B4
Windermere Ho **3**
  E3 ....26 B1
Windermere Point **3**
  SE15 ....50 B3
Windermere Rd N19 ..4 B2
Winders Rd SW11 ..168 A2
Windham Rd TW9 ..54 B4
Windlass Pl SE8 ......41 A2
Windlesham Gr
  SW19 ....69 C3
Windmill WC1 ......106 C3
Windmill Alley **7**
  W4 ....38 A2
Windmill Cl SE1 ....153 C4
  3 SE13 ....52 B1
Windmill Ct NW2 ..10 A2
Windmill Dr SW4 ..61 A2
Windmill Hill NW3 ..2 B1

Windmill Hill continued
1 NW3 .....11 B4
Windmill Ho SE1 ....121 C1
Windmill La E15 ....19 C2
Windmill Pas 10
  W4 .....38 A2
Windmill Rd W4 ....38 A2
  SW18 .....38 C1
  SW19 .....69 A1
Windmill Row
  SE11 .....149 B1
Windmill Sq 5 SE2 ..62 A2
Windmill St W1 ....105 B3
Windmill Wlk SE1 ..121 C1
Windrose CI SE16 ...40 C4
Windrush W4 .....45 B3
  SW11 .....59 C3
Windrush Ho NW8 ..101 C4
Windsock CI 1
  SE16 .....41 B2
Windsor Ct W2 ....114 A4
  SW11 .....144 B2
  NW3 .....10 C4
  20 SE16 .....32 C1
  SW6 .....58 A4
  4 SW18 .....58 C2
  2 SW4 .....61 B3
Windsor Gdns W9 ..23 C1
Windsor Ho N1 ....87 A2
  N4 .....92 B4
  NW2 .....10 A2
  4 E2 .....25 C2
  4 W4 .....37 B1
Windsor PI SW1 ...147 A4
Windsor Rd N7 .....5 A1
  Richmond TW9 .....44 B1
  N8 .....5 B4
Windsor St N1 .....86 B4
Windsor Terr N1 ...97 A4
Windsor Way W14 ..140 A4
Windsor Wlk SE5 ..48 C1
Windspoint Dr SE15 ..50 A4
Windus Rd N16 .....7 B3
Windus Wlk N16 ....7 B3
Wine CI E1 .....32 B2
Wine Office Ct
  EC4 .....107 C2
Winfield Ho SW11 ..167 C3
Winford Ct 15 SE15 ..49 C2
Winford Ho E3 ....18 B1
Winford Ho SE10 ...52 B2
Winfrith Rd SW18 ..71 B3
Wingate Ho 3 N16 ..15 C4
  20 E3 .....27 A2
Wingate Rd W6 ....39 A3
Wingfield Ho NW6 ..78 A2
  E2 .....98 C3
Wingfield Mews
  SE15 .....64 C4
Wingfield St SE15 ..64 C4
Wingford Rd SW2 ..62 A1
Wingham 3 NW5 ..12 C2
Wingmore Rd SE24 ..63 B4
Wingrad Ho 14 E1 ..32 B4
Wingrave Rd W6 ...47 C4
Wingrave Ho NW8 ..90 B2
Wingreen NW8 .....78 B4
Winifrede Paul Ho 7
  NW5 .....13 A4
Winkley St 3 E2 ...25 A3
Winkworth Cotts 13
  E1 .....25 B1

Winnett St W1 .....119 B4
Winnington Ho 8
  SE5 .....48 B3
Winscombe St N19 ..4 A2
Winsham Gr SW11 ..60 C2
Winsham Ho NW1 ..93 C4
Winslade Rd SW2 ..62 A2
Winslade Mews
  W2 .....101 B2
Winsland St W2 ...101 B2
Winsley St W1 ....105 A2
Winslow SE17 .....152 A1
Winslow Ho 5
  SW15 .....57 C1
Winslow Rd W6 ....47 B4
Winstanley Rd
  SW11 .....59 C4
Winston Ho N16 ...15 C4
Winston Wlk 4 W4 ..37 C2
Winter Box Wlk
  TW10 .....54 B2
Winter Lo 3 SE16 ..40 A1
Winterbourne Ho
  W11 .....112 A3
Winterbrook Rd
  SE24 .....63 B1
Winterfold CI SW19 ..70 A2
Winterleys 7 NW6 ..23 B3
Winterslow Ho 20
  SE5 .....48 B1
Winterton Ho 15 E1 ..32 B3
Winterton PI
  SW10 .....157 A4
Winterwell Rd SW2 ..62 A2
Winthorpe Rd SW15 ..58 A3
Winthrop Ho 10
  W10 .....23 A2
Winthrop St 5
  E1 .....32 A4
Winton Prim Sch
  N1 .....84 C1
Wirrall Ho 15 SE26 ..76 C1
Wisden Ho SW8 ...163 A3
Wise Rd E15 .....19 C4
Wiseley Ho SW17 ..72 B2
Wiseton Rd SW17 ..147 B2
Wisley Ho SW1 ...147 B2
Wisley Rd SW11 ...60 C2
Wisteria Rd SE13 ..67 C3
Wistow Ho 14 E2 ..24 C4
Witan St E2 .....25 A2
Witanhurst La N6 ..3 C3
Witchwood Ho 6
  SW9 .....62 C4
Witcombe Point 13
  SE15 .....49 C2
Witham Ho 3 SE5 ..48 B1
Witherington Rd
  N5 .....14 C3
Withers PI EC1 ....97 A2
Withy Ho 4 E1 ....25 C1
Withy La 3 SW2 ...74 B4
Witley Point 8
  SW15 .....69 A3
Witley Ho N19 ....4 C1
Wittering Ho
  SW11 .....169 A2
Wivenhoe CI SE15 ..65 A4
  6 Prim Sch SW4 ..61 A3
Wix's La SW4 .....61 A3
Woburn Ct 12 SE16 ..40 A1
  Richmond TW9 .....54 B4
Woburn Ho NW1 ..93 C3
Woburn Sq WC1 ..93 C1
Woburn Wlk WC1 ..93 C3
Wodehouse Ave
  SE5 .....49 B2
Wodehouse Ct 10
  W3 .....37 B3

Woking CI SW15 ...56 B3
Wolcot Ho N1 .....83 A1
Wolfe Cres 24 SE16 ..40 C4
Wolfe Ho 19 W12 ..30 A2
Wolfson Ct SE1 ...139 A4
  1 NW11 .....1 A4
Wolftencroft CI
  SW11 .....59 C4
Wollaston CI SE1 ..150 C4
Wolsey Ave SW18,
  SW19
Wolseley Gdns W4 ..45 A4
Wolseley Rd W4 ...37 B2
Wolseley St SE1 ...139 A3
Wolsey Ct NW6 ....11 B1
Wolsey Mews NW5 ..13 B2
Wolsey Rd N1 .....15 C3
Wolsey St E1 .....32 B4
Wolverley St 2 E2 ..25 A2
Wolverton SE17 ...152 A2
Wolverton Gdns
  W6 .....39 C2
Wontner CI 8 N1 ..15 B1
Wontner Rd SW12,
  SW17
Wood CI E2 .24 C1 99 B2
Wood Dene 8 SE5 ..50 A2
Wood Field NW3 ..12 B3
Wood Ho SW4 ....171 C2
  6 NW6 .....23 C3
Wood La W12 .....30 B2
Wood Lane Sch
Wood Point 8 E16 ..35 C4
Wood St EC2 .....109 A2
  W4 .....38 A1
Wood Vale SE22 ...65 A1
Wood Wharf SE10 ..52 B4
Wood's Mews W1 ..117 B4
Wood's PI SE1 ....138 B1
Wood's Rd E15 ....19 C1
Woodberry Down N4 ..6 B4
  Woodberry Down JMI
Woodberry Gr N4 ..6 B4
Woodbine Terr 9 E9 ..17 B2
Woodborough Rd
  SW15 .....57 A3
Woodbourne Ave
  SW16 .....73 C1
Woodbourne CI
  SW16 .....74 A1
Woodbridge CI 10 N7 ..5 B2
Woodbridge St EC1 ..96 B2
Woodbridge St EC1 ..96 A2
Woodchester Sq
  W2 .....100 A4
Woodchurch Ho
  SW9 .....173 B4
Woodchurch Rd
  NW6 .....11 A1
Woodcock Ho 4
  E14 .....33 C4
Woodcote Ho 4
  SE8 .....51 B4
Woodcott Ho 1
  SW15 .....68 C4
Woodcroft Mews
  SE8 .....41 A2
Woodfall Rd N4 ...5 C2
Woodfall St SW3 ..144 C1
Woodfarrs SE5 ....63 C3
Woodfield Ave
  SW16 .....73 C1
Woodfield Gr SW16 ..73 C1
Woodfield PI W9 ..23 B1

Woodfield Rd W9 ..31 B4
Woodger Rd W12 ..39 B4
Woodhall NW1 ....92 C3
Woodhall Ave SE21 ..76 B1
Woodhall Dr SE21 ..76 B1
Woodhall Ho SW18 ..59 C1
Woodheyes Rd NW10 ..8 A3
Woodhurst Rd W3 ..28 B2
Woodison St E3 ...26 A1
Woodland Cres
  18 SE16 .....40 C4
  SE10 .....53 A4
Woodland St 8 E8 ..16 B2
Woodland Wlk NW3 ..12 A3
  SE10 .....43 A1
Woodlands Ave W3 ..28 A1
Woodlands Ct
  NW10 .....22 C4
Woodlands Gr SE10 ..43 A1
Woodlands Gr SW15 ..58 B2
Woodlands Park Rd
  SE10 .....43 A1
Woodlands Rd
  SW13 .....56 B4
Woodlands St SE13 ..67 C1
Woodlands The N5 ..15 B4
Woodlands Way
  SW15 .....58 B2
Woodlawn CI SW15 ..58 B2
Woodlawn Rd SW6 ..47 C2
Woodlea Rd N16 ..7 A1
Woodleigh Gdns
  SW16 .....74 A1
Woodmans Gr NW10 ..8 B3
Woodmans Mews
  W12 .....30 A4
Woodquest Ave
  SE24 .....63 B2
Woodruff Ho 2
  SW12 .....73 B4
Woodrush CI 4
  SE14 .....51 A3
Woodseer St E1 ...111 A4
Woodsford SE17 ..151 B1
Woodsford Sq
  W14 .....126 B4
Woodsome Rd NW5 ..4 A1
Woodspring Rd
  SW19 .....70 A2
Woodstar Ho 3
  SE15 .....49 C3
Woodstock Ave
  NW11 .....1 A4
Woodstock Ct
  SE11 .....149 A2
  SE12 .....97 B3
Woodstock Gr W12 ..39 C4
Woodstock Ho 2
  N5 .....15 B4
Woodstock Mews
  W1 .....103 C3
Woodstock Rd NW11 ..1 B3
  N4 .....5 C3
  W4 .....38 A3
Woodstock St W1 ..104 A1
Woodstock Terr
  E14 .....34 A2
Woodsyre SE26 ....76 B1
Woodthorpe Rd
  SW15 .....57 A3
Woodview CI N4 ...6 B4
Woodville Ct 3
  SE10 .....52 B2
Woodville Ho SE1 ..138 C2
Woodville Rd NW11 ..1 A4
  N16 .....16 A3

Woodville Rd continued
  NW6 .....23 B3
Woodwarde Rd
  SE22 .....64 A1
Woodwell St SW18 ..59 B2
Woodyard CI NW5 ..12 C3
Woodyard La SE21 ..76 A4
Woolcombes Ct 4
  SE16 .....32 C1
Wooler St SE17 ...151 C2
Woolf CI 24 N1 ....41 B3
Woolley Ho SW9 ..63 A4
Woollon Ho 1 E1 ..32 B3
Woolmore JMI Sch
  E14 .....34 B2
Woolmore St E14 ..34 B2
Woolneigh St SW6 ..166 A1
Woolpack Ho 5 E9 ..17 B2
Woolridge Way E9 ..17 B1
Woolstaplers Way
  SE16 .....153 B4
Woolstone Ho 7
  E2 .....24 C4
Woolven Ho 6 SE3 ..53 B4
Woolwich Rd SE10 ..43 B1
Wooster Gdns E14 ..34 C3
Wootton St 5
  SE1 .....121 C1
Worcester Dr W4 ..38 A4
Worcester Gdns
  SW11 .....60 B2
Worcester Ho W2 ..100 C1
  SE11 .....135 B1
  9 SW15 .....57 C2
Worcester Mews 2
  NW6 .....11 A2
Wordsworth Ho
  NW6 .....23 C2
Wordsworth PI 11
  NW5 .....12 B3
Wordsworth Rd
  N16 .....16 A4
  SE1 .....153 A3
Worfield St SW11 ..158 B1
Worgan St SE11 ..148 C2
  SE16 .....40 C2
Working Men's Coll
  NW1 .....83 A2
World's End Pas
  SW10 .....157 B2
World's End PI
  SW10 .....157 A2
Worlidge St W6 ...39 B1
Worlingham Rd
  SE22 .....64 B3
Wormholt Park Prim
  Sch W12 .....29 C2
Wormholt Rd W12 ..29 C1
Wormwood St EC2 ..110 A2
Wornington Rd
  W10 .....31 A4
Wornum Ho 3
  NW6 .....23 A3
Woronzow Rd NW8 ..80 A3
Worple St SW14 ...55 C4
Worple Way TW10 ..54 A3
Worship St
  EC2 .....97 C1
Worsopp Dr SW4 ..61 B2
Worth Gr SE17 ...151 B1
Worthington Ho
  EC1 .....95 C4
  18 SW2 .....74 C4
Wotton Rd 18 SE8 ..51 B4

Wouldham Rd E16 . . .35 B1
Wray Cres N4 . . . . .5 B2
Wray Ct N4 . . . . .5 B2
Wray Ho ⑪ SW2 . . . .74 A3
Wrayburn Ho SE16 139 C3
Wren Ave NW2 . . . . . . .9 B4
Wren Cl E16 . . . . .35 B1
Wren Ho SW1 . . . . . .147 B1
  ⑰ E3 . . . . .26 A3
Wren Landing E14 . .33 C1
Wren Rd SE5 . . . . . . .48 C2
Wren St WC1 . . . . . . .95 A2
View View N6 . . . . .4 B3
Wrentham Ave
  NW10 . . . . .22 C3
Wrestlers Ct EC3 . .110 A2
Wrexham Rd E3 . . . . .26 C3
Wrigglesworth St
  SE14 . . . . .50 C3
Wright Cl SE13 . . . . .67 C3
Wright Ho SW15 . . . .57 A2
Wright's Gn SW4 . . . .61 C3
Wright's La W8 . . . .128 A2
Wright's Rd E3 . . . . .26 B3
Wrotham Ho SE1 . .137 C2
Wrotham Rd ⑪
  NW1 . . . . .13 B1
Wrottesley Rd
  NW10 . . . . .21 C3
Wroughton Rd
  SW11 . . . . .60 B1
Wroxton Rd SE15 . . .50 B1
Wulfstan St W12 . . . .29 B3
Wyatt Cl SE16 . . . . . .41 B4
Wyatt Dr SW13 . . . . .47 A3
Wyatt Ho NW8 . . . . . .89 C1
  SE3 . . . . .53 B1
Wyatt Park Mans ⑪
  SW2 . . . . .74 A2
Wyatt Park Rd SW2 .74 B2
Wyatt Rd N5 . . . . .6 B1
Wybert St NW1 . . . . .92 C2

Wycherley Cl SE3 . . .53 B3
Wychwood End N6 . . .4 B4
Wychwood Ho N4 . . . .6 B4
Wyclif Ct EC1 . . . . . .96 A3
Wyclif St EC1 . . . . . .96 A3
Wycliffe Ho ⑱ N16 .16 A4
Wycliffe Rd SW11 .169 C1
  ⑦ SW11 . . . . .60 C4
Wycombe Ct SE3 . . . .53 C3
Wycombe Gdns
  NW11 . . . . .1 C2
Wycombe Ho NW8 . .90 A2
Wycombe Pl SW18 . .59 B1
Wye St SW11 . . . . . .167 C1
Wyersdale Ho N4 . . . .6 B4
Wyfold Rd SW6 . . . .154 A1
Wyke Rd E3 . . . . .18 C1
Wyldes Cl NW11 . . . . .2 B3
Wyleu St SE23 . . . . . .66 A1
Wyllen Cl E1 . . . . . . .25 B1
Wymering Mans ⑥
  W9 . . . . .23 C2
Wymering Rd W9 . . . .23 C2
Wymond St SW15 . . .57 B4
Wynan Rd E14 . . . . . .42 A1
Wynard Terr SE11 . .149 A2
Wyndham Cres N19 . .4 B1
Wyndham Deedes Ho ⑰
  E2 . . . . .24 C3
Wyndham Ho SW1 145 B3
Wyndham Mews
  W1 . . . . .102 C3
Wyndham Pl W1 . . .102 C3
Wyndham Rd SE5 . . .48 B3
Wyndham St W1 . . .102 C4
Wyndham Yd W1 . . .102 C3
Wyneham Rd SE24 . .63 C2
Wynford Ho N1 . . . . .85 A2
Wynford Rd N1 . . . . .85 A2
Wynne Ho SE14 . . . . .50 C2
Wynne Rd SW9 . . . .173 B1
Wynnstay Gdns
  W8 . . . . .127 C2

Wynter Ho SW9 . . . .173 A1
Wynter St SW11 . . . . .59 B3
Wynton Pl W3 . . . . . .28 A3
Wynyard Ho SE11 . .149 A2
Wynyatt St EC1 . . . . .96 A4
Wytham Ho NW8 . . . .89 C1
Wythburn Ct W1 . . .102 C2
Wythburn Pl W1 . . .102 C2
Wyvil Prim Sch
  SW8 . . . . .162 B2
Wyvil Rd SW8 . . . . .162 A2
Wyvis St E14 . . . . . . .34 A4

Y

Yabsley St E14 . . . . . .34 B1
Yaldam Ho SE1 . . . .152 A3
Yalding Ho ⑳ E5 . . .17 A3
Yalding Rd SE16 . . .153 B4
Yale Ct NW6 . . . . .11 A3
Yardley St WC1 . . . . .95 B3
Yarmouth Pl W1 . . .118 A1
Yarnfield Sq ⑭
  SE15 . . . . .49 C2
Yarrow Ho W10 . . . . .30 B4
  ⑩ E14 . . . . .42 B3
Yates Ct NW2 . . . . . . .9 C2
Yates Ho E2 . . . . .99 C4
Yatesbury Ct E5 . . . . .18 A3
Yatton Ho W10 . . . . .30 B4
Yeadon Ho W10 . . . . .30 B4
Yearby Ho W10 . . . . .22 B1
Yeate St N1 . . . . .15 C1
Yeats Cl NW10 . . . . . .8 A2
Yeldham Ho W6 . . . . .39 C1
Yeldham Rd W6 . . . . .39 C1
Yelverton Rd
  SW11 . . . . .167 C1
Yeo St E3 . . . . .34 A4
Yeoman Cl SE27 . . . . .75 A1
Yeoman Ho SE1 . . . .153 A2
Yeoman St SE8 . . . . .41 A2
Yeoman's Row
  SW3 . . . . .130 B1
Yeoman's Yd E1 . . . .125 A4

Yeovil Ho N7 . . . . .5 B2
  W10 . . . . .22 B1
Yerbury Prim Sch
  N19 . . . . .4 C1
Yerbury Rd N19 . . . . .4 C1
Yesodey Hatorah Gram
  Sch N16 . . . . .7 B4
Yew Gr NW2 . . . . .9 C4
Yew Ho SE14 . . . . . . .51 B1
Yew Tree Rd W12 . . .29 B2
Yewfield Rd NW10 . . .8 B2
Yoakley Rd N16 . . . . .7 A2
Yoke Cl N7 . . . . .14 A2
Yonge Pk N4,N7 . . . . .5 C1
York Ave SE17 . . . . .151 A2
  SW14 . . . . .55 B2
York Bldgs WC2 . . . .120 B3
York Bridge NW1 . . .91 B2
York Cl ⑰ SE5 . . . . .48 B1
York Gate NW1 . . . . .91 C1
York Gr SE15 . . . . . . .50 B2
York Hill SE27,SW16 .75 A1
York Ho N1 . . . . .84 C1
  W1 . . . . .102 C4
  W8 . . . . .128 A4
  SE1 . . . . .135 A1
  SW3 . . . . .145 A2
  ⑧ N1 . . . . .13 C2
  N5 . . . . .14 C3
  W3 . . . . .28 B2
  Richmond TW9 . . . .44 C2
  Richmond TW10 . . .54 C2
York House Pl W8 . .128 A4
York Mans W1 . . . . .103 B4
  SW11 . . . . .169 C4
York Mews NW5 . . . .13 A3
York Pl WC2 . . . . . . .120 B3
  SW11 . . . . .59 C4
York Place Mans
  NW1 . . . . .103 A4
York Rd SE1 . . . . . . .135 A4
  W3 . . . . .28 C3
  ④ Richmond TW10 . .54 A2

York Rd Bsns Ctr
  SW11 . . . . .167 C1
York Rise NW5 . . . . . .4 A1
York Sq ⑭ E14 . . . . .33 A3
York St W1 . . . . .103 A4
York St Chambers
  W1 . . . . .102 C4
York Terr E NW1 . . . .91 C1
York Terr W NW1 . . . .91 B1
York Way N1 . . . . .84 B3
  N1 . . . . .14 A1
  N1,N7,NW1 . . . . . . .14 A1
Yorkley Ho W10 . . . . .22 B1
Yorkshire Cl N16 . . . .7 A1
Yorkshire Grey Yd
  WC1 . . . . .106 C3
Yorkshire Rd E14 . . .33 A3
Yorkton St E2 . . . . . .24 C3
Young St W8 . . . . . .128 A3
Young's Bldgs EC1 . .97 A2
Youngs Ct SW11 . . .169 C3
Yoxall Ho W10 . . . . . .22 B1
Yukon Rd SW12 . . . . .73 A4
Yuletide Cl NW10 . . . .8 A2

Z

Zampa Rd SE16 . . . . .40 B1
Zander Ct E2 . . .24 C2,99 C4
Zangwill Ho NW6 . . .23 B3
Zealand Ho ⑪ SE5 . .48 B1
Zealand Rd E3 . . . . . .26 A3
Zennor Rd SW12 . . . .73 B3
Zenoria St SE22 . . . . .64 B3
Zetland Ho W8 . . . . .128 A2
Zetland St E14 . . . . . .34 B4
Zion Ho ⑥ E1 . . . . . . .32 B3
Zoar St SE1 . . . . .122 C2
Zodiac Ho ⑧ E3 . . . .26 C1
Zoffany St N19 . . . . . .4 C2

List of numbered locations

This atlas shows thousands more place names than any other London street atlas. In some busy areas it is impossible to fit the name of every place.

Where not all names will fit, some smaller places are shown by a number. If you wish to find out the name associated with a number, use this listing.

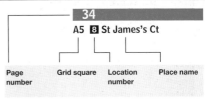

| Page number | Grid square | Location number | Place name |

1

B1
1 Mortimer Cl
2 Sunnyside Ho
3 Sunnyside
4 Prospect Pl
B4
1 Berkeley Ct
2 Exchange Mans
3 Beechcroft Ct
4 Nedahall Ct
C1
1 Portman Hts
2 Hermitage Ct
3 Moreland Ct
4 Wendover Ct

4

B1
1 Hunter Ho
2 Fisher Ho
3 Lang Ho
4 Temple Ho
5 Palmer Ho
B2
1 Flowers Mews
2 Sandridge St
3 Bovingdon Cl
4 Laurel Cl
5 Forest Way
6 Larch Cl
7 Pine Cl
8 Alder Mews
10 Aspen Cl
B3
1 Calvert Ct
2 Academy The
3 Whitehall Mans
4 Pauntley St
5 Archway Hts
6 Pauntley Ho
C1
1 Melchester Ho
2 Norcombe Ho
3 Weatherbury Ho
4 Wessex Ho
5 Archway Bsns Ctr
C2
1 Bowerman Ct
2 Hargrave Mans
3 Church Garth
4 John King Ct
C3
1 Louise White Ho
2 Levison Way
3 Sanders Way
C4
1 Eleanor Rathbone Ho

2
2 Christopher Lo
3 Monkridge
4 Marbleford Ct
5 High London
6 Garton Ho
7 Hilltop
8 Caroline Martyn Ho
9 Arthur Henderson Ho
10 Margaret Mcmillan Ho
11 Enid Stacy Ho
12 Mary McArthur Ho
13 Bruce Glasier Ho
14 Keir Hardie Ho
15 Monroe Ho
17 Iberia Ho
18 Lygoe Ho
19 Lambert Ho
20 Shelbourne Ho
21 Arkansas Ho
22 Lafitte Ho
24 Shreveport Ho
25 Packenham Ho
26 Orpheus Ho
27 Fayetville Ho
28 Bayon Ho

5
A1
1 Northview
2 Tufnell Park Mans
A2
1 Christie Ct
2 Ringmer Gdns
3 Kingsdown Rd
4 Cottenham Ho
5 St Paul's Ct
6 Rickthorne Rd
7 Stanley Terr
A3
1 Beeches The
A4
1 Marie Lloyd Gdns
2 Jessie Blythe La
3 Leyden Mans
4 Lochbie
B2
1 Berkeley Wlk
2 Lazar Wlk
3 Thistlewood Cl

3
4 Tomlins Wlk
5 Andover Ho
6 Barmouth Ho
7 Chard Ho
8 Methley Ho
9 Rainford Ho
10 Woodbridge Cl
11 Allerton Wlk
12 Falconer Wlk
13 Sonderburg Rd
B3
1 Lawson Ct
2 Wiltshire Ct
3 Hutton Ct
C2
1 Brookfield
2 Churnfield

6
B4
1 Finmere Ho
2 Keynsham Ho
3 Kilpeck Ho
4 Knaresborough Ho
5 Leighfield Ho
6 Lonsdale Ho
7 Groveley Ho
8 Wensleydale Ho
9 Badminton Ct
C2
1 Chestnut Cl
2 Sycamore Ho
3 Lordship Ho
4 Clissold Ho
5 Beech Ho
6 Laburnum Ho
7 Ormond Ho
8 Selwood Ho
9 Mendip Ho
10 Ennerdale Ho
11 Delamere Ho
12 Westwood Ho
13 Bernwood Ho
14 Allerdale Ho
15 Chattenden Ho
16 Farningham Ho
17 Oakend Ho

7
A1
1 Gujarat Ho
2 Marton Rd
3 Painsthorpe Rd
4 Selkirk Ho

3
5 Defoe Ho
6 Edward Friend Ho
7 Sheridan Ho
8 Barrie Ho
9 Arnold Ho
10 Macaulay Ho
11 Stowe Ho
12 Carlyle Ho
13 Shaftesbury Ho
14 Lillian Cl
15 Swift Ho
16 Dryden Ho
17 Scott Ct
18 Kingsfield Ho
19 Uhura Sq
A3
1 Godstone Ct
2 Farnham Ct
3 Milford Ct
4 Cranleigh Ct
5 Haslemere Ct
6 Belmont Ct
7 Hockworth Ho
8 Garratt Ho
9 Fairburn Ho
B1
1 Lawrence's Bldgs
2 Cottage Wlk
3 Batley Pl
B2
1 Garnham St
2 Garnham Ct
3 Sanford La
4 Sanford Wlk
B3
1 Stamford Hill Mans
2 Montefiore Ct
3 Berwyn Ho
4 Clent Ho
5 Chiltern Ho
6 Laindon Ho
7 Pentland Ho
B4
1 Regent Ct
2 Stamford Lo
3 Holmwood Ct
C1
1 Ravenscourt
2 Mellington Ct
3 Rendlesham Ho
4 Florence Ct
5 Burnaston Ho
C2
1 Cazenove Mans
2 Chedworth Ho
3 Aldergrove Ho
4 Abbotstone Ho

3
5 Briggeford Cl
6 Inglethorpe Ho
7 Ashdown Ho
C3
1 Stamford Grove E
2 Stamford Mans
3 Grove Mans
4 Stamford Grove W

8
C2
1 Regency Mews
2 Tudor Mews

10
A1
1 Fountain Ho
2 Kingston Ho
3 Waverley Ct
4 Weston Ho
5 Mapes Ho
6 Athelstan Gdns
7 Leff Ho
B1
1 Alma Birk Ho
2 Brooklands Ct
3 Brooklands Court Apartments
4 Cleveland Mans
5 Buckley Ct
6 Webheath
C1
1 Dene Mans
2 Kings Wood Ct
3 Embassy Ho
4 Acol Ct
5 Kings Gdns
6 Douglas Ct
7 King's Gdns
8 Carlton Mans
9 Smyrna Mans
10 New Priory Ct
11 Queensgate Pl
12 Brondesbury Mews
C2
1 Dene Mans
3 Sandwell Cres
4 Sandwell Mans
5 Hampstead West
6 Redcroft
C3
1 Melaris Mans
2 Walter Northcott Ho
3 Polperro Mans
4 Lyncroft Mans
5 Marlborough Mans

12 Jethou Ho
14 Upper Caldy Ho
15 Caldy Ho
16 Alderney Ho
17 Marquess Rd S
18 Oronsay Wlk
19 Upper Gulland Wlk
20 Gulland Wlk
B3 1 Pearfield Ho
2 Larchfield Ho
3 Beresford Ter
4 Pondfield Ho
5 Ashfield Ho
6 Elmfield Ho
B4 1 Fountain Mews
2 Woodstock Ho
3 Henson Ct
4 Taverner Sq
C2 1 John Kennedy Ct
2 John Kennedy Lo
3 Ball's Pond Pl
4 Haliday Wlk
5 Mason Bradbear Ct
6 Ramsey Wlk
7 Rona Wlk
8 Threadgold Ho
9 Wakeham St
10 Saffron Ct
11 Callaby Terr
12 Tilney Gdns
13 Westcliff Ho
14 Ilford Ho
15 Ongar Ho
16 Greenhills Terr
17 Romford Ho
C4 1 Ledo Ho
2 Salween Ho
3 Prome Ho
4 Arakan Ho
5 Rangoon Ho
6 Mandalay Ho
7 Karen Ho
8 Wingate Ho
9 Jubet Ho
10 Orde Ho
11 Chindit Ho
12 Mabel Thornton Ho
13 Crawshay Ho
14 Avon Ho
15 Connaught Mans
16 Jonson Ho
17 Herrick Ho
18 Donne Ho
19 Grasmere Ho
20 Thirlmere Ho

16
A1 1 Dorchester Ct
2 Wareham Ct
3 Dorset Ct
4 Stratton Ct
5 Swanage Ct
6 Blandford Ct
7 Portland Ct
8 Oscar Faber Pl
9 Lancaster Cl
A2 1 Kingsland Gn
2 Kingsland Pas
3 Metropolitan Benefit Societies Almshouses
4 Nimrod Pas
5 De Beauvoir Ct
A3 1 Hewling Ho
2 Matthias Ho

3 Port Royal Pl
4 Cressington Cl
5 King Henry's Yd
6 Bronte Ho
7 Sewell Ho
8 Lydgate Ho
9 Patmore Ho
10 Congreve Ho
11 Elton St
12 Conrad Ho
13 Southwell Ho
14 Neptune Ho
15 Campion Ho
16 Webster Ho
17 Meredith Ho
18 Beckford Ho
19 Ashley Ct
20 Hayling Cl
21 Millard Cl
22 Lydford Cl
23 Salcombe Rd
24 Truman's Rd
25 Templeton Cl
26 John Campbell Rd
27 Gillett Pl
28 Bradbury St
A4 1 Londesborough Ho
2 Knebworth Ho
3 Knebworth Rd
4 Bransby Ct
5 Imperial Ave
6 Leonard Pl
7 Shakspeare Mews
8 Binyon Ho
9 Shelley Ho
10 Browning Ho
11 Burns Ho
12 Andrew Marvell Ho
13 Wycliffe Ho
14 Blake Ho
15 Marlowe Ho
16 Fletcher Ho
17 Chaucer Ct
B1 1 Hilborough Rd
2 Shoreditch Ct
B2 1 Prospect Ho
2 Woodland St
3 Crosby Wlk
4 Kirkland Wlk
5 Bowness Cl
6 Carlisle Wlk
7 Skelton Cl
8 Camerton Cl
9 Buttermere Wlk
10 Houghton Cl
B3 1 Miller's Terr
2 Chow Sq
3 Drysdale Flats
4 Gateway Mews
5 Birkbeck Mews
6 Winchester Pl
B4 1 Coronation Ave
2 Morris Blitz Ct
3 Shacklewell Ho
4 Alexandra Ct
C1 1 Aldington Ct
2 Bayton Ct
3 Rochford Wlk
C3 1 Kingsdown Ho
2 Glendown Ho
3 Moredown Ho
4 Blakeney Cl
5 Beeston Cl
6 Benabo Ct
7 David Devine Ho
8 Kreedman Wlk

9 Hermitage Row
10 Grafton Ct
11 Lushington Terr

17
A1 1 Fortescue Ave
2 Pemberton Pl
3 Weston Wlk
4 Bayford St Ind Ctr
5 Bayford St
6 Sidworth St
7 Helmsley St
A2 1 Bohemia Pl
2 Graham Mans
3 Marvin St
4 Boscobel Ho
5 Royal Oak Rd
6 Colonnades The
7 Sylvester Ho
8 Sylvester Path
9 Doctor Spurstowe Almshos
10 Great Eastern Bldgs
11 Sojourner-Truth Cl
A3 1 Birchington Ho
2 Bicknor Ho
3 Boxley Ho
4 Adisham Ho
5 Cranbrook Ho
6 Marden Ho
7 Broome Ho
8 Crandale Ho
9 Cheriton Ho
10 Ditton Ho
11 Langley Ho
12 Dymchurch Ho
13 Elham Ho
14 Bodney Mans
15 Pembury Ho
16 Downs Ct
17 Perrywood Ho
18 Stapelhurst Ho
19 Pegwell Ho
20 Yalding Ho
21 Northbourne Ho
22 Monkton Ho
23 Milsted Ho
24 Athlone Cl
25 Clarence Pl
26 Gould Terr
27 Quested Ct
28 Brett Pas
29 Marcon Ct
A4 1 Sutherland Point
2 Embley Point
3 Downs La
4 Gaviller Pl
5 Robert Owen Lo
6 Apprentice Way
7 Arrowe Ct
8 Gilwell Ct
9 Sutton Ct
10 Kinnoull Mans
11 Rowhill Mans
12 Sladen Pl
13 Mothers Sq The
14 Richborough Ho
15 Sandgate Ho
16 Sheppey Ho
B1 1 Pitcairn Ho
2 Lyme Grove Ho
3 Shakespeare Ho
4 Upcott Ho
5 Loddiges Ho

6 Parkinson Ho
7 Sloane Ho
8 Vanbrugh Ho
9 Cambridge Pas
10 Lyttelton Ho
11 Victoria Park Ct
12 Tullis Ho
13 Fairchild Ho
14 Forsyth Ho
15 Tradescant Ho
16 Mason Ho
17 Capel Ho
18 Cordwainers Ct
19 Bridgeman Ho
20 St Thomas's Pas
21 Barclay Ho
22 Clayton Ho
23 Danby Ho
24 Sherard Ho
25 Catesby Ho
26 Petiver Cl
27 Leander Ct
28 Philip Turner Est
29 Grendon Ho
30 Shore Mews
31 Shore Bsns Ctr
32 Kendal Ho
33 Classic Mans
34 Tudor Ho
35 Park Ho
B2 1 Woolpack Ho
2 Elvin Ho
3 Thomas Ho
4 Hockley Ho
5 Retreat Ho
6 Butfield Ho
7 Brooksbank Ho
8 Cresset Ho
9 Brooksbank St
10 Lennox Ho
11 Milborne Ho
12 Collent Ho
13 Middlesex Ho
14 Devonshire Hall
15 Brent Ho
C1 1 Stuart Ho
2 Gascoyne Ho
3 Chelsfield Point
4 Sundridge Ho
5 Banbury Ho
C2 1 Musgrove Ho
2 Cheyney Ho
3 Haynes Ho
4 Warner Ho
5 Gilby Ho
6 Gadsden Ho
7 Risley Ho
8 Baycliffe Ho
9 Sheldon Ho
10 Offley Ho
11 Latimer Ho
12 Ribstone Ho
13 Salem Ho
14 Fieldwick Ho
15 Lever Ct
16 Matson Ho
17 Wilding Ho
18 Rennell Ho
19 Dycer Ho
20 Granard Ho
21 Whitelock Ho
22 Harrowgate Ho
23 Cass Ho
C4 1 Cromford Path
2 Longford Ct
3 Overbury Ho

6 Heanor Ct
7 Wharfedale Ct
8 Ladybower Ct
9 Ilkeston Ct
10 Derby Ct
11 Rushmore Cres
12 Blackwell Cl

18
A2 1 Wick Mews
2 Wellday Ho
3 Selman Ho
4 Vaine Ho
5 Trower Ho

19
C4 1 Mulberry Ct
2 Rosewood Ct
3 Gean Ct
4 Blackthorn Ct
5 Cypress Ct

20
1 Fitzsimmons Ct
2 Bernard Shaw Ho
3 Longlents Ho
4 Mordaunt Ho
5 Wilmers Ct

22
C2 1 Westfield Ct
2 Tropical Ct
3 Chamberlayne Mans
4 Quadrant The
5 Queens Park Ct
6 Warfield Yd
7 Cherrytree Ho

23
A1 1 Sycamore Wlk
2 Westgate Bsns Ctr
3 Buspace Studios
4 Bosworth Ho
5 Golborne Gdns
6 Appleford Ho
7 Adair Twr
8 Gadsden Ho
9 Southam Ho
10 Norman Butler Ho
11 Thompson Ho
12 Wells Ho
13 Paul Ho
14 Olive Blythe Ho
15 Katherine Ho
16 Breakwell Ct
17 Pepler Ho
18 Edward Kennedy Ho
A2 1 Onslow Ho
2 Slomon Ho
3 Stansbury Ho
4 Tilleard Ho
5 Tolhurst Ho
6 Selby Ho
7 Severn Ho
8 Mundy Ho
9 Macfarren Ho
10 Mounsey Ho
11 Courtville Ho

12 Croft Ho
13 Batten Ho
14 Bantock Ho
15 Banister Ho
A3 1 Lancefield Ct
2 Verdi Ho
3 Wornum Ho
B2 1 Boyce Ho
2 Farnaby Ho
3 Danby Ho
4 Purday Ho
5 Naylor Ho
6 Novello Ho
7 Leeve Ho
8 Longhurst Ho
9 Harrington Ct
10 Mulberry Ct
11 Quilter Ho
12 Romer Ho
13 Kilburn Ho
B3 1 Claremont Ct
2 William Saville Ho
3 Western Ct
4 Bond Ho
5 Crone Ct
6 Wood Ho
7 Winterleys
8 Carlton Ho
9 Fiona Ct
10 Kilburn Ho
C1 1 Westside Ct
2 Sutherland Ct
C2 1 Masefield Ho
2 Austen Ho
3 Fielding Ho
4 Park Bsns Ctr
5 John Ratcliffe Ho
6 Wymering Mans
C3 1 Wells Ct
2 Cambridge Ct
3 Durham Ct
C4 1 Ryde Ho
2 Glengall Pass
3 Leith Yd
4 Daynor Ho
5 Varley Ho
6 Sandby Ho
7 Colas Mews
8 Bishopsdale Ho
9 Lorton Ho
10 Marshwood Ho
11 Ribblesdale Ho
12 Holmesdale Ho
13 Kilburn Vale Est
14 Kilburn Bridge

24

A1 1 Bracer Ho
2 Scorton Ho
3 Fern Cl
4 Macbeth Ho
5 Oberon Ho
6 Buckland Ct
7 Crondall Ho
8 Osric Path
9 Caliban Twr
10 Celia Ho
11 Juliet Ho
12 Bacchus Wlk
13 Malcolm Ho
14 Homefield St
15 Crondall Pl
16 Blanca Ho

17 Miranda Ho
18 Falstaff Ho
19 Charmian Ho
20 Myrtle Wlk
21 Arden Ho
22 Sebastian Ho
23 Stanway Ct
24 Jerrold St
25 Rosalind Ho
26 Cordelia Ho
27 Monteagle Ct
28 John Parry Ct
29 James Anderson Ct
30 Ben Jonson Ct
A4 1 Portelet Ct
2 Trinity Ct
3 Rozel Ct
4 St Helier Ct
5 Corbiere Ho
6 Kenning Ho
7 Higgins Ho
8 Cavell Ho
9 Girling Ho
10 Fulcher Ho
11 Francis Ho
12 Norris Ho
13 Kempton Ho
14 Nesham Ho
15 Crossbow Ho
16 Catherine Ho
17 Strale Ho
18 Horner Hos
19 Stringer Hos
20 Whitmore Ho
21 Nightingale Ho
22 Fletcher Ho
23 Arrow Ho
24 Archer Ho
25 Meriden Ho
26 Rover Ho
27 Bowyer Ho
28 Longbow Ho
29 Tiller Ho
30 Canalside Studios
31 Bishopgate
32 Holburn
33 Fenchurch
B3 1 Queensbridge Ct
2 Godwin Ho
3 Kent Ct
4 Brunswick Ho
5 Weymouth Ct
6 Sovereign Mews
7 Dunloe Ct
8 Cremer Bsns Ctr
9 James Hammett Ho
10 Allgood St
11 Horatio St
12 Cadell Ho
13 Horatio Ho
14 Shipton Ho
B4 1 Hilborough Ct
2 Scriven Ct
3 Livermere Ct
4 Angrave Ct
5 Angrave Pas
6 Benfleet Ct
7 Belford Ho
8 Orme Ho
9 Clemson Ho
10 Longman Ho
11 Lowther Ho
12 Lovelace Ho
13 Harlowe Ho

14 Pamela Ho
15 Samuel Ho
16 Acton Ho
17 Loanda Cl
18 Phoenix Cl
19 Richardson Cl
20 Thrasher Cl
21 Mary Secole Cl
22 Canal Path
23 Pear Tree Cl
24 Hebden Ct
25 Charlton Ct
26 Laburnum Ct
27 Mansfield Ct
C3 1 London Terr
2 Sturdee Ho
3 Maude Ho
4 Haig Ho
5 Jellicoe Ho
6 Ropley St
7 Guinness Trust Bldgs
8 Ion Sq
9 Moye Cl
10 Morrel Ct
11 Courtauld Ho
12 Drummond Ho
13 Atkinson Ho
14 Gurney Ho
15 Halley Ho
16 Goldsmith's Sq
17 Ken Wilson Ho
18 Shahjalal Ho
19 Crofts Ho
20 April Ct
21 Sebright Ho
22 Beechwood Ho
23 Gillman Ho
24 Cheverell Ho
25 Besford Ho
26 Dinmont Ho
27 Wyndham Deedes Ho
28 Sheppard Ho
29 Mary James Ho
30 Hadrian Ct
31 Blythendale Ho
32 George Vale Ho
33 Lion Mills
34 Pritchard Ho
C4 1 Broke Wlk
2 Rochemont Wlk
3 Marlborough Ave
4 Rivington Wlk
5 Magnin Cl
6 Gloucester Sq
7 Woolstone Ho
8 Marsworth Ho
9 Cheddington Ho
10 Linslade Ho
11 Cosgrove Ho
12 Blisworth Ho
13 Eleanor Ct
14 Wistow Ho
15 Muscott Ho
16 Boxmoor Ho
17 Linford Ho
18 Pendley Ho
19 North Church Ho
20 Debdale Ho
21 Broadway Market Mews
22 Welshpool Ho
23 Ada Ho

25

A1 1 Rochester Ct
2 Weaver Ct
3 Greenheath Bsns Ctr
4 Glass St
5 Herald St
6 Northesk Ho
7 Codrington Ho
8 Heathpool Ct
9 Mocatta Ho
10 Harvey Ho
11 Blackwood Ho
12 Rutherford Ho
13 Bullen Ho
14 Fremantle Ho
15 Pellew Ho
16 Ashington Ho
17 Dinnington Ho
18 Bartholomew Sq
19 Steeple Ct
20 Orion Ho
21 Fellbrigg St
22 Eagle Ho
23 Sovereign Ho
24 Redmill Ho
25 Berry Ho
26 Grindall Ho
27 Collingwood Ho
A2 1 Charles Dickens Ho
2 Adrian Bolt Ho
3 William Rathbone Ho
4 Southwood Smith Ho
5 Rushmead
6 William Channing Ho
7 John Cartwright Ho
8 Charles Darwin Ho
9 Thomas Burt Ho
10 John Fielden Ho
11 Gwilym Maries Ho
12 Joseph Priestley Ho
13 Wear Pl
14 John Nettleford Ho
15 Thornaby Ho
16 Stockton Ho
17 Barnard Ho
18 Gainford Ho
19 Stapleton Ho
20 James Middleton Ho
21 Kedleston Wlk
22 Queen Margaret Flats
23 Hollybush Ho
24 Horwood Ho
25 Norden Ho
26 Newcourt Ho
27 Seabright St
28 Viaduct Pl
A3 1 Dinmont St
2 Marian St
3 Claredale Ho
4 Bradley Ho
5 Connett Ho
6 Winkley St
7 Temple Dwellings
8 Argos Ho
9 Helen Ho
10 Lysander Ho

11 Antenor Ho
12 Paris Ho
13 Nestor Ho
14 Hector Ho
15 Ajax Ho
16 Achilles Ho
17 Priam Ho
18 Peabody Est
19 Felix St
20 Cambridge Cres
21 Peterley Bsns Ctr
22 Beckwith Ho
23 Parminter Ind Est
24 Ted Roberts Ho
25 Cambridge Ct
26 West St
27 Millennium Pl
28 William Caslon Ho
29 Hugh Platt Ho
30 Mayfield Ho
31 Apollo Ho
A4 1 Welshpool St
2 Broadway Ho
3 Regents Wharf
4 London Wharf
5 Warburton Ho
6 Warburton St
7 Triangle Rd
8 Warburton Rd
9 Williams Ho
10 Booth Cl
11 Albert Cl
12 King Edward Mans
13 Victoria Bldgs
B1 1 Annie Bldgs
2 Donegal Ho
3 Frederick Charrington Ho
4 Wickford Ho
5 Braintree Ho
6 Doveton Ho
7 Doveton St
8 Cephas Ho
9 Sceptre Ho
10 Stothard Ho
11 Stothard St
12 Redclyf Ho
13 Winkworth Cotts
14 Ryder Ho
15 Hadleigh Ho
16 Hadleigh Cl
17 Amiel St
18 Stathard Ho
19 Barbanel Ho
20 Colebert Ho
21 Kenton Ho
22 Ibbott St
23 Stannard Cotts
24 Rennie Cotts
25 Rickman St
26 Rickman Ho
27 Pemell Cl
28 Pemell Ho
29 Leatherdale St
30 Gouldman Ho
31 Lamplighter Cl
32 Hamilton Lo
33 Cleveland Gr
34 Montgomery Lo
35 Bardsey Pl
36 Cromwell Lo
37 Colin Winter Ho
38 Mayfield Ho
B2 1 Mulberry Ho
2 Gretton Ho
3 Merceron Ho

4 Montfort Ho
5 Westbrook Ho
6 Sugar Loaf Wlk
7 Museum Ho
8 Burnham Est
9 Globe Terr
10 Moravian St
11 Shepton Hos
12 Mendip Hos
13 Academy Ct
14 Pepys Ho
15 Swinburne Ho
16 Moore Ho
17 Morris Ho
18 Burns Ho
19 Milton Ho
20 Whitman Ho
21 Shelley Ho
22 Keats Ho
23 Dawson Ho
24 Bradbeer Ho
25 Forber Ho
26 Hughes Ho
27 Silvester Ho
28 Rogers Est
29 Pavan Ct
30 Stafford Cripps Ho
31 Sidney Godley (VC) Ho
32 Butler Ho
33 Butler St
34 Thorne Ho
35 Bevin Ho
36 Tuscan Ho
B3 1 Evesham Ho
2 James Campbell Ho
3 Thomas Hollywood Ho
4 James Docherty Ho
5 Ebenezer Mussel Ho
6 Jameson Ct
7 Edinburgh Cl
8 Roger Dowley Ct
9 Sherbrooke Ho
10 Calcraft Ho
11 Burrard Ho
12 Dundas Ho
13 Ponsonby Ho
14 Barnes Ho
15 Paget Ho
16 Ponsonby Ho
17 Maitland Ho
18 Chesil Ct
19 Reynolds Ho
20 Cleland Ho
21 Goodrich Ho
22 Rosebery Ho
23 Sankey Ho
24 Cyprus Pl
25 Royston St
26 Stainsbury St
27 Hunslett St
28 Baildon
29 Brockweir
30 Tytherton
31 Malmesbury
32 Kingswood
B4 1 Halkett Ho
2 Colville Ho
3 Fane Ho
4 Christ Church Sq
5 Swingfield Ho
6 Greenham Ho

7 Dinmore Ho
8 Anstey Ho
9 Weston Ho
10 Carbroke Ho
11 Layton Ho
12 Smetheton Ho
13 Dawnay Ho
14 Wakelyn Ho
15 Villiers Ho
16 Paveley Ho
17 Manneby Ho
18 Kidron Way
19 Georgian Ct
20 Park Cl
21 Regency Ct
22 Norris Ho
C1 1 Raynham Ho
2 Pat Shaw Ho
3 Colmar Cl
4 Withy Ho
5 Stocks Ct
6 Downey Ho
7 Bay Ct
8 Sligo Ho
9 Pegasus Ho
10 Barents Ho
11 Biscay Ho
12 Solway Ho
13 Bantry Ho
14 Aral Ho
15 Pacific Ho
16 Magellan Ho
17 Levant Ho
18 Adriatic Ho
19 Genoa Ho
20 Hawke Ho
21 Palliser Ho
22 Ionian Ho
23 Weddell Ho
C2 1 Stubbs Ho
2 Holman Ho
3 Clynes Ho
4 Windsor Ho
5 Gilbert Ho
6 Chater Ho
7 Ellen Wilkinson Ho
8 George Belt Ho
9 Ayrton Gould Ho
10 O'Brian Ho
11 Sulkin Ho
12 Jenkinson Ho
13 Bullards Pl
14 Sylvia Pankhurst Ho
15 Mary Macarthur Ho
16 Trevelyan Ho
17 Wedgwood Ho
18 Pemberton Ct
19 Walter Besant Ho
20 Barber Beaumont Ho
21 Brancaster Ho
22 Litcham Ho
C3 1 Kemp Ho
2 Piggott Ho
3 Mark Ho
4 Sidney Ho
5 Pomeroy Ho
6 Puteaux Ho
7 Doric Ho
8 Modling Ho
9 Longman Ho
10 Ames Ho
11 Alzette Ho
12 Offenbach Ho

13 Tate Ho
14 Norton Ho
15 St Gilles Ho
16 Harold Ho
17 Velletri Ho
18 Bridge Wharf
19 Gathorne St
20 Bow Brook The
21 Palmerston Ct
22 Lakeview

26
A1 1 Formosa Ho
2 Galveston Ho
3 Arabian Ho
4 Coral Ho
5 Anson Ho
6 Lindop Ho
7 Moray Ho
8 Azov Ho
9 Sandalwood Cl
10 Broadford Ho
A3 1 Bunsen Ho
2 Bunsen St
3 Beatrice Webb Ho
4 Margaret Bondfield Ho
5 Wilmer Ho
6 Sandall Ho
7 Butley Ct
8 Josseline Ct
9 Dalton Ho
10 Brine Ho
11 Ford Cl
12 Viking Cl
13 Stanfield Rd
14 Ruth Ct
15 School Bell Cloisters
16 Schoolbell Mews
17 Medhurst Cl
18 Olga St
19 Conyer St
20 Diamond Ho
21 Daring Ho
22 Crane Ho
23 Exmoor Ho
24 Grenville Ho
25 Hyperion Ho
26 Sturdy Ho
27 Wren Ho
28 Ardent Ho
29 Senators Lo
30 Hooke Ho
31 Mohawk Ho
32 Ivanhoe Ho
B2 1 Trellis Sq
2 Sheffield Sq
3 Howcroft Ho
4 Astra Ho
5 Byas Ho
6 George Lansbury Ho
7 Regal Pl
8 Coburn Mews
9 Cavendish Terr
10 Buttermere Ho
11 Tracy Ho
12 Coniston Ho
13 St Clair Ho
14 Verity Ho
15 Icarus Ho
16 Whippingham Ho
17 Winchester Ho

18 Hamilton Ho
19 Longthorne Ho
B3 1 Roman Square Mkt
2 John Bond Ho
3 McKenna Ho
4 Dennis Ho
5 McBride Ho
6 Libra Rd
7 Dave Adams Ho
8 Tay Ho
9 Sleat Ho
10 Ewart Pl
11 Brodick Ho
12 Lunan Ho
13 Mull Ho
14 Sinclairs Ho
15 Driftway Ho
16 Clayhall Ct
17 Berebinder Ho
18 Stavers Ho
19 Barford Ho
20 Partridge Ho
21 Gosford Ho
22 Gullane Ho
23 Cruden Ho
24 Anglo Rd
25 Dornoch Ho
26 Dunnet Ho
27 Enard Ho
28 Fraserburgh Ho
29 Forth Ho
30 Ordell Ct
B4 1 Hampstead Wlk
2 Waverton Ho
3 Elton Ho
4 Locton Gn
5 Birtwhistle Ho
6 Clare Ho
7 Cavan Ho
8 Antrim Ho
9 Tait Ct
10 Ranwell Ho
11 Ranwell Cl
12 Tufnell Ct
13 Pulteney Ct
14 Vic Johnson Ho
C1 1 Fairmont Ho
2 Healey Ho
3 Zodiac Ho
4 Buick Ho
5 Consul Ho
6 Bentley Ho
7 Cresta Ho
8 Daimler Ho
9 Riley Ho
10 Jensen Ho
11 Lagonda Ho
12 Ireton St
13 Navenby Wlk
14 Burwell Wlk
15 Leadenham Ct
16 Sleaford Ho
C2 1 Jarret Ho
2 Marsalis Ho
3 Lovette Ho
4 Drapers Almshouses
5 Mallard Point
6 Creswick Wlk
7 Bevin Ho
8 Huggins Ho
9 Williams Ho
10 Harris Ho
11 Marina Ct
12 Electric Ho
13 Matching Ct

14 Wellington Bldgs
15 Grafton Ho
16 Columbia Ho
17 Berkeley Ho

27
A1 1 Broxbourne Ho
2 Roxford Ho
3 Biscott Ho
4 Stanborough Ho
5 Hillstone Ct
A2 1 Bradley Ho
2 Prioress Ho
3 Alton Ho
4 Foxley Ho
5 Munden Ho
6 Canterbury Ho
7 Corbin Ho
8 Barton Ho
9 Jolles Ho
10 Rudstone Ho
11 Baxter Ho
12 Baker Ho
13 Insley Ho
14 Hardwicke Ho
15 Glebe Terr
16 Priory St
17 Sadler Ho
18 Ballinger Point
19 Henshall Point
20 Dorrington Point
21 Warren Ho
22 Fairlie Ct
23 Regent Sq
24 Hackworth Point
25 Priestman Point
26 Wingate Ho
27 Nethercott Ho
28 Thelbridge Ho
29 Bowden Ho
30 Kerscott Ho
31 Southcott Ho
32 Birchdown Ho
33 Upcott Ho
34 Langmead Ho
35 Limscott Ho
36 Northleigh Ho
37 Huntshaw Ho
38 Chagford Ho
39 Ashcombe Ho
40 Shillingford Ho
41 Patrick Connolly Gdns
42 Lester Ct
43 Franklin St
44 Taft Way
45 Madison Ct
46 Elizabeth Ho
47 William Guy Gdns
48 Denbury Ho
49 Holsworthy Ho

28
A1 1 Lantry Ct
2 Rosemount Ct
3 Moreton Terr
4 Acton Central Ind Est
5 Rufford Twr
6 Narrow St
7 Mount Pl
8 Sidney Miller Ct

B1
1 Mill Hill Terr
2 Rectory Rd
3 Derwentwater Mans
4 Market Pl
5 Hooper's Mews
6 Cromwell Pl
7 Locarno Ct
8 Edgecote Cl
9 Harleyford Manor

B3
1 Avon Ct
2 Bromley Lo
3 Walter Ct
4 Lynton Terr
5 Acton Ho
6 Fells Haugh
7 Springfield Ct
8 Tamarind Ct
9 Lynton Ct

C3
1 Rosebank Gdns
2 Roseabank
3 Edinburgh Ho
4 Western Ct
5 Kilronan

30

A2
1 Abercrombie Ho
2 Bathurst Ho
3 Brisbane Ho
4 Bentinck Ho
5 Ellenborough Ho
6 Lawrence Cl
7 Mackenzie Cl
8 Carteret Ho
9 Calvert Ho
10 Winthrop Ho
11 Auckland Ho
12 Blaxland Ho
13 Havelock Cl
14 Hargraves Ho
15 Hudson Cl
16 Phipps Ho
17 Lawson Ho
18 Hastings Ho
19 Wolfe Ho
20 Malabar Ct
21 Commonwealth Ave
22 Charnock Ho
23 Canning Ho
24 Cornwallis Ho
25 Champlain Ho
26 Grey Ho
27 Durban Ho
28 Baird Ho
29 Campbell Ho
30 Mitchell Ho
31 Denham Ho
32 Mackay Ho
33 Evans Ho
34 Daws Ho
35 Mandela Cl

C1
1 Katherine's Wlk
2 Dorrit Ho
3 Pickwick Ho
4 Dombey Ho
5 Saunders Ho
6 Mortimer Ho
7 Nickleby Ho
8 Stebbing Ho
9 Boxmoor Ho
10 Poynter Ho
11 Swanscombe Ho
12 Darnley Terr
13 Norland Ho
14 Hume Ho

C2
1 Frinstead Ho
2 Hurstway Wlk
3 Testerton Wlk
4 Grenfell Wlk
5 Grenfell Twr
6 Barandon Wlk
7 Treadgold Ho
8 St Clements Ct
9 Willow Way
10 Florence Ho
11 Dora Ho
12 Carton Ho
13 Agnes Ho
14 Marley Ho

C3
1 Kelfield Ct
2 Downing Ho
3 Crosfield Ho
4 Robinson Ho
5 Girton Villas
6 Ray Ho
7 Walmer Ho
8 Goodrich Ct
9 Arthur Ct
10 Whitstable Ho
11 Kingsnorth Ho
12 Bridge Cl
13 Prospect Ho
14 Whitchurch Ho
15 Blechynden Ho
16 Waynflete Sq
17 Bramley Ho

31

A3
1 Malton Mews
2 Lancaster Lo
3 Manning Ho
4 Galsworthy Ho
5 Hudson Ho
6 Cambourne Mews
7 Camelford Ct
8 Camelford Wlk
9 Talbot Grove Ho
10 Clarendon Wlk
11 Kingsdown Cl

A4
1 Murchison Ho
2 Macaulay Ho
3 Chesterton Ho
4 Chiltern Ho
5 Lionel Ho
6 Watts Ho
7 Wheatstone Ho
8 Telford Ho
9 Golborne Mews
10 Millwood St
11 St Columb's Ho

B3
1 Tavistock Mews
2 Silvester Ho
3 Melchester
4 Clydesdale Ho
5 Pinehurst Ct
6 Colville Sq Mews
7 Denbigh Ho

B4
1 Blagrove Rd
2 Tavistock Ho
3 Leamington Ho

C3
1 Shottsford
2 Tolchurch
3 Casterbridge
4 Sandbourne
5 Anglebury
6 Weatherbury
7 Westbourne Gr Mews
8 Rosehart Mews
9 Viscount Ct
10 Hereford Mans
11 Hereford Ho

C4
1 Ascot Ho
2 Ashgrove Ct
3 Lockbridge Ct
4 Swallow Ct
5 Nightingale Lo
6 Hammond Lo
7 Penfield Lo
8 Harvey Lo
9 Hunter Lo
10 Barnard Lo
11 Falcon Lo
12 Johnson Lo
13 Livingstone Lo
14 Nuffield Lo
15 Finch Lo
16 Polesworth Ho
17 Oversley Ho
18 Derrycombe Ho
19 Buckshead Ho
20 Combe Ho
21 Culham Ho
22 Dainton Ho
23 Devonport Ho
24 Hanwell Ho
25 Truro Ho
26 Sunderland Ho
27 Stonehouse Ho
28 Riverford Ho
29 Portishead Ho
30 Mickleton Ho
31 Keyham Ho
32 Moulsford Ho
33 Shrewsbury Mews
34 St Stephen's Mews

32

A1
1 China Ct
2 Wellington Terr
3 Stevedore St
4 Portland Sq
5 Reardon Ho
6 Lowder Ho
7 Meeting House Alley
8 Farthing Fields
9 Oswell Ho
10 Park Lo
11 Doughty Ct
12 Inglefield Sq
13 Chopin's Ct
14 Welsh Ho
15 Hilliard Ho
16 Clegg St
17 Tasman Ho
18 Ross Ho
19 Wapping Dock St
20 Bridewell Pl
21 New Tower Bldgs
22 Tower Bldgs
23 Chimney Ct
24 Jackman Ho
25 Fenner Ho
26 Franklin Ho
27 Frobisher Ho
28 Flinders Ho
29 Chancellor Ho
30 Beechey Ho
31 Reardon Path
32 Parry Ho
33 Vancover Ho
34 Willoughby Ho
35 Sanctuary The
36 Dundee Ct
37 Pierhead Wharf
38 Scandrett St

A2
1 Newton Ho
2 Richard Neale Ho
3 Maddocks Ho
4 Cornwall St
5 Brockmer Ho
6 Dellow Ho
7 Bewley Ho
8 Artichoke Hill

A3
1 Jacob Mans
2 Wicker St
3 Langdale St
4 Walford Ho
5 Welstead Ho
6 Peter Best Ho
7 Sly St
8 Barnett St
9 Kinder St
10 Richard St
11 Sarah Ho
12 Mellish Ho
13 Dickson Ho
14 Joscoyne Ho
15 Bridgen Ho
16 Wilton Ct
17 Silvester Ho
18 Greenwich Ct
19 Tylney Ho
20 Damien Ct
21 Siege Ho
22 Melwood Ho
23 Colstead Ho
24 Hungerford St
25 Burwell Cl
26 Chapman Ho
27 Tarling Ho
28 Sheridan St
29 Brinsley St
30 Dunch St
31 Luke Ho
32 Turnour Ho
33 Norton Ho

B1
1 John Rennie Wlk
2 Malay Ho
3 Wainwright Ho
4 Riverside Mans
5 Shackleton Ho
6 Whitehorn Ho
7 Wavel Ct
8 Prusom's Island

B2
1 Gosling Ho
2 Vogler Ho
3 Donovan Ho
4 Knowlden Ho
5 Chamberlain Ho
6 Moore Ho
7 Thornewill Ho
8 Fisher Ho
9 All Saints Ct
10 Coburg Dwellings
11 Lowood Ho
12 Solander Gdns
13 Chancery Bldgs
14 Ring Ho
15 Juniper St
16 Gordon Ho
17 West Block
18 North Block
19 South Block

B3
1 Woollon Ho
2 Dundalk Ho
3 Anne Goodman Ho
4 Newbold Cotts
5 Kerry Ho
6 Zion Ho
7 Longford Ho
8 Bromehead St
9 Athlone Ho
10 Jubilee Mans
11 Harriott Ho
12 Brayford Sq
13 Clearbrook Way
14 Rochelle Ct
15 Winterton Ho
16 Sheridan Ho
17 Brinsley Ho
18 Dean Ho
19 Foley Ho
20 Robert Sutton Ho
21 Montpelier Pl
22 Masters Lo
23 Steel's La

B4
1 Fulneck
2 Gracehill
3 Ockbrook
4 Fairfield
5 Dunstan Hos
6 Cressy Ct
7 Cressy Hos
8 Callahan Cotts
9 Wexford Ho
10 Sandhurst Ho
11 Colverson Ho
12 Beckett Ho
13 Jarman Ho
14 Wingrad Ho
15 Armsby Ho
16 Miranda Cl
17 Drake Ho
18 Louise De Marillac Ho
19 Sambrook Ho
20 St Vincent De Paul Ho
21 Jean Pardies Ho
22 Clichy Ho
23 Le Moal Ho
24 Odette Duval Ho
25 Dagobert Ho
26 Charles Auffray Ho
27 Boisseau Ho
28 Paymal Ho
29 Ewhurst Ho

C1
1 Clarence Mews
2 Raleigh Ct
3 Katherine Cl
4 Woolcombes Ct
5 Tudor Ct
6 Quayside Ct
7 Princes Riverside Rd
8 Surrey Ho
9 Tideway Ct
10 Edinburgh Ct
11 Falkirk Ct
12 Byelands Ct
13 Gwent Ct
14 Lavender Ho
15 Abbotshade Rd
16 Bellamy's Ct
17 Blenheim Ct
18 Sandringham Ct
19 Hampton Ct
20 Windsor Ct
21 Balmoral Ct
22 Westminster Ct

C2
1 Barnardo Gdns
2 Roslin Ho
3 Glamis Est
4 Peabody Est
5 East Block
6 Highway Trad Ctr The
7 Highway Bsns Pk The
8 Cranford Cotts
9 Ratcliffe Orch
10 Scotia Bldg
11 Mauretania Bldg
12 Compania Bldg
13 Sirius Bldg
14 Unicorn Bldg
C3
1 Pattison Ho
2 St Thomas Ho
3 Arbour Ho
4 Bladen Ho
5 Antill Terr
6 Billing Ho
7 Dowson Ho
8 Lipton Rd
9 Chalkwell Ho
10 Corringham Ho
11 Ogilvie Ho
12 Edward Mann Cl
13 Lighterman Mews
C4
1 Roland Mews
2 Morecambe Cl
3 Stepney Green Ct
4 Milrood Ho
5 Panama Ho
6 Galway Ho
7 Caspian Ho
8 Darien Ho
9 Rigo Ho
10 Flores Ho
11 Taranto Ho
12 Aden Ho
13 Frances Grey Ho
14 Master's St
15 Searle Ho
16 Diggon St

33
A2
1 St Georges Sq
2 Drake Ho
3 Osprey Ho
4 Fleet Ho
5 Gainsborough Ho
6 Victory Pl
7 Challenger Ho
8 Conrad Ho
9 Lock View Ct
10 Shoulder of Mutton Alley
11 Frederick Sq
12 Helena Sq
13 Elizabeth Sq
14 Sophia Sq
15 William Sq
A3
1 Coltman Ho
2 Repton Ho
3 Causton Cotts
4 Delmane Ho
5 Culpepper Ho
6 Shaw Ho
7 Williams Ho
8 Jerome Ho
9 Darnley Ho
10 Mercer's Cotts
11 Troon Ho
12 Ratcliffe Ho

13 Wakeling St
14 York Sq
15 Anglia Ho
16 Cambria Ho
17 Caledonia Ho
18 Ratcliffe La
19 Bekesbourne St
20 John Scurr Ho
21 Regents Canal Ho
A4
1 Waley St
2 Edith Ramsay Ho
3 Andaman Ho
4 Atlantic Ho
5 Pevensey Ho
6 Solent Ho
7 Lorne Ho
8 Cromarty Ho
9 Hearnshaw Ho
10 Hawksmoor Ho
11 Hemlington Ho
12 Greaves Cotts
13 Donaghue Cotts
14 Ames Cotts
15 Maroon Ho
16 Blount Ho
17 Wilkinson Ho
18 Aylward Ho
B2
1 Hamilton Ho
2 Imperial Ho
3 Oriana Ho
4 Queens Ct
5 Brightlingsea Pl
6 Faraday Ho
7 Ropemaker's Fields
8 Oast Ct
9 Mitre The
10 Bate St
11 Joseph Irwin Ho
12 Padstow Ho
13 Bethlehem Ho
14 Saunders Cl
15 Roche Ho
16 Stocks Pl
17 Trinidad Ho
18 Grenada Ho
B3
1 Dora Ho
2 Flansham Ho
3 Gatwick Ho
4 Ashpark Ho
5 Newdigate Ho
6 Midhurst Ho
7 Redbourne Ho
8 Southwater Cl
9 Aithan Ho
10 Britley Ho
11 Cheadle Ho
12 Elland Ho
13 Butler Ho
14 Fitzroy Ho
15 Leybourne Ho
B4
1 Wearmouth Ho
2 Elmslie Point
3 Grindley Ho
4 Stileman Ho
5 Baythorne St
6 Wilcox Ho
7 Robeson St
8 Couzens Ho
9 Perley Ho
10 Whytlaw Ho
11 Printon Ho
12 Perkins Ho
13 Bowry Ho
14 Booker Cl
15 Tunley Gn
16 Callingham Cl

18 Tasker Ho
C2
1 West India Ho
2 Birchfield Ho
3 Elderfield Ho
4 Thornfield Ho
5 Gorsefield Ho
6 Arborfield Ho
7 Colborne Ho
8 East India Bldgs
9 Compass Point
10 Salter St
11 Kelly Ct
12 Flynn Ct
13 Mary Jones Ho
C3
1 Landin Ho
2 Charlesworth Ho
3 Gurdon Ho
4 Trendell Ho
5 Menteath Ho
6 Minchin Ho
7 Donne Ho
8 Dennison Ho
9 Anglesey Ho
10 Gough Wlk
11 Baring Ho
12 Hopkins Ho
13 Granville Ho
14 Gladstone Ho
15 Russell Ho
16 Pusey Ho
17 Overstone Ho
18 Stanley Ho
C4
1 Bredel Ho
2 Linton Ho
3 Matthews Ho
4 Woodcock Ho
5 Limborough Ho
6 Maydwell Ho
7 Underhill Ho
8 Meyrick Ho
9 Ambrose Ho
10 Carpenter Ho
11 Robinson Ho
12 Bramble Ho
13 Bilberry Ho
14 Bracken Ho
15 Berberis Ho
16 Busbridge Ho

34
A2
1 Westcott Ho
2 Corry Ho
3 Malam Gdns
4 Devitt Ho
5 Leyland Ho
6 Wigram Ho
7 Willis Ho
8 Balsam Ho
9 Finch's Ct
10 Poplar Bath St
11 Lawless St
12 Storey Ho
13 Abbot Ho
14 Landon Wlk
15 Goodhope Ho
16 Goodfaith Ho
17 Winant Ho
18 Lubbock St
19 Goodwill Ho
20 Martindale Ho
21 Holmsdale Ho
22 Norwood Ho
23 Constant Ho
A3
1 Colebrook Ho
2 Essex Ho

3 Salisbury Ho
4 Maidstone Ho
5 Osterley Ho
6 Norwich Ho
7 Clarissa Ho
8 Elgin Ho
9 Shaftesbury Ho
10 Shepherd Ho
11 Jeremiah St
12 Elizabeth Cl
13 Chilcot Cl
14 Fitzgerald Ho
15 Vesey Path
16 Ennis Ho
17 Kilmore Ho
A4
1 Sumner Ho
2 Irvine Ho
3 David Ho
4 Brushwood Ho
5 Limehouse Cut
6 Colmans Wharf
7 Foundary Ho
8 Radford Ho
B2
1 Discovery Ho
2 Mountague Pl
3 Virginia Ho
4 Collins Ho
5 Lawless Ho
6 Carmichael Ho
7 Commodore Ho
8 Mermaid Ho
9 Bullivant St
10 Anderson Ho
11 Mackrow Wlk
12 Robin Hood Gdns
B3
1 Langdon Ho
2 Balfron Twr
3 Tabard Ct
4 Delta Bldg
5 Kilbrennan Ho
6 Thistle Ho
7 Heather Ho
8 Tartan Ho
9 Trident Ho
C3
1 Lansbury Gdns
2 Thesus Ho
3 Adams Ho
4 Jones Ho
5 Sam March Ho
6 Arapiles Ho
7 Athenia Ho
8 Jervis Bay Ho
9 Helen Mackay Ho
10 Gaze Ho
11 Ritchie Ho
12 Circle Ho
13 Dunkeld Ho
14 Braithwaite Ho
15 Rosemary Dr
16 Sorrel La
17 East India Dock Road Tunnel

35
B1
1 Newton Point
2 Sparke Terr
3 Montesquieu Terr
4 Crawford Point
5 Rathbone Ho
6 George St
7 Emily St
8 Fendt Cl
B2
1 Radley Terr
2 Rathbone Mkt
3 Thomas North Terr

4 Bernard Cassidy St
5 Mary St
6 Hughes Terr
7 Swanscombe Point
8 Rawlinson Point
9 Kennedy Cox Ho
10 Cooper St
C1
1 Capulet Mews
2 Pepys Cres
3 De Quincey Mews
4 Hardy Ave
5 Tom Jenkinson Rd
6 Hanamel St
7 Kennacraig Cl
8 Charles Flemmell Mews
9 Gatcombe Rd
10 Badminton Mews
11 Holyrood Mews
12 Britannia Gate
13 Dalemain Mews
C2
1 Clements Ave
2 Martindale Ave
C4
1 Odeon Ct
2 Edward Ct
3 Newhaven La
4 Ravenscroft Cl
5 Douglas Rd
6 Ferrier Point
7 Harvey Point
8 Wood Point
9 Trinity St
10 Pattinson Point
11 Clinch Ct
12 Mint Bsns Pk

36
A1
1 Burford Ho
2 Hope Cl
3 Centaur Ct
4 Phoenix Ct
C1
1 Surrey Cres
2 Forbes Ho
3 Haining Cl
4 Melville Ct
5 London Stile
6 Stile Hall Par
7 Priory Lo
8 Kew Bridge Ct
9 Meadowcroft
10 St James Ct

37
A1
1 Churchdale Ct
2 Cromwell Ct
3 Cambridge Rd S
4 Oxbridge Ct
5 Tomlinson Cl
6 Gunnersbury Mews
7 Grange The
8 Gunnersbury Cl
A4
1 Cheltenham Pl
2 Beaumaris Twr
3 Arundel Ho
4 Pevensey Ct
5 Jerome Twr
6 Anstey Ct
7 Bennett Ct
8 Gunnersbury Ct
B1
1 Arlington Park Mans
2 Sandown Ho

3 Goodwood Ho
4 Windsor Ho
5 Lingfield Ho
6 Ascot Ho
7 Watchfield Ct
8 Belgrave Ct
9 Beverley Ct
10 Beaumont Ct
11 Harvard Rd
B2 1 Church Green Ho
2 Bell Ind Est
3 Fairlawn Ct
4 Dukes Gate
5 Dewsbury Ct
6 Chiswick Terr
B3 1 Blackmore Twr
2 Bollo Ct
3 Kipling Twr
4 Lawrence Ct
5 Maugham Ct
6 Reade Ct
7 Woolf Ct
8 Shaw Ct
9 Verne Ct
10 Wodehouse Ct
11 Greenock Rd
12 Garden Ct
13 Barons Gate
14 Cleveland Rd
15 Chapter Cl
16 Beauchamp Cl
17 Holmes Ct
B4 1 Belgrave Cl
2 Buckland Wlk
3 Frampton Ct
4 Telfer Ct
5 Harlech Twr
6 Corfe Twr
7 Barwick Ho
8 Charles Hocking Ho
9 Sunninghill Ct
10 Salisbury St
C1 1 Chatsworth Lo
2 Prospect Pl
3 Townhall Ave
4 Devonhurst Pl
5 Heathfield Ct
6 Horticultural Pl
7 Merlin Ho
8 Garth Rd

38
A1 1 Glebe Cl
2 Devonshire Mews
3 Binns Terr
4 Ingress St
5 Swanscombe Rd
6 Brackley Terr
7 Stephen Fox Ho
8 Manor Ho
9 Coram Ho
10 Flaxman Ho
11 Thorneycroft Ho
12 Thornhill Ho
13 Kent Ho
14 Oldfield Ho
A2 1 Chestnut Ho
2 Bedford Ho
3 Bedford Cnr
4 Sydney Ho
5 Bedford Park Cnr

6 Priory Gdns
7 Windmill Alley
8 Castle Pl
9 Jonathan Ct
10 Windmill Pas
11 Chardin Rd
12 Gable Ho
A3 1 Fleet Ct
2 Ember Ct
3 Emlyn Gdns
4 Clone Ct
5 Abbey Ct
6 Ormsby Lo
7 St Catherine's Ct
A4 1 Longford Ct
2 Mole Ct
3 Lea Ct
4 Wandle Ct
5 Beverley Ct
6 Roding Ct
7 Crane Ct
B1 1 Miller's Ct
2 British Grove Pas
3 British Grove S
4 Beresford Rd
5 North Eyot Gdns
B2 1 Flanders Mans
2 Stamford Brook Mans
3 Linkenholt Mans
4 Prebend Mans
5 Middlesex Ct
B3 1 Stamford Brook Ho
2 Hauteville Court Gdns
3 Ranelagh Gdns
C2 1 Hamlet Ct
2 Derwent Ct
3 Westcroft Ct
4 Black Lion Mews
5 St Peter's Villas
6 Standish Ho
7 Chambon Pl
8 Court Mans
C4 1 Becklow Gdns
2 Victoria Ho
3 Lycett Pl
4 Kylemore Ct
5 Alexandra Ct
6 Lytten Ct
7 Becklow Mews
8 Northcroft Ct
9 Bailey Ct
10 Spring Cott
11 Landor Wlk
12 Laurence Mews
13 Hadyn Park Ct
14 Askew Mans

39
A2 1 Albion Gdns
2 Flora Gdns
3 Lamington St
4 Felgate Mews
5 Galena Ho
6 Albion Mews
7 Albion Cl
8 King Street Cloisters
9 Dimes Pl
10 Clarence Ct
11 Hampshire Hog La
12 Marryat Ct

A4 1 Westbush Ct
2 Goldhawk Mews
3 Sycamore Ho
4 Shackleton Ct
5 Drake Ct
6 Scotts Ct
B1 1 Bridge Avenue Mans
2 Bridgeview
3 College S
4 Beatrice Ho
5 Amelia Ho
6 Edith Ho
7 Joanna Ho
8 Mary Ho
9 Adela Ho
10 Sophia Ho
11 Henrietta Ho
12 Charlotte Ho
13 Alexandra Ho
14 Bath Pl
15 Elizabeth Ho
16 Margaret Ho
17 Peabody Est
18 Eleanor Ho
19 Isabella Ho
20 Caroline Ho
B2 1 Phoenix Lodge Mans
2 Samuel's Cl
3 Broadway Arc
4 Brook Ho
5 Hammersmith Broadway
B4 1 Verulam Ho
2 Grove Mans
3 Frobisher Ct
4 Library Mans
5 Pennard Mans
6 Lanark Mans
7 Kerrington Ct
8 Granville Mans
9 Romney Ct
10 Rayner Ct
11 Sulgrave Gdns
12 Bamborough Gdns
C3 1 Grosvenor Residences
2 Blythe Mews
3 Burnand Ho
4 Bradford Ho
5 Springvale Terr
6 Ceylon Rd
7 Walpole Ct
8 Bronte Ct
9 Boswell Ct
10 Souldern Rd
11 Brook Green Flats
12 Haarlem Rd
13 Stafford Mans
14 Lionel Mans
C4 1 Vanderbilt Villas
2 Bodington Ct
3 Kingham Cl
4 Clearwater Terr
5 Lorne Gdns
6 Cameret Ct
7 Bush Ct
8 Shepherds La
9 Rockley Ct
10 Grampians The
11 Charcroft Ct
12 Addison Park Mans
13 Sinclair Mans

40
A1 1 Hockney Ct
2 Toulouse Ct
3 Lowry Ct
4 Barry Ho
5 Lewis Ct
6 Gainsborough Ct
7 Renoir Ct
8 Blake Ct
9 Raphael Ct
10 Rembrandt Ct
11 Constable Ct
12 Da Vinci Ct
13 Gauguin Ct
14 Michelangelo Ct
15 Monet Ct
16 Weald Cl
17 Jasmin Lo
18 Birchmere Lo
19 Weybridge Ct
20 Florence Ho
21 Gleneagles Cl
22 Sunningdale Cl
23 Muirfield Cl
24 Turnberry Cl
25 St Andrews Cl
26 Kingsdown Cl
27 St Davids Cl
28 Galway Cl
29 Edenbridge Cl
30 Birkdale Cl
31 Tralee Ct
32 Woburn Ct
33 Belfry Cl
34 Troon Cl
35 Holywell Cl
A2 1 Market Pl
2 Trappes Ho
3 Thurland Ho
4 Ramsfort Ho
5 Hambley Ho
6 Holford Ho
7 Pope Ho
8 Southwell Ho
9 Mortain Ho
10 Radcliffe Ho
11 Southwark Park Est
12 Galleywall Road Trad Est
13 Trevithick Ho
14 Barlow Ho
15 Donkin Ho
16 Landmann Ho
17 Fitzmaurice Ho
18 Dodd Ho
A3 1 Perryn Rd
2 Chalfont Ho
3 Prestwood Ho
4 Farmer Ho
5 Gataker Ho
6 Gataker St
7 Cornick Ho
8 Glebe Ho
9 Matson Ho
10 Hickling Ho
A4 1 Butterfield Cl
2 Janeway Pl
3 Trotwood Ho
4 Cranbourn Ho
5 Cherry Garden Ho
6 Burton Ho
7 Morriss Ho
8 King Edward The Third Mews

9 Cathay St
10 Rotherhithe Ho
B2 1 Damory Ho
2 Antony Ho
3 Roderick Ho
4 Pedworth Gdns
5 Beamish Ho
6 Gillam Ho
7 George Walter Ho
8 Richard Ho
9 Adron Ho
10 Westlake
11 McIntosh Ho
B3 1 Blick Ho
2 Neptune Ho
3 Scotia Ct
4 Murdoch Ho
5 Edmonton Ct
6 Niagara Ct
7 Columbia Point
8 Ritchie Ho
9 Wells Ho
10 Helen Peele Cotts
11 Orchard Ho
12 Dock Offices
13 Landale Ho
14 Courthope Ho
B4 1 Mayflower St
2 St Mary's Est
3 Rupack St
4 Frank Whymark Ho
5 Adams Gardens Est
6 Hatterick St
7 Hythe Ho
8 Seaford Ho
9 Sandwich Ho
10 Rye Ho
11 Winchelsea Ho
12 Kenning St
13 Western Pl
14 Ainsty St
15 Pine Ho
16 Beech Ho
17 Larch Ho
18 Seth St
19 Turner Ct
20 Risdon Ho
21 Risdon Ho
22 Aylton Est
23 Manitoba Ct
24 Calgary Ct
25 Irwell Est
26 City Bsns Ctr
C2 1 John Kennedy Ho
2 Brydale Ho
3 Balman Ho
4 Tissington Ct
5 Harbord Ho
6 Westfield Ho
7 Albert Starr Ho
8 John Brent Ho
9 William Evans Ho
10 Raven Ho
11 Egret Ho
12 Fulmar Ho
13 Dunlin Ho
14 Siskin Ho
15 Sheldrake Ho
16 Buchanan Ct
17 Burrage Ct
18 Biddenham Ho
19 Ayston Ho
20 Empingham Ho
21 Deanshanger Ho
22 Codicote Ho
C4 1 Schooner Cl

2 Dolphin Cl
3 Clipper Cl
4 Deauville Ct
5 Colette Ct
6 Coniston Ct
7 Virginia Ct
8 Derwent Ct
9 Grantham Ct
10 Serpentine Ct
11 Career Ct
12 Lacine Ct
13 Fairway Ct
14 Harold Ct
15 Spruce Ho
16 Cedar Ho
17 Sycamore Ho
18 Woodland Cres
19 Poplar Ho
20 Adelphi Ct
21 Basque Ct
22 Aberdale Ct
23 Quilting Ct
24 Chargrove Cl
25 Radley Ct
26 Greenacre Sq
27 Maple Leaf Sq
28 Stanhope Cl
29 Hawke Pl
30 Drake Cl
31 Brass Talley Alley
32 Monkton Ho
33 James Ho
34 Wolfe Cres

41
A2 1 Trafalgar Cl
2 Hornblower Cl
3 Cunard Wlk
4 Caronia Ct
5 Catinthia Ct
6 Freswick Ho
7 Graveley Ho
8 Husbourne Ho
9 Crofters Ct
10 Pomona Ho
11 Hazelwood Ho
12 Cannon Wharf Bsns Ctr
13 Bence Ho
14 Clement Ho
15 Pendennis Ho
16 Lighter Cl
17 Mast Ct
18 Rushcutters Ct
19 Boat Lifter Way
B1 1 Gransden Ho
2 Daubeney Twr
3 North Ho
4 Rochfort Ho
5 Keppel Ho
6 Camden Ho
7 Sanderson Ho
8 Berkeley Ho
9 Strafford Ho
10 Richman Ho
11 Hurleston Ho
12 Grafton Ho
13 Fulcher Ho
14 Citrus Ho
B2 2 Windsock Cl
3 Linberry Wlk
4 Lanyard Ho
5 Golden Hind Pl
6 James Lind Ho
7 Harmon Ho

7 Pelican Ho
8 Bembridge Ho
9 Terrace Ho
10 George Beard Rd
C2 1 Olympian Ct
2 Aphrodite Ct
3 Mercury Ct
4 Poseidon Ct
5 Neptune Ct
6 Artemis Ct
7 Hera Ct
8 Ares Ct
9 Cyclops Mews
10 Magellan Pl
11 Britannia Rd
12 Deptford Ferry Rd
13 Ironmonger's Pl
14 Radnor Wlk
15 Ashdown Wlk
16 Rothsay Wlk
17 Dartmoor Wlk
18 Ringwood Gdns
C3 1 St Hubert's Ho
2 John Tucker Ho
3 Clare Grant Ho
4 Gilbertson Ho
5 Bowsprit Point
6 Scoulding Ho
7 Cord Way
8 Cressall Ho
9 Alexander Ho
10 Kedge Ho

42
A2 1 Brassey Ho
2 Triton Ho
3 Warspite Ho
4 Rodney Ho
5 Conway Ho
6 Exmouth Ho
7 Akbar Ho
8 Arethusa Ho
B2 1 Betty May Gray Ho
2 Castleton Ho
3 Urmston Ho
4 Salford Ho
5 Capstan Ho
6 Frigate Ho
7 Galleon Ho
8 Barons Lo
B3 1 Cardale St
2 Hickin St
3 John McDonald Ho
4 Thorne Ho
5 Skeggs Ho
6 St Bernard Ho
7 Kimberley Ho
8 Kingdon Ho
9 Lingard Ho
10 Yarrow Ho
11 Sandpiper Ct
12 Nightingale Ct
13 Robin Ct
14 Heron Ct
B4 1 Llandovery Ho
2 Rugless Ho
3 Ash Ho
4 Elm Ho
5 Cedar Ho
6 Castalia Sq
7 Alice Shepherd Ho
8 Oak Ho
9 Ballin Ct
10 Martin Ct

11 Grebe Ct
12 Kingfisher Ct
C2 1 Verwood Lo
2 Fawley Lo
3 Lyndhurst Lo
4 Blyth Cl
5 Farnworth Ho
6 Francis Cl

43
A1 1 Bellot Gdns
2 Thornley Pl
3 King William La
4 Bolton Ho
5 Miles Ho
6 Mell St
7 Sam Manners Ho
8 Hatcliffe Almshouses
9 Woodland Wlk
10 Earlswood Cl
B1 1 Baldrey Ho
2 Christie Ho
3 Dyson Ho
4 Cliffe Ho
5 Moore Ho
6 Collins Ho
7 Lockyer Ho
8 Halley Ho
9 Kepler Ho
C1 1 Layfield Ho
2 Westerdale Rd
3 Mayston Mews

44
A4 1 Ferry Sq
2 Wilkes Rd
3 Albany Par
4 Charlton Ho
5 Albany Ho
6 Alma Ho
7 Griffin Ct
8 Cressage Ho
9 Tunstall Wlk
10 Trimmer Wlk
11 Running Horse Yd
12 Mission Sq
13 Distillery Wlk
B2 1 Primrose Ho
2 Lawman Ct
3 Royston Ct
4 Garden Ct
5 Capel Lo
6 Devonshire Ct
7 Celia Ct
8 Rosslyn Ho
9 Branstone Ct
10 Lamerton Lo
11 Kew Lo
12 Dunraven Ho
13 Stoneleigh Lo
14 Tunstall Ct
15 Voltaire
C2 1 Clarendon Ct
2 Quintock Ho
3 Broome Ct
4 Lonsdale Mews
5 Elizabeth Cotts
6 Sandways
7 Victoria Cotts
8 North Ave
9 Grovewood
10 Hamilton Ho
11 Melvin Ct
12 Power Ho

46
B1 1 Melrose Rd
2 Seaforth Lo
3 St John's Gr
4 Sussex Ct
5 Carmichael Ct
6 Hampshire Ct
7 Thorne Pas
8 Brunel Ct
9 Beverley Path

47
C4 1 Cobb's Hall
2 Dorset Mans
3 St Clements Mans
4 Bothwell St
5 Hawksmoor St

48
A1 1 Langport Ho
2 Iveagh Ho
3 Newark Ho
4 Edgehill Ho
5 Hopton Ho
6 Ashby Ho
7 Nevil Ho
A2 1 Fairbairn Gn
2 Hammerton Gn
3 Foxley Sq
4 Silverburn Ho
5 Butler Ho
6 Dalkeith Ho
7 Turner Ct
8 Bathgate Ho
9 Black Roof Ho
A4 1 Faunce Ho
2 Garbett Ho
3 Harvard Ho
4 Doddington Pl
5 Kean Ho
6 Jephson Ho
7 Cornish Ho
8 Bateman Ho
9 Molesworth Ho
10 Walters Ho
11 Cruden Ho
12 Brawne Ho
13 Prescott Ho
14 Chalmer's Wlk
15 Copley Cl
B1 1 Bergen Ho
2 Oslo Ho
3 Viking Ho
4 Jutland Ho
5 Norvic Ho
6 Odin Ho
7 Baltic Ho
8 Nobel Ho
9 Mercia Ho
10 Kenbury Gdns
11 Zealand Ho
12 Elsinore Ho
13 Norse Ho
14 Denmark Mans
15 Dane Ho
16 Canterbury Cl
17 York Cl
18 Kenbury Mans
19 Parade Mans
20 Winterslow Ho
21 Lilford Ho
22 Cutcombe Mans
23 Bartholomew Ho
24 Guildford Ho

25 Boston Ho
26 Hereford Ho
27 Weyhill Ho
28 Lichfield Ho
29 Lansdown Ho
30 Honiton Ho
31 Pinner Ho
32 Baldock Ho
33 Widecombe Ho
34 Nottingham Ho
35 Witham Ho
36 Barnet Ho
B2 1 Bertha Neuberg Ho
2 Mornington Mews
3 Badsworth Rd
4 Sycamore Ct
5 Elm Tree Ct
6 Samuel Lewis Trust Dwellings
7 Valmar Trad Est
8 Keswick Ho
9 Mitcham Ho
B3 1 Boundary Ho
2 Day Ho
3 Burgess Ho
4 Carlyle Ho
5 Myers Ho
6 Thompson's Ave
7 Palgrave Ho
8 Winnington Ho
9 Brantwood Ho
10 Lowell Ho
11 Lamps Ct
12 Otterburn Ho
13 Crossmount Ho
14 Venice Ct
15 Bowyer St
16 Livingstone Ho
17 Gothic Ct
18 Coniston Ho
19 Harlynwood
20 Carey Ct
21 Finley Ct
22 Grainger Ct
23 Hayes Ct
24 Moffat Ho
25 Marinel Ho
26 Hodister Ct
27 Arnot Ho
28 Lamb Ho
29 Kipling Ho
30 Keats Ho
31 Kenyon Ho
32 New Church Rd
C1 1 Selborne Rd
2 Hascombe Terr
C2 1 Joiners Arms Yd
2 Butterfly Wlk
3 Cuthill Wlk
4 Colonades The
5 Artichoke Mews
6 Peabody Bldgs
7 Brighton Ho
8 Park Ho
9 Peabody Ct
10 Lomond Ho
11 Lamb Ho
12 Kimpton Ct
13 Belham Wlk
14 Datchelor Pl
15 Harvey Rd
C3 1 Masterman Ho

6 Reginald Pl
7 Fletcher Path
8 Frankham Ho
9 Cremer Ho
10 Wilshaw Ho
11 Castell Ho
12 Browne Ho
C4 1 Dryfield Wlk
2 Blake Ho
3 Hawkins Ho
4 Grenville Ho
5 Langford Ho
6 Mandarin Ct
7 Peregrine Ct
8 Bittern Ct
9 Lamerton St
10 Armada St
11 Armada Ct
12 Benbow Ho
13 Oxenham Ho
14 Caravel Mews
15 Hughes Ho

52
A3 1 Finch Ho
2 Jubilee The
3 Gordon Ho
4 Haddington Ct
5 Maitland Ct
6 Ashburnham Retreat
B1 1 Ellison Ho
2 Pitmaston Ho
3 Windmill Cl
4 Hermitage The
5 Burnett Ho
6 Lacey Ho
B2 1 Penn Almshouse
2 Jarvis Ct
3 Woodville Ct
4 Darnell Ho
5 Renbold Ho
6 Lindsell St
7 Plumbridge St
8 Trinity Gr
9 Hollymount Cl
10 Cade Tyler Ho
11 Robertson Ho
B3 1 Temair Ho
2 Glaisher St
3 Prince of Orange La
4 Lombard Ho
5 St Marks Cl
6 Ada Kennedy Ct
7 Arlington Pl
8 Topham Ho
9 Darnell Ho
10 Hawks Mews
11 Royal Pl
12 Swanne Ho
13 Maribor
14 Serica Ct
B4 1 Greenwich Mkt
2 Turnpin La
3 Durnford St
4 Sexton's Ho
5 Bardsley Ho
6 Wardell Ho
7 Clavell St
8 Stanton Ho
9 Macey Ho
10 Boreman Ho
C4 1 Frobisher Sq

2 Hardy Cotts
3 Palliser Ho
4 Bernard Angell Ho
5 Corvette Sq
6 Travers Ho
7 Reade Ho
8 Maze Hill Ho

53
B3 1 Westcombe Ct
2 Kleffens Ct
3 Ferndale Ct
4 Combe Mews
5 Mandeville Ct
6 Heathway
7 Pinelands Cl
C3 1 Mary Lawrenson Pl
2 Bradbury Ct
3 Dunstable Ct
C4 1 Nethercombe Ho
2 Holywell Cl

54
A1 1 Lancaster Cotts
2 Lancaster Mews
3 Bromwich Ho
4 Priors Lo
5 Richmond Hill Ct
6 Glenmore Ho
7 Hillbrow
8 Heathshot
9 Friars Stile Pl
10 Spire Ct
11 Ridgeway
12 Matthias Ct
A2 1 Lichfield Terr
2 Union Ct
3 Carrington Lo
4 Wilton Ct
5 Egerton Ct
6 Beverley Lo
7 Bishop Duppa's Almshouses
8 Regency Wlk
9 Clearwater Ho
10 Onslow Avenue Mans
11 Michels Almshouses
A3 1 St John's Gr
2 Michel's Row
3 Michelsdale Dr
4 Blue Anchor Alley
5 Clarence St
6 Sun Alley
7 Richmond Adult Coll
8 Thames Link Ho
B1 1 Chester Cl
2 Grosvenor Ct
3 Queen's Ct
4 Russell Wlk
5 Charlotte Sq
6 Jones Wlk
7 Hilditch Ho
8 Isabella Ct
9 Hobart St
10 Damer Ho
11 Eliot Ho
12 Fitzherbert Ho
13 Reynolds Pl
14 Chisholm Rd
B2 1 Alberta Ct
2 Beatrice Rd
3 Lorne Rd

4 York Rd
5 Connaught Rd
6 Albany Terr
7 Kingswood Ct
8 Selwyn Ct
9 Broadhurst Cl
B3 1 Towers The
2 Longs Ct
3 Sovereign Ct
4 Robinson Ct
5 Calvert Ct
6 Bedford Ct
7 Hickey's Almshouses
8 Church Almshouses

55
A3 1 Hershell Ct
2 Deanhill Ct
3 Park Sheen
4 Furness Lo
5 Merricks Ct
C4 1 Rann House
2 Craven Ho
3 John Dee Ho
4 Kindell Ho
5 Montgomery Ho
6 Avondale Ho
7 Addington Ct
8 Dovecote Gdns
9 Firmston Ho
10 Glendower Gdns
11 Chestnut Ave
12 Trehern Rd
13 Rock Ave

56
B1 1 Allenford Ho
2 Swaythling Ho
3 Tatchbury Ho
4 Penwood Ho
5 Bramley Ho
6 Shalden Ho
7 Dunbridge Ho
8 Denmead Ho
9 Charcot Ho
10 Portswood Pl
11 Brockbridge Ho
12 Hurstbourne Ho
C2 1 Theodore Ho
2 Nicholas Ho
3 Bonner Ho
4 Downing Ho
5 Johsen Ho
6 Fairfax Ho
7 Devereux Ho
8 David Ho
9 Leigh Ho
10 Clipstone Ho
11 Mallet Ho
12 Arton Wilson Ho

57
B2 1 Inglis Ho
2 Ducie Ho
3 Warncliffe Ho
4 Stanhope Ho
5 Waldegrave Ho
6 Midmay Ho
7 Mullens Ho
C1 1 Balmoral Cl
2 Glenalmond Ho
3 Selwyn Ho

4 Keble Ho
5 Bede Ho
6 Gonville Ho
7 Magdalene Ho
8 Armstrong Ho
9 Newnham Ho
10 Somerville Ho
11 Balliol Ho
12 Windermere
13 Little Combe Cl
14 Classinghall Ho
15 Chalford Ct
16 Garden Royal
17 South Ct
18 Anne Kerr Ct
19 Ewhurst
C2 1 Geneva Ct
2 Laurel Ct
3 Cambalt Ho
4 Langham Ct
5 Lower Pk
6 King's Keep
7 Whitnell Ct
8 Whitehead Ho
9 Halford Ho
10 Humphry Ho
11 Jellicoe Ho
C3 1 Olivette St
2 Mascotte Rd
3 Glegg Pl
4 Crown Ct
5 Charlwood Terr

58
A2 1 Claremont
2 Downside
3 Cavendish Cl
4 Ashcombe Ct
5 Carltons The
6 Draldo Ho
7 Millbrooke Ct
8 Coysh Ct
9 Keswick Hts
10 Lincoln Ho
11 Avon Ct
B2 1 Burlington Mews
2 Cumbria Ho
3 St Stephen's Gdns
4 Atlantic Ho
5 Burton Lo
6 Manfred Ct
7 Meadow Bank
8 Hooper Ho
C2 1 Pembridge Pl
2 Adelaide Rd
3 London Ct
4 Windsor Ct
5 Westminster Ct
6 Fullers Ho
7 Bridge Pk
8 Lambeth Ct
9 Milton Ct
10 Norfolk Mans
11 Francis Snary Lo
12 Bush Cotts
13 Downbury Mews
14 Newton's Yd

59
A2 1 Fairfield Ct
2 Blackmore Ho
3 Lancaster Mews
4 Cricketers Mews
B4 1 Molasses Ho
2 Molasses Row

1 Cinnamon Row
2 Calico Ho
3 Calico Row
4 Port Ho
5 Square Rigger Row
6 Trade Twr
7 Ivory Ho
8 Spice Ct
9 Sherwood Ct
10 Mendip Ct
11 Chalmers Ho
C3 1 Burke Ho
2 Fox Ho
3 Buxton Ho
4 Pitt Ho
5 Romsey Ho
6 Beverley Cl
7 Florence Ho
8 Linden Ct
9 Dorcas Ct
10 Johnson Ct
11 Agnes Ct
12 Hilltop Ct
13 Courtyard The
14 Old Laundry The
15 Oberstein Rd
16 Fineran Ct
17 Sangora Rd
18 Harvard Mans
C4 1 Benham Cl
2 Milner Ho
3 McManus Ho
4 Wilberforce Ho
5 Wheeler Ct
6 Sporle Ct
7 Holliday Sq
8 John Parker Sq
9 Carmichael Cl
10 Fenner Sq
11 Clark Lawrence Ct
12 Shaw Ct
13 Sendall Ct
14 Livingstone Rd
15 Farrant Ho
16 Jackson Ho
17 Darien Ho
18 Sheppard Ho
19 Ganley Ct
20 Arthur Newton Ho
21 Chesterton Ho
22 John Kirk Ho
23 Mantua St
24 Heaver Rd

60
A4 1 Kiloh Ct
2 Lanner Ho
3 Grifton Ho
4 Kestrel Ho
5 Kite Ho
6 Peregrine Ho
7 Hawk Ho
8 Inkster Ho
9 Harrier Ho
10 Eagle Hts
11 Kingfisher Ct
12 Lavender Terr
13 Temple Ho
14 Ridley Ho
15 Eden Ho
16 Hertford Ct
17 Nepaul Rd

C1
1 Rayne Ho
2 St Anthony's Ct
3 Earlsthorpe Mews
C4
1 Shaftesbury Park Chambers
2 Selborne
3 Rush Hill Mews
4 Marmion Mews
5 Crosland Ct
6 Craven Mews
7 Wycliffe Rd
8 Basnett Rd
9 Wickersley Rd
10 Tyneham Cl

61
A4
1 Turnchapel Mews
2 Redwood Mews
3 Phil Brown Pl
4 Bev Callender Cl
5 Keith Connor Cl
6 Tessa Sanderson Pl
7 Daley Thompson Way
8 Rashleigh Ct
B1
1 Joseph Powell Cl
2 Cavendish Mans
3 Westlands Terr
4 Cubitt Ho
5 Hawksworth Ho
6 Normanton Ho
7 Eastman Ho
8 Couchman Ho
9 Poynders Ct
10 Selby Ho
11 Valentine Ho
12 Gorham Ho
13 Deauville Mans
14 Deauville Ct
B2
1 Timothy Cl
2 Shaftesbury Mews
3 Brook Ho
4 Grover Ho
5 Westbrook Ho
6 Hewer Ho
7 Batten Ho
8 Mandeville Ho
9 George Beare Lo
B3
1 Polygon The
2 Windsor Ct
3 Trinity Ct
4 Studios The
5 Bourne Ho
B4
1 Clapham Manor Ct
2 Clarke Ho
3 Gables The
4 Sycamore Mews
5 Maritime Ho
C1
1 Parrington Ho
2 Savill Ho
3 Blackwell Ho
4 Bruce Ho
5 Victoria Ct
6 Victoria Ho
7 Belvedere Ct
8 Ingram Lo
9 Viney Ct
10 Bloomsbury Ho
11 Belgravia Ho
12 Barnsbury Ho
C3
1 Kendoa Rd
2 Felmersham Cl

3 Abbeville Mews
4 Saxon Ho
5 Gifford Ho
6 Teignmouth Cl
7 Holwood Pl
8 Oaklands Pl
C1
1 Chelsham Ho
2 Lynde Ho
3 Greener Ho
4 Towns Ho
5 Hugh Morgan Ho
6 Roy Ridley Ho
7 Lendal Terr
8 Slievemore Cl

62
A2
1 King's Mews
2 Clapham Court Terr
3 Clapham Ct
4 Clapham Park Terr
5 Queenswood Ct
A3
1 Morris Ho
2 Gye Ho
3 Clowes Ho
4 Thomas Ho
5 Stuart Ho
6 Storace Ho
7 Bedford Ho
8 Ascot Ct
9 Ascot Par
10 Ashmere Ho
11 Ashmere Gr
A4
1 Callingham Ho
2 Russell Pickering Ho
3 Lopez Ho
B2
1 Beatrice Ho
2 Florence Ho
3 Evelyn Ho
4 Diana Ho
5 Brixton Hill Ct
6 Austin Ho
7 Manor Ct
8 Camsey Ho
9 Romer Ho
10 Gale Ho
11 Byrne Ho
12 Farnfield Ho
13 Marchant Ho
14 Rainsford Ho
15 Springett Ho
16 Mannering Ho
17 Waldron Ho
B3
1 Freemens Hos
2 Roger's Almshouses
3 Gresham Almshouses
4 Exbury Ho
5 Glasbury Ho
6 Dalbury Ho
7 Fosbury Ho
8 Chalbury Ho
9 Neilson-Terry Ct
10 Pavilion Mans
11 Daisy Dormer Ct
12 George Lashwood Ct
13 Marie Lloyd Ct
14 Trinity Homes
B4
1 Turberville Ho
2 Thrayle Ho
C1
1 Eccleston Ho
2 Scarsbrook Ho
3 Purser Ho

4 Rudhall Ho
5 Hardham Ho
6 Heywood Ho
7 Haworth Ho
8 Birch Ho
9 Lonsdell Ho
10 Lomley Ho
11 Laughton Ho
C2
1 Crownstone Ct
2 Brockwell Ct
3 Nevena Ct
4 St George's Residences
5 Hanover Mans
6 Fleet Ho
7 Langbourne Ho
8 Turnmill Ho
C3
1 Electric Mans
2 Electric La
3 Connaught Mans
4 Clifton Mans
5 Hereford Ho
6 Chaplin Ho
7 Brixton Oval
8 Lord David Pitt Ho
9 Marcus Garvey Way
10 Montgo Ct
11 Bob Marley Way
12 Leeson Rd
C4
1 Buckmaster Ho
2 Barret Ho
3 Albermarle Ho
4 Goodwood Mans
5 Angell Park Gdns
6 Fyfield Rd
7 Howard Ho
8 Harris Ho
9 Broadoak Ct
10 Burgate Ct
11 Witchwood Ho
12 Blacktree Mews
13 Chartham Ct
14 Chilham Ct
15 Northgate Ct
16 Westgate Ct
17 Dover Mans

63
A3
1 Mahatma Ganhi Ind Est
2 Dylan Rd
3 Bessemer Park Ind Est
4 Pablo Neruda Cl
5 Langston Hughes Cl
6 Walt Whitman Cl
7 James Joyes Wlk
8 Alice Walker Cl
9 Louise Bennett Cl
10 Chaddacre Ho
11 Burwood Ho
12 Pyrford Ho
13 Wangford Ho
14 Ashford Ho
15 Kenwood Ho
16 Moyne Ho
17 Elveden Ho
18 Sussex Wlk
19 Carrara Wlk
20 Broughton Dr
21 Angela Davis Ind Est
A4
1 Mallams Mews

2 Amberley Ct
3 Harper Ho
4 Leicester Ho
5 Station Ave
6 Wellfit St
7 Loughborough Ct
8 Belinda Rd
9 Higgs Ind Est
C3
1 Shaftesbury Ct
2 Mayhew Ct
3 Morris Ct
4 Swinburne Ct
5 Perth Ct
6 Tayside Ct
7 Matlock Ct
8 Hunter Ct
9 Turner Ct

64
A2
1 Velde Way
2 Delft Way
3 Arnhem Way
4 Isel Way
5 Kempis Way
6 Terborah Way
7 Steen Way
8 Deventer Cres
9 Nimegen Way
10 Hilversum Cres
A4
1 Harfield Gdns
2 Karen Ct
3 Seavington Ho
4 Appleshaw Ho
5 Birdsall Ho
6 Whitney Ho
7 Wheatland Ho
8 Wilton Ho
9 Walcot Ho
10 Whadden Ho
11 Melbrook Ho
12 Ledbury Ho
13 Tidworth Ho
14 Riseholme Ho
15 Ringmer Ho
16 Petworth Ho
17 Stagshaw Ho
18 Ivybridge Ho
19 Inwood Ho
20 Gatcombe Ho
21 Gatebeck Ho
22 Felbridge Ho
23 Cowdray Ho
B3
1 Dulwich Mews
2 St James's Cloisters
C2
1 Dorothy Charrington Ho
2 Keswick Ct
3 Kendall Ct
4 Halliwell Ct

65
A4
1 Tilling Ho
2 Goodwin Ho
3 Citron Terr
4 Cheam St
5 Linden Ho
C3
1 Laxton Path
2 Barlings Ho
3 Bayfield Ho
4 Coston Wlk
5 Coverham Ho
6 Gateley Ho
7 Dereham Ho
8 Greenwood Ho

9 Hilton Ho
10 Goodall Ho
11 Horsley Ho
12 Jordan Ho

68
1 Farnborough Ho
2 Rushmere Ho
3 Horndean Cl
4 Highcross Way
5 Timsbury Wlk
6 Foxcombe Rd
7 Ryefield Path
8 Greatham Wlk
9 Gosport Ho
10 Stoatley Ho
11 Milland Ho
12 Clanfield Ho
13 Fareham Ho
14 Grayswood Point
C4
1 Woodcott Ho
2 Lyndhurst Ho
3 Wheatley Ho
4 Allbrook Ho
5 Bordon Wlk
6 Chilcombe Ho
7 Vicarage Ct
8 Shawford Ct
9 Eastleigh Wlk
10 Kings Ct

69
A3
1 Ramsdean Ho
2 Purbrook Ho
3 Portsea Ho
4 Blendworth Point
5 Eashing Point
6 Hindhead Point
7 Hilsea Point
8 Witley Point
9 Buriton Ho
10 Grately Ho
11 Hascombe Ho
12 Dunhill Point
13 Westmark Point
14 Longmoor Point
15 Cadnam Point
B4
1 Cumberland Ho
2 Devonshire Ho
3 Cornwall Ho
4 Norfolk Ho
5 Leicester Ho
6 Warwick Ho
7 Sutherland Ho
8 Carmarthen Ho
9 Worcester Ho
10 Rutland Ho
C3
1 Sandringham Cl
2 Eastwick Ct
3 Oatlands Ct
4 Banning Ho
5 Grantley Ho
6 Caryl Ho
7 Duncombe Ho
8 Chilworth Ct
9 Kent Lo
10 Turner Lo
11 Marlborough
12 Parkland Gdns
13 Lewesdon Cl
14 Pines Ct
15 Ashtead Ct
16 Mynterne Ct
17 Arden
18 Stephen Ct

10 Marsham Ct
20 Doradus Ct
21 Acorns The
22 Heritage Ho
23 Conifer Ct
24 Spencer Ho
25 Chartwell
26 Blenheim
27 Chivelston
28 Greenfield Ho
29 Oakman Ho
30 Radley Lo
31 Simon Lo
C4 1 Brett Ho
2 Brett House Cl
3 Sylva Ct
4 Ross Ct
5 Potterne Cl
6 Stourhead Cl
7 Fleur Gates
8 Greenwood

70
A3 1 William Harvey Ho
2 Highview Ct
3 Cameron Ct
4 Galgate Cl
5 Green Ho The
6 King Charles Wlk
7 Florys Ct
8 Augustus Ct
9 Albert Ct
10 Hertford Lo
11 Mortimer Lo
12 Allenswood
13 Ambleside

72
C2 1 Upper Tooting Park Mans
2 Cecil Mans
3 Marius Mans
4 Elmfield Mans
5 Holdernesse Rd
C3 1 Heslop Ct
2 St James's Terr
3 Boundaries Mans
4 Station Par
C4 1 Hollies Way
2 Endlesham Ct

73
A3 1 Holbeach Mews
2 Hildreth Street Mews

3 Coalbrook Mans
A4 1 Meyer Ho
2 Faraday Ho
3 Hales Ho
4 Frankland Ho
5 Graham Ho
6 Gibbs Ho
7 Dalton Ho
8 Anslie Wlk
9 Rokeby Ho
10 Caister Ho
11 Ivanhoe Ho
12 Catherine Baird Ct
13 Marmion Ho
14 Devonshire Ho
B4 1 Limerick Ct
2 Homewoods
3 Jewell Ho
4 Glanville Ho
5 Dan Bryant Ho
6 Olding Ho
7 Quennel Ho
8 Homan Ho
9 West Ho
10 Neville Ct
C3 1 Sinclair Ho
2 MacGregor Ho
3 Ingle Ho
4 Riley Ho
5 Bennett Ho
6 White Ho
7 Rodgers Ho
8 Dumphreys Ho
9 Prendergast Ho
10 Hutchins Ho
11 Whiteley Ho
12 Tresidder Ho
13 Primrose Ct
14 Angus Ho
15 Currie Ho

74
A1 1 De Montfort Par
2 Leigham Hall Par
3 Leigham Hall
4 Endsleigh Mans
5 John Kirk Ho
6 Raeburn Ct
7 Wavel Ct
8 Homeleigh Ct
9 Howland Ho
10 Beauclerk Ho
11 Bertrand Ho
12 Drew Ho
13 Dowes Ho
14 Dunton Ho
15 Raynald Ho

10 Sackville Ho
11 Thurlow Ho
12 Astoria Mans
A2 1 Wyatt Park Mans
2 Broadlands Mans
3 Stonehill's Mans
4 Streatleigh Par
5 Dorchester Ct
A3 1 Beaumont Ho
2 Christchurch Ho
3 Staplefield Cl
4 Chipstead Ho
5 Coulsdon Ho
6 Conway Ho
7 Telford Avenue Mans
8 Telford Parade Mans
9 Wavertree Ct
10 Hartswood Ho
11 Wray Ho
A4 1 Picton Ho
2 Rigg Ho
3 Watson Ho
4 MacArthur Ho
5 Sandon Ho
6 Thorold Ho
7 Pearce Ho
8 Mudie Ho
9 Miller Ho
10 Lycett Ho
11 Lafone Ho
12 Lucraft Ho
13 Freeman Ho
14 New Park Par
15 Argyll Ct
16 Dumbarton Ct
17 Kintyre Ct
18 Cotton Ho
19 Crossman Hos
20 Cameford Ct
21 Parsons Ho
22 Brindley Ho
23 Arkwright Ho
24 Perry Ho
25 Brunel Ho
26 New Park Ct
27 Tanhurst Ho
B1 1 Carisbrook Ct
2 Pembrook Lo
3 Willow Ct
4 Poplar Ct
5 Mountview
6 Spa View
B3 1 Charwood Ho
2 Earlswood Ho
3 Balcombe Ho
4 Claremont Cl
5 Holbrook Ho

6 Gwynne Ho
7 Kynaston Ho
8 Tillman Ho
9 Regent Lo
10 Hazelmere Ct
11 Dykes Ct
B4 1 Archbishop's Pl
2 Witley Ho
3 Outwood Ho
4 Dunsfold Ho
5 Deepdene Lo
6 Warnham Ho
7 Albury Lo
8 Tilford Ho
9 Elstead Ho
10 Thursley Ho
11 Brockham Ho
12 Capel Lo
13 Leith Ho
14 Fairview Ho
15 Weymouth Ct
16 Ascalon Ct
C3 1 Valens Ho
2 Loveday Ho
3 Strode Ho
4 Ethelworth Ct
5 Harbin Ho
6 Brooks Ho
7 Godolphin Ho
8 Sheppard Ho
9 McCormick Ho
10 Taylor Ho
11 Saunders Ho
12 Talcott Path
13 Derrick Ho
14 Williams Ho
15 Baldwin Ho
16 Berkeley Ct
17 Churston Cl
18 Neil Wates Cres
19 Burnell Ho
20 Portland Ho
C4 1 Ellacombe Ho
2 Booth Ho
3 Hathersley Ho
4 Brereton Ho
5 Holdsworth Ho
6 Dearmer Ho
7 Cherry Cl
8 Greenleaf Cl
9 Longford Wlk
10 Scarlette Manor Wlk
11 Chandlers Way
12 Upgrove Manor Way
13 Ropers Wlk
14 Tebbs Ho
15 Bell Ho

16 Worthington Ho
17 Courier Ho
18 Mackie Rd
19 Hamers Ho
20 Kelyway Ho
21 Harriet Tubman Cl
22 Estoria Cl
23 Leckhampton Pl
24 Scotia Rd

75
A1 1 Thanet Ho
2 Chapman Ho
3 Beaufoy Ho
4 Easton Ho
5 Roberts Ho
6 Lloyd Ct
7 Kershaw Ho
8 Wakeling Ho
9 Edridge Ho
10 Jeston Ho
11 Lansdowne Wood Cl
C2 1 Coppedhall
2 Shackleton Ct
3 Bullfinch Ct
4 Gannet Ct
5 Fulmar Ct
6 Heron Ct
7 Petrel Ct
8 Falcon Ct
9 Eagle Ct
10 Dunnock Ct
11 Dunlin Ct
12 Cormorant Ct

76
C1 1 Tunbridge Ct
2 Harrogate Ct
3 Bath Ct
4 Leamington Ct
5 Porlock Ho
6 Cissbury Ho
7 Eddisbury Ho
8 Dundry Ho
9 Silbury Ho
10 Homildon Ho
11 Highgate Ho
12 Richmond Ho
13 Pendle Ho
14 Tynwald Ho
15 Wirrall Ho
16 Greyfriars